I0754352

Congregational Council.

DEBATES AND PROCEEDINGS

OF THE

NATIONAL COUNCIL

OF

CONGREGATIONAL CHURCHES,

HELD AT

BOSTON, MASS., JUNE 14—24, 1865.

FROM THE PHONOGRAPHIC REPORT BY

J. M. W. YERRINTON AND HENRY M. PARKHURST.

BOSTON:
AMERICAN CONGREGATIONAL ASSOCIATION,
23 CHAUNCY STREET.
1866.

PREFACE.

WHEN the Congregational Churches of the United States were about to assemble in National Council in the year 1865, the Committee of Arrangements, in Boston, — Rev. Andrew L. Stone, of Boston, chairman, — secured the services of a phonographic reporter for the entire session of the Council. This arrangement was officially sanctioned by the Council itself; and a complete report of the debates and proceedings, made by men of eminent ability in that work, was thus obtained. Their manuscripts, with the original records and papers, were, by vote of the Council, placed on perpetual deposit with the Directors of the American Congregational Association; and the Directors were "authorized to publish a volume of proceedings and debates."

The Directors believed that a volume containing the acts and discussions entire would be of permanent historical value as well as of present interest to the churches. They determined to publish it, and appointed Rev. Alonzo H. Quint, Rev. Isaac P. Langworthy, Rev. Henry M. Dexter, Edward S. Tobey, Esq., and Rev. Rufus Anderson, D. D., to edit the work and carry it through the press. That committee placed it in the hands of a sub-committee, consisting of Rev. A. H. Quint, and Rev. Isaac P. Langworthy, who have superintended the publication of this volume.

In the execution of this duty, the main object has been to give to the public a faithful and exact copy of the phonographic report. That report has been varied from only in the following particulars: Statements introductory to items of business have been occasionally modified to secure uniformity in style; the names of members have been corrected when misstated; for occasional abstracts of votes, the full official language has been substituted, and a few changes have been found necessary on comparison with the record of the secretaries; and manifest errors in phraseology (extremely rare) have been corrected, although only upon the suggestion of those whose authority was unquestionable. The fidelity of the phonographers has proved to be worthy of special mention.

It was also thought desirable to insert an account of the various proceedings of different ecclesiastical bodies preliminary to, and resulting in, the assembly of the Council; and to add freely any explanatory notes which seemed needed, to make a complete historical record. The list of members, with their nativity, prepared by Rev. Increase N. Tarbox, and inserted at the close of the work, will doubtless be appreciated. As a matter of historical interest, a brief account of the several Synods or Councils, general or nearly so, which have been held by the American Congregational Churches, has been prefixed; and full indexes of topics and names are added at the close.

The committee trust that this work will be of permanent historical value; as well as meet the wishes of that large body of Christian churches which felt called by God to deliberate upon new duties in a day marked by the downfall of treason, and the deliverance of millions from human slavery,

ALONZO H. QUINT,
ISAAC P. LANGWORTHY,
HENRY M. DEXTER,
EDWARD S. TOBEY,
RUFUS ANDERSON,
Committee.

Boston, Massachusetts, May, 1866.

CONTENTS.

PREVIOUS SYNODS OR COUNCILS

HELD BY THE

AMERICAN CONGREGATIONAL CHURCHES.

GENERAL SYNODS have been few in the history of American Congregationalism. In the denial of any central human authority,— a principle fundamental in this polity,— they have been convened only by mutual consent; and, necessarily, only when some matter of "common concern" seemed to the churches to be of sufficient importance to require such a proceeding. It is hardly necessary to say, that

> "The proper function of a synod is not to legislate for the churches, nor to determine imperatively any question which is not already determined by the Scriptures, but by inquiry and brotherly conference, with prayer for divine illumination, to obtain and hold forth light on such matters as the churches have referred to its deliberations."[1]

The first Synod was held in 1637. It was called after consultation of "sundry elders and brethren,"[2] in consequence of the disturbances caused by the speculations of John Wheelwright, Mistress Anne Hutchinson, and others. It met on the thirtieth day of August, 1637, at Newtown, now Cambridge, Mass.; consisted of "all the teaching elders through the country,"[3] and of "messengers from the churches,"[4],—"about twenty-five godly ministers of Christ, besides many other graciously-eminent servants of his;"[5] chose Rev. Peter Bulkley, of Concord, and Rev. Thomas Hooker, of Hartford, moderators; examined and condemned "eighty [eighty-two] erroneous

[1] Page 124.
[2] Cotton's Way of the Congregational Churches Cleared. Ed. 1648, p. 40.
[3] Winthrop's Journal, Savage's Ed. 1853, I. 285.
[4] Cotton's Way, p. 40.
[5] The number of churches then existing, appears to be as follows: Massachusetts Bay, thirteen; Plymouth, four; Connecticut, two; total, nineteen. Possibly two or three others, whose dates are doubtful, may have been in existence.

opinions," and nine "unwholesome expressions," and decided a few points of church order; and dissolved on the twenty second day of September.

The erroneous opinions and unwholesome expressions, are, almost entirely, minute subdivisions of alleged errors regarding the doctrines of justification and sanctification.[1]

The second Synod convened at Cambridge, on the first day of September, 1646; after "about fourteen days," adjourned to the eighth day of June, 1647, "in regard of winter drawing on, and few of the elders of other colonies were present;"[2] met on the day appointed, but almost immediately adjourned, on account of an "epidemical sickness;" met again on the fifteenth of August, 1648; and "ended in less than fourteen days."[3]

This Synod was called by the General Court of Massachusetts,[4] upon the suggestion of "some of the elders;" the proposed order of the court being changed to a "desire," on account of the scruples of some in regard to the right of civil magistrates to "assemble the churches." The Synod confined itself to a Declaration of Faith, and a Platform of Church Discipline. For the former: —

> "This Synod having perused and considered (with much gladness of heart, and thankfulness to God) the Confession of Faith published of late by the Reverend Assembly [the Westminster] in *England*, do judge it to be very holy, orthodox, and judicious in all matters of Faith; and do therefore freely and fully consent thereunto, for the substance thereof."[5]

For Church Discipline, it set forth what is known as the "Cambridge Platform," which was mainly from the pen of Richard Mather. Their result was submitted to the General

[1] They are found in "A short Story of the Rise, Reign, and Ruin of Antinomians, Familists, and Libertines, that infected New England," a documentary kind of work with preface by Rev. Thomas Weld, published in 1644; and are reproduced in Felt's Ecclesiastical History of New England, I. 315–8. Mr. John Higginson was employed by the synod to report its proceedings in short-hand, and prepared the copy for the press; but it was not printed. Mass. Records, II. 52.

[2] The number of churches then existing appears to have been, — in Massachusetts Bay, twenty-nine; in Maine, one; in New Hampshire, three; in Plymouth, ten; in Connecticut, ten; total, fifty-three.

[3] Winthrop's Journal, of the dates specified.

[4] Mass. Records, III. 70–2.

[5] Results of Three Synods. Ed. 1725, p. iii.

Court, which, in 1649, commended it to the "judicious and pious consideration of the several churches." It was generally approved; was endorsed by subsequent councils, and became the exponent of the Congregational polity.

There was no general synod or council from that of 1648 to the Convention at Albany in 1852. But there were partial synods at several times, whose results were so important as to require notice.

The Synod of 1662 was confined to Massachusetts. It was called by the General Court's "order and desire," as declared on the thirty-first day of December, 1661, and met at Boston, consisting of above seventy elders and messengers, on the tenth day of March, 1662. On the next day, finding that the questions before them required more time than could be then given, the Synod adjourned to the tenth day of June. It then met, and again adjourned on the fourth day of July; assembled on the ninth day of September, and soon closed its sessions.

The two questions submitted to this Synod by the General Court, were, 1. Who are the subjects of baptism? 2. Whether, according to the word of God, there ought to be a consociation of churches, and what should be the manner of it?[1] In reply to the first, the synod recommended the disastrous "half-way covenant;" by which, persons baptized in infancy, and therefore members of the church, might "own the covenant," if not scandalous in their lives, without coming into full communion; and might thus be entitled to have their children baptized. It met with strong opposition, and never universally prevailed. Upon the second question, the Synod recommended nothing materially different from the Platform of 1648.

The result was submitted to the General Court in October, 1662, was ordered to be printed, with a preface by Mr. Mitchell, and was commended "unto the consideration of all the churches and people of this jurisdiction."[2]

The Synod of 1679–80, known as the "Reforming Synod," was also confined to Massachusetts. It was called by the General Court, at its session of May, 1679, upon "a motion made by some of the reverend elders,"[3] and met at Boston, on the

[1] Mass. Records, v. IV. part II. 30. [2] Same, p. 60, 62.
[3] Mass. Records, V. 215.

tenth day of September. Rev. John Sherman and Rev. Urian Oakes were moderators. The questions before it were, 1. What are the evils that have provoked the Lord to bring his judgments on New England? 2. What is to be done, that so these evils may be reformed? The Synod held two sessions; unanimously approved the Platform of 1648; spent "several days"[1] in discussing the questions presented; and adjourned on the 19th. The result, which was drawn up by Increase Mather, was presented to the General Court, October 15, 1679,[2] which commended them to the "serious consideration of all the churches and people of this jurisdiction," and ordered the report to be printed.

The same Synod held a second session, on the twelfth of May, 1680,—Increase Mather, moderator,—and "consulted and considered of a Confession of Faith."[3] It adopted, with slight variations, the Confession consented to by the Congregational Churches of England, at the Savoy, in 1658, which was, "for the most part, some small variations excepted, the same with that which was agreed upon first by the Assembly at Westminster, and was approved of by the Synod at Cambridge, in New England, Anno 1648.[4] "That little variation," says the Synod, "which we have made from the one, in compliance with the other, may be seen by those who please to compare them." This Confession was ordered, by the General Court,[5] to be printed.

The Synod, which met at Saybrook, in 1708, was confined to Connecticut. It was called, May 24, 1708, by the Legislature, which had been "made sensible of the defects of discipline in the churches of this government, arising from the want of more explicit asserting of the rules given for that end in the Holy Scriptures, from which would arise a permanent establishment among ourselves, a good and regular issue in cases subject to ecclesiastical discipline, glory to Christ our head, and edification to his members." The Legislature directed that the ministers of the several counties should meet at the county towns, with such messengers as the churches should send, consider and agree upon methods and rules of ecclesiastical discipline, and

[1] Results of Three Synods, Ed. 1725, p. vi.
[2] Mass. Records, V. 244.
[3] Preface to Result.
[4] Ibid.
[5] Mass. Records, V. 287.

appoint two or more of their number to meet at Saybrook; there to "draw a form of ecclesiastical discipline," to be laid before the Legislature at its October session.

The Synod met at Saybrook on the ninth of September. Rev. James Noyes, of Stonington, and Rev. Thomas Buckingham, of Saybrook, were moderators. The first act of this Synod was to accept the Confession of Faith set forth by the Massachusetts Synod of 1680. The second, was to "agree, also, that the Heads of Agreement assented to by the United Ministers, formerly called Presbyterian and Congregational, be observed by the churches throughout this Colony;" the Heads of Agreement adopted in London, in 1691. The main work, however, was the adoption of fifteen "Articles of Discipline," which established the consociation system. The entire platform was reported to the Legislature, at its October session; which ordained "that all the churches within this government, that are, or shall be, thus united in doctrine, worship, and discipline, be, and for the future shall be, owned and acknowledged established by law."[1]

More than two hundred years had elapsed before the American churches again met in council. The third general Synod,[2] known as "a Convention of Ministers and Delegates of Congregational Churches in the United States;"[3] met "in accordance with a call issued by direction of the General Association of New York." It assembled in Albany, N. Y., on the fifth day of October, 1852; consisted of four hundred and sixty-three elders and messengers from churches in seventeen States; chose Rev. William T. Dwight, D. D., of Maine, President, and Rev. Noah Porter, D. D., of Connecticut, and Rev. Asa Turner of Iowa, Vice-Presidents; and dissolved on the eighth day of October.

[1] See Historical Discourse, by Rev. Leonard Bacon, D. D., in Contributions to the Ecclesiastical History of Connecticut.

[2] Proceedings.

[3] The number of churches then existing in the United States has not been computed with accuracy. They numbered, probably, not far from two thousand. An estimate by Rev. Joseph S. Clark, D. D., in 1847, made the number to be one thousand five hundred and ninety-five, at that date. Careful statistics found in 1858, two thousand three hundred and eighty-five. In the year 1865, that of the National Council at Boston, the number was two thousand seven hundred and twenty-three (not including, of course, the churches outside the limits of the United States), with two hundred and sixty-three thousand two hundred and ninety-six members; and of ministers, two thousand eight hundred and two.

The main subjects upon which the Convention acted, were, 1. The subject of aiding feeble churches at the West, in building church edifices. 2. The construction and practical operation of the "Plan of Union between Presbyterians and Congregationalists," agreed upon by the General Assembly of the Presbyterian Church and the General Association of Connecticut in the year 1801.

Upon the first, the Convention adopted a plan for raising the sum of fifty thousand dollars at once, and for its apportionment and use.

Upon the second, the Convention found that the Plan had been repudiated by the General Assembly before the schism of 1838, but was acknowledged as in force by one branch of that church; that although so acknowledged, it was not maintained in its integrity, and that its operation was now "unfavorable to the spread of and permanence of the Congregational polity, and even to the real harmony of these Christian communities;" and therefore unanimously declared its continuance to be inexpedient.

It will thus be seen that the Council, whose proceedings are published in this volume, is the fourth General Synod or Council in the history of the American Congregational Churches.

Debates and Proceedings.

PRELIMINARY PROCEEDINGS.

THE PROPOSAL.

THE circumstances of the country, emerging as it was from the war by whose success the existence and safety of the nation were to be assured, had led to a wide-spread feeling that the Congregational Churches of the United States ought to consult together upon their duties and opportunities. Suggestions to this effect were repeatedly made. Recognizing this feeling, THE CONVENTION OF THE CONGREGATIONAL CHURCHES OF THE NORTH-WEST, — a body organized with special reference to the Chicago Theological Seminary, — at its Triennial Meeting held in April, 1864, adopted the following: —

WHEREAS, By the present war, the structure of society and of ecclesiastical organization is being dissolved or greatly changed through a large section of the United States, and the shackles are being struck from millions of slaves; and

WHEREAS, Thus vast regions and populations are being opened to free thought, speech, and free missions, that have heretofore been sealed against them; and

WHEREAS, Ideas and emigration from the Free States are likely to follow the triumph of the Union cause southward; therefore be it

Resolved, 1. That it is the duty of the Congregational churches of the United States to inquire what is their duty in this vast and solemn crisis, such as comes only once in ages, and what new efforts, measures, and policies they may owe to this condition of affairs, — this new genesis of nations.

Resolved, 2. That the crisis demands general consultation, co-operation, and concert among our churches, and to these ends, requires extensive correspondence among our ecclesiastical associations, or the assembling of a National Congregational Convention.

Resolved, 3. That we believe no ecclesiastical order has a right to exist which has not also the right and duty of self-extension, nor will any such order prosper that does not recognize and assert such right and duty.

Resolved, 4. That it is due the principles of church order which we hold, and our convictions of their vital value and vast benefits, that we aim by all proper means to diffuse them; and that recognizing no restrictive limit of section or race, we believe them to be the universal right and property of the church of Christ, and the race of man.

Resolved, 5. That we believe it due to our principles, especially in this present crisis, that there be a more general and thorough indoctrination in them of our Theological Seminaries, our Ministry, and our Churches, and that more of general and national concert and co-operation should, by correspondence and convention, be secured among us, — especially for missionary and aggressive action, — an action which shall bear, together with the gospel, those ideas and principles of church order which we believe best adapted to diffuse with evangelical truth, evangelical liberty, and most beneficially to organize both church and society.

THE GENERAL ASSOCIATION OF ILLINOIS, at its session held in Quincy, May 27, 1864, upon consideration of the above proposal, adopted the following, which had been reported by Rev. J. M. Sturtevant, D. D., chairman of a committee to whom the subject had been referred: —

WHEREAS, This Association adopts the sentiments and views in said resolutions expressed, and desires to see them carried into practical effect; therefore,

Resolved, 1. That a National Convention of Congregationalists be invited to assemble at Springfield, Mass., or Albany, N. Y., on the first Tuesday, the 6th day of September next, or at such other time and place as may be agreed upon after correspondence with the brethren in other parts of the country.

Resolved, 2. That a Committee of three be appointed by the Association to lay this proposition before other General Associations, Conferences and Conventions hereafter to meet, and to act with any Committees which they may appoint, in fixing definitely the time and place of meeting, and in making all other necessary arrangements for the same.

Resolved, 3. That this Association recommend, as the basis of the Convention, the following, viz.: That each Orthodox Congregational Church in the United States, and the British Provinces of North America, be invited to send as delegates their acting pastor or pastors, and one other member; and to provide, if necessary, for paying their expenses to and from the Convention.

Resolved, 4. That copies of this Minute be transmitted to religious newspapers of our denomination, for insertion.

THE CONGREGATIONAL CONFERENCE OF OHIO, at its session held in Springfield, June 10, 1864, approved of the proposal, and adopted also the following: —

Resolved, That the Ohio Congregational Conference, in accordance with the wishes of the pastors and delegates of the Cleveland churches represented here, tender a cordial invitation to the churches of our faith and order throughout the country, to meet at Cleveland, at whatever time may be determined by general correspondence.

These papers were forwarded to the General Associations and Conferences throughout the country, and met with an almost unanimous approval by these bodies at their several sessions. The General Association of Indiana ratified the proposal, May 20; the General Association of Michigan, May 21; the General Association of Iowa, June 3; the Congregational Conference of Rhode Island, June 15; the General Conference of Maine, June 21; the General Association of Connecticut, June 23; the General Convention of Vermont, June 23; the General Association of Massachusetts, June 30; the General Association of New York, September 20; and the General Conference of Minnesota, October 14. The General Association of New Hampshire, August 25, put on record that it had "failed to appreciate the reasons for the call of such a convention, especially in the present juncture of affairs, and respectfully decline further action with reference to it;" but the united sentiment of the churches of that State was subsequently found to be in hearty co-operation with the proposal. The several bodies appointed committees to represent them, with power to unite in calling the proposed convention.

Upon the suggestion of such delegates as met at New Haven, in July, 1864, on the occasion of the annual commencement of Yale College, the Trustees of THE AMERICAN CONGREGATIONAL UNION invited the several committees to meet in conference in the Broadway Tabernacle Church, in the city of New York; to which end, their committee issued the following letter:—

NEW YORK, October 1st, 1865.

DEAR SIR:—As a Committee of the American Congregational Union, we invite you to attend a conference of the State Committees, appointed with reference to a NATIONAL CONGREGATIONAL CONVENTION, to be held at the Broadway Tabernacle Church, in this city, on Wednesday, the 16th day of November next, at 10 A. M.

The time and place of holding the Convention, the basis of representation in the body, the subjects proper to be mentioned in the call as a guide to its deliberations, are topics that demand careful thought and mature counsel. In this view, the preliminary conference has been appointed at a time remote from any general ecclesiastical preoccupation, and at a place where ready communication can be had with the officers of such benevolent societies as are directly interested in the Convention and its objects. In the present condition of the country, this movement is so important to the future of Congregationalism that we earnestly hope every member of each State committee will come to the conference in November, even at great personal inconvenience.

We can not doubt that the State bodies will reimburse the traveling expenses of their representatives, upon this momentous errand of the churches; and, in behalf of the Broadway Tabernacle Church, we cordially proffer you their hospitality during the session of the conference. Please send an immediate answer, that you may be advised in season where you will be entertained.

Respectfully yours,

William G. Lambert.
William Allen.
Joseph P. Thompson.

P. S. — Please address,

"Wm. G. Lambert, *Chairman, &c.*,
81 Worth Street, New York."

The committees, unanimously accepting the invitation, met at that time and place.

THE CONFERENCE OF COMMITTEES.

The various committees having assembled in the Broadway Tabernacle Church, New York, November 16, 1864, Rev. Joseph P. Thompson, D. D., of New York, called the conference to order, and made statements regarding the origin of the meeting.

THE ROLL.

It appeared that the following persons were present, either as members of committees, or representing churches in States where no general organizations exist: —

Maine — Rev. George E. Adams, D. D., Brunswick; Rev. Alfred E. Ives, Castine; Dea. Simon Page, Hallowell.

New Hampshire — Rev. Nathaniel Bouton, D. D., Concord; Rev. Henry E. Parker, Concord; Rev. William T. Savage, Franklin.

Vermont — J. G. Stimson, Esq., Waterbury.

Massachusetts — Rev. Alonzo H. Quint, New Bedford; Rev. Emerson Davis, D. D., Westfield; Rev. Isaac P. Langworthy, Chelsea; Rev.

Joshua W. Wellman, Newton; Rev. Nathaniel H. Eggleston, Stockbridge.

RHODE ISLAND — Rev. Constantine Blodgett, D. D., Pawtucket; Rev. Alexander H. Clapp, Providence.

CONNECTICUT — Rev. Leonard Bacon, D. D., New Haven; Rev. William T. Eustis, Jr., New Haven; Rev. Joel Hawes, D. D., Hartford; Rev. John P. Gulliver, Norwich.

NEW YORK — Rev. Ray Palmer, D. D., Albany; Rev. William I. Budington, D. D., Brooklyn; Rev. Joseph P. Thompson, D. D., New York; Rev. Jeremiah Butler, Fairport; Rev. L. Smith Hobart, Syracuse.

NEW JERSEY — Rev. William B. Brown, Newark.

OHIO — Rev. Israel W. Andrews, D. D., Marietta; Rev. James A. Thome, Cleveland; Douglas Putnam, Esq., Harmar.

MICHIGAN — Rev. Philo R. Hurd, Romeo; Rev. Sereno W. Streeter, Union City; Rev. James S. Hoyt, Port Huron.

ILLINOIS — Rev. Julian M. Sturtevant, D. D., Jacksonville; Rev. Flavel Bascom, Princeton; Charles G. Hammond, Esq., Chicago.

WISCONSIN — Rev. W. DeLoss Love, Milwaukee; Dea. Edward M. Danforth, Oconomowoc; George E. Sickles, Esq., Waukesha.

MISSOURI — J. B. Turner, Esq., St. Louis.

MINNESOTA — Rev. William R. Stevens, Rochester.

PENNSYLVANIA — Rev. Burdett Hart, Philadelphia; Rev. Edward Hawes, Philadelphia.

Other brethren present were afterwards invited to sit as Honorary Members, viz.: —

Rev. Milton Badger, D. D., New York; Rev. David B. Coe, D. D., New York; Rev. Daniel P. Noyes, New York; Rev. Theron Baldwin, D. D., New York; Rev. Absalom Peters, D. D. New York; Dea. William G. Lambert, New York; William Allen, Esq., New York; Seth B. Hunt, Esq., New York; Rev. William Clift, New York; Rev. Henry G. Ludlow, Oswego, N. Y.; Rev. Michael Strieby, Newark, N. J.; Rev. George Whipple, Newark, N. J.; Rev. Increase N. Tarbox, Boston, Mass.; Rev. Rufus Anderson, D. D., Boston, Mass.

ORGANIZATION.

Rev. Isaac P. Langworthy, Rev. L. Smith Hobart, and Rev. Julian M. Sturtevant, D. D., were appointed a committee to nominate the permanent officers of the conference.

This committee reported Rev. Leonard Bacon, D. D., for moderator; Charles G. Hammond, Esq., for assistant moderator; Rev. Philo R. Hurd for scribe; and Rev. Nathaniel H. Eggleston for assistant scribe. The report was accepted and adopted. The conference was opened with prayer by Rev. Joel Hawes, D. D.

Rev. George E. Adams, D. D., Rev. John P. Gulliver, Rev. Flavel Bascom, Rev. Joseph P. Thompson, D. D., and Rev. Julian M. Sturtevant, D. D., were appointed a business committee.

The following resolution was adopted: —

Resolved, That since this body is composed of committees appointed for free consultation in relation to the matters referred to them, we deem it important that there should be a distinct understanding that their business is of a private nature, and that it would be considered wholly improper that any report of its proceedings should be made public, except by the direction of the body itself.

Rev. Ray Palmer, D. D., Rev. Isaac P. Langworthy, and Rev. Nathaniel H. Eggleston, were appointed a committee on Credentials and Invitations. This committee reported the following resolutions, which were adopted: —

Resolved, 1. That this body is understood to be composed of the committees regularly appointed by the General Associations and Conferences of the several States and Territories, with such other persons as, by a liberal construction, may be regarded as representing the churches in the States or Territories from which they came.

Resolved, 2. That the Secretaries of the American Home Missionary Society, of the American Missionary Association, of the Education Society, and of the Society for the Promotion of Collegiate and Theological Education at the West, be invited to sit and deliberate with this conference.

Rev. Absalom Peters, D. D., Rev. William Clift, Dea. William G. Lambert, and William Allen, Esq., being present, were invited to sit as honorary members; and the same invitation was afterwards extended to Rev. Henry G. Ludlow, Rev. Rufus Anderson, D. D., and Seth B. Hunt, Esq.

The Business Committee reported a docket of subjects proposed for the consideration of the conference.

THE HOLDING OF A CONVENTION — ITS BASIS, CALL, AND BUSINESS.

The question, Shall there be a National Congregational Convention? was unanimously answered in the affirmative.

In regard to the mode of constituting the convention, the following resolution was adopted: —

Resolved, That the convention be based upon a representation of Congregational churches, having a recognized fellowship in doctrine and order; and that a committee be appointed to prepare and report the terms of such representation.

Rev. Alonzo H. Quint, Rev. Isaac P. Langworthy, and Rev. Julian M. Sturtevant, D. D., were appointed that committee; to which Rev. John P. Gulliver was afterwards added. The question of the time and place of holding the convention was also referred to this committee.

Rev. Leonard Bacon, D. D., Rev. Julian M. Sturtevant, D. D., and Rev. Alfred E. Ives, were appointed a committee to prepare a call for the convention.

The moderator, Rev. Leonard Bacon, D. D., Rev. Julian M. Sturtevant, D. D., Rev. William I. Budington, D. D., Rev. Joseph P. Thompson, D. D., and Rev. Alonzo H. Quint, were appointed a committee to nominate suitable persons to present to the National Convention, when it shall assemble, the topics which may be suggested by this conference, for its consideration.

The conference adjourned to meet on Thursday morning, at 9½ o'clock.

Thursday Morning.

The conference met, according to adjournment. The meeting was opened with prayer by Rev. Constantine Blodgett, D. D.

The minutes of the previous meeting were read and approved.

TOPICS.

The conference entered upon an inquiry relative to the topics which it should recommend for the consideration of the National Convention; and it was voted, that the call for the convention suggest the following subjects, to wit: —

1. The work of evangelization, in the West and South, and in foreign lands.

2. Church-building.

3. Education for the ministry, — in colleges, theological seminaries, or otherwise; and ministerial support.

4. Local and parochial evangelization.

5. The expediency of issuing a statement of Congregational church polity.

6. The expediency of setting forth a declaration of the

Christian faith, as held in common by the Congregational churches.

7. The classification of benevolent organizations to be recommended to the patronage of the churches.

TERMS OF REPRESENTATION. — TIME AND PLACE OF MEETING.

The committee on the terms of representation in the convention, and on the time and place of its meeting, made the following report, which was accepted and adopted: —

WHEREAS, the Congregational churches recognize two, and only two, fundamental principles of church polity, viz. (1,) That the local church is the only organized and authoritative ecclesiastical body established by Christ and his apostles, complete in itself for all church purposes, and with an authority which can not be delegated; and (2,) That all churches hold relations of fellowship one with another, under which it is one of their duties and privileges to meet for counsel in cases of general moment; therefore,

Resolved, 1, That the National Council now proposed is wholly destitute of any power or authority whatever over individuals, churches, or other organizations; and, (2,) That the churches are to meet in the proposed council, to consider the present exigencies and opportunities of the kingdom of Christ.

Resolved, 2, That the National Council of Congregational Churches, now to be called, be selected by the churches, assembled, for convenience as to numbers, in local conferences; and be made up of pastors and delegates of churches, according to the following ratio of representation: that the churches represented in each district, conference, or association of churches, select in conference one pastor and one delegate, or two delegates, for each ten churches, and for any remaining fraction greater than one-half of that number; each conference or association of churches being allowed at least one pastor and one delegate.

Resolved, 3, That in localities where no such bodies exist, representing churches, the committees constituting this conference be requested to secure a representation of the churches within such districts, on the above basis.

Resolved, 4, That the committee from each State be authorized and requested to issue, at an early time, prior to the meeting of conferences, circular letters, embodying the call for the council, and pointing out in what manner the delegates are to be selected in each State or Territory, in accordance with the above basis of representation, to be forwarded to each church for action, as well as to the several conferences; and that they use their best endeavors to secure a complete representation.

Resolved, 5, That the Council meet in the city of Boston, Mass., or in such other place as the committee of arrangements may designate, on the second Wednesday of June, 1865.

The following resolutions were adopted: —

SPECIAL SERVICE FOR DEVOTION.

Resolved, That it be recommended to the National Council of Congregational churches, when assembled, to appoint, early in its session, a special service of devotion, for the acknowledgment of the marvelous and merciful dealings of Almighty God with the nation, in connection with the war, and for supplicating a gracious dispensation of the Spirit of God upon the land, that our restored national unity may be consecrated in righteousness, and in the peace and joy of the Holy Ghost.

COLLECTION FOR EXPENSES.

Resolved, That we recommend to all our churches to take up a collection, on or near the second Sabbath in May, before the meeting of the proposed Council, to assist in paying the traveling expenses of ministers coming from a considerable distance who may need such aid, and also to defray the incidental expenses of the Council itself; the avails of these collections to be distributed by a committee of the proposed Council; and any surplus that may remain, to be placed in the hands of the Congregational Union, in aid of church-building.

COMMITTEES ON TOPICS.

The following persons were appointed committees to present to the Council the subjects suggested for its consideration: —

On Evangelization in the West and South.

Warren Currier, Esq., St. Louis, Mo.; Rev. Julian M. Sturtevant, D. D., Jacksonville, Ill.; Rev. Reuben Gaylord, Omaha, Neb. Ter.; Rev. Thomas E. Bliss, Memphis, Tenn.; Rev. Flavel Bascom, Princeton, Ill.

Parochial Evangelization.

Rev. Daniel P. Noyes, New York; Rev. Henry M. Dexter, Boston, Mass.

Education for the Ministry.

Rev. Ray Palmer, D. D., Albany, New York; Rev. John P. Gulliver, Norwich, Conn.; Rev. Franklin W. Fisk, Chicago, Ill.

Ministerial Support.

Rev. George Shepard, D. D., Bangor, Me.; Charles G. Hammond, Esq., Chicago, Ill.; Gov. William A. Buckingham, Norwich, Conn.; Samuel Holmes, Esq., New York; Douglas Putnam, Esq., Marietta, Ohio.

Statement of Church Polity.

Rev. Leonard Bacon, D. D., New Haven, Conn.; Rev. Alonzo H.

Quint, New Bedford, Mass.; Rev. Henry M. Storrs, D. D., Cincinnati, Ohio.

Declaration of Christian Faith.

Rev. Joseph P. Thompson, D. D., New York; Rev. George P. Fisher, Yale College; Rev. Edward A. Lawrence, East Windsor Hill, Conn.

Systematizing Benevolent Contributions.

Rev. Israel W. Andrews, D. D., Marietta, Ohio; Rev. Ray Palmer, D. D., Albany, N. Y.; Rev. Henry E. Parker, Concord, N. H.; William G. Lambert, Esq., New York.

The following persons were appointed a Committee of Arrangements for the meeting of the Council: —

Rev. Andrew L. Stone, D. D., Boston; Rev. Edward N. Kirk, D. D., Boston; Rev. George W. Blagden, D. D., Boston; Rev. Henry M. Dexter, Boston; Rev. Elihu P. Marvin, Medford; Rev. Rufus Anderson, D. D., Roxbury; Rev. Isaac P. Langworthy, Chelsea; Rev. Joshua W. Wellman, Newton; Charles Stoddard, Esq., Boston; Julius A. Palmer, Esq., Boston; Edward S. Tobey, Esq., Boston; J. Russell Bradford, Esq., Roxbury; Henry Hill, Esq., Saxonville.

PUBLICATION OF THE CALL.

Rev. Daniel P. Noyes, Samuel Holmes, Esq., A. S. Barnes, Esq., and William Allen, Esq., were appointed a committee to print the call, and to supply the State committees with copies for distribution, and to secure a representation of the churches in those States and Territories which are not represented by committees in this body.

REPORT ON THE CALL.

The committee on the call for the Council made a report, which was accepted and adopted for substance, and was recommitted for completion.

PREACHER.

Rev. Joseph P. Thompson, D. D., Rev. John P. Gulliver, Rev. Alonzo H. Quint, and Rev. Flavel Bascom, were appointed a committee to nominate a preacher to open the Council with a sermon. The committee reported the name of Rev. Julian M. Sturtevant, D. D., of Jacksonville, Ill., as principal, and Rev. Truman M. Post, D. D., of St. Louis, Mo., as alternate. The report was accepted and adopted.

PUBLICATION OF DOINGS.

The following resolution was passed: —

Resolved, That the proceedings of this conference be published in such newspapers as may desire to publish them, and in the Congregational Quarterly; and that the publishers of the Quarterly be requested to print one thousand copies extra for the use of the Council. Also, that all the restrictions heretofore imposed upon the publication of the proceedings of this conference be removed.

TREASURER.

Henry Hill, Esq., of Saxonville, Mass., was appointed the treasurer of the contingent fund to be raised for the expenses of the delegates and of the Council.

THANKS.

The following resolution of thanks was unanimously adopted: —

Resolved, That the heartfelt thanks of this conference are tendered to Rev. Joseph P. Thompson, D. D., William G. Lambert, Esq., and William Allen, Esq., and to the members of the Broadway Tabernacle Society, for their wise arrangements and generous and ample provision for the accommodation and comfort of this body during its deliberations.

ADJOURNMENT.

The conference adjourned. Concluded with prayer by Rev. Ray Palmer, D. D., and the benediction by the moderator.

LEONARD BACON, *Moderator*.
CHAS. G. HAMMOND, *Assist. Moderator*.

PHILO R. HURD, *Scribe*.
NATH'L H. EGGLESTON, *Assistant Scribe*.

LETTERS OF INVITATION.

The committee intrusted with that duty prepared the following invitation, which, after being submitted to and approved by all the members of the preliminary conference, was sent to the churches by the instrumentality of the several State committees, who placed a sufficient number of copies in the hands of the scribes of the several local conferences (or other parties where no conferences exist), to reach each church: —

INVITATION.

Those Congregational churches in the United States of America which are in recognized fellowship and co-operation through the General associations, conferences, or conventions in the several States, are hereby respectfully and affectionately invited to meet by their representatives in a National Council at Boston, Massachusetts, on the fourteenth day of June, A. D. 1865, at 3 o'clock, P. M., in the Old South Meeting-House.

This invitation is the result of a request proceeding from a representative convention of Congregational churches in the North-west. It has been considered and approved in a meeting of committees representing the Congregational churches and ministry associated for fellowship and co-operation in the several States; and on us whose names are undersigned, has been devolved the duty of convening the Council, of defining the mode in which the churches may be conveniently and equally represented, and of proposing to the churches, and through them to their assembled delegates, the subjects which require at this time the deliberate attention and advice of such an assembly.

Inasmuch as the Congregational churches acknowledge and hold that the local church is the only ecclesiastical body established by Christ and his apostles, — a body complete in itself, and invested with an authority under Christ which can not be delegated; and, at the same time, that the churches thus constituted are in relations of fellowship one with another, under which it is their duty and their privilege to meet for mutual counsel in cases of general interest and common responsibility; it will be universally understood that the National Council now proposed is destitute of all power or authority over individuals or churches, or over other organizations, and that the churches complying with this invitation will meet by their pastors and other messengers only for the purpose of considering the present crisis in the history of our country and of the kingdom of Christ, and the responsibilities which the crisis imposes upon us who have inherited the polity and the faith of our Pilgrim Fathers.

As it is impossible for every church to be directly represented in any national assembly, we propose that neighboring churches, within such districts as may be found convenient, meet by their pastors and delegates in particular councils or conferences for the purpose of designating the elders and brethren who shall assemble in the National Council; and that the ratio of representation be two delegates (one of them a pastor if convenient) for every ten churches, and for every remaining fraction greater than half that number.

We propose that where county or district conferences or other like associations of churches have been instituted, the churches of each conference or association meet according to their usual method, and elect their delegates in the ratio above mentioned, — it being understood that the churches of every such conference, though less than ten in number, may be represented by a pastor and another delegate.

We propose that where the churches are not accustomed to meet statedly in organized conferences, they be invited to meet in special councils for this purpose.

The subjects on which it seems to us desirable that a National Council of our churches should deliberate and advise at the present crisis are these: —

First, The work of home evangelization devolving on our churches, — a work including all the efforts which they are making, or ought to make, for the complete Christianization of our country; particularly by planting churches and other institutions of Christian civilization at the West and at the South; by co-operating in labors for the instruction and elevation of the millions whose yoke of bondage GOD has broken; by helping to build houses of worship in destitute places; by encouraging and guiding each other in parochial plans and labors for Christ; and by providing the wisest and most efficient methods for the supply and support of an able, learned, and godly ministry.

Secondly, The setting-forth of a simple declaration or testimony concerning the evangelical faith and the ecclesiastical polity, which are the actual basis of mutual confidence and helpfulness, and of co-operation, among the Congregational churches of the United States. The expediency and desirableness of such a declaration — how far it may tend to make the continued orthodoxy of our churches, and the apostolic simplicity and efficiency of their polity, more widely and clearly understood among Christians not in our connection, and how far it may tend to a more complete harmony and co-operation among ourselves, as well as to a more just conception of our system in its capability of expansion and of progress — will be the more wisely considered by the Council, if, in the meantime, the matter shall have been duly considered by the churches.

Thirdly, The responsibilities of these churches in relation to spreading the gospel through the world. It can not be forgotten that the work of missions from the United States to the heathen in foreign lands, was first undertaken by the American Board of Commissioners for Foreign Missions, originating in the General Association of Massachusetts, appealing to the Congregational churches for their contributions, and serving them as their agent and almoner. Nor should we cease to praise God that the same institution, now venerable with the years of more than half a century, and illustrious with the success which it has gained by the favor of God's providence and the outpourings of his Spirit, is still the medium of a visible and most fraternal co-operation not only among our churches, but also between us and those Presbyterian churches which are most nearly related to our own in their ecclesiastical traditions and their evangelical sympathies; and that, even in these times of national conflict, it has been enabled to carry on its work without interruption or curtailment, and has been gaining a stronger hold on the confidence of those who pray continually

"Thy kingdom come." But if we believe that in the new era which the termination of the present conflict must inaugurate, our country, relieved of the shame that has impaired its influence and the burthens that have impeded its progress, is to stand in new relations to the world, we can not but recognize the crisis as summoning our churches to inquire, devoutly, and with careful and extended consultation, as well as with mutual incitements to love and zeal, what God would have them do, henceforward, in the work of preaching to all nations the gospel of his kingdom.

While we commend these subjects to the attention of the churches and of the Council which we invite them to constitute, we may also commend to the Council, when assembled, the fitness of appointing, early in its sessions, a special service of praise and prayer, for the acknowledgment of the marvelous and the merciful dealings of God with the nation in connection with the war, and for supplicating a gracious dispensation of the Spirit of God upon the land, that our restored national unity may be consecrated in righteousness, and in the peace and joy of the Holy Ghost.

In communicating to the churches this proposal for a National Council, we may be permitted to express our hope that they will seriously consider the occasion on which it is addressed to them, and the subjects on which the Council is invited to deliberate and advise. We ask that the proposal may be in the churches, as it has been in our consultations, a subject of humble and earnest prayer; and especially that on the second Lord's day in the month of May next, there may be united supplication throughout our country, and among our missionaries also in foreign lands, beseeching the God of all grace to pour out his Holy Spirit on the Council then so soon to meet, so that the result may be a great reviving and advancement of his work.

It is also requested that on or near the day just mentioned, May 14, contributions be received in the churches generally to a contingent fund for the incidental expenses of the Council, and for relieving the traveling expenses of ministers who may attend as delegates from distant parts of the country, — it being understood that the fund thus created shall be distributed by a committee of the Council itself, and that any remainder shall be entrusted to the Congregational Union, in aid of the church-building charity conducted by that Society. Henry Hill Esq., has consented to serve as treasurer of the contingent fund; and it is important that contributions, when made, be promptly remitted to him at No. 28 Cornhill, Boston, Mass.

We have only to add that we have made arrangements to lay before the Council, when assembled, such statements of facts, and such suggestions, concerning the matters referred to it, as shall afford material for intelligent deliberation, and facilitate the dispatch of business.

This invitation was agreed upon in a consultation of committees at the Chapel of the Broadway Tabernacle, in the city of New York, on the seventeenth day of November, A. D. 1864. In testimony whereof we have hereunto subscribed our names.

George E. Adams, *Brunswick*, Alfred E. Ives, *Castine*, Simon Page, *Hallowell*, Samuel Harris, *Bangor*, Woodbury Davis, *Portland*,	Committee of the General Conference of Maine.
Nathaniel Bouton, *Concord*, Henry Parker, " William T. Savage, *Franklin*,	Committee of Hopkinton Association, New Hampshire.
J. G. Stimson, *Waterbury*, Silas Aiken, *Rutland*, Jonathan Clement, *Woodstock*,	Committee of General Association of Vermont.
Alonzo H. Quint, *New Bedford*, Emerson Davis, *Westfield*, Isaac P. Langworthy, *Chelsea*, Joshua W. Wellman, *Newton*, Nath'l H. Eggleston, *Stockbridge*,	Committee of the General Association of Massachusetts.
Constantine Blodgett, *Pawtucket*, A. Huntington Clapp, *Providence*,	Committee of the Congregational Conference of Rhode Island.
Leonard Bacon, *New Haven*, William T. Eustis, Jr., *New Haven*, Joel Hawes, *Hartford*, John P. Gulliver, *Norwich*, Joseph Eldridge, *Norfolk*,	Committee of the General Association of Connecticut.
Ray Palmer, *Albany*, William I. Budington, *Brooklyn*, Joseph P. Thompson, *New York*, Jeremiah Butler, *Fairport*, L. Smith Hobart, *Syracuse*,	Committee of the General Association of New York.
William B. Brown, *Newark*,	New Jersey.
Israel W. Andrews, *Marietta*, James A. Thome, *Cleveland*, Douglas Putnam, *Harmar*, Henry M. Storrs, *Cincinnati*,	Committee of the General Conference of Ohio.
Philo R. Hurd, *Romeo*, Sereno W. Streeter, *Union City*, James S. Hoyt, *Port Huron*,	Committee of the General Association of Michigan.
Julian M. Sturtevant, *Jacksonville*, Flavel Bascom, *Princeton*, Charles G. Hammond, *Chicago*,	Committee of the General Association of Illinois.
Wm. DeLoss Love, *Milwaukee*, Edward M. Danforth, *Oconomowoc*, George E. Sickles, *Waukesha*,	Committee of the General Convention of Wisconsin.
J. B. Turner, *St. Louis*,	Missouri.
Wm. R. Stevens, *Rochester*,	Committee of the General Association of Minnesota.
Burdett Hart, *Philadelphia*, Edward Hawes, "	Pennsylvania.
Asa Turner, *Denmark*, Jesse Guernsey, *Dubuque*, Ozro French, *Blairstown*,	Committee of the General Association of Iowa.

In addition to the above, the following paper was signed by the several State committees, and forwarded to the several churches with the invitation : —

To the *Church in*

Brethren,

We transmit to you, for your consideration and action, a copy of the invitation which has been issued for a National Council of Congregational Churches to be convened at Boston, on the 14th day of June next.

If you approve the proposal, and desire to be represented in the Council at Boston, you are hereby invited to be present by your delegates in a conference of churches which will be held at on the day of at o'clock, for the purpose of uniting in the choice of Messengers to the National Council aforesaid.

The other churches invited to this conference are:—

. . . .

Should it be impracticable for a delegation from you to be present, we earnestly hope that you will certify by letter your desire to be represented according to the method proposed in the accompanying invitation, and will authorize the conference to act in your behalf.

Your brethren in the Lord,

} *Committee.*

P. S.—We enclose with this letter, for your convenience, a form of a certificate accrediting your delegates to the conference.

The form of certificate just alluded to was as follows:—

THIS CERTIFIES that the Church in desiring to be represented in the NATIONAL COUNCIL OF CONGREGATIONAL CHURCHES which is invited to assemble at Boston, in Massachusetts, on the 14th day of June, A. D. 1865, has appointed and its representatives to a conference of churches to be held at on the of for the choice of messengers to the National Council aforesaid.

Should the brethren above named be unable to attend, the delegates present in conference from other churches are hereby authorized to act for this church.

In behalf of the church,

Dated at 1865.

Still further to secure uniformity and promote convenience, the following form of credentials to the Council was prepared and distributed, to be signed and returned by the several scribes of conferences:—

THIS CERTIFIES that at a conference of churches held at on the of A. D. 1865, in which the following churches, to wit:—

. . . .

were represented by delegates elected to act as their representatives (or by letters authorizing the conference to act for them) in the choice of messengers to the NATIONAL COUNCIL OF CONGREGATIONAL CHURCHES which is to meet in Boston, in Massachusetts, on the 14th day of June next, the following brethren were chosen to be the messengers of the churches aforenamed in said National Council, to wit:—

By vote of the Churches in Conference,

Scribe.

RESPONSE FROM BOSTON.

The proposal to hold the session of the Council in Boston received a welcome answer from the churches in that city, and the following expression of their feelings was widely circulated:—

BOSTON, Jan. 16, 1865.

The Committee of Arrangements, appointed by the conference of State Committees held in New York in November last, to make arrangements for the Council of the Congregational Churches of the United States, which it appointed to meet in Boston on the 14th of June next, have corresponded with the Congregational churches in Boston in regard to holding the Council in this city. They have received a cordial response from them all, and have adopted the following minute of welcome to the National Council:—

"We regard the proposed Synod or General Council as an indispensable means of meeting our present responsibilities as a branch of the Church of Christ. The reasons for calling such an assembly appear to be weighty and urgent. To us, indeed, the call appears to have come from the Captain of our Salvation, who is summoning his churches to prepare for new services and new sacrifices.

"Averse to centralized power as is the genius of Christianity, yet it equally favors all that is expressive of the unity of faith and purpose in the Christian brotherhood. And when our Lord calls us to new forms of action, new enterprises, new expressions and applications of our distinctive principles, it is most becoming in us to convene our best and ablest men, both ministers and lay brethren, to confer on matters of common interest.

"In view of these considerations, this committee, representing the churches of this city, and in their behalf, invite the General Council to hold its sessions in Boston; cordially offering to it the use of our church edifices, and extending to its members the offer of our Christian hospitalities so long as the Council shall continue its sessions.

"We respectfully express our desire that the opening services may be held in the Old South Church, on account of its association with the sacred memory of the elders who 'by faith obtained a good report.'

"And may the Lord bestow upon each member of the council a full measure of his Spirit, that the body may be full of light, having discernment of the Master's will, simplicity of faith, largeness of heart, a full sense of responsibility in these peculiar times, wisdom in deliberation, and decision and power in uttering words of counsel and appeal to quicken and guide the churches.

"May this assembling of the representatives of the entire body of Congregationalists in our country be attended with the richest spiritual blessings to all our churches and to the country. We rejoice in the prospect of meeting our brethren, and the master in the midst of them."

ANDREW L. STONE,	JOSHUA W. WELLMAN,
EDWARD N. KIRK,	CHARLES STODDARD,
GEO. W. BLAGDEN,	JULIUS A. PALMER,
HENRY M. DEXTER,	EDWARD S. TOBEY,
ELIHU P. MARVIN,	J. RUSSELL BRADFORD,
RUFUS ANDERSON,	HENRY HILL,

ISAAC P. LANGWORTHY.

DEBATES AND PROCEEDINGS

OF

THE NATIONAL COUNCIL

OF

CONGREGATIONAL CHURCHES.

AT BOSTON, JUNE, A. D. 1865.

FIRST DAY, WEDNESDAY, JUNE 14, 3 P. M.

THE NATIONAL CONGREGATIONAL COUNCIL, convoked by delegation from the Congregational churches of the United States, in response to letters-missive agreed upon in a consultation of committees at the chapel of the Broadway Tabernacle, in the city of New York, on the seventeenth day of November, A. D. 1864, assembled in the Old South Meeting-house, in the city of Boston, Mass., on Wednesday, 14th June, 1865, at 3 o'clock, P. M.

The Council consisted of delegates from the churches (with their respective places of residence), as follows: —

CALIFORNIA.

Jacob Bacon, San Francisco.
Rev. Milton Badger, D. D. [of N. Y., representing Cal.]
Luther P. Fisher, Oakland.
Rev. Kinsley Twining, San Francisco.

COLORADO TERRITORY.

Rev. William Crawford, Central City.
Samuel Cushman, Jr., Black Hawk.

CONNECTICUT.

Dea. Charles Adams, Litchfield.
Rev. Walter S. Alexander, Pomfret.
Rev. Hiram P. Arms, D. D., Norwich Town.
Albert Austin, Suffield.
Rev. Frederick D. Avery, Columbia.
Rev. Leonard Bacon, D. D., New Haven.
Hon. Walter Booth, Meriden.
Hon. John Boyd, Winsted.
Gov. William A. Buckingham, Norwich.
Rev. Davis S. Brainerd, Old Lyme.
Rev. Enoch F. Burr, Lyme.
Dea. Philander Button, Greenwich.
Rev. Louis E. Charpiot, Stratford.
Rev. Amos S. Chesebrough, Glastenbury.
Rev. Malcolm M. G. Dana, Norwich.
Rev. Oliver S. Dean, Roxbury.
Rev. Andrew C. Denison, Portland.
Hon. Benjamin Douglas, Middletown.
Rev. Samuel W. S. Dutton, D. D., New Haven.
Rev. John Edgar, Falls Village.
Rev. Joseph Eldridge, D. D., Norfolk.
Rev. William T. Eustis, Jr., New Haven.
Rev. Thomas P. Field, D. D., New London.
Rev. Edwin R. Gilbert, Wallingford.
Rev. Leverett Griggs, Bristol.

Rev. John P. Gulliver, Norwich.
Hon. Henry P. Haven, New London.
Dea. Willis Hemingway, Jr., Fair Haven.
Rev. Jonathan L. Jenkins, Hartford.
Henry M. Knight, M. D., Salisbury.
Rev. Orpheus T. Lanphear, New Haven.
Prof. Edward A. Lawrence, D. D., East Windsor Hill.
Rev. Robert C. Learned, Plymouth.
Rev. Joel H. Linsley, D. D., Greenwich.
Hon. Samuel Miller, New Haven.
Rev. David Murdoch, New Milford.
Rev. George B. Newcomb, Bloomfield.
Rev. George A. Oviatt, Somers.
Rev. Levi L. Paine, Farmington.
Prof. Noah Porter, Jr., D. D., New Haven.
Dea. Selden M. Pratt, Center Brook.
E. Beecher Preston, Rockville.
Daniel C. Robinson, Esq., Brooklyn.
Dea. George W. Shelton, Birmingham.
Ralph D. Smith, Guilford.
Rev. George Soule, Hampton.
Dea. John Stevens, Cromwell.
Hon. Henry G. Taintor, Hampton.
Dea. Chester Talcott, North Coventry.
Rev. Jeremiah Taylor, D. D., Middletown.
Dudley R. Wheeler, North Stonington.
Rev. Elisha Whittlesey, Waterbury.
Rev. Samuel G. Willard, Willimantic.
Rev. Francis Williams, Chaplin.
Dea. John B. Woodford, Windsor.

DELAWARE.

Dea. Abner H. Bryant, Canterbury.

ILLINOIS.

Marshall Ayres, Griggsville.
Prof. Samuel C. Bartlett, D. D., Chicago.
Rev. Flavel Bascom, Princeton.
Rev. Edward Beecher, D. D., Galesburg.
Rev. Frederick W. Beecher, Kankakee.
Dea. Philo Carpenter, Chicago.
Rev. William Carter, Pittsfield.
Rev. N. Catlin Clark, Elgin.
Rev. Henry M. Daniels, Winnebago.
Rev. Andrew J. Drake, Atlanta.
Rev. Richard C. Dunn, Toulon.
Rev. Samuel Hopkins Emery, Quincy.
Rev. Henry M. Goodwin, Rockford.
Hon. Charles G. Hammond, Chicago.
Prof. Joseph Haven, D. D., Chicago.
Levi T. Hewins, M. D., Loda.
Rev. George B. Hubbard, Aurora.
Rev. Elisha Jenney, Galesburg.
Rev. Edwin N. Lewis, Ottawa.
Dea. Nelson Mason, Sterling.
Rev. Milo N. Miles, Geneseo.
Rev. Lucius H. Parker, Galesburg.
Rev. George C. Partridge, Batavia.
Rev. William W. Patton, D. D., Chicago.
Dea. Moses Pettengill, Peoria.
Rev. Lemuel Pomeroy, Wethersfield.
Rev. Samuel F. Porter, Wheaton.
Rev. George S. F. Savage, Chicago.
Joel K. Scarboro, Payson.
Dea. Brainerd Smith, Normal.
S. D. Stinson, Esq., Sandwich.
Pres. Julian M. Sturtevant, D. D., Jacksonville.
Rev. Lathrop Taylor, Farmington.
Rev. Henry M. Tupper, Waverly.
Prof. John C. Webster, Wheaton.
Rev. John W. White, Morrison.
Rev. Martin K. Whittlesey, Ottawa.
Martin Wright, Lee Center.
Rev. Samuel G. Wright, Dover.

INDIANA.

Rev. Nathaniel A. Hyde, Indianapolis.
Rev. John L. Jenkins, Kokomo.
Dea. A. G. Willard, Indianapolis.

IOWA.

Rev. Harvey Adams, Farmington.
Caleb B. Atkins, Glenwood.
Rev. George Bent, Burr Oak.
Rev. Henry L. Bullen, Durant.
Rev. Cornelius S. Cady, Maquoketa.
Rev. Joshua M. Chamberlain, Des Moines.
Rev. Samuel D. Cochran, Grinnell.
Rev. William L. Coleman, Mitchell.
Rev. Miner W. Fairfield, Lyons.
Dea. John G. Foote, Burlington.
Rev. Charles H. Gates, Oskaloosa.
Rev. James B. Gilbert, Lansing.
Rev. Jesse Guernsey, Dubuque.
Rev. Lemuel Jones, Bellevue.
Rev. Daniel Lane, Eddyville.
Rev. Orville W. Merrill, Anamosa.
Rev. John K. Nutting, Bradford.
Richard J. Patterson, M. D., Mount Pleasant.

Rev. Giles M. Porter, Garnavillo.
Dea. John Porter, Cedar Falls.
Rev. Julius A. Reed, Davenport.
Seth Richards, Bentonsport.
Rev. Alden B. Robbins, Muscatine.
Rev. Isaac Russell, Bowen's Prairie.
Rev. William Salter, D. D., Burlington.
Rev. Samuel P. Sloan, McGregor.
Fitch B. Stacy, Stacyville.
Rev. Chauncy Taylor, Algona.
Rev. Thomas Tenny, Plymouth.
Rev. John Todd, Tabor.
Rev. Asa Turner, Denmark.
Alfred Woods, Iowa Falls.

KANSAS.

Rev. Lewis Bodwell, Wyandotte.
Rev. Richard Cordley, Lawrence.
William Crosby, Grasshopper Falls.
Rev. James D. Liggett, Leavenworth.
Hon. Samuel C. Pomeroy (U. S. S.), Atchison.
William H. Watson, Leavenworth.

MAINE.

Rev. Geo. E. Adams, D. D., Brunswick.
Rev. Uriah Balkam, Lewiston.
Rev. Smith Baker, Jr., Veazie.
Rev. Joseph Bartlett, Buxton.
Dea. Jacob Blanchard, Blanchard.
Josiah Brown, Bethel.
Rev. Elbridge G. Carpenter, Houlton.
Rev. Benjamin C. Chase, Foxcroft.
Rev. Albert Cole, Cornish.
Rev. Temple Cutler, Skowhegan.
Rev. Edward F. Cutter, Rockland.
Rev. John Dinsmore, Winslow.
Dea. Elnathan F. Duren, Bangor.
Rev. Franklin E. Fellows, Kennebunk.
Rev. John O. Fiske, Bath.
Hon. Robert Goodenow, Farmington.
Prof. Samuel Harris, D. D., Bangor.
Rev. Josiah T. Hawes, Bridgeton Center.
Rev. Alfred E. Ives, Castine.
Rev. Seth H. Keeler, D. D., Calais.
Charles A. Lord, Portland.
Hon. Seth May, Auburn.
Rev. Wellington Newell, Brewer Village.
Dea. Simon Page, Hallowell.
Rev. Wooster Parker, Belfast.
Dea. Charles C. Sawyer, Saco.
Rev. Rufus M. Sawyer, York.
Rev. David Shepley, Yarmouth.
Rev. William T. Sleeper, Patten.
Charles A. Stackpole, Gorham.
Francis K. Swan, Calais.
Nathaniel T. Talbot, Rockport.
Joseph J. Taylor, New Castle.
Rev. Sewall Tenny, D. D., Ellsworth.
Hon. William W. Thomas, Portland.
Dea. Joseph Titcomb, Kennebunk.
Rev. Horace Toothaker, New Sharon.
Rev. George Leon Walker, Portland.
Rev. Benjamin G. Willey, East Sumner.

MARYLAND.

Rev. Edwin Johnson, Baltimore.
Nathaniel Noyes, "

MASSACHUSETTS.

Ebenezer Alden, M. D., Randolph.
Rev. Ebenezer Alden, Jr., Marshfield.
Rev. George Allen, Worcester.
Rev. Rufus Anderson, D. D., Boston.
John S. Andrews, M. D., Ashby.
Rev. George N. Anthony, Marlboro'.
Dea. Horace Armsby, Millbury.
Rev. Rowland Ayres, Hadley.
Rev. James M. Bacon, Essex.
Rev. William M. Barbour, South Danvers.
Rev. Willam Barrows, Reading.
Rev. Thomas C. Biscoe, Grafton.
Rev. Amos Blanchard, D. D., Lowell.
Dea. Wm. S. Bradbury, Westminster.
Rev. Samuel G. Buckingham, Springfield.
Timothy W. Carter, Chicopee.
Wm. C. Chapin, Lawrence.
Hon. Linus Child, Boston.
Hon. Henry H. Childs, Pittsfield.
Dea. John Clary, Conway.
Rev. Robert Crawford, D. D., Deerfield.
Dea. Walter Crocker, West Barnstable.
Rev. Christopher Cushing, North Brookfield.
Rev. J. Jay Dana, Cummington.
Rev. Emerson Davis, D. D., Westfield.
Joseph A. Denny, Leicester.
Rev. Henry M. Dexter, Boston.
Hon. Allen W. Dodge, Hamilton.
Rev. John Dodge, Harvard.

Rev. Edmund Dowse, Sherborn.
Dea. Nathaniel Eddy, East Middleboro'.
Rev. Zachary Eddy, D. D., Northampton.
Rev. Nathaniel H. Eggleston, Stockbridge.
Rev. Alfred Emerson, Fitchburg.
Rev. Joshua Emery, Weymouth.
Constantine C. Esty, Framingham.
Dea. Phinehas Field, East Charlemont.
Dea. John A. Fitch, Hopkinton.
Allen Folger, Gardner.
Jonathan French, Braintree.
Rev. Nahum Gale, D. D., Lee.
Timothy Gordon, M. D., Plymouth.
Dea. Jabez R. Gott, Rockport.
Rev. John W. Harding, Longmeadow.
Dea. Ivory H. Harlow, Middleboro'.
Jacob Haskell, Fitchburg.
Dea. Henry Haynes, Sturbridge.
Dea. Wm. E. Hinsdale, Blandford.
Moses Howe, Haverhill.
Dea. Geo. W. Hubbard, Hatfield.
Rev. Jacob Ide, D. D., West Medway.
Dea. Galen James, Medford.
Charles A. Jessup, Westfield.
Rev. James P. Kimball, Falmouth.
Rev. Edward N. Kirk, D. D., Boston.
Dea. Samuel M. Lane, Southbridge.
Rev. Isaac P. Langworthy, Chelsea.
Rev. Charles Lord, Buckland.
Rev. Erastus Maltby, Taunton.
Rev. Abijah P. Marvin, Winchendon.
Rev. Elihu P. Marvin, Medford.
Rev. James T. McCollom, Bradford.
Rev. James B. Miles, Charlestown.
Hon. Henry Morris, Springfield.
Rev. Osborne Myrick, Provincetown.
Dea. Lorenzo S. Nash, Granby.
Rev. Theophilus Packard, Sunderland.
Rev. William P. Paine, D. D., Holden.
Prof. Edwards A. Park, D. D., Andover.
Rev. Ariel E. P. Perkins, Ware.
Rev. Ralph Perry, Agawam.
Rev. John Pike, Rowley.
Joseph G. Pollard, Woburn.
Zebulon Pratt, North Middleboro'.
Rev. Alonzo H. Quint, New Bedford.
Dea. Edgar H. Reed, Taunton.
Dea. Josiah Reed, South Weymouth.
Nathaniel C. Robbins, Salem.
Rev. Reuben T. Robinson, Winchester.
Rev. Ezekiel Russell, D. D., East Randolph.
Rev. Lewis Sabin, D. D., Templeton.
Marshall S. Scudder, Grantville.
Rev. John S. Sewall, Wenham.
Dea. John Smith, Andover.
Pres. William A. Stearns, D. D., Amherst
Dea. Charles Stoddard, Boston.
Rev. Seth Sweetser, D. D., Worcester.
Henry W. Taft, Lenox.
Rev. Eli Thurston, Fall River.
Dea. William Thurston, Newburyport.
Rev. John Todd, D. D., Pittsfield.
Rev. Edwin B. Webb, Boston.
Rev. Joshua W. Wellman, Newton.
Dea. Albert D. Whitmore, Housatonic.
Rev. John Willard, Fairhaven.
Rev. William H. Willcox, Reading.
Hon. Samuel Williston, Easthampton.
Rev. Thomas Wilson, Stoughton.
Bartholomew Wood, Newton.
Dea. Luther Wright, Easthampton.

MICHIGAN.

Rev. Joshua W. Allen, Franklin.
Dea. Sherman S. Barnard, Detroit.
Rev. Henry Bates, Grass Lake.
Hon. J. Webster Childs, Augusta.
Rev. Geo. H. Coffey, Jackson.
Hon. Wm. I. Cornwell, Newaygo.
Dea. Samuel F. Drury, Olivet.
Rev. Hiram Elmer, Clinton.
Dea. Allen Fish, Port Huron.
Rev. Thomas F. Hicks, Alpena.
Homer O. Hitchcock, M. D., Kalamazoo.
Rev. James S. Hoyt, Port Huron.
Rev. Philo R. Hurd, Romeo.
Rev. Thomas Jones, Olivet.
Rev. Adam S. Kedzie, Somerset.
Rev. James A. McKay, Lamont.
Rev. Henry Mills, Kalamazoo.
Rev. John C. Myers, Saugatuck.
George K. Newcombe, Esq., East Saginaw.
Rev. John Patchin, Owosso.
Rev. Herbert A. Read, Marshall.
Rev. Charles Spooner, Greenville.
Rev. Alanson St. Clair, Croton.
Rev. James F. Taylor, Chelsea.
Hon. James B. Walker, Benzonia.
Rev. Le Roy Warren, Elk Rapids.

MINNESOTA.

Rev. Edward Brown, Zumbrota.
Rev. David Burt, Winona.

Rev. Richard Hall, St. Paul.
Rev. Abel K. Packard, Anoka.
Dea. Oliver Pendleton, Wabasha.
Rev. Charles C. Salter, Minneapolis.
Rev. Charles Seccombe, St. Anthony.
Rev. Charles Shedd, Wasioja.
Rev. James W. Strong, Faribault.
Rev. Edwin S. Williams, Northfield.

MISSOURI.

Warren Currier, Esq., St. Louis.
Rev. Truman M. Post, D. D., St. Louis.
Rev. Julian M. Sturtevant, Jr., Hannibal.

NEBRASKA.

Rev. Reuben Gaylord, Omaha City.
Rev. Elisha M. Lewis, Nebraska City.

NEW HAMPSHIRE.

Rev. George M. Adams, Portsmouth.
Rev. Zedekiah S. Barstow, D. D., Keene.
Rev. Nathaniel Bouton, D. D., Concord.
Stephen Brown, Kensington.
Dea. Sampson W. Buffum, Winchester.
Dea. Orrin Bugbee, Lake Village.
Rev. Erastus B. Claggett, Lyndeboro'.
Rev. Edward W. Clark, Claremont.
Dea. Horace Childs, Henniker.
Rev. Josiah G. Davis, Amherst.
Dea. Archibald H. Dunlap, Nashua.
Dea. Andrew A. Farnsworth, Peterboro'.
Hon. Asa Freeman, Dover.
Rev. William L. Gaylord, Fitzwilliam.
Hon. Milan Harris, Harrisville.
Rev. Henry A. Hazen, Plymouth.
Hon. Thomas J. Melvin, Chester.
Dea. Abel K. Merrill, Haverhill.
Rev. Charles E. Milliken, Littleton.
Prof. Daniel J. Noyes, D. D., Hanover.
Dea. Daniel H. Parker, Dunbarton.
Rev. Henry E. Parker, Concord.
Rev. Ebenezer G. Parsons, Derry.
William Ramsdell, Milford.
Rev. Moses T. Runnels, Orford.
Rev. William T. Savage, Franklin.
Rev. Josiah H. Stearns, Epping.
Rev. Benjamin P. Stone, D. D., Concord.
Rev. Alvan Tobey, Durham.
Rev. Cyrus W. Wallace, Manchester.
Albert E. Wellman, Cornish.
Rev. Horace Wood, Ossipee Corner.
Rev. John K. Young, D. D., Laconia.

NEW JERSEY.

Rev. John M. Holmes, Jersey City.
Lowell Mason, Jr., Orange.

NEW YORK.

Rev. Stephen A. Barnard, Willsborough.
Rev. Henry Ward Beecher, Brooklyn.
Henry C. Bowen, Esq., Brooklyn.
Dea. Edson Boyd, M. D., Ashville.
Rev. John Bradshaw, Crown Point.
Dea. Albert G. Bristol, M. D., Rochester.
Rev. Wm. I. Budington, D. D., Brooklyn
Rev. Jeremiah Butler, Fairport.
Rev. Edward D. Chapman, Sinclearville.
Dea. Wm. H. Childs, Niagara City.
Rev. Oliver E. Daggett, D. D., Canandaigua.
Dea. Lorenzo D. Dana, Morrisville.
Rev. Edward Davies, Waterville.
Rev. Morgan L. Eastman, Lisbon.
Rev. George L. Entler, Meredith.
Rev. Griffith Griffiths, Utica.
Rev. Henry M. Hazeltine, Sherman.
Rev. L. Smith Hobart, Syracuse.
Rev. John C. Holbrook, D. D., Homer.
Charles Hopkins, Norwich.
Dea. Hiram Hulburd, Stockholm.
Rev. Samuel Johnson, Chenango Forks.
Rev. Seneca M. Keeler, Guilford Center.
John M. Kinsman, North Potsdam.
Rev. Joshua Leavitt, D. D., New York.
Dea. Thomas Marvin, Walton.
Rev. Samuel Miller, Eaton.
Rev. John H. Nason, Smyrna.
Rev. Richard Osborn, Champion.
Rev. Ray Palmer, D. D., Albany.
Rev. Samuel T. Richards, Spencerport.
Rev. Thomas H. Rouse, Jamestown.
Rev. Aaron Snow, Miller's Place.
Daniel S. Tarr, Gloversville.
Rev. Jos. P. Thompson, D. D., New York.
Rev. Warren W. Warner, Lawrenceville.
Rev. Moses H. Wilder, Gaines.
Rev. Edwin E. Williams, Warsaw.
David S. Williams, Flushing.
Rev. Horace Winslow, Binghamton.
Hon. Arden Woodruff, Strykersville.

OHIO.

Rev. Alex. Bartlett, Austinburg.
Rev. Henry S. Bennett, Wakeman.
Rev. Loren W. Brintnall, York.
Dea. Asa Cady, East Cleveland.
Dea. Charles Clark, Cuyahoga Falls.
Rev. George Darling, Hudson.
Rev. Thomas W. Davies, Youngstown.
Prof. James H. Fairchild, Oberlin.
Rev. Heman Geer, Wayne.
Dea. Abram Griswold, Gustavus.
Rev. John C. Hart, Kent.
Rev. Lysander Kelsey, Columbus.
Andrew J. Knapp, Wauseon.
Rev. Thomas E. Monroe, Mt. Vernon.
Dea. Thomas W. Painter, Weymouth.
Chas. W. Palmer, Esq., Cleveland.
Hon. Francis D. Parish, Sandusky.
Hon. Douglas Putnam, Harmar.
Rev. Edward W. Root, Springfield.
Rev. John Safford, Bellevue.
Rev. S. Willard Segur, Tallmadge.
Hon. Lester Taylor, Claridon.
Rev. James A. Thome, Cleveland.
Rev. Charles W. Torrey, Madison.
Joseph P. Walker, M. D., Cincinnati.
Evander S. Warner, Kelloggsville.
Rev. Wm. Watkins, Newburgh.
Rev. Thomas Wickes, D. D., Marietta.
Rev. Samuel Wolcott, D. D., Cleveland.
Dea. Wm. W. Wright, Oberlin.

OREGON.

Rev. Geo. H. Atkinson, Portland.

PENNSYLVANIA.

Rev. Davis R. Barker, Guy's Mills.
Geo. B. Delamater, Esq., Meadville.
Rev. Edward Hawes, Philadelphia.
Rev. Philip Peregrine, Blossburg.
Rev. George W. Smiley, D. D., Philadelphia.
Rev. Roderick R. Williams, Pittsburg.

RHODE ISLAND.

Hon. Amos C. Barstow, Providence.
Rev. Constantine Blodgett, D. D., Pawtucket.
Rowland Hazard, Esq., Peace Dale.
Rev. Leonard Swain, D. D., Providence.

TENNESSEE.

Rev. Thomas E. Bliss, Memphis.

VERMONT.

Hon. James D. Bell, Walden.
Rev. Nelson Bishop, Windsor.
Rev. Lewis O. Brastow, St. Johnsbury.
Rev. Ezra H. Byington, Windsor.
Rev. Calvin B. Cady, Alburgh.
Charles Carpenter, W. Charleston.
Edward Conant, Randolph.
George H. Crane, Northfield.
Rev. Theodore M. Dwight, Putney.
Benj. Fairchild, M. D., Milton.
Rev. Clark E. Ferrin, Hinesburgh.
Rev. James T. Ford, Stowe.
Geo. F. French, Lunenburg.
Hon. Ira Goodhue, Westminster.
Rev. Henry M. Grout, W. Rutland.
Rev. L. Ives Hoadley, Craftsbury.
Rev. Azariah Hyde, Pawlet.
Dea. Samuel James, Jr., Weybridge.
Rev. Isaac Jennings, Bennington.
Dea. Freeman Keyes, Newbury.
Hon. Wm. C. Kittredge, Fairhaven.
Rev. Benjamin Labaree, D. D., Middlebury.
Rev. Silas McKeen, D. D., Bradford.
Rev. Wm. Stratton Palmer, Wells River.
Rev. Charles C. Parker, Waterbury.
Rev. Sidney K. B. Perkins, Glover.
Dea. Henry W. Robinson, Johnson.
Dea. Edward D. Selden, Brandon.
Gov. James G. Smith, St. Albans.
Dea. Gilbert M. Sykes, Dorset.
Rev. Charles C. Torrey, Chester.
Rev. George P. Tyler, D. D., Brattleboro'.
Josiah B. Wheelock, Coventry.
Samuel D. Winslow, Townshend.

WISCONSIN.

Rev. Asa S. Allen, Black Earth.
Rev. Charles Boynton, Watertown,
Dea. Russell Cheney, Emerald Grove.
Rev. Dexter Clary, Beloit.
Dea. Orris K. Coe, Watertown.
Rev. Joseph Collie, Delavan.
Rev. Isaac N. Cundall, Rosendale.
Rev. Franklin B. Doe, Appleton.
Timothy Dwight, Esq., Beloit.

Rev. Solomon A. Dwinnell, Reedsburg.
Asahel Finch, Esq., Milwaukee.
Rev. Joseph W. Healey, Milwaukee.
Hon. Edward D. Holton, Milwaukee.
Dea. Guerdon Judson, Raymond.
Rev. David M. Jones, Arena.
W. Wallace Jones, La Crosse.
Rev. William DeLoss Love, Milwaukee.
Rev. Charles T. Melvin, Elk Grove.
Rev. William E. Merriman, Ripon.
Rev. Edward G. Miner, Whitewater.
Rev. Henry A. Miner, Menasha.
Rev. Lucius Parker, Palmyra.
Rev. Philo C. Pettibone, Beloit.
George W. Pratt, River Falls.
Rev. John C. Sherwin, La Crosse.
Rev. George Spaulding, W. Eau Claire.

HONORARY MEMBERS.

The following persons were subsequently made honorary members, most of them on account of their appointment to special service by the preliminary conference at New York. Many members of those committees are not named here, from the fact that they were delegates, and are on the roll proper.

Rev. Israel W. Andrews, D.D., Marietta, O.
Rev. Geo. W. Blagden, D. D., Boston.
J. Russell Bradford, Esq., Boston.
Hon. Samuel A. Chapin, Nevada.
Prof. Geo. P. Fisher, New Haven, Ct.
Prof. Franklin W. Fisk, Chicago, Ill.
Henry Hill, Esq. (Saxonville P. O.), Framingham.
Dea. Samuel Holmes, New York.
Rev. Daniel P. Noyes, Boston.
Dea. Julius A. Palmer, Boston.
Rev. Joseph E. Roy, Chicago, Ill.
Prof. George Shepard, D. D., Bangor, Me.
Rev. Andrew L. Stone, D. D., Boston.
Edward S. Tobey, Esq., Boston.

The following persons were received as delegates from foreign countries: —

Congregational Union of England and Wales. — Rev. Robert Vaughan, D. D.; Rev. Alexander Raleigh, D. D.; (Rev. James W. Massie, DD., LL. D., honorary.)

Glanmorganshire Association, Wales. — Rev. John Thomas, D. D.; C. R. Jones, Esq.; J. Griffith, Esq.

North Staffordshire Congregational Union. — Rev. S. R. Asbury.

Union of Evangelical Church of France. — Rev. Theodore Monod.

Congregational Union of Canada. — Rev. Edward Ebbs; Rev. Henry Wilkes, D. D.; Rev. John Wood; Rev. E. J. Sherrill; Rev. Archibald Duff; Rev. D. C. Frink; Theodore Lyman, Esq.

Congregational Union of Nova Scotia and New Brunswick. — Rev. W. H. Daniels.

The membership of the Council, therefore, was as follows: —

Whole number of delegates,	502
Honorary members,	14
Delegates from Foreign Countries,	16
Total membership,	532

REV. ANDREW L. STONE, D. D., of Boston, chairman of the

local committee of arrangements, called the council to order, and welcomed the delegates in the following address: —

Brethren of the Council: I will take the liberty of calling you to order, and of asking your attention for a moment, before suggesting a temporary organization, while I report briefly on behalf of the Committee of Arrangements, what we have done as your servants, in preparing for your coming.

I have been persuaded that it is not inappropriate for me officially to utter to you this first voice of public salutation. We are glad to welcome to-day our *fathers* and brethren, the representatives of the churches of our faith and order through the land, to this cradle of the Congregational order, and of Puritan principles. We would have you feel that you have come *home*, and that all the doors and hearts of the old home are open to your return. We should rejoice to find you able to make the associations under whose shadow you are come, and in the midst of which you shall walk and sit for these days or these weeks of your abiding among us, the tender and sacred associations of a domestic scene, from which you once went forth, and to which you have now come back.

Be at home with us, feel at home, and take the warmth of a home greeting.

And we do not forget that there are some among you who have crossed international lines, and others who have crossed dividing seas, brethren of the same language, of the same faith, and of the same remoter forefathers, to partake of the fellowship, and to share in the deliberations of this body. We extend to you on the shores of this *New* England the right hand of Christian brotherhood. May those international lines and those dividing seas between these two great nations and their dependencies, never be crossed by the armies and armaments of war,— never but as now, by the envoys and messengers of peace!

It seems to us well, apart from all our personal pleasure and profit in the matter, that this Council should assemble in Boston, where, or in the immediate vicinity of which, in other days, the grand synods of our church order have met in grave epochs of our history; as the synod of 1637 in Cambridge (then Newtown), which gave its crushing deliverances concerning the heresies of Mistress Anne Hutchinson; the synod of 1648, which issued the Cambridge Platform, after two years of incubation; the synod of 1662, — 203 years ago, — which sat in the first church in this city, gathering in March, adjourning to June, and afterwards to September, and determined so disastrously upon the subjects of "baptism and the consociation of churches." By these memorable precedents, this is naturally and historically the Jerusalem of our tribes, whither they should go up for the high festivals of their progress and story.

We have thought it fitting, too, that your first assembling should be within the walls of this old, historic meeting-house; kindly granted us by the church and society for this purpose. This house was built thirty-six years before the "Declaration of Independence." It is now 135 years old. It has been closely identified with all the important civil changes in this city and commonwealth, and with the whole growth of civil liberty. Here were celebrated, through those six years pending the Declaration of Independence, the anniversaries of the King Street tragedy, in which Crispus Attucks and four others were shot by an insolent royal soldiery, and year after year the voices of Otis and Warren and Adams made the place echo with their indignant patriotism. For many years after, the anniversary of the 4th of July was kept here by oration and civic ceremony. Here were the popular gatherings when the public mind surged into strong remonstrance against the Stamp Act. Here, too, in the Revolutionary days, British officers galloped for their own training and exercise, and that of their war steeds, while royalist spectators looked down upon them from the galleries.

Here, also, have been scenes of memorable religious interest. The echoes, that resounded to the voices of patriot orators, awoke also to the tones of Whitefield, on each of his visits to this city. They gave their responses to the words of Thatcher and Willard and Sewall, and almost all the great New England divines of the last century.

But I must not detain you by such reminiscences. We had thought it would be grateful to you to assemble here, even if you should find it necessary to adjourn to some place with more quiet surroundings for your daily sessions. We have taken the liberty to provide such a place. The Mount Vernon Church, in a cordial note which I shall lay upon your table, tender you the use of their house in Ashburton Place for your deliberations.

We have remembered your coming in our domestic arrangements, and have provided you guest-room in the city and in our suburban homes.

We have remembered you in our cities for prayer, and have, by concerted intercession, besought God to meet you, and to greet you with the baptism of the Holy Ghost, and to make your work here the fountain of richest spiritual blessings to our land and to our times, both, in these great days, calling upon us all for the utmost Christian wisdom, energy, and consecration.

I repeat the suggestion which I have made, that the Council organize at first by the choice of temporary chairman and secretary; giving time for the full assembling of your body, and a more deliberate permanent organization.

And suggesting only, at this point, one thing more, — that it seems to your Committee of Arrangements, that the opening sermon would be more happily listened to to-morrow morning, at 9 o'clock, than amid the confusion and disorder and business of this first evening, — I will take the liberty of nominating CHARLES STODDARD, of this city, a delegate, as I know, to the National Council, to act as your temporary moderator during the initial services of the Council.

The nomination was unanimously ratified.

In accordance with the request of the temporary moderator, prayer was offered by Rev. Edward Beecher, D. D., of Illinois.

The moderator then nominated Rev. Henry M. Dexter, of Boston, as temporary secretary, and he was unanimously appointed.

Deacon Julius A. Palmer, in behalf of the Committee on Hospitality, reported in reference to places of entertainment. The committee would be in attendance in the chapel of the Old South Church after adjournment, and on Wednesday evening until 7½ o'clock, to wait upon delegates; and afterwards every day in the chapel of the church where the sittings would be held. Arrangements had been made for meetings in the Mount Vernon Church, where the body of the church would be reserved for delegates and foreign visitors. It was suggested that the daily sessions be held from 9 A. M. to 1 P. M., and from 3 P. M. to 5 P. M., two hours being allowed for dinner. It was advised that no evening sessions be held. Mr. Palmer stated that some of the delegates had been provided for in adjoining towns, on account of the absence from the city of many families who would otherwise have furnished accommodations.

On motion of Rev. Isaac P. Langworthy, of Massachusetts, it was —

Voted, That the moderator appoint a committee (to be composed of one member from each State represented here) to nominate permanent officers of the Council.

The moderator appointed that committee as follows: —

Massachusetts — Hon. Linus Child; *Maine* — Rev. George E. Adams, D. D.; *New Hampshire* — Rev. Benjamin P. Stone, D. D.; *Vermont* — Rev. Benjamin Labaree, D. D.; *Rhode Island* — Hon. Amos C. Barstow; *Connecticut* — Rev. Samuel W. S. Dutton, D. D.; *New York* — Rev. Joseph P. Thompson, D. D.; *New Jersey* — Rev. John M. Holmes; *Pennsylvania* — Rev. Davis R. Barker; *Delaware* — Abner H. Bryant, Esq.; *Maryland* — Nathaniel Noyes, Esq.; *Ohio* — Judge Francis D. Parish; *Indiana* — Rev. Nathaniel A. Hyde; *Illinois* — Hon. Charles G. Hammond; *Michigan* — Hon. William I. Cornwell; *Wisconsin* — Timothy Dwight, Esq.; *Iowa* — Dea. John Porter; *Minnesota* — Rev. Charles C. Salter; *Missouri* — Warren Currier, Esq.; *Nebraska* — Rev. Reuben Gaylord; *Kansas* — Hon. Samuel C. Pomeroy; *Colorado* — Samuel Cushman, Jr., Esq.; *Oregon* — Rev. George H. Atkinson; *Tennessee* — Rev. Thomas E. Bliss; *California* — Jacob Bacon, Esq.

Rev. Julian M. Sturtevant, D. D., of Illinois, moved that a committee be appointed to report Rules of Order. After some discussion, the motion was carried, and the following gentlemen were chosen to constitute that committee, viz.: —

Rev. Julian M. Sturtevant, D. D., of Ill.; Rev. John P. Gulliver, of Ct.; Henry C. Bowen, Esq., of New York.

On motion of Rev. William W. Patton, D. D., of Ill., a committee of five was appointed to receive the credentials of members, and report who are entitled to membership in this Council, consisting of—

Rev. William W. Patton, D. D., of Ill.; Rev. Alonzo H. Quint, of Mass.; Rev. Edward Beecher, D. D., of Ill.; Dea. Allen Fish, of Mich.; Hon. Douglas Putnam, of Ohio. Rev. Mr. Quint declining to serve, Jacob Haskell, of Mass., was appointed instead; and on request of the committee, it was subsequently enlarged by the addition of Rev. Robert C. Learned, of Ct., and Rev. Samuel Wolcott, D. D., of Ohio.

Hon. Linus Child, from the committee on Permanent Organization, reported as follows: —

That the permanent officers of the Council consist of a moderator, two assistant moderators, and five scribes; and that those officers be the following: —

Moderator — His Excellency Gov. William A. Buckingham, of Conn.

Assistant Moderators — Hon. Charles G. Hammond, of Ill.; Rev. Joseph P. Thompson, D. D., of New York.

Scribes — Rev. Henry M. Dexter, of Mass.; Dea. Samuel Holmes, of New York; Rev. Philo R. Hurd, of Michigan; Rev. Alonzo H. Quint, of Mass.; Caleb Atkins, of Iowa.

Rev. Alonzo H. Quint, of Mass., declined being a candidate for the position of scribe; and Rev. Martin K. Whittlesey, of Ill., was nominated in his place.

It was —

Voted, To accept and adopt the report of the committee; and the Council was permanently organized by the choice of this moderator, assistants, and scribes.

Hon. Linus Child, of Mass., and Rev. Dr. Dutton, of Conn., conducted the moderator to the chair, when he addressed the Council as follows: —

GENTLEMEN OF THE COUNCIL: I assume the responsibilities of this position with some hesitation, distrusting my ability to perform them properly; and I rely with confidence upon your kind co-operation and assistance to aid me and support me in their performance. We are the representatives of three thousand Congregational churches of the United States of America, who recognize the responsibility of each member, his accountability to Christ, the great Head of the Church, and the importance of uniting together for the purpose of extending the interests of the Redeemer's kingdom. You will be called upon, perhaps, in the first place, to determine whether you will put forth a declaration of evangelical faith and of church polity, and again whether you will adopt some plan for the purpose of uniting all these churches who are in one common faith, in measures for the purpose of extending the Redeemer's kingdom, and especially for evangelizing this nation, which needs more than ever to be instructed in the first principles of that commandment, "Thou shalt love the Lord thy God with all thy heart, and thy neighbor as thyself." [Applause.]

The meeting is now open for the consideration of these and of any other questions which may come before you for consideration.

On motion of Rev. Dr. Dutton, of Connecticut, and after some discussion, it was —

Voted, That the opening sermon be delivered in the Mount Vernon Church, in Ashburton Place, to-morrow, at 9, A. M.

On motion of the temporary scribe, it was —

Voted, That, until otherwise ordered, the sessions of this Council be from 9, A. M. to 1, P. M., and from 3, P. M. to 5, P. M.

An invitation to the Council to visit the General Theological Library was read by the secretary; after which, on motion of Hon. Linus Child, of Massachusetts, it was —

Voted, To adjourn to to-morrow morning, at 9 o'clock, to meet in the Mount Vernon Church, in Ashburton Place.

Adjourned.

SECOND DAY, THURSDAY, JUNE 15.

The Council met in the Mount Vernon Church (Rev. Dr. Kirk's), Ashburton Place, at 9 o'clock, A. M., the moderator, Governor Buckingham, in the chair.

PUBLIC WORSHIP.

Rev. Dr. Vaughan, of England, read the hymn commencing,

"Let children hear the mighty deeds;"

which was sung by the congregation; after which, Rev. Dr. Vaughan read the cxliv. Psalm, and the second chapter of the First Epistle to the Thessalonians, and offered prayer; and after the congregation had sung the psalm, —

"Glorious things of thee are spoken," —

the sermon was preached by Rev. Julian M. Sturtevant, D. D., President of Illinois College.

SERMON.

JEREMIAH vi. 16. — "Thus saith the Lord, Stand ye in the ways, and see, and ask for the old paths, where is the good way, and walk therein, and ye shall find rest for your souls."

It would perhaps not be difficult to find circles of opinion, in which the selection of such words as these for the theme of discourse would be thought to require an apology. Indeed, judging from some of the givings-forth of the periodical press, I deem it not improbable that there may be such a circle in this goodly city of Boston. There are, I fear, not a few persons among us who, though by no means deficient in natural gifts or generous culture, are greatly wanting in reverence; men who would regard the exhortation of our text, when applied to our own times, with something of indignation and contempt, as though it were a suggestion that the enlightened present should disown her wisdom, and go to school to the blind and stupid past. Such men seem to have forgotten that the past is ever the parent of the present; that other men have labored, and we are entered into their labors; that, whatever superiority we may have attained over those who have gone before us, we owe to the principles which our fathers established, to the institutions which they founded, and the lessons which they taught.

But I am fairly entitled to assume that no such apology is necessary in addressing the representatives of the Congregational churches of the United States, assembled here around the old hearth-stone, and the cradle of our political and religious institutions; not only from the hills and valleys where the New England fathers sleep, but from the basin of the lakes, the banks of the Mississippi and its branches, the glens of the Rocky Mountains, and the shores of the Pacific.

Nor this alone. From beyond the St. Lawrence, brethren beloved are here; and from that beautiful island of the ocean, which is the mother of us all, — a revered and honored mother, who, though in these late years she hath chided her eldest American daughter with a little unmerited severity, will yet honor her ancestral bravery, and her fidelity to her precious inheritance of liberty.

This audience, assembled on this spot, surely needs not be told that there are principles coeval with the founding of these New England colonies, which sustain such a relation to our whole social and religious life, that we can never have any sound and healthful growth except by their free and natural development, — principles which sustain the same relation to our entire nation, however great it may become in future ages, which the little germ enclosed in the acorn does to the sturdiest monarch of the forest.

I am sure of the hearty sympathy of this audience, in "standing in the ways, to ask for the old paths." Our fathers were but men. We claim for them no exemption from the errors and follies to which all this poor humanity is ever subject. But God was with them, and did guide their feet into paths of wisdom, which led them to the attainment of a condition of freedom and social order, which richly compensated them for all the danger and sufferings of the wilderness, and is destined to confer untold blessings on their descendants for ever. And it is well worthy our most earnest endeavor to trace out those same paths, through all the intricacies and sorrowful confusions of the present; and perfectly safe for us to walk in them. They conducted our fathers to prosperity and happiness in circumstances seemingly the most unpropitious and forbidding, and they will not fail to conduct us to the same.

We propose no servile imitation of the fathers. We will adhere to no principle and no custom because it was theirs. "Prove all things, hold fast that which is good," shall be our motto. We intend to look backwards, not because we think innovation a crime, but because we know that all true national growth is the development of first principles; and that the principles of any nation's life are to be learned, not from the agitations of the passing moment, but from the study of its history. We think it wise to ask the fathers what is the seminal principle of our national life, by the development of which we may attain to the growth and strength and beauty and productiveness of which God hath made us capable.

Nor am I wrong in looking to the early history of New England for the seeds of our national life. The French De Tocqueville, not a Puritan, not a Protestant, says: —

> "The two or three main ideas which constitute the basis of the social theory of the United States were first combined in the Northern British colonies, more generally denominated the States of New England. The principles of New England spread at first to the neighboring States; they then passed successively to the more distant ones; and at length they imbued the whole confederation. They now extend their influence beyond its limits over the whole American world. The civilization of New England has been like a beacon lit upon a hill, which, after it has diffused its warmth around, tinges the distant horizon with its glow."

What, then, are the principles of social life which are indicated in the early history of New England? In the foreground of the picture meets us the fact, that our fathers believed in their heart of hearts that God had revealed himself to the soul of man, and that it is the privilege and the duty of every man to receive and obey for himself that revelation. With clear and mighty conviction they rejected, as unsatisfactory and untrue, that interpretation and social expression of the divine will which kings and nobles and bishops had imposed with tyrant power on every foot of English soil. That they might find some spot of earth on which — some arch of sky beneath which — they might individually and socially worship God according to their own understanding of his will, not only brave and strong men, but timid old age, and delicate womanhood, and helpless infancy, dared encounter the ocean, the wilderness, and the savage. This is certainly the foremost fact in the history of New England, nay, of North America.

Next meets us the fact, that, when they reached their desolate home on these ice-bound shores, they were as far removed from the government which should have protected their persons and their rights, as from the step-mother church that would impose on them her ceremonies and her superstitions. If under those stern winter skies they were free to worship God, they were also under a necessity of providing for their own protection from cold and famine, and the violence of bad men.

It needs no argument to show, that, from such a history, must necessarily have been born a "Church without a bishop, and a State without a king." The family, with all its God-given authorities, sacred subordination, and delicate dependencies, had been transported across the ocean, and stood unimpaired and unshaken on the shores of a new world. And never has it been more revered, or more honored, than by the fathers and mothers of New England. But all else of the religious and political authorities of the Old World had been left on the other side of the ocean. The individual man, the family tie, and the golden chain that binds each individual man to "the throne and monarchy of God," were all that remained of the organic forces of society. These men are social beings, and therefore they will reconstruct religious and political society. But they will construct both only for the protection of individuals and families, in the enjoyment of their God-given rights, and to aid them in performing their divinely-appointed duties and achieving their allotted destiny. The recognition of the rights, the duties of individual human beings, as the direct subjects of the government of God, *will*, MUST be the germinant principle of all social arrangements. The principle will become recognized and crowned and enthroned, that every individual has rights which God gave him when he made him in his own image, and owes an allegiance to the Supreme Ruler which is superior to all human enactments, and which rights and duties no earthly power can over-ride in the smallest degree, without incurring the righteous displeasure of God. If, from these feeble beginnings, a nation shall grow up, which shall stretch from ocean to ocean, and cover a continent with the emblems of its power, that nation must rest on this simple principle, as its mountains rest on their foundations of everlasting granite; and if at any point in its future history, in the pride of its prosperity and power, it shall violate this sacred principle, an earthquake will shake its strongest structures, and volcanic fires will burst up from beneath its foundations, and, like Sodom of old, it will be consumed with a storm of fire and brimstone, unless it repents in sackcloth and ashes, and puts away the national iniquity.

That this principle must be seminal to our national life, no thoughtful man surely will deny; and in searching for the true pathway of our progress, we are only to seek for the just and rational development of it. Is it not, then, equally obvious, that, in constructing society on this principle, the largest amount of liberty will be reserved to the individual which is consistent with provision for his social wants; and that, in all social arrangements, local provisions will be preferred to the provincial, the national, or the imperial, except in cases where the latter are found to be essential to the general welfare? The individual will not commit to a society what he can better take care of as an individual; and local communities will not commit to general societies what they can better understand and better provide for than any more general society can do it for them. Individuals will enjoy the largest liberty, local communities will surrender the smallest portion of their independence, consistent with the general good; and imperial power will only be permitted to meddle with those interests in which all the millions of a great nation are alike concerned. I need not argue before this audience to show, that as this results directly and necessarily from our national history, so it is a true enunciation of the characteristic principle of American institutions as they exist in fact; and that the more perfectly this principle is carried out, the more harmonious and beneficent is the working of our social machinery.

What, then, is the development of this principle in the direction of religion? I need not prove that earnest faith in the gospel must and always will have a social development. It follows inevitably from the nature of the religion, and the social affections to which it is largely addressed. Persons living in each other's neighborhood, reading the Bible in the same mother tongue, and believing with the heart its revelations of God and Christ, and redemption and forgiveness, and the life everlasting, will find themselves drawn into social relations by irresistible attractions. They will organize themselves into a religious society for mutual sympathy, edification, instruction, and co-operation, as naturally and necessarily as the loving pair unite in marriage bonds, or as beings possessed of human nature unite in civil society.

And, consistently with the conditions which the Pilgrim Fathers brought with them to the shores of New England. consistently with the fundamental principles of our social life. they will organize those societies, independent[1] of all dictation or control in discipline, worship, and doctrine. except that of the one divine Head of the Church of God. Had not our fathers accepted a home in this great and terrible wilderness, that they might enjoy the doctrine, the discipline, the worship, which they

[1] The author of this discourse is quite well aware that the Congregationalism of our fathers recognizes two principles as fundamental, — the *self-government* and the *fellowship* of the churches: and if, in advocating the former as against ecclesiastical centralization, he has given it chief prominence in this discourse, it is not because he does not hold, or undervalues, the latter.

approved? And should they now construct any authority of bishop or council or presbytery, empowered to interfere with their enjoyment of this dear-bought privilege? And why should any society of Christian men and women, associated for these religious purposes, subject themselves to any such control of human power and invention? They want religious teaching; are they not competent to select their own religious teachers, in the fear of the Lord? They want to exclude from their society the irreligious, the unbelieving, the scandalous, the profane; are they not better qualified to estimate the character of the men and women among whom they live than any distant church authority? They want a doctrine and a worship conformed to the divine word; must they not themselves prove all things, and hold fast that which is good? Can they delegate the judgment of these matters to other fallible men like themselves? Does not their individual allegiance to God imply their individual right to try the teaching they hear, and the worship in which they engage, by the standard of God's revealed will, and themselves to judge what is right? What bishop, council, presbytery, synod, can decide for them?

While thus claiming that the doctrine of the independency of the local church was a most natural result of the circumstances and the religious convictions of the fathers of New England, I do not forget the fact, that the Pilgrims of Plymouth had been instructed in the principles of Congregational independency by that truly great and good man, John Robinson, before they left the mother country, and during their residence in Holland, and were therefore rooted and grounded in them before they embarked for America. Nor do I forget the still more weighty fact, that Robinson himself was but the humble pupil of the apostles themselves; that the churches which Paul and Peter and their fellow-apostles founded from Jerusalem to Rome were, by the agreeing judgment of the ablest writers on ecclesiastical history, independent local churches; and that, whatever other men may say of the fathers, independency is sustained by the uniform practice of the apostles.

Such were the churches which our fathers planted amid the primeval forests of New England; such were the churches of Plymouth and Salem and Boston; and as their settlements encroached farther and farther upon the domain of the oak, the pine, and the fir, they covered the territory which they reclaimed from the wilderness with a complete network of such churches. It was the function of each of these churches to care for the intellectual and religious culture of the entire population within their respective boundaries. Thus, at every step of their advance, the Christian teacher and the schoolmaster accompanied them, and every child was taught the rudiments both of secular and of divine knowledge. This was a true development of the principle of our national life; and we may well challenge any intelligent denial, that in application to such a State as Massachusetts only, and as it actually exists in practice at the present moment, it is a grand development; and that applied in its entireness to a great nation, extending from the Atlantic to the Pacific, it would be as sublime and glorious as it is free and simple. If it would have been as quiet and tranquil as sunshine, it would also have been as potent and life-giving.

Such was the conception of the fathers of New England; and that conception they did make an actual reality in every settlement which they formed. And the network of Congregational churches, with which they covered over much the larger portion of New England, presented a completeness and symmetry of organization for the religious instruction and spiritual nurture of a free people, never attained to elsewhere in this country, and probably not even in the world. An unobstructed development of their principles would have covered our whole territory with such a chain of organizations from ocean to ocean. At least, on every six miles square of our inhabited territory, they would have planted such a society, not cared for and governed by some distant ecclesiastical authority, but by its own living forces, and efficiently caring for the intellectual, moral, and spiritual necessities of the entire population within its limits; nor for these alone, but supplying the physical necessities of all the sick, the poor, and the afflicted.

And such a religious organization is essential to our national life and health. It is one of the great vital forces of all free society. There can be no better future, no millennium, either political or religious, without it. We do but grievously deceive ourselves if we imagine a sublime superstructure of freedom can be reared up, covering a continent, and enduring for ages, if this element is wanting. Some men among us glory in the superiority of this generation over our simple-minded fathers. But we are sadly fallen from the grace of such an organization for the religious culture of the people; and it is a grievous fall. Many of the stars are fallen even from the sky of New England, and no other luminaries have taken their places; and many others are sadly dimmed in their luster and are reeling from their orbits. In most of the country which lies west and south of the Hudson, we have abandoned the conception itself, as impracticable and impossible. An eminent divine of one of the Middle States, alike well known for his fervid eloquence and his burning zeal for the Christian cause, who thought I loved New England better than I ought, once sent this message to me in my distant home in the West: "Tell Mr. S. he can not make New England in the West." Alas! thus far it is true; and it is this very element of New England which we have been unable to transplant. But I have not ceased, and shall not cease, to try, till I despair of my country and the Church of God.

It would be greatly to the purpose of the present occasion to exhibit an exhaustive view of the causes which have prevented the realization of this simple but grand conception west and south of the Hudson. The time, however, which can be allotted to this discourse would be entirely insufficient for such a presentation. But there are four of these causes which seem to me imperatively to demand the consideration of the National Council. They are, —

1. Want of homogeneity in our population.
2. Negro slavery.

3. Undue reliance on temporary, superficial, and inorganic efforts for home evangelization; and,

4. Want of sufficient tenacity in adhering to our own polity.

In naming the first of these, want of homogeneity in our population, I do not chiefly refer to the fact that everywhere there is a portion, and in some communities a very large portion, of the population, who are not believers in the gospel, who are either indifferent or hostile to that faith which is the basis of all living and permanent church organizations. However deeply we must deplore this fact, this unbelieving portion of the population is not numerous enough to throw any insuperable obstacles in the way of a ubiquitous organization of the church on Congregational principles. It rarely or never occurs in any American community, that, if the gospel is preached in its purity, such multitudes will not embrace it in the love of it, as to render the organization and sustentation of a Christian Church easy. And this remains true, after we have made ample allowance for those forms of semi-Christian belief and worship which reject that gospel which we have received. That gospel which consists in repentance toward God, and faith in our Lord Jesus Christ, will still find adherents, who will be both able and willing to sustain an organized church with all its ordinances. At least, within the circle of my observation, this has rarely, if ever, failed to be true. Aid they might need, while struggling with the first difficulties of a new settlement. But when these were a little over, I have seldom or never known a community in which there was not enough of earnest and devout Christians to sustain the institutions, of social religion, if they were united in their endeavors; or, at least, in which, if the gospel were for a little time faithfully preached, it would not win converts, and make the problem of the church easy. There are few communities, East or West, in which a Christian teacher may not preach as Paul did at Corinth, with the assurance that the Lord "has much people" there.

But the heterogeneousness of which I speak is of another kind. Almost everywhere west and south of the Hudson, the descendants of New England have met a religious population, holding, in a greater or less degree of purity and simplicity, the same religious faith as themselves, who yet are not willing to accept their conception of the Church. Everywhere beyond the western boundary of New England, they meet not only the divisions which have arisen among Independents on the mode and subjects of baptism, but, in its almost endlessly multiplied modifications, the Presbyterianism of Geneva, Holland, and Scotland, and the various offshoots of the modified Episcopacy of the Wesleys. The inevitable consequence is, a conflict of rival conceptions of the church, which renders impossible the construction of any such system of religious organization as the Congregational conception of the church has produced in New England. It is not only true that no one of these Christian denominations is able to construct a ubiquitous system for the instruction of the people in the things of God, but that their mutual rivalries render it impossible that such a system should exist, either by the efforts of any particular denomination, or of all together. This is not a random assertion, but it is capable of demonstration; and if true, it is surely worthy of the most serious consideration, not only of the Congregational churches, but of all men of every denomination that love our country and the kingdom of God.

In cities and large towns, all the different religious denominations that exist in our country may be represented by religious organizations, embodying each its own conception of the church; and in this way provision may be made, in some sort, for the religious instruction of the population. But it is quite essential to the great social experiment which we are trying on a scale so gigantic, that our rural civilization should attain to a completeness never known in any other land. The means of intellectual, moral, and religious culture must not be shut up in cities: they must be carried to every square mile of our territory, and brought within easy reach of every human habitation. Every six miles square of the entire habitable surface of our country must contain such permanent and effective institutions for the instruction of the people, and the whole people, that the man who has never traveled beyond the limits of his own native township may yet have a noble education, and be a truly cultivated and civilized being, the product of all the centuries that are past. In order to this, I need not prove to this audience that it is indispensable that the Christian sanctuary shall be built there, and that on each successive Lord's day the assembled people shall feel the influence of social worship, and of the clear, lucid, and earnest exhibition of evangelical truth.

What I affirm is, that the heterogeneousness of our population, in the sense in which I have defined it, renders it impossible to effect any such religious organization; but that, on the contrary, vast regions and multitudinous populations are by it doomed to religious destitution and a moral desolation, like some great Sahara, with only here and there a blooming oasis.

Subtracting from the sum total of our population the population of our cities and large towns where religious institutions can be maintained in some sort, in spite of the causes of which I am speaking, the remainder of course will be our rural population; and it will not be found to exceed some twenty-eight to the square mile, or about one thousand souls to each township of six miles square. Let us then bear in mind, that in each of these townships will be found the usual amount of indifference to religion, and misbelief and unbelief, and that all this must be counted out, in estimating the capability of the township to sustain social religion. After then subtracting from the one thousand souls that inhabit the township all persons of this character, the remainder can not be presumed to exceed six or seven hundred, of all ages, from the cradle to the grave, and of both sexes. If these were united, you could not expect of them more than that they would be able to sustain one church with energy and efficiency. What then can we hope for, if they are to be divided between Presbyterians, in all their diversities of Dutch, Scotch, and American origin; Wesleyan Episcopacy, in all its modifications; and Independency, with the divisions which have arisen respecting the mode and subjects of baptism? What but the impossibility of sustaining any religious organization whatever?

And yet what I have supposed is but the stern and terrible fact over vast districts of our territory; and the result is religious destitution and religious anarchy, from which we can not only discern no deliverance in the immediate future, but we do also clearly see, that, in the present line of things, deliverance is impossible; that the evil must wax worse and worse with each successive generation for ever. Sects will multiply and unbelievers will multiply, and the house of David will wax weaker and weaker. We might as well hope that the barrenness of the Arabian desert will be healed, while yet the clouds refuse to pour their rain upon it. Religious men of New England birth and education have impressed upon the very substance of their souls the conception of a religious organization of society, which will bring the influence of a regular Christian sanctuary within easy reach of every dweller on the soil. And they know well that by such an arrangement only can the education of the people be provided for. And I thank God, that, in the hope of realizing this noble conception, they will, if need be, pour out their money like water, in sustaining home missionary societies, in founding schools and colleges, and in educating young men for the Christian ministry; and they will give their own sons and daughters to this work in a spirit of as true heroism as ever poured out life in the defence of liberty, or endured martyrdom for the truth as it is in Jesus. And I shall never cease to thank God that it is so.

But we are in duty bound to look the stern facts of the case full in the face; and, if we do so, we shall acknowledge and feel to our heart's center, that obstacles at present exist over the whole West and South, which render the realization of the noble conception which inspires this glorious Christian heroism as impossible as to cover the ice-fields of the polar circle with the luxuriant vegetation of the tropics.

It is often asserted, and seldom or never contradicted, that this want of homogeneity of which I speak is the inevitable result of religious freedom, acting through the permanent laws of the human mind. If that is so, the prospects of our country for a high religious civilization are gloomy enough. But I thank God, the assertion, often as it is made, is made gratuitously. Nobody has, so far as I know, ever proved it; and to me it seems not only unproved, but most clearly untrue. The whole history of this country, from the landing of the Pilgrims until now, furnishes no proof, or ground of suspicion, that religious men, in the full enjoyment of religious liberty, would ever have invented any other church polity than independency. I know not that any centralized system of church government ever originated in this country, or any other country enjoying full religious liberty. Our Presbyterianism all sprung from the State churches of Geneva, Holland, and Scotland. It was originally constructed as an ecclesiastico-political system, through which a State church could exert its power of control over all the religious interests of a nation. Organization did not begin with the people and grow up into the General Assembly, but with the General Assembly, and extended its radii of administration downwards to the church sessions. If any one doubts this, I commend to his especial study the history of the church of Scotland, and would especially recommend as a text-book the work of that stanch Presbyterian, Mr. Hetherington. Presbyterianism has greatly multiplied its sects in this country. But it has been only by subdivisions of itself, of which it has an unlimited capacity. They have all arisen from the attempt to carry out its principles in an atmosphere of freedom. But the system itself, freedom never generated in any country, and there is no proof that it could. With no propriety can it be claimed as any necessary product of a religious liberty, however numerous its offshoots may be in a free atmosphere.

There is just as little reason to believe that the Wesleyan polity could have originated from a condition of perfect religious liberty. Mr. Wesley's aim certainly was to organize an army of brave soldiers for Christ, and so to command it in the name of the Lord as to secure its efficiency. But the principles of organization by which that command was to be exercised were derived from the Episcopal hierarchy of the church of England, which he never ceased to love and cherish. The seminal principle of the system is not that of the people propagating that gospel which they have received, but that of the rulers converting and governing the people in the name of the Lord.

I am free to affirm, that to begin with a free, self-governing Christian people, and develop from it either the Wesleyan or the Presbyterian polity, seems to me as impossible as to create an aristocracy by the free votes of democrats. Give us nothing but liberty and Christianity to begin with, and if we ever have any ecclesiastical centralization, it must be imported from some other clime.

As to the Papal and Episcopal systems of government, the case is still plainer. If we can find them taught in the inspired Word, of course we can account for their existence. But, as most of us are unable to see that the Holy Scriptures lend them any support, we can only recognize them as offshoots from the civil and military systems of imperial Rome and the middle ages, transplanted to this land of freedom, and here endeavoring, with what success time must determine, to maintain themselves in the midst of all the forces of universal and absolute religious liberty.

The assertion, then, that the heterogeneous character of our population is the inevitable result of our perfect religious liberty, is without any foundation at all. The conflicting systems by which our population is divided and distracted are, for the most part, not the products of religious liberty, but of the church and state systems of Europe, transplanted to American soil, and here trying the very interesting experiment, whether their existence and their power can be propagated in the midst of the absolute religious liberty of the United States. If, in the all-wise providence of God, they are destined to succeed in this great ecclesiastical experiment of the nineteenth century, then must every system of effort for establishing a symmetrical and efficient system for the religious instruction of the whole people necessarily be a failure.

The whole history of the church, from the great schism of the Eastern and Western churches to the last disruption of American Presbyterianism, shows, with the certainty of demonstration, that centralized church governments, whenever they are liberated from state control, and are free to act out their own nature, will always indefinitely multiply rival church governments and sects by their own internal convulsions. They all exhibit the phenomenon of a government claiming and exercising the right to command, without the power to compel obedience. They are all perpetually in the condition in which our Federal Government would have been, if the doctrine of the democratic party at the outbreak of the Rebellion had prevailed, that the Federal Government has no right to coerce a State. We should now have had as many nations as States. Every centralized church government acts under these impossible conditions, and consequently is liable to be divided into two rival governments, whenever the majority or the governing power commands what any portion of the membership are unwilling to obey. It is therefore true, that, as things now are, we not only have so great a multiplication of rival ecclesiastical powers as to render efficient religious organization impossible, but also the certainty of an indefinite increase of their number in the future.

Want of homogeneity in our population is, then, one potent cause which has hindered, and is hindering, such a religious organization of our whole country as would have resulted from the development of the ideas of our New England fathers. And it is an obstacle of giant magnitude with which we have still to contend.

2. Another fatal hinderance to the realization of the great conception of our New-England fathers has ever been negro slavery. On this point I need not detain you long, for the principles of the case are too familiar to require much illustration. Slavery degrades one half the population to the condition of beasts of burden, and denies them any place in society as independent and personally responsible human beings. Our conception of the church, on the contrary, is founded on the equal brotherhood of the human race. It can not be supposed that the proud and lordly master can ever admit his slave to equality in church relations, and recognize his independent manhood as a Christian brother. A higher power may admit both to the church, and govern both; but the master will never admit the slave to an equal share with himself in the government of the church, on principles of democratic equality. If churches of our polity exist in such circumstances, their membership must be confined either to the enslaving or to the enslaved class. Among the latter, in the Baptist connection, they have existed in great numbers. But driven out from all the fountains of knowledge, and deprived day by day of the earnings of their own hands, what could these poor people do for the spiritual enlightenment of the communities under whose oppressions they and their fathers before them lived and groaned?

Nor could the principles of our polity develop themselves with any better effect in the enslaving class. The white population of the slave-holding States has always been divided into two classes, which are separated by an immense distance from each other, — the wealthy and aristocratic slave-holders, and the poor white men, reduced, both in respect to property and intelligence, to a position scarcely less wretched than that of the slave himself; and this latter much the more numerous class. A population thus degraded, and reduced to ignorance and barbarism, would furnish but poor materials out of which to construct such Congregational churches as those which the fathers planted in the wilderness of New England. Many of this class have been organized into Baptist churches, and much has thus been achieved for their spiritual benefit. But little could be hoped from them in the way of a religious organization to supply the moral wants of a great people. Poverty and ignorance have been their leading characteristics, accompanied, of course, by a degrading servility to the proud and selfish aristocracy that is above them.

The wealthy slave-holding class, on the other hand, could not be expected to choose a system of church government founded on the idea of an equal Christian brotherhood. It is impossible that such a polity as ours should be successfully developed, in a community thus divided by artificial and unjust legislation, into classes so widely removed from each other. When English aristocrats learn to love and cherish English Independency, you may expect our American slave-holding aristocrats to love and cherish the Congregationalism of New England. In both cases, the Congregational polity is sure to be rejected with scorn and contempt. We need, therefore, feel no surprise that our polity has no existence among the intelligent and wealthy classes of the South, and that the Congregational churches which once existed in South Carolina and Georgia have long since been swallowed up in those organizations in which the Christian brotherhood is less distinctly recognized. It may therefore be assumed, that, while slavery continued in the South, our polity was possible there only among the slaves and the most degraded and ignorant of the white population; and that there it would be quite powerless to provide a system of religious instruction for a great, free, and enlightened people.

And it should be remarked, that this obstacle to the progress of our polity has been felt much beyond the limits of the slave-holding States. Slavery has attacked, with terrible effect, that doctrine of fraternal equality which the gospel teaches, not only in the slave-holding States, but in all parts of our country, and especially in those portions of it to which emigrants from the South have gone in large numbers. It has fearfully assailed the fundamental principle of our free institutions, both civil and ecclesiastical, and, if God had not come to our aid in the destruction of slavery, would ere long have subverted the republic itself. And the weakening of this principle shows itself earlier and more strikingly in the church than in the state. Thousands, who would not acknowledge themselves aristocrats, would feel a decided aversion to joining a church which was governed by the vote of the majority, and in which the vote of a poor man would be worth as much as their own.

And that the growth of this aristocratic spirit has been greatly fostered and extended by the influence of a slave-holding aristocracy on our society, and that tastes have thus been generated which incline strongly to the less democratic forms of church polity, I cannot for a moment doubt. He who has watched the causes which, for the last thirty years, have resisted the progress of our polity in the North-west, will not need proof of this proposition.

3. Another obstacle which has greatly hindered our organic work is undue reliance on modes of effort which are inorganic, and necessarily temporary and superficial.

I must tell you frankly, fathers and brethren; this has been a very painful subject to many of your frontier laborers during the last thirty years. We have seen great, and in their design truly Christian, societies, having the ear of all our churches, and holding the very highest place in their regard, founding their plea for large pecuniary contributions upon the assumption, that the founding of the church, the sustaining of an enlightened Christian ministry, the rearing-up of the permanent institutions of Christian learning, is too slow a process; that the results are too remote; that these efforts can not reach the people, and that, therefore, other and speedier methods must be adopted. You must send the colporter with his Bibles, his tracts, and Christian books, and thus carry the word of life to the people at their own homes. And this logic has been accepted, — accepted against the solemn and clearly uttered protest of the very men whom you have sent there to build up the institutions of a Christian civilization on the frontier; and not only accepted, but most vigorously acted upon. While it has been a matter of the greatest difficulty to get a few hundred dollars to aid a feeble new congregation in building a house of worship; while heroic home missionaries, and their still more heroic wives, have been called to endure the severest privations and the greatest and most distressing hinderances in their work; while fields the most inviting of organic missionary enterprise could not be entered for the want of means; and while those colleges which your far-seeing liberality has founded were left so feeble and inadequately provided with the needful resources as often to fill the hearts of those who labored in them with shame and deep despondency, — while all these things and more were going on before our eyes, on those very same fields, funds derived from the sacred treasury of Christian benevolence were expended by tens of thousands in the circulation of tracts and printed volumes, which few cared to read, and multitudes could not read if they would. I should not be surprised to learn, that for many successive years more money was annually expended in Illinois, in peddling religious books, than the entire cost of sustaining all the colleges which Christian liberality has founded there.

I do not say that all this has done no good. But I do say, that, having been constantly for more than thirty-five years in the heart of the great North-west, I have never had but one view of it. It has always seemed to me very bad economy. As I have looked at these things, I have never doubted that the children of this world are in very deed, in their generation, wiser than the children of light. To found institutions as the vital organs of Christian society is our first business, and let us never be cheated into forgetting it. And there is no substitute for them, any more than for eyes and ears and lungs in the body. Let us build such institutions if we do nothing else. And let us put our books and our tracts and our Sunday-school libraries into the hands of our missionaries, as their munitions of moral warfare.

And I must ask any man, well informed and of sound judgment, what, beyond the permanent institutions we have founded, we have to show for the evangelical labors of the last thirty-five years in the North-west. I would ask him too, if we had, in the respects now indicated, used our money more wisely, these results might not have been far more abundant than they are; whether, if we had used the funds we have spent in forcing the circulation of printed books, in founding and building up our churches and our colleges, our churches might not have been far stronger and more numerous; and whether our colleges might not have been far nearer than they are to the attainment of the great destiny intended by their founders. For my part, I have no doubt of it.

Let us learn by experience; let us put these more superficial and temporary agencies in their proper place, and address ourselves to our great organic work, and determine to do that, whatever else we neglect, and to trust in God that the seed we thus sow shall yield a glorious harvest for millions yet unborn. If we could learn this lesson, one of the greatest obstacles with which we contend would be overcome.

4. The only remaining obstacle of which I shall speak is the want of sufficient tenacity in adhering to our principles.

I do not mean that Congregationalists are tired of their mode of government, and desirous to change it for another. This is far from being true. As a general rule, and in its ordinary and normal working, our system in a good degree satisfies the taste of an intelligent, active-minded people, both for tranquillity and freedom. There is movement enough to give consciousness of life; freedom enough to give opportunity for individual development; and tranquillity enough to content even quiet and conservative spirits. In all these important respects, the history of the system gives abundant indications of a capability of enduring for ever.

But it has been the glory of our churches, that under their influence men have always learned to put the gospel immeasurably higher in regard and honor than any mere forms and ceremonies and governments. And may they retain that glory for ever! And yet out of this very characteristic has grown one of the chief obstacles in the way of our realizing that grand organic conception with which our fathers subdued the wilderness.

As the men of New England emigrate westward, they would always, if left to their own tastes and wishes, organize the church after the pattern of the fathers. And the sons of New England have pitched their tents toward the setting sun in sufficient numbers, and with sufficient preponderence of intellectual and moral weight, to have exerted, if they had adhered to their own polity, an irresistible formative influence on the religious institutions of our country, from the Hudson to the shores of the Pacific. And I do not see how an enlightened, thoughtful New-Englander, acquainted with what has happened and is happening in our country, can help regretting that they did not do it. But the past is unalterable, and regret is useless. The reason why they did not do it is obvious. They held, as a sacred article of their faith, that the gospel is primary, and government secondary. They met other streams of emigration, not of New England, holding the same precious faith with themselves, but tenacious of quite another system of polity. For the sake of securing the co-operation of these good men in planting the church in the wilderness, they were induced, sometimes at a single step, sometimes by little and little, to surrender the polity of their fathers, and accept that of Calvin and Knox in its stead. They did not prefer the change; it cost them a struggle; but, for the sake of unity and co-operation, they thought it best. And so the fathers of New England taught their emigrant sons, and it came to be understood, that the difference between the Congregationalism of John Robinson, and the Presbyterianism of John Knox, was a mere difference of longitude; that to cross the Hudson would make a good Presbyterian of any Congregationalist. Worse than this; when, a little more than thirty years ago, young men who went out from you to plant the gospel on the banks of the Mississippi, began to feel a decided longing for the polity of the Mayflower, and to organize churches on that platform, they were met by their fathers and brothers here with a frown, and often treated by the leading men of New England as men wanting in sober sense and sound judgment. I am uttering the experience of more than one man in this audience. That state of things has, thank God, passed away, never, we trust, to return.

But the evil is not yet cured; or, if I may not assume that it is an evil, this obstruction to the progress of our church principles, in the regions which lie toward the going-down of the sun, is not yet removed. Need I say, that to this hour Presbyterianism grows more from Congregational roots than from its own? that multitudes of the most gifted men whom the New England churches rear for the Christian ministry treat this question of polity as one involving no principle at all? — do not hesitate a moment to accept the highest positions in the Presbyterian Church, and to become its standard-bearers "and champions for the spread of its most distinctive and denominational peculiarities, in advance of all others"? I need not say that this same facility of abandoning our polity is constantly exhibited by our emigrant laity, as well as by our ministry. New England men, making their homes in the West, will, without hesitation, turn their backs on Congregational churches that need their help, to unite themselves with Presbyterian churches, for no higher motive than to secure customers to their business, or to attain to a higher social position.

The progress of the Congregational polity in the North-west during the last twenty-five years has been truly wonderful, unsurpassed certainly by that of any other religious denomination. But it has all been accomplished in spite of the existence of this obstacle in greater or less degree over all that field. It has achieved much, very much; but for this obstacle, it would have accomplished vastly more. Many churches which are now weak would have been strong, and many which have been absorbed by the centralization of the Presbyterian Church would have remained in the simpler and freer polity of the fathers.

I can not doubt, that by this process the organic power of the emigration from New England has been greatly diminished: its power to multiply churches where churches are needed; its power to endow and sustain schools and colleges; its power to train up a Christian ministry; its power to multiply and strengthen all the institutions of a Christian civilization; its power to transplant whatever is precious in New England to the West, and the South, and the shores of the Pacific.

It is now quite time I draw this discourse to a conclusion by a brief consideration of one great practical inquiry: What is, to the churches represented in this Council, now the line of practical wisdom and Christian duty?

1. We must never abandon that grand conception of a symmetrical and ubiquitous religious organization for the moral and spiritual care and culture of the whole people. To abandon this is to abandon the experiment of American liberty as a miserable failure. We can not, *we can not* succeed in this grandest social experiment of the age, except through the high intellectual and religious culture of the whole people. Our mother country, England, is governed by her upper and middle classes: to these classes, therefore, she applies the forces of a high and noble culture, that they may be fit to govern, and leaves the lower classes in a great degree uncared for. This is, at least, consistent. We are governed by the people, the whole people, and therefore to the whole people we must apply all the forces of intellectual and moral culture, that all may be qualified to wield that share in the government which the law accords to them. Nothing but ruin can come of elevating the masses to the position of rulers, while we do not so teach and train them as to qualify them to rule well. And, in order to this end, we must have a ubiquitous rural civilization, purified and exalted by the influences of free Christian worship and instruction.

And to conclude that a system of perfect religious freedom can not give us such a religious organization, that it will necessarily produce such a conflict of religious sects as to render it impossible for rural districts ever to establish the permanent institutions of religious instruction and worship, is to admit that the experiment of religious liberty is a failure, and that we must go back to some church and state system, which can, by the compulsory power of law, divide the country into parishes, and maintain in every one of them the means of religious as well as of secular instruction. We must solve this problem *by a free system*, or acknowledge, in the face of exultant Europe, that our Protestantism and our voluntaryism have signally failed. It is the trial-question of American religious freedom, whether by it we can provide for the religious culture of our whole people. The Congregational churches must not be the first to pronounce this experiment a failure. God forbid!

2. We have a far better prospect of success through our own polity than through any other to which we might be induced to lend our co-operation. He who should adopt any form of centralized church government, with the hope of effecting through it a universal religious organization for our country, would certainly choose an instrument very ill adapted to his ends. Rival governments, each claiming jurisdiction over the whole territory, in face of every other, may in this way be multiplied indefinitely, and be brought into more and more intense rivalship with each other; and that is all we can expect from that instrument, however vigorously used. This is about as hopeful for securing a religious organization for our country, as to favor State rights and no coercion was of perpetuating our national unity. It can only aggravate the evil indefinitely, and drive us farther from the end we wish to reach.

But if we will, even now, be true to the polity of our fathers, there is hope of ultimately attaining to complete success. The independency of the local church is, as we have shown, a true development of the seminal principle of our national life. All centralized church government is contradictory to it. The events of the last five years have taught us, as with a voice from heaven, that that principle is to be developed in the whole social life of this great nation; and that any and all principles which are contradictory to it are, sooner or later, to be eradicated through the agitations and convulsions which they themselves occasion. I affirm, that the principle of centralized church government does constantly demonstrate its opposition to the foundation principles of American society, by the agitation, confusion, and anarchy which it causes. In this conflict, I think it reasonable to believe that the principle itself will sooner or later be overturned and destroyed.

This state of things can not exist always. Men will see at last that these evils must be remedied, or the gospel itself must perish, and the light of the Sun of Righteousness go out. Men will cease at length to make labored apologies for the ceaseless conflict of the sect system, and begin to look around them for some platform on which the whole church of God on earth can stand together, and make war on one another no more. And when they do begin in earnest to inquire after such a platform, they will find it in the independency of local churches, built on the everlasting foundations of the simple truth as it is in Jesus; each disciple as an equal brother receiving every other, and putting no yoke on his neck which the Master hath not imposed.

I have no wish to claim any especial glory for New England. The history of New England is not above criticism, and the men of New England, I hope, are not yet too wise to learn. But the principles which found their way to these shores in the cabin of the Mayflower are evidently destined to prevail over this continent from ocean to ocean, and to give character to all our social systems, both in church and state. I can see no reason why men who hold that conception of the church, which was one of the most remarkable characteristics of that Pilgrim band, should despair of its power to overspread the continent. That the tendency of American society is to localize the government even of the most centralized churches, is apparent to every well-informed man. Presbyterianism can not be the same in America that it is in Scotland. Neither Presbyterianism nor Methodism can be the same in the presence of active and efficient Congregational churches, that it is in the absence of any such influence. In such circumstances, their central forces are always weakened, and their local and individual forces strengthened. Why, then, should we doubt that a force which is always active and potent, and springs up from the very source of our national life, will ultimately prevail? In such circumstances, can we doubt for a moment that independency is the fittest instrument of religious organization in this free country?

One of the obstacles which has hitherto effectually resisted our progress over half our territory has been destroyed by a mighty earthquake from God. Babylon the great is fallen. Negro slavery shall no longer resist the organization of the church on the basis of the equality of the Christian brotherhood over half our country. Another of the four obstacles which I have mentioned will be entirely removed when we, and all the churches represented here, adhere to our principles of ecclesiastical freedom with a zeal corresponding to their preciousness. The rivalship of opposing forms of church governments is the only serious one that remains. In respect to this we may reasonably assume that there is deliverance in the not distant future.

> "The day of freedom dawns at length,
> The Lord's appointed day."

We have only to select that one of the conflicting systems in which all men are most likely to find harmony and fraternity, under the full-orbed influence of American freedom, evangelical truth, and the Spirit of the Lord, and to adhere to it. For my part, I am at no loss to choose.

3. We must teach and defend the principles of our polity. Such has not been our custom. Some may have done it; many have neglected it. We have not seldom trained our sons and the people of our charges, from infancy to gray hairs, without their ever once having heard one earnest and thorough statement of the reasons why they are, and should continue to be, Congregationalists. We have even inculcated upon ourselves and our brethren the notion, that a minister of the gospel can hardly be worse employed than in defending the ecclesiastical polity to which, after all, he thinks it his duty to adhere. And then we are surprised and shocked that our brethren treat the matter of church polity, not as a question of principle, but of mere convenience and worldly advantage. And as things have been over three-fourths of our territory, there are far more motives of convenience and worldly advantage inclin-

ing a man to be a Presbyterian, than a Congregationalist. There are hundreds in this assembly who could testify to the truth of this from their own experience. If there are reasons why we should adhere to our polity at all, the same reasons would prove that our practice in respect to teaching and defending our system should undergo a speedy and total change.

I imagine, however, I hear an objector inquiring, What! would you abandon that glorious characteristic of all our past history, that the gospel alone is primary, and all questions of mere polity, by a great remove from it, merely secondary? Bishop Butler has very truly said, "It is one of the peculiar weaknesses of human nature, when, upon the comparison of two things, one is found to be of greater importance than the other, to consider this other as of scarce any importance at all." I must add that it seems to me that this is pre-eminently "the peculiar weakness" of us Congregationalists. We have a polity, the glory of which is that it immeasurably exalts the spiritual truths and moral precepts of the gospel above all questions of mere polity; and therefore we never teach our people the excellence of this polity at all, or even explain to them its principles, but leave them without any instruction on the subject, to be swallowed up by other polities, under the influence of which they will be very sure to acquire, and transmit to their children after them, an intense spirit of proselytism, which is alike foreign to our history and to Christianity. Would it not be well to draw a little of the attention of our people to questions of polity, to guard them against such a danger?

There is, at the present time, a tacitly understood truce among the various denominations in respect to the open advocacy of their peculiarities of faith and order, especially the latter, entered into for the sake of peace and good feeling. We are told that the minor questions which divide evangelical Christians are not important enough to justify the agitation and the disturbance of good feeling and Christian charity, which might result from the open discussion of our differences. These differences are assumed to be important enough to justify our rending the body of Christ asunder for the sake of them; important enough to justify us in demanding for every little community in Christendom at least six church organizations, when one only can be supported, and thus entailing on the whole Christian cause, division and weakness before its enemies, and religious anarchy; they are important enough to justify Christian men, and, still more, Christian women, in plying with unresting activity all the arts, all the social influences, all the motives, both religious and secular, of the most intense proselytism, to build up each his own denomination; but not important enough to justify us in a little honest outspoken defence of what we really think to be important truth, and clear and fair refutation of what we think to be erroneous and injurious.

Indeed, fathers and brethren, I have, in some sense, taken my life in my hand in delivering such a discourse as this on the present occasion. I am in danger of being thought to have violated established inter-denominational law, and thereby to have criminally disturbed the peace of those high contracting ecclesiastical powers which at present assume to divide Protestant Christendom among them. Nor need I limit the statement to Protestant Christendom. The truce, when once fairly established, will necessarily embrace Romanism itself. We have, in recognizing such a truce to the extent we have recognized it, erected a false standard of judgment, by which any Christian minister would be sure to be condemned as a bigot and a bitter sectarian, who should truly represent to his congregation the falsehoods, the delusions, and the despotism of Popery. That great red dragon is to-day greatly protected from the merited and healthful indignation and abhorrence of a free Christian people by this truce among our Christian denominations. We can not agree not to rebuke one another, without imposing restraint on ourselves in respect to rebuking other and perhaps more heinous sinners.

This truce proceeds upon the assumption that the present divided condition of Protestant Christians is an inevitable result of religious freedom, and destined to be perpetual, and that therefore we must divide up every Protestant community among the existing powers ecclesiastical as quietly as possible. The advocates of those centralized church governments, which, like the Presbyterian and Methodist, are not exclusive, generally not only accept this state of things as inevitable, but apologize for it as desirable and beneficial to the interests of Christ's kingdom. I am glad to say that I have met very few Congregationalists who take this view of it. They generally deplore it as a great and intolerable evil. If, however, we would be truly prepared for our great work, we must go one step farther, and believe that the Lord has deliverance for his people; that they are not perpetually to wander thus bewildered and confounded; that the Lord will at last appear, and lead his people over Jordan into the promised land of freedom and blessed fellowship. And, amid all the confusion of the present, we must seek light from God to guide us in the true path by which he will lead his people to this blessed consummation, and point out that path to all over whom we have any influence, and exhort them to pursue it.

For myself, I must frankly declare, that, to me, the whole beauty and preciousness of the Congregational system lies in this,—that it is a method by which the whole church of God under heaven may stand in blessed moral unity, on the basis of the gospel, the whole gospel, and nothing but the gospel, divided and distracted by no forms or ceremonies or governments which man hath devised. And I think, in the midst of such a scene of religious anarchy as that in which I have lived, such a polity is worthy of being explained, defended, and adhered to, till God shall call me hence.

4. We must make this ecclesiastical question one of principle, otherwise we can not be efficient laborers for the evangelization of this continent and the world. If our gifted and strong young men regard the present confused and anarchical condition of religious society in the valley of the Mississippi as necessary and inevitable; if they are taught that there is no question of principle at issue between the Protestant denominations, and that all which a pastor can do is, in the general rivalship of churches,

to build up his own as well as he can, by the power of his eloquence, the attraction of his own social character, and the social influences which he can gather round him, and by the excellence of his organ and his choir, without any appeal to the principles and convictions of the people, — I say if strong and vigorous-minded young men see that churches are chiefly to be built up by such influences as these, they will feel little attraction in the pastoral office, and seek some other profession; or, if they enter the ministry, a sense of these difficulties will weaken their hands, and sicken their hearts, and crush their spirits. And this, my brethren, is one of the most potent causes which is thinning the ranks and impairing the energies of the Christian ministry.

Let us have done with all this. Let us bring before our minds the grand conception of a continent to be overspread with a network of Christian institutions. Let us, with devout earnestness, inquire what ecclesiastical system is the fittest instrument for achieving this great result; and, when we have chosen it with full conviction, we shall wield it with hearty good will; we shall see and feel the giant obstacles that oppose us; but we shall believe that the truth and spirit of God are strong enough to overcome them. We shall not be intolerant or exclusive. We shall meekly instruct those who oppose themselves; but we shall instruct them, and not dodge them by any cunning artifices. We shall have principles to defend, and we shall defend them, and we shall put our brethren of other denominations on the defense of theirs; and if the truth is with us, our cause will go up, and theirs will go down; if with them, theirs will go up, and ours go down. In either case, we shall have labored successfully, and the truth will have triumphed.

If we mean to be efficient, we must not purpose to hold our own in a conflict of sects, admitted to be interminable and inevitable; but in all things we must be the advocates of principles which are true, and therefore, through God, mighty, and destined to overcome and exclude all opposing error. And it is infinitely important that this spirit be infused into the Independent churches all over the world. English Independency is suffering the same paralysis, only in a far higher degree. It is but too content to be the religion of the middle class. It is expected, if a family becomes rich and great, it will desert "the Chapel," and go to "the Church." English Independency must have done with this. It must recognize its principles as true for all men, and fitted to rule the world, and wield them with the expectation of overturning the proud hierarchy which has so long crushed them down, and establishing, in face of the aristocracy of England, the doctrine of the equal brotherhood of the disciples of Christ. It must demand for its sons a culture as large and as generous as Oxford and Cambridge give to the sons of nobility and the state church. It must claim to speak in the name of the Lord, alike to high and low, rich and poor. When this spirit fully possesses English Independency, bishops will hold their miters and their revenues by a very frail and transient tenure. Fathers and brethren, both in this country and in England, any polity is worthy of being advocated and defended thus, or it is not worthy of being adhered to at all. If it is true, let it triumph and reign; if false, let it go into oblivion as soon as possible.

Finally, we must be in earnest. God never gave to any other people such a problem to be solved as that which he has given to the Christian people of our country, — to plant the gospel under the full-orbed sunlight of civil and religious freedom, from the Atlantic to the Pacific, and from the eternal snows of the Arctic to the eternal verdure of the Tropic. In these last few months, he has come with his own terrible earthquake, and shaken down and utterly destroyed the only political barrier which obstructed our progress. The land is now before us, and the sunshine of freedom is on it all. And God is calling us, as by a voice speaking to us from out of the sky, Arise and build; rear up the Church of Christ on the foundation of apostles and prophets, Jesus Christ being the chief corner-stone, over all those hills, amid all those valleys, that it may teach to all the millions that shall soon dwell there, in your own dear mother-tongue, these wonderful works of God; that it may be so ubiquitous that no human being shall fail to hear its melodious summons every Sabbath morning to the house of Christian prayer and praise; that all those dark places of the land that have been cursed by the abominations of slavery may be purified, and filled with light, and covered over with a population as peaceful, as free, as enlightened, and as religious, as the inhabitants of the sweetest valley that nestles among New England hills; in one word, to found and nurture the institutions of learning, freedom, and religion, for a mighty nation, very soon to surpass in population the empire of China; and in wealth and ubiquitous influence the empire of Britain.

And shall we deal lukewarmly, coldly, and in a worldly spirit with the elements of such a problem? Shall we not, in such a cause, pour out our wealth like water, and give our sons and daughters to the work, as freely as patriots ever gave their sons to their country, and offer our own selves as freely as our adorable Redeemer gave himself for us?

The minutes of yesterday's proceedings were read and approved.

CREDENTIALS.

Rev. Dr. Patton, of Illinois, from the committee on Credentials, offered a partial report.

Dr. Patton said the documents submitted to the committee were very imperfect in many cases. In some instances, there was no indication of the State to which the individuals designated as delegates, belonged. In many cases, there was an omission properly to fill out the blanks, so as to enable the committee to judge whether the churches had acted properly in determining the number of delegates to which they were entitled, according to the basis of representation. It was intended that every conference should not only certify that such and such individuals were their delegates, but that such a number of churches were represented, and fill in their names, that it might be put beyond all question that they were entitled to that number of delegates. That had been omitted in a large number of instances; and of course the committee had not been able to judge perfectly with reference to the matter submitted to them. Then the documents, in some instances, had the names of the principals and alternates; in other cases, the names of the principals alone. Of course, it would have been impossible to make out a list giving the alternates and principals, and the committee had not attempted to do it. In the next place, there was no indication as to which of the appointees were present, and which absent; and it was impossible to tell whether the principals were all present, or whether part of them were absent, and their places filled by alternates. The committee took it for granted that the principals were present, unless they were notified to the contrary.

The committee further reported that credentials had been presented from foreign bodies; but, as it was not for them to settle the status which these delegates should hold in the body, they had simply reported their names. They had included in the list the delegates from Canada, although a literal construction of the Call, which was issued to the "United States," would exclude them. But, inasmuch as the committee expected the United States to include Canada at no distant period [laughter], they did not deem it expedient to raise the question with reference to the propriety of their admission to the floor.

The list of delegates was then read by the several members of the committee on credentials, opportunity being afforded for additions and corrections. The report was then recommitted to the committee, for the purpose of securing greater fullness and accuracy.

INVITATIONS.

Rev. Mr. Dexter, of Massachusetts, read the following letters of invitation: —

BOSTON, June 14, 1865.

Delegates to the National Congregational Convention are invited to participate, as a body, in the Temperance Festival to be held on the Common in this city, on Saturday, the 17th inst., at 9 o'clock, A. M. A place in the procession will be assigned to the Convention, on the reception of an affirmative answer.

For the Committee,

(Signed,) HENRY HOYT.

CHARLESTOWN, June 14, 1865.

TO THE MODERATOR OF COUNCIL:

Dear Sir, — I beg leave, in behalf of the ancient First Church of this city, — the oldest of the churches of the New World represented in this body, — to extend to the Council a most cordial invitation to hold, whenever agreeable to them, their contemplated special service in honor of the "marvelous and merciful dealings of Almighty God with the nation," in our sanctuary. I may be permitted to say, that the location of our church edifice is upon Harvard Hill, conveniently near to this place; a spot around which cluster many patriotic and sacred associations; where the sainted Governor Winthrop and his fellow-Christians, two hundred and thirty-five years ago, established the worship of God, and quite near to that eminence upon which, ninety years ago next Saturday, occurred the first great battle of the American Revolution.

It affords me great pleasure herewith to transmit to the Council the enclosed communication from Hon. Geo. W. Warren, President of the Bunker Hill Monument Association; and also to add, that I am requested by Rear Admiral Silas H. Stringham, Commandant of the Navy Yard in this place, to convey to the members of the Council, from him, a cordial invitation to visit the Yard and the government works at such time as may suit their convenience.

Most respectfully and sincerely,

(Signed,) JAMES B. MILES,

Pastor First Church, Charlestown.

---

42 COURT STREET, June 14, 1865.

Dear Sir,—Understanding that there is to be, during the present week, a Convention in Boston of the National Congregational Council, and that it is their purpose to hold, during their session, a patriotic service of thanksgiving for the overthrow of the rebellion, I beg leave to request you to extend to the Council, on behalf of the Bunker Hill Monument Association, an invitation to visit Bunker Hill and the Monument at such time as may suit their convenience.

Yours most respectfully,

(Signed,) G. WASHINGTON WARREN.

Rev. JAMES B. MILES.

On motion of Rev. Dr. Thompson, of New York, it was

Voted, That the Council acknowledge the courtesy of the invitation to join in the Temperance celebration on the 17th inst., and express its sympathy in the object, but respectfully decline to participate, on account of the pressure of its own business.

On motion of Rev. Mr. Dexter, of Massachusetts, the other invitations were referred to the Business Committee to be hereafter appointed.

On motion of Rev. Mr. Langworthy, of Massachusetts, it was

Voted, That a committee of five be appointed, to nominate the various committees of the Council.

Adjourned.

THURSDAY, P. M., JUNE 15.

The Council met at three o'clock, the moderator in the chair.

The committee on Nominations was announced as follows: —

Rev. Isaac P. Langworthy, Massachusetts; Gov. James G. Smith, Vermont; Rev. Milton Badger, D. D., California; Rev. Flavel Bascom, Illinois; Asahel Finch, Esq., Wisconsin.

DISPATCH TO THE PRESIDENT.

On motion of Mr. Bowen, of New York, it was ordered that a telegraphic dispatch be sent to the President of the United States, as follows: —

TO HIS EXCELLENCY, ANDREW JOHNSON,
President of the United States, Washington, D. C.

The National Congregational Council, now in session in this city, representing nearly three thousand churches, in all sections of the country, desire to present you their Christian salutations, to assure you of their profound sympathy in your great and trying labors, to promise you their loyal support and their prayers, and to express their solemn conviction that the hundreds of thousands embraced as worshipers in our churches will most heartily co-operate with you in extending the institutions of civil and religious liberty throughout the land.

MOUNT VERNON CHURCH, Boston, June 15, 1865.

On motion, it was

Voted, That the dispatch be signed by the moderator, and transmitted to the President.

RULES OF ORDER.

Rev. Mr. Gulliver, of Connecticut, from the committee on Rules of Order (in the absence of the chairman, Rev. Dr. Sturtevant), submitted their report as follows: —

RULES OF ORDER.

I. Each morning, at the time to which the Council is adjourned, the moderator shall open the meeting with prayer, and the scribe shall read the minutes of the preceding day, that any needful correction may be made.

II. In case of an equal division of votes, the moderator shall have a casting vote.

III. Whilst the moderator is putting any question or addressing the body, no one shall walk out of or across the house; nor in such case, or when a member is speaking, shall entertain private discourse, or read any printed book or paper; nor whilst a member is speaking shall pass between him and the chair.

IV. When any member, in debating or otherwise, shall transgress the rules of the body, the moderator shall, by his own authority, or at the request of any member, call him to order; and if a question shall arise concerning his being in order, it shall be decided by an appeal to the body.

V. Every member, when he wishes to speak, shall address the moderator, who shall announce his name. When two or more rise at once, the moderator shall name the member who is first to speak.

VI. No member shall speak more than twice to the merits of the question in debate, except by special permission of the body; nor more than once until every member choosing to speak shall have spoken.

VII. Every motion, except for adjournment, shall be reduced to writing, if the moderator or any two members desire it.

VIII. When a motion is regularly made and seconded, and has been stated by the moderator, it cannot be withdrawn or modified by the mover without the consent of the body.

IX. No vote can be reconsidered except on the day of its passage, or the next succeeding, and on motion of one who voted with the majority.

X. When a question is under debate, no motion shall be received, but to adjourn, to lay on the table, for the previous question, to postpone to a day or hour certain, to commit, to amend, to postpone indefinitely, which several motions shall have precedence in the order in which they are arranged. On a motion for adjournment, for laying on the table, for indefinite postponement, or for the previous question, there shall be no debate.

XI. The effect of a negative of the previous question is to allow further debate and the issue of the subject in due order; the effect of adopting the previous question is to put an end to debate, and to bring the Council to a direct vote upon pending amendments, if any, and then upon the original question.

XII. If a question under debate contains several parts, any member may have it divided, and the question taken on each part.

XIII. Every committee shall consist of three members, unless expressly ordered otherwise by the body, and shall be nominated by a committee appointed for the purpose.

XIV. If the report of a committee contains nothing more than matters of fact for information, or matters of argument for the consideration of the Council, the question is, *Shall the report be accepted?* and that question, unless superseded by a motion to reject, to recommit, to postpone, or to lay upon the table, shall be taken without debate.

Such a report, if accepted, is placed upon the files of the Council, but not being an act of the Council, is not entered on the minutes.

If the report is in the form of a vote or resolution, or of a declaration, expressing the judgment or testimony of the Council, the additional question arises, *Shall the report be adopted?* and motions for amendment are in order. Such a report, if adopted, with or without amendment, is the act of the Council, and is entered on the minutes.

If a report gives the views of the committee on the matter referred to them, and terminates with the form of a resolution or declaration in the name of the Council, the adoption of the report is the adoption only of the resolution or declaration; and while the report at large is placed on file, that part of it which has become an act of the Council is entered on the minutes.

XV. It shall be the duty of the business committee to prepare a docket for the use of the moderator, upon which shall be entered all items of business which members of the Council may desire to bring before the body, and, except by special vote of the Council, no business shall be introduced which has not in this manner passed through the hands of the committee.

The report was adopted, and ordered to be printed.

PRESENTATION OF FOREIGN DELEGATES.

REV. DR. BLAGDEN, of Massachusetts. I have a duty to perform, sir, as one of the Committee of Arrangements, who by their vote have assigned to me that duty; and it strikes me that the subject to be brought before the Council, in the fulfillment of that duty, had better be presented now, before the Council shall engage in any of the regular business that succeeds the reception of the credentials of delegates.

It is known to the Council that there are gentlemen present from foreign bodies, and the Committee of Arrangements appointed me to introduce two of the brethren from the Congregational Union of England and Wales, in a few words. Those brethren are present, sir, and I am glad to hear and to know that there are others present from other bodies. The two brethren to whom I refer are the only brethren from abroad who were mentioned as attendants upon the Council at the time of the last session of the Committee of Arrangements; and it will not preclude that attention which the Council would wish to pay to others if I, in the discharge of that particular duty, present only those two brethren at this time.

With these few remarks, I have the honor to introduce to the Council Rev. Dr. Robert Vaughan and Rev. Dr. Alexander Raleigh, of England, delegates to this body, as I understand, from the Congregational Union of England and Wales.

HON. MR. HAMMOND, of Illinois. I am informed that there are some documents which have been presented by these gentlemen, which they would like to have read.

Dr. Patton of Illinois, read the following letter and documents: —

NORTH STAFFORDSHIRE CONGREGATIONAL UNION.

Spring Meeting held in the Congregational Church, Stoke-on-Trent, April 17th, 1865. *Henry Pidduck, Esq., Mayor of Hanley, in the Chair.*

The following resolution was proposed by the Rev. R. McAll, of Hanley, seconded by the Rev. S. Jones, of Longton, and unanimously carried: —

"That the North Staffordshire County Association of Congregational Churches and Pastors is happy to take the opportunity of nominating the Rev. S. R. Asbury, B. A., as a delegate to the National Congregational Council, meeting at Boston on the 14th of June, 1865, and would thus express the earnest wish that Congregational principles may further advance in the United States.

"And they would also express the hope that the churches of England may soon have to rejoice with their brethren in America over the removal of the curse of slavery from that continent, and the restoration of true peace."

(Signed,) HENRY PIDDUCK, *Chairman.*
J. HANKINSON, *Secretary,*
And Pastor of the Congregational Church, Leek.

SHEFFIELD, N. B., 1st June, 1865.

TO THE NATIONAL COUNCIL OF CONGREGATIONAL CHURCHES, BOSTON.

Dear Brethren, — Though widely separated in our fields of labor, and though under different forms of civil government, and among people differing much in their social and domestic habits, yet we are members of the same family of the church on earth, — identified as brethren by a common faith and by our scriptural form of church polity.

The Congregational Union of Nova Scotia and New Brunswick is a small body, numbering only twelve churches. We are spread over a wide territory, and no possibility exists of our coming together except at our annual gatherings. This difficulty has presented an insuperable barrier to our appointing a delegate to represent us in your "National Council." The Rev. W. H. Daniels, who has labored in the city of St. John, N. B., for a number of years, purposes being present with you; and it is with the greatest pleasure, as Secretary of our Union, that I introduce him to your notice.

Our Union does not meet till the 21st of next month; but if an opportunity had existed, I am confident it would have been the cordial and unanimous desire of all our members and churches that our beloved brother Daniels should have appeared as our delegate at your Council.

If, under these circumstances, he can not be allowed to take part in your proceedings, I have no doubt he will be cordially welcomed by you, and be at your sittings an interested hearer and spectator.

I am dear brethren, yours in the best of bonds,

ROBERT WILSON,
Secretary of the Home Missionary Society and Congregational Union of Nova Scotia and New Brunswick.

FROM THE CONGREGATIONAL UNION OF ENGLAND AND WALES.

This assembly, while uniformly cherishing the liveliest interest in the Congregational churches of the United States, and always desirous of cultivating friendly relation with those churches, is constrained to give a prompt and special expression of these sentiments and feelings in the present unparalleled crisis of American history.

The assembly, therefore, dispensing with the formality of a regular invitation, requests the Rev. R. Vaughan, D. D., the Rev. A. Raleigh, D. D., and the Rev. George Smith, D. D., to proceed as delegates from this Union, to attend the Convention of Congregational churches, to be held next month in the city of Boston.

This assembly instructs the deputation to convey its cordial greetings to the ministers and churches represented at the said conference, and to assure them of its earnest prayers for their continued welfare and growing prosperity; its high appreciation of the great services rendered by them to the interests of our common Christianity, and of human progress; its cordial acknowledgment of the anti-slavery principles held and advocated by those churches; its hearty congratulations on account of the great work of emancipation thus far accomplished, and, it is fully believed, under God, completely and finally secured; its profound sympathy with them and their fellow countrymen generally in the fearful losses and agonizing trials of the four years' civil war; and, especially, in the foul assassination of the upright, patient, and noble-hearted Abraham Lincoln; its intense delight at the prospect of peace and re-union, without compromise on the slave question; its profound thankfulness to Almighty God for the spirit of moderation and clemency hitherto displayed on the victorious side; its full confidence in the efforts that will now be made to meet the physical, intellectual, and moral necessities of four millions of human beings in their sudden transition from the degradation of slavery, to the privileges and responsibilities of freedom; and finally, its readiness, in every appropriate way, to co-operate with their American brethren in these philanthropic labors, and in all future endeavors tending to promote the complete triumph of evangelical truth, religious equality, and universal peace.

UNION DES ÉGLISES EVANGELIQUES DE FRANCE.

PARIS, 27th April, 1865.

TO THE PRESIDENT OF THE CONVENTION OF THE CONGREGATIONAL CHURCHES OF AMERICA.

Reverend and dear Sir, — The Union of Evangelical Churches of France was invited, in your name, to send a representative to your great

Convention. We are very happy to be able to answer your kind invitation. We send, as our delegate to your Convention, our dear friend, the Rev. Theodore Monod, who succeeded his excellent and lamented father, the Rev. Dr. Monod, in his church at Paris. M. Monod is a bond of union between France and America; for, as he was born for the first time in Paris, he was born again in your great revival, and, although Pastor in our metropolis, he has studied and has been ordained in your country.

When we decided to send him to your assembly, we charged him with a message of exultant joy over the triumph of the cause of union and liberty. That final and splendid victory, secured after an amount of energetic efforts and of sacrifice hitherto unequalled, filled us French Protestants with a delight and an enthusiasm which words can not describe. If it had been our own cause, we should not have felt more. And it was indeed our own cause which had been imperiled; our own cause which, for four years, had been contemned and abused, when all the enemies of political, civil, and religious liberty prophesied scornfully that your union would be broken, and that your flag, upon which is inscribed all that which is dear to us, would lose for ever all its prestige. Now the Lord be praised; we have much prayed for you; we thank our God with you from the deepest of our heart.

But now, we are filled with mourning and awe; and our representative, M. Monod, will tell you under what gloom was held the anniversary of our Evangelical Society, which began just at the hour when the frightful news of Mr. Lincoln's assassination was known in Paris. Oh, you might have seen how much your cause is ours, by the universal lamentation which it excited among us all. But, in our deep sorrow, we did not for a moment fear for the ultimate result. We know that the more the Lord chastises us, the greater are the blessings which he keeps for us. M. Monod will convey to you our deepest sympathy in that bereavement which affects every one of us.

May the Lord, Mr. President, give to your great Convention an immense efficacy for the spread of His truth, and for the temporal and spiritual welfare of your great nation. May the fruits of that assembly ripen even after the removal of our generation for a better world; may your children and your children's children have to bless the day of your meeting.

In the name of the Commission Synodale,

G. Fisch, *President.*

T. Armand Delille, *Pastor*, *Secretaire.*

Rev. Dr. Thompson, of New York, read the following communication and address from the Welsh brethren:—

(TRANSLATION.)

At the annual meeting of the Glamorganshire Association of Congregational ministers and churches, held at Mountain Ash, Aberdare, May 31, 1865, it was unanimously resolved,—

1. That this Conference, representing 150 churches, 102 ministers, 81 lay preachers, and more than 20,000 communicants, rejoices to hear that an important Convention of the Congregational churches of the United States of America is to meet next month at Boston; earnestly prays that the Lord's blessing may rest on their deliberations; and appoints the Rev. John Thomas, Tabernacle, Liverpool, C. R. Jones, Esq., Llanoyllin, and Mr. John Griffiths, London, to represent this association at the Boston Convention.

2. That this Association greatly rejoices at the termination of the war in America; gratefully acknowledges the persistent and successful efforts of the North to extirpate the hateful curse of slavery; hails the restoration of the Union with joy and thankfulness; deeply sympathizes with the people and the government of the United States in their sorrow for the cruel and base assassination of one of the *wisest, noblest, most honest*, and most tender-hearted men that ever governed the United States, or any other country; admires the quiet and firm manner in which the government was carried on at so dangerous a crisis, and notwithstanding a catastrophe so unexpected and appalling; and earnestly trusts that the future of the Union will be worthy of the glorious history to which the American people can lay claim, from the first landing of the Pilgrim Fathers on the shores of the Western Continent, until now; and desires its representatives to convey this resolution to our beloved brethren at the Boston Convention.

THOMAS REES, D. D., Chairman. [*diff.*
JOHN DAVIES, *Mount Stuart Chapel, Car-*
HENRY OLIVER, B. A. (*Lond Univ.*), *Pan-*
JOHN REES, *Canaan, Swansea.* [*typudd.*
THOMAS THOMAS, *Landore, Swansea.*
JONAH ROBERTS, *Summerfield, Neath.*
HERBERT DANIEL, *Port-y-Pool.*
JOHN JONES, *Zoar, Maestey.*
JOHN MATTHEWS, *Neath.*
RHYS SWESYN JONES, *Merthyr Tydfil.*
JOHN LLOYD JAMES, *Whitchurch.*
JOHN JONES, *Rudery.*
JAMES EVANS, *Carmel,* [*dare.*
WILLIAM WILLIAMS, *Abercrombay, Aber-*
S. D. JONES, *Heolgenig, Merthyr.*
J. M. DAVIES, *Maesycwmur.*
PRYSE HOWELL, *Xnysgan Chapel, Merthyr.*
R. WHITTINGTON, *Freherbert.*
STEPHEN DAVIES, *Soar, Aberdare.*
MORGAN MORGAN, *Bethesda-y-pro.*
WILLIAM MORGAN, *Saron Troedyrhiew.*
JAMES THOMAS, *Carmel, Bonvilstone.*
JOHN BENAN, *Warmarluyd, Swansea.*
ROBERT JONES, *Craigyfargod.*
JOHN DAVIES, *Tailierion,*
JOHN JONES, *Carmel.*
RICHARD WILLIAMS, *Bryn.*
JOSIAH THOMAS JONES, *Aberdare.*
JOSUAH THOMAS, *Salem, Aberdare.*
THOMAS DAVIES, *Horeb, Morriston.*
JOHN GRIFFITHS, *Glantaf.*
JONAH MORGAN, *Cwmbach, Aberdare.*
WILLIAM WILLIAMS, *Hirwaen, Aberdare.*
REES MORGAN, *Addaldy, Glynneath Neath.*
DAVID EVANS, *Briton Ferry, Neath.*
DAVID JONES, *Wind Street Chapel, Neath.*
THO'S LLEWELYN, *Mountain Ash, Aber-*
JOHN DAVIES, *Pontygof, Ebbw Vale.* [*dare.*
WILLIAM EDWARDS, *Aberdare.*
WILLIAM WATKINS, *Maesteg.*
WILLIAM MORGANS, *Maesteg.*
DAVID PRICE, *Silsa, Aberdare.*
EVAN PRITCHARD, *Glandur.*
JOHN EVANS, *Maendn.*
ELLIS HUGHES, *Penmain.*
DAVID DAVIES, *Newinn.*
WILLIAM GRIFFITHS, *Llanharhan.*
RICHARD GRIFFITHS, *Cefucoedcymer.*
R. ROWLANDS, *Aberaman.*
DAVID RICHARDS, *Caerphilly.*

The following address to the Convention of the American Congregational Union, assembling in the city of Boston, Massachussetts, on the

14th of June, 1865, from ministers, deacons, and members belonging to the Welsh Congregational churches in the towns of Liverpool and Birkenhead, and a number of friends from London, and the Principality, at a public breakfast given May 30th, 1865, to their friends and brethren, the Rev. J. Thomas, Liverpool, C. R. Jones, Esq., Llanfyllin, and Mr. J. Griffith, London, on their departure on a visit to America:—

Moved by the Rev. N. Stephens, Liverpool; seconded by the Rev. W. Ambrose, Portmadoc (Secretary of the Carnarvonshire Association); supported by the Rev. O. Evans, Wrexham (Secretary of the Association of the Counties of Denbigh and Flint).

To the President of the Convention of
the American Congregational Union.

Honored Sir,—We, ministers, office-bearers, and members of the Welsh Congregational Churches, in Liverpool, Birkenhead, and elsewhere, who have assembled together on this 30th day of May, 1865, desire, through you, to express our fraternal love and regard for our American brethren, of the same faith and order, assembled at your convention, and the American churches and people in general. We feel assured, that the numerous Welsh Congregational churches in the Northern States, and thousands of our countrymen resident there, will be rejoiced to hear the expression of sympathy and affection towards their adopted country, from friends and brethren in their native land.

Our ministers in Liverpool have had the privilege of presenting an address to your eminent brother and countryman, the Rev. H. Ward Beecher, at a public breakfast given him by the friends of the Federal Union and negro emancipation, in this town, on his departure from our shores, after his recent visit to this country; expressing their profound sympathy with the government and people of the Northern States, in their great struggle to crush the infamous rebellion of the slaveocracy of the South.

In that address, they had the confidence to affirm it as their conviction, that had opportunities been afforded them, almost all the ministers and churches of our denomination in the principality of Wales—nearly eight hundred in number—would have cordially concurred in the sentiments therein contained. Subsequent information fully sustained that conviction.

Sir, we have watched the progress of the desolating war, which for the last four years afflicted your country, with the deepest solicitude. Our best sympathies were with your cause; our prayers were also in your calamities; and now those calamities being overpast, we are anxious to embrace the opportunity afforded by the assembling of your Convention to offer you our hearty congratulations on the happy termination of the unhappy strife. We rejoice in your rejoicings. We congratulate you, that, through the mercy of an overruling Providence, your Federal Union has ridden triumphantly through the terrific tempests which at one time threatened to overwhelm it; that it has come out of the fiery ordeal like gold purified in the furnace, having the plague spot of slavery wiped off entirely, and for ever, we trust, from its fair escutcheon.

The sacrifice, which you were called upon to make, indeed, was great and costly; but the blessings obtained, — the liberation of four millions of human beings from bondage and oppression as cruel as ever disgraced the earth; the eradication of the cancer which ate the vitals of the political Constitution of the Union; the removal of the hateful incubus which rested on the churches, and disfigured the fair face of Christianity in the land, — must be esteemed as a fair compensation.

Sir, we rejoice in the fact that the Congregational body in America has never, so far as our knowledge goes, participated in the actual guilt of negro slavery. We bless God that you have been enabled to keep aloof from the accursed thing, and to raise your voices against it, maintaining the spirit and traditions of your noble Pilgrim fathers, who

> —— "planted freedom's sacred tree
> Two hundred years ago"

on the rock of Plymouth.

We confidently trust that the universal cry of horror and indignation, raised simultaneously by all parties in England, at the atrocious deed of assassination by which your late honest, amiable, and virtuous President was cut off in the hour of triumph and rejoicing; the words of tender and heartfelt sympathy and condolence sent by our beloved widowed Queen Victoria to the sorrowing widow of your illustrious Abraham Lincoln; the warm sympathy expressed by our Government and Houses of Parliament with your Government and people on that mournful occasion, — will serve to calm and to soothe the offended feelings of our American brethren toward the mother country, on account of the sympathy shown by a certain party, and a portion of our public press, with the late rebellion, and be the means of uniting both countries together in a closer union, and deeper mutual affection, than ever before. May it ever be regarded as a most sacred duty, by ministers and Christian men in both countries, to use all possible endeavors to influence their respective governments to maintain peace and amity between Great Britain and America; so that they go forth hand in hand to confer upon the world the blessings of peace, civilization, and religion.

Finally, we rejoice in the benevolent and Christian object which your Union is contemplating; that of returning blessing upon the South for the curse which its slave oligarchy has brought upon your land; by establishing educational and religious institutions there, for the temporal and spiritual benefit of the poor and neglected negro races, to whom the late war brought the inestimable boon of emancipation; yea, to preach the gospel of peace and good-will to those who have been so long and so cruelly oppressed and to those who oppressed them, — to make of both, who till lately stood in the anomalous relation of master and slave to each other, "one new man, making peace." "Out of the South came the whirlwind" of rebellion and devastation upon your land. Out of the North also came the cold which blasted that rebellion; and now it may be added, "Fair weather cometh from the North," when its right hand is extended toward its fellow-countrymen in the South, to bestow upon them the blessings of the gospel of the grace of God, irrespective of race or color.

May the eye of the great Head of the church be upon you, to guide and direct your deliberations. May the spirit of the Lord rest upon your convention, "the spirit of wisdom and understanding, the spirit of counsel and might, the spirit of knowledge and of the fear of the Lord."

WILLIAM REES, *Chairman.*

The documents were accepted.

INSTRUCTIONS TO THE NOMINATING COMMITTEE.

On motion of Rev. Mr. Eustis, of Connecticut, it was

Voted, That the Nominating Committee be requested to bring before the Council the nominations for committees on business, finance, printing, and devotional exercises.

On motion of Rev. Dr. Bacon, of Connecticut, it was

Voted, That the Nominating Committee be authorized to nominate as many persons on each of these committees as they think best.

Rev. Mr. Dexter stated that Mr. Atkins, one of the scribes, asked to be excused, and moved that the Nominating Committee be requested to nominate a scribe in his place. Carried.

THE CANADA DELEGATION.

Rev. Dr. Bacon, of Connecticut, inquired if the names of the delegates from Canada had been inserted in the list as members of the Council, or whether they stood on the same footing as the brethren from England.

Dr. Patton said that was for the Council to decide.

Rev. Dr. BACON. I want the question presented now. I received, some time ago, a communication, indirectly, in regard to the representation of some Canadian churches in this National Council; and I made reply, that the terms of invitation to this Council made it not an Ecumenical nor an International Council, but simply a National one. The call is addressed to all those Congregational churches in the United States of America which are in recognized fellowship and co-operation, through general associations, general conferences, and conventions. Canada is not in the United States; and I therefore suggested that representatives from those churches would be gladly, I had no doubt, received here on the same footing with representatives from Great Britain and from France, as delegates from foreign churches, with which we are in fellowship. I move that those brethren who present credentials from various bodies of Congregational ministers and churches in foreign countries be received as honorary members of this National Council.

The motion was carried.

Rev. Dr. Budington, of New York, inquired if any documents had been presented to the committee on Credentials with regard to the Rev. Dr. Massie, of London, who was present.

Rev. Dr. Patton, of Illinois, said that no credentials had been presented to the committee.

Rev. Dr. Bacon, of Connecticut, said that Dr. Massie had formerly visited this country, and was known as our stanchest friend in times of trial; and he would move that he be invited to sit as an honorary member of this Council.

Carried.

WELCOME TO THE FOREIGN DELEGATES.

The moderator then addressed the foreign delegates as follows: —

Christian Brethren, — In behalf of the Council, I greet you with a cordial welcome. It is true, as has been stated in one of the documents which have been presented to this Council, that for the last four or five years, the condition of this country has been unparalleled in its embarrassment. We have been contending, as we feel, not for ourselves merely, but for the interests of humanity and the interests of Christianity throughout the civilized world. [Applause.] It has required all the energies of our minds and our hands, and all the sympathies of our hearts; but, in the exercise of these powers, we have suppressed the rebellion, and to-day we have peace. [Applause.] In securing that peace, it is true, we have laid our sons and brothers upon a hundred battle-fields in death; it is true that our honored President has been struck down by the assassin's hand, and mourning and sorrow have spread all over our land, and reached our brethren in foreign lands. But to-day, blessed be God, we turn from that past which has occupied our attention, with cheerful hearts, to engage in a cause more welcome to our hearts, — quite as dear and quite as important to the interests of Christianity as those duties in which we have hitherto been engaged. And we meet in council to-day to take measures to plant New England, with all her educational and all her Christian institutions, in the great West, and in the South, and in all parts of this land, in spite of the obstacles which stand in our way, which were presented so eloquently and ably by the gentleman [Rev. Dr. Sturtevant] who addressed us this morning. [Applause.] We are grateful that in such an hour as this, the minds of Christian brethren in our mother-country, and in other countries, are turned with interest toward us; and we are happy to greet you here to-day, and to receive from you those messages of sympathy and Christian affection which we know come from those whom we love, holding, with us, Christ as the common head of the living church. We shall be happy, brethren, to listen to you at this hour, and to receive from your own lips such words as you shall be pleased to utter.

REPLY OF REV. ROBERT VAUGHAN, D. D., OF LONDON, ENGLAND.

My dear and honored Brethren, — I have come very far to see you, to look you in the face, to shake you by the hand, and to tell you of the friendly thoughts, and of the honest sympathies, which are cherished toward you by multitudes in the land that I have left. Our assembly, representing the Congregational churches of England and Wales, appointed my friend Dr. Raleigh and myself as delegates to this body, — calling us from our homes and our work, solely that we might appear in your midst; and we are here, rejoicing in the thought that in you we see the representatives of nearly 3,000 American Congregational churches ; and we feel thankful in being able to assure you, that in us you see the representatives of nearly the same number of churches of the same faith and order in the old country. [Applause.] Those churches have deputed us to express to you on this occasion their most cordial greeting. They have laid it upon us to assure you of their sincere sympathy with every thing touching your welfare as American Congregationalists, and with every thing pertaining to the social and to the religious interests of your great country. I ought to assure you that the members of the Congregational Union of England and Wales are men who always have been, and are now, so far as my knowledge goes, to a man, opposed to the slave system, — men who have pronounced it to be an unchristian, unrighteous, and iniquitous system, that should die, that must perish. [Applause.] They did not all of them see, as you may perhaps have been aware, in the earlier stages of your struggle, what policy was the best for your country and for the slave; but there was no difference in them, arising from one portion being friends of your country, and the other not. No such difference existed. They were all your friends, whether mistaken in judgment or right in judgment; and now, to a man, they receive the issues of your great struggle, looking upon them as having come to pass under the influence of a higher hand than the hand of a man. They congratulate you upon the extinction of that system that brought on the war, and rejoice in the prospect of the better days which they believe to be waiting humanity here and humanity every where, through you. [Applause.]

Mr. Chairman, in brief, there are not upon God's earth — no, not upon God's earth — hearts beating more truly toward this country, more as a brother's heart should beat, than the hearts of the men who constitute the Congregational Union of England and Wales. [Applause.] Being confident of this, I feel it laid upon me truly to say it.

And now, sir, when I look upon this vast assembly, and remember what is represented by it, I have some memories rushing upon me, — thoughts which I should like to find words to express, but which I am sure I can not find words to express adequately. I must, however, venture to remind our friends that this Congregationalism, of which we have been hearing so much, is distinctly and emphatically ENGLISH. [Loud laughter and applause.] I mean what I say. Its revival in the modern church was left to be brought about by English thought and English piety, after it had been lost to the church for more than a thousand years. The men who were to discover this were men — a small band — devoted and brave in their generation. The mediæval Christianity that prevailed in England before the Reformation, as you all know, came from Rome. The Church of England, too, as we now have it, good people as there are in it, is an establishment that may fairly be described as greatly more mediæval than Protestant. And even Presbyterianism is an exotic in England; it did not grow there; it can hardly be said to ever have had any root there; it has tried to live there, but has found it very hard to do so. [Laughter.] But there was to be a body of men, as I have said, in the time of Elizabeth, and subsequently, separating from the established church. The men who became exiles under Queen Mary, and returned under Elizabeth, brought Presbyterianism from Frankfort and Geneva, and they tried to give it root in the country; but it could not be made to take root there, — it could not be made permanent there. But the separatists were men who began to thirst for that larger kind of liberty which our Congregationalism gives to the human spirit. That thirst rose within them, they scarcely knew how; but Congregationalism was to them like the waters of Bethlehem to the parched lips of David: they must have it or die. [Applause.] What God did in them as spiritual men, and what circumstances did around them, persecuting them at all points, fitted them for going to the New Testament, and discovering there the very polity which they felt they needed, as the polity of the first churches bearing the apostolic sanction.

Now, you know very well, for you have heard it to-day, that a portion of those holy men, worn and wearied by the trials of that country that would not give them liberty, came to this land in search of a home. Not far from this did they put their feet for the first time upon these shores; and here they were, as you know, to create a great future. A portion of those men remained in England; and there they had to make, and did make, a history for themselves, — a history of which we who have descended from them are by no means ashamed. [Applause.] The man does not deserve the name of Englishman, who is not proud of that period in his nation's history, when the high-souled thought and passion of a great people went forth through the genius of a Cromwell and a Milton. [Loud applause.] We are doing something now in England to bring up these old names, associated with these principles of Congregationalism, and marvelously chagrined are many around us at the thought that we can plead such a noble ancestry; but we mean to hold to it. [Applause.]

But, sir, I see in this bit of history, in which we are now both interested, something that presents itself to my imagination like the flow of some ancient river. I see its waters up in some far back territory, divided into two streams, and these two streams widen their way apart, through their separate beds, until, after a long space, they are seen verging toward each other, and finally the waters meet and are one again; and then roll on with greater force than ever, as if joyous at the meeting. Here are the two streams: your stream of Congregationalism in America, our stream in England; and to-day, sir, the two come together, and we are one. [Loud applause.] Will you excuse me if I ask you to give me your hand in token of this union? [The moderator and the speaker clasped hands amid enthusiastic applause.] This is a happy day, to me, sir! May the power be powerless and fall, come whence it may, that would ever divide men whom God has joined together by a common blood and a common faith! [Applause.]

But, my friends, our Congregationalism is an infant in years compared with what it is to be. It has, beyond all other systems, pronounced upon the grand question of the union of church and state. The early settlers of this country, indeed, were placed in peculiar circumstances, and if they did not see every thing in relation to this principle at once, it was sure to be seen; and at this moment I could, were this the place for doing it, direct your attention to what is passing in Europe, which shows very clearly that the first order of minds in Europe are beginning to find their way to our principle of English independency, as presenting the grand secret by means of which to put an end to that broil of ages, — the mingling of the ecclesiastical with the civil. We have Emperor marshaled against Pope, and Pope against Emperor; we have hierarchies rising against nationalities, and nationalities rising against hierarchies. We have men coming forth not merely from schools of theology, but from the departments of high statesmanship, — such men as Guizot and Laboulaye, — and affirming, in their own way, that the great principle by which an end is to be put to this protracted strife is the principle by which men learn to give unto God the things which are God's, while they give unto Cæsar the things that are his. Our friend, M. Monod, can tell you a little how French thought is working in this direction; what M. Bersier and M. Pressensé and others, are doing to illuminate the French mind upon this great principle. Then there is M. Vinet, a man who, coming out from an order of things very unlike ours, was brought, by the influence of light, to embrace the principle we hold. The great Cavour learned to take up the maxim, "A free church in a free state," as what the people want. "Very good as far as it goes," say some, more enlightened yet. "Free *churches* in a free state — that is what we want." [Applause.] You can never have *one* church in any state that would not be a favoritism to some, and a wrong to others. You must look to a grand tolerance of variety, more or less, if there is to be really a system of liberty for men; and our principles go in that direction.

But, sir, I will not detain you longer. I should not have said this much but that, when a man comes across the Atlantic to speak half an hour, perhaps he may have it. [Laughter, and calls of "Go on."]

Your country has passed through trouble; but let it be remembered, dear brethren, that since those dark days of the war of independence, you have known nothing of what trouble means. Through that long interval, until within the last three or four years, your history has been one unbroken flow of prosperity. And will you bear with me in saying, that it is not in the power of prosperity alone to raise a nation to all the greatness of which a nation is capable? Individuals and communities are ripened by other influences into higher forms of manhood. It is very instructive, as you know, to see what the fruits are that a good man brings out of his trouble, — the broader thought, the calmer self-possession, the wiser patience and considerateness, the higher development of the richer tones of man's nature. Nations may have that, — God means that you shall have it. He is doing by you as he does by many more. The result will be that for which your children will be grateful. We sympathize with you in what you have had to bear. Misconceptions of all kinds have been brought against you, — some in quarters where you might have expected them, others in quarters where you might have expected better things: you have had to bear these. Malignity, in all forms and grades, has leveled its envenomed shafts at you, and that, too, in your hour of trial: you have had to bear that. And the dastard villanies of assassination have been allowed to place their ingredients in the cup which you have had to drink. But be of good cheer, brethren! The dark day is past, and the day to come will be brighter. Many who did not see your case at first, could not see it as it really was, have come to see it as it is. Many who prophesied that if a strain like that which has come upon your institutions were once to come upon them, they would snap asunder, and proclaim their emptiness and worthlessness to the world, have proved false prophets, as you know. The strain has come; the snap has not taken place; the institutions are here on a more solid rock than before. And this takes place in the sight of all the nations. It has gone forth wherever a freeman is found, or the friends of freedom, like a new song of hope for humanity; and it has gone to the homes of the oppressor like a knell of despair. Your victory is ours; your progress is ours. Man's fate is bound up not a little with your fate. Never forget that. You have now coming upon you new duties. Your armies have gained victories that have placed you in the foremost rank of nations in that respect. What so fitting now as that you show that you are capable of realizing the victories of peace, if need be, at a cost as great as that which has been involved in the victories of war? Let this be done, and the reputation, the honorable name of your country will be greater than ever, and institutions like yours have a fairer chance of becoming the institutions of men than they have ever possessed in the history of the world. Count it not a hard thing to be summoned to this work. It is because the God of your fathers means to make you honorable and useful in the earth that he has summoned you to it. That luxuriant South has destroyed the Spaniard, from the day when he first put his foot upon the soil down to now, while this hardy North has reinvigorated the Anglo-Saxon. Nations are wasted, swept away as worthless, by being allowed to live in ease and indulgence. They are made strong by being compelled to do, to dare, and to suffer. If these things be so, then have you not encouragement? Your ship has weathered this storm, as that old ship from whose deck I have just come has weathered many a storm before, and she is none the worse for it. No, that land is far better to-day than it has been since the days of which I was speaking just now, — the days of our Cromwell and Milton. When you were brought into your trouble by the high tory faction, — a church and king tyranny, — that rule was extended over us, and far into the present century; but it is gone, gone forever. Then we were under the regime of the Corporation and Test Acts, which excluded every Englishman from every office in which he could serve his country, unless he were prepared to take the sacrament according to the forms prescribed by the Church of England. That impious tyranny is no more. The Catholic then asked, and asked from year to year, without a prospect of success, to be allowed to have a voice, through men of his faith, on the floor of the House of Commons. That exclusion, too, no longer exists. Our House of Commons, too, through the influence of our peers, in their nomination boroughs, could be so packed by nobles as to be the peers' house rather than the people's house. The great Reform Bill has made all our statesmen understand, that to create a majority in our House of Commons is the work of the people, and that where that majority is, there the power of the realm is to be found. Our municipal corporations were all close, consisting of men who had passed through the Test-Act process to get there, and who filled up vacancies among themselves. Now, our townsmen and citizens choose all these functionaries by fair and open suffrage; and the consequence is, that the municipal power of the country has passed, to a large extent, into the hands of the Congregationalists. So, too, it has been in other ways. Education has advanced marvelously beyond what it was. Cheap and good literature is flooding the country to an extent that is almost incredible, and the result is, we have working-classes now so well educated, that, if we were to be a republic to-morrow, we should have nothing to fear. [" Hear, hear," and applause.] This is everywhere obvious to those who know what our country is. Really, paradoxical as it may sound, I can venture to say, *old* England was never so *young* as at this day. [Laughter.]

Why do I touch upon this? Is it in mere boastfulness? O, God forbid! God forbid! It is from God, not from any desert of ours, that I am able here, upon your platform, to speak thus of that dear home of mine. God has done it for us, and will do more. Our march began with the early years of this century, and take care that we do not catch you before the end of it. [Laughter and applause.] But I will only now say, sir, that the grand mission, I think, that God is showing to us, — your country and ours, — is that we shall demonstrate that we have been made free that we might delight to make others free. All that I have said has been intended to show to you how admirably the two countries are mated for this great mission; and if it should be given to us to see that this is what Providence would seem to have devolved upon us, who can tell the result? But my last word to you is this: This will not be but as the good men of this land, and the good men of our land, resolve that with God's help it shall be. There will be bad men with you, there will be bad men with us, and we must not lean upon the consciousness that our cause is good, and allow the bad to triumph. We must feel that we have to watch against it, to neutralize it, and to endeavor in every possible way to secure amity between England and America, that they may be one for no selfish purpose, but one for God and humanity. The Union Jack and the Stars and Stripes must float in every harbor of the world; the commodities of your country and of mine must be exposed in competition in all the markets of the globe; and one only needs to look back to the history of England and Holland two hundred years ago, to perceive how much there must be in the relations of two such nations, calling on both sides for a superiority to all little irritating things, and for a breadth of manhood that will not be offended by trifles, but will know how to subordinate them to great principles and to duty. [Loud applause.]

BUSINESS COMMITTEES.

Rev. Mr. Langworthy, chairman of the committee on Nominations, reported the following as the committees of the Council: —

COMMITTEE ON BUSINESS.

Rev. Alonzo H. Quint, of Massachusetts; Rev. Samuel Wolcott, D. D., of Ohio; Rev. Benjamin Labaree, D. D., of Vermont; Dea. Philo Carpenter, of Illinois; Dea. Samuel F. Drury, of Michigan.

COMMITTEE ON DEVOTIONAL EXERCISES.

Rev. Edward N. Kirk, D. D., of Boston; Rev. Wm. De Loss Love, of Wisconsin; Rev. Asa Turner, of Iowa; Rev. George E. Adams, D. D., of Maine; Dea. Daniel H. Parker, of New Hampshire.

COMMITTEE ON FINANCE.

Dea. Charles Stoddard, of Massachusetts; Henry C. Bowen, of New York, E. Beecher Preston, of Connecticut; Hon. Douglas Putnam, of Ohio; Dea. Moses Pettengill, of Illinois.

COMMITTEE ON PRINTING.

Rev. James B. Miles, of Massachusetts; Rev. John C. Holbrook, D. D., of New York; Dea. Elnathan F. Duren, of Maine.

ADDITIONAL SECRETARY.

Rev. Elihu P. Marvin, of Massachusetts, in place of Mr. Atkins.

ADDRESS OF REV. ALEXANDER RALEIGH, D. D., OF LONDON, ENGLAND.

Rev. Dr. Raleigh, having been called upon to address the convention, said: —

Mr. Moderator, — I am perfectly sensible of the value of the time of this assembly, and therefore I am loath to present myself, especially after my venerated friend, Dr. Vaughan, has spoken so long and so well;

but I, too, have come across the Atlantic to say something, if I may be allowed a very short space of your time, for others, as well as for myself; for others, because they are pleased to judge that in the main my thought would be theirs.

It is impossible to meet you here without thinking and speaking of the last four years. Those years speak themselves so loudly, and lead so far into future time, that unless one shall catch some of their voice, and chime in with their solemn and grand tones, it is a mere impertinence to profess to speak at all. I want to speak to you for a few minutes of those last four years; and to tell you, if I can, how intense an interest has been in the hearts of many of us, in all you have been doing, attempting, achieving, suffering; what a joy we have sometimes had, and sometimes what an agony of sympathy we have felt, as your fortunes have been rising or falling during those memorable years. It is literally true that we have had you in our hearts. Perhaps no single day of those four years has passed, in which some of our best and most sacred thoughts, — thoughts ever ready to melt into feeling or rise into prayer, — have not been with you here, upon this side of the Atlantic. We have serenaded your president, a martyr now. Peace to his ashes, eternal honor to his memory. We have camped with your soldiers upon the banks of the Potomac, listening to the rippling of the river, and looking up into the glittering stars. We have watched the dark tide of battle rise and fall upon those blood-red fields to which you have given undying names. We have rejoiced with you in your victories. We have wept with you over your slain.

I know some of you say, in a kindly way, — I have heard it more than once since I came — "If this is so, we are sorry we did not know it more fully." [Applause.] Well, I shall be honest: I am sorry too. [Renewed applause.] I am sorry you did not know it more fully and more seasonably; but I give you the word of an honest man that it is not the less true upon that account. We did not understand your circumstances; and I do not think you have quite understood ours.

The truth is, — and I do not suppose any of us have the least interest in concealing the truth, — we have not all been of one mind in reference to some of the exterior aspects of your question; and we have taken the English and American liberty of expressing our thoughts and opinions. A great many of us have been with you from the beginning, and through and through. [Applause.] We have believed that your cause was right, and that you were promoting it, in the main, in the right way, — in the only way in which it could be effectually promoted under the circumstances. We have thought your end good, and we have thought your means necessary. We have judged that you were fighting for us, as well as for yourselves; for liberty against slavery; for good government against political misrule; for morality against many social shames; for peace over this continent, and through the whole earth. Instead of falling in with the vulgar and hypocritical cry against the "War Christians," which some newspaper correspondents upon this side of the water have attempted to raise against you, we have judged that if the war be in itself just and necessary, it would better be in the hands of Christians than in the hands of other men. [Applause.] And why? Because we have felt that they will conduct it without personal animosity; that they will soothe its inevitable horrors and miseries with Christian sympathy; that they will treat the vanquished with humanity; that they will soothe the agonies of the dying, and bury the dead with honor. We have felt that they might be trusted, on the one hand, not to cease from the war so long as it should be necessary, and thus betray interests far more precious to humanity than a few years of human life; and, on the other hand, not to continue it one hour beyond the time when with safety and honor it might cease. These have been our views.

Others among us, feeling not less kindly to you, have had many difficulties, — really you should not be surprised at this, for you have had them among yourselves, — difficulties with regard to state rights, and what not; in relation to your central federal power, and in relation to accomplishing good by means of evil. Those doubts have been hanging upon the minds of some of our thoughtful and serious men. I am thankful I never shared them to any appreciable extent myself. I saw your way — just the way you have taken — in all these difficulties, just as I saw my way in faith and hope through some of the thick fogs through which we passed upon the Atlantic in coming to your hospitable Western shores. But I claimed the liberty for those who had these doubts to have them if they felt they must; and temperately to express them, and to hold them until, by human argument or by Divine Providence, they should be disputed and set aside. "Charity believeth all things, hopeth all things, endureth all things."

Now we want to strike hands in peace, friendship, and co-operation in our great Master's work. We all yield to the logic of events. We all accept the facts of the present hour. I think I may say that now we are all glad that you have triumphed. Dr. Vaughan has borne true testimony that there is not a man among us Congregationalists, that would have had a thought of any thing but sorrow and shame at the triumph of the South over you. We are all glad that you have triumphed; glad that you did not give up your work until it was done; glad that you refused to listen to those alluring overtures of peace proffered to you by men among your own ranks and by others from abroad, while yet there lay in the very heart of the South the principles of eternal rebellion and war; and glad, above all, to recognize, as my venerated friend has so fully done, the action of a superior Power; glad to think how much God has taken this matter into his own hands. It was in his providence, if not by his direct ordination, that there came so early in this struggle this partial chill of some portion of British sympathy. You were taught by this a precious lesson, — a lesson you will never forget, and for which the whole world will be the better, — the lesson of complete self-reliance in doing that which you felt was necessary to be done. [Applause] And your great enemy was thus, I believe, led on and on, until he put all upon the final cast, and brought on the overwhelming and glorious end. Oh, He is wonderful in counsel and excellent in working.

I wish I could tell you with how much cordiality we have been sent to you, and with how much earnest and loving desire we came. I have attended many meetings of the Congregational Union of England and Wales, and I have seen, in my time, some pleasant excitements, some enthusiasms; but I cannot remember any thing at all approaching the unbounded enthusiasm and the excitement with which the subject of our relation to you and your churches was entertained and settled at the meeting of the last month. It was as if long pent-up waters had escaped at last. It was as if our love — we hardly know how, strangely to some of us, and not with our will — had been kept in by restrictions; but the hour came at length; and then I only wish you could have been there to see how that sober, quiet, deliberative assembly became in a few minutes like your Niagara. We seemed to have solved the problem of the Atlantic telegraph before it had been laid; and it seemed that we were sending waves of cordiality to your shores, instead of a few solitary men like my friend and myself.

Receive us. We come in truth and sincerity. "We be true men; thy servants be no spies." [Applause.] We come to behold neither the nakedness nor the fullness of your land. We rejoice in the beneficence of your constitution, the stability of your laws, the loyalty of your citizens, the indomitable courage of your soldiers, the education of your common people, the increase of your population. We rejoice — I do, for I love every growing thing — in your vast plains, although we have not seen them yet, your wide-stretching prairies, every wind of which sings the song of freedom. We rejoice in your mountains and rivers and lakes and seas. God has brought you into a goodly land; fountains and depths springing out of valleys and hills; a land of wheat and barley, and vines, and fig-trees, and pomegranates; a land of oil and wine. [See Deut. 8: 8.] Only beware, — we say this with sorrowful memory of our own failures, — beware lest thou forget the commandments of the Lord thy God, which he doth command thee again this day in the solemn hour of trial, and under the solemnities of Sinai itself.

Receive us, I say; and make with us a covenant of peace, this day; and let us go home, and say we know you have made it in your hearts. Oh, my heart trembles and is afraid, when I draw with the finger of imagination the scenes that would rise upon an astonished world if these two great people were to fall into deadly strife. My heart trembles, not with any craven fear. I am an Englishman; at least I am a Scotchman, and that is still better. [Applause.] But I know my countrymen; and I know that like yours they are incapable of fear, in a matter which touches the honor or the life of the nation. We are of your own metal. Now judge our hearts by that, and test them. Judge by that what a war must be, if there be the pith of England upon the one side, and the resources of America upon the other: too shocking a thing to be imagined. I want peace with my whole heart. I know it is vain to say, "Peace, peace," when there is no peace. "First pure, then peaceable." Justice comes before peace, and must be its base. If in any thing we have wronged you, and if you can make it good before the judgment of mankind, or even to our own moral consciousness, we will use all our influence that your wrongs may be righted, whatever they may be. [Applause.] And if you have wronged us, you must do the same. [Renewed applause.] This we can do. We can resolve that all such difficulties — and I shall not allude to them more particularly — shall be taken up and considered in the spirit of Christian justice and charity. A war need not be. A war cannot be without great mutual sin.

What can any man propose by such a war? What can any statesman propose to gain? What could we do to each other? I will tell you what we could do. We could sweep the commerce of both nations from the sea. We could ensanguine the waves that usually roll so peacefully between us. We could add to the already too long list of the world's battle-fields. We could multiply widows and orphans, and swell the dark tide of misery in both lands. We could cast into the unknown future, seeds of evil, which our children and children's children will certainly reap when we are in our graves. But what benefit of any kind could be proposed by such a strife, how it could be thought in any way to help justice, fairness, humanity, or religion, I cannot tell. May the God of peace bruise Satan under our feet shortly. May He turn the heart of England to America, and the heart of America to England, lest He come and smite the earth with a curse.

Finally, I may say again, like my venerated brother, we bid you God speed in your blessed work. It is a work that will require all your wisdom, all your patience, all your love; and sure I am that if you continue it with that persistent tenacity, which has been commended to you so nobly in the eloquent discourse of this morning, you will at length spread over this whole continent righteousness and love: and the fruits of righteousness shall be peace and quietness forever. Now blessed be the Lord God, the God of Israel, who only doeth wondrous things; and blessed be His name for ever; and let the whole earth be filled with His glory. Amen and amen.

ADDRESS OF REV. JAMES W. MASSIE, D. D., OF ENGLAND.

Rev. Dr. Massie, of England, being called upon, addressed the convention as follows: —

Mr. Moderator, — I feel as if I were renewing the intercourse with my American brethren which terminated eighteen months ago, after one of the most pleasant scenes I ever witnessed or took part in. My fellowship with American Christians and ministers of religion at that time gave me assurance that not only were you ready to accomplish a great work, but were willing to accomplish it in fellowship with English Christians. I rejoice in the testimony that my brethren have borne concerning the denomination to which they and I belong; and especially do I rejoice in the testimony that Dr. Raleigh has presented as to the enthusiasm which pervaded our Congregational assembly upon the nomination of those two excellent brethren, when it was proposed and carried. I think that, if this assembly had heard our friend, Dr. Raleigh, in the speech he uttered upon that occasion, there would be indeed what he has described as the bursting tide of Niagara, even here. I felt then constrained to say that the triumph of your cause was as manifest in the city of London as it had been in the city of Richmond. [Applause.]

I come here with credentials from no association, though there are associations that requested me to come. Those associations gave me my credentials upon my former visit; but inasmuch as they were for union and for emancipation, for the freedmen of America, — the freedmen's aid commissions of England, — I did not think it would be suitable to present these credentials, which I have in my pocket, to a council of Congregational ministers. But I came that I might witness the welcome that you would give to my brothers; to witness the testimony they would bear of the country from which I come; and that, if I might be a humble instrument, I might yet increase the tide of sympathy and affection that flows between the American and the English people.

I feel that we are not two nations. I feel that we are one people; that my best kindred, in collateral lineation, dwell with you; that your kindred dwell with us; that your language is my language; that your religion is mine; and that your laws, and the spirit of your laws, may be said to be congenial with our laws and the spirit of our laws. Your missions and our missions flow in the same channel, and pervade the same fields of action. You are generously sustaining us, while we are seeking honorably to sustain you, in extending the knowledge of the gospel of Christ to all lands. I rejoice in that sympathy between us. I am sure that Dr. Raleigh's fears will never be realized; for, were war to prevail between England and America, not only would priestcraft send forth a howl of rejoicing, and the aristocracy and oppressors of mankind mingle together their hisses of applause, but the very devils in hell itself would rejoice; because the instruments capable of the greatest work of regeneration and evangelization in the earth, would be shattered and rendered unfit for operation. Let England and America be one in their religion, and in co-operation, and all the tyrannies of the world will quail before them. Let their one language girdle the earth, and be the channel of religious instruction and sympathy and love, and heathenism will submit, and our God shall be all and in all.

Rev. Theodore Monod was called upon to speak in behalf of France; but stated that he wished to read, in the course of his remarks, a letter, which he had not with him, and would prefer to speak to-morrow morning. This arrangement was agreed to by the Council.

ADDRESS OF REV. HENRY WILKES, D. D., OF MONTREAL, CANADA.

Rev. Dr. Wilkes, being called upon, said: —

I perceive, Mr. Moderator, that I have only seven minutes left before the hour fixed for the adjournment, and I shall therefore be brief. After the expression of the sentiments of my learned friends and brethren from the fatherland, the truth of which it was not at all necessary that I should endorse, because their own character is quite sufficient, I need not have said any thing upon that point; but I was at a meeting of the Congregational Union in 1862, one year after the commencement of your struggle, at a time when in that country its success was by no means very promising, even in the estimation of many among you; and I may perhaps venture to say, that at that time, mingling with my brethren there, and listening to them in their churches, in May, June, July, and August, 1862, there was throughout the Congregational churches in England, — I am speaking of them, and not of the "Times" newspaper at all, for that is a very different thing, — I unhesitatingly say, that in all the Congregational churches in England, there was a deep, deep sympathy with this nation, and a sympathy upon the right side. I know that at that time the Union recommended that on the second Lord's day in June, there should be special prayer offered throughout the kingdom, and that special prayer was offered, not merely that the Lord would restore peace, but that the Lord would bless you in the great work in which you were engaged in overthrowing that fearful system, as it has been so emphatically done to-day.

Now, sir, I come to Canada. Canada has been very unpopular with you, particularly during the last year. These raids have vexed you very much; and I am not surprised at it. But I am not to speak so much for Canada as for the Congregational churches of Canada. They are but a small band of churches, about ninety; but those churches, east and west, without a single exception, have been with you most heartily and lovingly in the strife in which you have been engaged. [Applause.]

To the proof, — for there is nothing like the proof. A newspaper, which has two or three times the circulation of any other in Montreal, is owned by a deacon of my church, and has a very powerful influence in that city and throughout a large part of the country. That paper has been uniformly, from the commencement of the strife until now, on the side of truth and righteousness, on the side of freedom, on the side of what we call the North. Another press in the city has opposed it most bitterly, — a press which has been fed, I suppose, and in part edited by Southern refugees who are in the city, who have doubtless awakened sympathy among certain classes in our community, and particularly with those who do not sympathise with us in our holy religion. You know we have something else in Canada. We have a Popish religion there. Protestantism is, I was going to say, an exotic with us. But not merely our own denomination, but the people generally holding Protestant views, are upon your side.

It seems to be supposed, in many parts of your country, that because a police judge, who happens not to be a man qualified to declare upon international law, makes a decision to release the raiders, and because there were hurras in the court-room, Canada is responsible. I remember well the mourning and lamentation, when that decision was arrived at, among the merchants and other respectable men whom I met in the streets, who uniformly regarded it as a mistake, and about which they sincerely grieved. I think it is due to Canada to declare this honestly and openly. I have been there thirty years, and profess to know something about the feeling of that community. I met a man, and asked him, "Why don't you come to church?" "Why," said he, "you always pray for the United States." "Well," said I, "ought I not to pray for the United States?" "I can tell that you sympathize with the North, and I don't." And what I have done in my church is done by all my brethren.

When that terrible thing occurred, the assassination of your noble President, I happened to be in Boston and Hartford at the time, and therefore could mingle with you in the very midst of your mourning; but I know that our country was filled with distress, that our pulpits were draped, and that men of all denominations wept and prayed together, and prayed that God would have mercy, and overrule an event so fearful as this for good. They expressed an intense sympathy, from the very heart of hearts of the people, in this affliction, and an abhorrence and utter detestation against the act and those who applauded it.

I will now close by saying, that I bring to you the fraternal congratulations, and the expression of the warm affection, of the churches, as represented in our Congregational Union this week and last week. I left Toronto at half past five o'clock on Monday, when they were assembled, and they instructed me to express to you our most cordial affection. We have a feeling of oneness with you, — oneness in politics, oneness in the faith once delivered to the saints, oneness in the longing desire for the spread of the great principles of our holy religion throughout your land and ours. Having said this, I will retire, praying that all your deliberations may be under the divine guidance, and may be richly blessed by the Head of the church, for the welfare of his own kingdom, the glory of God, and blessings upon your country. [Applause.]

Rev. Mr. Quint, of Massachusetts, chairman of the Business Committee, reported a recommendation of the order of business for to-morrow as follows: —

That immediately after the address of Rev. Mr. Monod, the committee on Credentials have time to report, after which the papers prepared by the committees appointed by the conference in New York should be read in the following order: —

1. Declaration of Christian faith.
2. Statement of church polity.
3. Evangelization in the West and South.
4. Church-building.

He reported, also, the following recommendations: —

1. That the time from eleven, A. M., to half past eleven, A. M., be daily assigned to devotional exercises.

2. That the contracts made by the Committee of Arrangements, with phonographic and other reporters, be ratified by the Council.

3. That the reports originating with committees outside of the Council be referred to special committees immediately on their acceptance by the Council, and without debate on their merits; all debate to take place when these special committees report to the Council.

The report was adopted.

The hour of five o'clock having arrived, the Council adjourned until to-morrow morning, under the rule.

THIRD DAY, FRIDAY, JUNE 16.

The Council was called to order and opened by prayer, at 9 o'clock, A. M., by the moderator.

The record of yesterday's proceedings was read by the scribe, Rev. Mr. Dexter, and approved.

Rev. Dr. Patton, of Illinois, reported from the committee on Credentials a recommendation that all chairmen of committees directed to present special reports to the Council preparatory for business, by the preliminary meeting held in New York, but who are not members of the Council, be invited to sit as corresponding members.

Rev. Dr. Harris, of Maine, moved to amend by inserting "members" instead of "chairmen."

The amendment was seconded.

Rev. Mr. Dexter moved to amend by including the committee on Arrangements, and Dr. Harris accepted the amendment.

The amendment, as amended, was agreed to.

Rev. Dr. Patton, of Illinois, read the following paper: —

"At the annual meeting of the General Association of Illinois, held at Peoria, Ill., May, 1865, the following action was had, concerning the subject of church-building: —

"'*Whereas*, By an unintentional oversight, the preliminary conference at New York did not appoint a committee to report upon the topic of church-building, which had been adopted in the programme of subjects to be presented before the Boston Council; and

"'*Whereas*, By the request of the nominating committee of the conference, through the secretary of the Congregational Union, Rev. J. E. Roy has prepared a report upon this enterprise:

"'*Resolved*, That Brother Roy be requested to read the same before this association after the sermon, this (Thursday) evening.'

"His essay having been read according to request, it was

"'*Resolved*, That, in the omission of the preliminary conference to appoint a committee to report on the subject of church-building, Rev. J. E. Roy be requested to proceed to Boston to lay before the National Council, in the name of the General Association of Illinois, the paper he has just read.'

"By order of the Association,

"RICHARD C. DUNN, *Scribe.*

"PEORIA, May 27, 1865."

It was moved further to amend the report by including the name of Rev. J. E. Roy, of Illinois.

Rev. Dr. PATTON, of Illinois, said there would be no objection to that, although the language of the report was intended to include him.

Rev. Dr. BACON, of Connecticut. In regard to the statement just read, of the omission with regard to church-building, it strikes me as altogether a mistake. I think that the document prepared by Mr. Roy ought to be handed to some committee already appointed.

Rev. Dr. PATTON, of Illinois. As one of those who took action in Illinois, I would like to observe that we were informed that it was entirely by oversight that no special committee was appointed. The subject of church-building was separately named as one of the subjects to be brought before this body; and Brother Roy, being familiar with the whole subject, was desired, by request from the East, to prepare a document upon it. Allow me to observe, also, that any respectable body of Congregational ministers and laymen, in requesting a report to be presented to this body, stand perfectly upon a level with that preparatory conference in New York; for I take it upon me to say that that conference was not specially expected beforehand to appoint these committees, or to have these reports prepared, although the thing done may have been a wise thing in itself. But any other body of Congregationalists had a perfect right to prepare a report on any subject to come before the Council, and this body has a perfect right to receive such report on a level with any other report from any quarter. We are a free body. Those preparatory committees are not committees of this body, but of the conference, and any other body may send reports here.

Rev. Dr. BACON, of Connecticut. All of which I acknowledge, *ab imo pectore;* but I say, that as a free body we have a right to say that the report of Mr. Roy shall come to us through the committee we have already recognized, upon evangelization in the West and South.

Rev. Dr. PATTON, of Illinois. That committee has not included it in their report, but have left it for Brother Roy to present.

Rev. Dr. BACON, of Connecticut. They can make this a part of their report.

Rev. Mr. QUINT, of Massachusetts, dissented from the view taken by the chairman of the committee, and maintained that no other body could stand in the same relation to this Council as the preliminary conference in New York, and that the paper presented by Mr. Roy could not be properly called a report. The paper ought to be received; but the rules adopted by the convention provided for the case of such papers, and he desired that they be adhered to.

Rev. Dr. HARRIS, of Maine, suggested that the pending question was not the disposition of the report, but whether Mr. Roy should have the privilege of a seat upon the floor, and of speaking in the Council.

The motion was agreed to, and the report of the committee was adopted.

Rev. Dr. Patton further reported: —

That the committee had added to the roll such further names as had been received since yesterday morning.

Also, that application had been made to admit a delegate appointed by a church which was omitted from the letters missive sent to the neighboring churches, and which thus had no opportunity to act with them in conference. The committee, acknowledging the injustice of the omission, did not feel that it was within their province to attempt to rectify it, but reported the case for the action of the Council.

Rev. Dr. HARRIS, of Maine, conceived it to be impossible for the Council to rectify the omission in this or in similar cases; and therefore moved that the consideration of that part of the report be indefinitely postponed.

The motion was agreed to.

Rev. Dr. Dutton, of Connecticut, under the impression that the matter was not fully understood by the Council, moved a reconsideration of the last vote.

The Council refused to reconsider, by a vote, on division, of ayes 94; noes 126.

Rev. Mr. Quint, from the committee on Business, made a report, recommending, —

That to-morrow, June 17, be set apart as the time recommended by the preliminary committees as a special service of devotion for the acknowledgment of the marvelous and the merciful dealings of Almighty God with the nation in connection with the war, and for supplicating a gracious dispensation of the Spirit of God upon the land, that our restored national unity may be consecrated in righteousness, and in the peace and joy of the Holy Ghost; and that the invitation of the First Church in Charlestown, to hold service in their meeting-house on Harvard Hill, be accepted, and that the Council meet there at three o'clock, P. M.

On motion of Dr. Bacon, of Connecticut, the report was referred to the committee on devotional exercises.

6

FOREFATHERS' ROCK.

Rev. A. L. Stone, D. D., of Massachusetts, chairman of the Committee of Arrangements, extended an invitation to members of the Council to visit in a body the Forefathers' Rock at Plymouth, free of all charge, and participate in a collation there to be provided.

He thought such an excursion would be no mean element in the history of the Council. Arrangements would also be made by which others could participate in the trip at a small expense. The day of the excursion would be fixed hereafter, but could not well be before Thursday of next week.

Rev. Dr. Todd, of Massachusetts, moved to accept the invitation.

Rev. Dr. THOMPSON, of New York, expressed his hearty sympathy with the proposition, and hoped it would be possible to comply with the arrangement, but called attention to the great amount of business to be done, and thought it better to carry out Plymouth-Rock principles, upon which all could unite, than to visit the Rock itself, where no two men could stand at the same time. [Laughter.]

Rev. Dr. ADAMS, of Maine, was fully persuaded that the work of the convention would not be hindered by taking next Thursday for such an excursion.

The motion to accept the invitation was agreed to.

Rev. Mr. Byington, of Vermont, stated that Gov. Smith of Vermont, in consequence of illness, would be unable to perform his duties on the committee on Nominations, and wished to be excused from further service upon that committee; and nominated Rev. Clark E. Ferrin, of Vermont, to take his place.

The motion to excuse Gov. Smith, and appoint Rev. Mr. Ferrin, was agreed to.

Rev. Mr. Langworthy, of Massachusetts, moved that a committee be appointed to prepare resolutions in reference to the condition of the country, and to report the same for the action of the Council.

The motion was agreed to.

On motion, at the suggestion of the chairman of the committee on Nominations, the rule of the Council, limiting the number to be appointed upon committees to three, was modified, so as to allow the committee to appoint in each case such number as in their judgment seemed best.

The orders of the day were called for, the preliminary business having been completed; the first of which was the address of Rev. Mr. Monod.

ADDRESS OF REV. THEODORE MONOD, OF PARIS, FRANCE.

Rev. Mr. Monod, having been called upon, in pursuance of the order of yesterday, said, —

Mr. Moderator, Christian Fathers and Brethren, — If I were in Paris to-day, I would wish I was in Boston; and wherever I might be, in the Old World or the New, to-day, I would wish I was in Boston. It is to me a pleasure I cannot express, and something more than a pleasure, for there is a solemn feeling about it, to find myself before such an assembly at such a time. It is well understood, here at least, that America, now-a-days, is in the vanguard of the world. It is equally well understood that New England is in the vanguard of America; and I venture to say that such a body of ministers and laymen as this is in the vanguard of New England. I therefore feel that I am now standing before the very first ranks in the great army of liberty and of progress and of Christ.

When I think of this, I can hardly believe that I myself, who am not old, was in this country at a time that seems now to be about as far behind us as the Crusades, — it was in 1859, when the South was ready to claim any thing, and when the North seemed to be ready to give up any thing; and when it appeared to be generally admitted that every white man had an equal right to the pursuit of happiness and of runaway negroes. [Laughter and applause.]

All that is now behind us. You have now proved to the world that you are a nation, and not a kind of town-meeting. You have proved to the world that you could get rid of slavery; or rather, God has proved that he could sweep it out of the land; and you have proved to the world that a democratic government "is as good as another, and a great deal better too." [Applause.]

I bring to you the congratulations of the Union of Evangelical Churches in France. That body was formed sixteen years ago. Before that, there were in France a few free churches, scattered here and there; but there was no bond of union between them. In 1849, when Frederic Monod, my father, with Count Agénor de Gasparin, pastor Armand Delille, and some others, left the established church of France, they at once set to work to organize, not exactly into one body, certainly not into one church, but into one union, those scattered free churches. They invited them to send representatives to Paris, which they did; and thus was formed what we called the constituting synod. That synod voted for a constitution, which was sent to the churches; and now most of the free churches in France have accepted that constitution, and belong to that union. That body does not bear the name of Congregationalist; neither does it bear the name of Presbyterian. It is not strictly the one nor the other; yet it is nearer Congregationalism than any thing else. This is its first article: —

"The evangelical churches in France, composed of members who have explicitly and individually professed their faith, and who recognize in religious matters no other authority than that of Christ, the only and sovereign Head of the church, associate with one another to glorify God, by manifesting the union of his children, to labor in common for the edification of the body of Christ, and to unite their efforts for the extension of the kingdom of God."

The distinctive feature of difference between them and your churches is, that they have, every other year, what they call a synod, composed of representatives from the churches, whose decisions are accepted by the churches. If a church does not accept its decisions, then it ceases to belong to the body. I may say here, that, when we in France look back to the fathers to know what "the old paths" were, we receive for an answer, *Presbyterianism:* our history, our traditions, point us to that form of church polity. And as to the future, even if we could to-day have the whole of the French Protestants organized into separate churches, and if you were there in France, I am persuaded that, looking at the condition of the people, at their habits of mind and of action, you would come to the conclusion that they can not have there and now exactly the system that you have here in New England. I know that some people say that if a man wants to learn to swim, he must not be afraid to jump into the water; and that we shall never learn self-government, without any central authority, unless we try it. But it takes some education to come to that point. If you saw a man who did not know at all how to swim, and who, beside. had considerable stiffness in all his joints, you would not throw him into the water before you had taken time to get his limbs a little more supple.

From these churches, I bring you most hearty congratulations. I bring them to every evangelical church in America. I have had the privilege of bearing them myself to the General Assembly in Pittsburg, to that in Brooklyn, to the General Synod in New Brunswick, and now I bear them to you; and I do so with special pleasure, because I know that you feel, and you deserve to feel, a special happiness in the great joy of the nation, because it is the consummation of the great work upon which you have set your hearts from the beginning, and to which you have adhered, not only of late, but when it was a work attended with great difficulty and with much obloquy; and therefore we congratulate you first and most of all.

And now, about our feeling toward you during the war, I can only say of our churches what some of the brethren yesterday said of theirs, that, whatever may have been the feeling of others, the feeling of Protestant France was with you almost altogether. And, when I come to the free churches, I can take the "almost" away; for the free churches, as far as known to me, were with you, to a man, to a woman, to a child. As to the general feeling in France, even that was better than you probably think, and I will touch upon the point presently. In our churches, I repeat it, the feeling has been thoroughly for you, from the beginning, before the beginning, and all the way through.

In 1861, where did that movement come from, that brought you a letter of cheer and of sympathy in your darkest hour? It originated with us, — with three hundred French Protestant pastors. Then it went over into England, and received four thousand signatures there; and then Dr. Massie brought it over to you. When any proclamation came from President Lincoln, it was always put into our religious newspapers; and I had almost said that there was hardly any thing in those papers that was more religious, and did us more good. We were so well acquainted with him, that one lady who did not know him personally, and had never come to this country, said to me, speaking of his death, "Somehow this Lincoln seemed to belong to us." When a day of fasting and prayer was appointed here in 1863, we gave notice in our Protestant papers, at least in one of the oldest of them, requesting Protestant Christians to unite with you in their families upon that day, in special prayer for you and your country. During the last Presidential campaign, we were waiting for the news, as they that watch for the morning; and there was great rejoicing among us when the news did come. And when the news of the fall of Richmond came, your friends there did not know what to do with themselves. One pastor, instead of following the plan he had laid out for himself that afternoon, went to the next telegraphic station, and sent to Dr. Sunderland a dispatch which embodied the feelings of us all: — "Glory to God, and three cheers for the Union." [Applause.] And, as I told them in Brooklyn the other day, there was a young physician in Paris, a Frenchman and a Protestant, who when he got the news, felt he must shake hands with an American, in fact, that he must kiss an American; and, as he could not find an American to kiss, he kissed me as the next best thing. [Applause and laughter.]

I am very thankful to you, gentlemen, for the sympathy you express; and it brings me to the next point. We can not make so much noise as that in our synod, because we are not so numerous; but we did make all the noise we could when Dr. Cleaveland spoke to us last November about the war — how it was going on and what would be the end of it. We are not in the habit of applauding; but we did applaud then, and stamped too, and did every thing in our power to express our sympathy.

If you want to know the feeling of France in 1862 and 1863, ask those who were among us then; ask Mr. Cuyler, — you know him well, though he is a Presbyterian; or ask Mr. Woodruff or Mr. Beecher; and they can tell you what were the prayers in our families, and what were the prayers from our pulpits, during that time. It can all be embodied in this fact, that our representative man in the matter is Count de Gasparin.

Now I have a letter to read to you. I am sorry to take up your time, but you must remember that there is only one delegate from France: now suppose there were three, I will only take up as much time as two of them. The letter comes from the General Conference of Protestant

Pastors, that takes place in Paris every year, during the week of the anniversaries of our religious societies, in May or June. At those conferences, every shade of Protestantism is represented. You find there the Established Church Reformed, the Established Church Lutheran, and both parties in those churches, — the evangelical, and also those who call themselves the liberal party. Furthermore, you find there the Methodist Church and the Baptist Church. All are represented there. In their meeting this year (and first in the conference special to the established churches), several letters were unanimously voted: one to the American people, one to Mrs. Lincoln, one (by the General Conference) to the ministers of the gospel in the United States. The latter, I will read entire; of the former, I will give only a few extracts, the sentiments being substantially the same in them all. First, from the letter to Mrs. Lincoln. Speaking of the assassination, it says : —

"That horror was still wanting to slavery, that consecration to victory, that halo to the brow of the defender of liberty. We will not seek, madam, to comfort you by the thought of the glory now attached to the name of your husband, whom future generations will place, as we do now, among the benefactors of mankind. But directing your thoughts and ours higher still, we will adore the mysterious will of God, who has been pleased to make Abraham Lincoln one of those mighty workers whom he uses for the fulfillment of his purposes, and who has allowed him to be called from us, after the labors and sorrows of the conflict. We sympathize, from the depths of our heart, with your grief, which is not only a national grief, but one which reaches all humanity. . . . . We hope that the indignation excited by that abominable crime will not alter in any thing the thoughts of charity that were to crown the work of freedom."

Again, one of the committees of the French Evangelical Alliance addressed a letter to President Johnson, from which I will read only two lines: —

"The gospel makes it our duty, Mr. President, to pray for princes, and for those who have authority over the people: we will not forget that duty toward the present President of the United States."

Mr. Bigelow, your minister to France, acknowledged the reception of that letter as follows: —

"Legation of the United States, Paris, May 1st, 1865.

"To Rev. M. S. Descombay, President of the Evangelical Alliance of Lyons.

Mr. President, — I have received your touching and sympathetic address to the President of the United States, and I will, with painful satisfaction, transmit it to him. The horrible crime that has called him to succeed to the first martyr in the list of our presidents, will make him peculiarly thankful for your sympathies and your prayers. The profound emotion that our national grief has created everywhere, and particularly in France, shows that the assassin who has deprived us of the precious counsels of President Lincoln has given him the immortality of the martyr, and has illumined with fadeless light that rare example of courage and of Christian patriotism.

"Be pleased, sir, to receive for yourself and your reverend colleagues, the assurance of my profound veneration.

"JOHN BIGELOW."

I now come to the letter which is directed to you, and which I therefore must read to you. I received the paper containing it on the very day when I left New York for Boston. By the way, I do not know whether it is proper for an editor to say any thing about his paper; but this is the oldest paper in France. It is now in its forty-eighth year. It was edited by my father for about forty-two years; and now my colleague, M. Duchemin, and myself, are editing it. It is a weekly paper, called the "Archives du Christianisme au Dix-neuvième Siècle." This number also contains a letter from our General Pastoral Conference, to all the Protestant ministers in France, and in countries where the French language is spoken. The object of the letter is to urge them to labor in behalf of the freedmen. Let me give you a few extracts:—

"Dear brethren, two years ago, seven or eight hundred French pastors, of every denomination, signed a letter addressed to all the pastors in England, in favor of the triumph of the holy cause of emancipation in the United States. That letter received an answer signed by four thousand English pastors,—magnificent echo of our appeal. Both letters were carried to the United States by Dr. Massie, secretary of the Emancipation Society in London, and were read in Washington by Dr. Sunderland, chaplain of Congress, before a large assembly, by which they were received with enthusiasm. The wish we then expressed is now fulfilled."

The letter then goes on to show what has been effected for the abolition of slavery, what are the present necessities of the freedmen, and what the American government and the American people are doing for them. They conclude as follows:—

"Our brethren in America have come to solicit their friends in Europe to give them some assistance in that gigantic work of charity, such as does not present itself twice in a century. They say to us: 'You have justly reproached us for slavery, and the sufferings of these people; you have prayed for their emancipation. Now that we have broken their fetters, or rather now that God has answered you, and has delivered them, chastising us as we deserved, will you not help us to save them from death, to form them for liberty, for civilization, to make them citizens and Christians? The work will not be long, so great is their zeal to work as freemen and support themselves, and, we might add, so great is the ardor of many of them to be instructed in the knowledge of salvation. We must help them through the terrible crisis through which God leads them and our whole nation, to create a new people, where there shall be neither white nor black, but one family of fellow citizens and brethren, presenting to the world the spectacle of one of the most magnificent reparations that it has ever witnessed.'

"Dear brethren, let us hearken to those moving appeals, and invite every one of our churches, and every one of our parishioners, to help, according to their ability, those four millions of slaves, whose tears and blood have so long ministered to the sustenance and to the opulence of Europe. May the God who delivered Israel from bondage, and who gave his Son to abolish, with the servitude of sin, every other servitude, unite in that labor of love the nearts and hands of all our churches."

Collections for that purpose are doubtless going on in our churches at this time. The funds will be forwarded through those societies that have sent delegates to us,—the National Freedmen's Relief Association, in New York, and the Western Freedmen's Aid Society, in Cincinnati.

It is time that I should read the letter addressed to yourselves.

"TO THE PASTORS AND MINISTERS OF THE GOSPEL OF EVERY DENOMINATION IN THE UNITED STATES.

"PARIS, May 2, 1865.

"*Brethren in the Faith of the Lord Jesus, and in the Ministry of the Gospel,*—A meeting of some two hundred pastors, ministers, and elders, or active members of Protestant churches from every part of France, and, together with them, pastors and elders from Belgium, Switzerland, and other countries, feel constrained to express to you their deep and ardent sympathy. That sympathy, three days ago, would have been one of gratitude to God and of holy joy: to-day, it is also one of grief, and almost of stupor.

"We were praising God for the progress of the great cause of the emancipation of the slaves in the United States, and we were giving thanks to him for the powerful help that the Christian pulpit in America has given to that work, — precious answer to our prayers for the American churches and their pastors! — when the fearful news reached us of the assassination of Lincoln, that noble emancipator of the slaves. It seems as though it had been God's purpose to seal with that precious blood, as with that of a martyr, the victory of the cause for which he fought and suffered. With you, with the whole world, we weep over the loss of that great man and that great Christian. But, while weeping, we remember the beautiful words he spoke on the day of his second inaugural, and that expressed with so much force and simplicity his confidence in God. We render thanks to God for the admirable work that it was given to Abraham Lincoln to accomplish in four years; and we ask and expect comfort from on high for his widow, for his family, for the people who had known how to select such a man and to place him at their head, for the churches and pastors who had part in that choice, and who gave him the support of the sanctuary in the fulfillment of his providential task.

"In the name of the General Conference of Protestant pastors, elders, and laborers for the gospel, met together in Paris.

M. M. VAURIGAUD, Pastor at Nantes (Reformed church), *President.*
FISCH, Pastor at Paris (Free church), *Vice-President.*
VALLETTE, Pastor at Paris (Lutheran church).
MONTANDON, Pastor at Paris.
GUILLAUME MONOD, Pastor at Paris."

I shall be most happy to tell them that that letter of theirs was delivered directly to you on this day.

You will have perceived in this letter, and also in the letter of the French Emancipation Society to President Johnson, published a few days ago, and bearing the names of M. Guizot, M. Laboulaye, Prince de Broglie, and others, something said about the strong desire in France that the President's death should alter in no respect his purposes of charity. I am well aware that it would be utterly out of place for me to say any thing to you looking at all like counsel on a subject which is emphatically your own business; but I also feel that I should not be doing my duty toward the churches that have sent me, nor toward you, if I did not tell you, as a matter of fact, how they feel on that important matter. They have a right to expect me to state it, and you have a right to expect it of me. . . . . As a matter of fact, the Protestants of France, all of them, and perhaps your best friends more than any others, and the whole liberal party of France, will not lift so much as a finger in the way of expostulation or of blame, if every man who can be proved to have aided and abetted assassination in any shape — assassination by the bullet, assassination by the yellow fever, or assassination by starvation — shall suffer the utmost penalty of the law. [Applause.] But if any man or men should be proven guilty of no other crime than that of having rebelled against the government, and having endeavored to set up an independent government for themselves, and if for that crime only, he or they should be put to death, it would be a matter of deep regret to your friends in France, and, I think I may say, to your friends in Europe everywhere. The penalty of death for such offenses has been abolished in France. We do not wish to see it established in America. Besides, it would put into the hands of every despot, who is threatened with any thing like a popular movement against him, a dreadful arm, enabling him to look to America for a pattern in dealing with those who may oppose his government. On the other hand, if, under such provocation as you have suffered, and such sacrifices as you have undergone, you should still deem it compatible with the present dignity and with the future safety of the nation (I do not enter into that question) not to execute the sentence pronounced upon men as guilty of treason, such an exhibition of clemency would be looked upon as highly honorable to democracy and as an example to all governments.

Now I come to the point of the feeling in France outside of our churches. I know that there are some in this country who are ready to interpret our felicitations somewhat after this wise: "Seeing that you have the best of it, we congratulate you; if you had the worst of it, we would congratulate ourselves." That is not so. It may have been so with the government. You must distinguish between the government, with the circle around it, and France. They are not the same thing, — not at all. [Applause.] The last time our Emperor wrote to the legislative body, he spoke about things all round the world; but somehow it quite escaped him that there was such a place as the United States of America. He did not utter one syllable about them. Well, we said nothing; we never say anything. [Applause.] But we supposed that very likely the government was like the dustman's parrot, that he wanted to sell: "It does not speak much, but it keeps up a heap of thinking." What it was thinking about, I do not know; perhaps Maximilian knows.

But as to the sentiments of our people. I wish I could do now what I did a few days ago in New York, at a special meeting for the purpose, reading extracts from our leading periodicals during the last four years, on American affairs. I can only sum up the matter in a few words. The paper which has the largest circulation in France is the *Siécle;* that has always been for you. Then there is the *Temps*, another daily paper, which has been for you all the while. Then there is the *Journal des Débats*, which goes among the more refined and cultivated portion of society. That has constantly been for you also. The *Opinion Nationale*, the *Presse*, and the *Courier du Dimanche* are for you. I speak only of the Parisian newspapers. There have been some against you, it is true. There is the *Pays*, and the *Patrie*, and the "*Daily News*" — no, that was on *this* side. [Great laughter and applause.] Well, I was saying that we had some papers that opposed the Union cause: I might name others,— the *Constitutionnel*, the *Moniteur*. The government party, of course, was against you; and there were some whose pecuniary interests were upon the Southern side, who leaned that way. Then, again, we had those who thought the cause of the North was good, but could never be successful; they forgot that "what is impossible with man is possible with God."

Now, if I come to our reviews, you will find them strongly on your side. The *Revue Nationale*, — I will not say anything about that, except that Edward Laboulaye writes for it constantly; the *Revue des Deux Mondes*, which is known the world over, was for you. I wish to read you a paragraph from its pages in a few moments. The *Revue Chrétienne*, our Protestant review, has been for you as much as the "Independent," could be. The *Correspondant*, a Catholic but liberal review, was for you. In fact, I believe that every paper read by the more intelligent classes, and edited by the ablest men, was for you all the while.

That was all we could do, — talk about it, and write about it, gently enough, so as not to provoke the government, and especially pray about it. As to doing any thing else; as to advertising it in the streets and getting up a little demonstration, I would like to see you come over and try it. [Laughter and applause.] Why, the other day, they would not let twelve hundred young men go to Mr. Bigelow's to express their sympathies upon the occasion of the death of Lincoln. It would not do.

I said I would read you one extract. I do not take it from the *Revue Nationale:* that was too thoroughly on your side, and its opinion would therefore not have so much weight for my present purpose; but there is an article from the pen of M. Auguste Langel, in the *Revue des Deux Mondes*, — our leading review, — that does not publish any thing unless it is pretty certain to meet with acceptance. The article is dated October, 1863: —

" The civil war in the United States will take its place in history as one of the greatest events of the 19th century: for it is not only a war; it is a revolution. Whatever Lord Russell may have said, if the South fights for " independence," the North does not fight for " empire," in this sense, that it does not fight for provinces, for frontiers, for military positions; it fights for the principles that in less than a century have made a nation on the other side of the Atlantic, and have carried it to a degree of prosperity unheard of; it fights for its laws, for its constitution, and, it may be said without exaggeration, for its very existence; for democratic government becomes impossible when minorities cease to accept the will of majorities, and when majorities are no longer able to make their sovereignty respected. * * * * * * *

" The friends of human liberty have reason to congratulate themselves on the political results of the war in the United States; and would do wrong if they took an exaggerated view of the perils of the future. Liberty will heal the wounds made by slavery; a democracy that has displayed such energy, such resources, such patriotism, such intelligence, will not let the work of the last two years be lost, and will secure itself against the return of a revolutionary crisis. The hostilities can not end by simple treaties of peace; they must end in acts that consecrate the final ruin of slavery: but let not the States now most favorable to that institution be alarmed at such a result, for the ruin of slavery will be to them the beginning of a new life."

This was written, remember, in 1863.

I can not express to you the feeling at the death of your President. It was a sudden blow and a dreadful one. It came to us in the evening papers, just as we were on our way to the annual meeting of the Evangelical Society. I did not see the paper myself, but learned the news from the lips of a friend; and such was the expression on his face when he came to me with the intelligence, that I thought that perhaps some near relative had died. We could not believe the news till it was confirmed; and the sorrow was greater on the second day than on the first. That sorrow was all over our land, and all over Europe. You may see in this week's " Independent," an account of the feeling in Prussia. I received a letter a few days ago from a brother of mine, who, although the subject was no longer new, speaks of it again in the most affecting terms, speaks of the sorrow all over Europe, and ends with the remark, " There is yet hope for the nations that can find tears over the grave of Abraham Lincoln." [Applause.]

Let me tell you a word said about Lincoln that probably has not been published, and that may interest you. It comes from M. Cochin, who is a member of our French Academy, and one of our most able men, and a faithful, serious, and earnest man, belonging to the Roman Catholic Church. He has published a book on the results of the emancipation of slaves everywhere. It was my privilege to be present at a meeting, held a few weeks ago, in M. Laboulaye's house, to organize a French Emancipation Society for the relief of your freedmen. M. Cochin said we must do all we can at once, using our means, our pens, our tongues, because wherever the work of emancipation has been done, it has hardly been accomplished before there were people ready on every side to prove that it would have been better that it had not been done, for the emancipated people were better off before they were freed. Now we must go to work and help the American people to disprove, here and everywhere, those statements. And about President Lincoln, he spoke in these terms (we had not then heard of his death): "I propose," he said, "that we should send a letter to that great man, that honest great man, who, in the highest station that the world could give him, not only did not lose his mind, but lost nothing of his heart." [Applause.]

And now I only want to call your attention to one fact; which is, that what you are doing here, while it will exert a great influence on your own country, does not concern your people only, but concerns the world. No man liveth for himself, and no nation liveth for itself, and yours least of all. Europe is turned toward you now. There was a time when American affairs were of little interest in Europe. Such is not the case now. What has taken place here has riveted our attention. It is a little the fault, too, of our government. They have kept telling us for the last four years, "Look over there to America, if you want to see the effects of a democratic government; look at their fighting; how awful it is; and look at their anarchy." Just as the old Spartans got a man intoxicated, and told the children to look at him and take warning; so our government told us to look over here. And we did look; and what did we see? We saw that you could raise armies, and make war, and furthermore that you could win. We saw that you could have great generals, and that you could show such a spirit of patriotism and self-sacrifice as was unheard of before. We saw that you were one nation, with one heart. We saw that you could be guided by a President who defended liberty and union at the same time; who allowed such an amount of freedom against him and his administration, at his very doors, as would not have been tolerated in any other land; and yet in spite of it the good cause went forward. We saw that that man was re-elected in the very midst of the war. We saw, at last, your courage and perseverance crowned with success. We saw that after the foulest murder ever committed had plunged your country into the depths of sorrow, your government was unmoved, unshaken. We looked, and saw all this, and we mean to keep looking. But now the government says, "What are you looking over there for? Look at home." [Laughter and applause.] The Emperor's cousin looks, and says, "I declare, that is a grand sight;" whereupon the Emperor says to him, "I declare, you had better hold your tongue." [Renewed laughter.]

Now that you are (I was about to say whether you will or no, but I think you are willing enough) occupying such a position, you have and will have a growing influence upon Europe. You will have an influence upon your Protestant brethren in France. I can not allow myself now to speak to you of the state of religion in France, though my heart is full of the subject. I hope that I may have an opportunity, before your session closes, of making some statements on that topic in a special meeting; for I am also delegated by the Evangelical Society, the domestic missionary society of our free churches. But let me tell you that our principles are growing every year, every week, every day. The principle of the separation of church and state — and I must say a word upon that point, for Dr. Vaughan announced to you yesterday that I would — is in France the order of the day, with three different parties, — the Protestants, the Catholics, and the Philosophers. Of course, in each camp there are two sides; but the battle is fought in every one of these three camps.

As to the Protestants, we have the free churches upon one side, M. de Pressensé, carrying out the teachings of *Vinet*, his master. Then there is in the national church, a considerable party of evangelical men, who see, with increasing clearness, that the only remedy for their troubles is to cut themselves aloof from the state. Again, in that same established church, you have those among the evangelicals who do not wish for the separation of church and state, because they are afraid for the church; they think it needs the protection of the state; they are attached to the existing state of things, and unwilling to alter it. The position of the *Liberals* is singular, and well worth mentioning. You would think that they who called themselves Liberals, — who want every man to preach in our pulpits whatever he pleases, so much so that the evangelicals had to discuss with them the question whether any man has such a right or not, that the men who insist upon it that there must be no general synod of the church, would all be for perfect independence and for separation; but they insist upon it, though in a somewhat embarrassed manner, that they do not want the church to be separated from the state. They know, if there should be a separation, the Liberals would immediately find themselves separated from the Evangelicals, thus losing much of their influence, and having to organize a church of their own, standing upon its own merits, and supported by their own people; and that is what they do not want.

Among the Catholics, there is, of course, a strong party against the separation of church and state; and it is represented by the ultra-montanists, who would like the church to swallow the state. Then there is another party, headed by Cochin and others, who think that the Roman Catholic Church would have more prosperity if it had more liberty.

And finally, among the Philosophers, there are those, with M. Laboulaye at their head, — I call him a philosopher although he is also a Catholic, — a serious, earnest man, and I think an honest believer in

Christianity, who are for the separation of church and state. The *Temps*, a very able, though unfortunately not a Christian paper, is very strongly on that side. Finally, we have a democratic school, of a peculiar kind, in which the *Opinion Nationale* is the chief exponent. They want freedom for everybody, except for those whom they consider as the enemies of liberty, for instance the Roman Catholic Church. They want them to be supervised and restrained. Others do not want the church to be separated from the state, because they are afraid for the church; but these men do not want it, because they are afraid for the state. That is, as you well know, neither true religion nor true democracy.

But we shall come to the point when every man will wish for separation between the churches and the state, with perfect freedom for the churches, and perfect freedom for the state.

Now I have only to thank you for your attention and sympathy, to beg you to excuse the time I have consumed, and to express my earnest desire and prayer that God's spirit may rest upon you, and upon all that you may do during your sessions, and upon your beloved country, that I love as my own. While the eyes of the world are fixed upon you, let your eyes be fixed upon Christ, and all will be well. [Applause.]

Rev. Dr. THOMPSON stated that upon consultation with the Welsh delegation, three in number, it had been determined that Rev. Dr. Thomas should respond in their behalf.

ADDRESS OF REV. JOHN THOMAS, D. D.

Rev. Dr. Thomas, of Liverpool, England, said:—

I shall detain the meeting but a very few moments. The Welsh churches are so well represented here by the deputation from the Congregational Union of England and Wales, headed by the venerable Dr. Vaughan, whom we claim as a Welshman, that it may appear very unnecessary for us to stand before this great convention as a distinct deputation. But, sir, the Welsh people are a peculiar people. We live in a peculiar country. We speak a peculiar language. We possess a peculiar warmth of feeling, which no English deputation can properly represent. [Applause.] We have in connection with our body, in the principality of Wales, 802 churches, 405 ministers, about 95,000 communicants, upwards of 100,000 hearers, and 86,000 Sunday-school scholars. In the document read by Dr. Thompson yesterday, you can learn the feeling of the Welsh Congregational Churches as a body. I may say a word as regards, not only the Congregationalists in Wales, but the Welsh people generally. Our sympathy was entirely with you in all your troubles. Hundreds of young Welshmen died bravely upon your battle-fields. We have mothers in Wales, sorrowing for their sons. And I can add that the Welsh press—quarterlies, monthlies, and weeklies—was entirely upon your side. Not a single quarterly, or monthly, or weekly paper dared to side with the rebellion. [Applause.] It is true that some did not approve of your proceedings; but as to the rebellion, they had no sympathy with it, and they denounced the curse of slavery in the strongest language. I bring to this convention to-day the best wishes of the Welsh people generally; and you will allow me to say in conclusion, in the language of my own countrymen: —

"Dymunwch heddwch Jerusalem llwydded y rhai ath hoffant. Heddwch fyddo ofewn dy ragfur a ffyniant yr dy balasan. Er mwyn fy mrodyr am cyfeillion y dywedaf yr awr heddwch fyddo i ti. Er mwyn ty yr Arglwydd rin Duw yeisiaf i ti ddaione."

[*Translation.* "Pray for the peace of Jerusalem, they shall prosper that love thee. Peace be within thy walls, and prosperity within thy palaces. For my brethren and companions' sakes, I will now say, peace be with thee. Because of the Lord thy God, I will seek thy good."]

Rev. Henry Ward Beecher, of New York, in behalf of the Business Committee, presented the following resolution: —

"Whereas the attitude of various religious bodies in Europe toward the United States during the past five years requires a careful discrimination and statement, —

"*Resolved*, That a committee of five be appointed to prepare a suitable reply from this Council to the delegates from foreign bodies who have been heard before it."

Mr. BEECHER said: If our cause has been a cause involving every moral principle which the world has wrought out since the coming of Christ, — and we hold that it is, — then the attitudes of prominent Christian bodies in regard to this matter are not insignificant. They reach very far in toward fundamental questions. If they have been right, it is a matter of signal gratitude; and, if they have been wrong, it is an instance of the inability of good men to form a sound moral judgment upon facts patent to all the world, which we are not at liberty ourselves to pass by or to hoodwink in any way. It seems to me, therefore, that respect to ourselves not alone, but the duties which we owe to the cause of Christ, requires that any reply made should be made considerately, Christianly, and discriminately; and that therefore a committee of this kind would far better answer the ends of love and justice than any possible extemporized reply.

The resolution was agreed to.

DECLARATION OF FAITH.

Rev. Dr. Thompson, of New York, in behalf of the committee, read the following paper: —

The committee appointed by the preliminary conference to prepare a Declaration of Faith, to be submitted to the Council, respectfully report: —

That, in the light of the discussions of that conference upon the expediency of such a Declaration, and also of the general principles of our polity, they could not regard it as their function to prepare a Confession of Faith to be imposed by act of this, or of any other body, upon the churches of the Congregational order. "It was the glory of our fathers, that they heartily professed the only rule of their religion, from the very first, to be the Holy Scriptures;"[1] and particular churches have always exercised their liberty in "confessions drawn up in their own forms."[2] And such has been the accord of these particular confessions, one with another, and with the Scriptures, that we may to-day repeat, with thankfulness, the words of the fathers of the Savoy Confession, two centuries ago; while "from the first, every, or at least the generality of our churches, have been, in a manner, like so many ships, — though holding forth the same general colors, — launched singly, and sailing apart and alone in the vast ocean of these tumultuous times, and have been exposed to 'every wind of doctrine,' under no other conduct than the Word of the Spirit," . . . . . . yet "let all acknowledge that God hath ordered it for his high and greater glory, in that his singular care and power should have so watched over each of these, as that all should be found to have steered their course by the same chart, and to have been bound for one and the same port; and that the same holy and blessed truths of all sorts, which are current and warrantable amongst all the other churches of Christ in the world, are found to be our lading."[3]

Whatever the diversities of metaphysical theology apparent in these various confessions, they yet, with singular unanimity, identify the faith of the Congregational churches with the body of Christian doctrine known as Calvinistic; and hence such Confessions as that of the Westminster divines, and that of the Savoy Synod, have been accredited among these churches as general symbols of faith.

It has not appeared to the committee expedient to recommend that this Council should disturb this "variety in unity" — as Cotton Mather happily describes it — by an attempted uniformity of statement in a Confession formulating each doctrine in more recent terms of metaphysical theology. It seemed better to characterize, in a comprehensive way, the doctrines held in common by our churches, than thus to individualize each in a theological formula. The latter course might rather disturb the unity that now exists amid variety. Moreover, little could be gained in this respect beyond what we already possess in the ancient formulas referred to, which, being interpreted in the spirit in which they were conceived, answer the end of a substantial unity in doctrine, and have withal the savor of antiquity and the proof of use.

In the language of the Preface to the Savoy Declaration, a Confession is "to be looked upon but as a meet or fit medium or means whereby to express a common faith and salvation, and no way to be made use of

[1] Preface to the Confession adopted at Saybrook, Conn., 1708.

[2] Cotton Mather, Preface to "Faith professed by the Churches of New England."

[3] Preface to the Savoy Declaration, in Hanbury's Historical Memorials, iii. 523; see, also, *infra*, p. 2.

as an imposition upon any. Whatever is of force or constraint in matters of this nature causes them to degenerate from the name and nature of confessions, and turns them from being confessions of faith into exactions and impositions of faith!"[1] Yet a common confession serves the important purpose — the "neglect" of which the Savoy fathers sought to remedy — of making manifest our unity in doctrine, and of "holding out common lights to others whereby to know where we are."[2]

With these views, as the result of prolonged and careful deliberation, the committee unanimously recommend that the Council should declare, by reference to historical and venerable symbols, the faith as it has been maintained among the Congregational churches from the beginning; and also that it should set forth a testimony on behalf of these churches, for the Word of Truth now assailed by multiform and dangerous errors; and, for this end, they respectfully submit the following

RECITAL AND DECLARATION.

When the churches of New England assembled in a general synod at Cambridge, in 1648, they declared their assent, "for the substance thereof," to the Westminster Confession of Faith. When, again, these churches convened in a general synod at Boston, in 1680, they declared their approval (with slight verbal alterations) of the doctrinal symbol adopted by a synod of the Congregational churches in England, at London, in 1658, and known as the "Savoy Confession," which in doctrine is almost identical with that of the Westminster Assembly. And yet again, when the churches in Connecticut met in council at Saybrook, in 1708, they "owned and consented to" the Savoy Confession as adopted at Boston, and offered this as a public symbol of their faith.

Thus, from the beginning of their history, the Congregational churches in the United States have been allied in doctrine with the Reformed churches of Europe, and especially of Great Britain. The eighth article of the "Heads of Agreement," established by the Congregational and Presbyterian ministers in England in 1692, and adopted at Saybrook in 1708, defines this position in these words: "As to what appertains to soundness of judgment in matters of faith, we esteem it sufficient that a church acknowledge the Scriptures to be the Word of God, the perfect and only rule of faith and practice, and own either the doctrinal part of those commonly called the Articles of the Church of England, or the Confession or Catechisms, shorter or larger, compiled by the Assembly at Westminster, or the Confession agreed on at the Savoy, to be agreeable to the said rule."

And now, when, after the lapse of two centuries, these churches are again convened in a General Council at their primitive and historical home, it is enough for the first of those ends enumerated by the synod at Cambridge, — to wit, "the maintenance of the faith entire, within itself," — that this Council, referring to these ancient symbols as embodying, for substance of doctrine, the constant faith of the churches here represented, declares its adherence to the same, as being "well and fully grounded

[1] Hanbury's Historical Memorials, iii. 517.
[2] Hanbury's Historical Memorials, iii. 523.

upon the Holy Scriptures,"[1] which is "the only sufficient and invariable rule of religion."[2]

But having in view, also, the second end of a public confession enumerated by the Cambridge Synod, — to wit, "the holding forth of unity and harmony both amongst and with other churches," — we desire to promote a closer fellowship of all Christian denominations in the faith and work of the gospel, especially against popular and destructive forms of unbelief, which assail the foundations of all religion, both natural and revealed; which know no God but nature; no Depravity but physical malformation, immaturity of powers, or some incident of outward condition; no Providence but the working of material causes and of statistical laws; no Revelation but that of consciousness; no Redemption but the elimination of evil by a natural sequence of suffering; no Regeneration but the natural evolution of a higher type of existence; no Retribution but the necessary consequences of physical and psychological laws.

As a testimony, in common with all Christian believers, against these and kindred errors, we deem it important to make a more specific declaration of the following truths: —

There is one personal God, who created all things; who controls the physical universe, the laws whereof he has established; and who, holding all events within his knowledge, rules over men by his wise and good providence and by his perfect moral law.

God, whose being, perfections, and government are partially made known to us through the testimony of his works and of conscience, has made a further revelation of himself in the Scriptures of the Old and New Testaments, — a revelation attested at the first by supernatural signs, and confirmed through all the ages since by its moral effects upon the individual soul, and upon human society; a revelation authoritative and final. In this revelation, God has declared himself to be the Father, the Son, and the Holy Ghost; and he has manifested his love for the world through the incarnation of the Eternal Word for man's redemption, in the sinless life, the expiatory sufferings and death, and the resurrection of Jesus Christ, our Lord and Saviour; and also in the mission of the Holy Ghost, the Comforter, for the regeneration and sanctification of the souls of men.

The Scriptures, confirming the testimony of conscience and of history, declare that mankind are universally sinners, and are under the righteous condemnation of the law of God; that from this state there is no deliverance, save through "repentance toward God, and faith in the Lord Jesus Christ;" and that there is a day appointed in which God will raise the dead, and will judge the world, and in which the issues of his moral government over men shall be made manifest in the awards of eternal life and eternal death, according to the deeds done in the body.

JOSEPH P. THOMPSON.
EDWARD A. LAWRENCE.
GEORGE P. FISHER.

BOSTON, June 14, 1865.

[1] Preface to the Savoy Confession, as adopted at Saybrook in 1708.
[2] Ditto.

DEVOTIONAL EXERCISES.

The hour of eleven having arrived, the Council spent half an hour in devotional exercises, singing several hymns, and prayer being offered by Rev. Dr. Post, of Missouri, Rev. Mr. Guernsey, of Iowa, and Rev. Henry Ward Beecher, of New York.

DECLARATION OF FAITH.

The consideration of the report of the committee on a Confession of Faith, was resumed.

Rev. Dr. WOLCOTT, of Ohio. The Council have concurred with the recommendation of the business committee, that the papers presented to this body, which did not originate in the body, and were not matured by committees appointed by the body, should, after being read here, without discussion of the subject matter of the reports, be referred to the appropriate committees. They can be referred, sir, with or without instructions. I rise to move that this report be referred, with instructions, — instructions which do not involve a discussion of the merits of the paper; and with your leave, sir, before offering the motion, which I have put into writing, I will make a remark or two which will explain it.

This Council originated in an overture from the General Association of Illinois. That association, adopting a resolution or resolutions passed by the Triennial Convention of the Congregational Churches of the North-west, which has the Theological Seminary of Chicago in charge, issued a letter to the Congregational churches of other States, asking them to unite with them in a preliminary convention, for the purpose of calling a National Council. That proposal was responded to by the several State bodies. The Ohio State Conference passed a resolution expressing their concurrence in the recommendations and the reasoning of the overture, and, *for the purposes therein specified*, appointed a committee to meet the committees of the other State bodies. Their resolution was purposely thus guarded. The delegation that went from our State Conference were not authorized to introduce into the programme of the Council any topic that was not specified in the overture of the General Association of Illinois. I regret not to find that paper embodied in the proceedings of the preliminary meeting of the State committees, of which it was the basis; but it will not be questioned, I suppose, by any, that that preliminary meeting did a larger preliminary work than they were expected or appointed to perform, or than they themselves anticipated when they came together. The general exigencies and opportunities of Christ's kingdom in this country, with general reference to which the Council was to be called, appeared to them, on a survey, to embrace points which were not in the contemplation of the State conferences when they were appointed. I am sure that it would not be possible to select from our churches a company of men, ministers and laymen, in whose judgment the churches would repose more entire confidence than in the judgment of the brethren who formed that preliminary convention. But still it is true, sir, that the State bodies represented by those committees were not committed by that convention to any thing that was not contained in the original overture from the General Association of Illinois. Had the question, sir, of issuing a declaration of faith to the churches been coupled with the other recommendations of that overture, I doubt whether it would have met with general favor from the churches. That jealous regard for individual liberty, for the rights of conscience and of private judgment, which is our original legacy and birthright as Congregationalists, that traditional repugnance toward even the seeming introduction of any rule or standard other than that of the word of God, would have led them to regard a document of this character, whatever the disclaimers, in that aspect.

Rev. Dr. BACON, of Connecticut. I call the brother to order. He is entering into a debate of the question, which is to be referred to the committee.

Rev. Dr. WOLCOTT, of Ohio. I think it will be seen that what I have said has a bearing upon the motion.

Rev. Dr. BACON, of Connecticut. Undoubtedly it has, — a great bearing; but it is debate.

Rev. Dr. WOLCOTT, of Ohio. The resolution I have to offer, is this: —

Resolved, That the report be referred to the appropriate committee, with instructions to consider the propriety of submitting to the Council a declaration of the common faith of our churches, and, if thought advisable, to report such declaration.

If this document were sent to the committee without instructions, they would be authorized, I suppose, either to report it back, or to revise it; and it would be satisfactory, I know, to many members of this body, if the propriety of the issuing of such a declaration could be considered by the committee.

Hon. Mr. DOUGLAS, of Connecticut. I understand that this report has been printed; but it has not been distributed among the members in this vicinity. I think it proper that it should be distributed before we are called upon to act upon it.

Rev. Mr. BURR, of Connecticut. I would respectfully inquire whether the reference of this document to a new committee will not delay, unnecessarily, the proceedings of this Council. If, sir, as it seems to me but fair to presume, the committee to be appointed shall have given no more attention to this matter than most of us, very considerable time would be required for them to do justice to the subject in a formal report.

Rev. Dr. PATTON, of Illinois. I call the brother to order. We settled that matter yesterday. If he wishes to proceed, he must move a reconsideration of that vote.

Rev. Mr. BURR, of Connecticut. I was not aware of it, sir; and I know there are other members here who were not aware of it. I would plead that there was a misconception, on the part of a large number of the delegates, as to this matter. If I had known this report was to be referred in the manner proposed, I certainly should have spoken. I don't think it ought to be referred.

Hon. Mr. HAMMOND, of Illinois. My understanding was, that all the documents ordered by the preliminary meeting at New York, which was only for the purpose of bringing subjects before this Council, should be read, and then referred to special committees appointed for each.

Rev. Dr. BACON, of Connecticut. I submit that the document has already been referred by the action of the Council yesterday, and that all the Council has to do is to appoint its committee.

The question was then taken on the resolution offered by Dr. Wolcott, and it was adopted.

REPORT ON RELIGIOUS EXERCISES.

Rev. Dr. Kirk, of Massachusetts, from the committee on Devotional Exercises, reported as follows: —

Whereas, the Council has already appointed daily religious exercises, and whereas, so much time has already been occupied with preliminary business; therefore, the committee recommend: —

1. That they be permitted to report in part, and continue their sessions.

2. That each day's exercises be terminated with the use of the doxology.

3. That in compliance with the recommendation of the provisional committee, for a special service of devotion, "for the acknowledgment of the marvelous and merciful dealings of Almighty God with the nation in connection with the war, and for supplicating a gracious dispensation of the Spirit of God upon the land, that our restored national unity may be consecrated in righteousness, and in the peace and joy of the Holy Ghost," the Council meet in the house of worship of the First Church in Charlestown, to-morrow afternoon, at three o'clock, — the services to continue one hour.

The report was accepted and adopted.

CHURCH POLITY.

The moderator called upon the committee appointed at the preliminary meeting to prepare a statement of church polity, for their report.

Rev. Mr. EUSTIS, of Connecticut. I understand that this report is a long one, in different chapters, and has been printed. The question with me is, whether it had not better be distributed, and, when it comes from the committee, be read in sections, and be acted upon in sections, rather than be acted upon now. I defer, however, to the opinion of the committee.

Rev. Dr. BACON, of Connecticut. My impression upon that subject is, that the report ought to be heard by the hearing of the ear: it ought to enter the mind of every member of the Council through that channel, — the ear. Then it should be distributed, and put into the hands of every member of the Council, that he may read it with his eyes, and get access to it through another medium. After that, I apprehend it will not be necessary to read it, either in sections or otherwise, again. Each chapter can be read by its title.

Rev. Dr. Bacon, from the committee on Church Polity, then read Parts I. and II. of the report, as follows: —

TO THE NATIONAL COUNCIL OF CONGREGATIONAL CHURCHES,
CONVENED AT BOSTON, JUNE 14, 1865.

Fathers and Brethren, — In the preliminary conference which made arrangements for this National Council, the undersigned and the Rev. Dr. Storrs, of Cincinnati, now in England, were appointed to bring before the Council " the expediency of issuing a statement of Congregational polity." We, therefore, ask leave to present for the consideration of this venerable assembly, *first*, the fitness and desirableness of such a measure; *secondly*, the principles which ought to determine the character and contents of the document to be issued; *thirdly*, the kind and degree of authority with which such a document, proceeding from this Council, would be invested; and, *fourthly*, the form of a statement, to be adopted with or without amendment, or to be rejected, as the Council shall see fit.

I. The fitness and desirableness of a statement from this Council, describing the polity of the Congregational churches, may appear from these considerations: —

1. In issuing such a statement, we only follow the example of ancient Congregational synods. The Cambridge Synod, as it is commonly called, which assembled in 1646, and was continued by successive adjournments till 1648, and to which all the churches of the New England colonies were invited, left, as a perpetual memorial of itself, that statement of Congregational polity which has ever since been called the Cambridge Platform. The synod of Congregational churches which was convened under the patronage of the English government in 1658, at the Savoy in London, issued a "Declaration of the Faith and Order owned and practised in the Congregational churches of England." The synod of the churches in the colony of Connecticut, which was convened at Saybrook in 1708, gave out that scheme of a modified Congregationalism, which, though never formally adopted elsewhere than in that

State, has had its influence on our churches in almost all parts of our country. And more recently, the meeting in which the Congregational Union of England and Wales was instituted, though it was not properly a synod or council of churches, issued a declaration, or statement, describing the faith and order of the Congregational churches in that country.

2. A document which shall exhibit, with more authority than can belong to any individual or local testimony, the system of order actually held by the Congregational churches in the United States, is greatly needed. The churches need it for their own information and guidance. Pastors and home missionaries, and indeed all our ministers, need it. Young men in theological schools, who are preparing themselves for the service of the churches, need it. Many whose ecclesiastical connection is with other portions of Christ's universal church need it, that their minds may be disabused of misinformation or of prejudice. Especially is it needed in the new States and Territories, where ecclesiastical institutions are yet to be formed; and in the recovered States, so lately ravaged by rebellion, where ecclesiastical reconstruction, disembarrassed of all connection with a Christianity apostate from the first principles of righteousness, is hardly less important to the future welfare of society than a new political and social order.

3. No ancient document can be wisely referred to as being in all respects sufficient for our present need. The Cambridge Platform was made more than two hundred years ago, when American Congregationalism was in its infancy; and it is now more valuable as a means of showing how little our churches have departed from the original principles and methods of their polity, than as a guide to the manner in which those principles are applied and administered in the practice of our churches at the present day. Indeed, there are portions of it which, to readers not versed in our ecclesiastical history, nor familiar with the technical terms of a logic now obsolete, are hardly intelligible without a commentary.

II. What sort of a statement will best supply the existing need, is a question which seems to answer itself. There is no need of an argumentative or rhetorical defense of Congregationalism to be issued by this assembly. Such expositions of our polity may proceed more fitly from individuals than from any representative body. On the other hand, a simple statement of the two or three first principles which constitute the radical difference between Congregationalism and other theories of church government, would not be sufficient. Those first principles are only the points of divergence between differing systems; and how wide the divergence is, can not be shown but by tracing out the application of the principles. A simple and perspicuous statement, not only of the principles on which our polity is founded, but also of the usages and arrangements which those principles have established among us, and in which, by common consent, they are applied and made practical, will be, it is believed, of great use to our churches, both in their internal administration and in their fellowship with each other.

III. The authority of any document issued by this assembly of elders and messengers is wholly unlike the authority which is claimed for the canons enacted by the various assemblies of clergy and delegates which assume to govern the particular churches under them. It is little more than a truism to say that this Council has no legislative power to ordain a new constitution for the Congregational churches, or to make any new law, and no judicial power to establish precedents which inferior judicatories must follow. All that a council like this can do is to inquire, to deliberate, and to testify. The testimony of this assembly concerning what is and what is not the Congregational polity, cannot but have whatever authority belongs to the testimony of competent witnesses, assembled in a great multitude, well informed concerning the matter in question, and representing all "those Congregational churches in the United States of America which are in recognized fellowship and coöperation through the general associations, conferences, and conventions in the several States." Whatever authority the Cambridge Platform has as testifying what the Congregational polity of our fathers was in 1648, just that authority a similar statement, proceeding from this assembly, will have as testifying what American Congregationalism is in 1865.

IV. The undersigned, therefore, respectfully submit the accompanying form, or draught, of a statement to be issued by this Council, together with a briefer document stating substantially the same points. We have not presumed to insert any novelties, nor to express our individual preferences, but only to state the usages of the churches. A comparison of our draught with the Cambridge Platform will show how closely we have followed that time-honored instrument in the general plan, in the arrangement of topics, and in language, and, at the same time, how freely we have departed from it, whether for the sake of increased perspicuity, or for the sake of exhibiting the Congregational polity as it is in fact to-day, instead of exhibiting it as it was in theory when our fathers, more than two hundred years ago, were beginning to build on this continent the living and ever-living temple of our God.

LEONARD BACON.
ALONZO H. QUINT.

BOSTON, June 14, 1865.

THE GOVERNMENT AND FELLOWSHIP PRACTISED BY THE CONGREGATIONAL CHURCHES IN THE UNITED STATES.

PART I. — PRELIMINARY PRINCIPLES.

CHAPTER I. — DEFINITION AND RULE OF CHURCH POLITY.

1. The first principle from which the polity of the Congregational churches proceeds, is, that the Holy Scriptures, and especially the Scriptures of the New Testament, are the only authoritative rule for the

constitution and administration of church government; so that no other rule than those which are warranted by Christ and his apostles can be imposed on Christians as conditions of membership and communion in the church.

2. Ecclesiastical polity, therefore, or church government and discipline, is that *association of believers* for united worship and spiritual communion, in order to the visibility, the purity, the advancement, and the perpetuity of Christ's kingdom, which God has prescribed by the teaching of the Holy Spirit in the Scriptures.

CHAPTER II. — THE CATHOLIC CHURCH AND A PARTICULAR CHURCH.

1. Christ's catholic or universal church is the great company of God's elect, redeemed and effectually called from the state of sin and death into a state of reconciliation to God.

2. The church universal is either triumphant or militant. They who have come out of the great tribulation, and have entered into the joy of their Lord in heaven, are the church triumphant. They who are still serving Christ on the earth, and contending with the powers that rule the darkness of this world, are the church militant.

3. The universal church on earth is not invisible merely, as discerned by God who searches the hearts and knows the relation of every individual soul to Christ, but is visible, also, as including all who profess to believe in Christ, and do not wholly contradict that profession by ungodliness in their lives, or by denying the essential truths of the gospel.

4. The visible church catholic, as it includes all visible Christians, comprehends not only such particular churches as are constituted and governed according to the word given in the Holy Scriptures, but also all assemblies of Christian believers and worshipers, even though, in things not essential to the Christian faith, they err through the force of tradition or the infirmity of human judgment; and it is governed, not by the pretended vicar of Christ, nor by any human authority assuming to have jurisdiction over all particular churches, but only by Christ himself through his word and spirit.

5. As we renounce the notion of an organized and governed catholic church, which has no warrant from the Scriptures; so we renounce the equally unwarranted action of a national church, having jurisdiction over the particular churches in a nation. Under the gospel, the organized and governed church is not ecumenical, nor national, nor provincial, nor diocesan, or classical, but only local or parochial, — a congregation of faithful or believing men, dwelling together in one city, town, or convenient neighborhood.

6. A local or Congregational church is, by the institution of Christ, a part of the militant visible church, consisting of a company of saints by calling, united into one body by a holy covenant, for the public worship of God, and their own mutual edification, in the fellowship of the Lord Jesus.

7. All particular churches, being the one body of Christ, and having

one Lord, one faith, one baptism, one God and Father of all, are bound to maintain and hold forth the catholic communion of saints, endeavoring, in their intercourse and relations one with another, to keep the unity of the Spirit in the bond of peace.

PART II. THE CHURCH: ITS FORM, ORGANIZATION, AND GOVERNMENT.

CHAPTER I. — HOW A PARTICULAR CHURCH IS ORGANIZED.

1. The visible church consists of those who belong to Christ, and are, therefore, in the phrase of our ancient platform, "saints by calling," and who, being holy by their calling and profession, are gathered out of the ungodly world, and united in a holy fellowship.

2. Those who visibly belong to Christ are, *first*, such as have not only attained a knowledge of the principles of religion, and are free from gross and open scandals, but also do profess their personal faith and repentance, and walk in blameless obedience to the word; and, *secondly*, their children, who, being children of the covenant, are also holy.

3. The members of one church ought ordinarily to dwell in such vicinity to each other that they can meet in one place; so that every city, town, or convenient neighborhood, shall have its own church complete and distinct. And ordinarily the members of one church ought not to be more in number than can conveniently meet for worship in one assembly, and manage their affairs by one administration. Yet, if there be many congregations, distinct from each other, in one town or city (whether their several parishes be distinguished by geographical lines or otherwise) they ought to regard themselves and each other as so many branches of Christ's one catholic church in that place.

4. Those believers who dwell together in one place become a particular and distinct church, by their recognition of each other, and their mutual agreement, express or implied, wherein they give themselves unto the Lord to the observing of the ordinances of Christ in the same society. Such a recognition and agreement is usually called the church covenant.

5. Different degrees of explicitness in such an agreement do not affect the being of the church, or the duties and responsibilities of membership. The more explicit and solemn the act of covenanting, the more are the members reminded of their common and mutual duties, and the less room is there for uncertainty in distinguishing between those who are members and those who are not. Yet the whole essence and meaning of the covenant are in fact retained, where the agreement of certain believers to meet constantly in one congregation for worship and edification, is expressed only by their *practice* of thus meeting, and their actual use and observance of Christ's ordinances in their assembly. However explicit the covenant may be, it can reasonably and rightfully express nothing more than a mutual agreement to observe all Christ's laws and ordinances as one church; and, however informal the agreement may be, it can mean nothing less.

6. All believers, having the opportunity, should endeavor to become members, every one, of some particular church, that they may honor Christ by their professed conformity to the order and ordinances of the gospel, and that they may have the benefits of visible union and fellowship with the church, which is the communion of the saints. These benefits are, *first*, a participation in the promise of Christ's special presence with his Church; *secondly*, their increased activity and enjoyment in the Christian life by the combination of their affections and their endeavors, and by their inciting each other to love and good works; *thirdly*, watchful and fraternal help to keep each other in the way of God's commandments, and to recover, by due admonition and censure, any that go astray; and, *fourthly*, aid in the Christian nurture and training of their children, that their households may be holy, and their posterity be not cut off from the privileges of the covenant. Should all believers neglect this duty of voluntarily entering into organized Christian fellowship, to which duty they are moved by all the impulses of a renewed and holy mind, Christ would soon have no visibly associated and organized church on earth.

CHAPTER II. — GOD'S INSTITUTED WORSHIP IN THE CHURCH.

1. Believers joined to each other and to Christ, in a church relation, are builded together for a habitation of God through the Spirit, on the foundation of the apostles and prophets, Jesus Christ himself being the chief corner-stone; in whom all the building, fitly framed together, groweth into a holy temple of the Lord.

2. The worship of God in his spiritual temple, the church, includes prayer, the singing of psalms and hymns and spiritual songs, the ministry of the word, the sacraments, and the contribution of gifts and offerings for the service of Christ.

3. Prayers offered in the church should be grave and earnest, lifting up the thoughts and desires of the assembly to God; they should be offered not in any prescribed and inflexible form, but freely, according to the vicissitudes of need and trial, and of joy or sorrow, in the church or in its households; they should be offered for all men, for those who are in authority, for the welfare of the civil state, and for the universal church of Christ on earth; and in the matter and manner they should be conformed to such models as the Scriptures give, and, above all, to that model which Christ himself gave to his disciples that he might teach them how to pray.

4. Singing in the church is not for the delight of the sense as in places of amusement, but for the union of voices and hearts in worship, and for spiritual edification. The Psalms which God gave by the Holy Spirit in the Old Testament are sanctioned for us by Christ and his apostles, and remain in the church for ever, to be used in praising God. There is warrant, also, in the New Testament for the use of hymns and spiritual songs, but not to the exclusion or neglect of the Psalms.

5. The ministry of the word in the church is by the reading of the

Scriptures, with such exposition as may aid the hearers in their personal and family searching of the Scriptures; and also by preaching and teaching, that the truths and principles which God has revealed in his law and in the gospel of his grace may be set forth distinctly in their manifestation of the glory and government of God, in their relations to each other, and in all their applications to the duties of men and to the salvation of sinners.

6. The two sacramental institutions of the New Testament, representing significantly, and commemorating through all ages, the two-fold grace of God offered in the gospel, as they are to be observed by all believers, are also to be administered in every church. Baptism, wherein the purifying element of water signifies and holds forth the inward washing of regeneration and renewing of the Holy Ghost, which God shed on men abundantly through Jesus Christ our Saviour, is most becomingly administered in the church, whether on converts from without or on the children of the covenant, and should be administered in simplicity, with no addition of vain or superstitious ceremonies. In like manner, the Lord's Supper, wherein his disciples, partaking of the bread and cup, partake of his body which was broken for us, and of his blood which was shed for many for the remission of sins, is to be celebrated in all simplicity, according to the recorded words of the institution, without any mixture of human inventions.

7. In the place of the tithes and the offerings, which were part of God's instituted worship before the coming of Christ, are the free gifts of Christ's disciples to his suffering brethren and to his cause and service. The contribution in the church is not a secular thing, intruded into the house of God for mere convenience' sake, and adverse to spiritual edification, but is itself an act of grateful homage to Christ as well as of communion with his brethren.

CHAPTER III. — CHURCH POWER.

1. Church power, under Christ, resides primarily, not in the officers of the church, nor in any priesthood or clergy, but in the church; and it is derived through the church, to its officers from Christ.

2. Church power is not legislative, but only administrative. It extends no further than to declare and apply the law of Christ. No church has any lawful power to make itself other than simply a church of Christ, in which the mind of Christ, as made known in the Scriptures, shall be the only rule of faith and practice. As no church may lawfully add any thing to the sum of Christian doctrine, or take any thing therefrom; so no church may lawfully add any thing to, or take any thing from, the rules of Christian living, and the conditions of Christian fellowship, which the Scriptures prescribe.

CHAPTER IV. — CHURCH OFFICERS.

1. Though church officers are not necessary to the mere existence of a church, yet to its well-being, and to the performance of its functions,

officers are necessary. Therefore they are appointed by Christ's institution, and are counted among the gifts of his triumphal ascension to glory.

2. The powers and functions of church-officers are not to be confounded with the powers and functions of the apostles and other extraordinary ministers of Christ, who were sent forth at the beginning of the gospel. Nor are any church officers to be recognized as holding their official power in the succession from the apostles, or as having any of that authority over all the churches with which the apostles were invested.

3. Church officers, according to the arrangement which the apostles instituted in every church, are of two sorts, — bishops, or elders, and deacons.

4. The office of elder, or bishop, in the church is two-fold: to labor in word and doctrine, and to rule. As laboring in word and doctrine, elders are pastors and teachers, for the perfecting of the saints, for the work of the ministry, for the edifying of the body of Christ; and in order to this, they are rightly to divide the word of truth, and to administer those sacramental ordinances in which the grace of the gospel is visibly set forth and sealed. Like all whom God has put into the ministry of his gospel, they are to preach the word, and are to be instant in season and out of season, reproving, rebuking, exhorting, with all long-suffering and patience, holding forth the faithful word, that they may be able by sound doctrine both to exhort and to convince the gainsayer. As ruling in the church, they are to be not lords over God's heritage; but being the servants of all, for Jesus' sake, they are to watch for souls as they that must give account. They are to open and shut the doors of God's house by the admission of members approved by the church, by ordination of officers approved by the church, by excommunication of obstinate offenders denounced by the church, and by restoring penitents forgiven by the church. They are to call the church together when there is occasion, and seasonably to dismiss them again. They are to prepare matters for the hearing of the church, that in public they may be carried to an end with less trouble and more speedy dispatch. They are to preside in the meetings of the church, whether for public worship or for the transaction of church business. They are to be guides and leaders in all matters pertaining to church administration and church actions; but they have no power to perform any church act save with the concurrence and by the vote of the brotherhood. They are to care for the spiritual health and growth of individual members, and to prevent and heal such offenses in life or doctrine as might corrupt the church; and they are to visit and pray over their brethren in sickness when sent for, and at such other times as opportunity shall serve.

5. The number of elders, or bishops, in a particular church is neither prescribed nor limited, but is to be determined by the discretion of the church itself, in view of its ability and its need. In the primitive churches, a plural eldership seems to have been the rule, and not the exception. In the American Congregational churches, at the beginning, it was thought needful that every church should have at least three elders, of whom two were to labor in word and doctrine, and the other

was to be associated with them in all their work as bishops, or overseers of the flock. While no church is rightfully subjected to any presbytery exterior to itself, every church should have its own presbytery. The modern usage, concentrating all the powers and responsibilities of the eldership in one person, is founded on convenience only, and is exceptional rather than normal. Whether, instead of one elder, who under the title of pastor performs the whole work of the eldership in a church, there shall be two or three, or more, among whom the work of public preaching and the work of ruling and oversight shall be divided, is a question which every church may determine for itself, without infringing any principle of order.

6. Inasmuch as the duty of contributing for the poor saints, for the support and advancement of the church, and for the spread of the gospel, is incumbent on all disciples of Christ according to their ability, and is essential to the communion of saints; and inasmuch as the Lord's Day is especially designated as a day for such contributions; the church is provided with officers for that service. Deacons are chosen in every church to help the elders, not by taking part in the public ministry of the word, nor by ruling in the church, but chiefly by serving tables. Their office is to receive the contributions and whatever gifts are offered to the church; to keep the treasury of the church; and to distribute from it for the relief of the poor, especially of those in communion, for the supply of the Lord's table, and, if needful, for the support of the ministry. As almoners of the church, they are to care for the poor, to know them personally, to inquire into their wants and afflictions, and to be the organ of communication between them and the brotherhood.

7. Other officers than bishops and deacons are not provided for the church by any precept or example in the Scriptures. Yet it is in the power of the church to designate any member or members to the performance of a certain work, such as that of a scribe or clerk and keeper of the records, or that of the superintendents or teachers in a Sabbath-school, or that of a committee for some inquiry. In designating fit persons to perform such duties, it institutes no new order of church officers, but only distributes among its members certain duties which are common to the brotherhood.

CHAPTER V. — ELECTION AND ORDINATION OF CHURCH-OFFICERS.

1. Though no man may assume an office in the church but he that is called of God, the call of bishops and deacons is not, like that of the apostles, immediately from Christ, but mediately through the church.

2. Those who are to bear office in the church should first be proved by thorough acquaintance and trial, and should be known and well reported of as having not only the needful gifts, but also those graces and virtues which the Scriptures prescribe as qualifications of bishops or of deacons.

3. A church, being free, can not become subject to any but by a free

election; yet when such a people do choose any to be over them in the Lord, then do they become subject, and most willingly submit to the divinely authorized ministry of those whom they have chosen.

4. Church officers are not only to be chosen by the church, but are also to be *ordained* by laying-on of hands and prayer, with which, at the ordination of elders, fasting is also to be joined. This ordination is the solemn and public induction of the chosen officer into his place and office, like the inauguration of a magistrate in the commonwealth. Such ordination of a pastor or teacher is his induction into the work of ministering in the word; and if he be afterwards dismissed from his eldership in that church, and be called to a like office in another church, it is not deemed necessary that his installation in his new place be with the laying-on of hands. Yet we protest against the superstitious notion, that consecration to the ministry by imposition of hands introduces the person into a hierarchal or priestly order, and so may not be repeated.

5. In a church which has elders, the laying-on of hands in ordination is to be performed by those elders. But if the church be destitute of elders, then other fit persons, elders of other churches, or ministering brethren not in office, or (if need be) brethren who have not been called and set apart to minister in the word of God, may be deputed by the church to perform this service; and the laying-on of their hands, with prayer and fasting, is a fit and sufficient induction of the chosen elders or bishops, not less than of deacons, into the office to which they have been designated.

6. Neither a deacon, nor an elder or bishop, is an officer in any other church than that which elected him to his office; nor can he perform official acts in another church, otherwise than at the invitation of that church, and by a power derived through them from Christ; for as no church has authority over another church, so no church can invest its officers with authority over other churches.

CHAPTER VI. — MAINTENANCE OF CHURCH OFFICERS.

1. The duty of every church to provide a sufficient and honorable support, according to its ability, for the officers who give their time and strength to its service, is evident in itself, and is expressly enjoined by the Scriptures. Every member of the church in his place, and in the measure of his ability to contribute, is responsible for this duty.

2. Inasmuch as not only the covenanted members of the church, but all who are taught, may be reasonably expected, and should be encouraged, to bear their part in the expense of building the house of God and sustaining the ministry of the word, the civil incorporation of ecclesiastical societies, or parishes, in connection with churches, is a natural arrangement of Christian civilization in a free commonwealth. The form in which a society may be incorporated, for the legal ownership of ecclesiastical property and the support of public worship, is determined by the laws of the state; but the church, as a spiritual fellowship, electing

and ordaining its own officers, and worshiping God according to the New Testament, holds its charter only from Christ, and may not surrender its spiritual rights and powers to any civil corporation. Therefore, the independence of the church in the choice of its own officers, and in all its discipline, and in the conduct of its worship, must be steadfastly guarded. At the same time, the right of the parish or ecclesiastical society, as a legal corporation (including or representing all who in any equitable manner aid in the support of public worship), to control, within the limits of its trust, the use and expenditure of its own property, must be recognized. While the church is at liberty to elect whom it will, and as many as it will, to be church officers, it can not, by its own authority, require the parish to assume the burden of supporting them. Thus, in the election and settlement of a pastor or other officer who is to be supported by the parish, the concurrent votes of the church and the parish are necessary.

CHAPTER VII. — ADMISSION OF MEMBERS INTO THE CHURCH, AND DISMISSION OF MEMBERS FROM ONE CHURCH TO ANOTHER.

1. The things which are requisite in all church members are repentance from sin, and faith in Jesus Christ; and, therefore, these are the things whereof men are to be examined at their admission into the church, and which then they must profess and hold forth in such sort as may satisfy rational charity that the things are there indeed.

2. The weakest measure of faith is to be accepted in those that desire to be admitted into the church, because weak Christians, if sincere, have the substance of that penitent faith and holiness which is required in church members; and such have most need of the ordinances for their confirmation and growth in grace. Such charity and tenderness are to be used, that the weakest Christian, if sincere, may not be excluded or discouraged.

3. It is not needful that the profession of repentance and faith should be always in the same form of words; but it must always be in such words as are satisfactory to the church, and must be accompanied by a professed engagement to walk with the church according to the gospel.

4. Such personal profession is required not only of those who have not been before in any church relation, but also those who, having been born and baptized in the church, may be considered as in some sort hereditary members; for they, too, must credibly show and profess their own repentance toward God and faith toward our Lord Jesus Christ, before they come to the Lord's table or are recognized as members in full communion.

5. A church member, removing his residence to another place, does not thereby throw off his responsibility to the church with which he is in covenant. If his removal is permanent, he ought to seek, and, unless he is liable to some just censure (in which case he must be dealt with as an offender), he has a right to receive, a letter of dismission and commendation to an evangelical church in the place of his new residence; or, if

there be no such church in that place, to any such church with which he can have communion statedly in Christian ordinances. But his dismission can not take effect till he shall be received, as a member, by the church to which he has been commended.

6. A church is not bound to receive a member merely because of his dismission and commendation from another church; but if it find any just ground of objection to him, it may remit the case to the consideration of the church from which he came, and of which he is still a member.

CHAPTER VIII. — THE METHOD OF DEALING WITH OFFENDERS.

1. The censures of the church are appointed for the prevention and removal of offenses and the recovering of offenders; for purging out the leaven which may infect the whole lump; for vindicating the honor of Christ and of his church, and the profession of the gospel; and for preventing the displeasure of God, that may justly fall upon the church if they suffer his covenant, and the seals thereof, to be profaned by notorious and obstinate offenders.

2. Censures of the church are of two sorts,— admonition and excommunication.

3. If an offense be private, one brother trespassing against another, the offender is to go and acknowledge his repentance of it unto his offended brother, who is then to forgive him. But if the offender neglect or refuse to do this, then (1) the brother offended is to go and admonish him privately, between themselves. If thereupon the offender be brought to repent of his offense, the admonisher hath won his brother. But if the offender hear not his brother, then (2) the offended is to take with him one or two more, that in the mouth of two or three witnesses every word may be established, whether the word of admonition, if the offender receive it, or the word of complaint, if he refuse. (3) If the offender be not recovered by that second admonition, the offended brother is then to tell the church. If the church find that the complaint is well founded, it admonishes the offender; and then if he hear the church, and penitently confess his fault, he is recovered and gained, and is to be forgiven. But if, after being admonished by the church, he be not yet convinced of his fault, and ready to profess, frankly, his repentance of it, he remains under the censure of admonition, which of itself excludes or suspends him from the holy fellowship of the Lord's Supper, till either the offense is removed by his penitent confession, or the church, after reasonable forbearance, proceed to cast him out by excommunication.

4. When the offense is already public and notorious, and is of such a character as to be infamous among men, a more summary proceeding is authorized by the Scriptures. The church, without waiting for an individual complaint, or for the effect of private admonition, may take notice of the notorious fact, and cast out the offender without delay, for the mortifying of his sin, and the saving of his soul in the day of the Lord Jesus, as well as for the vindication of the gospel which he has dishon-

ored. Yet no offender may be censured without trial and the opportunity of being heard.

5. In dealing with an offender, great care is to be taken that we be neither too rigorous nor too indulgent. Our proceeding ought to be with a spirit of meekness, considering ourselves lest we also be tempted. Yet, the winning and healing of the offender's soul being the end of these endeavors, we must be earnest and thorough, not healing the wounds of our brethren slightly.

6. While the offender remains excommunicated, the church is to refrain from all communion with him in spiritual things, and also from all familiar communion with him in civil things, further than the necessity of natural, domestic, or civil relations may require. Yet, while there may be any hope of his recovery, we are to be kindly watchful for signs of repentance in him; not counting him an enemy, but admonishing him as a brother.

7. If the censure be made effectual by the grace of Christ, so that the excommunicated person repents of his sin, and with confession desires to be restored, the church is thereupon to forgive him; and as the censure was public, he is to be publicly absolved or loosed from the censure, and restored to full communion.

8. It is doubtless of great importance to the welfare of the church, that profane and scandalous persons be not permitted to continue in its fellowship, and to partake at the Lord's table; and the church which neglects to deal with such members, and to use the discipline of the Lord's house for their reformation or their exclusion, is greatly to be blamed. Yet such a church is not therefore to be immediately forsaken and renounced by those who would live godly in Jesus Christ. Nor is it reasonable that any individual member of that church should therefore withdraw himself from the Lord's table. In so doing, he wrongs his own soul by denying to himself the appointed means of grace, and wrongs the church by adding another scandal to that which he would rebuke. Let him rather endeavor, modestly, and seasonably, according to his power and place, that the unworthy may be duly proceeded against by the church to whom that duty belongs.

CHAPTER IX. — RELATION OF THE CHURCH TO CIVIL GOVERNMENT, AND THE CONFLICT OF LAWS.

1. The right of the church to assemble for worship, to observe Christ's ordinances, to hold forth the word of life by public preaching and by private communication, to receive into its communion those who give evidence of repentance and faith, and to admonish offenders or exclude them, is not a mere concession from the civil power, but is part of that religious liberty which Christ, by commanding his gospel to be preached to every creature, challenges for all men, and which no human government can suppress or violate, without incurring the displeasure of God.

2. The law which the church administers in its discipline is not merely the law of the land, nor the law of common use and opinion, but the

higher law of God as revealed in the Scriptures; for that which is highly esteemed among men conformed to this world may be abominable to God and to men enlightened by his word and spirit. If wickedness go unpunished in the civil State, or be even honored by public opinion, it is not therefore to be tolerated in the church. If the law of the land require of any man, under whatever penalties, that which the law of God forbids him to do, or if it forbid him to do what the law of God requires, it is better to obey God rather than men; and the church is to require of all its members obedience to the higher law of God. Yet, inasmuch as the Scriptures require of every Christian soul subjection to existing powers in the civil State, whether Christian or anti-Christian, the duty of loyalty to government, of conscientious obedience to every law which does not positively require what God forbids, or forbid what God requires, and of patient submission to persecution or other injustice when there is no lawful redress, is a duty of religion which the discipline of the church must honor and maintain.

3. With matters properly and exclusively political, the church has no concern; for Christ's kingdom is not of this world. But with matters of morality and religion, the church, in the administration of its discipline, and in the testimony which it is to give for God, has much to do. Especially in a free commonwealth, where the government proceeds continually from the people, the church is bound to testify, in its discipline and in its teaching, against wicked laws and institutions, not fearing to assert and apply the law of God, as revealed in the Scriptures, whatever may be the contradiction of sinners, and whatever the conflict between that supreme law of Christ's kingdom and the laws ordained of men, or the institutions and usages of society. Thus, the moral sense of communities and nations must be corrected and enlightened, and must be made to advance with the progress of the church, till Christ shall be honored in all lands as King of kings, and Lord of lords, the blessed and only Potentate. [Continued on page 118.]

At this point, the hour of adjournment having nearly arrived, Dr. Bacon paused, and said that, as it would be impossible to conclude the report this forenoon, he would not enter upon the third part, but would read the remainder of the document, with the leave of the Council, in the afternoon.

A motion was made that the hour of adjournment in the afternoon be six o'clock, instead of five.

Rev. Mr. Wellman, of Massachusetts, suggested that five and a half o'clock would be a better hour, inasmuch as six would interfere with the convenience of many delegates who lodged out of the city. He moved to amend the motion, so that it should read five and a half o'clock, instead of six.

The amendment was accepted by the mover.

Rev. Dr. Todd, of Massachusetts, opposed the motion. He thought six hours a day were as much as they could profitably sit at this season, and that they would probably accomplish as much in that time as they would if they should make the change proposed.

The question was put, and the motion lost.

LETTER FROM MASSSACHUSETTS CONVENTION OF CONGREGATIONAL MINISTERS.

Rev. Mr. DEXTER, of Massachusetts. I have a communication to read, and I desire to say, as preliminary, in order that all present may understand how it comes here, that the Massachusetts Convention of Congregational Ministers is a body that had an existence before the days of Unitarian separation; that it had funds in its possession for the widows of poor ministers; and that, on account of that peculiar condition of things, the convention has continued to exist until this day, and includes all Congregational ministers in Massachusetts, whether Orthodox or Unitarian in their faith. This communication comes from that body:—

"TO THE MODERATOR OF THE NATIONAL COUNCIL OF CONGREGATIONAL MINISTERS.

"*Dear Sir*,—Will you please lay before the Council the following resolution, passed at a meeting of the Massachusetts Convention of Congregational Ministers, held in Boston, May 31, 1865:—

"*Resolved*, That the National Council of Congregational Churches, to be held in this city on the 14th of June next, be respectfully requested to use such language, in their official procedures as a Trinitarian Congregational Council, as shall recognize the fact that there are Unitarian and other Congregational churches in this Commonwealth.

"Very respectfully,

[Signed] "JAMES H. MEANS,

"*Scribe of the Convention.*

"DORCHESTER, June 12, 1865."

Rev. Mr. QUINT, of Massachusetts. As this is a communication which should be respectfully received, and the subject to which it refers carefully considered, I move that it be referred to a special committee of three, to draft an appropriate reply.

Rev. Mr. GULLIVER, of Connecticut. I wish to propose that the committee also take into consideration the very great necessity and importance of making a distinction, in our minutes and in all our phraseology, between Baptist and Pedobaptist Congregational churches. The cases are entirely parallel, and I wish the committee would report upon both of them.

Rev. Dr. DUTTON, of Connecticut. And also the Universalists.

Rev. Dr. BUDINGTON, of New York. I hope that the suggestions which have now been made will not be pressed upon the committee.

THE MODERATOR. I supposed they were suggestions only.

Rev. Dr. BUDINGTON. If they are suggestions, simply, I will not occupy the time of the Council by remarking upon them. There are very grave considerations at the bottom of this communication, and I trust they will be very prayerfully and carefully considered, as they deserve to be.

The motion of Rev. Mr. Quint was then put, and carried.

Adjourned.

AFTERNOON SESSION.

The Council was called to order at 3 o'clock, by the moderator.

Rev. Mr. Quint, from the Business Committee, reported the following as the programme for the afternoon: —

That after the reading of the papers upon the evangelization of the West and South, and Church Building, the next business in order be the Report on Ministerial Education, and that the Rev. Edward A. Walker, who has just returned from Italy, desiring to speak upon Congregationalism in that country, the reading of papers be suspended at twenty minutes before five, in order to afford him an opportunity to do so.

The report was accepted and adopted.

CHURCH POLITY.

Rev. Dr. Bacon then resumed the reading of the report on church polity, as follows: —

PART III. — THE COMMUNION OF CHURCHES.

CHAPTER I. — PRINCIPLES AND SPECIFICATIONS.

1. Although churches are distinct, and therefore may not be confounded one with another, and equal, and therefore have not dominion one over another; yet all the churches ought to preserve church communion one with another; because they are all united to Christ as integral parts of his one catholic church-militant against the evil that is in the world, and visible in the profession of the Christian faith, in the observance of the Christian sacrament, in the manifestation of the Christian life, and in the worship of the one God of our salvation, the Father, and the Son, and the Holy Ghost.

2. The communion of churches with each other is manifested in various acts of fraternal courtesy, correspondence, and helpfulness: —

(1.) In mutual recognition; one organized congregation of Christian worshipers acknowledging another to be a visible church of Christ, and each professing a readiness to interchange with the other all reasonable acts of Christian courtesy and love.

(2.) In admitting members of one church to commune, as such, at the Lord's table in another church, and refusing to admit them if they are under censure.

(3.) In permitting and inviting ministers of the word, recognized and accredited as such by one church, to speak for Christ in another church.

(4.) In the dismission and reception of members, when for any sufficient reason they pass from one church to another.

(5.) In giving and receiving advice when one church desires counsel of another and of many others.

(6.) In giving and receiving help; as when one church gives of its members that another may be supplied with officers; or as when one church receives outward support from the contributions of another or of many others.

(7.) In consultation and co-operation for each other's edification and prosperity, or for the common interest of the gospel.

(8.) In giving and receiving admonition; as when there is found in a church some public offense which it either does not discern, or neglects to remove; for though churches have no more authority one over another than one apostle had over another, yet as one apostle might admonish another, so may one church admonish another, and yet without usurpation; in which case, if the admonished church refuse to hear its neighbor churches and to remove the offense, it violates the communion of churches.

3. The Congregational churches in the United States of America, as integral portions of Christ's catholic church, maintain all practicable communion with all other portions of the church universal. While other churches differ from us in their internal polity, in their relations and connections with each other, in their forms of worship, or in the uninspired statements and definitions of doctrines disputed among Christians, and while we disown their schemes of hierarchal or synodical government, we acknowledge as particular churches of Christ all congregations of Christian worshipers that acknowledge the Holy Scriptures as their supreme rule of faith and practice, and Christ as the Lamb of God who taketh away the sin of the world. We pray for their peace and prosperity. We invite their members to occasional communion with us in worship and in sacramental ordinances. We receive their letters of dismissal and commendation, and, in return, dismiss our members, as occasion may require, with letters of commendation to them. We are ready to be edified by their ministers; and, in all reasonable and hopeful methods, we are ready to consult and co-operate with them for the advancement of the gospel.

4. As some acts of the communion of the churches are due, in one degree and another, to all the integral parts of Christ's catholic church, so other acts of communion are specially due from churches instituted and governed according to the Congregational polity to other churches instituted and governed according to the same polity. Certain acts of communion are not practicable between churches congregationally governed and churches that are under a hierarchal or synodical government; and certain acts of communion are not practicable between

churches which seriously differ from each other in the system of doctrine which they declare, respectively, from the Scriptures, even though they recognize each other as holding that faith which is necessary to salvation. A church desiring the approbation and assistance of other churches, in the ordination of its officers, can not wisely or courteously ask such approbation and assistance from churches in whose professed theory of government all ordinations must be by a prelate, or in whose theory the power of ordination is given only to a presbytery ruling over many congregations. In like manner, if it desire counsel in any case involving questions of doctrine, it can not, wisely or courteously, ask such counsel of churches not accepting that general system of doctrines which is the well-known basis of mutual confidence and intimate communion among churches of the Congregational polity.

5. The more intimate communion existing among these churches is exercised in asking and giving counsel, in giving and receiving admonition, in various acts of helpfulness toward churches needing help from others, and in conferences and consultations for the parochial revival and prosperity of religion, or the general advancement of Christ's kingdom.

CHAPTER II. — COUNCILS.

1. Councils of churches, orderly assembled to declare the opinion of the churches on any matter of common concern, are an ordinance of Christ, and are necessary to a communion of the churches. That scriptural example, where the church at Antioch sent messengers to the church at Jerusalem, for consultation and advice in a difficult question, is a sufficient warrant for such councils.

2. The churches invited to assist in a council are represented by messengers or delegates, chosen by them for the particular occasion. By ancient usage, the pastor of a church, having been duly recognized as its presiding elder or bishop, is always expected to be one of its messengers; and the letters convening the council invite each church to be represented by its pastor and delegate. Yet in the council, when convened, there is no distinction of authority between the pastor and other delegates.

3. It is manifest, from the reason of the case, that in ordinary cases a council ought to be made up chiefly of churches in the near vicinity. But when a council is called to advise in some personal or parochial controversy which involves strong sympathies and interests in the surrounding region, it may be expedient to ask counsel from more distant churches, rather than exclusively from those near at hand.

4. A council is to be called only by a church, or by an aggrieved member or members in a church which has unreasonably refused a council, or by a competent number of believers intending to be gathered into a church. In a difficulty or controversy between the church and its elder or elders, or between the church and some other person or party in the church, if a council is desired, and the church consents, the churches to constitute the council are selected by agreement between the parties, and are invited by letters-missive from the church; and this is

called a mutual council. If a church unreasonably refuses to call a mutual council, then an *ex parte* council may be invited, by letters-missive from the aggrieved member or members.

5. An *ex parte* council, properly called, has the same standing, and is entitled to the same respect, as a mutual council; for it were unreasonable that, in case of grievance, either party should be deprived, by the obstinacy of the other, of such relief as the neighboring churches could give. But, that it may be properly convened, it is requisite, (1) that there be proper ground for calling a council; (2) that one party, properly requested, has unreasonably refused to join in calling a mutual council; (3) that the *ex parte* council is called upon the statement of the original grounds for asking a council, and of the unreasonable refusal of the other party to join; and, (4) that the churches invited be impartially selected. When assembled, the *ex parte* council should first offer itself to the refusing party, as a mutual council.

6. Councils consist solely of such churches as are invited, with the occasional addition of persons whose advice is especially desired. After being called, no church or person can be added to or taken from the proper members in any manner. For the letters-missive having specified the churches and persons invited, each church appointed its delegates upon that knowledge of those with whom it was asked to associate.

7. Councils are not to be convened upon every ground of dissatisfaction with a church, nor in cases of light moment. They are proper only upon some matter of common interest to the churches, such as the relations of fellowship between churches; or the relation of a member to the communion of other churches; the relation of pastors and churches; the reputation of the brotherhood of churches, as affected by the acts or condition of a church; or matters of general interest to the cause of Christ. They are in no such sense such courts of appeal that they may alter or rescind any act of a church. Yet, in cases of censure, if the proceedings complained of are found to have been in gross violation of the rules given in the Scriptures, the council may advise and declare, that, in its judgment, the censure complained of is wrong, and may commend the censured person to be received by some other church, as a member in full communion.

Particular occasions for councils are such as these: —

(1.) When a competent number of Christian brethren propose to unite in a church covenant, and desire to be recognized as a church in the more intimate communion of Congregational churches, the ordinary and most orderly method of obtaining such recognition is by an ecclesiastical council, invited for that purpose by their letters to a convenient number of churches, and especially of churches in the near vicinity. Having given to that council, when assembled, a satisfactory statement of their faith and order, and of the reasons for their becoming a distinct church, together with sufficient evidence, not only of their Christian character, but also of their fitness in respect to gifts and numbers, for performing the duties of a church, they receive, as a church, the right hand of fellowship extended to them by the council, in behalf of all the churches.

(2.) The induction of a pastor or teacher into his office, in any church, or, on the other hand, the dismission of such an officer from his place, concerns the communion of the churches. Therefore an ecclesiastical council is convened for the ordination or installation of a pastor, and, in like manner, for his dismission at his own request. A due respect to the communion of the churches requires that no man assuming to be a pastor of a church shall be acknowledged as such by other churches, unless, at or after his entrance on the duties of the office, he has been publicly recognized, by receiving the right hand of fellowship from neighboring churches, through a council convened for that purpose. The welfare of the churches, in their intimate communion with each other, requires this safeguard. In like manner, the communion of churches requires that no minister dismissed from his charge shall be regarded as having sufficient credentials of his good standing, unless he is duly commended by a council convened on the occasion of his dismission.

(3.) When difficulties, whether internal or external, threaten the peace and spiritual prosperity of any church, and are not likely to be adjusted without aid, or when any question arises on which the church needs advice for the guidance and correction or confirmation of its own judgment, that church has a right to ask the advice of other churches with which it is in communion. To such an advisory council the trial of a difficult case is sometimes referred. The council examines the questions referred to it, whether questions of fact or questions of principle and duty; it pronounces its conclusions, but it has no power to inflict any church censure, or to absolve from censure. It can only advise the church; and the church, by accepting and adopting the result of the council, carries the advice into effect.

(4.) When a member against whom charges have been preferred requests the calling of a council for the trial of those charges, and the church consents to the request, or when, in any manner, parties have arisen who desire a council for the hearing of the questions between them, the churches to constitute the council are mutually agreed upon between the parties. Yet a mutual council is not convened in the name of the parties, but in the name of the church. But in such cases a refusal on the part of the church to agree to call a council before trial, does not give any occasion for an *ex parte* council.

(5.) When a member, having been censured by the church, conscientiously protests that the censure is not according to the facts, or that it is not warranted by the word of God, he may respectfully ask the church to join with him in calling a mutual council for a new hearing of his case; and, that request being denied by the church without sufficient reason, he may appeal to other churches for advice, and for such relief as they may find reason to give him, and may invite them to meet in an *ex parte* council. Or when a portion of any church has been seriously aggrieved by such action of the church as causes public scandal to the cause of Christ, and their request for a council has been denied by the church, they may in like manner appeal to other churches for a hearing of their cause and for advice concerning their duty.

(6.) When a member liable to no just censure has requested letters of dismission and recommendation to some other recognized church, and the request is refused, he may request the church to invite a council to hear the case; and, if the church refuses, he may himself ask a council to give him relief.

(7.) When a pastor or other ordained minister in any church is charged with offenses which would render it proper that he be deposed from the ministry, then the church should invite a council to examine the charges; if they be proven, the council should advise that fellowship be withdrawn from him, and that he be no longer recognized as a Christian minister.

8. The council, when assembled, organizes itself by the choice of a moderator and scribe, that its proceedings may be orderly and deliberate, and may be duly written down for the use of those whom the result concerns. If half of the churches invited be not represented, those present ought not to proceed to act, unless the party inviting consents. Being a representative body, its functions are limited to the subjects specified in the letters-missive. In voting, it was an ancient and laudable custom that each church give its voice as a church, and not that the messengers vote as individuals; but this custom is not universal. Having properly deliberated, and made up its decision, the council is forthwith to be dissolved; and the scribe is to convey a copy of its proceedings and advice to the parties concerned.

9. The decision of a council is only advisory. Yet it is to be received, with reverence and submission, (unless inconsistent with the Scriptures) as the voice of the churches, and as an ordinance of God appointed thereunto in his word. In cases of difference, therefore, the party adopting the advice of council is entitled to the sympathy and commendation of the churches, rather than the one rejecting it.

10. When a council, properly convened and orderly proceeding, whether mutual or *ex parte*, has pronounced its advice, a second council, upon the substance of the same questions, or upon the advice of the first, is manifestly improper. If *both* parties desire further light, they may agree thereto. But, if one refuse, an *ex parte* council is in that case not warranted, and is manifestly disorderly.

11. A council orderly assembled to advise concerning the acts and administrations of a church, and finding that such church deliberately receives and maintains doctrines which subvert the foundations of the Christian faith, or that it wilfully tolerates and upholds notorious scandals, or that it persistently disregards and contemns the communion of churches, may, after fit admonition, advise the churches to withhold from that erring church all acts of communion till it shall give evidence of reformation. And any church, after due admonition, may call a council.

12. Some Congregational churches, neighboring to each other, are confederated, more or less strictly, for mutual assistance in cases which require a council. Such confederations, whether under the name of

consociation or convention, may be useful if they duly recognize and guard the principle that the power of inflicting church censures and of absolving from censure, and the power of choosing and ordaining officers and of removing them from office for good cause, reside under Christ, in the particular church, and not in some ecclesiastical authority extrinsic to the church; and the cognate principle that councils, however constituted, are for the communion of churches with each other, and not for government over the churches.

CHAPTER III. — CONFERENCES OF CHURCHES.

1. It is fit and convenient for the churches of a neighborhood to meet, sometimes, by their pastors and delegates, for the purpose of reporting to each other their spiritual prosperity and progress, and of consulting together how to advance the cause and kingdom of Christ. Such meetings are commonly called conferences of churches, and are distinguished from councils in that they have nothing to do with giving advice to any particular church concerning the ordination or dismission of any of its officers, or concerning the administration of its government. They meet only for mutual information and inquiry, that through them the churches may provoke each other to love and good works.

2. Conferences of churches are either occasional or stated. Any church may invite the neighboring churches, more or fewer, at its own discretion, to meet with it for mutual edification and inquiry. Or a number of churches may associate to hold such conferences at fixed periods and under definite regulations. Stated conferences of the churches have been greatly useful in promoting zeal and Christian activity, and in making the gifts of one church subserve the edification of others.

3. In some States the several conferences are associated in a general conference or association of churches, which institutes a careful inquiry every year, and makes its report concerning the general prosperity and progress of the churches throughout the State.

CHAPTER IV. — SYNODS, OR NATIONAL COUNCILS.

1. Occasions may arise, in the progress of Christ's kingdom, when a representative assembly of churches, coming together for consultation and agreement, and for testimony, is required; an assembly which shall be larger in its numbers than any council, such as a single church can convene for its own need, and larger in its constituency than any stated conference of churches. Such synods were required, and were held at sundry times, when the fathers of the American Congregational churches were laying the foundations on which many generations were to build.

2. A synod can not be constituted by any number of unauthorized individuals assuming to represent the churches. The express consent of the churches, acting severally, in their self-government under Christ, recognizing the call, and sending forth their elders and other messengers, is what constitutes the synod as a representative body. An assembly thus constituted by the joint action of many churches, and coming together

not for strife and contention, but for devout and earnest consultation concerning things that pertain to the kingdom of God, may be expected to have much of those gracious influences and of that guidance by the Holy Comforter, in which Christ fulfills his promises: "Lo, I am with you alway, even unto the end of the world;" and, "Where two or three are gathered together in my name, there am I in the midst of them."

3. The calling of such a synod ought not to proceed from the mere will or motion of unauthorized individuals, nor from the mere motion of any one church acting without consultation. When the elders and other messengers of any considerable body of churches, coming together in a representative assembly, such as the general conference or general association of a State, are convinced that an occasion has arisen which requires a national synod or council, they may reasonably institute inquiries by correspondence with other similar bodies; and if, after such correspondence and conference as may conveniently be had, the conviction is strengthened and extended, that, in the providence of God, there is a call upon the churches to confer with each other in a national council, the arrangements may be made, and the invitation issued by such persons as shall have been designated to that service, by common consent in the preliminary consultations. The invitation should be addressed, not to associations or conferences purporting to represent the churches, but distinctly to each several church, so that the ultimate determination of the question shall proceed directly from the churches themselves; and every church shall have the opportunity of consenting or withholding its consent, according to the wisdom given to it from above.

4. The proper function of a synod is not to legislate for the churches, nor to determine imperatively any question which is not already determined by the Scriptures, but by inquiry and brotherly conference, with prayer for divine illumination, to obtain and hold forth light on such matters as the churches have referred to its deliberations. A synod, as a great cloud of witnesses, may properly testify in behalf of the constituent churches not only their common faith in Christ their Saviour, but what is the system of Christian doctrine, and what the system and theory of ecclesiastical administrations, which are the basis of their special communion one with another, as churches walking in the order of the New Testament.

CHAPTER V. — CONFESSIONS OF FAITH.

1. Neither Christ nor his apostles prescribed any form of words to be imposed on disciples, or on churches, for the confessing of their faith. Had such a form been given, it would have become a part of the canonical Scriptures.

2. Every church is to judge for itself whether the form of words offered or adopted as a confession of faith by any who desire admission to its holy communion, is a satisfactory profession of faith in Christ and his gospel.

3. When a council is assembled for the ordination or recognition of a

pastor, or for the ordination of a missionary or other minister at large, the candidate for ordination or recognition may reasonably be required to make a more ample declaration of his religious belief, holding forth to the church and the council, not only his personal faith in the Saviour of sinners, but also his doctrinal soundness as a preacher of the word. Such confession of faith should be in words deliberately and accurately chosen, and the council must judge for itself whether the confession is sound and sufficient.

4. Every church desiring to share in the fellowship of the churches should make some adequate declaration of its fidelity to the doctrine which is according to godliness. It is therefore fit that every church set forth, in the form of a confession or catechism, the system of truth which it receives as the faith once delivered to the saints, which its fathers and teachers maintain by their ministry, and in which it trains its children.

5. Any assembly of elders or messengers, representing a body of churches, local or national, is competent to testify, in the form of a confession, what system of doctrines is received and maintained in the churches which it represents. Or any body of Christian men, being called thereto in the providence of God, may frame and publish, as a confession of their faith, a declaration of the truths which they receive as revealed from God by his word and Spirit. Such confessions of faith have often been useful for the refutation of injurious reproaches, or for the confirmation of the truth.

6. The right use of confessions of faith is not for separation and mutual exclusion among Christians, but rather for mutual information and confidence, and the manifestation of unity. For this purpose, inasmuch as the Scriptures are often perverted, and doctrines subversive of the faith once delivered to the saints are brought in among the churches, it sometimes becomes reasonable and fit for churches, or for representative assemblies, not only to testify and confess, but also to bear witness against doctrines contrary to the gospel of Christ, and dangerous to the souls of men. For Christian unity is not to be maintained by compromises with doctrines which corrupt the word of God, but only by adherence to the truth as it is in Jesus. Yet no confession of faith or testimony against error is to be set up in place of the Scriptures, which are the only standard and unerring rule of faith, and with which all human formularies are to be constantly and diligently compared.

PART IV.—THE MINISTRY.

CHAPTER I.—THE PREACHING OF THE WORD.

1. While those whom the church chooses and ordains to be its pastors and teachers are, by virtue of their office, preachers of the gospel, laboring in word and doctrine, the Congregational churches have always acknowledged that the work of preaching is not exclusively a function of church officers. Fit men, not bearing office in any church, but giving

themselves to the work of preaching, have always been recognized among us as ministers of the word.

2. The necessity for a recognized class of ministers, not holding office in any church, is manifold. (1.) In preaching the gospel to every creature, there is much to be done which can not be done by elders or bishops of churches, whose proper work is parochial, and not missionary. (2.) There is, and ever must be, need of ministers, recognized as such, who can supply, by occasional and temporary ministration, the lack of service in churches that have no preaching elders. (3.) Those who are to teach and train men for the ministry must needs be ministers, recognized as such among the churches, and esteemed for their zeal and power in holding forth the word of life; and yet they can not ordinarily be at the same time officers in the churches. (4.) Under every theory of church order, there must be, in fact, a class of men accredited in some way, and recognized as qualified by natural endowments, by learning and study, and by the work of the Holy Spirit on their souls, to preach the word; among whom the churches may find fit men to be their pastors and teachers. (5.) Nor can the churches consent that when a pastor, for any good reason, resigns his office, and is discharged with commendation as a good and faithful servant of Christ in the gospel, he shall thenceforth cease to be reputed and recognized as a minister of the word. (6.) It is abundantly evident from the Scriptures, that, in the beginning, there were many ministers of the word, beside the elders who were ordained in every church; and that while the distinctive work of the apostles was essentially extraordinary, ceasing with their lives, and transmitted to no successors, the work of ministers, not holding office in the churches, was a work which continues, and must continue, till Christ's catholic church on earth shall cease to be militant.

3. Such ministers of the gospel, not being apostles, nor successors of the apostles, are invested with no apostolic authority; and, not being elders or bishops, they have no official place or power in any church (except when temporarily invited by any church); but each one, in the church with which he is in covenant, is only a member till the church shall call him to office either as a deacon or as an elder; and if he be called to office as an elder, laboring in word and doctrine, then the communion of the churches will require that his induction into office shall be approved by a Council before he can be recognized as pastor by the neighbor churches.

4. A minister who is not a member of some Congregational church is not in fact, and ought not to be, counted a minister in connection with the churches and ministry of the Congregational order, though he may be worthy of confidence and fellowship by virtue of his responsible connection with some other body of evangelical churches.

CHAPTER II. —CALL AND ORDINATION TO THE MINISTRY.

1. As it was in the church at Antioch that Barnabas and Saul received their special call to the missionary work among the Gentiles, so, by parity of reason, the call of any brother to the work of a minister at

large ought always to proceed from some church cognizant of his gifts and graces, and therefore competent to judge, in the first instance, whether he is called of God; nor ordinarily should the call proceed from any other church than that in which he is, or in which he is to be a member.

2. As Barnabas and Saul, when sent from the church at Antioch on a mission to the Gentiles, were separated to their work by ordination; so it is fit, that, after reasonable trial, those who are called to minister in the word of God without holding the office of elders or bishops in any church, be solemnly commended to the grace of God, and, by the laying-on of hands and prayer, be separated to the work whereunto he hath called them. No church ought to ordain any without the approval of neighbor churches assembled in a council. Yet it should be remembered that the ordination or installation is the act of the church, and that the duty of such council is not to exercise jurisdiction or authority over the church, but simply to advise and assist, and to express the fellowship of other churches in the transaction. We therefore commend the ancient custom, now too much disused, of calling on the church, before the prayer of consecration and the giving of the charge, to renew their choice and call, and on the candidate to renew his acceptance of the call, in the presence of the approving council and the witnessing assembly. Thus the ordination or installation will proceed by the authority which Christ has given to that church; and the council, as representing neighbor churches, will give, in their behalf, the right hand of fellowship.

3. When a minister, without pastoral charge, is accused of any scandal dishonorable to the ministry with which he is intrusted, or with teaching that which is contrary to the gospel, and dangerous to the souls of men, the church of which he is a member should seek the assistance of an ecclesiastical council in the trial of the case, and, if he be found guilty, should declare him to be deposed from the ministry, and then deal with him by admonition and excommunication, as with any other member.

CHAPTER III. — ASSOCIATIONS OF MINISTERS.

1. The experience of our churches, from the beginning, has proved that the frequent consultation of ministers with each other, so that the watchmen may see eye to eye, is of great importance to their efficiency in their work; and the formal association of pastors, not excluding other ministers, for mutual counsel and helpfulness, is an arrangement which has been greatly blessed of God for the welfare of the churches and the advancement of religion.

2. An association of ministers has no jurisdiction or authority over the churches. It may give advice to its own members, or to any other persons asking its advice, on questions of church order or questions of doctrine; but it can neither inflict nor remove any church censure. It forms its own rules concerning the qualifications and conditions of membership, and in accordance with those rules it can admit members and exclude them; but it can ordain no man to the ministry, nor can it depose any man from the ministry. If one of its members, whether a pastor or a minister without pastoral charge, is guilty of an offense for which he

should be deposed from the ministry, it may not only exclude him from its fellowship, but may bring the matter to the notice of the church to which he is responsible. Or if any minister or professed minister of scandalous or heretical character is presuming to officiate in the churches of the vicinity, the association may take measures to bring the matter to the notice of the proper ecclesiastical authority, or, if necessary to the protection of the churches and the vindication of the ministry, may give public notice that he is not in their fellowship.

3. By the common consent and ancient usage of our churches, the recognized associations of pastors and other ministers are intrusted with the duty of examining those who are to preach as candidates for the ministry, and of commending them to the churches by letters of approbation, so that untaught or otherwise unfit persons may not intrude themselves into the work of preaching.

4. The associations of Congregational ministers, throughout the United States, have their own methods of correspondence with each other, and of mutual recognition, through general associations in the several states, or otherwise.

CHAPTER IV. — CANDIDATES FOR THE MINISTRY; THEIR EDUCATION, AND THE TRIAL OF THEIR GIFTS.

I. Inasmuch as the work of ministering in the word of God, to the edification of the churches and to the advancement of religion, requires not only natural gifts of intelligence and discretion, and of utterance, but also a personal experience of the gospel as the power of God unto salvation, a hearty love to Christ and to the souls of men, and a comprehensive knowledge of the Holy Scriptures and of the system of truth which they reveal, our fathers, at the beginning, made great endeavors and sacrifices to establish colleges consecrated to Christ and the church, that a faithful and competently learned ministry might be provided for their posterity, and for the country which they were redeeming from the wilderness. Colleges under Christian influence and control, and founded primarily for the education of men whom the churches may call to the ministry, are among the foremost of the voluntary institutions which accompany the prosperity of churches walking in the faith and order of the gospel; and the work of presiding and teaching in such institutions is a work in which consecrated ministers of the gospel may make full proof of their ministry, and may obtain a place among those who have turned many to righteousness.

2. In later times, the progress of society, and the increase and wide diffusion of knowledge, having changed in some degree the course of education in the colleges, so that other and special studies are now necessary to a full preparation for the ministry, theological seminaries have been founded, that those who offer themselves to the service of Christ, in the preaching and defense of his gospel, and who have been disciplined by liberal studies and enriched with general knowledge, may be instructed in all kinds of sacred learning, and, under the guidance of teachers who are also able and faithful preachers of the word, and experienced in the

care of souls, may, by God's blessing on their endeavors, prepare themselves for the largest usefulness in the churches that may call them to office, and in the work of preaching the gospel to every creature.

3. The credentials which a young man may receive from a college or a theological seminary are not sufficient for his introduction to the churches as a preacher. Still less may his own desire to preach, or the desire of his friends, and the commendation he receives from them, authorize him to offer himself as a candidate for the ministry, or make it safe for congregations to employ him for the trial of his gifts. Even at the beginning, when the churches were few, and not far distant from each other, it was soon found needful to institute some well-considered arrangement for the examination of candidates, and their orderly introduction to the churches. And inasmuch as it devolves on the pastors and teachers of churches to feed the several flocks of which the Holy Ghost hath made them overseers, and to take heed whom they severally introduce to preach the word, it was agreed that neighboring pastors should jointly exercise their right of examination and inquiry, before recognizing or commending a candidate as qualified to preach in public. It is therefore a long-established usage in the communion of our churches, that no man is to offer himself as a candidate for the ministry, or is to be received as such, without having been examined and approved by some recognized association of pastors.

4. In the examination of a candidate, the association, having received evidence of his standing as a member in full communion of some evangelical church, with other testimonials to his blamelessness of life and his attainments in knowledge, inquires of him concerning his experience of the power of godliness, the reasons of his desire and choice to preach the gospel, the studies he has pursued, his knowledge especially of the system of doctrines contained in the Scriptures, and his readiness in the exposition and application of the word of God; and, having obtained satisfactory evidence of his fitness to preach in the churches for the trial of his gifts, the pastors and other ministers in that association assembled certify their approbation in a written testimonial.

5. The person thus accredited is not yet recognized as a minister of the gospel, but is only a candidate for the ministry, temporarily commended to the churches, that they may make trial of his fitness for that sacred work; and till he shall be duly ordained to the ministry, the testimonial given to him may be withdrawn whenever that association, for any good reason, is no longer willing to be responsible for him.

The remaining portion of the report was then read by Rev. Mr. Quint, of Massachusetts, of the same committee.

EPITOME OF CHURCH GOVERNMENT AND FELLOWSHIP.

I. — GENERAL PRINCIPLES.

I. Ecclesiastical polity, or church government, is that form and order which is to be observed in the Church of Christ.

II. The Holy Scriptures are the sufficient, exclusive, and obligatory rule of ecclesiastical polity. Church powers, therefore, are only administrative, not legislative.

III. For government, there is no one visible, universal church; nor are there national, provincial, diocesan or classical churches; but only local churches, or congregations of believers, and responsible directly to the Lord Jesus Christ, the one Head of the Church universal, and of every particular church.

IV. Each local church is complete in itself, and has all powers requisite for its own government and discipline. But all churches, being in communion one with another, have such mutual duties as grow out of the obligations of fellowship.

II. — OF A CHURCH.

I. Of its matter and form.

1. A church is always to be composed of such as are judged to belong to Christ, and of none others.

2. A church is a society of professed believers, united by a covenant, express or implied, whereby all its members agree with the Lord and with each other, to observe all the ordinances of Christ, especially in united worship, and in mutual watchfulness and helpfulness.

3. It is the duty of all believers in Christ to unite in church fellowship.

4. Believers are added to the church by entering into covenant, upon the vote of the brotherhood, after due trial of their repentance from sin, and faith in the Lord Jesus Christ.

5. Members cease to be such, when they are recommended to, and received by some other recognized church; to which dismission and commendation they are always entitled, unless liable to some just censure.

II. Of the officers of a church.

1. Though officers are not necessary to the being of a church, they are to its well-being.

2. The officers appointed by Christ's institution are bishops (or pastors and teachers) and deacons. Other persons, appointed for special duties, constitute no order of church officers.

3. Church officers are to be chosen exclusively by the church to which they are to minister; and they may be dismissed, for cause, by the same authority. Yet, in the choice or dismission of a pastor, neighboring churches should be consulted, — both for advice, and for the sake of fellowship among the churches.

4. No man may be a pastor but one that is called of God to the work of the ministry. But the church judges of his fitness by due trial of his faith, grace, and abilities.

5. Church officers are to be ordained, or solemnly inducted into their several offices; and the ordination of a pastor involves his consecration to the ministry of the gospel.

6. The work of a pastor is to labor in word and doctrine; and to rule, not as a lord over God's heritage, but with the consent of the brethren.

The work of a deacon is to assist the pastor, not by ruling or teaching, but chiefly by "serving tables."

7. The church should provide proper maintenance for the pastor. It is right also, that not only members of the church, but all who are taught in the word contribute to his support. When incorporated societies assume the maintenance of a pastor and teacher, it is also right that they have concurrent voice with the church in his election.

III. Of church censures.

1. It is the right and duty of every church to preserve its purity by the prevention and removal of offenses, and the recovery of offenders. This duty it can not depute to others, neither can others rightly assume it.

2. In the treatment of offenses, the object is both to reclaim offenders, and to preserve the purity of the church in faith and practice.

3. Church censures are of two sorts, — admonition and excommunication.

4. If one brother offend another, and does not acknowledge his fault, it is the duty of the brother aggrieved to follow the course which Christ has prescribed in the eighteenth chapter of Matthew, in the hope of winning his brother. If the grievance come before the church, the church should endeavor to recover the offender; and, failing that, it should admonish him, which of itself suspends him from church communion until the offense be removed.

5. If an offense be public and scandalous, the church may proceed without such gradual steps, to try the offender, and, if it find cause, admonish or excommunicate him.

6. When an offending brother makes penitent confession to the church, to its entire satisfaction, he is recovered and gained. If not fully satisfied, the church should admonish him. If, in any case of admonition, the offender prove obstinate, he is, after reasonable delay, to be excommunicated by vote of the brotherhood.

7. While one lies under the censure of excommunication, he is not to be received to spiritual communion in any church. But, upon repentance, he may be absolved of the censure and restored.

8. Inasmuch as the first object is to reclaim the offender, all things should be done in a spirit of gentleness and meekness. In the trial of one who is accused, all proceedings should be conducted with equity and patience; and, in the decision, unnecessary harshness is not less to be avoided than remissness.

9. If a brother claims to be aggrieved by any censure affecting his communion with other churches, or if a letter of dismission and recommendation is unreasonably refused, he may ask the church to join with him in requesting advice of the neighboring churches; and, if the church refuse, may of himself request the churches to assemble by their messengers to inquire into his case, and to give him advice.

III. — OF THE COMMUNION OF THE CHURCHES.

I. Although churches are distinct and equal, yet they ought to preserve fellowship one with another, being all united to Christ their head.

II. When a company of believers propose to unite in a distinct church, it is requisite that they ask the advice and help of neighboring churches; particularly that those churches, being satisfied with their faith and order, may extend to them the hand of fellowship.

III. Communion is to be exercised by recognizing each other's rights, by due regard to each other's welfare, and by consultation before acts of common concern.

IV. Councils are the ordinary and orderly way of consultation among churches, and are proper in all cases where the communion of the churches is involved.

1. In councils, the churches meet for consultation, usually by messengers (pastors and delegates) chosen for the special occasion.

2. Councils are properly called of churches in the near vicinity, except when matters which excite strong local sympathies render the advice of distant churches necessary.

3. Councils are called only by a church, or an unauthorized party in case of disagreement, when the church unreasonably refuses to join; that is, by a church desiring light or help; by a church and pastor (or other member or members) in case of differences, when it is styled a mutual council; or by either of these parties when the other unreasonably refuses to unite, when it is styled an *ex parte* council; which *ex parte* council, when properly convened, has the same standing as if it had been mutual.

4. Councils consist solely of the churches invited by the letters-missive, to which no member can be added, and from which none can be removed.

5. Councils are convened when a church desires recognition; when a church asks for advice or help; when differences are to be composed; when men whose call of God is recognized by the church are to be separated to the ministry; when pastors are to be inducted into office or removed; when a brother claims to be aggrieved by church censure; when letters of dismission are unreasonably refused; when a church or minister is liable to just censure; and when matters of common moment to the churches are to be considered.

6. The decision of a council is only advisory. Yet, when orderly given, it is to be received as the voice of the churches, and an ordinance of God appointed in his word, with reverence and submission, unless inconsistent with the word of God. But councils cannot overrule the acts of churches, so far as they are within the church, nor exercise government over them.

7. When in any case of difference, a council properly convened, whether mutual or *ex parte*, has given its judgment, neither party can demand that another council be called, whether to re-examine the substance of the question referred to the first, or to judge of its advice. An *ex parte* council in such case is manifestly disorderly, and without warrant.

V. Fellowship should be withdrawn from any church which is untrue to sound doctrine, — either by renouncing the faith or continuing to hear a teacher declared by council to be heretical; or which gives public scandal to the cause of Christ, or which wilfully persists in acts which break fellowship. When one church finds such acts in another, it should admonish, and, if that fail, invite a council to examine the alleged offense.

VI. Conferences of churches are allowable and profitable; but they hear no appeals, give no advice, and decide no question of church or ministerial standing.

IV. — OF THE MINISTRY.

I. The ministry includes all men called of God to that work, and orderly set apart by ordination.

II. When ordination of a pastor is to be performed, the church in which he is to bear office invites a council to examine as to faith, grace, and ability, that, if he be approved, they may extend the hand of fellowship. If the ordination be in view of any other sphere of labor, the request for a council ought to come from the church of which he is a member.

III. A pastor dismissed does not cease to be a minister; but he can not exercise any official act over a church until orderly replaced in office, except when particularly invited by a church.

IV. In case a pastor offend in such a way that he should no longer be recognized as a minister, the church should request a council to examine the charges, and, if it find cause, to withdraw all fellowship from him, so that his ministerial standing shall cease to be recognized. If a minister who is not a pastor be the offender, the church to which he belongs, or the church nearest his residence, should take the same course.

V. Associations of ministers are useful for mutual sympathy and improvement. They can exercise no sort of authority over churches or persons, save to prescribe the rights and duties of their own membership. But common consent has recognized that their examination of candidates for introduction to the churches is a wise safeguard.

On motion, the report was accepted.

Rev. Mr. Langworthy, of Massachusetts, from the committee on Nominations, reported the following committees: —

Committee on the State of the Country. — Rev. Truman M. Post, D. D., Missouri; Hon. Seth May, Maine; Hon. James D. Bell, Vermont; Hon. Milan Harris, New Hampshire; Hon. A. C. Barstow, Rhode Island; Hon. Dudley R. Wheeler, Connecticut; Judge Henry Morris, Massachusetts; Rev. Oliver E. Daggett, D. D., New York; Rev. John M. Holmes, New Jersey; Rev. Edward Hawes, Pennsylvania; Dea. Abner H. Bryant, Delaware; Rev. Edwin Johnson, Maryland; Rev. James A. Thome, Ohio; Rev. John C. Webster, Illinois; Dea. Allen

Fish, Michigan; Hon. Edward D. Holton, Wisconsin; Rev. Alden B. Robbins, Iowa; Rev. Charles Seccombe, Minnesota; Hon. Samuel C. Pomeroy, Kansas; Rev. Elisha M. Lewis, Nebraska Territory; Luther P. Fisher, Esq., California; Rev. Geo. H. Atkinson, Oregon; Rev. Wm. Crawford, Colorado.

Committee on Declaration of Faith. — Rev. John O. Fiske, Maine; Prof. Daniel J. Noyes, D. D., New Hampshire; Rev. Nahum Gale, D. D., Massachusetts; Rev. Joseph Eldridge, D. D., Connecticut; Rev. Leonard Swain, D. D., Rhode Island; Dr. Albert G. Bristol, New York; Rev. John C. Hart, Ohio; Dea. Sherman S. Barnard, Michigan; Rev. George S. F. Savage, Illinois.

Committee on Communication from Massachusetts Convention of Congregational Ministers. — Rev. Alonzo H. Quint, Massachusetts; Rev. William T. Eustis, Connecticut; Asa Freeman, Esq., New Hampshire.

Committee on Platform of Church Polity. — Rev. John P. Gulliver, Connecticut; Prof. Samuel Harris, Maine; Rev. Nelson Bishop, Vermont; Rev. Edwards A. Park, D. D., Massachusetts; Rev. Josiah G. Davis, New Hampshire; Rev. Joshua Leavitt, D. D., New York; Prof. Samuel C. Bartlett, Illinois; Rev. Jesse Guernsey, Iowa; Rev. Charles C. Salter, Minnesota; Judge Lester Taylor, Ohio; Rev. James S. Hoyt, Michigan; Rev. James D. Liggett, Kansas.

Committee on Response to Foreign Delegations. — Rev. Leonard Bacon, D. D., Connecticut; Rev. Henry Ward Beecher, New York; Rev. Julian M. Sturtevant, D. D., Illinois; Rev. Rufus Anderson, D. D., Massachusetts; Hon. James B. Walker, Michigan.

These several reports were accepted and adopted.

Rev. Dr. Kirk, of Massachusetts, in behalf of the churches of Boston, though without any official authorization, invited the members of the Council, so far as convenient to them, to be present in the church meetings, held in the city this evening. He also stated that a book written by the Rev. Horatius Bonar, D. D., called, "Words to the Winners of Souls," had been reprinted by the American Tract Society, and that a copy would be presented to every member of the Council, through the liberality of distinguished friends of the church and the ministry who had made a special donation for that purpose.

EVANGELIZATION IN THE WEST AND SOUTH.

The moderator called on the committee upon "Evangelization in the West and South" for their report; and it was read by Warren Currier, Esq., of Missouri (the rule fixing the hour of adjournment at 5 o'clock being suspended, on motion of Hon. C. G. Hammond, in order that the reading might be completed this afternoon), as follows: —

The subject on which this committee is required to report presents itself to their minds under two distinct aspects, each of which will properly and almost necessarily, in a greater or less degree, engage the attention of the National Council.

Foremost meets us the great fact, which has been a sublime characteristic of our whole history as a people, that our population is always spreading itself over vast regions hitherto unoccupied by civilized man, and requiring the unceasing activity of all Christian people to accompany the emigrant to the wilderness, with Christian instruction, and make the institutions and influences of the religion of Christ coëxtensive with our physical civilization.

To this fact, at the moment when we are called together to consider the greatest crisis in our nation's history, is added another of a still more solemn and momentous import: that, over one half of our hitherto peopled territory, Christian institutions, though once existing in a greater or less degree of purity and efficiency, have been corrupted by slavery, and well-nigh obliterated by the ravages of war connected with the slaveholders' rebellion.

Regions of country larger than a great European empire are thus left in moral desolation, imposing on the Christian people of our nation the imperative and most urgent duty of building again, in these waste places, the institutions of a Christian civilization.

In this view of the home missionary work now devolved upon us, there is nothing denominational. It appeals to the whole American church, and to every American Christian, simply as such.

But there is another aspect of the subject, which is not without its importance, and which we believe the National Council can not altogether disregard.

We are as sure that God chose and called the early fathers of New England to be the founders of this nation, as we are that he chose Abraham to be the founder of his ancient people. They were men whom he had trained and qualified for the work to which they were appointed. And it ought not to be assumed, without proof, that the peculiar conception of the church which they brought with them to the shores of New England, and which was the seed from which have sprung all the churches represented in this Council, had no value in the estimation of the Divine Architect of our national edifice. This Council is bound by the most solemn obligations rightly to estimate the value of that unique conception, and to recommend to the churches such a system of home evangelization as shall fully recognize its importance as a universal and permanent element of American society.

During a considerable portion of our history, our home missionary arrangements have been such as apparently to concede that the Congregational idea of the church was of no especial value, — well enough in New England, where it was already established, but, west of the Hudson, for the most part inapplicable and impracticable. If that view was sound and just, then all effort to plant distinctively Congregational churches in the new regions of our country is worse than useless. If Congregationalism has no mission except to add one to the number of religious sects, which divide and distract the household of faith, then far better confine itself within the limits of New England, and consign at once all its emigrant population to the care of those centralized church governments which always stand ready to receive and assimilate them. But if the Congregational conception of the church is true and precious, — if it is as well fitted to all latitudes and longitudes as to New England, and is really an important element of American civilization, and of the brighter and better ages of the promised future, — then these Congregational churches are bound to be true to their fundamental principles. In this system of home evangelization, they are bound to put forth their strength, not only to accompany our emigrant population with the gospel of Christ, but to plant the church, after the conception of the Pilgrim Fathers, wherever they make their home on the borders of the wilderness.

We trust the Council will have in view both these aspects of the case, in all the advice it may give to the churches.

In order to present a survey of our home missionary work with as much clearness as possible, we shall divide it into four parts.

First. Those portions of the West and North-west in which numerous churches have been already planted by our missionary efforts, many of which are still dependent, in part, on missionary funds for their support.

Second. Certain districts of the same States, in which our missionary efforts have hitherto been attended with little success, and in which few churches are now receiving our aid.

Third. The new States and Territories of the West and North-west toward which the tide of emigration is now setting, and is likely to flow in the immediate future.

Fourth. The States of the South and South-west which have been the principal theater of the great rebellion.

Of the *first* of these divisions, the committee have little to say: not because the work of evangelization in that section of our field is complete, nor because what remains to be done is not vastly important, but only because the condition of other sections of the field is so critical, and their claims so urgent. In respect to these more favored parts of our home missionary field, it should not be forgotten, that there yet "remaineth much land to be possessed." The prominent centers of influence are, for the most part, occupied. The towns and villages along the thoroughfares of travel and traffic are generally supplied with gospel ministrations. But, in the wide intervals between the railroads, and remote from the villages, a great majority of the population is beyond the influence of the churches we have planted, and is very inadequately supplied with religious privileges. Unless this rural population is brought more directly under gospel influences, and their children and youth are furnished with better opportunities for Christian education, we have great reason to fear the results which must follow. These wide fields, neglected, will become moral wastes, whose population will have no sympathy with the sentiments and institutions which have been the glory of our land.

To meet the wants of this part of our field, Sabbath-schools, prayer-meetings, family visitation, and colportage ought to be sustained by the voluntary efforts of the self-denying men and women of adjacent churches. But, in addition to this instrumentality, we need a class of missionaries who go forth, not to seek eligible settlement in a community that is prepared to welcome and support them, but who, in the spirit of Paul, are willing to build where no man has yet laid a foundation.

There is scarce a county, even in the most favored portion of the North-west, that does not contain waste places which would repay the best religious culture we could bestow upon them.

The *second* division embraces large portions of Southern Illinois and Indiana, and probably, also, important districts in other States, with which the committee are less accquainted.

In these districts, so far as the knowledge of the committee extends, our home missionary efforts in the past have been crowned with little success, and at present, and for several years just past, we are scarcely attempting any thing. They are passed by as fields for which, at present, little or nothing can be done. But they are not passed by because there is no need of doing any thing for them.

It *may* be said that *other* denominations have the ground, and therefore for us, as Congregationalists, there is no room.

If other denominations do have the ground, they occupy it most inefficiently and unsatisfactorily. The people are not taught. The Sabbath is not made a day of religious rest and instruction. Ignorance, both of things secular and divine, widely prevails. In all these respects, a state of things exists which can not extensively prevail in our country, without disqualifying us to continue long a free people. The truth of the case is, that the districts in question are not in such a sense preöccupied by other denominations as to relieve us from the obligation of further effort, until, by a fair experiment, it is proved that there is nothing more which we can do.

If our home missionary effort must be limited to the organization of churches from materials found ready to our hands, and to the aiding of churches so formed till they become self-sustaining, then it is difficult to see what more can be done for these districts than we are now doing. But why must our efforts be circumscribed to such limits? Why should we wait till some church or community is ready to invite a missionary to labor with them, and to assume a part of the responsibility of his support? Why should we rather not send forth into such districts devoted men, with their support fully guaranteed, to labor where they can find a field, and to preach Christ where they can find hearers, — leaving it to their judgment to bestow their labors where the best results are to be expected, and to organize churches where there is promise of permanence and usefulness? That in this way sinners can be converted to Christ, and churches founded and multiplied, which will prove blessings to generations yet unborn, no believer in the adaptation and power of the gospel is at liberty to doubt.

In this section of which we are speaking, there are certain points of great and growing importance, where the population is already large and is rapidly increasing; but religious people are few, and religious privileges scarce and meager. At such points, the committee believe, missionaries should at once be stationed and sustained, till they can gather around them congregations able to support them. Houses of worship should also be provided in such fields, either wholly by the Congregational Union, or partly by them and partly by such contributions as liberal men on the spot are willing to make.

Enterprises thus commenced should be adequately sustained till they can stand alone. It would perhaps be invidious and unwise to name particular places which should be thus occupied. But the committee are of the opinion, that places may be found in these districts where enterprises of this sort have already been delayed years too long. Until such efforts have been made and have failed, it is the judgment of the committee, that the conclusion is premature that nothing can be done for these districts. Till such attempts are made, the few brethren now scattered over these regions, and struggling almost alone against prejudice and abounding wickedness, will not cease to feel and to lament their lack of the earnest and efficient co-operation of the churches in more favored sections of the country.

Our *third* division of the field consists of those new States and Territories toward which the tide of emigration is now setting in great force.

It will be no easy matter for the members of the National Council to bring their minds up to a conception of the vastness and urgent importance of this field of Christian effort.

North of the south line of Kansas, extended to the Pacific, and west of the Mississippi, excluding Missouri, there is an area of territory belonging to the United States of one million three hundred thousand square miles. Embraced in this area are the States of Iowa, Minnesota, Kansas, Oregon, Nevada, and a part of California, and the Territories of Nebraska, Dacotah, Colorado, Utah, Washington, Idaho, and Montana. Within these limits are four tenths of the entire territory of the United States, equal to twenty times the area of New England, twenty-six times that of the State of New York, and one hundred and sixty times that of Massachusetts.

In 1860, the above States and Territories had a population of one million three hundred and eighty-five thousand one hundred and fifty-three, which now undoubtedly exceeds two millions. Until 1859, the population was confined mostly to the States on the Mississippi and the Pacific, and those parts of Kansas and Nebraska contiguous to the Missouri River. The whole mountain region, aside from the Mormon settlements in Utah, was uninhabited, and, to a great extent, unexplored. Since that time, many thousands have made houses, either temporary or permanent, in the mountains, and four new Territories have been organized, since 1861, along the mountain ranges. The great Platte Valley, stretching eastwardly from the mountains to the Missouri River, a distance of five or six hundred miles, has become an immense thoroughfare of travel and transportation to the mountain Territories and Pacific States. This results, in a great measure, from the discovery of the precious metals in various localities, over a large extent of country. This first caused the settlement of California, and is now, with equal rapidity, peopling the fastnesses of the Rocky Mountains. Wherever gold has been found, cities and villages are springing up with marvelous rapidity. There is no longer any doubt as to the richness and inexhaustibleness of the gold deposits in these regions. And as gold has always proved a mighty motive power, we may infer, with certainty, that with increasing facilities for reaching the mining localities, with improved machinery for obtaining the precious metals, and with the aid of the surplus capital of the Eastern States, the tide of emigration will increase in volume from year to year. The vast agricultural regions of Kansas, Nebraska, and Iowa will find a remunerative market for their productions in this mining region. Thus the one will help the other, and both will develop together.

Such are the elements of growth and progress which this wide region contains within itself; and we can not doubt it will soon be occupied with a multitudinous population. The foundations of those future States are now being laid; and their character and influence will, to a great extent, be determined by these early beginnings.

Another very material fact in its bearings on the growth of these new States and Territories is the construction of the great Union Pacific Railroad. Chartered by Congress, and liberally endowed by the general government, this road is to connect the Missouri River with the Pacific Ocean, and carry the facilities for travel and commerce through all the vast interior. This work is actually in process of construction at both ends of the line. And such is the influence of railroads in developing the resources of a country, in stimulating enterprises, increasing the value of property, and contributing to the growth of towns and cities, that we doubt not the completion of this road to the mining region will, in a brief period, quadruple its population, while, at the same time, it will add greatly to the population and wealth of the Missouri and Mississippi Valleys.

Emigration to the mountains tends strongly to concentrate in cities, thus affording greater facilities for preaching the gospel, and rendering delay in sending it more perilous. This population is enterprising and energetic, and ready to aid liberally in the support of the gospel, and in building houses of worship. And yet they are exposed to many and peculiar temptations, and, without the influence of the gospel, they are exceedingly exposed to the worst vices which corrupt society.

Among the inhabitants of these new States and Territories are not a few members of Congregational churches, and many sons and daughters of New England, who love her simple church polity, and believe it better fitted to develop and elevate man than any other. From the "Congregational Quarterly" of January, 1865, we learn that these numerous States and Territories, with their two millions of people, had, one year ago, two hundred and seventy Congregational churches, with an aggregate membership of a little more than ten thousand. They had, also, one hundred and eighty-two ministers, either supplying these churches, or laboring in new settlements, where churches were not yet organized. In the four mountain Territories and the State of Nevada we have, by report, but three churches, and an equal number of ministers. Yet the population to-day probably exceeds two hundred thousand, with the certain prospect of a very large increase.

It seems to the committee that this portion of our home missionary field ought to be most seriously considered by all the churches represented in this Council. Here is a call for new zeal and increased efficiency in the prosecution of the home missionary work, in order to carry it forward upon a scale commensurate with the vastness of the field to be cultivated.

The other portion of the home missionary field, which demands our attention, embraces the States that have just been redeemed from slavery, and are thus opened to a pure gospel, and to churches founded on the principles of Congregational freedom.

In the survey of this field, the first feature which arrests our attention is the peculiar condition of the four millions of people now emerging from slavery into manhood and the light and liberty of the sons of God. Deprived hitherto of all opportunities for education, they now hunger and thirst after learning. Never before did any people manifest such eagerness to acquire the rudiments of education, and the knowledge of God's word. In Virginia, North and South Carolina, and along the banks of the Mississippi, they began, early in the war, to come within our lines, and were immediately provided with schools and teachers by the American Missionary Association. In the progress of the war, this work has continually grown in magnitude and importance, until, by the overthrow of the rebellion, the whole colored population of the South are soon to be brought within the reach of Christian teachers and missionaries. Never was a missionary field more inviting. The soil is rich and mellow, and all prepared for the "good seed of the kingdom." Blessed are they that shall so cultivate this field as to reap the rich harvest of which it is capable.

How far the way is open for home missionary labors among the white people of the South, the committee is unable to speak with much definiteness, for the want of accurate information. But we rejoice to know that hostile armies no longer overrun those States. The rebellion is crushed, and the way is prepared for a thorough and accurate survey of the moral desolation which slavery and war have left in their track. Let such survey speedily be made, and the result laid before the churches. In the mean time, the following facts, reported from certain portions of the field, which have been longer under Federal control, and therefore better known, may be taken as specimens of the whole.

Missouri, in its general condition and history, may be taken as representing, in the main, the region of country under consideration, and is, in position, territory, and population, no inconsiderable part of it. In 1860, it had the largest white population of any of the slave States, and is, in territory, larger than the whole of New England, and much richer in natural resources. But, from its earliest settlement, slavery has been there, paralyzing its energies, depressing its industry, corrupting its politics, perverting its theology, and poisoning the whole surrounding atmosphere. From this blighting curse, the State is now delivered, by a war undertaken in the interest of slavery, and having for its object its perpetuation and lasting domination over a continent.

While emancipation in Missouri is a consequence of the war, it is a consequence wrought out through conviction, — a radical change in the opinions and feelings of the people. It is not the result of military coercion operating upon the elections. It rests on the deliberate choice of the people, ascertained through the ballot-box, and that, too, by a most decisive and significant majority. "An ocean of changed thought and feeling" has rolled over the State in these last four years. And what has happened in Missouri in this respect, we believe will be found, to a considerable extent, to be true in the other slave States.

Missouri came into the Union in a convulsive struggle that shook the nation. New England protested; but her protest was unavailing, and for the time slavery triumphed. This was forty-five years ago. On the 11th day of January last, she was born again, amid the rejoicings and congratulations of millions of freemen, from the Atlantic to the Pacific.

In January, 1852, there was not a Congregational church in this State. Nine years later, at the outbreak of the slaveholders' rebellion, there were two, and the only two in the slave States, — one at St. Louis, and one at Hannibal, both situated on the eastern boundary line of the State, and together containing scarcely more than three hundred members. At this date ten are reported, and the door is wide open for the planting of as many more as Christian zeal and enterprise may elect. Old temples and altars have been thrown down. The priests of slavery, with their followers, are scattered and gone, or are fast going. The society of Missouri is no longer suited to their tastes. They prefer a hiding-place anywhere else to the scene of their former pride, where all is now so changed, and where the friends of the Union and the enemies of slavery are in the popular ascendant.

What has been said indicates, in general, the state of things in Missouri. To a great extent, except in a few counties, it is, in respect to religious organizations, a mighty waste. We give an example or two, by way of illustration: Jefferson City, the capital of the State, is situated on the south bank of the Missouri River, one hundred and twenty-five miles west of St. Louis, with which it is connected by railway. It has a population of about four thousand. In 1861, it had four churches, representing as many different denominations, viz., Presbyterian (O. S.), Baptist, Episcopal, and Methodist (South). All these churches are now, or were as late as March last, closed. No services have been held in the Presbyterian church for four years, and only occasionally, if at all, in the three others, during the same period. A Methodist church (North) has, in the mean time, been organized, and a small house of worship erected, of dimensions to accommodate, perhaps, a hundred and fifty persons. This is the only Protestant house of worship now in use in the capital of the State of Missouri, although it has been constantly within the Federal lines, and in daily connection with St. Louis.

If such a state of things exist in the protected capital, it is not to be imagined that religious institutions are in a more satisfactory condition where bushwhackers and guerillas have roamed at large.

In a growing town of some two thousand inhabitants, on the Pacific Railroad, west of Jefferson City, no church organization or house of worship exists. An agent of the American Missionary Association visited it last summer, and was much encouraged by the friendly temper of the people, and their readiness to hear. His chief difficulty, during his short stay, was to find a room large enough to accommodate those who wished to attend upon his services.

It is believed that these are only specimens, tending to give a true idea of the condition of a large part of the State. And, as far as the committee can judge from the information in their possession, they believe a very similar state of things exists in all the States, which, at the outbreak of the rebellion, were under the controlling influence of slavery. Religious organizations existing previous to the rebellion are overturned. The church, in its various denominations, was as thoroughly pervaded and corrupted by slavery as the State, and as completely involved in the rebellion, and consequently has been equally dissolved and destroyed by the overthrow of slavery and the rebellion. And, if the work of political reconstruction is to tax the mind and heart of the nation to the utmost, the reconstruction of religious society in the South is a work no less difficult and momentous. If the restoration of government in the South on the basis of universal freedom is the trial question of our political institutions, the restoration of religious society on the basis of the gospel of Christ is no less the trial question of our Protestant Christianity.

No graver question at present demands the attention of the churches which we represent, than the inquiry, "What part in this mighty work belongs to those men and those churches which adhere to that conception of the church which found its way to this continent in the cabin of the May-flower?" The committee certainly is not prepared fully to answer this question. But to say, that, in all this, Congregationalism is to have no share, seems to us like saying that the principles of that polity are not worthy of what our Pilgrim Fathers suffered for them, nor of the tenacity with which we hold them. If we have a conception of the church which must be laid aside before we can enter upon the greatest Christian enterprise of the nineteenth century, the sooner we discard it everywhere the better, that we may take up some other polity, which is capable of universal application.

In reconstructing religious society at the South, it seems to the committee as most obviously important, to adopt a policy analogous to that pursued in military affairs. There are many cities and large towns which are as truly strategic points in our moral as in our carnal warfare. No time should be lost in taking possession of them in the name of our Great Captain, and in erecting in them fortresses of evangelical truth, furnished with all the munitions of spiritual warfare. Persons who, in connection with the army, have had opportunity to study the South, testify on this point with great unanimity and earnestness.

Commencing at Cairo, Illinois, every considerable town on the Mississippi and its tributaries, quite down to the Gulf, should receive early and earnest attention.

At Memphis, an organization has already been effected, under favorable auspices, and a self-sustaining church established.

In New Orleans, a handful of men, noble and true, are already soliciting our co-operation. Congregational polity was once at home in Charleston, and in Savannah, and other parts of Georgia. Is it not our duty to make haste to rebuild what slavery has corrupted and destroyed?

In Wilmington, Norfolk, Richmond, Baltimore, and Washington, and doubtless in many less prominent cities of the Atlantic States of the South, we may soon expect openings for the introduction of a pure gospel, and the establishment of permanent religious institutions, by our instrumentalities, for home evangelization. In the prosecution of this great work, why should we not imitate the example of the apostolic age? The apostles of Christ were appointed to plant the Christian church, not for the Roman Empire, but for the world; not for one age, but for all time. They began, indeed, at Jerusalem; but, as soon as they began to go abroad from that center, they hastened to the centers of that influence which controlled the world, — the cities that lay around the Mediterranean Sea. In them they preached the gospel, and planted churches; and from Ephesus and Philippi and Thessalonica and Corinth and Rome, the gospel spread into the surrounding populations.

The Valley of the Mississippi is the Mediterranean region of this continent; and in the great centers of influence in this valley our work must begin. These strategic points must be speedily garrisoned for Christ; and it must be done by hands that are clear of all participation in the great rebellion.

To no portion of the Christian people of the United States does the call to engage in this great religious enterprise come more imperatively than to the churches represented in this Council. In this connection, the committee deem it proper to call attention to the following passage, from "Bancroft's History of the United States," volume i., pp. 467–8. "I have dwelt the longer on the character of the early Puritans of New England," says the historian, "for they are the parents of one third of the white population of the United States. In the first ten or twelve years, — and there was never afterward any considerable increase from England, — we have seen that there came over twenty-one thousand two hundred persons, or four thousand families. Their descendants are now (1834) not far from four millions. Each family has multiplied, on the average, to one thousand souls. To New York and Ohio, where they constitute one half of the population, they have carried the Puritan system of free schools; and their example is spreading it through the civilized world."

If this calculation be brought down to the present time, it will be found that the descendants of the early Puritans of New England now number about ten millions, and that they have not only carried the Puritan system of free schools to New York and Ohio, but that they have carried these, and all the ideas and institutions of a society founded on the doctrine of the equal rights of man, beyond the Great Lakes, beyond the Mississippi and the Missouri, to the banks of the Columbia, and the shores of the Pacific. It is patent to every observant eye, that that great current of opinion which made the lamented Lincoln President of the United States, and overturned the iniquitous system of slavery, and with it the whole structure of Southern society, followed every where along the ramifications of this stream of New England emigration. It is no wonder that the rebels and their Northern allies proposed to leave New England out in the cold. New England ideas were found utterly incompatible with the continued existence of slavery.

What, then, so fit as that, in reconstructing society at the South on the basis of freedom and Christianity, large room should be given to the spirit, the principles, and the modes of organization, of these Puritan Fathers. It is not the business of the committee to urge this matter. But we religiously believe and honestly affirm, that, if our Puritan Fathers had brought to New England a centralized church government, they never could have exerted their mighty and benignant influence on the destinies of their country and the world. And we can assign no reason why their ideas are not just as precious and just as potent in restoring society at the South as they were in constructing it in New England. Bible principles never grow old, and their value and their adaptation undergo no change.

The committee cannot refrain from expressing their full conviction, that, in this work of religious reconstruction, an indispensable condition of success is our hearty recognition of our equal brotherhood with the colored man, and our earnest endeavor to raise him to the full enjoyment of all the privileges of the gospel. God has overturned society in the South for the crime of trampling on the rights of the negro, and let no one think to restore it without fully recognizing his equal rights with the white man to citizenship, both under our government and in the kingdom of God.

He who is no respecter of persons will surely frown on all such attempts, however cunningly conceived and zealously prosecuted.

Such then is the vast work to which the providences of God call the churches and people represented in this council. And what shall we say of the machinery needed to accomplish it? On this point we have but little to suggest. We see no necessity for any new organization. The American Home Missionary Society and the American Missionary Association, those noble institutions through which we have been accustomed to act in the work of home evangelization, seem, in the good providence of God, to be raised up especially for this very time. They have a prestige, an experience, and an adaptation, that commend them to universal confidence.

The American Home Missionary Society, formerly the organ of another denomination as well as of our own, has, without its own seeking or ours, been released from any obligation which would have restrained its action in promoting the church polity of our Puritan Fathers. In the progress of events, the way seems now prepared for the universal acceptance of the anti-slavery principles which the American Missionary Association has always maintained. Both societies have therefore an open field, and both enjoy largely the confidence and sympathy of the churches.

Nor do we find any difficulty in recognizing the respective spheres of these two societies. For while no separation is or can be made by a geographical line, and still less by any invidious distinction of color, we yet discover, in the past labors of the American Missionary Association, among the colored people of America, the West India Islands, and Africa, and in the ready facility with which it has adapted itself to the peculiar condition of this people at the South, an instrumentality providentially prepared for their evangelization. We therefore commend to the churches this association for the work at the South, with special reference to the freedmen.

The American Home Missionary Society, on the contrary, is limited by its constitution to one specific work of aiding destitute communities and feeble churches to sustain the preaching of the gospel. For this distinctive work, it will find comparatively little preparation among the freedmen; but its glorious history, endearing it to the affections of all the churches, points it out still as the chosen instrumentality for its specific home missionary work in all parts of our country, in the South, as far as the door may be opened, as well as in the North and Great West.

With these limitations of special adaptation and constitutional provision, each organization has a distinct work; and the field is so large, and the relation of the two societies so friendly, that each can expend its utmost energies without rivalry and collision.

In this connection, we recognize the important mission of the Congregational Union, but forbear discussion of it here, since its claims are to be submitted outside of this report.

It is not, then, new machinery which we want, but to give greatly increased efficiency to the machinery which we have, by supplying a vastly greater moving power. The great question before this body is, how can this be done? It is perfectly obvious that our missionary societies cannot carry out the policy recommended in this report, without a large increase of their resources. They will need a yearly income of not less than half a million of dollars. Our resources for church building, and all the other auxiliary instrumentalities, will need also to be proportionably increased.

How can such an increase be obtained? That is the question of this occasion. One thing the committee will suggest in answer to this inquiry. We must determine, in good solemn earnest, to do the work whereunto God has called us. No man who has borne a part in the work of evangelization in any of our new States and Territories within the last ten or fifteen years can have failed to see, and with sickness of heart to feel, that the American churches, after all, are not half in earnest in this work. In times of prevailing worldly prosperity, men of the noblest endowments of mind and heart, who have given themselves to this sacred cause in the true spirit of self-sacrifice, have found themselves left, like soldiers in the field, without arms, without ammunition, and without rations. If this state of things is to continue, the hope of accomplishing the glorious work which now invites our efforts will prove utterly fallacious and delusive. The spirit of Christian self-sacrifice must not be confined to a few missionaries, teachers, and colporters, while the thousands of our Israel dwell in their ceiled houses, and suffer the house of God to lie waste. If we enter on this enterprise with some such all-pervading earnestness as that with which we undertook the work of subduing the great rebellion, there will be no difficulty in obtaining the needful resources. It will be as it has been in the war. When men are needed, they can be had; and, when money is wanted, it will be poured out like water.

In closing this report, the committee present the following summary of the results to which they have come.

1. In addition to the work to which our Home Missionary Societies have, for the most part, confined their labors, — that of planting and fostering churches where materials are found ready to their hand for forming them, — there is an imperative necessity that able and devoted men should be sent to labor for Christ where no churches exist and no materials are ready for their formation. At whatever cost of men and money, the great centers of influence should at once be occupied by men divinely endowed for such a work; and their support should be drawn from missionary funds, till their congregations are able to sustain them.

2. That the time for efficient action is emphatically the present. In the West and North-West, our emigration is spreading itself over a field vaster than ever before; and immediate and most efficient action is necessary to overtake and keep pace with this ever-swelling tide of population, in founding the institutions of Christianity, learning, and freedom. In all the late domain of slavery, society is dissolved, ecclesiastical organizations are broken up or paralyzed. By their sanction of human chattelism, and their complicity with the rebellion, the churches have become utterly demoralized, and are like salt that has lost its savor. Church edifices and school-houses are abandoned, and in wide districts the institutions of education and religion have no practical existence. In all these regions, now or never is the time to arise, and build the temple of the

Lord. If we neglect to occupy this inviting field of labor to which God now calls us, he may, we trust he will, raise up others who will cultivate and possess it for him. But, for us, it will be an opportunity for ever lost, a harvest season never to return.

3. We can not perform our part in this work without a vast increase in earnestness, zeal, and self-denial in our churches. Without this, it will be impossible to command either the men or the money for the work. The resources and the strong young men of any community will always be where its heart is. If the heart of the church is in the world, her sons and her wealth will be there also; and she will be as powerless in promoting the cause of Christ, at home or abroad, as Samson was to meet the Philistines when his locks were shorn.

Three questions the committee must leave unanswered, pressing, we trust, on the hearts of the National Council.

1. How can the requisite spirit of earnestness and self-consecration be imparted to the churches?

2. How can our young men be induced, by thousands, to consecrate their lives to this holy cause?

3. How can we raise the requisite pecuniary resources for a religious enterprise so vast, and so imperatively demanding immediate action?

The American church is in much the same relation to this great crisis that our government was to the rebellion at its outbreak. From whence will the Lord send deliverance?

WARREN CURRIER,
JULIAN M. STURTEVANT,
REUBEN GAYLORD,
THOMAS E. BLISS,
FLAVEL BASCOM,
} *Committee.*

At twenty minutes before five o'clock, the reading of the report was suspended, to afford Rev. Mr. Walker an opportunity to speak on the subject of the churches in Italy, in accordance with the recommendation of the Business Committee; but that gentleman not being present (through a misunderstanding as to the assignment), the reading of the report was resumed, and at its conclusion, it was accepted.

The Doxology, "Praise God from whom all blessings flow," was then sung, and the Council adjourned.

FOURTH DAY, SATURDAY, JUNE 17.

The Council was called to order at 9 o'clock, by the moderator. Prayer was offered by Hon. Mr. Hammond, of Illinois.

The minutes of yesterday were read, amended in some few particulars, and then approved.

On motion of Rev. Mr. Bascom, of Illinois, Rev. Wm. Crawford, of Colorado, was added to the committee on the State of the Country.

Rev. Mr. Quint, of Massachusetts, from the committee on Business, reported the order for to-day, as follows: —

That after the report of the committee on Credentials, and statements by the chairmen of other committees, and by the scribe, the business consist in reading the papers on "Ministerial Support," "Ministerial Education," "Church Building," "Parochial Evangelization," and the "Systematizing of Benevolent Contributions." That so many as can be read this morning be read, and the remainder be made the order for Monday.

The committee also recommended that the following resolutions, which had been placed in their hands, be passed: —

Resolved, That, for the correction and certification of the list of delegates to this Council, the roll shall be called by the scribe after reading the minutes on Monday morning, and members who do not answer to their names, or whose presence is not attested by delegates, shall be stricken from the list.

Resolved, That, in making up the roll of members of this Council, the committee on Credentials be requested and instructed to record the churches which they severally represent, and the residence of delegates, both ministers and laymen.

Resolved, That the committee on Credentials be directed, when recording the names of members, to insert the first name in full.

Rev. Mr. PERKINS, of Massachusetts, said, in reference to the first resolution, that he thought some other time than Monday morning, when a great many would be unable to be present, would be better for calling the roll. He suggested Tuesday morning.

Hon. Mr. HAMMOND, of Illinois, suggested Tuesday, at 12 o'clock, as the time.

The amendment was accepted by Mr. Perkins.

Rev. Mr. EUSTIS, of Connecticut, said it was desirable to have the list of delegates completed as soon as possible, with reference to the proposed trip to Plymouth. He therefore moved to amend by substituting Monday, at 12 o'clock, in the place of Tuesday.

Rev. Dr. BACON, of Connecticut, suggested that there was a surer way yet, which was by appointing a committee of one from each State and Territory, who should report a full roll of the delegates from that State or Territory. He thought there were delegates present from New Jersey and Connecticut, and from other States, who could tell the names of all the members from those States.

Rev. Mr. PERKINS said there was no one from Massachusetts who could tell the names of all the delegates.

Mr. AYRES, of Illinois, moved to amend by substituting 12 o'clock to-day as the time for calling the roll.

This amendment was carried by a vote of 175 to 90.

Rev. Mr. ALLEN, of Massachusetts, said that one of the reasons given for calling the roll, was, that the body might know what churches were represented. He supposed the Council were not to determine that matter. He took it that the credentials which came from the different bodies settled that.

Rev. E. P. MARVIN, of Massachusetts, said he believed it almost impossible to make out an accurate list of delegates from the credentials. The committee had found a large number of them in duplicate, and, in some cases, three copies of the same credentials. In looking over two letters of the alphabet, he found, at one time, twenty duplicates. Many of those names were yet on the roll, and the committee wanted very much to find who of the persons whose names were on the roll were here, and, unless they could resort to this method, they should be obliged to circulate printed slips all through the house, which would take up a great deal more of the time than to call the roll.

It was moved to amend the resolution by adding, that the names to which no response is made on the call of the roll to-day be called again on Monday, at 12 o'clock.

This motion prevailed, by a vote of 86 to 75 and the motion, as amended, passed.

The second resolution submitted by the Business Committee was then considered, to wit: —

Resolved, That in making up the roll of members of this Council, the committee on credentials be requested and instructed to record the churches which they represent, and the residence of delegates, both ministers and laymen.

Dr. PATTON, of Illinois. I wish, in behalf of the committee on credentials, to say, that that committee have never understood themselves to be the scribes of this body. All our business, as we suppose, is to see that persons who present proper credentials are allowed to come in as members of the body, and report their names; and then our duty is ended, it being the duty of the scribes to make up the roll. The credentials are in such a shape, that it would be impossible to tell what churches are represented. We have credentials from Pennsylvania, for instance, certifying that so-and-so, from the Congregational churches of Pennsylvania, are entitled to seats, having been elected by conferences in the proper towns. In that State, they had a central committee, to which the conferences reported, and that central committee made out the credentials for all.

Rev. Mr. QUINT, of Massachusetts. In regard to that matter, I differ from our friend. In the first place, it is very important that we should know, from our record, what churches are represented in this body. That is the essential point. If persons coming here are without any credentials certifying how many churches and what churches they represent, it is, to begin with, evidence that they are not entitled to seats; and, to show that they are entitled to seats, they must bring additional facts, because the call is very explicit. But allowing that to pass, it is perfectly practicable to get this list; and any committee with a sufficient degree of energy, though they will have some work to do, will find it so. In the next place, although it is not the work, *primâ facie*, of the committee on credentials, the person who drew the proposal up (for it did not originate with the business committee) thought that, inasmuch as they had had the papers, and understood the matter better than anybody else, it would be better to instruct them to do it. If that committee prefer not to do it, it is perfectly easy to appoint another committee to perform that work.

Rev. Dr. TODD, of Massachusetts. The point that is obscure in my mind is this. Does that resolution mean that I shall report myself as pastor of my church, and representing one fourth part of seventeen other churches, and that my fellow-delegates shall report that they represent each one fourth part of seventeen churches? or what does it mean? I do not understand it. I can tell you the church of which I am pastor, and I can tell you the churches which are represented by our delegations; but there are four in the delegation.

Rev. Mr. WHITTLESEY, of Illinois. As one of the scribes, I want to make one remark in reference to this matter. I have spent two days of hard labor in getting this roll arranged in alphabetical order, under the States; now, I think, from my experience, that it will take at least three or four days for any man, or any committee of this body, to do the work proposed in that resolution, and I do not think there is anybody here who has three or four days to spend on it. I move you, therefore, that that resolution be laid on the table.

This motion prevailed, and the resolution was laid on the table.

The third resolution submitted by the Business Committee was then taken up for consideration, to wit: —

Resolved, That the committee on Credentials be directed, when recording the names of members, to insert the first name in full.

Rev. Mr. WHITTLESEY, of Illinois. I have taken great pains to get the full names, so far as it is possible; but, sir, the Council will see that it is a very great labor to get the full names of more than six hundred members. Whenever they are on the list I have put them down, and I have put down a great many that are not on the list. I appreciate the remarks of Mr. Quint, who, you all know, is a prince in statistics; and I should be very glad to get the full names of the members, if I could; and if anybody whose name does not appear upon the roll in full will give it to me, I will insert it, but I will not engage to go round and find out the name of every man. I move that that resolution be laid on the table.

The motion prevailed, and the report of the Business Committee on the order for the day was then accepted.

Rev. Mr. QUINT, of Massachusetts. The committee to whom the duty was assigned of presenting a report on the work of evangelization in the West and South, and in Foreign Lands, having, through inadvertence, reported only on the home department, I desire to offer this resolution: —

Resolved, That a committee be appointed to report upon the work of evangelization in foreign lands, that properly devolves upon the Congregational churches of the United States.

On motion of Rev. Dr. Beecher, of Illinois, the motion was adopted.

Rev. Mr. Dexter, of Massachusetts, moved the appointment of a committee to arrange in regard to the supply of pulpits in this vicinity, so far as the pastors of churches desire to receive assistance from the members of the Council.

Rev. Dr. Thompson, of New York, moved that the matter be referred to the committee on Devotional Exercises.

Rev. Mr. Dexter accepted this suggestion, and the motion, in that form, passed.

Rev. Dr. PATTON, of Illinois. The committee on Credentials desire to present a question for the consideration of the Council, to wit: What shall be done when a primary has taken his place in this body, been enrolled, and taken part in the proceedings, but leaves before the close of the session, and then the substitute appears, and wishes to occupy the seat for the remainder of the time? Many such cases exist, and are to exist, according to arrangements that are being made, and the committee on credentials recommend the adoption of the following resolution: —

Resolved, That when a delegate has appeared, and taken his seat in the body, but leaves before the close of the session, his alternate may occupy his place.

Thus much I report as chairman of the committee. In my individual capacity, I propose to offer an amendment, — to add, "provided, that the traveling expenses of but one shall be paid from the appropriate fund."

Rev. Mr. TAYLOR, of Illinois. Is it designed, that the names of both primary and substitute shall appear upon the list?

Rev. Dr. PATTON. That question has not been considered. I am aware, sir, that it is an awkward arrangement at best; but we were disposed to favor those who had come here from a distance, as much as we consistently could.

Rev. Prof. BARTLETT, of Illinois. It seems to me that the adoption of this resolution would involve us in inextricable confusion, — make us a constantly fluctuating body. When men come here to do business, they are bound to do it, and do it through, and not commit it to other parties. I move the resolution be laid on the table.

The motion prevailed, and the resolution was laid on the table.

Rev. Dr. BEECHER, of Illinois. I wish to move the appointment of a committee to accomplish the object suggested by the chairman of the business committee,—that is, to obtain the names, in full, of the churches represented. I have approved of what has been done, in laying the motions, in their existing form, upon the table, because I did not suppose it was the duty, either of the committee on credentials, or of the scribes, to accomplish this purpose; and yet the value of the record of the doings of this body, as an historical document for future ages, will be very greatly affected by the consideration, whether we have the names of the churches represented, and the names of the members, in full, or not. It will be of less value, and of less interest all over the Union, if the names are not given in full, and also the churches represented; and yet, as the credentials were handed in, it was impossible for the committee on credentials to do it; it is impossible, with these credentials, for the clerks to do it. If it is done at all, it must be done by a committee from each State and Territory. I move, therefore, that a committee be appointed, from each State and Territory represented, to report, in full, the names of the pastors and delegates of such States and Territories, present in this Council, and also the names of the associated churches which they respectively represent.

Rev. Mr. DAVIS, of New Hampshire. The names of churches are much more important than the names of members. We can have the names of the churches, with a little care; and if we do not, we have no record of the authority by which we act.

The question was then put, and the motion of Dr. Beecher carried.

Hon. Mr. Douglas, of Connecticut, offered the following resolution:—

Resolved, That the committee on Declaration of Faith, with the aid of the committee on platform, be instructed to report to this body, for its consideration and action, a catechism, compiling, in the most simple form, for the use of children, the faith and polity of the Congregational churches.

Rev. Mr. GULLIVER, of Connecticut. I object to the introduction of the resolution in this form. We have adopted rules which were drawn up for the express purpose of preventing the introduction of business in this way. I like the resolution, and like Mr. Douglas, as he knows, very much; but if we allow these things to be brought in here in this way, there will be no end to the confusion in which we shall be involved.

THE MODERATOR. It was read for information.

Rev. Mr. GULLIVER, of Connecticut. Yes, but if everything is read for information, it will lead to confusion. The rule is, that no business shall be brought up here until it has been before the business committee.

Hon. Mr. DOUGLAS, of Connecticut. I know of no other way to get it before the committee. This is the legitimate, parliamentary way, in my mind to get it to the committee. I move its reference to the committee.

THE MODERATOR. The motion is not in order. It can be presented to the chairman of the business committee, without being brought before this body, and it may be considered by the committee whether it shall be presented or not.

Rev. Mr. GULLIVER, of Connecticut. No, sir; the committee have no discretion in the matter. They are obliged to present the resolution. They simply arrange the order in which business shall be presented. We must entirely do away with the rule before this can be done.

Rev. Mr. BISHOP, of Vermont. If that is really the rule, that the business committee has no discretion, then I move that it be amended.

Assistant Moderator Hammond read the rule, as follows:—

"XV. It shall be the duty of the Business Committee to prepare a docket, upon which shall be entered all items of business which members of the Council may desire to bring before the body, and except by special vote of the Council, no business shall be introduced which has not in this manner passed through the hands of the committee."

Rev. Mr. BISHOP, of Vermont. I move that that rule be so amended, that the Business Committee present only what they deem proper.

A delegate inquired if that motion was in order, whether it ought not to go to the Business Committee? [Laughter.]

The chair ruled the motion out of order.

Rev. Dr. Stone of Massachusetts, from the committee on Hospitalities, announced that the contemplated excursion to Plymouth would take place on Thursday of next week.

Rev. Mr. Gulliver, of Connecticut, from the committee to whom was referred the report on church polity, stated that the committee had held two meetings, but had been unable to procure a copy of the report,—the one read to the Council having been taken by the scribe and pasted into the minutes.

After some discussion, the scribe was instructed, on motion of Rev. Dr. Patton, to deliver the report to the committee.

On motion of Dea. Stoddard, of Massachusetts, it was—

Voted, That the addresses on letters to the members be read here, but that they shall not be delivered here, but in the room below.

MINISTERIAL SUPPORT.

The report on "Ministerial Support," was then called for, and it was read by Rev. Prof. George Shepard, of Maine, chairman of the committee, as follows: —

The committee appointed to present to the Council the topic of Ministerial Support hereby report: —

We find the most concise and comprehensive axiom on this subject, — uttered by the Lord in connection with the sending forth of the seventy disciples, — "The laborer is worthy of his hire." The laborer here pronounced upon is the servant of Christ, the minister and messenger of his gospel, the bearer of spiritual blessings to the lost race of man.

We have here a class of men set apart to a service deemed of vital importance to the welfare of the world, — a class extending down the centuries, — their permanence affirming their indispensableness. They are appointed and commissioned of God, — consecrated to a single and peculiar service. That they may the most largely compass the benefits of this, they are set apart from the ordinary and gainful pursuits of life; all their capabilities held to and absorbed in a ministry of beneficence, not to get good, but confer good.

We find the *order* and the principle in the opening of the Mosaic dispensation. First, The *separation* and *consecration* of the sons of Levi: "Behold, I have taken your brethren, the Levites, from among the children of Israel; to you they are given as a gift from the Lord." Secondly, The *obligation* on the part of the people to them. "Wherefore forsake not the Levite as long as thou livest upon the earth." Under the old and the new dispensation, the principle of service and support is the same, a principle of support meant to conduce to the highest measure of service, and service the most effective in quality.

The *principle* of support to those who preach the gospel, the *obligation* to support those who consent to be separated to this service, we find put by the apostle Paul in a peculiarly terse and satisfactory way,— as is the manner of that apostle to put things, — in a sort of closing-up fashion, as though the brief word he used, held within itself the finality of all argument. He says, linking his conclusion with the arrangement divinely made ages before, "Even so hath the Lord ordained, that they which preach the gospel should live of the gospel." So far as *authority* can settle this principle, the arranging and commanding of the Supreme Lord settle the principle that preachers derive their living from the people whom they serve.

There are *good reasons*, statements which come to the people with the *authority* of reason, why what the Saviour so explicitly enjoins should be done, — namely, the laborer in this field have his hire; that the preacher of this gospel be furnished a living in it.

The first is, he is *a laborer;* what he does is labor. An apostle pronounces it a good work. Every undertaker of it, who with a soul of zeal aims at any tolerable fidelity in it, is satisfied of one thing, that it is *work;* work various, multiform, ever-crowding, never finished; reaching to the inmost sensibilities of life; drawing off its most ethereal quality, its finest capital. No man could bear the strain and intensity of this toil, only as he felt and was allowed to say, it is a *good* work.

2. It is a work which, to get ready to do, fit, qualified to do, takes years of laborious preparation, and expenditure in the preliminary, *exceeded* in no other human function, equaled by a very few. It is a work which can not be worthily done, unless done by a class prepared by the discipline of study and grace; to them committed; themselves consecrated to it, and made responsible for it; their *life's* work, and all the work of life they are allowed to do.

3. It is a work most vital in its bearing upon all human interests. Society could hardly subsist without it. It has an essentially modifying influence upon all branches of industry; makes even the fields more prolific, the houses more tasteful and comfortable. It elevates and makes purer the whole course of morals; holds in check the wasteful propensities; inclines toward harmony the conflicting passions; advances the character in all worthy attributes; greatly quickens and strengthens the intellect; lifts the heart to the divine and heavenly; nullifies or turns into positive benefit the most formidable powers of evil.

It is admitted, because *demonstrated*, that the work of the minister adds largely to a people's worldly prosperity, to their literal enrichment; brings a gain in character, in happiness, in possession, in items of benefit innumerable, beyond the count of gold.

This is admitted, confessed to, by Christian people, that the support of these workers is a just due, enjoined by the Lord, earned by hard, exhausting, and invaluable service; yet their hire is kept back in part; as a general thing they are not at all adequately paid; the average of pay is decidedly below a proper standard of compensation. This I may safely assume; no Christian mind will question it. There is no time to array facts in confirmation of this. They abound — are every where; they are humiliating — are positively disgraceful to our Christianity.

In some instances, this inadequate support arises from the *inability* of the people to do more. These discharge themselves from blame by doing what they can, — all that they can. In other instances, and these probably the more common, the inadequate compensation for service grows out *of a prevalent low estimate of the value of the service.* It is service in the department of religion, which, as many conceive, if not wholly without cost, is proximately so. And men of this way of judging justify themselves in crowding all estimates in the direction of a cipher. The very economical argument is, — the Master opened by giving himself. And then his salvation is put without price. And the men sent to dispense it are supposed to be above all self-seeking; bound to be mortified in all their desires; the whole living they aspire to is simply a partial deliverance from starvation. There is here furnished to the people a promising field for cheapening; and the minister's work is sometimes cheapened with a vengeance. If it were some other branch of service, — stood in some likely or prolific connection with increase, — had to do with hoarding money, rather than garnering souls, — the standard of compensation and expenditure would be set higher at once; a larger price proffered and paid, because greater *value* is assigned to the service.

All the causes of depressed pay we can not run over or even hint. *This low appreciation of the things of God* may be clearly set down as prominent among them. That there is ever downright *fraud* — the hire of *these laborers* kept back of fraud — we like not to think; we recoil from making so grave a charge; yet the eye that sees through all *may* see even this. We choose the rather to assume that the people do not consider; and that they will do better when they perceive the obligation in its true light, — will be disposed to do what is equable and just, when they see what that is.

And what is it? What is the just measure of a minister's compensation or support?

This is a quantity we can state in no fixed formula of figures. It is a variable quantity, — changes with times, circumstances, places. It is not pay for his work as men in other callings are paid. It is not, of course, the highest pay his measure of talent is capable of commanding, — not the most liberal pay he may win, by consenting to be the tool of competing churches, and swayed by their bids on his coveted gifts. He degrades the office, shows himself not worthy of the office, if he consents to forsake a place where God has put him, where he is largely useful, where generous hearts surround him, are ready to give him, actually *do* give him, all he needs, and attempts the perilous grade that promises to take him higher in the scale of emolument or notability.

We can fix the just measure of a minister's support only by the statement of a principle. It is that measure of support which conduces to the highest effectiveness in his work. *That* is an *average* quantity, — a *medium* quantity. The flush of gain, the excitement of rolling up property, can only be damaging to him. The harassments of poverty will necessarily cramp and deaden the life of all noble endeavor. What meets the case is an easy competence; that he have what he needs to make him comfortable, — to set him free from corroding anxiety, — to give him a tone of assurance favorable to vigorous work; a sense of manly independence; a deliverance from a feeling of meanness, — from a subjected and cringing spirit, as one afraid to affirm and press obligation. We strike a conception of the quantity as that which puts him in the best condition for his work. On the one hand, it is that which does not, by largeness of emolument, or any item of worldly attraction, draw, by unworthy motives, aspirants into this field; and does not, on the other hand, by rigor of place, or unjust severities of treatment, repel from the office those who ought to enter it, and in this way deplete the ranks of competent Christian laborers.

This, then, the measure of support in the place or office; that it is a position in which those who enter it are assisted, enabled, by the compensation rendered, to live on a scale which shall be a full average, if not a little above the average, of the community they serve; a position, therefore, in which they can assuredly live, and be largely useful.

The reasons, in addition to those already given, for furnishing this measure of support, press on *interest*, *conscience*, *sensibility*. They so throng, that we can do little more than make a naked statement of them. The minister, then, should be thus equably supported: —

1. That he *may be enabled to give himself wholly to his work*. This work is sufficient to tax all his powers, and absorb all his time. Few men, for any reason, even for the necessities of a living, can go outside of it without detriment. Paul did; but he is the grand exception and anomaly of the ages. The man who truly desires this work, so desires it, that he will lay down all other work for this alone, — will choose to make this his sole work; and the savor of his example, and the measure of his usefulness, will turn almost entirely upon the singleness of his consecration to it.

2. That he may keep himself *in the best condition for his work;* which means that he be not tempted to over-work by a necessity laid upon him to do other things; which also means that he be able to command the reasonable means of recuperation, by diversion, travel, rest.

3. That he may *furnish himself with the indispensable helps to his work;* that it be put in his power to purchase, in books and otherwise, the materials of thought, argument, exposition; whatever will feed and replenish his own mind, bring to it strength and opulence, and make it a storehouse of varied and exhaustless supply to the minds of the people. If the people but understood how solid and good books, put into the hands of their ministers, find their terminus in themselves, they would load his arms and shelves with them, or give him the means to do it.

4. That he *may be respectable and appear respectable*. In house, in furniture, in the dress and culture of his children, he must come up to a certain standard, or he drops in the public estimation and influence. If his bearing is mean, his words will be despised.

5. That *he may be honest*. To a just measure, *he* must be paid, that he may pay, — may stand in that pecuniary supremacy Paul commends in the words, "Owe no man anything." The minister should have the power of standing on this high vantage-ground, that there may be nothing between him and the hearts and the consciences of his people; that he may enforce, by word and deed, all the claims of integrity, and lead the people to "love one another."

6. That he *may be liberal;* take the lead; be an example in Christian giving. One of his hardest functions, everywhere, will be to train his flock worthily to the grace of giving. No argument or eloquence of speech alone will do it, so terribly and deeply knotted and intrenched, even in *Christian* hearts often, is the lust of getting and laying up. He must lead the way, like that old hero of a weaponless fight, Gideon; he must be in a condition to say to the people, when they come together to deal blows against this master lust, so loath to die, — with Gideon, let him say, "Look on me and do likewise." No one thing is so important to a minister's efficacy in this respect, as that he be in a condition that will enable him thus to be an *example of giving* to the people.

7. That *he may have some prudent forecast and providing* for the loved

ones he will be called to leave. Some may think faith will dispense with this; yet humanity demands this, that he leave something for the helpless behind.

8. *That the favor of the Master may be conciliated toward* his churches. Just and liberal in their treatment of the servants he sends to them, the like the style and measure of his dispensation to them. If it is a course of withholding on the part of any of the churches; a niggardly policy, depressing and grinding down the promulgers of this free and most generous gospel, making them compulsory patterns of self-denial, and fleshly mortification; then, probably, receive they in the like, from the Divine Source. It proves a ministry of leanness to them, on the principle, that their reaping is according to their sowing. We have here, doubtless, the explanation of numberless parched and arid fields. It is a grand law of God's treatment,—with the merciful he will show himself merciful; with the froward he will show himself froward.

9. There is another reason for yielding an equable support, according as we have defined it; namely, if it *be not done*, ministers *will not be* to be supported. It is possible that there be a treatment of them that shall not only diminish, but threaten to run the class out.

Christian men, appointed to do God's service, will stand forth ready to bear, cheerfully, any severity of lot GOD may appoint for them. But the stint, and the mean withholding of *men*,—they will not so degrade themselves as to put up with that; but with a self-respecting independence, will they be tempted to say to these men, too niggardly to pay in support of God's free gospel of saving, in the words of Paul, "Thy money perish with thee." Any hardship *God* ordains in the fulfillment of his commission, let the servant of this gospel rejoice and glory to bear. Let no servant shun the service because of the hardship. Be this ever and supremely the motive which draws into this field the highest and noblest talent,—*the privilege to serve Christ* in the ministry of his gospel, though in the want of all things.

When the naked work or office ceases to have the power to draw the men, then it is a function, an office, which can no longer find men; the absence of them being proof that the race of *fit* men no longer exists.

The above constitute what one rightly calls the economic reason why the church should worthily support its ministry.

There is another and higher, we have previously touched, which is the moral reason,—that which shows it to be eternally right that the preacher of the gospel be compensated for his service. It is the reason the Lord gives, "The laborer is worthy of his hire;" a statement of principle which makes it infinitely just, that he be paid for the value of services rendered,—services which are literally invaluable, lying beyond the power of money to measure.

We come to another department of the topic, namely,

The mode of payment. This is of importance, as well as the measure. It is a satisfaction to the minister, after he has wrought and deserved and earned, to receive what he needs in equity, as a matter of just due. He knows, and the people also, that it *is* matter of just debt. He feels a more manly sentiment when it comes regularly, punctually, cheerfully, as what is due him. If it is looked upon, in any sense, as charity; if his support is made, by contract, inadequate, through avarice, when the people are abundantly able to make it a sufficiency, and then they supplement, piece out the stipend, for *this reason* deficient, by donations, in visits and otherwise; though in the end he may receive as much, yet the *mode* is somewhat degrading to him, — degrading, that he has to take as a gift what is so ascendantly his due. If the people choose to make gifts to their ministers, over and above a just compensation for service, it is all amiable, — honorable to both parties. If they put to him, as a *present*, what they owe to him as a *debt*, it is not honorable to either of the parties. These sunny-side chapters, found weekly in our religious papers, *if established* as the people's mode, in part, of paying their minister, then brood they over the future of our Zion in most ominous shape. They are admissible only as setting the pastor by an emergency, which comes by a *temporary* rise of prices.

We lay down this as indispensable in the arrangement of the minister's support, namely, that *there be a legally constituted corporate body responsible for his support.* Then, if *individuals* fail, this body stands as good, held according to the contract. We deprecate the practice of bringing a minister, at the beginning, and annually ever after, to the test of a subscription paper, the figures of which, in the putting down, are the votes for his call or his continuance. The failure to cancel any of these subscriptions, in some cases, is set to the minister's account, — made detractions from his stipulated pay.

We like the theory, and are clear in commending it where circumstances favor, — *the theory of no individual property* in the house of God. All contributions to build it are gifts to the church for this purpose; the house held by the church for God and his worship; and the minister's support provided for by the rentals of the place. This comes as near to a free church as is feasible or desirable. It is desirable and important, as a means of spiritual benefit from the service, that all responsible members of the body be instructed, encouraged, and expected to bear *some part, help in some form* of payment the body to meet the expenses of sustaining the worship and ordinances of God.

It is a principle most will admit, that the *primal obligation to support the minister* lies with the church he serves, in such form as they may choose. Each church, as a general thing, held solely responsible for its own minister. While this is valid and true, it is also true, that the able churches are *bound to help support* the weak, — the ministers of the weak churches. Here lies the argument and appeal for home missions.

Another point, which may not be passed in this discussion, is, *the minister's function and responsibility in the matter of his own support.* It being a contract between him and the people, of course there is a side for him to fulfill.

The main consideration here is, that he do his work to the extent of his ability, — all he has consecrated to the service of God, in promoting the highest interests of his people. His right to a support, as a minister, depends upon the fact that he is a minister *only.*

As another item of duty resting upon him, let him *keep young and fresh*, that he may do the work a long time; keep young, by continuing to grow, intellectually as well as spiritually, even up to length of years. For every man has a claim to be held as young so long as he keeps growing. Fresh and full of fire, let him make the people forget that he is an old man, even when he is beginning to be one. Let the people also bear with the offense which their minister can not wholly avoid taking on, namely, some of the outer signs of age. There is a wrong done to some of the best and most useful men of the pulpit, by a judgment, or demand, which cuts short, many years, their term of service, and takes away their breath, — men in the acme of their strength and their usefulness, but for the inevitable signs just alluded to. Moses, at eighty, said, "I can not speak, for I am a child." The people now sometimes reverse his plea against speaking, and hurl it into the face of the veteran: you can not speak — not *fit to speak*, because you are growing *old*. "Milk for babes," says Paul, in substance. The people say now, Babes to dispense the milk. There is coming to be almost an insane demand for *young* ministers, — nearer to boys the better. Still, there is another, and a conflicting taste abroad, which demands that they pause a while at Jericho. For we have come to a time when a man's hair is an essential part of him.

Another item in the minister's responsibility in his own support is, that he be a man, and his wife a woman, *of stable and frugal ideas* as to *what constitutes* a living. While they should not be subjected to live meanly, they should be willing to live moderately, — in that medium condition which, doubtless, is the most conducive to comfort, respectability, and usefulness. It is the case with some ministers, that they are not supported because they are not supportable; good ministers, in most regards, only they have not the faculty to come down to a minister's stipend of living. They are given to fancies and fashions which overleap all the regular estimates of the people. It is important that the minister regulate and adjust his expenditures to a tolerably fixed scale, in order that the people may know, right along, the probable limit of their responsibility in this regard.

There is still another department of the minister's function in his own support. It is *incumbent on him to educate his people to integrity* and benevolence, — make them honest and benevolent. The first done, they will pay as they agree. The second done, they will agree to furnish him a reasonable amount.

The minister, to do this part of his work thoroughly, must be on his guard against the prevalent fallacy, that converting men — making them Christians — *of course* makes them honest and benevolent. Frequent and painful facts show that it does not *of course*. Christians we must believe we have, and, notwithstanding the grace of God, not strictly, purely, honest; certainly not free to give and do for the cause of God and the saving of men.

Let the minister put in, clearly and *specifically*, truth, precept, instruction, for the grace of God to vivify. And let him persist to do this, and be still more faithful and specific, till the conscience is brought up to a point of enlightenment, and measure of fidelity, where, so far as his flock is concerned, not only himself, but all other men, will be paid what is due to them, if to pay is possible.

Doctrine, duty also, line upon line, on the other *cardinal virtue*, benevolence, — the disposition to disburse freely for all good objects. To the doctrine, the instruction, precept, which here, too, must lead, let practice be made to follow closely and perpetually. Nothing like giving, to make people love giving.

There is a hurtful fallacy here to be guarded against, — that giving depletes the resources, and so reduces the ability of a Christian man or body. The minister, in a circle of small means, in a parish of limited strength, is liable to reason directly wrong, namely, thus: If I am to be supported, I must be on the watch, and use my influence to keep the money mainly at home. He does so, and he takes the high road to starvation. And he deserves to.

Let him change his policy, and throw wide open his heart, — take into it the whole world, and make it his glad rule to help, personally and through his people, all good objects, — thus lead his people, in acts of giving, till they attain to a hearty love of giving; that minister's support has a basis equal to the strength of two Gibraltars, — one the integrity of his people, the other the benevolence of the people.

GEORGE SHEPARD,
CHARLES G. HAMMOND,
W. A. BUCKINGHAM, } *Committee.*
SAMUEL HOLMES,
DOUGLAS PUTNAM.

The report was accepted and referred under the rule to the appropriate committee.

On motion of Rev. Mr. Langworthy, of Massachusetts, for the committee on Nominations, the following members were added to the committee on the Declaration of Faith: —

Prof. Samuel Harris, of Bangor; Prof. Edwards A. Park, of Andover; Prof. Edward A. Lawrence, of East Windsor; Prof. Noah Porter, Jr., of New Haven; Prof. James H. Fairchild, of Oberlin; Prof. Joseph Haven, of Chicago.

The hour of 11, A. M., having arrived, prayer was offered by Rev. Dr. Hopkins, of Massachusetts, and by Rev. Dr. Massie, of England, and appropriate hymns were sung.

On motion of Rev. Mr. Langworthy, for the committee on Nominations, the following committees were appointed: —

ON EVANGELIZATION IN THE WEST AND SOUTH.

Rev. Samuel W. S. Dutton, D. D., of Connecticut; Rev. Joseph P. Thompson, D. D., of New York; Hon. Samuel Williston, of Massachusetts;

Rev. Benjamin P. Stone, D. D., of New Hampshire ; Rev. Lucius H. Parker, of Illinois ; Rev. Dexter Clary, of Wisconsin ; Judge Francis D. Parish, of Ohio ; Rev. Jesse Guernsey, of Iowa ; Rev. William Crawford, of Colorado ; Jacob Bacon, of California ; Rev. George H. Atkinson, of Oregon.

ON THE RELATION OF FOREIGN MISSIONS TO THE CONGREGATIONAL CHURCHES.

Rev. W. Ives Budington, D. D., of New York ; Rev. Zachary Eddy, D. D., of Massachusetts ; Rev. Charles C. Parker, of Vermont ; Rev. William Carter, of Illinois ; Hon. Benjamin Douglas, of Connecticut.

ON THE ROLL.

Rev. Edward Beecher, D. D., of Illinois ; Dea. Elnathan F. Duren, of Maine ; Rev. John K. Young, D. D., of New Hampshire ; Rev. Ezra H. Byington, of Vermont ; Rev. J. W. Harding of Massachusetts ; Rev. William Barrows, of Massachusetts ; Rev. Robert C. Learned, of Connecticut ; Rowland Hazard, Esq., of Rhode Island ; Rev. L. Smith Hobart, of New York ; Rev. Edward Hawes, of Pennsylvania; Rev. Edwin Johnson, of Maryland ; Rev. Lysander Kelsey, of Ohio ; Rev. Adam S. Kedzie, of Michigan ; Rev. S. Hopkins Emery, of Illinois ; Rev. Joseph W. Healey of Wisconsin ; Rev. Julius A. Reed, of Iowa ; Rev. Richard Hall, of Minnesota ; Rev. Julian M. Sturtevant, Jr., of Missouri ; Rev. Lewis Bodwell, of Kansas ; Rev. Reuben Gaylord, of Nebraska ; Rev. William Crawford, of Colorado ; Rev. Kinsley Twining, of California ; Rev. John M. Holmes, of New Jersey.

MINISTERIAL EDUCATION.

Rev. Ray Palmer, D. D., of New York, chairman of committee, read the following : —

By the conference of committees from the principal ecclesiastical bodies representing the Congregational churches in the United States, which met at New York, in the chapel of the Broadway Tabernacle Church, on the seventeenth of November, 1864, the undersigned were appointed a committee to call the attention of the National Council to be assembled at Boston on the fourteenth of June, 1865, to the subject of the education of young men for the Christian ministry, and to make such suggestions as might facilitate the thorough consideration and discussion of the topic. The duty so imposed has seemed to them a difficult one. The magnitude of the matter in itself ; its relation to various questions pertaining to the state and duty of the churches, — to the condition and prospects of our colleges, and especially of our theological institutions, — to the work of home evangelization and that of foreign missions, and the new aspects under which it is just now providentially presented; render it no easy thing to exhibit it so concisely that it can be comprehended at a single view, and yet so fully that it shall make, in its details, anything like the desired impression. The committee, accordingly, have not been able to make their statement so brief as they desired; but they have not been willing, for the sake of brevity, to omit any thing that seemed necessary to be said in order to a just view of the subject. If they have succeeded in bringing it fairly before the Council for discussion, they suppose that this is all that was expected of them. They, therefore, respectfully submit the following paper.

SECTION I.

FACTS BEARING ON THE SUBJECT OF THE EDUCATION OF YOUNG MEN FOR THE MINISTRY.

1. From the day when the Pilgrims landed on Plymouth Rock, it has been the settled conviction of our Congregational churches, that for the high and responsible work of the Christian teacher a thorough intellectual discipline and culture, a truly liberal education, is, as the rule, imperatively demanded. No other view could be expected to prevail in churches whose earliest pastors were many of them men of eminent learning and wore the honors of the highest scholarship in the English universities. To provide the means of raising up for themselves an educated ministry, was, it is well known, one of the first things connected with their settlement here on which they bestowed anxious care and thought. Our standard of ministerial education has, therefore, always been relatively high; for the last fifty years it has been rising steadily; and it is no longer a question with us whether it should be carried to the highest practicable point.

2. The number of young men in a course of preparation for the ministry, as compared with the whole number of persons pursuing liberal studies, has for the last twelve or fifteen years been on the whole materially *diminishing.* The inducements offered to Christian young men to enter into secular pursuits, the growing respectability of teaching as a profession, the increasing profitableness of literature, the attractions of the political arena, the new enterprises opened on every hand and promising rapid gains, — all the stimulants, in short, which are fitted to stir an honorable ambition in gifted minds, have exerted an effective influence in diverting from the sacred office those who might naturally have been expected to desire to enter it. A mistaken impression has also prevailed that the ranks of the ministry were already over-full, and by this error many have doubtless been turned aside. The demands of the war just closing have called great numbers of young men not only to leave their studies, but to lay down their lives, for the sacred cause of national unity and freedom. By these and other causes, it has come to pass that the number of students in our colleges and seminaries, who are looking forward to the service of Christ in the pulpit, is *painfully small,* just when the need of men in this holy work is becoming every day more urgent.

3. While in general scholarship and theological training the Congregational clergy, as a body, are probably unsurpassed by any equally numerous clerical body in the world, it is quite plain that they are but

partially meeting the spiritual necessities of our advancing population. Even in New England, where our churches originally had the ground, and where it would seem that they ought to have kept pace with the social growth, there are now great numbers who are not reached in any effectual manner by the stated means of grace. Not only in the large cities and manufacturing towns into which many of foreign birth have gradually introduced themselves, but also in the country towns and villages, where the people are still chiefly of native Puritan descent, it is undeniably true that a very considerable, and, it is to be feared, an increasing portion of the whole population are not reached by the ministry so as to feel the power of the gospel of Christ. Many such are relapsing into religious ignorance and spiritual death in the very sight of Christian sanctuaries.

4. There are to be found, in New England itself, not a few towns and villages in which Congregational churches were once planted and had full possession of the field, but in which such churches have become nearly or quite extinct, and the ground has been occupied by others, sometimes by unevangelical churches or congregations, and sometimes by churches whose ministry has been far inferior in educational culture to our own. While, in the largeness of our liberality, we have supplied to one branch of the Presbyterian church no inconsiderable portion of its clergy, and even a greater portion probably of its laymen; while we have sent forth multitudes of Christian missionaries, and of pioneers, who, in the newer parts of the country, have planted churches, established colleges, and laid the foundations of a Christian civilization, and have given our hearty support to all forms of Christian effort; we have yet, with all our advantages, failed to hold and to strengthen, in the interest of our Lord, positions that once were ours. We have lost them for want of care to sustain the weak, and of fidelity and zeal in relation to the unimposing details of Christian duty.

5. In our statistical tables, a great number of feeble churches are reported, which for the larger part of the time are without pastors, or any regular supplies, and so are becoming more and more feeble. *Less than one third of our churches have pastors settled over them.* Something more than another third have only stated supplies; leaving something a little less than a third of the whole with no steady supply at all. Most of these are unable to procure any, unless it be for brief and uncertain periods, and often, for years together, suffer a dearth of the word of life. They are in the sad condition of sheep without a shepherd.

6. While such a state of things exists even in New England, the case is still worse, much worse beyond these limits. The newer States, including the vast regions of the West, now extending to the Pacific and opening to receive the flood-tide of population, present almost innumerable points at which churches have been planted and are yet in a feeble state, or must be planted to struggle up from feebleness amidst the embarrassments and hardships of a forming social condition. To these illimitable fields are now added the Border and Southern States, in which, as the result of our great contest, society is to a great extent to

be reorganized. Over these extensive regions are to be scattered, for a long time to come, a great number of churches which will not present inviting parishes, nor afford a liberal ministerial support. Yet it is of the utmost importance to the cause of evangelical religion, and to the future well-being of our country, that these positions should be taken and held by faithful Christian ministers, and that the church should grow up side by side with other institutions from the first.

7. From various parts of the foreign missionary field there are soon to be heard the most earnest calls for efficient re-enforcements. For the last four years no enlargement of operations has been attempted. To avoid disastrous curtailment, to weather the financial storm without a wreck, has been the grand anxiety. But four years, in which little more has been done than just to hold our ground, will render imperative a vigorous advance so soon as circumstances will permit. The day is now at hand. The missionary brethren, who have uncomplainingly borne excessive burdens, and have patiently endured the troubles arising from straitened means, must speedily see others coming to their aid. Where the seed has been sown through tedious years, the harvest that at last has ripened must be reaped; and at many a new post must the banner of our Lord be planted. The educational institutions must be manned, the work of translation and of creating Christian literatures must go forward, and the presses must be kept effectively at work. For men to go forth and enter into all these labors, in every quarter of the world, we shall very soon hear strong appeals. They come indeed already.

Such are a few of the material facts that meet us at the threshold in the consideration of the subject now before us.

BEARING OF THESE FACTS AS REGARDS THE MINISTRY.

It is of the utmost importance that these acknowledged facts should be set distinctly before both ministers and churches, and should be carefully and seriously considered. We, as a denomination, have sought to disencumber Christianity of the machinery of a sensuous ecclesiasticism. We have had faith in its spiritual power, and so have returned to the simple forms and usages of the primitive church. We have believed that the gospel, in the naked simplicity in which Christ and his apostles originally proclaimed it, is the divinely appointed means for the renewing of individual man, and for the elevating and purifying of the social and religious condition of the world. We have understood that Christ has given his followers solemn charge to apply it faithfully for the accomplishment of these great ends, and that he has pledged himself, so far as this is done, to make it effectual by his co-operative providence and grace. In the full enjoyment, as a people, of civil and religious freedom, we have nothing external to embarrass us in so applying it. Never, on the face of the earth, has there been offered a fairer opportunity than here exists for the direct and thorough preaching of the gospel to the masses of the people, and the infusing of its peculiar influences into all the relations and institutions of social life. It would seem, therefore, that here there should be furnished to the whole world an instructive and stimulating example of what a pure, free gospel, preached by a learned and godly ministry, can do to renovate and exalt a people, and to adorn society with the charm of general intelligence, refinement, and virtue. If evangelical Christianity fail here to fulfill its mission, where is it likely to succeed? What, then, is to be said in view of the facts to which we have referred? What, in particular, are the *wants*, as regards the Christian ministry, which they forcibly suggest?

SECTION II.

PRESENT WANTS AS REGARDS THE MINISTRY.

1. First of all, there is wanted for the general needs of our Congregational churches a ministry in the ranks of which shall be found *the broadest and most thorough scholarship*, — a scholarship no where to be surpassed. It is indeed not necessary that every individual minister shall attain, or attempt to attain, the highest eminence of learning. But surely it would ill become us, who, from our earliest denominational history, have set so high a value on clerical education, and whose form of church organization and government supposes intelligence and free thought, to lack in our pastors and educators the best learning, the most finished culture, which the present age in any country can produce. At a time when the most momentous questions in theology, in philosophy and morals, in philology and criticism, in science and in social and civil economy, are engaging constantly the popular as well as the educated mind, we must have men to fill the more important positions in our institutions and our churches, who can bring to the discussion of these questions not only the highest power of thought, but the most ample wealth of knowledge. We have such men. We have always had them. Not only some of the ablest thinkers, but some of the most accurate philologists and most comprehensive scholars, living, may probably be found among our clergy. The higher periodical literature among us, and other publications connected with sacred learning, the result of the labors of such men, compare well with the best of other countries. But it must be admitted that such men are by far too few. Many more such are called for by the exigencies of the time. We want them to repel the assaults, so confidently made on critical, scientific, and speculative grounds, on the very foundations of the Christian faith. We want them for many and rapidly multiplying positions, which none but the best scholarship can creditably fill. We want them at the head of all our collegiate and theological institutions. We want them in our pulpits, and on our platforms, to teach pretentious error to be modest. We want them in the newer portions of our country, where the foundations of learning for many generations must be laid, and the forming thought of society be shaped. We want them abroad, where translations of the Scriptures must be made, and many difficult tasks be performed with the nicest scholarly care. Without such men in our ministry, we can neither maintain our ancient prestige, nor meet the necessities of the educated and thoughtful mind with which we have to deal.

2. *A much larger number* of men are at the present moment wanted in the ministry; and this want is sure to become every day more pressing. The carefully arranged statistical tables in the "Congregational Quarterly" for January, 1865, abundantly justify this statement. The total of Congregational churches is there given at twenty-eight hundred and sixty-five; the whole number of *nominal* ministers, at twenty-eight hundred and sixty-two. Of these ministers, *seven hundred and fifty-six are known not to be in the pastoral work.* Besides these, there are reported one hundred and forty whose status is not ascertained. Probably the greater part of these are not actually engaged in the work of the ministry. Adding say one hundred of these to those *known* not to be so engaged, we have eight hundred and fifty-six, who really have no relation whatever to the supply of the churches, to be deducted from the total of twenty-eight hundred and sixty-three given in the tables; leaving but two thousand and six persons who are in the pastoral work for the supply of the twenty-eight hundred and sixty-five churches. If, therefore, every minister, better or worse, who is at this time engaged in preaching, were to-day placed over a church, there would remain *eight hundred and fifty-nine churches for whom no minister could be supplied.* The fact that many of these churches are feeble, so far from weakening the force of this statement, only gives it *greater* force, by showing that their need of pastors is most urgent. The duty of providing these eight or nine hundred churches with pastors, and aiding them, if need be, to sustain them, is clearly pressing now upon us. To this we must also add, that for the exploring of the vast regions in which churches ought to be formed at once, or must speedily be formed, and also for the various departments of the foreign missionary service, many, very many more ministers are urgently demanded.

3. But, further, the want which is becoming every day more pressing, extends beyond mere numbers. We want men, who, *by their natural endowments and their special training, are adapted to the work that now is not accomplished.*

We are not now called upon, it is conceived, as churches, to make any special efforts and sacrifices to raise up pastors for the well-paying and prosperous parishes. These will, of course, need a steady succession of thoroughly educated, able, and earnest ministers. But the supply of the pulpits of such parishes may safely be left to take care of itself. With due care to supply the proper facilities for education, and in view of the number of Christian young men who are coming forward, it is quite certain that those positions in the ministry, which are in themselves pleasant and desirable, will be desired and sought. It may occasionally happen that a particular church, though every way attractive, will have some temporary difficulty in finding the man it wants; but this may arise from unreasonable expectations, or from the number of candidates proposed, or some such incidental embarrassment. In general, however, it may safely be calculated on, that, as regards the more eligible places, the supply will keep pace with the demand. In saying this, we are casting no reproach on either the churches or the ministry. The prosperous churches are not to be blamed for desiring the best pastors they can obtain. Ministers, when called by the churches to responsible charges, where, though the labors are great, the circumstances are congenial, are not to be blamed for undertaking those charges. The simple fact to be noticed is, that the law which holds in all other departments of social life is likely to hold here, — namely, that what is in itself worth seeking, somebody will certainly be found to seek. It is not in this direction that the attention and the efforts, especially the charitable efforts, of the churches should now be turned. It is not about the men required for these positions that there is occasion specially to concern ourselves.

We are specially called on to bring forward into the ministry, as soon as possible, from eight hundred to one thousand young ministers, who are fitted to the particular work *of raising up the feeble churches of New England, and the new churches in other parts of our wide country*, that must be feeble for a time. It is plain, that, for this service, men of a certain type are needed. It is not disparaging the ministry, as a class, to say, that, on all ordinary principles of calculation, it must be expected, that, out of a given number who enter the sacred office, there will be a certain per cent. who can not be successful. It is so in all other pursuits in which men are accustomed to engage, and, without a perpetual miracle, it will always be so in this. Some will lack in part, and some almost wholly, after all the processes of education, the peculiar powers and qualities which give influence over men.

It has, probably, been one of the practical errors of the past, to imagine that *this* class of ministers might meet the wants of the churches that are suffering from chronic weakness, and of those that have been newly planted. On the contrary, inasmuch as the work to be done for these is peculiarly difficult, the men to do it must be men of special force and tact. Only men of physical energy, of gristle, nerve, and pluck, — men whom hard work, hard fare, and hard usage of all sorts, will not kill, — can be expected to meet the exigencies of such a service. There must be, also, an intellectual adaptation not less positive and marked. We live in stirring times. All the pulses of social life beat quick and strong. The minds of people of remotest places are reached by all sorts of stimulating influences, and thought and feeling are intensified to a high degree. Whoever is to exert a molding influence on a people in such a state, must be himself alive, flexible, vigorous, sympathetic, human, as well as scholarly, intellectual, and pious. He must have quickness to plan, and enthusiasm to execute; must know how to find access to the hearts even of the prejudiced and hostile; and be sagacious in discerning, and prompt in meeting, the exigencies that every day will bring. It is young men, who have the capacity for all this, that are demanded. What we here say, in regard to the kind of men demanded for the missionary work at home, is not less true in respect to those wanted for the missionary work abroad. They must be men whom God, by their natural endowments, has fitted to force and grapple with the arduous and peculiar difficulties which that work of necessity involves.

4. But we must go still farther. The men now wanted in the ministry

must be men who, along with force of natural character, possess also *the higher force which eminent faith and the deepest Christian earnestness* supply. With the facts of the case before us, it is plain that ministers are demanded who will be *willing to enter, and willing to stay in* the most trying and difficult fields, if so the Master in his providence directs. To go into obscure and feeble parishes, or into destitute regions to plant new churches, or into the isolation and trials of a home among pagans, and to be able and willing patiently to labor there, requires a vigorous hold on things unseen, and a deep baptism into the spirit of self-sacrifice. To do these things men must be had to whom the pleasures of filling a conspicuous position, of preaching to refined and appreciative hearers, of being surrounded by agreeable society, and even of having a comfortable support, will hardly be taken into the account in accepting a field of labor. They must be men who, not in some highly figurative sense, but literally, count all things but loss in comparison with the privilege of imparting the knowledge of Christ *to those whose need of it is greatest ;* who feel that a woe is on them if they preach not the gospel, and are determined to preach it, paid or unpaid, with comforts or without comforts, and have even a holy ambition to work in the darkest and most cheerless places where work is to be done. Is it doubted whether it can be the duty of Christian young men to give themselves to the preaching of the word at such a cost? Paul and the first preachers of Christianity did. There have been those in all ages of the Christian church who have done it. If Francis Xavier, and Ignatius Loyola, and others like them in the Romish church, could rise to such a heroic self-devotion as they exhibited, is it too much to hope, that, under the clearer light and higher inspirations of spiritual Christianity, men may be raised up to emulate, in doing the work of Christ, their zeal, their self-denials, their patient endurance of suffering? Without *such* men to meet the present and prospective need, it is clear that our own country can not be brought fully under the power of Christ's religion, still less can the world ever be won to God. It will be of little use to increase the number of young ministers, or even to bring the most gifted and energetic of our sons into the sacred office, if, after all, they have not the sublime self-devotion which will make them willing to go any where, and to face any discouragements whatever for Christ's sake. Without this in the ministry, the work that now lies undone will still lie undone; moral wastes will multiply; churches will become extinct; and we as a Christian denomination shall appear to have lost the spirit of our godly fathers, whose faith and polity have come down to us as a goodly heritage. Apostolic faith and zeal, and unflinching readiness to do or suffer,—nothing short of a ministry possessing these high spiritual endowments, will meet the present want.

5. We want likewise, it must be added, men for the ministry *who understand and heartily approve the system of faith and the ecclesiastical principles of the Fathers of New England.* It is the just glory of our churches that they are of all churches the most truly catholic. This arises from the fact, that according to the teaching of Christ and the

apostles, and in opposition to corrupt ecclesiastical traditions, we have placed *vital Christianity*, the renewing and saving power of the gospel and the cross, first and highest in our religious system, and have made modes of worship and forms of administration subordinate to life. While others have deemed organic unity, an outward consolidation of churches, a thing to be desired, our fathers saw in it, and we see in it, only a peril to the liberties and to the purity of the Christian brotherhood. It has appeared to us, that, of all men on the earth, Christian men are most likely to be capable of self-government; and it has seemed that the freedom and the responsibilities of self-government must tend to develop individual Christian activity, and to make church membership a real commitment of each disciple to a practical and working piety. We can not but think that our principles, as sanctioned alike by reason and the Scriptures, are, for our own sakes and our children's, worth maintaining; and also, that, faithfully maintaining them, we shall exert a most salutary influence on the large bodies of consolidated churches with which we come in friendly contact, in the way of infusing into them a more liberal spirit than naturally belongs to their own systems, and by in some sort constraining them to respect the rights of individual believers and those of the local churches. With these views of our polity, it appears to us a sacred trust committed to the children of the Puritans for the good of the churches of all names, not less than for their own.

The men, therefore, whom the wants of our churches, in their present rapid multiplication, urge us to bring into the ministry, must be men who are the sons of the Pilgrim Fathers, not by birth or in name merely, but as grasping the same great effective principles which made them the successful founders and vindicators of civil and religious freedom, and breathing the same spirit of devotion to the authority of the Scriptures, to earnest and progressive religious thought, and to a piety of deep experience. Men who do not understand and love our principles, and can not teach our churches to understand and love them; men who have in them no sympathy with the great ideas that cluster historically about old Plymouth Rock, — who do not see that it is very much through the force of these ideas that there is so much of Christian liberality, and so much genuine catholic feeling among the evangelical churches of all names throughout our country, — are not the men to do the work that presses on our hands. The hearts of great numbers of the people, in all parts of the land, are open all the more to receive our scriptural theology, because they see it allied to a church organization and government so peculiarly in accord with the progressive and practical spirit of the time. In such a state of things, we want ministers who have positive convictions as to the truth and the value of our principles; ministers, in a word, who are *Congregationalists in heart*, to take the oversight of our churches, and to conserve and make yet more perfect the precious religious heritage we have received from ancestors whose names are among the most honored of mankind. It is such men that the churches, and particularly the new churches, are more and more imperatively requiring.

Such seem to the committee to be the chief wants, as regards the supply of a fit ministry, which, in view of the facts referred to in the beginning, are forcing themselves on the attention of the churches. We are brought, then, to the inquiry, *What shall be done*, to the end that these wants may be effectually met?

SECTION III.

WHAT OUGHT NOW TO BE DONE?

1. In accordance with the well-known views of the fathers of New England, and our own convictions as to the value of thorough theological education, our theological seminaries should, as soon as possible, *be placed in a position to offer all facilities which the highest scholarship in this department may require.*

At present, none of our theological seminaries are properly endowed. The number of professorships is wholly inadequate to the work that should be done; the necessary consequence of which is, that the professors are often over-worked, and, after all, the course of study is too narrow. The libraries are comparatively meager, and fall far short of meeting the wants both of the professors and the students. The provision for the pursuit of those branches of learning, which, while not strictly included in the study of theology, are collateral and auxiliary to it, amounts to almost nothing. As a large part of the presidents and professors of our colleges and seminaries at home, and of the men who must master foreign languages and literatures, and be the translators and the educators at our foreign missionary stations, must be trained in our theological institutions, the deficiencies which exist are the more to be regretted. It has hitherto been a necessity, that those who have wished to pursue their studies up to the highest range of scholarship should go to Germany, or elsewhere abroad, in order to find the requisite facilities. To this there are very grave objections; and such a course would no longer be needful were our own institutions such as they ought to be. It is far better that those who are to be at the head of our literary institutions, who are to shape the thought, and, to a great extent, to determine the spirit and character of our churches, should be educated in the moral atmosphere of our own country, than where influences prevail which are not in harmony with the principles and habits which we have inherited from our noble ancestors, and which have been a chief source of our national power and glory. We *can* have, we *ought* to have, we MUST have, theological institutions *unsurpassed by any in the world* in the largeness and completeness of the advantages they offer, and, at the same time, thoroughly imbued with the spirit of the Pilgrims. They must lack nothing in the way of men or endowments or books, but must be thoroughly equipped. To this important matter, it is conceived, immediate attention should be given. It has been neglected already quite too long.

2. It is also greatly to be desired, it is, indeed, an imperative necessity, that the advantages of our theological seminaries, made thus ample, *be placed within the reach of all suitable candidates for the Christian ministry.*

It will avail but little to urge Christian parents to consecrate their sons, or young men of piety and talents to devote themselves to Christ's service in the ministry, if the way is not fairly open for them to get the needed preparation. The whole subject of charitable aid, in some form, to those preparing for the ministry, must be taken up anew in the light of experience, and with due regard to the change of circumstances which the past few years have wrought. The expenses of living at any of our seminaries are at least treble what they were thirty years ago. The trifling assistance which could at that time be rendered to deserving young men, and which then but barely enabled them to struggle through, is wholly insufficient now. While the standard of scholarship has materially risen, and the student can *less* than ever afford to have his studies interrupted by efforts for his own support, he is *more* than ever under the necessity of interrupting them if he will avoid the burden of hopeless debt. Our own institutions — a strange thing to be true in view of our past history — are more deficient in the means of rendering aid than those of other denominations with whom we affiliate. Because of this, a very considerable number of our young men, within the last few years, have naturally been induced, by the hope of more liberal assistance, to turn away from the seminaries in which our own doctrines and polity are taught; and so, educated in another atmosphere, and forming other associations, they have many of them been lost to us. We rejoice in the thought that they carry somewhat of the free and catholic spirit of New England, and of our communion as a whole, into churches where it is likely to be useful; but to us as a fellowship of churches, the suffering of this process to go on is suicidal. We want our own young men. We ought to retain them for the service of our own churches and for the manning of our own missions. But the only way to retain them is to enable our own institutions to give them the help they need. In order to this, the wealthy members of our churches must be induced to endow scholarships, the avails of which may be granted, by examinations held, to good attainments and general promise; so that every young man, who is qualified by his talents, diligence, and piety to enter the sacred office, may be enabled, without the interruptions and distresses of poverty, to pursue a thorough course of study. The same provision, or something equivalent to this, should also be made in the colleges, that there as well as in the theological schools, young men of the right character may be helped forward toward the ministry, instead of sinking under discouragements, or turning to other courses of life. An adequate number of scholarships, supplemented by the American Education Society, and perhaps, also, by some associations for the supply of clothing, and for the care of students who may be sick, would place our institutions in an entirely different position from that which they now occupy in respect to students. They would, in this way, be able to offer their advantages freely to all suitable persons who might be inclined to profit by them. Without such liberal provision we must expect to continue to lose many of our best young men.

3. While such provision is made for the assistance of those who wish

to prepare themselves thoroughly for the ministry, pious and promising young men, whose circumstances absolutely forbid a full course of study, *must be brought forward by a shorter process, and must be allowed to resort to the theological seminaries for such limited periods and such partial studies* as may seem expedient in each case.

In past years, it has been felt that there were strong objections to the admission of students to the privileges of the theological schools unless they could proceed in the regular order of study to the end. It was feared that to allow any to enter the ministry with any thing *short* of the established course of study might tend to lower the general standard of ministerial education. But necessity is an efficient teacher. In view of the great and urgent wants of our country, as well as of the world, it has become quite certain that it will not be possible to furnish a sufficient number of highly-educated ministers to supply the demand. At the same time there are found young men of good ordinary education, good sense, or even superior natural abilities, who, owing to something peculiar in their circumstances, *can not* go through the regular course of study, and yet, with a more limited preparation, might be exceedingly useful as preachers of the gospel. It is believed that the time has now fully come when such young men should be permitted to enjoy the advantages of our theological institutions for the purpose of taking *any such partial course* as the exigencies of each case may render proper, and should, with this, be commissioned and sent forth. Men of this class, like the first disciples that went every where preaching the word, may do excellent service as faithful witnesses for Christ. Leaving to their more thoroughly educated brethren the higher offices of the Christian teacher, they may, *perhaps with some advantage from their less scholastic tastes and modes of thinking*, come into close sympathy with common people, and testify to them the truth as it is in Jesus. If it be true, as some have thought, that—not necessarily it may be, but really—the high culture of our ministers has tended to place them sometimes too far above those whom they should reach and save, a moderate number of earnest, judicious men, with less of the spirit of the schools, might do a special service in the way of counteracting such a tendency, and maintaining a vital contact, a practical community of feeling, between the clergy as a body and those who need the gospel. Certainly they may help to make up the deficiency in numbers; and a warm-hearted Christian preacher and pastor, though lacking the best scholarship, may be owned of God to the saving of many souls that must otherwise have been left to perish. With due care, there seems to be no need to fear that the admission of some men of special adaptation to the work of preaching Christ, with an abbreviated course of preparatory study, will either lower the standard of general theological education, or deteriorate the general character of the ministry. We may safely, in this case as in others, obey the call of the providence of God.

4. Yet further: a general and earnest effort should at once be made *to awaken in the churches a new enthusiasm for the work of the Christian ministry.*

To the accomplishment of this, the religious press may effectively contribute; but the chief reliance must be on faithful presentations of the subject by the pastors. Many of us can well remember when, through the burning words of Porter, Griffin, Cornelius, and others of like ardor, a fire was kindled in the hearts of Christian parents and Christian young men that glowed with a notable intensity. It led godly fathers and mothers with prayers and tears to consecrate their children from their birth to Christ's service in the gospel, in the hope that he would call them to it; and to a conscientious and careful training of them with reference to the sacred office. Possibly, at that time, too little discrimination was used in advising young men to enter on a course of preparation for the ministry, — an error to be carefully avoided; but this was certainly no reason why the whole subject should have been dropped, as we fear it has been, to a great extent at least. We must come back again — the pastors must carry the churches back — to the old conviction, or even a deeper conviction, of the value of the Christian ministry, and of the honor and blessedness of the work, in spite of all its crosses, when undertaken and performed in a truly Christian spirit. Young men must be persuaded, by cogent arguments and stirring appeals, that to be a good minister of Jesus is to occupy a position than which there is none more worthy to be aspired to, none higher and nobler in the world. Such an ardor as we have seen move the young men of the country to enlist in the loyal service for the attainment of the grandest of earthly ends must be awakened in the minds of the sons of Christian parents; an eagerness to enlist in the army of the Son of God, as leaders of the host that is going forth at his command to put down the great rebellion against his throne. Every pastor has a personal responsibility to see that this is done within his own particular circle. Each must become an earnest recruiting agent, using of course all due care to enrol those only who have the requisite gifts and capabilities for the service. The presidents and professors in our colleges have equally a duty to perform. It will no longer do to leave this subject to take care of itself. The most attractive objects of ambition, the most inviting prospects of wealth and worldly greatness and distinction, present themselves to our young men on every side, and must be expected to engage them in secular pursuits, unless they can be made to see that the claims of Christ on them are paramount, and that his rewards surpass infinitely all that earth can offer. Until the churches are thoroughly aroused to this great matter, so that our pious young men, sharing in the common impulse, *shall be inspired with the spirit of a truly Christian chivalry*, with the healthful enthusiasm of a loyalty to Christ that shall make his service the best and highest to their thought, the ranks of the ministry are not likely to be filled with the choicest sons of believing parents.

5. It is not less important, likewise, that those whose attention is directed toward the ministry, should be led, from the outset, and by the whole drift and spirit of their education, to regard it *as eminently demanding a self-devoting and world-renouncing spirit.*

Where the church is organically connected with the State, and so is directly related to political and civil life, the tendency, necessarily, is, to regard the ministry simply as a profession, — as offering agreeable employment, a respectable position, opportunity for literary culture, a comfortable livelihood, and, with all these, a prospect of advancement. It is but natural, that to those who enter the ministry with such a view of it as this, — who choose it, as others choose the profession of law or medicine, for the sake of the worldly advantages it offers them, — it should seem entirely proper to desire, and habitually to seek to reach, the highest and the best positions. But it will be a sad day for the interests of pure religion in our churches, when our young men generally shall think of the pastoral office as they think of the secular professions, and seek, in entering it, chiefly the gratification of their own tastes, and their own comfort and respectability in life. Any approach to such a state of things may well excite alarm. Christ does not call men into the ministry, as into a mere profession, in which to make agreeable provision for themselves. He calls them into it as into a high and holy service, in which, with disinterested devotion to his person, to toil, to contend, to suffer, if need be, for the saving of men's souls, and for the honor of his name. To seek one's own pleasure in entering the ministry; to indulge, when in it, an ambitious and worldly spirit, — to be dissatisfied with the position in which Christ has placed one, because it is obscure, or because the people are not refined, or because one's sphere seems circumscribed; in short, to be intent on personal advantages, and disposed to get away from difficulties, instead of facing them with courage, is to mistake, sadly and totally, the nature of the work which has been given in charge to his ministers by the ascended Lord. All this is, in general terms, admitted.

But is there not need to make the *necessity of self-sacrifice far more prominent*, when the claims of the ministry are pressed upon the young men of our churches, than it has been hitherto? If it is for the home missionary work and for the foreign missionary work that we are now specially concerned to raise up ministers, *care must be taken to educate them into such views and such a spirit* as will fit them for these forms of Christian labor. From the first, our pious sons must be taught to dismiss the romantic notion, that they may look forward to the ministry as affording a position in which to gratify their literary tastes, and to enjoy intelligent and refined society. They must be led to regard an entrance into the sacred office as committing them to a service, high indeed and honorable, divinely appointed, and connected with the sublimest satisfactions and rewards; but yet attended, or liable to be attended, with privations and trials, and even with personal sufferings, analogous to those of which the life of Christ himself, and of Paul and his fellow-apostles, were so full. To this education of pious young men to higher and more spiritual conceptions of the work of the ministry, and to purer and more disinterested aims, Christian parents and the Christian pulpit must contribute. College officers must make conscience of lending all their influence to help it on. Above all, our theological seminaries must give *a very marked prominence to spiritual* culture, in its course of training, and must be pre-eminently pervaded by a warm, vitalizing and inspiring Christian atmosphere. Even the most ample learning and the most complete dogmatic knowledge will fail utterly to give us the ministry we need, if not steeped in devout affection, and consecrated by the baptism, and rich indwelling, of the Holy Spirit of God. It is for the churches to look to this, and to insist that *the cultivation of a fervent personal piety* shall not only be distinctly recognized as a prominent part of the work to be accomplished in the theological seminary, but *shall be made subordinate to nothing else.* We believe it wrong to say, as has been sometimes said that there is less of a devotional spirit among theological students than among the average of Christians elsewhere. We think it especially wrong to blame the few and overtasked professors, whose attention must necessarily be very largely occupied with their several departments, for not doing all that is needed to produce, with steadiness, an elevated tone of Christian feeling. *Particular provision* ought to be made, in every theological institution, for the spiritual training of all connected with it; to this should be added habitual and earnest prayer for the young men themselves, and their instructors. Then we may expect that the end desired will be attained. So long as but little is done, or thought necessary to be done, to produce, among those who are designing to enter the ministry, an *apostolic spirit,* — a holy self-consecration like that which made Brainerd, and the great Edwards, even, willing to preach the gospel to poor Indians in the wilderness, — so long we shall lack the men whom the present wants of the Christian cause, and of our own denomination, urgently demand. We can not reasonably expect to bring forward a ministry of eminent spiritual earnestness, of self-sacrificing and heroic zeal and energy, *unless we seriously propose this, and adapt our methods of training to effect it.*

6. While those who look forward to the ministry are taught to do it in a spirit of self-sacrifice, the churches must be made to feel, far more deeply than they have generally done hitherto, *the necessity of a just and liberal support of those who are in the work.*

As the subject of ministerial support is referred to another committee, which will, doubtless, present it fully, we do not propose to speak of it here at length. Yet, standing, as it does, in very important relations to the difficulties connected with the work of bringing young men into the ministry, we can not properly omit to notice it. When we insist that our young men must be ready to do and to suffer anything for Christ, we do not mean to imply that ministers are under a different law of self-consecration, from that which binds the members of the churches generally. If it is their duty cheerfully to meet all the trials, and even hardships, which are *necessary,* it is the sacred duty of the churches to see to it that they suffer none that are unnecessary, — none that an honest readiness to render unto them a due reward of their labors would prevent. It can not be doubted, that the want of justice in the adequate support of those who serve at Christ's altars in word and doctrine, — a want of justice often so palpable that it is seen and known of all, — is one of the most powerful among the causes which operate to turn the most gifted young men from the ministry to other pursuits. Is it strange, if a young man sees, that after having spent ten years in hard study, and expended three or four thousand dollars for his education and the beginning of a library, the churches will not, on the average, pay him any more salary than is given to a respectable clerk in a mercantile establishment, he is not able to see it to be his duty to consent to such injustice? Is it strange that he concludes that he has the same liberty as other men, to employ his talents and his acquisitions in such a way that he may reap the fruits of his industry and toil? Say that it would be wise in him to commit himself to Christ, and leave the matter of recompense to him; but this does not relieve the wrong, on the part of the churches, of wishing ministers to serve them without reasonable compensation; and, further, when young men are called to decide the question of their future course, they are commonly *young* in Christian experience, as well as years. They can not be expected to take such views of the subject as might be taken by one who had attained to the highest life of Christian faith. It is clear that the members of the churches must be willing to share the burdens and self-sacrifices of the ministry, and must honestly and fairly do what they can to diminish these, if they will have the service of the young men whom God has endowed with the choicest gifts in the pastoral work. They can not expect, and ought not to expect, if they are not willing to do this, that the gifted sons of Christian parents will be eager to give themselves to the sacred office.

7. Let us add, still further, more systematic and faithful effort should be made *to enkindle in the churches, and especially in the children of the churches, a heartier love for the simple worship and admirable polity* from which we have derived such precious spiritual benefits.

That there has been great neglect among us in respect to transmitting the views and spirit of the fathers to the children, there is no need, we suppose, to prove. For the last fifty years or more, pastors and churches, colleges and theological seminaries, appear to have bestowed very little direct attention on the matter. No provision has been made in the theological curriculum for thorough instruction as to the history, the principles, and the practical advantages of our church order. While our simple forms admit of being made — *all the more from their simplicity* — pleasing to a healthful taste, attractive to the heart, and solemnly impressive, they have been too often made to appear barren and uninviting, by a careless, slovenly, and perfunctory manner, in the administrations of God's house. It has seemed to be too much forgotten, in the leading of the praise and worship of the public assembly, and in the administration of Christian ordinances, that with these things should always be associated a sacred comeliness and grace, so that it should be felt by all, that, as in the days of old, strength and beauty conjoined were in the sanctuary. The result of these things has obviously been some degree, at least, of decay of interest in our distinguishing peculiarities, of which others have been, and are now, ready to take advantage; and some of Puritan descent have been led to place themselves again under the same systems of ecclesiastical authority from which it cost their liberty-loving ancestors long struggles, and, in many instances, sufferings unto death, to break away.

Plainly, then, it is high time that a new interest in this subject were awakened. Are our ecclesiastical principles, as a denomination, true, scriptural, and of great practical importance? Were they *worth* contending for, when for them so many of our venerated forefathers wore out their best years in filthy prisons, or went to barbarous deaths to vindicate them for the sake of their posterity? Then are we recreant and degenerate, indeed, if we fail to teach them to our children from their early years, and to hold them dear to our own hearts. While writing these pages, it has been stated to us that it has become a common practice in a section of New England to send to the theological institutions of another denomination for students to supply, during their vacations, destitute churches. We trust there may be some mistake in this singular statement; and yet such an occurrence might not seem an altogether improbable illustration of the indifference which has silently stolen over us. Surely there is need to revive the spirit of John Robinson, of Shepard, Hooker, and Davenport. We must reassert their principles. They should be inculcated at the fireside. They should be taught in the pulpit. They should be embodied in popular tracts, and sown all over the land. Especially should every theological institution have a professorship, or at least a lectureship, which should thoroughly discuss them; and every theological student should be required, as one of the conditions of licensure to show himself able and willing to defend them. When there shall be such a revival of the spirit, and such a return to the principles, of the men to whom, under God, we owe our best religious blessings, we may expect to have a ministry adapted to our wants as lovers of the largest healthful religious freedom.

8. Finally: the committee will only suggest further, that, in view of the existing and the prospective necessities of the churches, as regards the ministry, it becomes an urgent duty *to labor and pray more earnestly for the conversion of young men.*

"Pray ye the Lord of the harvest that he will send forth laborers," said our blessed Lord. Pastors and teachers were among the gifts which, at his ascension, he received power to bestow on men; and these, like other gifts, are dispensed under the law of prayer. The hinderances to piety in the case of young men are, at this time and in a country such as ours, so very great, that unless direct and special effort is made for their early conversion, and that with strength of faith and persistency of prayer on their behalf, we can not expect to see them devoting their lives from the outset unto God. It is needful to call attention *very frequently* to this matter. Especially in connection with the observance of the annual day of prayer for colleges should the whole subject of the early conversion of young men, in all its interesting relations, be set faithfully before the churches. Such a solicitude in respect to this should be kept alive in the hearts of all who are engaged in the instruction of young men, as shall lead them to propose it distinctly to themselves, as an essential part of the best education of the precious sons of the church, to win their hearts to Christ. Every thing, in a word, that *can* be done, should be done diligently and on system, to bring those especially who are pursuing courses of liberal study under the full influence of Christian truth. No college officer should feel that he is doing his whole duty if he is not striving to accomplish this. Revivals of religion in our churches and our colleges, so deep and powerful in their effects that far greater numbers than have hitherto been reached may be gathered unto God, should be desired and sought with an earnestness that will not be denied. If the measure of God's bestowment, both in the light of reason and the Scriptures, is seen to be — *according to your faith be it unto you* — there should be a new kindling-up of holy confidence in Christ, the Head of the church and the dispenser of all grace, — a new spirit of intercession for the sending forth of the Holy Ghost to renew unto repentance and Christian life the choicest of our sons, and a deeper and more general consecration, on the part of Christian parents, of their children to the work of the gospel ministry. When fathers and mothers plead, and the united churches plead, and a faithful ministry plead, — when the hearts of all Christ's servants are set on the consecration of the brightest jewels of their households unto God, — we need not doubt that divine power will indeed work wonders, and that the ranks of the ministry will find a multitude prepared to enter them. It is not enough that we know this and say it; in good earnest we must ACT AS IF OUR INMOST HEARTS BELIEVED IT. There is no need to enlarge on this.

CONCLUDING REMARKS.

The committee have thus endeavored, so far as they were able, to bring the more important aspects of the great subject referred to them to the notice of the Council. They have not deemed it becoming in them to indicate the particular action to be taken by this body. They have supposed that this should be left to be determined by the Council itself, after full discussion had. They can not doubt that it will seem to the fathers and brethren here assembled, that such measures should be adopted by those representing the churches here, in regard to a matter so vitally connected with our entire religious system, as will secure the inauguration of a new era in our history, and lead speedily to the attainment of the desired practical results. The urgency of our need and of the time forbids delay, and demands that something effectual be done. Whatever difficulties attend the subject, it calls us to face them without flinching, and promptly, as ministers and churches, to address ourselves to the work which God is imposing on us. By some it has been suggested that a plan be devised to induce each self-sustaining church to pledge itself to secure the education of a number of young men *at least equal to the number of ministers required for its own supply;* since any church failing to do so much as this, in fact, enjoys its ministry at the expense, in part or altogether, of other churches. Some have suggested, also, the creation of a *Bureau of Clerical Education*, at the head of which should be placed one of the wisest, ablest, and most practical men to be found among our pastors, who should devote his best and undivided energies to the work of stimulating, enlightening, and guiding the efforts of the churches, and setting forward, in all practicable ways, and throughout the whole country, the momentous work that is needful to be done. The Society for the promotion of Collegiate Education at the West has contributed largely, by its wise and efficient action, to the supply of an educated ministry in that vast opening region, where the present and prospective need is greatest. To that society, vigorously sustained, we must look for yet greater results in the era that now opens. It may be possible for the Council to give some new impulse to the action of this noble society. The committee may, perhaps, offer a brief supplementary report, with special reference to this. Other methods will, doubtless, be suggested by the wisdom of this body.

Let, then, the Council determine that the things which, it has been seen, we are as churches called to do, shall resolutely be done. Let them indicate the course to be pursued, and take the initiative at once. Not a day is to be lost. We are like men standing on the shore when the flood-tide is sweeping in; we must move forward, or be overwhelmed. The well-being of our churches is waiting on us. The cause of true religion in our land is waiting on us. The salvation of our country, which the blessed gospel alone can save, is waiting on us. The providence of God itself is waiting on us. Here, for a century to come, and much longer, it may be, must be waged, between the kingdom of Christ and that of the prince of darkness, a mighty moral conflict which shall be as the great battle of Armageddon, and will involve results which our thought endeavors in vain to grasp. If, in past years, our hearts have been stirred at the consideration of the work which we saw before us and our children, much more should we now be aroused to comprehend the greatness, the sublimity, of the coming struggle, and to address ourselves to it with manly earnestness and in the strength of God. Let our faith be firm, that he who hath carried us successfully through the perils, blood, and tears of the stupendous war just closed, — who has placed four millions of freedmen within the reach of Christian influence, — who has caused our glorious flag — more glorious now than ever — to float peacefully over the whole land, so that every part is open to the gospel, — will crown with his abundant blessing the efforts of his servants to make Christianity here triumphant, to the exaltation and happiness of this great people. If now we show ourselves equal to the crisis, our country, *powerful*, *regenerate*, *and free*, shall also stand, for coming ages, illustrious, among the nations, as THE HOME OF INTELLIGENCE, VIRTUE, AND RELIGION.

RAY PALMER,
FRANKLIN W. FISK, } *Committee.*
JOHN P. GULLIVER,

At twelve o'clock, the reading of the above paper was suspended, for the purpose of calling the roll, which was read over and corrected.

Rev. Dr. Kirk, of Massachusetts, read a list of persons to officiate in religious services to-morrow, in various Congregational churches in Boston and vicinity.

On motion of Rev. Dr. Wolcott, for the Business Committee,

Resolved, That a committee of five be appointed by this Council, to consider the subject of securing, for the permanent use of our denomination, a house of worship in the City of Washington; and, if they deem it expedient for the churches of our order to engage in such a movement, that the said committee be requested to report to this Council a plan for its accomplishment.

Rev. Mr. Langworthy, from the committee on Nominations, reported the following members, as the committee on the above subject: —

Henry C. Bowen, of New York; Dea. Charles Stoddard, of Massachusetts; Rev. Leonard Bacon, D. D., of Connecticut; Hon. Douglas Putnam, of Ohio; Hon. Samuel C. Pomeroy, of Kansas.

The report was adopted.

Rev. Mr. Quint, from the Business Committee, reported the following papers, with recommendation of reference, as follows: —

Papers regarding Lincoln College, presented by Hon. Mr. Pomeroy: to be referred to a special committee on collegiate education, hereafter to be appointed.

Memorial respecting civil government as an ordinance of God: to be referred to the committee on the state of the country.

Resolution respecting the declaration of faith, and the propriety of having a catechism: to be referred to the committee on the Declaration of Faith.

Communication respecting temperance: to be referred to a special committee on temperance, hereafter to be appointed.

Papers presented by Rev. Dr. Post, in regard to the church in Utah: to be referred to the committee on Evangelization in the West and South.

Communication prepared by Rev. Rufus W. Clark, respecting an American Protestant Assembly: to be referred to a special committee upon that subject, hereafter to be appointed.

Communication from California: to be referred to the committee on Evangelization in the West and South.

The recommendations were adopted.

It was also

Voted, That a special committee be appointed, who shall consider and report to this Council, what deliverance, if any, it ought to make on the subject of temperance.

CHURCH POLITY.

Rev. Mr. Langworthy, of the committee on Nominations, reported the name of Rev. Enoch F. Burr, of Connecticut, as an additional member of the committee on church polity.

The report was adopted.

The convention then adjourned, under the previous order, to meet at Charlestown, at three o'clock, P. M., in the First Congregational Church.

AFTERNOON SESSION.

In accordance with the vote of the Council yesterday the afternoon session was held in the First Church, Charlestown, to comply with the recommendation of the preliminary meeting of state committees, that a special service of devotion be held, "for the acknowledgment of the marvelous and merciful dealings of Almighty God with the nation, in connection with the war."

The chair was taken at three o'clock by Rev. Dr. Thompson, of New York, assistant moderator, who said: —

The hour has arrived to which the Council adjourned to meet in this place. In the absence of Gov. Buckingham, who has been called to Connecticut, and of Col. Hammond, who is elsewhere engaged, it devolves upon me to take the chair, though the general direction of the meeting will be in the hands of Dr. Adams, in behalf of the committee on devotional exercises. The Council will remember that we are now convened under a special order for "A service of devotion for the acknowledgment of the marvelous and merciful dealings of Almighty God with the nation, in connection with the war, and for supplicating a gracious dispensation of the Spirit of God upon the land, that our restored national unity may be consecrated in righteousness, and in the peace and joy of the Holy Ghost." Let us hear, then, the word of the Lord, as it is written in the 105th Psalm.

The 20th Psalm was also read, and a portion of the 12th chapter of Revelation.

The 1115th hymn was then sung, commencing, —

"Oh, God, beneath thy guiding hand,
Our exiled fathers crossed the sea,
And when they trod the wintry strand,
With prayer and psalm they worshiped thee."

Rev. Dr. ADAMS, of Maine. As Dr. Thompson has remarked that, after the introductory exercises, the general direction of the meeting will be left with myself, acting in behalf of the committee on devotional exercises, I will now fulfill my vocation, and give this direction to the meeting: it is left to itself. No provision, so far as I know, has been made for particular persons to speak. It is, as I understand it, a meeting for the free and spontaneous utterance of exultation one to another, and of desire in prayer to God; and the hope is, that the short time that we may spend together will be occupied, in very small portions, by a great number of individuals. Will Dr. Edward Beecher lead in prayer?

Rev. Dr. BEECHER, of Illinois. I wish to say one word before we unite in prayer. It is desirable that our devotions be not formal, but that they may be the simple expressions of the feelings of the heart. I presume there is no brother here who can not, in going back through the war, recall meetings in which, with his Congregational brethren, the burden of the nation was upon his soul. I recollect a meeting in Burlington, when the General Association of Iowa had appointed an hour for prayer. I was struck with the deep current of feeling there. It was like that expression which you will find in Romans, — "We know not what we should pray for as we ought, but the Spirit itself maketh intercession for us with groanings which can not be uttered." Our armies were then around Vicksburg, and soldiers from all the churches scattered around through that whole country were at that time engaged in deadly conflict, and we knew not what we should hear next. Who can tell what a depth of feeling there was then? — what a movement of the Holy Ghost?

Now, brethren, who of us is there who can go back during the time of the war and not remember some such scenes? Remember what burdens the providence of God laid upon us; remember with what intense anxiety we looked into the future, and remember what tides of emotion flowed through our souls; take your stand-point there, and think how we felt, how we prayed, how we wrestled, how we desired, how we longed, and with that state of feeling compare what we are now and where we are! Oh, what expressions of gratitude there ought to be! How our hearts should overflow! There is no language that can express what God hath done for us. So high, so deep, so long, so broad, so great are his mercies, that words can not utter them.

Take one other instance: our feelings at the time of the election. When, all over this land, we felt that it was possible the control of the interests of this nation might pass into the hands of such men as made the Chicago platform, that such a man as Vallandigham might be appointed minister of war, — then the voice of prayer went up from the church of God; and I believe that that election was as much controlled by prayer as any revival of religion ever was, — that there was as manifest an outpouring of the Spirit of God upon this nation. Let us go back and think with what deep emotions the triumph which we then achieved, in the providence of God, was received. How it filled our thoughts! We have become somewhat used to these things; but let us refresh the recollection in our minds, and wake up our souls to utterance, that the voice of prayer and praise and thanksgiving may go up to God as the real expression of the Congregational body. And, without intending to flatter, but simply intending to speak the truth, those who have lived in the Mississippi valley know, that with regard to this great movement of loyalty, that with regard to the great principles that have been brought up and impressed upon the government, the voice of our associations and the voice of our churches have always been in advance; that they have held up that principle, which has been carried out; and we ought to thank God that there is a record in regard to the position of our churches on these great questions, as they have come up, which we are not ashamed to read to-day. And let us thank God that the spirit of his Christ has been upon us, to enable us, in this hour, to be faithful to our God and to our country. Let us pray.

At the conclusion of the prayer, Rev. Dr. Todd, of Massachusetts, addressed the assembly. He said: —

I have a claim to a moment of the time of my brethren, which perhaps no other brother here has. When I came in at the door this afternoon, I found myself coming nearer and nearer the pulpit; and when I say that, in my boyhood, if I ever knew any thing about the religion of Christ and the mercy of the Redeemer, I learned it here; that on this spot I consecrated myself publicly, by uniting with this ancient church, and on this spot devoted myself to the work of the ministry, if the Master would accept me, you will understand why I did so. My memory goes back to the time when Jeremiah Evarts walked these aisles as one of the deacons of this church, and to the time when, later, Prof. Morse, the inventor of the telegraph, and his family were baptized. I recall the image of old Dea. Miller, whom President Monroe, when he came on to visit us, took with him as a guide, to tell him all about the battle; and in the course of his investigations, he said, "What about that, Mr. Miller?" — "What about that?" — and "What about this?" "Well," said the deacon, "Mr. President, I feel a little ashamed, that I can not tell you more, but the fact is, I was very busy on the day of Bunker Hill." [Laughter.] We have been so busy that we have hardly kept sight of the influences that have gone forth from this spot, this old mother of us all. Just before this church was organized, just before our fathers came here, there was a colony planted on the James River, and another colony here on the banks of the Charles River, that we have just crossed, — the principles of the two colonies differing entirely. The one sought to make the gospel free to all, — to build upon the foundation of the apostles and prophets, Jesus Christ himself being the chief corner-stone, — to make labor honorable to every man, and to establish the principle, that if any man would not work, neither should he eat. The other colony was planted on the principle, that if any man would eat, another should work for him and earn his bread. The principles of these two colonies have been in conflict from that day to this. They have struggled whenever and wherever they have met, and the result has been, as you know, dear brethren, that there was no end to the conflict, until at last we met upon the battle-field. The sons of New England here and throughout all the West accepted the issue, and we are met together this afternoon to congratulate ourselves and to thank God that the principles of the Charles River colony, the principles of the Puritan fathers, the principles of this ancient church, have prevailed, and the land is free — is puritanized, or will be puritanized, from one end to the other.

Our errand here is to meet before God; and no more suitable place could be selected than this sanctuary, where there has been much prayer offered, — from whence many noble saints have gone, whose influence, I hope and believe, has but just begun. Here, feeling that we can almost feel the warm breath of our fathers, — we meet to rejoice, to thank God, to take courage, and to go forth, dear brethren, feeling that we and our churches and our church polity and our nation now are joined to the plans of the great Redeemer; and wherever his chariot-wheels shall go, we shall be near them.

Rev. James B. Miles, pastor of the church, was then introduced. He said: —

Mr. Moderator, and Fathers and Brethren of this Congregational Council: — The committee of arrangements thought it fitting that the pastor of this church should say a word of welcome to the fathers and brothers who come up to this ancient shrine of liberty and of religion this afternoon. I might well shrink from the thought of occupying a single moment of the exceedingly precious time of this Congregational Council; but, fathers and brethren, if you will allow me a few moments at this time, you may feel assured that I shall not again, during the session of the Council, trespass upon your patience, unless I shall discover that you are in danger of departing from the soundness of the faith and from the order of the fathers. If, at any moment, I shall discover that, I shall feel bound, as one in the regular apostolic succession, to rise, and protest against any defection from the "faith once delivered to the saints," or any departure from the order of the primitive churches of New England.

I am oppressed with a sense of the inadequacy of any words that I can command, upon the impulse of the moment, to express the delight of these Christian men and women, the members of this old church in Charlestown, on welcoming you to our church edifice this afternoon. In the name of all these devoted men and women, I welcome you to this hallowed spot at this hour. Yea, in the name of all the churches in the immediate neighborhood of this city of Charlestown, who have honored me by sending me as their delegate to this Council, I welcome you to Harvard Hill, this afternoon. Yea, in the name of the sons of Bunker Hill, without distinction of sect, who are here, crowding these galleries and the side-slips of the church, I welcome you to this renowned historic city. For, fathers and brethren, these Christian men and women, these sons of Bunker Hill, have already, over in the city of Boston, felt the spell of your fervid eloquence; they have heard the expressions of your devoted love of country; and they have heard those eloquent, those warm words of salutation, and those expressions of love for America, that have fallen from the lips of our distinguished and reverend brethren who have come to us from the good old mother-country, from England, from France, and from Canada, — and they welcome you all, with hearts full of gladness and joy, to Bunker Hill this afternoon. Would that it were in my power, Mr. Moderator, to reciprocate, adequately, these expressions of fellowship and love. Standing on this hallowed spot, — the most sacred spot, I believe, on this continent, — I desire to take you by the hand, and to extend, through you, to the members of this Council, to these brethren from the regions beyond the Hudson River, who have come to us from the great West, — to these brethren from Tennessee, and from Maryland, and from Delaware, and from the Pacific Coast, — to these fathers and brethren who have come to us from the mother-country, from France, and from Canada, — to all the brethren who are in this Council, I wish, through you, sir, to extend this right hand of Christian fellowship, and to welcome you all, and all the churches you represent, to this old home of Puritanism, of Congregationalism, and of Republicanism. [Loud applause.]

America's great statesman and orator, when standing on Plymouth Rock, said, "The genius of the place awes and inspires us;" and we, brethren, may feel that the genius of this place awes and inspires us. Reminiscences, I must not speak of. They crowd into my mind, and I should occupy all the time appropriated to this meeting, were I to enter upon them. Suffice it to say, that, two hundred and thirty-five years ago, that noble and sainted man, John Winthrop, — a nobler Christian, I believe, has rarely lived than he, — and his companions, immediately after landing, bowed, in worship and reverence, before Almighty God, under the spreading branches of an oak-tree that stood upon this hill; and ever since that hour, with the exception of about three years, when the town was burned, at the time of the attack upon it by the British, the worship of Almighty God has been continued on this spot, without interruption, and Christian men and women have come up hither to pay their vows to the Most High. Christ and Him crucified have been preached here. And let me say to you, who love our Congregational polity, that you see, I believe, in the perpetuity of this church down to the present time, through all the mutations of states and empires, an illustration of the nobility, of the sublimity, of our simple Congregational church polity. Upon this spot a pure, Christian republic has been maintained, from that hour down to the present; and though convulsions have shaken the nation, though the house of worship in which the Christians met was burned, yet the bush was not consumed. The members of the church were obliged to disperse, but the church lived, and when it was safe to return to their desolate homes, they came back to this hill, and here, in a rude block-house, erected by the enemy, they celebrated the dying love of their Lord Jesus Christ. Down to the present hour, without any other interruption, the worship of God has been maintained here. The faithfulness of Almighty God, — this church is a monument of that; the nobility, the sublimity of simple republican Congregational church government, — this church bears eloquent testimony to that.

Now, beloved fathers and brethren, we have come together on this spot, to-day, — on this proud, high day for the sons of Bunker Hill; for this is our patriotic and religious anniversary. You see the stars and stripes floating from these flag-staffs, — you hear the strains of martial music; it is a proud, high day for the sons of Bunker Hill; and we welcome you with joy on this day, praising and blessing Almighty God, that that independence which, ninety years ago, was practically achieved by the battle on the eminence yonder, has been maintained, that those precious rights and privileges and institutions have been rescued and preserved, and we come together with joy, that we may praise Almighty God, who has wrought this great deliverance for us.

My friends, after a few moments, you will be invited, by the president of the Bunker Hill Monument Association, to look upon that shaft, which uplifts its form in majesty on yonder eminence; and I beseech you, as you look upon its uninscribed surface, to look intently, and see if you can not read an inscription there. You may not discover any at first; but we, who live beneath its shadow, and daily look upon it, in its majesty, and in its simple, plain beauty and grandeur, read many inscriptions there; we have read many during the past eventful four years. Sometimes, when have come to us the sad tidings that our sons and brothers have been slain by hundreds upon the battle-field, and the hearts of mothers, fathers, and brothers, have sunk within them, — then, through our tears, we have looked at that plain, but noble, shaft, and while we have read lamentation and weeping and mourning inscribed there, yet, on looking a little longer, there have come out, clear and legible, the inspiring words, "Liberty and Union, now and forever, one and inseparable!" [Applause.] When the hearts of strong men failed, when rebels were insolent and boastful, when our noble heroes were driven back upon the battle-field, and people all about were saying, "It may be, that our government must fall," we have looked at that noble shaft, to see if it trembled or tottered, — but firm and immovable has it stood, and its language has been, "Liberty and Union, now and forever, one and inseparable!" And when the saddest of all tidings came to us over the wires, "Abraham Lincoln, president of the United States, has been assassinated," and this whole community was crushed down, as if by a blow of the Almighty, we looked through our fast-streaming tears, and we saw the same inscription. Though the shaft seemed to be clad in deepest mourning, we could yet distinctly read, "Liberty and Union, now and forever, one and inseparable!" And to-day, as the bright and glorious morning of peace dawns, — as our heroes, the sons of Bunker Hill, who have fought shoulder to shoulder with the noble and brave heroes of New England, of the West, and of all the loyal States, are returning to their homes, and we are wreathing their brows with chaplets of undying honor, — to-day, I say, as you go up on that eminence, and look upon that shaft, methinks you will see this inscription, having taken upon itself new luster and beauty, and shining with dazzling glory, — "LIBERTY AND UNION, NOW AND FOREVER, ONE AND INSEPARABLE!" [Loud applause.]

We are glad to welcome the representatives of old Mother England — good Mother England. With all her faults, we love her still; and we feel that they need not have any unpleasant feelings to-day, as they stand upon that spot. It is true, that, ninety years ago, Old England and Young America met in dire and deadly conflict there; but it was only a misunderstanding between mother and daughter. Mother loved daughter too well, and was not willing that daughter should depart from her care and watchfulness, and daughter felt that she had reached the period of womanhood, and could be her own mistress. So there was a misunderstanding, — a falling-out, — and daughter prevailed. We will not be particular to say we won a great victory there, for the champions of the mother-country say it was a defeat for us. We admit, it was a defeat for us; but we add, with a great deal of confidence and gratification, that it was one of those defeats which is better than a victory; and the immortal Daniel Webster, who stands, in enduring bronze, in front of our State Capitol at this hour, said, "All that is noble and valuable in the independence of America was bound up in that battle of Bunker Hill. When the sun of that day went down, the independence of America was decided." It was a decisive battle; but we welcome the representatives of old Mother England to-day. We welcome the representatives of France. FRANCE! — we speak her name with joy, as we think of Bunker Hill; for the illustrious and immortal Gen. Lafayette, in 1825, on stepping upon that spot, said, "I feel a profound reverence, as I tread upon this hallowed ground." We owe a debt of gratitude to Gen. Lafayette. We feel kindly toward France; we welcome her messengers and representatives to Bunker Hill. We welcome all to Bunker Hill, — to its noble associations.

But, dear brethren and fathers, I must not protract these remarks. I will simply say, that, as I look over this congregation, and the thought occurs to me of what is represented here, — three thousand churches on this continent, and as many more in other countries, — a vision of glory comes before my mind. You know, that some of the ablest astronomers feel and believe that there is one central body or point in the system of the universe, and that all the fixed stars, and the milky way, even, revolve round that one central point, receive their law from it, and are controlled by it. I say, it is a grand and surpassingly sublime conception, giving us noble ideas of God, who, in wisdom, has made this universe. But, as I look over this assembly, and remember of what it is composed, a sublimer vision is before my mind, — a more transcendent and surpassingly noble conception; and that is, of individual Christian churches, of the same faith and order as this, — "one faith, one Lord, one baptism," — scattered over our land, and, in the progress of pure Christianity and of republican principles, destined to prevail through the length and breadth of the land, — all over the South, as well as New England and the West; and when I think that, in the progress of the simple faith of the New Testament, these churches are to be established, not only on this great continent, but all over the world, and look upon them as independent bodies, they seem to me to be revolving about one central point, — one central sun, — and that is, the Sun of Righteousness, — the Lord Jesus Christ. No sovereignty but the sovereignty of Jesus. That central point is not Pope Pius the Ninth, nor any pope, but the Lord Jesus. All stand upon the same level. "One is your Master, even Christ, and all ye are brethren." And my prayer is, that "the baptism of the Holy Ghost, sent down from heaven," may come down upon us; that Jesus may come down into our hearts; that we may go from this place with a new baptism, ready to labor, to spend and be spent for Jesus; so that the day may speedily come, when there shall be neither Englishman nor American, neither Frenchman nor Canadian, neither Northern man nor Southern man, neither bond nor free, but Christ shall be all in all. May God hasten that great and glorious consummation, and honor us as the instruments of its accomplishment, and praise shall be to His name for ever!

The 1038th hymn (Sabbath Hymn Book) was then sung, commencing: —

"Oh, where are kings and empires now,
Of old that went and came?
But Lord, thy church is praying yet,
A thousand years the same."

Rev. Dr. Adams, of Maine. I was reminded by the first verse of the hymn, as well as by the remarks of Dr. Todd, of some reminiscences connected with this church. Dr. Todd's claim to prominence here is greater than mine in one particular, for he says he was born again on this spot. Mine is greater than his in another, for I was here before his time. Nearly fifty years ago, I sat in this house with my venerable father and mother, who are long since dead; my father's brothers, prominent men in this congregation, also long since dead; Jeremiah Evarts, before he was deacon; Dea. Miller and Dea. Frothingham, then old men. The Sabbath school connected with this church was established mainly by the concurrent efforts of Jeremiah Evarts and my own father. We have these personal reminiscences, which it is almost impertinent to mention, and yet they mingle in well perhaps with those higher considerations to which reference has been made.

Rev. Milton Badger, D. D., of New York, then led in prayer.

THE MODERATOR. Although in strictness, the hour assigned for this service has expired, yet, if some brother, from the East or the West will speak in brief, earnest words, or will offer up brief, earnest prayer, I am sure that another half hour can be spent with pleasure and profit. You have the largest liberty of a Congregational prayer-meeting.

Rev. Dr. BUDINGTON, of New York. I can not claim the right to speak here, as my friend and brother Dr. Todd does, for I am younger than he is, and have no right to claim the attention of this honored body; and yet, as the tone of remark hitherto has been in the way of reminiscence, perhaps I shall be pardoned for expressing the feeling that pervades my soul at this moment. I think there is no spot on this continent, all things considered, where a Congregational Christian should be more deeply impressed than on this. Next to Plymouth Rock in political significance, this is most important; and it seems to me, that standing where we do to-day, between the heroic past and that future for the contemplation of which and for the preparation for which we are assembled in Council, it is a solemn moment. It is now ninety years since the flames of war and devastation swept over this devoted place, and the steeple of this church fell foremost among the dwellings over which it had been guardian and sentinel; emblem of the fact that it was the Christianity of New England that met the foe at the outset, and emblem of the fact that I believe will characterize the history of this country to the last, that with the church of God will stand, and with the church of God will fall, this republic. [A voice — "It will never fall!"] Never! Half of the republic has fallen, because the church first apostatized and fell with it. We must remember to-day, that half of this country would never have presented at this hour a spectacle for men and for angels such as was never given to them before since Adam stood in Paradise, but for the fact that our brethren in the faith, ministers who officiated at the altars of God, forsook the truth of the gospel, trampled upon the rights of humanity, and when the hearts of their fellow-citizens were rightfully shrinking back from the impending conflict, goaded them forward, and madly plunged them into the abyss of ruin. [Cries of "Shame! Shame!"] Near my residence in Brooklyn, the other day, one of the truth-speaking ministers from Tennessee rose up in the General Assembly and said that, in the view of every loyal Christian man in East Tennessee, every minister of the gospel there came before them with the blood of at least twelve of their martyred sons staining their hands; and, said he, "It is the unanimous declaration of all our people, never, *never*, NEVER will we listen to the word of God from their lips again; never shall our children look up to them as shepherds of the flock." [Loud applause.]

Well, I recur to the remark that I made: Brethren, it depends upon us, it depends upon the Spirit of God in our hearts, it depends upon our fellow-Christians and the Spirit of God in their hearts, what the church in this country is to be, and I am thankful to stand here, as I never expected to stand, on the spot of my youthful ordination. Here, five and twenty years ago, last April, I received the charge of this people, and for fifteen of those years I ministered to them in the name of God. Here I took up the blessed, the holy sacramental furniture from this table, — furniture which was borne aloft in the hands of that man of God whose name has been mentioned through the fire and the storm of bullets in this town, and then brought back again with the return of peace, — bearing, upon the solid silver, names that are memorable alike in our church and in our state, — names that take us back to the days of Winthrop, — names that are baptized with the blood and tears that made us a nation. I am glad to stand here with you, my brethren, for it seems to me that, standing on this soil, we imbibe something of that spirit which I believe in God is the only spirit which is to make us faithful and successful ministers of the Lord Jesus Christ. This hill is consecrated to the memory of suffering. When our fathers came here they were called upon to suffer in as large proportion as fell upon their sons on Bunker Hill, or the more fatal fields of the South and the South-west. They *died* in laying the foundations of this church and this State, and we are assembled to-day over their forgotten graves. John Harvard, who gave his name to yonder University, was buried here, and when that storm swept over the town, it buried his humble memorial so that "no man knoweth unto this day his place of sepulture." This town was buried in the terrible struggle that gave birth to the nation, and between 1861 and 1865, the sons of this town have been just as prominent in the war of redemption, as it may well be called, as their fathers were in that war of revolution — the war of our birth-pangs.

My dear friends, we are standing midway between the heroic past and the grand future, — a solemn tie of connection between our dead Puritan fathers and the mighty hosts of God who, in their intelligent and hearty reception of those Puritan principles, are to spread them to the Pacific shores, and down through all the ages of time to come; and I believe that the influences of this day are to tell largely upon the faithfulness with which that work is accomplished.

President Andrews, of Ohio. As you have invited speakers from the West, sir, allow me to say, that as I heard this morning the firing of guns and crackers, and the ringing of bells, I asked my host the meaning of it, and he said, "It is the 17th of June;" and in my simplicity, I said, "What is the 17th of June?" [Laughter.] He told me it was an anniversary. "Then," said I, "It is like the 7th of April." On the 7th of April, 1788, there landed upon the banks of the Muskingum, a colony formed in Massachusetts, and headed by an old General of the Revolution, composed of revolutionary officers who had lost their property in the war, and who went to the West to build themselves new homes. It has been my lot to labor for twenty-five years in that Plymouth of the West, where the first landing was made, and my home is the old capital of the North-west Territory, where the first Governor had his residence, where the first courts were held, and where the first laws were enacted; and this 17th of June is like the 7th of April, for we celebrate that day.

It gives me great pleasure to come back to New England, to meet these brethren, and to feel that it has been my lot, for a quarter of a century, to endeavor to establish, and to carry out the principles of New England, in a literary institution which lies nearer the equator than any other founded after the New England model; and I rejoice to know that the same principles, which those brethren carried from this place, are there yet; that the descendants of those old sires are there yet; that there was established the first Congregational church in the West, and that we worship in an edifice that was built at the very beginning of the century. It is pleasant for me to reciprocate these words of kind feeling, and I believe that, as the result of this National Council, those of us who have come up from the West and from the South-west, — who have been laboring to establish these principles which you love, and this polity which you revere, — will go back, to labor more zealously, more faithfully, feeling better assured, I may say, of the commendation, of the encouragement, of the heartfelt love of our brethren of New England, than we have sometimes felt.

My brethren, I can not forget that, thirty years ago, in Massachusetts, in the same class-room with me, in one of your colleges, there sat two men, who have made themselves men of mark. One of them preached that memorable sermon at New Orleans, on Thanksgiving Day, in 1860, in which he made the declaration, that the mission of the South was, to conserve and extend slavery; and the other has been, for two years, in Toronto, and the evidence brought out on the assassination trial brings in his name in connection with that detestable scheme to introduce the yellow fever into the United States. These men, I am thankful to be able to say, were not members of our communion. Perhaps they might have been, and perhaps they might have done as they have done if they had been; but, I thank God, they were not.

Rev. Mr. Gaylord, of Nebraska. As the West has been invited to take part in these services, as well as the East, I desire to say a few words. I will take but a moment or two simply to say to you, brethren and friends, that I come from about the center of the United States, — from the banks of one of those great rivers that reach from north to south, across the entire country; and I rejoice to say to you, that the same principles which were planted here in the early history of our country, are being transplanted, not only across the "Father of Waters," but also across the "Big Muddy," — for that is the familiar name by which the Missouri River is known among us. As we stand upon the banks of that river, there are some suggestive thoughts that rush upon our minds. As we look down to the landing, and see, as we did last year, the men of Wisconsin and Minnesota, from Lacrosse, all the way down to St. Louis, and then up the Missouri River, a distance of twenty-six hundred miles, to Fort Benton, at the head of navigation, on their way to the Rocky Mountains, we have some little conception of the vastness of our great western country. And then, as we look off toward the setting sun, away up that valley of which you have so often heard, coming down, as it does, for a distance of more than six hundred miles, in an almost easterly direction, from the Rocky Mountains, — a valley which is the great thoroughfare of travel and of commerce across the continent, and up which the iron horse is already preparing to go forth, bearing the civilization and the population of this part of the continent across the Rocky Mountains to the Pacific States, — I say, when we look out upon those vast stretches, they open up before the mind the greatness of the work which devolves upon the church, demanding her energies and her activity in this day of miracles and of wonders; and we feel that there is laid to the hands of the American church a work such as no people and no nation has ever before been invited to perform. But I will not dwell upon this.

THE MODERATOR. It has been thought necessary to draw this meeting to a conclusion now, by singing the 1111th hymn.

This familiar hymn, "God bless our native land," &c., was then sung, after which prayer was offered by Rev. Dr. Bacon.

Rev. Mr. Miles then said: —

You will remember that a certain high functionary in what was called the "Southern Confederacy," once promised, with a great deal of assurance, that he would call the roll of his slaves in the shadow of Bunker Hill. I have the pleasure of introducing to you, Hon. GEO. WASHINGTON WARREN, President of the Bunker Hill Monument Association, who will conduct you to that spot.

Dr. KIRK, of Massachusetts. Mr. Toombs is not there, — is he?

Mr. MILES. I will say, that the president of the association and myself reside near that locality, and we are not aware that that promise has been fulfilled. We presume that it has not; and such are the circumstances of the country to-day, that we have good reason to believe it never will be fulfilled. Men very often promise what they do not perform.

Dr. BACON, of Connecticut. I trust we shall not adjourn here, but proceed from this place to Bunker Hill, and make our adjournment there.

Rev. Dr. KIRK, of Massachusetts. With the doxology.

Hon. G. W. Warren then addressed the Council, as follows: —

Mr. Moderator and Gentlemen of the Congregational Council: — I am happy to do my humble part in welcoming so honored a body to these interesting scenes. You are here assembled, as you have been told, in the house of worship of the first church of Massachusetts Bay, — here, where Winthrop and his associates first gathered their flock together, and from whence they afterward went to constitute the first church of Boston. From this place, too, and about forty years thereafter, was formed the Old South Church, in Boston, in whose temple your convention was organized. Here was the scene of trial, where sickness and suffering, for many a long and dreary day, thinned the number of those devoted pilgrims who first landed and formed a settlement upon the banks of the Charles. This hill, and the fields below, were strewed with the graves of our forefathers. They brought here the two grand principles which have molded us into a great and flourishing country: the principle of the separation of Church and State, and the principle of Congregationalism, — of the independence of each individual church and society. These were the principles which they maintained and these principles were the foundation of our republic. "*Hic*, HIC, *cunabula gentis*." [Applause.] You do well to go from here in a body, without adjournment, to that other mount of sacrifice, which, no less than this hill, and in the same spirit of devotion, has made Charlestown immortal. There you will behold the monument erected by the children of those men of the Revolution who staked their lives and their honor for the doctrines of the Declaration of American Independence, which that battle ushered in. You will see, sir, in that monument, not an Egyptian obelisk, — not a monolith, hewn out of the solid rock, by the labor of an oppressed people; but you will observe many massive stones, welded together into one graceful shaft, reminding you of the "*E Pluribus Unum*," and of that conglomerated body which we love to call the people of the United States of America. [Loud applause.] That monument was erected by the voluntary efforts and subscriptions of the people from every part of the United States. Every one of those here present has an interest in it; and I am glad that the East and the West are come together to-day, to join in heartfelt and devout recognition of the services rendered by our fathers on that spot, and also of the heroic services rendered by our sons in defence of the principles there first maintained. [Applause.] I trust you will not complain of the heat of this day in that visit. It was, sir, about this hour, and, as history informs us, on the hottest day of the season, that the Battle of Bunker Hill was fought. And, more than all, it was on Saturday, — this very day of the week, — and ninety years ago to-day, that that memorable action took place. [Applause.] It will give me great pleasure to conduct you to Bunker Hill, from the top of which you will observe a beautiful panorama, exhibiting the growing prosperity of the metropolis and its environs, and many of our national flags waving in the skies, on this day of triumph, vying with the many spires built by a church-going people, in grateful recognition of their dependence upon Heaven for its continued blessing upon our common country.

Rev. Dr. THOMPSON, of New York. In the name of the Council, I cordially accept this courteous invitation, and thank you, sir, for the privilege of enjoying such heroic and memorable associations. Indeed, it is a special felicity that this service, which was contemplated six months ago, in our preliminary conference, "in special acknowledgment of the marvelous and merciful dealings of Almighty God with us as a nation, in connection with the war," should have brought us to-day into harmony with your commemorative anniversary, on this historic ground. We are thus carried back through all the period of the ninety years since that 17th of June when our national independence was virtually proclaimed upon this hill. Indeed, sir, in these past four years, we have been living through all those ninety years, and not only so, — there have been moments in which we have seemed to live through all the centuries that are gone, — to live over again in our own experience all that was great and heroic and memorable in the past, — and to see all that was grand and merciful in the illustrative providence of God repeated before our eyes. But especially have we felt ourselves linked with the heroic men who here fought and died for liberty. We have felt their blood tingling through our veins and kindling our hearts in this new conflict for the life of the nation and for the rights of man. We will go with you gladly, sir. We, who are the sons of Bunker Hill, the representatives of the principles of the original founders of Charlestown, the representatives of the principles of the heroic defenders of independence and nationality here, coming up from all this broad land, — we will go with you gladly to visit that spot where they made the first stand for that independence which God has honored and maintained, not only against foreign foes, but against the severer trial of internal rebellion. And as we go, there will go with us another and a mightier host, — that invisible host of their followers, who, like them, not counting their own lives dear unto themselves, were willing to give up all for the life of the nation, that God has given us again through them. We go with that invisible host to gather around that silent finger-post of the heroic past, which ever points upward to the God of our fathers, — the God of their children and their children's children, from generation to generation. [Applause.]

The Council then formed in procession, and, escorted by the President of the Monument Association, marched to Bunker Hill, where Mr. Warren gave an interesting account of the events of the ever-memorable 17th of June, 1775, and pointed out the various localities to which special interest is attached from their connection with the great battle of that day. At the close of this explanation, the moderator said: —

Brethren of the Council, — We are honored with an invitation from Admiral Stringham, who has done good service to the country in its time of peril, to visit the Navy Yard. It has been suggested, however, that it would be better for us to bring our session, as a Council, to a close on this spot; and with renewed thanks to our kind friend, Judge Warren, for the instructive and interesting explanation he has given us of its memorable scenes, and following out the suggestion made in the church, I would request you to unite in singing the first stanza of the familiar hymn, "My country, 'tis of thee," &c., and we will close with the Doxology, in long meter.

At the conclusion of the singing, it was, on motion of Dea. Stoddard, of Massachusetts, —

Voted, That the Council adjourn to meet in the Mount Vernon Church, Boston, on Monday morning, at nine o'clock.

Rev. Dr. Hopkins, of Massachusetts, then pronounced the benediction.

FIFTH DAY, MONDAY, JUNE 19.

In the absence of the moderator, the meeting was called to order by Hon. C. G. Hammond, first assistant moderator, and was opened with prayer by Rev. Dr. Thompson, of New York.

The journal of yesterday was read by the scribe, and approved.

Rev. Dr. Thompson, of New York, resigned his place upon the committee on Evangelization in the West and South, and his resignation was accepted.

Rev. Dr. Wolcott, of Ohio, in behalf of the Business Committee, reported the order of business for the day. The report was adopted.

Also, the following resolution: —

Resolved, That the committee to whom was referred the Declaration of Faith be instructed to report to the Council one or more samples of a creed for the use of churches for doctrinal and not for controversial purposes, embodying as far as may be, in the language of the Scriptures, the leading doctrines thereof as held by all Congregational churches.

On motion, the resolution was laid upon the table.

Rev. Mr. Marvin, of Massachusetts, moved that the order in reference to filling vacancies in the Council be taken from the table.

The motion was not agreed to.

Rev. Dr. Palmer, of New York, resumed and concluded the reading of the report on Ministerial Education, contained in yesterday's proceedings. Referred under the rule.

On motion of Rev. Dr. Todd, of Massachusetts,

Resolved, That the Council render thanks to Rev. Dr. Sturtevant for the sermon preached at the opening of the Convention, and request a copy for publication.

On motion of Rev. Mr. Langworthy, on behalf of the committee on nominations, Rev. George Darling, of Ohio, was added to the committee on the roll.

CHURCH BUILDING.

Rev. J. E. Roy, of Illinois, read the following paper, which was then referred under the rule: —

The first instance in this country of aid in building a meeting-house was that when the Pilgrim Church made its first contribution for any object outside of its own wants to assist the Second Congregational Church of America in erecting its house of worship. The example thus set has been followed in many individual cases since. But the enterprise, as a systematic policy, was inaugurated in 1852, by the Albany Convention. When, in that assembly, the brethren of the East perceived the grace that was given unto the churches of the West in the inheritance of the Faith and Order of the Apostles and Puritans, they gave unto them the right hands of fellowship ; and, as a token of affection, animated by the magnificent proffer of the mover of the project, they resolved to put into those right hands the sum of fifty thousand dollars to aid those churches in the erection of sanctuaries. Upon the same Sabbath day, under an impulse of love, as when of old the people brought more than enough for the service of the sanctuary, this offering of sympathy produced an overplus of eleven thousand eight hundred and ninety-one dollars. That fund aided two hundred and thirty missionary churches in building houses of worship.

So blessed were the results of that ministration of charity, and so great was the pressure for additional aid of this kind, that a second offering was called for on Forefathers' Day in 1856. It was a pious effort to build a monument in memory of the Pilgrims, not in a single pile of elaborate architecture, but in sanctuaries that should perpetuate their spirit and their principles. This effort resulted in a collection of about ten thousand dollars, by which about forty feeble churches were helped to homes. Conviction was now confirmed of the need of some organic method in this business. Whereupon the Congregational Union, according to a provision in its constitution, to wit, — "to promote plans of co-operation in building meeting-houses and parsonages," — assumed superintendence of the work, under the care of its board of trustees and of its secretary, who has prosecuted this enterprise with such wisdom, tact, and zeal as entitle him to the grateful confidence of the supporters of that institution and to the affectionate esteem of its hundreds of beneficiary churches. Under these auspices, during the eight years past, — and those the years of our financial revulsion and of our all-engrossing war, — the "Union," while meeting the difficulties and the prejudices incident to its newness, has raised the sum of sixty-five thousand four hundred and seven dollars, and has aided therewith in building one hundred and fifty-seven churches, an average of twenty per year, while the "Union" is now pledged to thirty-two more, for which the money is in hand. Thus that which was originated in an impulse of fellowship has been transferred into an institution; the waters flowing from the smitten rock are still following our Christian Israel.

In the aggregate, four hundred and twenty-seven meeting-houses have been built, — an average of thirty-five per year, — at an expense of one hundred and forty-nine thousand two hundred and ninety-eight dollars. But these sums total convey no adequate conception of the extent of good accomplished. To arrive at this, even approximately, we must gain an estimate from each church so aided, — its necessities met, its hopes inspired, its influence and usefulness extended. Some of these results may be generalized, as follows: —

I. This enterprise has secured the erection of many houses of worship which would not otherwise have been built. It is astonishing how much of stimulus is furnished by that sure amount of cash. It often starts the work. Frequently the hope of aid is the first thing presented to inspire courage to rise up and build. It furnishes the money for the necessary articles of purchase, while much of the material and labor are subscribed in kind. It sustains during the tedious progress of the work; it stimulates to the last grand effort of hope against hope to cover the final gap between present possibility, already twice or thrice exhausted, and the condition of freedom from debt. It often saves a church that would otherwise die out. At Lincoln, the county seat of Logan county, Illinois, a town of three thousand five hundred population, and named for our late beloved president, a Congregational church had lived four years in a small and unpleasant hall. Making no progress, the brethren began to be discouraged and to talk of disbanding. "No," said the missionary, "*we must build.*" "Impossible," said they. Meeting called; disheartenment complete. The "Union" proffers five hundred dollars. Hope is rallied. The house is built at a cost of two thousand dollars. Since the dedication, one year ago, the membership and the congregation have been doubled, and the Sabbath school trebled. A revival has brought in twenty hopeful converts. And the pastor writes me: "We owe our continued existence and prosperity to-day to the encouragement the Congregational Union gave us in our hour of need." This is but a specimen, and no uncommon case. Of the twelve Congregational meeting-houses built in Northern Illinois during the last fifteen months, all of which but one had aid from the "Union," eight were incited to build by the proffered help; — the remainder could not have built alone without incurring the incubus of debt. The agent of the American Home Missionary Society for Minnesota, says: "I can think of thirteen churches, which now have houses of worship, that in the first instance were undoubtedly stimulated to build by the proffer of aid. Without it, building in each case would have been delayed longer than it was, and in several cases it would not have been accomplished at all." The agent for Kansas says: "But for such help, nine of these sixteen churches, built with aid from the Union, would now be incomplete, probably not begun; four would have been put off for months, perhaps for years; and but three at the utmost would have been built without aid." And these sixteen are all the Congregational meeting-houses there are in that martyr State. The agent for North-western Wisconsin says: "I am sure the prosperity, if not the continued existence, of several of our more useful churches is largely due to the fact that houses of worship were secured soon after their organization; while several churches within my field, in villages of considerable importance, are now threatened with extinction because they are not provided with places of worship wholly their own." From many years of observation, and after consultation with other persons well informed upon these matters, I am confident that of the four hundred and twenty-seven churches aided, one half would now be without houses of worship, and one quarter would yet be burdened with debt or with unfinished enterprises, had it not been for such assistance.

II. Church building has been an efficient *auxiliary of Home Missions.* The Home Missionary Societies and the Congregational Union have to deal with the same churches, the young and the feeble. One is the Commissary department; the other, the Quartermaster's. All that can be said of the influence of the sanctuary any where may be said of the missionary church, while to it are thereby secured peculiar advantages. In the East, churches could get along better without houses than at the West. Here the people are assimilated; there they are heterogeneous, and society lacks the attraction of cohesion. This want the church edifice largely helps to meet. In the rude community it becomes a visible representative of the gospel. It is a garner of generated religious influences. So important to the children of Israel during their period of training was the sanctuary, that, through divine wisdom, they were furnished with the traveling tabernacle. Many persons going West make it an excuse for absenting themselves from the temporary places of worship because there is no church edifice. When a house has been secured, such in large numbers have been brought under the influence of the gospel. A meeting-house ordinarily doubles the congregation, the pecuniary resources, and the power of the missionary church. It lessens the amount of aid needed; it cuts short the period of dependence; and often, at once, lifts it into self-support. Three such churches in Illinois, aided by the "Union" in building, have just dedicated their houses of worship, the slips of which were at once rented for an amount to cover increased salaries and incidental expenses, — thus relieving the treasury of home missions, while the excess over the former income came mainly from those who had been non-supporters. We find that in Illinois *thirteen* missionary churches, thus helped to sanctuaries, soon after dedication, became self-supporting; in Wisconsin, *twelve;* in Michigan, *five;* in Minnesota, *three;* in Northern Iowa, *four;* in Kansas, *three.* The secretary of the "Union" reports that to five churches the sum of one thousand five hundred and fifty dollars was appropriated to pay "last bills" on houses of worship, and that each of these at once became a self supporting and a giving church; thus saving to the treasury of home missions the annual appropriation of one thousand seven hundred dollars for the support of preaching there. A pastor, now in the East, formerly in the West, writes to the same secretary: "I consider your cause as one of the *most important*, as it increases immensely the efficiency of the home missionary enterprise." In the June number of the *Home Missionary*, a minister in Iowa, reporting the dedication of a house of worship after three years of tugging and lifting, and referring to the three hundred dollars secured from the "Union," calls it "the truest helper to the home missionary that could possibly be invented." The actuaries of the American Home Missionary Society, whose function it is, on their respective fields, to explore destitutions, to organize and to nurse the young and feeble churches, who are brought into pastoral sympathy with the weakest flocks, and under whose eye all applications for aid in church building pass, are unanimous and enthusiastic in their appreciation of this enterprise as the right-hand helper of home missions. Their last resort, sometimes, in efforts to save a church, is to propose to build, while the first incentive they use is the prospect of aid. They understand that by thus securing church edifices they are doing the most efficient home missionary work, knowing that in many such cases not to build is to die. The secretary of the Old School Presbyterian Board of Church Extension, writes: "We find that the completion of a sanctuary, free from debt, almost uniformly adds largely to the congregation, at least, on an average, doubles it; that revivals of religion are very frequent in such churches; that ministerial support is largely increased, and the period of self-sustentation greatly hastened, by securing an unincumbered church."

III. The church-building enterprise has proved itself one of true *economy in benevolence.* Its economy in saving the funds of home missions we have already noticed. Then by its appropriations usually *seven times* as much is developed by the applicant churches. It was found that the sixty-one thousand eight hundred and ninety-one dollars of the first fund stimulated the raising of three hundred and thirty-seven thousand seven hundred and four dollars. At the same average, the aid granted to the four hundred and twenty-seven churches in all must have called forth six hundred and twenty-six thousand eight hundred and sixty-three dollars from the beneficiaries. Then, again, this method has saved much over the old mode of self-appointed agencies for particular churches. It was truly said, in the Albany Convention, that such agents ordinarily received but little more than enough to pay their salaries and traveling expenses. The present plan obviates that waste. It saves the annoyance of such random calls. It saves pastors the trouble of investigating each case. It secures, by the agents and committees on the ground, a more rigid scrutiny into the merits of each application, and so saves unworthy appropriations. And then, as managed by a Central Board of Trust, the almoner of a sacred charity, confidence is inspired. The economy of this work appears also from the fact that the churches, thus helped to homes and so to self-support, become *givers.* In their state of dependence they are trained to systematic contributions by the American Home Missionary Society and the "Union," — a collection every year for these respective causes being the condition on which aid is granted; so that this habit of remembering other feeble churches will be likely to abide, and so too will every good cause be made the gainer by the increase of the number of *giving* churches. One church in Chicago, that was aided by the fifty thousand dollar fund, gave, the last year, besides a generous support of the gospel, one thousand eight hundred and ninety-nine dollars to objects of benevolence, and paid five thousand six hundred and fifty-two dollars on a subscription of thirty thousand dollars for its permanent edifice. Of the thirty-two churches that contributed to the Congregational Union in the quarter next to the last, *seven* had been aided from the same treasury. The district secretary of the Baptist Home Mission Society for New England, after a three months' reconnoissance at the West, said: "It is my profound conviction that rather than sustain two missionaries in two towns for five years, it were much better to sustain only one and build for him a good house of worship." One, who is acquainted with the Western churches, is greatly surprised, in reading over the list of those aided in building, to find how many that are now prosperous and generous, were so recently recipients of this Christian charity. Only to read in this place the roll-call of the churches thus helped out of weakness into strength, would be at once a testimony and an argument in favor of the economy of this policy.

IV. A precious result of aid in building sanctuaries is its influence in promoting in them *revivals of religion.* The entrance upon such a house has often been a signal for the manifestation of the Spirit; and such seasons of revival following upon the dedication services have not been few. At the consecration of the first church aided in Illinois by the Albany fund, the incense offered was that of the first love of several new-born souls, and this was followed in a few months by a work of grace that added some ninety persons to the company of believers. Of the six churches aided in Southern Ohio by that same fund, *all* received a baptism of the Spirit soon after dedication. Of those aided in Illinois up to the present time, *twelve* have enjoyed revivals soon after entering their new houses of worship; in Wisconsin, *seven;* in Minnesota, *five;* in Iowa, *fifteen.* Complete returns would show that very many of these new church edifices have become at once places of spiritual nativity. It is also noticeable that meeting-houses have frequently been built immediately after seasons of spiritual refreshing.

V. As a result of the church-erection scheme, it has contributed to an *increased prevalence of the principles and polity of the Puritans.* Since the Albany Convention, the number of Congregational churches in the West, including Ohio, has increased from five hundred and seventy-three to one thousand and eighty-four, and their membership from twenty-eight thousand two hundred and ninety-nine to fifty-nine thousand nine hundred and sixty-eight. If we make the increase of the last year, not yet reported, the same as the year before, then these churches will have more than *doubled* in number and in membership since the initiation of this enterprise. Various causes have contributed to this growth. One was the natural force of this free and simple polity; one was the anti-slavery position of these churches; another was the arousing, in some degree, of the people of this faith to the duty of disseminating the wisdom of the New Testament in regard to the church constitution; and not the least of these causes was the policy of church building. It is more than a coincidence that this era of the increase of churches corresponds with the era of systematic aid in erecting meeting-houses. Churches that would naturally take on the form of autonomy have, by this help in securing their houses, been saved from yielding to solicitation to assume an uncongenial polity in order to gain the needed aid in building. Not a few churches have been organized in places where a house seemed to be a prime necessity, and where the Congregational Union by its help has secured the organization of as many churches in important positions. Take an instance. At Kokomo, Indiana, a thrifty railroad town, a county seat, with a fine academy, with a population of two thousand, where was only a Methodist church and a Campbellite, each with a feeble administration, another church was seen to be needed, — one that should embody the small Calvinistic element of four different denominations. And though there was but one Congregational family in the place, and though some who proposed to come into the organization had never seen a Congregational minister before, yet it was found that this mixed material could be most readily affiliated under the polity of the brotherhood. But a house of worship was seen to be a *sine qua non*, inasmuch as two other efforts by other denominations had miscarried through a failure in church building. And so the proffer of aid from the American Home Missionary Society was accompanied with an assurance of help for a house. Upon that a church of seventeen members was organized, a minister secured, and now the sanctuary is drawing toward completion, while the membership has been doubled, and a rare position of influence and usefulness attained. Without such aid, that church, which has just now entertained the General Association of the State, and whose pastor is a member of this Council, would not have been brought into life.

VI. Our church-building enterprise has imparted a stimulus in the same direction to all the other denominations. Taking the idea from the Albany Convention, the New School Presbyterians, in 1853, raised a church-erection fund, which now amounts to one hundred and twenty-three thousand eight hundred and forty-six dollars, and has aided two hundred and twenty-eight churches. In 1854 the Baptist Home Mission Society undertook to raise a fund of one hundred thousand dollars, but has as yet secured only thirty-five thousand dollars of it. In 1855, the Old School Presbyterians, instead of their committee of the Board of Domestic Missions, set up a church-extension board, which calls for annual collections, and has thus far aided five hundred and sixty-six churches, besides the three hundred and eighty-two assisted by the old committee; while their receipts, the last year, have been thirty-eight thousand seven hundred and ninety-six dollars and ninety-eight cents, and the aggregate of collections for this object has been three hundred and twenty thousand nine hundred and ten dollars and ninety-three cents. The Methodists have just set up a church-extension board for the same purpose. Thus the denomination, nine-tenths of whose charities have been given for undenominational purposes, and not a little of that to build up another sect, imparts to all the others a stimulus in the idea and the plan of church erection. Not a little of the good done by the building of these eleven or twelve hundred church edifices in other communions, is due to the Albany scheme. Such, then,—not to speak of the binding of the East and the West together by this enterprise, not to speak of its relation to patriotism illustrated by the passage: "He loveth our nation and he hath built us a synagogue,"—such are some of the precious fruits of this undertaking. It has helped hundreds of churches to houses; it has been an auxiliary to home missions; it has increased economy in benevolence; it has promoted revivals of religion; it has disseminated Puritan ideas; it has led other branches of the church into a like work. How vast the amount of good accomplished by the outlay of so small an amount as one hundred and forty-nine thousand dollars! Such results become in themselves a sufficient argument for the prosecution of this enterprise, if, indeed, there be any thing more to be done in that direction.

What, then, are the present and prospective necessities in this matter? "The thing which has been is that which shall be." Read over the secretary's successive quarterly reports, and while you will be moved to grateful emotion in view of the good accomplished by this agency, you will also be oppressed with a sense of the vastness of the work left undone simply for want of means. The statement of so many applications, ten, fifteen, twenty, rejected for the lack of funds, becomes a painful recurrence. Nor are these the same ever-waiting supplicants. Baffled in their suit they retire,—some to struggle on with adversity, some to die; while others take their place at the suitors' stand, only to be kindly but peremptorily dismissed. Says one report: "But there are twenty-six churches now urgently pressing their claims for small appropriations, with many of which the question is 'to build or to disband;'" and another: "Still back of these are scores of others, whose only hope of success is to be found in our treasury;" and one of the very latest says: "From scores that are waiting and longing for aid we must hold back until the givers shall afford us the means of aiding them." It certainly must be a painful experience of the gentlemen who serve as the trustees and the secretary of this interest, to see these successive bands of Christ's disciples, in which are the elements of so much blessing, struggling for life upon the waves of adversity, while they are themselves powerless to respond to the cry for help.

Then we find that there are in Michigan, at the present time, *fifty* Congregational churches that have no houses of worship; in Illinois, *forty-four;* in Wisconsin, *thirty-nine;* in Minnesota, *forty;* in Iowa, *fifty-eight;* in Kansas, *sixteen;* and many in other States, so that, in all, as nearly as we can ascertain, there are *four hundred* of these families of the Puritan sisterhood without homes, all of which need to be brought into the holy habitation.

Then there is no reason why we may not expect that in the next twelve years, as in the last, the churches of this pattern will, at the West, double their number, raising it from one thousand and eighty-four to two thousand one hundred and sixty-eight, many of which, in embryo communities, will need aid in securing that first of all requisites in a new country, a place to live in. There will always be, along our ever-receding frontier, a cordon of such feeble churches, the outposts of our Christian civilization, which will appeal to our sympathy. The opening of the Pacific railway; the operation of the homestead law and of soldiers' warrants; the tremendous stimulus to new settlement afforded by the rich metals in all of the central mountain country; the flood of foreign emigration; the manufacturing interest, the seat of which is working westward, — all these influences will tend to hasten the filling up of our intercontinental empire, which must be brought into allegiance to Christ. The extent of that country yet to be filled with living souls we can but little realize. The half-way place on the parallel of New York is yet two hundred miles beyond the Missouri, seven hundred beyond Chicago, the gateway of the North-west, seventeen hundred west of Boston! The Territories upon the Rocky Mountains are already coming to their majority, and asking of the paternal authority their portion of goods. Unborn commonwealths are yet to come from that region to knock at the door of our national capitol for recognition. The extent of territory in those oncoming States staggers comprehension. And yet into that region of vast distances and possibilities, the enterprise of home missions is rapidly projecting itself, following in the path of the pioneer, the miner, the soldier. The Path-Finder threw out our glorious stars and stripes from the loftiest peak of those Rocky Mountains; and so the home missionary has unfurled the banner of Jesus upon the same Alpine range; even into the region and shadow of death has he borne it, setting up the claim of his King upon the adherents of that system of abomination which now occupies the heart of the continent. All over that region churches of the pilgrim faith will be born, and they must have homes. Their Redeemer is already there, "waiting to find room." And "as the mother of Jesus looked up wistfully to the guest-chamber that cold night, drawing her Holy Thing to her bosom," so will these new-born churches of Christ look longingly to our spacious and amply-furnished sanctuaries for hospitality and blessing.

Then, in the older portions of the missionary field, away from the original centers of population, away from the railway stations, in the isolated townships of well-to-do farmers, there is yet a vast work to be done. Many new churches are there to be organized; many new houses of worship to be built. If we are to profit by the experience of New England, and by its awakened interest in home evangelization, we must forestall the "waste places." Of this kind of work take an example: A banker in Michigan City, Indiana, goes out seven miles to a neglected neighborhood, cursed with a distillery, and starts a Sabbath school. A revival ensues. The distillery is turned into a flouring mill. A church is organized, and the superintendent becomes the lay-preacher. The old school-house is enlarged; a new one is built, and this is outgrown by the congregation and the aspiration of the brotherhood. A church must be built. People poor; prospect poorer. The "Union" proffers aid. A neat and commodious sanctuary is secured; and, through the "Union," a young man in the First Church of New Haven, Merritt W.

Barnes, as a dying gift appropriates three hundred dollars, his little all, to pay the last bills, — a legacy of love commemorated by a tablet set into the wall of that house of God. Last summer, during the vacation of the Chicago Seminary, one of the students, under commission of the American Home Missionary Society, relieved the lay pastor, and in the new house was permitted to welcome nine persons into that fellowship as the result of a spiritual refreshing in harvest time.

Then who can compute the demand for aid in church erection at the South? The angel of the Lord is now saying to the Philip of our evangelism: "Go toward the South . . . . which is desert." If we had come across this newly-discovered missionary field in any other part of the globe, it would thrill the heart of Christians to occupy it at once. Though their treason, in seeking the life of our nation, has slain our sons and brothers, and now our beloved President, yet thither we are bidden to go with the gospel, even as the disciples were directed by their Lord to begin at Jerusalem, the very city which had rejected and crucified him, and even as Philip was to carry the Evangel of Jesus to that same Philistia which had been the perpetual enemy of Israel. We are likewise under special obligation to propagate there that system of church-order, which, divinely appointed, like Christianity itself, is adapted to man as man in all parts of the earth, — which by its simple form and catholic spirit is well fitted to unite and assimilate that disorganized material which, by its affinity for freedom and its cleaner record, is suited to that *recoil* going on at the South in intelligent and conscientious minds, and which, in its reproduced style of Puritanism, though long rejected there, will be the most hopeful means of rescuing that fair land from its moral desolation.

Now, then, the churches which, among both the whites and the blacks, are there to spring up as by magic, must be *housed.* In that disrupted society a chaste, comfortable church edifice will be a powerful attraction. Said Dr. Lyman Beecher, in the Albany Convention: "If you want martins about your house you must put up a martin-box." In the South there will be special need of using the economy of church erection in order to take up this great work at its flood tide. Not as heretofore in the gradualness of the opening of the Home Missionary field, now whole States, to the number of one third of our Federal Union, already populated and seething with the antagonistic influence of irreligion, are thrown upon our hands, and God says, take these, reform them, Christianize them. In order to meet this exigency, we shall need all the attracting, sustaining influence of sanctuaries. When our soldiers went first into the service, in the abandon of heroism, they cared little for entrenchments; but, wiser by experience, they will now work cheerfully at every halt upon some simple breastwork. The soldiers of Christ going South, in order to save all their gain and to make irresistible their advance, must have their series of fortifications. Neglecting this, though they may gain important strategetic points, their safety and success will be in jeopardy. At Hannibal, Mo., the "Union" has fortified one such position, which has stood through the rebellion a rallying center for loyalty, has sent a stream of influence along the line of railway that crosses the State, and now with its membership of one hundred, its home Sabbath school of three hundred and thirty pupils, its mission school of one hundred and fifty, and its school of four hundred colored people, is accomplishing in that city a vast deal of work for Christ. Already applications are coming in from the South for more of such defenses.

Such being the demand for church building at the West and at the South, how grave must be the consequences of neglecting it! Imagine this work of the last twelve years undone, a large proportion of these four hundred and twenty-seven missionary churches left without sanctuaries, and some of them dead. What apology could satisfy the Head of the Church for such dereliction? Then imagine the four hundred families in our Christian sisterhood, yet without homes, deprived of all prospect of aid from this source in the future, many of them doomed to a protracted feebleness, which shall deaden hope and finally life itself. Then consider the hundreds of churches yet to spring up, many of which, if not planted in the house of the Lord, will droop and bear but little fruit. In the failure to provide these garners, vast harvests will go into the earth.

Then, as a consequence of neglecting this work, many of these Puritan flocks will be driven into folds not congenial. It would be a shame that the body of churches, which led the way in this scheme of benevolence, should fall behind in the enterprise, and actually turn its own people over to those of other faith and order for hospitality. It would be worse than a shame, — it would be a crime; for, "If any provide not for his own, and specially for those of his own house, he hath denied the faith and is worse than an infidel." These which, by lineal descent or by *adoption*, are the children of the Puritan family, have a right, by all principles of equity and of grace, to look to the parent for nurture and for protection. The two denominations which have learned to do this work the most efficiently are those that would make the most of a draft upon the Congregational material. We honor those branches of Christ's people; we wish them all success in bringing their feeble churches into the sanctuary. But we think that we have a more excellent way; that the people of the Puritan faith can do the most good under the forms of their own simple polity, and that the Congregational *swarms* will do the best in Congregational *hives*. We believe that, as a miracle was wrought to convince the apostles that the gospel was to go beyond their own nationality, so now God, by the marvelous revelations of war, is teaching us that the same gospel is to be carried in the same church order to all parts of our land, and that the crossing of no parallels of latitude or of longitude can justify an exchange of that system for any man-made establishment. And it will be neither with self-satisfaction nor with approval, human or divine, that we come to the confession, "They made me the keeper of the vineyards, but mine own vineyard have I not kept."

It is a favor of Providence that we have in the Congregational Union an organ of this enterprise, well-manned, skilled by experience, settled in its policies, and so, prepared for the crisis. Though its work is germane to that of the Home Missionary Societies, yet a wise division of the labor, which has an appalling magnitude, the certainty of raising more funds by a double appeal, and the mutual helpfulness of the two departments, will make it wise to continue the present arrangement. All the other denominations but one give to this cause a separate organ, and one of these changed to a double acting machinery after having tried the single. The established principle of annual collections has, over an invested fund, the advantage of keeping the cause fresh in the thought and sympathy of the churches, and of avoiding the risks of an accumulated capital, while, under the present demands upon benevolence, the raising of any competent endowment would seem to be out of the question. As to the amount that will be needed for church building, year by year, it will not do to put the estimate at any thing less than fifty thousand dollars.

But how can the treasury be kept in a condition equal to this draft? We believe that all that will be needed will be to afford every congregation in our fellowship the opportunity of making an annual offering to this cause, and that, in order to this, every church place this object upon its calendar. During the last reported year, only one hundred and fifty-five, or one in eighteen, of the Congregational churches contributed to this object. The secret of the success of the Old School Presbyterian Church Extension Board seems to have been in getting collections from a large number of churches. During the last year, seven hundred and fifty-one church-contributions were acknowledged; and these, if we leave out the gifts of two congregations in New York City, averaged only seventeen dollars and sixty-seven cents, while four hundred and nine of the churches gave but ten dollars and under. If but one half of the Congregational churches would simply "go through with the motions" of a collection for this cause, the treasury would not labor. But if, as one of the latest applicants, the Congregational Union can scarcely find room in the calendar, then it may be well for this Council to advise the churches to *make* a place for this feeder of all the other charities. In the plans recommended by the General Associations of Ohio, Michigan, Illinois, and Wisconsin, this cause has its specific month; the system is growing in favor, and this object meets with a peculiar appreciation. Indeed, it should be said for the encouragement of Eastern friends, who have given so freely to the West, that the seed thus sown is now coming to the harvest. A generous spirit is growing up in those Western churches, which will join the East in liberal giving for the New West and the South. That stream of New England theology and of Puritan ideas, which has been poured across the West, has given character to its institutions, and has thus magnified its power for good, as now the swelling current shall sweep down to the Gulf. And if the parental household, by the exhausting of itself for the welfare of its emigrating offspring, shall ever come to the need of succor, then with grateful, loving attention will the children, natural and adopted, delight to reciprocate the blessing.

But still, in order to the filling of this treasury, in common with those of all other benevolence, — in order to our rising to the sublimity of this providential occasion, — we need a national dispensation of the Spirit that shall lead to a consecration of property and of life wholly unto the Lord.

Half an hour was spent in devotional exercises, Rev. Mr. Turner, of Iowa, Rev. Mr. Clark, of Illinois, and others leading in prayer.

On motion of Rev. Dr. Wolcott, it was

Voted, That this body, having learned that His Excellency Governor Andrew, of Massachusetts, is in the city, and would take pleasure in paying his respects to this Council, and can not do so conveniently after to-day, will be pleased to receive him at 3 P. M.

Rev. John L. Jenkins, of Indiana, was added to the committee on the Roll.

Rev. Mr. Langworthy, on behalf of the committee on Nominations, reported the following committees. The reports were severally agreed to.

ON COLLEGES AND THEOLOGICAL EDUCATION.

Rev. Mark Hopkins, D. D., of Massachusetts; Hon. William W. Thomas, of Maine; Rev. Henry E. Parker, of New Hampshire; Rev. Silas McKeen, D. D., of Vermont; Rev. Thomas P. Field, D. D., of Connecticut; Rev. Thomas Wickes, D. D., of Ohio; Rev. Adam S. Kedzie, of Michigan; Rev. William Deloss Love, of Wisconsin; Rev. Elisha Jenney, of Illinois; William H. Watson, of Kansas; Jacob Bacon, Esq., of California.

ON AMERICAN PROTESTANT ASSEMBLY.

Rev. Jeremiah Taylor, D. D., of Connecticut; Rev. Edwin B. Webb, of Massachusetts; Rev. Moses H. Wilder, of New York; Rev. Abel K. Packard, of Minnesota; Rev. Philo C. Pettibone, of Wisconsin.

ON CHURCH BUILDING.

Rev. Samuel G. Buckingham, of Massachusetts; Dea. Henry P. Haven, of Connecticut; Rev. Franklin B. Doe, of Wisconsin; Dea. Philo Carpenter, of Illinois; Rev. Isaac Jennings, of Vermont; Rev. Joshua M. Chamberlain, of Iowa; Rev. Edwin Johnson, of Maryland.

ON TEMPERANCE.

Rev. Constantine Blodgett, D. D., of Rhode Island; Rev. Zedekiah S. Barstow, D. D., of New Hampshire; Charles A. Stackpole, of Maine; Dea. William Thurston, of Massachusetts; Dea. Lorenzo D. Dana, of New York; Dea. Abram Griswold, of Ohio; Rev. Joseph Collie, of Wisconsin.

ON PAROCHIAL EVANGELIZATION.

The committee appointed to introduce to the National Council of Congregational Churches the subject of parochial evangelization, report the following

STATEMENT.

The work of our churches divides itself into several departments. Efforts in behalf of other nations we call foreign missions; the founding of new churches and the assistance of such as are feeble, within the limits of our own country, we name home missions; while all churches exist for a particular work, styled, in the resolution appointing this committee, *parochial evangelization*, — a work which looks toward the reconciliation and sanctification of all the souls embraced within the communities that severally constitute the proper parishes of the churches, and which aims at a general and complete popular Christianization.

The object of the present paper is, to bring clearly to mind this glorious duty and privilege of the churches, with some of the ways of its fulfillment. To this end it is necessary briefly to recall the true idea and office of the church, and to consider, somewhat more at length, the modes in which its established services and its administration may be most efficient.

THE CHURCH UNIVERSAL.

It is the chief end of man to glorify God, and share his joy; and of the world, to be a place of nurture for souls thus fulfilling their end. The church on earth embraces all who have begun to glorify and enjoy God, and so is the essential realization of the end of creation; but, being the "body of Christ," wherein he dwells and whereby he works, it is also the means of its realization. The conquest of the world is its proper function; and it is no more really the natural quality of salt to save from corruption, or of light to annihilate darkness, of leaven to leaven the lump, or of a living seed to assimilate earth, air, water, and light, into its own body, according to its own law, than for the spirit of Christ, working in and through the church, to cleanse from moral corruption, disperse moral darkness, fill society with a divine leaven, and incorporate with its own body, and build up in heavenly beauty the alienated and lost souls that surround it. God ordained the churches for this end, and they must be esteemed equal to its accomplishment. In entering upon the consideration of our subject, we properly start with this assumption.

ORGANIC CHURCHES.

But, obviously, in order that our *organic* churches, which are, at best, but an imperfect realization of their idea, may justify such an expectation, they must be *really churches*, and must be nothing else.

To this end, it is necessary, first, that they should be composed of believers, — of those who have begun to love with Christ's love; a love in which they are holy and a brotherhood.

Furthermore, every church must needs embody its essential idea in its organization, and be a brotherhood in form as well as in spirit, — avoiding all semblance of such authority and subjection as are common in the world. No "greatest," and no "master," can be recognized here. As believers, we have one Master, and he is above: all we are brethren. The apostle disclaimed dominion, and aspired only to be a helper of joy to his fellow-disciples; and our blessed Lord specifically instructed his followers, with regard to the spirit and law of his church, when he washed their feet.

The structure of a society embodies ideas and fixes relations; and these ideas it is always teaching, and these relations are always shaping character and action. The church needs to have the true church form — of a brotherhood — or its organization will be subtly, or perhaps very openly, counterworking its work. Its very organization should be the birth of a love which annihilates caste and sense of hierarchy.

When churches have thus been organized of the right material, and in the right form, they need to be careful, thirdly, to confine themselves to their true end.

The one end of the church universal is the glory of God in human redemption; and the local church finds its one chief end in the same result, throughout the community which makes up its proper parish, — in other words, "parochial evangelization." It may not allow itself to be turned to any other object; nor can it safely unite with other churches as a constituent in societies, either secular or semi-secular, whose operations involve large material interests or weighty financial cares. One thing it has to do; and that is so immense and difficult, that it cannot give itself to anything else. In one precious and eternal bond is it united with all other churches of the Lord Jesus Christ; and it may not imperil this most sacred of all conceivable relations, so peculiarly delicate and sensitive, by grosser mixtures, so often fruitful of strife. It is essential that each church both hold fast to its exclusively spiritual end, and to its own separate identity and responsibility, maintaining, indeed, the closest possible spiritual union with other churches, in love, but refusing all corporate and business ties with them, all authority (in the worldly sense) and all subjection. This we hold to be essential to the prosecution of a thorough and universal parochial evangelization.

When churches have thus been organized of the right material, in the right form, and for the right end, it remains, fourthly, that they adopt the right methods for the accomplishment of this end. The end, as already stated, is the working out, under God, of human redemption from sin, into love, blessedness, and holy service; and the work of the church may be viewed in three aspects, — as related directly to God, to believers, and to man still in a state of alienation; thus having the three divisions of worship, edification, and conversion; and its efficiency in all these is necessary to its success in parochial evangelization.

THE CHURCH-WORK.

WORSHIP.

The first great duty of the church is *worship*. This is God's due; and it is essential that every church render a pure and acceptable worship before the throne of the Divine Majesty. But inasmuch as God is most glorified by that which is so ordered as to be also the greatest blessing to his children, its method may appropriately be considered when we come to treat of what is essential to Christian edification.

EDIFICATION.

The second great object of the church, prominent in its work of parochial evangelization, is the *edification of its members in the divine love.*

By Worship.

The first means by which it furthers this aim is a *worship* in which it becomes a channel of divine grace to all participants, and offers itself, as such, to all witnesses of its act.

Worship is rendered (1) when the hearts and minds of a devout assembly are reverently yielded to the guidance of *Holy Writ* — records of the divine dealings, breathings of penitence, prayer, and thanksgiving, and the story of redemption — motions of minds moved by the Holy Ghost. This is the river which makes glad the city of God. We need to go back ever to these flowings of the primal springs.

There are two ways in which this benefit of Scripture may be enjoyed by a worshiping congregation; namely, listening to an expressive reading, which re-clothes the sacred words with their original life; and chanting. It is to be regretted that the latter is no more in use among us; as, with singing, it is almost the only way in which an assembly can properly join in the outward expression of worship through the lips. Our congregations will probably never satisfactorily realize and appropriate the meaning and preciousness of the most ancient songs of the Church until they have learned to chant them, and this in more reverent and less hurried style than prevails elsewhere. We should not be altogether wide from the truth, if we were to say, that it requires the strength of a great multitude to bear into our hearts the weight and sense of these words of God. Our children ought, from the beginning, to be made to feel the grandeur and the gladness, the lowliness and the tenderness, of these inspired Psalms. Each church needs them in the evangelization of its parish.

The two methods that have been mentioned are the only seemly and proper methods in which congregations can use the Scriptures in the public services of the sanctuary.

(2.) The "service of *song*" in the Lord's house, it is now generally conceded, needs to be chiefly rendered by the whole congregation, led by a choir. But our churches have by no means, as yet, entered upon the exceeding riches of the inheritance of the saints, contained in this elevating, comforting, and transporting service — so full of blessing to devout hearts, in its nearness and sweetness of communion with our Lord, and so universally attractive and impressive. There is a mighty power of edification and of persuasion in rhythmic, melodious psalms and hymns and choral harmonies, which our churches and their schools have only begun to realize. It can unquestionably be made a powerful instrument in the evangelization of communities and of classes that now neglect the sanctuary; and, indeed, has already often been of great service in attracting children to the Sunday school, and their parents to the place of public worship.

(3.) As the mere reading of Scripture, in seemly style, becomes a way of worship, so the *preaching* of the divine word often leads the hearts of a congregation, in a contemplation of God and a beholding of his glory, to thanksgiving, adoration, confession, and yearnings of deepest aspiration and longing. If we dare look toward the Christianization of whole communities, — and what minister or church dares aim at any thing less, — how must we abjure all merely literary, logical, disputatious, denunciatory, or melodramatic and sentimental preaching, and strive to bring our hearers in view of the eternal mountains of God, the mighty truths whose foundations and whose summits are equally out of sight! In those mountains are peace and joy; they are homes of power; and from them flow the living waters. The deepest truth is most divine; and is not merely pleasant, beautiful, and moving, but awful, glorious, transforming, and transporting. It is our privilege to wield this truth; and, for our work, we need it. The people must worship while they hear. It were vain to think of the Christianization of communities if we were to forget this.

(4.) In public *prayer*, the most perfect union of hearts is probably reached when one man of fervent and devout spirit leads the multitude, in words, which, with his tones, are the birth of the moment, — the breathing of the Holy Ghost. But, that this may ordinarily be secured, even in moderate measure, it is necessary that the person who leads should be habitually in communion with God; and, furthermore, should be accustomed to turn his inward communings into words. The usage of our churches now lays this demand upon their ministers. It is a wholesome burden, and ought by no means to be removed. Having adopted the highest possible ideal, we ought to seek to rise to its demand. The effort, in our work of parochial evangelization, is to bring all souls into communion with God; and the Church maintains these public acts of communion, in part, from the hope that the spirit of devotion may spread, like leaven, from soul to soul, till all be leavened. But, that the leaven may spread, it must be real, and real at the time which is its opportunity.

By Instruction.

The second method in which a church promotes the edification of its members is by supplying *instruction.*

The instruction furnished in the church aims at the reconciliation and sanctification of souls, by bringing them face to face with God, in Christ;

that, beholding his glory, they may be changed into the same image. If it exhibit not that glory, it fails of its end. So far as it deals with other than eternal realities, and with thoughts lower than the thoughts of God, or is satisfied with a beauty inferior to that of Christ, it stoops from its state, and abases its sovereignty. It ought to unveil eternity; to unfold the mind of God; to take divine things, and show them unto men; to make plain the ways of a heavenly life here on earth; and to breathe something of the dignity native to souls regenerate and sanctified, — the dignity of a love like Christ's. While considering the methods of parochial evangelization, neither the ministry nor the churches may forget this.

In Organization.

But verbal instruction is not all. As has been already remarked, the very structure of the church, when what it should be, is mighty for the *instruction* of its members and of the community at large. But while, in its constitution and the general spirit of its administration, it needs to express and teach the Christian love, and while in its worship and the ministrations of its pulpit it must not fail to edify, it ought to do this, thirdly, by furnishing *special facilities and opportunities for the development among its members of an active love.*

Arrangements should be made by every church for bringing its members together, so that they should become acquainted, and acquainted as Christians. For this purpose the weekly prayer-meeting is of priceless value. So, too, are the smaller neighborhood prayer-meetings, and all social religious gatherings, and indeed all religious social assemblies, — in many places too much neglected. In every practicable way the church needs continually to strive to bring about among its members the fulfillment of the Saviour's prayer, that "they all may be *one.*" Upon this largely depends the possibility of an extended Christian influence and of the development of a system of church-work. The love is indispensable to union in labor; and for the awakening and cherishing of love, there must be acquaintance and intercourse. Our church members have all been welcomed with covenant vows of affection and help, which deserve to be better kept; and, to facilitate this, special arrangements are necessary.

But not alone in the delight and the impulse of love does the church need to build itself up; it should edify itself also in love's *wisdom,* — in that spiritual wisdom which only comes from living out Christ's precepts. These precepts involve the most fundamental and comprehensive principles, which principles must be studied in their application, and not simply heard of from a teacher, in order really to possess the soul. Accordingly, the church needs to throw upon its members the *responsibility of decision*, in the application of Christian principles, especially of those which are fundamental; and any church leader who undertakes to decide for his church, or, worse still, to force his judgment upon them, or, worst of all, to carry a judgment by intrigue or intimidation, misconceives his office. His office is to guide, not to dictate, — least of all to manipulate.

It is his privilege to lead his brethren in the study of the mind of the Spirit, so that they, all together, shall apprehend it, — not to declare it by authority. He is guide, not governor. No man can be a master in the church. And whoso departs from Christian simplicity, and assumes control, or uses "art," grieves the Spirit, sins against the brethren, and breaks the constitution of the church. In like manner, also, any church which submits to a dominion that dulls its life transgresses its fundamental law.

It is only by familiarizing men with the practical application of principles that they can be put in possession of them. This the church does when organized and administered faithfully after the New Testament model. When organized and governed after any other plan, its efficiency is necessarily impaired.

Again: not only must the responsibility of decision, especially in important questions, be thrown upon the members of the church, but for their own spiritual good they all need also a share in the responsibilities and the manifold benefits of *church-work*. So essential is this privilege, that we may even declare it indispensable. But of this we shall speak more at large under another head.

In Fellowship.

Again: each church needs to stand in suitable relations with other churches, — recognizing and feeling its oneness, not only with those of its immediate neighborhood and its own time, but with all true churches of every age. With its neighbors it should join in counsel and labor; and it has no right to allow any bonds of authority to divide it from such communion. All should be counted its neighbors with whom it can join, or whom it can reach, to bless. Nor should it lack a sense of unity with the churches of other lands, of other days, and other names. Great strength comes from a consciousness of the oneness of the Lord's kingdom; and this needs not at all a corporate unity, so sure to work disaster, and to defer the accomplishment of our Saviour's prayer, but can best exist without it.

In the Sacraments.

Finally: each church needs for its edification to cherish most solemnly and tenderly *a sense of union with the Lord.*

The unity of all true churches of Jesus Christ with one another, and of all believers with their Head, is commemorated, figured, ratified, and perpetuated, in the sacraments, — those universal signs and seals, which, shared by all, are a manifestation of their oneness from the beginning, — of their oneness with Christ. We can not hold in too dear affection, or celebrate with too loving and careful solemnity, these seasons of grace, in which all ages join and all disciples remember their only Lord. Churches which propose the Christianization of their parishes need to take all possible pains to secure the full blessing of these sacred opportunities.

Conversion.

The third great end of the church remains, namely, the *bringing into a state of reconciliation the souls that are alienated from God.*

We have, it is presupposed, a church composed of believers, — persons who have begun to love with a love like Christ's; organized a brotherhood; worshiping God; instructing and edifying its members in the wisdom, the power, and joy, of divine love; entering into sacred bonds of communion in the sacraments.

But the chief labor of Christ's militant church on earth has ever been the reconciliation of alienated souls, the saving of the lost. Not only do our churches find their principal *work* here, but they can not even be faithful toward their own members unless they engage them in efforts for the spiritual benefit of those who are still out of personal covenant with God. Very properly, therefore, is the inquiry urged home upon us: How can a church be faithful and successful in this momentous work?

Trust in God.

First of all, it needs to be keenly sensible of the fact, that the work of saving and sanctifying souls is the work of God; and that it is only, as in union with him, that men are privileged or able to engage in it.

The Doctrine of the Church.

In the *next* place, it is in a high degree important, that the church should understand its own nature and office. Its members need to be so well instructed in the *doctrine of the church*, that the thought of God's kingdom, and of his earthly kingdom and family, should occupy and thrill their minds. There are no truths more full of light and power than those which center here. Without them, churches will but imperfectly grasp the idea of what they have to do, and will lack both the courage and the faith indispensable to sustained activity and a comprehensive and permanent success.

Parishes.

In the *third* place, it is important that every church should definitely recognize and accept its own particular work, — *its parish*. The very form of the statement proposed for this Council's consideration, — the subject of "*Parochial* Evangelization," — seems to assume that this has already been done; and yet how seldom in our day, is it really done!

But, if a church is to do its work, it must know its work, — know it as a church. Nor can we reflect at all upon this matter, without perceiving that when once this work has taken definite form in the mind of the church, and has been solemnly acknowledged before God as his commission, one important step has been gained. The divine call now sounds clear, has been understood, and the church has answered, "Here am I."

Furthermore, so soon as a definite work has thus been recognized, its *parts* begin to be distinguished, — some, perhaps, very difficult, but others more immediately hopeful; and so an *order* begins to appear; and now, no sooner has it been determined where to commence, than *methods* suggest themselves, — a really intelligent beginning can be made, a beginning of the whole; and the motive drawn from the whole urges and helps the prosecution of each part; furnishing a great advantage to every working member, and especially to the pastor, whose duty it is to superintend and incite.

In most rural districts, and in some villages, the natural "parish" of the church is so obvious that no question can arise concerning its boundaries; and where two or more churches stand side by side, and draw their congregations from the same communities, the question is still one of no difficulty; for here the churches obviously have a *joint* parish; and, having agreed upon such division of labor as the case demands, may each go forward with its own; recognizing, in reference to the whole, a joint responsibility, while also owning a distinct care and duty. Nor, where churches of other denominations are found, does this bring in any serious complication. For, acknowledging with joy their work for the Lord, we shall find enough for our hearts and hands in caring for our own and for neglected families.

But it may be said that this system of parishes is impossible at the West, where missionaries sometimes have whole counties under their charge. On the contrary, it is quite as easily arranged there as elsewhere, and is, perhaps, of greater importance than in Eastern communities; in every case, there is a community that forms the proper parish of the church which the missionary makes his principal center. This is that church's field; the rest is the minister's *out-field*, over which he exercises inspection, and where he temporarily bestows a certain amount of labor, in preparation for other laborers who shall enter in and establish permanent centers and parishes. It is of the utmost importance that the young churches of the West, now in their formative period, be educated to the idea of *church responsibility for communities.*

The plan suggested may possibly be thought to be impracticable in cities. By no means; for it would supply what city churches so greatly need, — a definite object and mode of practical union; and, indeed, is absolutely necessary to the thorough occupation of their field. A certain geographical allotment will, it is believed, be found expedient in all our largest towns.

The Home Prayer-meeting.

But a church can not be expected permanently to keep in mind a corporate duty, unless in its corporate capacity it regularly recalls and considers it. Inevitably, interest will flag, and efforts will wane, unless the church holds regular meetings in behalf of its work. Wherefore it is evident, *fourthly*, that "the *home prayer-meeting*" — that is, a meeting devoted to prayer and counsel specifically in behalf of the church and its parish — is valuable, and perhaps indispensable, as a means of reminding the church of its duties, besides affording occasion for that fervent supplication which avails much.

Moreover, since all beginnings are in God, and all human beginnings leading to real success must be with God, it would seem impossible for any church to make any wiser commencement of new efforts for its parish than this, of regular prayer in its behalf. No church is so strong that it can afford to neglect prayer, nor is any so weak that it can not pray. If the difficulties that encompass it are so great that it sees no way whatsoever in which it can make any beginning of new labor, then, surely, it is called to lay the case before God, to study it in his presence, and with undoubting faith to await the guidings of his Spirit and providence.

Systematic Labor.

Fifthly. It is important that a church should prosecute its work upon *system.* It has already been remarked, that, so soon as the church has defined its parish, the several distinct *parts* of its work begin to appear. The community is at once resolved into four principal classes, comprising (1) the members of the church; (2) members of the congregation, and regular attendants who are not members of the church; (3) those in some sense *connected* with the congregation, but not regular or frequent attendants at the sanctuary; (4) families and individuals having no real connection with any Christian congregation, and who come under no stated religious influence.

Each of these classes, again, has a four-fold division, according to age; into children, youth, the mature, and the old. A watchful pastor undoubtedly carries the analysis further, and classifies the members of these subordinate portions in accordance with diversities of condition, character, and history, which indicate different ways in which Christian influences may be expected to reach them with good effect.

Although we are not here called to enter in detail upon a discussion of methods of church-labor, it may be proper to indicate certain points that invite special attention.

And, first, with regard to the religious education of *children.* We believe it possible, through the Sunday school and otherwise, to secure a larger amount of valuable Christian instruction at the children's homes; and that this is necessary.

This end would be promoted by giving a greater fullness and impressiveness to the mode of administering the baptism of children (which ought always to include a brief but solemn covenant, and an appropriate chant or hymn), by a more frequent and urgent preaching of this duty, and by a system of tender watchfulness, on the part of the church, over the baptized children of its charge, and over all the children of its congregation and Sunday school.

Furthermore, there is need of a competent revision of Scripture question books, of Sunday-school library and especially of Sunday-school music books, and the relentless exclusion of all that are not of really excellent quality. The amount of poor and bad material in our children's singing-books is appalling.

Secondly. In respect to the religious training of our *youth.* It is a question for those competent to decide, whether more pains may not wisely be taken to exhibit the gospel *in its glory*, so that the young, who are easily kindled with enthusiasm, may be led to feel that nothing else can possibly be so glorious as the truths and realities contained in this "gospel of the blessed God." Also whether, in addition to general instruction, special teachings for the purpose of guarding against prevalent errors might not be of use. Whether *succinct catechisms* might not be formed for this purpose; and whether lectures upon portions of church-history, and the history of opinions, could not be turned to advantage. Whether the influences of "society" may not be made more uniformly benignant and wholesome? Whether pastors are really faithful in following up with personal labors the effects of their preaching.

Thirdly. Are not persons of *adult* years often incorrectly presumed to be practically out of reach? And would not a more sedulous care — would not more *system* — in pastoral labor and administration, be fruitful of precious results?

It is certainly true that our churches do not study, methodize, and watch their work as they should; and important portions of it are often wholly neglected, while others suffer from the inattention necessarily consequent upon lack of system. Business is impossible without method; and a similar attention to system is indispensable to any complicated or long-continued work.

Fourthly. There are many *families* and individuals, and not a few distinct *communities*, unreached by any stated ministration of the word.

Within the parish bounds of many churches, in all the States, there are neighborhoods or districts the inhabitants of which belong to no Christian congregation, and are reached by no regular religious influence. These *outlying communities* require the attention of the churches.

Within the bounds of parishes, and often in the immediate neighborhood of the sanctuary itself, there are numbers of families and individuals, — some of foreign, others of native birth, — who are equally neglecters of the sanctuary. These *outlying classes* also demand the attention of the churches.

The circumstances of these neighborhoods and districts, and the character of these classes, are so various in the different parts of the country, that it would be unduly occupying the time of the Council to enter here upon their classification. The methods by which they are to be reached by effective Christian influence are also various; and the consideration of them, in detail, belongs to the churches themselves, and to local and State conferences, rather than to a National Council. The *leading methods*, however, are familiar to all: special visitation; systematic visitation, accompanied with a distribution of Bibles, tracts, and religious books and papers; branch Sunday schools; neighborhood prayer-meetings, in private dwellings or in school-houses; neighborhood preaching, — with regular services of worship; and to these may probably be added, what has been so well tried beyond the water, the employment of "Bible readers."

Unquestionably our "outlying communities" and our "outlying classes" can all be reached, if the churches will enter upon systematic, prayerful endeavors in their behalf. It was for such work that they were made. Let us not doubt that they can do it. Experience proves that a church that is in earnest, and tolerably well guided, will meet with encouraging success; and that a well-adjusted system makes many things possible that are otherwise hopeless.

Lay Evangelists.

We have been wont to speak of the foolishness of preaching as the power of God, and rightly. But we seem to have forgotten, that preaching needs not a pulpit or consecrated temple for its efficacy, but may do its deepest work by any fireside or wayside, in any workshop or field. Wherever a heart full of the divine love brings this love in the truths of the gospel to bear upon any other heart, there the gospel is preached, the "power of God to salvation." All faithful Christian parents, teachers, and friends are instruments of the word and Spirit of God.

It is a question, whether our churches may not safely set apart and "license" certain of their members — gifted with a suitable measure of wisdom, knowledge, and power of utterance — as *lay evangelists*, to superintend and carry on the Christian work, in out-stations, under the particular counsel and oversight of the church, through its committee and pastor. We are inclined to believe that an important portion of our work now waiting to be done, can be done in no other way.

Local Conferences.

Fifthly, This whole matter is peculiarly the proper and the principal theme of church conferences.

It would seem to require no argument to prove that the immediate work of the churches is properly their main concern. Would it not, indeed, be a strange mistake, if, when assembled in conference, they were to omit its consideration, or were to fail to give to it, ordinarily, the greater part of the time which they spend together? Our Sunday-school teachers find enough to interest large conventions in the details of a comparatively limited and simple task. How vastly more various, comprehensive, and difficult are the responsibilities which come upon the churches and their pastors! There can be no question that these demand a profounder and more general study; and, for the purpose of bringing them statedly before the churches, in judicious form and manner, and of securing an intelligent comparison and summary of methods and results, it would probably be well for local conferences to maintain standing committees on parochial evangelization. These conferences can, also, by means of public discussions and addresses, affect the movements of public opinion, and create currents of sentiment which will greatly assist each local church in its particular work.

State Conferences.

Sixthly, The larger conferences, embracing entire States, can render a similar service, appointing their commissions on popular Christianization, — gathering thus the results of the general experience for general benefit, and marking the general progress, from year to year, and decade to decade, in this process inevitably bringing into prominence questions of universal and permanent interest.

The American Congregational Association[1]

Now have under consideration a plan for securing reports, summaries, and discussions, that shall cover the labor of all the churches of the country, — our national work of popular Christianization. We trust that some arrangement to this end will be carried into effect.

GENERAL MINISTERIAL ASSOCIATIONS.

Another department of our subject merits more attention than can now be given it. Error and sin intrench themselves behind defenses of learning, while the truth itself is deep and wide, — a sea that no sounding-lines fathom — a continent which no armies subdue. Hence the importance, not only of a learned ministry, but also of ministerial associations, for concentrating the best wisdom of the ablest minds upon the exposition, inculcation, and defence of the truth. Whether the local associations, which are now universal in the older parts of the country, are all that we need, and whether larger " colleges," converging the learning and experience of the ministry of entire States, may not have a place in the best church system, are questions not yet answered. When we consider how much is implied in the thorough Christianization of any community, that the evangelization of our parishes not only involves the defeat of iniquity in its high places and its palaces, but also an increase in the average depth, and an elevation of the average tone, of popular thinking, we can not but be deeply impressed with the importance of securing, on the part of our ministry, a patient, united study of great religious themes and issues. We need to join our strength, in the endeavor to think the thoughts of God; to comprehend, expound, and defend the truth. Nor do we despair of this result, but are inclined to believe that ministerial associations, *general*, as well as local, have an important part to play in the grand work of popular Christianization.

OUR NEED AND OUR DUTY.

And now, if any are inclined to feel that your committee has dealt too much with general views, and has had too little to say of details, we reply: The details belong to the churches and their more local conferences; and, furthermore, the general doctrine, with the impulse which it breeds, is what the churches now most need. When they have come to estimate aright the sacred dignity, responsibility, and privilege which clothe the church, as God's kingdom and family, and the agency which he has ordained for the conquest of the world, they will assuredly find out for themselves the best methods of Christian labor.

Immense interests are dependent on the proper prosecution of this work of parochial evangelization. Unless the churches rise to a higher efficiency, not only must multitudes of souls from their own communities go down in hopeless paths of sin, but the work that calls to us from broad Territories and from newly opened States must fail in its very begin-

[1] Until recently, known as the " Congregational Library Association."

ning; and our institutions, flooded with a foreign tide, and penetrated with a hidden decay in their very foundations, must yet come to their fall. The hope of our land is in the success of its churches.

Our fathers expected to found a Christian people. This, their purpose, is our inheritance. Let us solemnly resume it in all its breadth; lift up a standard to the people, and cast up highways for their return, until they shall all have come in, a "holy people, the redeemed of the Lord."

In conclusion, your committee respectfully suggest the adoption of the following

RECOMMENDATIONS TO CHURCHES AND MINISTERS.

1. That, when possible, every church, taking counsel if necessary with neighboring churches, define for itself the territory embraced in its parish, and recognize a special responsibility to labor for the spiritual benefit of all Congregational and all neglected families and individuals within those bounds.

When churches are so near together that this is impossible, it is recommended that they accept the common territory as their *joint parish*, and, with a similar formal acknowledgment of responsibility, secure a good mutual understanding for the best prosecution of their work. But, even in cities, we counsel a geographical division, in reference to certain kinds of labor. In the newer portions of the country, when convenient, an *outfield* may be designated in connection with the parish proper.

2. We recommend to all churches to devote one prayer-meeting every month (or, perhaps, in the case of the feeblest country churches, one in each quarter), to the special object of the church and its work, — giving to this meeting the name of *The Home Prayer-Meeting.*

3. We would suggest that each church set before itself, as its work, the complete Christianization of its parish, and enter methodically upon the prosecution of this enterprise, — classifying the whole population intrusted of God to its care, and endeavoring to shape its instrumentalities so as to reach the whole; keeping, also careful records of all known labor, and all visible progress, and reporting the same, in proper form for record, to their neighbor-churches in conference.

4. That the churches maintain, through local conferences, *standing committees on parochial evangelization.*

5. That the churches, meeting in State conferences, create permanent *commissions on popular Christianization.*

6. We shall be gratified to learn that the American Congregational Association has perfected plans for the promotion of movements toward popular Christianization throughout the country.

7. That all ministers of churches (1) take special pains to instruct their people in the true *doctrine of the church;* bringing into special prominence (a) the character of its material — believers; (b) the form of its organization — a brotherhood; (c) the dignity of its three-fold end — God's glory in conversion, holiness, and worship; (d) the several methods whereby it accomplishes its end; making especially prominent the duty

of each church to be, within itself, a veritable family of God, and, for those without, a band of loving missionaries; and sedulously inculcating the doctrine of *church responsibility for communities.* (2) That the ministers systematize the work of their churches, apportioning it so that none of it shall be overlooked, and none unnecessarily neglected; and aiming to secure the effective employment of as many church-members as possible in some form of Christian effort.

8. It is furthermore suggested, that the churches, in their local conferences, take into consideration the expediency of endeavoring to meet the wants of such outlying districts as can not be statedly supplied with the services of ministers of the gospel, by the employment of *lay evangelists* regularly appointed by the church or its committee.

9. We suggest whether it may not be wise to test, by trial, whether a State ministerial association can not be of service as a professional body for professional ends, — a *college* for the promotion of Christian fellowship, and of the knowledge, wisdom, and skill requisite for the inculcation of the truth, the sagacious conduct of necessary controversies, and the successful administration of the pastorate, — thus rounding out, in full symmetry, our Congregational organization.

DANIEL P. NOYES, } *Committee.*
HENRY M. DEXTER, }

Boston, June 14, 1865.

Rev. Mr. Langworthy reported the following as the committee, and the report was adopted: —

ON PAROCHIAL EVANGELIZATION.

Rev. Reuben T. Robinson, of Massachusetts; Rev. Amos S. Chesebrough, of Connecticut; Rev. John M. Holmes, of New Jersey; Rev. Henry M. Goodwin, of Illinois; Rev. David Burt, of Minnesota; Rev. Richard Cordley, of Kansas; Rev. James T. Ford, of Vermont.

CLASSIFICATION OF BENEVOLENT ORGANIZATIONS.

Rev. Israel W. Andrews, D. D., of Ohio, read the following report, which was then referred under the rules: —

SYSTEMATIZING BENEVOLENT CONTRIBUTIONS.

The committee to whom was referred "the classification of benevolent organizations to be recommended to the patronage of the churches," have found themselves embarrassed by the difficulty of attaching precise ideas to the subject on which they were appointed to report. In the discussion of this topic at the preliminary meeting, three different classes of views were presented.

The first contemplated an examination of the existing benevolent organizations, with reference to re-arrangement and consolidation. The conviction was expressed that two or more societies might profitably be united into one, as having the same end in view; and that some others, in consideration of the urgent wants of the times upon which we are entering, should not be pressed upon the churches.

Another view gave prominence to the practical embarrassments to ministers and churches arising from the multiplicity of objects, and the confusion and conflict that sometimes result. The present workings of our benevolent system were declared to be satisfactory neither to the churches nor societies; and the belief was expressed that measures ought to be devised for their mutual relief.

The third view deprecated any consideration of the topic by the National Council, deeming it an interference with the work of the individual churches, and not likely to be productive of benefit. In accepting the duty assigned them, the committee must, of course, put themselves in opposition to this last view, though the responsibility belongs to the preliminary conference rather than to them; still, the existence of such an opinion adds to their embarrassment. If, in addition to this difference of opinion as developed at the preliminary meeting, and subsequently by consultation and correspondence, the sensitiveness of the churches on the one hand, and that of the benevolent societies on the other, be considered, it will be manifest that a duty has been assigned to the committee alike difficult and delicate. It would be vain, therefore, to expect that the views here presented would meet with universal favor. Whatever value may be attached to them, they are given as embodying the results to which the committee have been led by the best consideration they have been able to give to the subject.

The individual Christian, as well as the individual church, has a twofold duty to perform; he is to grow in grace himself, and to do good to others. And this latter duty is to be performed partly by personal effort and partly through the agency of others. Here is the sphere of what is commonly called *benevolence.* The Christian expends money to buy Bibles for himself and family; we do not term it benevolence. He pays for the support of his own minister; it is not a benevolent contribution. But money given to procure Bibles for distribution, to support a minister preaching to a feeble congregation, to send the living teacher to the heathen, is said to be for benevolent purposes. Possibly, Christians sometimes employ others to do what it would be better that they should do themselves. It may be easier in some cases to give money than personal effort. But the discussion of that topic belongs not to this committee. Assume that there are no shortcomings in the personal activity of the members of a church,—that no one of them performs by proxy the duty which he should perform in person; still, there is a boundless field in the cultivation of which others must be employed, and for this benevolent contributions are indispensable. It may be said, indeed, that the more of personal efficiency the Christian manifests, the more will he give for *objects* beyond his immediate reach; that the more perfectly he cultivates his local field, the more vividly will he see and feel the wants of the great field, the world.

The question, then, of benevolent contributions is one of great scope. It comprehends a large part of the work of the Christian, — of the churches. The giving of money is not enough; it should be given intelligently. To what causes shall our churches contribute? To what organizations shall they intrust the expenditure of their money? These are questions always important, always pertinent. Is there any thing in the peculiar circumstances of our country, or the world, that makes them specially important and appropriate at the present time? Has there been any change in the relative importance of different organizations? Even if nothing be said of the honesty, fidelity, and ability with which these organizations have been conducted, has not the progress of events, or rather the providence of God, rendered the claims of some more imperative, of others less so, than formerly? Has not this Council been convened to consider anew the fields of Christian labor, and to inquire how the work of Christian benevolence can be most successfully carried forward?

The subject of benevolent contributions is thus broad and comprehensive; and a discussion of it, while embracing, should by no means be limited to, the practical difficulties of which our ministers and churches complain.

These difficulties are, an undue multiplication of organizations; too many occasional contributions, which interfere with the regular causes; a want of discrimination, so that more important objects sometimes receive the smaller contributions; and, in general, an excess of friction in the working of the machinery. Perhaps the difficulties may be reduced to these two, — a lack of system in the organization of the benevolent societies, considered as a whole, and a lack of system in the arrangements for contributions in the individual churches. Has not too much been left to accident, as well in the formation of the societies as in providing the means for their operations?

Our benevolent machinery should be as simple as possible consistent with the highest efficiency. Two or more organizations ought not to be established or continued to perform a work for which one is sufficient. The churches have no surplus, either of men or money, for organizations which are not strictly necessary. It has been said that appeals have been made to our churches, for contributions in behalf of the Freedmen, by *twelve* different organizations. Besides the useless expenditure in keeping up so many associations, what confusion must be caused by such a multiplicity of appeals for the same object! Nothing is plainer than that no new society should be established without the most careful examination of the field to be cultivated, and of the agencies already engaged in the work. There should also be a wide consultation of intelligent, Christian men, both clerical and lay, before entering upon so important an undertaking as laying the foundations of a benevolent association, which is to be supported, if supported at all, by appeals to Christian churches.

Akin to this difficulty arising from the multiplicity of organizations is that from the numerous *occasional* calls for contributions. This evil is felt more in the cities and larger towns. Aid is needed for some object not coming within the province of any regular association, and to secure it, application is made to one or more churches where it is thought a hearing can be obtained. The applicant deems his cause to be meritorious in a high degree; and it is one, moreover, whose claims to immediate attention are imperative. It is often difficult thus to withstand the various influences brought to bear upon the pastors or officers of the church, and the number of calls of this character may become, in the aggregate, very great.

But shall a church absolutely close its doors to all appeals except from certain societies? By no means. With all our system, we can not so look into the future as to see all that a year will disclose. There are good objects to which aid must be rendered outside of the regular organizations. But the number will be small.

As it is, the churches complain, and with reason. Even if all these occasional calls were for worthy objects, their number is an evil. In some cases private liberality should be appealed to. In others, the aid should be given through one of the regular societies. Almost every large church takes collections each year for objects which come legitimately within the sphere of some one of the regular benevolent organizations. In the eyes of some men, *independence* is the cardinal virtue. They wish to do things in their own way. They care not to be hampered. If they raise the money which they think they need, directly from the churches, instead of receiving it from the treasury of a society, they are sure of a wide discretion in its expenditure. This feeling of independence, this impatience of restraint, will account for many of these occasional calls on the churches. Perhaps to the same source may be traced the formation of some of our numerous organizations.

As illustrating the great advantage to the churches of rendering aid through the channel of a regular society, rather than in response to individual appeals, reference may be had to the society established more than twenty years ago for aiding colleges and theological seminaries in the West. The churches were saved from a multitude of conflicting applications. What they had to contribute they could give with perfect confidence that it would be wisely appropriated. Substantial aid was thus furnished to institutions really worthy, while it was withheld from those that were not needed.

Some, at least, of these occasional appeals will be for unworthy objects. Yet it is often exceedingly difficult for the pastor, or the officers of the church, to distinguish at the time between the good and the bad. Even recommendations from men of the highest respectability are not always proof that the object recommended is deserving. Names are sometimes given without any expectation that they are to be used for such a purpose. Thousands of dollars may be collected at a distance, on the strength of recommendations from men who, living in the vicinity, and having personal knowledge, would neither give a dollar themselves, nor take a collection in their churches. But men should have more firmness, it is said. Of course they should; but the fact that all have not this desirable trait makes it the more difficult for the churches to know to which of these occasional calls they should respond.

This class of appeals should be subjected to the severest scrutiny. The churches have no funds to expend on unworthy objects; and when men discover that they have given to such, their confidence is shaken, and their general contributions are diminished.

In connection with these occasional calls outside of the regular benevolent organizations, allusion may be made to the taking-up of a *second collection* for a given cause in a single year. The exigency of the case is the reason assigned. But as there are many societies which need all the funds they can obtain, it is a question whether justice to others will allow any one to ask for a double opportunity. The precedent would be sure to be pleaded, and thus the difficulties from which the churches now seek relief would be increased. The *year* is the great unit of time for our benevolent societies, and there is eminent propriety in adhering to it.

These are some of the embarrassments under which the churches labor. The multiplicity of appeals for carrying forward the work of the regular societies, as well as for the objects lying beyond their sphere, tends to confuse the minds of the people, and subjects the pastors to a sore trial. But these are not the only parties from whom complaints are heard. The managers of our great charitable organizations are no better satisfied with the practical workings of the benevolent machinery. The conflict of application prevents a full development of Christian benevolence, and thus these organizations are often subjected to serious embarrassment in their work. Those upon whom devolves the duty of presenting these causes to the churches, find their work, which at best is never pleasant, to be doubly disagreeable.

It should never be forgotten that the churches and the societies are laboring for a common end, — that the latter are but the agents of the former. There should ever be the highest Christian courtesy between our ministers and churches on the one hand, and the officers and agents of our benevolent societies on the other. The many appeals, sometimes conflicting, that are made, coupled with the lack of system which prevails in too many of the churches, furnish ground for complaint, it may be, but not for the tone and manner in which that complaint sometimes finds expression. It is easy to find fault with agents, but the time for wholly dispensing with their services has not yet come. The number of pastors who are both able and willing to do in their own churches all that is usually done by agents is increasing every year; and just as far as the work can thus be done should other agencies be dispensed with. Nothing will tend more to hasten the day when extraneous help will no longer be needed than a wise classification of benevolent organizations, and the devising and executing in every church a thorough system of contributions.

The pastors of the churches and the officers and agents of the societies are laboring in the same great field. All desire that the benevolence of the churches should be so developed and directed as to accomplish the highest good. If this requires the consolidation of two or more societies into one, no personal or official considerations should be allowed to stand in the way of doing it. An organization may have been hitherto absolutely necessary, whose work can henceforth be done as efficiently and more economically by another. Great changes are taking place, new and wide fields of Christian enterprise have been thrown open; our benevolent operations must be adapted to the exigencies of the times, and to the demands which God is making upon us.

As already stated, one of the great ends for which this Council has been convened is to inquire what is the special duty of the churches which we represent in relation to the great fields of labor which the providence of God has opened to us. Having given this inquiry their most earnest and prayerful consideration, shall the Council then recommend to the churches the benevolent organizations through which these fields are to be cultivated? Your committee have no hesitation in giving an affirmative answer to this question. Not to make such a recommendation would be to leave their work but half accomplished. Nor is there any reason to fear that the churches will deem it an interference. If the members of an individual church are guided in great measure, as to the direction which their contributions shall take, by the suggestions of their pastor, who can doubt that the deliberate recommendation of this large body of ministers and delegates will carry with it great weight?

The Council should not be deterred from such a recommendation, either by a groundless fear of encroaching on the rights of the churches, or because of any apprehended insinuations of inconsistency from those who prefer some other polity. The Congregational churches have been so thoroughly pervaded with the spirit of catholicity, and so ready to do good wherever an opportunity offered itself, and to contribute money to sustain enterprises, no matter by whom controlled, that the absence of denominational feeling has come to be regarded as their denominational characteristic. And when action is proposed that has any look toward providing for our own, and especially for those of our own house, it is hinted within, and asserted without, that we are abandoning the old ways, and becoming like the nations around us.

The churches have sent up their delegates to deliberate on great questions. Shall the results of their deliberations be hermetically sealed, lest the churches shall know what has been done, and be influenced thereby? On the same principle, and with equal wisdom, suppress our *Congregational Quarterly*, and give up all our religious newspapers and periodicals.

The *ministry* is the chief instrumentality by which the world is to be converted to God. The gospel is to be preached at home and abroad. This is the great work. Others are important as they aid and supplement this. This is the principal; others are auxiliary. We call it the *missionary* work, *home* and *foreign*. But the missionary is a minister, and the importance of his work may be estimated by that of the pastors of our churches. Close the places of worship in these towns of New England, and remove the ministers from their people, and then expect the ways of Zion to rejoice, and the kingdom of Christ to be built up! When those whose field of labor is on our Western frontiers have looked over the wastes, and heard the importunate appeals for ministers, they may be pardoned if sometimes they have asked themselves whether the Christians of a county in Massachusetts or Connecticut would be quite satisfied to have, as their sole spiritual guide and teacher, a colporter. If nothing could be a substitute for the ministry here in New England, neither could it be in the West. Were the members of our churches to make an estimate of the amount invested in church edifices in the older States, as well as the sums annually expended in payment of salaries, and in defraying the other expenses incidental to sustaining public worship, they would have more sympathy with the feeble churches of the newer portions of our country, and their contributions to aid them would be greatly increased.

The Christian ministry is the great agency to be employed. Those churches which can not, unaided, support their pastor, must receive assistance. Young men must be brought into the ministry, and the churches must aid in defraying the expenses of their education. Houses of worship are necessary, and a helping hand must be given in erecting them. If permanent educational institutions have been found indispensable to the highest and truest religious progress in New England, and especially as training-places for the ministry, they should for the same reason be established elsewhere. So far as ministers and Christian laymen can make more available their efforts to do good, by the circulation of the word of God, or by the distribution of tracts and other printed matter, or by furnishing libraries to Sabbath schools, they should certainly avail themselves of these auxiliary means. But it is of no little importance that these associations, which are engaged in thus providing religious reading, should be regarded as merely supplementing the work of the ministry. The special wants of our seamen should not be overlooked, though the duty of making provision for their spiritual improvement seems to devolve chiefly upon the members of our churches on the seaboard. So, too, a class in our own country, that can not be reached directly by our domestic missionaries, may require special provision for a time; and, through the same channel, efforts may be made for bringing the gospel to those who dwell in papal countries. The people from whom the shackles of slavery have just fallen have a claim upon us for the gospel and the institutions of religion and civilization, which we have neither the right nor the desire to shake off. As yet, but a small portion of that work can be done by our Home Missionary Society; but another organization is already doing most efficient service, whose antecedents give it the highest confidence of that people.

So far, then, as it belongs to this committee to classify organizations to be recommended to the churches, we place first and foremost the two great missionary societies, — the American Board of Commissioners for Foreign Missions, and the American Home Missionary Society. If the important work of church building could be performed by the latter of these two societies, the churches doubling contributions, it would simplify to that extent our benevolent work. Whatever other causes are overlooked by any church, these two should always be remembered.

The cause of education for the ministry has a relation to the missionary work more intimate than that sustained by any other, and its importance should give it place in all our churches. In some of the States, an educational committee attends to the work of collecting funds, and in others the American Education Society has the matter in charge. Surplus funds might well be used, as in some other denominations, in establishing permanent scholarships.

As also directly connected with the missionary work, the Society for promoting Collegiate and Theological Education at the West should be named. Its work in the past has been most salutary, and through no other channel can liberal men do so much to advance, in the West, the interests of thorough intellectual culture, under the auspices of religion.

The American Missionary Association is understood to devote its chief — perhaps its entire — attention to the freedmen, and the committee take pleasure in referring to it as the fittest organization for that work.

The American Bible Society is too well known to need any special mention.

In regard to contributions for furnishing libraries to destitute Sabbath schools, the committee venture a single suggestion. It is, that a portion, at least, of the contributions made by the children of our Sabbath schools should take this direction, or that our churches, when raising funds for replenishing their own libraries, should, at the same time, contribute for feeble schools. Suitable books can be procured in many places, though none more suitable, nor on better terms, than from the Massachusetts Sabbath School Society.

Allusion has already been made to the American and Foreign Christian Union, and to the American Seamen's Friend Society.

Most of the organizations called into existence by the exigencies of the war will cease with the occasion which called them forth. The work for the Freedmen, however, must continue; and, as already suggested, the American Missionary Association seems to be the most desirable channel through which our churches should contribute.

There are many points to which the attention of the Council might be called, for the discussion of which the committee have not time. The importance of conducting the benevolent operations of the individual churches in a systematic and business manner, to which allusion has already been made, can not be urged too strongly. The nature of our polity makes this indispensable. While our churches abound with business men, it is to be feared that in cases not a few the contributions are managed with very little reference to business principles. Let it not be forgotten that benevolent contributions are a means of grace. The individual Christian who gives is benefited no less than he who receives. All proper means should then be employed to develop the benevolence of our churches. Among these means none is more important than the adoption of a well-digested plan, such as is already in operation in many churches. Suppose each church should, at the beginning of the year, determine to what causes they will contribute, specifying the months. The *church*, we say, not the pastor, or the pastor and deacons, for the members must be interested that they may act intelligently. The number of occasional contributions should be limited, for it is those which are responsible for most of the confusion. Let as little as possible be left to discretion, and nothing to accident. At the end of the year let a full report of the contributions be made to the church, and entered upon the church records. Let the appropriate committees, or the deacons, present the receipts of the treasurers of the societies as the proper evidence that the contributions have reached their destination. All other associations make their annual reports; why should not our churches? The members need to know what their church has done. In some churches this knowledge is in possession, but not in all. It is probable that our members know less of the operations of their individual churches, and less of what is done by the churches of their order throughout the land, than those of any sister denomination. To whatever cause this may be attributed, it is to be remedied only by systematic effort in the individual church.

The committee think that those churches which contribute to a regular cause each month will have no difficulty in completing the cycle each year. But no occasional cause should be allowed to crowd out one of those decided upon by the church. Where collections are taken less frequently, two plans may be adopted. One is to make contributions singly for the more important objects, and to group the others, that the list shall be completed each year. The other contemplates annual collections for the great causes, and biennial for the others. Each has its advantages. Where two or more causes are presented at once, and the collection divided, the impression must be less distinct and definite. The members should give intelligently, and clear statements should be made by agents or pastors of the nature and object and workings of every association for which funds are solicited. The pastors assume too much knowledge of our societies and their operations on the part of their congregations. They forget that young people are all the while coming forward, and that men are brought into the church from the world, with whom the American Board even is not a household word. It is our conviction that a clear, business-like statement of the condition and operations of a society, occupying ten or fifteen minutes, would be more potent with the men who give the money than an impassioned appeal of an hour.

In conclusion, the evils of which so much complaint has been made can be remedied by the pastor and the churches, and by them alone. The adoption of rigid system, as to contributions, is indispensable to the prosperity of every church. Irresponsible agents must be excluded, and churches must decide for themselves to what they will contribute. Their plans and the manner in which they are executed should be put on record. The history of the benevolence of a church is worthy of preservation. Because money is given for benevolent purposes, it does not follow that it should be given at random. Perhaps, by virtue of their office, the deacons should look after these matters; but if they do not, the minister must. Let him not fear a little contact with business details. Other things being equal, the more practical talent he possesses, the greater will be his success.

The field of benevolence is large and open. A great work is before us. God has given wealth to our churches, and, to some extent, they acknowledge their stewardship. What is specially needed is *system*, both in the individual churches and in the benevolent organizations considered as parts of one whole, and as doing a common work; it is needed in the former, that the treasury of the Lord may be kept always full; in the latter, that from every expenditure the best results may flow.

ISRAEL W. ANDREWS,
RAY PALMER,
HENRY E. PARKER, } *Committee.*

BOSTON, June 14, 1865.

It was accepted, and reference ordered to a special committee.

The convention then took a recess until 3 o'clock, P. M.

AFTERNOON SESSION.

The Council was called to order at 3 o'clock, Rev. Dr. Thompson in the chair.

The report of the committee on Evangelization in Foreign Lands was read by the chairman, Rev. Dr. Budington, as follows: —

EVANGELIZATION IN FOREIGN LANDS.

The committee appointed by the Council upon the work of evangelization in foreign lands, submit the following report: —

As Congregationalists we are not only committed to the prosecution of foreign missions, but our place is that of pioneers in the enterprise. We have taken the lead of all the denominations in our land in the origination of agencies, and the contribution of men and means. The American Board of Commissioners for Foreign Missions is the child of the Congregationalists of New England; and although instituted in the comprehensive spirit of catholic Christianity, and common to us with the Presbyterians, and formerly with the Reformed Dutch Church, it has all along been the favorite of our people; and there is no distinction which we cherish more fondly than this of having originated and been foremost in sustaining American missions to the heathen. New England was at the outset a mission. Our fathers came here on this distinct errand, as professedly and as really to preach the gospel to the Indians, and to extend the Redeemer's kingdom, as to make new homes for themselves, train up their children for God, and lay the foundations of a Christian State. Congregationalists, therefore, come legitimately by their zeal for foreign missions. We should be unworthy of our ancestry, and recreant to the trust we have received from them, if we should make the commandment of Christ to preach the gospel to every creature secondary to any other duty or interest. Especially incumbent is this declaration upon this *First National Congregational Council;* and not the less because we are assembled at a solemn juncture of our country's history to enter afresh upon the work of home missions, and adjust ourselves to the new openings the war has made for the establishment of free churches and a free gospel in the South. We are planning and praying for the enfranchisement and regeneration of our country; but we do not stop with this, — we wish to give our country to Christ, that through it the world may be the more speedily redeemed. A patriotism that ends in coldness or antagonism toward the rest of mankind is selfishness and crime. Our country, its reconstruction and evangelization, is just now our first solicitude; but so far from separating the home field from the foreign, we believe them to be one and indissoluble, and it is only as we are loyal to Christ that we can hope that he will be propitious to us.

Your committee, therefore, recommend that the Council, as representatives of the churches, do testify their deep sense of the importance of Foreign Missions, and their unabated devotion to the prosecution of the enterprise. We need it for ourselves. The work will die at home, if it languish abroad. It is the sign of our fellowship with Christ. It is the condition of his blessing. We need it in every sense, and for every reason. Our piety needs it. It is the purest form of benevolence on earth; and it sustains and intones every other form of benevolence in church or State. If we withhold from the heathen, God will withhold from us. If we keep back our sons and daughters from the remotest people for whom Christ died, the spirit will be wanting in them for the service of God in this our dearest country. For every true missionary of the cross who has died on the foreign field, God has poured the spirit of consecration into the hearts of our youth at home; and we have been the richer in spirit and material for every such loss. We can not afford to shut off this source of supply, now that we are entering a wider and more destitute field of missionary effort than was ever open to a Christian people before, and we need resources of men and money which nothing short of the Spirit of Christ in the best ages of missionary zeal can impart. For ourselves, then, and the work of home evangelization, we must cultivate the missionary spirit, and bound our sympathies only where Christ bounded his.

Besides this, God has so greatly blessed us, given us such success in regions so wide and inviting, so many populations are looking to us for the gospel, and by the tacit consent of Protestant Christians are left to us, and made dependent upon us, that we are beholden of God to prosecute the work. No branch of the church has missions relatively more important to the evangelization of the world than ours. Some of the most interesting peoples, and, when converted, the most influential, are ours to labor for, and by the blessing of God redeem. No missionaries from any land, in any part of the world, have won a more enviable name than the Congregational and Presbyterian missionaries connected with the American Board; nor has greater success been vouchsafed to any laborers than to them. The Turkish Empire is open to us as to no other nation, and the decayed Oriental churches are receiving almost entirely the gospel at our hands. And it is a pure gospel. The churches gathered among the Armenians are as worthy of confidence as those gathered by the apostles, and by the blessing of God may be made as efficient in spreading the truth. In India, we have a wide and most important field among the Mahratta and Tamil races. In Northern China the openings are more numerous than we can enter. In South Africa we have a limited but interesting field; and Western Africa affords to us one well fitted to call forth the energies and educate the Christian zeal of the Freedmen of our country, and it seems to have been held in reserve for us by God to meet the wants of our colored people, and assist in their development. Africa and America, whose destinies have been so strangely blended in the past, are to react upon each other in blessings that shall efface the memory of the wrongs and cruelties of the age of slavery. As to the islands in the ocean world, it is enough for us to point to the Hawaiian peoples whom our missions have given to the community of nations; and though they are in a transition state from dependence upon missionaries to a condition of self-support, we must defend them from invasion and injury by others till they shall be able to preserve, by their own intelligence, the free institutions we have given them. And there is also the Micronesian mission, a most hopeful enterprise, an offshoot of Hawaiian zeal, and doubly precious to us, as a seal of the true Christianity of those recently regenerated islands. How intimately, therefore, are we related by past labors and present commitments to the whole world of mankind, and how much is the speed and thoroughness of the world's evangelization dependent upon the continued activities of Congregational Christians! We can not, if we would, disengage ourselves from the work; we would not, if we could.

WM. IVES BUDINGTON,
ZACHARY EDDY,
C. C. PARKER,
BENJAMIN DOUGLAS,
WILLIAM CARTER, } *Committee.*

This report was accepted and adopted.

Rev. Dr. Wolcott, of Ohio, of the committee on Business, reported the following resolution, without any recommendation: —

Resolved, That the Committee on the Roll be instructed to report the names of those members only who furnish a list of the churches that actually participated in the vote by which they were chosen.

The resolution was adopted.

The committee also reported the following resolution: —

Resolved, That the Committeee to whom the Report on Home Evangelization was referred, be requested to consider the expediency of organizing some system of benevolent effort, by which in the various regions of the country where the education of the whole population is not provided for by law, teachers may be sent forth, in company with missionaries, and schools be established wherever churches are gathered.

The resolution was adopted.

At this point, His Excellency, Gov. Andrew, of Massachusetts, entered the church, accompanied by Rev. Dr. Kirk and Major Wm. L. Burt. On reaching the platform, he was welcomed by the Moderator, in the following address: —

We are very happy, Gov. Andrew, to welcome you on this occasion. I am happy to present your Excellency to this council, representing three thousand Congregational churches in our land — a body with whose constitution your Excellency is of course familiar. When fully organized, as at first, we are, in a sense, a Christian State as well, having for our head an honored Governor of a sister State, who has stood by you, sir, shoulder to shoulder, in our dark and terrible struggle. [Applause.] — That noble man, from whose live-oak the wisdom of Connecticut, for seven successive years, hath hewn out her pillars of State. [Renewed applause.] And yet, sir, when he sits here among us, it is not in his capacity as a governor, but as a deacon of one of these little Christian Commonwealths, and as a member of the body of Christ, serving with us under Him who is Head over all principalities and powers, and who is Head over all things to his church.

It is no new thing, sir, for a body of Christian men, of Congregational men, to tender their expression of loyalty and respect to the State. These are loyal men; they have been loyal to the nation from first to last; and, sir, they have been loyal to good old Massachusetts, acknowledging her lead in this dark and terrible conflict. [Applause.] And we have rejoiced to feel, sir, that that State, whose Quincy Adams and Charles Sumner were the first confessors in this great moral conflict, and whose noble sons, in the streets of Baltimore, were the first martyrs in this material conflict, has been so nobly led through this dark and terrible storm. [Applause.] We honor you, sir, while with you we honor Him who hath ruled over all these mighty deeds for the restoration of the land; who himself hath taught us that a great redemption from a great sin comes only by a great sacrifice. While we bow reverently, acknowledging the hand of God, we rejoice also to honor those who have been his honored instruments. We thank you, sir, for your promptitude, your energy, your firmness throughout all this struggle; and we thank you, especially, for words that have roused the hearts of the people, — words such as few of our public men have been gifted to utter in this conflict. [Applause.] Words, stirring words from your lips, flashing across the wires, have thrilled our hearts in other cities and other States; and you, sir, have taught us to apply the words of Scripture as mottoes of patriotism, charging us, as I well remember, in one of our darkest hours, to go forward in this conflict "with the high praises of God in our mouths and the two-edged sword in our hands." We remembered, sir, that Massachusetts had once more, according to her motto, drawn the sword, that she might have again the sweet repose of liberty, — a sword drawn, only for the defense of justice and liberty, — and we knew that when she drew it, it would never be sheathed until justice and liberty were won.

We welcome you to-day, sir, as the representative of Massachusetts, in that long line of illustrious governors, excelled by the record of no other States. Governor of Massachusetts, this Council tenders you its respects; this Council will remember you in its prayers; this Council now waits the pleasure of your words. [Loud applause.]

To this address, Gov. Andrew responded as follows: —

Mr. Chairman and Gentlemen:—You ought not to expect one of my experience, — I say nothing of my years, — to be embarrassed. [Laughter.] I took the liberty to inquire this morning, concerning the hours of the afternoon session of your Council, because, being under the necessity of visiting Western Massachusetts and Connecticut to-morrow and next day, I feared that your body might adjourn before an opportunity should come to me of seeing it in session, and of paying my personal and official respects to the gentleman who is the permanent President of the organization, — Governor Buckingham of Connecticut, with whom I have had, for several years, a most agreeable intercourse, and for whom I entertain the highest respect. I did not know, nor suspect, that in visiting the Council I should be placed in any situation where attention would be called to my person or presence, differing at all from that of any other visitor; but since it has pleased you, Mr. Chairman, and you, gentlemen of the Council, to recognize in the person of an official representative, the merits and worth and history and character of that grand old Commonwealth which it is my fortune to attempt to serve, I can not, either in respect to her or to your kindness, omit to respond, out of place as perhaps, in other respects, I might be upon your platform, with such poor words of my own as may be given me to say.

I thank you, Mr. Chairman, for the cordial words with which you have alluded to the history of Massachusetts, and to the public services of her public men. I am sure there is no man or woman in all our domain who does not catch with gratitude and sentiments of cordial reciprocity, every sincere and kind word looking either to our past, present, or to our future;

for we recognize in our Commonwealth of Massachusetts, only one of the representative States of the American Union, patient to follow, and also prepared to lead. [Loud applause.] If in the past, either as leaders or followers, we have been found faithful to the great ideas which characterize American liberty, to the great duty which Divine Providence has laid upon this people, to the great hopes foreshadowed for us and for all mankind in the principles of that very Gospel in whose service you are met, we are grateful to that great and good Being who is the Father of man and the Sovereign of nations, that he has given to us such measure of liberty, that he has given to us such measure of grace. And, more than all, sir, we are grateful for the opportunities of this present hour, which opens to the faithful, devoted servants of universal truth to-day, a work for mankind which it was never the province of the sword to accomplish. [Applause.]

Mr. Chairman, the hour has come when the duties of statesmanship are before us, transcending in importance a thousand times, either the duties or the hardships of war. War, sir, is a question of science; war presents a problem of mathematics; and almost any one can solve that problem by a shrewd guess in advance. Assure us on which side are the strongest and heaviest battalions; assure us that the side on which the strongest and heaviest battalions are will never give up, and mathematics prove to us who will win. Let us be assured, Mr. Chairman, that truth and justice are on our side, and I do not know that we will win, in this our day. The days of God are long — those of men are short. The work of God is in eternity — the work of men is in time. The question now presents itself to the American people whether they are capable, by reason of conviction, by reason of a firm purpose, by reason of a sufficiently intelligent comprehension of their own duty and their own case, to link themselves with the fortunes of eternity, and in the great moral battles of the universe, fight with God. [Loud applause.] And I trust, Mr. President, that the meetings of such associations as yours, that the convenings of men led and inspired by high conceptions of duty, whose hearts anchor themselves to the Eternal Throne, may help to encourage, instruct, and inspire the people. [Applause.]

I know not how far I agree or how far I differ with a majority of the gentlemen, or any one of the gentlemen present, upon questions of dogmatic theology, and I suppose that neither you nor any one else cares. But I do know that you, as faithful citizens and Christian men, do care whether the people of Massachusetts, and those to whom, for a time, it is given in any measure to represent Massachusetts, are grounded in those doctrines, principles and methods of the Bible upon which were originally founded the free commonwealths of America. [Applause.] In a common purpose, with a common hope, encouraged by the expectation of good in this life and the promise of supernal good in that which is to come, let us devote ourselves, with one heart and one mind, toward the realization of the highest hopes of humanity, toward the perfection of all that which distinguishes and characterizes us as a free people, that which inspires the song of angels, and adds to the beatitude of heaven. [Loud applause.]

Rev. Mr. Quint, in behalf of the Business Committee, submitted the following resolutions: —

Whereas, all true principles of civil and religious freedom have originated from the Bible, and can be established and sustained only by the general circulation of the Word of God through all the channels of popular education, whether in the school or in the sanctuary; therefore,

Resolved, That we honor the wisdom, as well as the piety of our Puritan fathers, in ordering the daily use of the Bible in the schools established for the education of the people.

That we regret any departure from this time-hallowed usage, as destroying the life-giving power of popular education, which has no true basis but in those great principles of human brotherhood and equality, taught alone in the Holy Scriptures.

That, in our efforts to promote the education of the people, and to train up an intelligent, patriotic, and Christian community, understanding their rights and duties, and prepared to carry out the great mission of freedom and religion opening before this nation, we pledge ourselves to maintain the right of the Word of God in the school as in the sanctuary, and to resist, steadfastly, any and every encroachment on that wise provision of our fathers which carried the Bible into the daily education of the people.

The resolutions were adopted.

The committee also presented the following resolution, which was referred to the committee on Declaration of Faith: —

Resolved, That, in the gathering of new churches in the West and South, the National Council recommend that only those essential doctrines of the Gospel in which evangelical Christians generally are agreed should be made the condition of church fellowship.

The following resolutions were also submitted by the committee, and severally laid on the table: —

Resolved, That a committee be appointed to report an order of public Sabbath services in our churches, that will relieve us from the present confusing diversity by some appropriate order of service that will secure, in the denomination, general harmony.

Resolved, That a committee be appointed to consider and report on the expediency of recognizing, as part of the Congregational system, a class of ministers specially devoted to the work of promoting revivals of religion, in connection with pastors.

Resolved, That inasmuch as the enemies of Christianity are at this day persistent in their attempts to overthrow the Bible through the medium of science, a special committee be appointed by this Council, to give utterance to our confident belief that the Bible will withstand all the assaults of its opponents.

Resolved, That a committee be appointed to which all historical and statistical documents shall be referred.

The Business Committee also presented the following inquiry to the Council, which had been submitted to them: —

"Is it according to Congregational principles for a minister, who is not a pastor, to represent a church in an Ecclesiastical Council?"

The question was referred to the committee on Church Polity.

The following resolution was also submitted by the same committee: —

Resolved, That a committee be appointed to consider, and, if they deem it expedient, report upon the relations and duties of our denomination in relation to religious books and tracts.

On motion of Rev. Mr. Gulliver, of Connecticut, the resolution was referred to a special committee of three.

The following letter was read by Rev. Dr. Wolcott, and, on motion of Rev. Dr. Sturtevant, referred to a special committee of three: —

The Synod of the Waldensian Church, of Italy, to the Christians of the United States.

Brethren in Christ: — The Synod of the Waldensian Church, lately assembled for its annual session at San Giovanni, Piedmont, has felt it behooved it as a Christian body, to record, in their acts, their sympathy for you in the loss you have sustained by the death of your late President, and has directed me to convey to you, in writing, an expression of their feelings.

Need we say, brethren, with what horror we received the news of the atrocious murder which deprived your nation of its chief magistrate?

We had watched the course of that great and good man; we had seen him raised, in the providence of God, to be the liberator of an oppressed race, and, after years of war, preparing to be the pacificator of his country, as full of clemency in the hour of the triumph of his cause as he had been steady in carrying on the deadly struggle. We were rejoicing with him and with you that at last peace was dawning again on your country, when suddenly we were called to mourn and weep with you.

May God sustain you in this national bereavement, and make all your afflictions fruitful of good for your people!

As to Abraham Lincoln, he neither lived nor died in vain. A Christian life like his, humbly devoted to the right and to humanity, made great by great and good deeds, and crowned with a martyr's crown, adds to the moral wealth of mankind, is an immortal honor to your nation, and an evidence of the truth and power of our common faith such as no words could ever give.

By order, and in the name, of the Waldensian Synod.

LEON PILATTE, *the President.*

May, 1865.

Rev. Mr. Langworthy, from the committee on Nominations, reported as follows:—

COMMITTEE ON MINISTERIAL SUPPORT.

Hon. Edward D. Holton, of Wisconsin; Rev. Hiram Elmer, of Michigan; Rev. Edwin N. Lewis, of Illinois; Marshall S. Scudder, Esq., of Massachusetts; Dea. Selden M. Pratt, of Connecticut; Rev. William Salter, D. D., of Iowa; David S. Williams, Esq., of New York.

COMMITTEE ON BENEVOLENT SOCIETIES.

Rev. William A. Stearns, D. D., of Massachusetts; Rev. Joel H. Linsley, D. D., of Connecticut; Rev. Wooster Parker, of Maine; Rev. Jeremiah Butler, of New York; Rev. Calvin B. Cady, of Vermont; Martin Wright, of Illinois; Rev. Henry A. Miner, of Wisconsin.

Rev. Dr. Hopkins, of Massachusetts, asked to be excused from serving as chairman of the committee on Collegiate and Theological Education, and by vote of the Council he was excused, and, on the recommendation of the nominating committee, Rev. Seth Sweetser, D. D., of Massachusetts, appointed in his place.

Rev. Henry Ward Beecher, of New York, in behalf of the Messrs. Hook, organ-builders, tendered an invitation to the Council to attend an exhibition of their last and best organ at the Church of the Immaculate Conception, to-morrow, at five o'clock.

Mr. Bowen, of New York, from the committee on the Establishment of a Congregational Church in the city of Washington, submitted the following resolution:—

Resolved, That the authorities of the American Congregational Union be advised and requested to take into consideration the importance of a well-sustained Congregational church in the city of Washington, and having ascertained what facilities there are for the establishment of such a church, and what aid will be necessary, to institute such arrangements, according to their best judgment and discretion, for building or purchasing a suitable edifice in the national capital, in which a Congregational church may maintain the preaching of the gospel and the public worship of God.

Rev. Dr. ANDERSON, of Massachusetts. It would be rather convenient if that resolution could lie on the table for a little while. There is another object, not in conflict with this, and yet upon which it might be well to consult before this matter is brought before the Council.

No objection being made, the resolution was laid on the table.

The committee on the State of the Country were then called upon for their report, and it was read by Rev. Truman M. Post, D. D., of Missouri, the chairman, as follows: —

Whereas, In the beginnings of our national history, the God of our fathers brought them, the confessors of civil and religious liberty, to these shores, and gave to them to plant the germs of a free Christian civilization for a new world; and,

Whereas, After the lapse of more than two centuries, during which that civilization has extended over vast regions, and to the shores of the Western Ocean; and at the close of a terrible civil war, we, the representatives of churches adhering to the religious faith and order of those fathers, and witnesses in our times of the marvelous judgments and deliverances of God, have been gathered by his hand, from the breadth of a continent, to this cradle of our national life, as a National Ecclesiastical Council, in a crisis of solemn moment for the future of our country and the kingdom of God: we, therefore, feel it befitting the capacity in which we are assembled, and the hour in which we stand, to make the following utterances in regard to our country in this juncture of its history.

First of all, humbling ourselves under the mighty hand of God in contrite acknowledgment of the righteousness of his awful judgments afflicting our entire people, we yet record our grateful trust in his infinite mercy and everlasting truth, and we do in his presence this day, thus

Resolve, First, That for the deliverance of our nation from the insurgent and anarchical power that treacherously and remorselessly sought its life; for the preservation of our Union and of the integrity of our territory; for the triumph of right over wrong, of liberty over slavery, and of lawful government over usurpation; for the redemption — though at a terrible cost — of our country from the curse of slavery, and for the emancipation of four millions of our fellow-men from bondage; for the faith and hope, the intrepidity and endurance, given to our people in the days of calamity; for their patient and unstinted sacrifice of blood and treasure for the right, and their unwearied labor and liberality in works of Christian sympathy and beneficence; and for the final, crowning victory granted to our arms; we do this day ascribe praise and glory to the Lord of hosts. We also render thanks to the Lord that he has given to the members of our government — administrative and legislative — a faith that has never despaired of the republic, and a patience, courage, and sagacity that have not only triumphantly upborne us in the agonism of this rebellion, but guided us safely through complications threatening us with foreign war.

We offer thanks to our brave defenders, by land and sea, whose heroism has, through the hand of the Lord, achieved for us the victory; and we invoke for them, living or lying with the glorious dead, the love and honor, and, for the widows and orphans of those who have fallen, the generous protection and fostering care, of a grateful people; and we regard the rendering of this in the light of a most sacred debt of the republic.

Resolved, That we profoundly sympathize with the grief and horror of the nation at the assassination of its late beloved chief magistrate, ABRAHAM LINCOLN, and with that sentiment of our countrymen and of the civilized world which now places him among the foremost in the ranks of the martyrs for liberty and humanity in the history of mankind.

Resolved, That we extend to his honored successor, President ANDREW JOHNSON, assurances of our earnest sympathy and hearty co-operation in the momentous and arduous work devolved on him, by God, of the restoration of order and tranquillity to the country after the shock and ruin of this war, and of reconstruction, where needed, on the eternal principles of truth, liberty, and justice; and of so closing up the bloody gulf of this rebellion that neither treason nor ambition shall ever reopen it.

Resolved, That we regard rebellion against a government so just, benign, and beneficent as ours; so incorporated with the essential rights of man and the hopes of human liberty; so created and administered by the people for themselves, and sheltering a prosperity so vast and so brilliant; as a crime transcending the enormity of treason recorded in the history of other countries, or of conspiracy against other forms of political order; as a crime against freedom, civilization, and human nature itself; and we feel that it is due from our government in its final adjudication upon this highest of crimes, that, while blending mercy with justice, it shall so deal with treason that the sense of its guiltiness be not impaired, and that of the majesty of law and the divine sanction of legitimate government be sustained in the mind of the nation.

Resolved, That wrongs committed against our people and our soldiers, beyond the measure of the laws of war, — such as assassination, arson, introduction of pestilence, the massacre of captives, and the deliberate and systematic slow murder of tens of thousands of prisoners by exposure and starvation, — are crimes that can find no shelter under the pretext of being "political offences," and are beyond the pale of amnesties, challenging upon their authors, whenever and wherever lawfully convicted, justice from our own government as well as the wrath of Heaven.

16

Resolved, That we regard the late civil war as the judgment of Heaven upon slavery, and upon a nation in complicity with its mighty wrongs; a judgment punishing our practical infraction of our social and political life-principles, and demonstrating that such infraction is national suicide.

Resolved, That justice, honor, the maintenance of loyal control in the lately revolted States, and the safety of the nation, and gratitude for their eminent military and other services rendered during the war, imperatively require that we deal in a spirit of Christian sympathy and charity, and of a generous humanity, with a race held by this people two hundred years in bondage, and now thrust upon the perils and trials of new liberty; and that we see to it that they be protected and fortified in their new status by intellectual and religious culture, and the rights of the elective franchise, and all the privileges of freemen.

Resolved, That while we hail with gratitude the fact, that, by the removal of slavery, and the social and ecclesiastical conditions allied with it, vast regions are newly opened to a pure and free gospel, we, moreover, believe that by this war the mind of the nation at large, having been stirred to its depths by passion and suffering and the manifest tokens of a present God and a divine government in human affairs, has been thereby prepared for profounder convictions of Christian truth, and larger effusions of the Holy Spirit, and for a vaster religious movement than in the past.

Resolved, That we also at the same time recognize with solicitude the hazard, that from the disturbance or dissolution of old order, and from the shock given to former habitudes and ideas, and from new practices and modes of thought and feeling generated by the war, conditions of the popular mind may arise, that, unless illumined and restrained and guided by education and Christian truth, may project us upon courses wild, revolutionary, and ruinous.

Resolved, therefore, That in view of the above facts, we regard the present as a crisis in this nation's life, demanding the immediate appliance of the most effective means of education and evangelization in our power, and that amid the agencies, creative and organic, of social and political reconstruction on the eternal foundations of Right and Liberty and Truth, we regard as most effective and beneficent the religious Faith and Order of our Forefathers, — agencies primordial to our national life, and approved in history as the most powerful of vitalizing and conservative forces; and we therefore deem it as due to the perpetuity of our national well-being, that the churches which inherit that Faith and Order should endeavor to diffuse them throughout the extent of our country, and especially to those sections now in social and political ruin.

Resolved, That we who are now placed on this hight of history, and who have been permitted to behold great and terrible things which our fathers have not seen, having emerged from the stormy deeps of a civil war, and standing on the verge of a vast and mysterious continent of the future, do this day lift the psalm of thanksgiving where our fathers lifted it, mingling, as did theirs, with the roar of the Atlantic surge, to Him that sitteth King and Lord for evermore; and we commit our beloved country to him in humble prayer, that as he has been the God of our fathers, so he will be our God and the God of our children and our children's children, — even till above our national starry emblem shall be seen in heaven the sign of the second coming of the Son of man.

Signed,	T. M. POST,	J. C. WEBSTER,
	SETH MAY,	A. FISH,
	JAMES D. BELL,	E. D. HOLTON,
	A. C. BARSTOW,	A. B. ROBBINS,
	DUDLEY R. WHEELER,	CHARLES SECCOMBE,
	HENRY MORRIS,	S. C. POMEROY,
	O. E. DAGGETT,	E. M. LEWIS,
	J. M. HOLMES,	L. P. FISHER,
	EDWARD HAWES,	GEO. H. ATKINSON,
	ABNER H. BRYANT,	W. W. CRAWFORD,
	EDWIN JOHNSON,	MILAN HARRIS,
	J. A. THOME,	*Committee.*

Rev. Mr. SAVAGE, of Illinois. We all of us believe that our beloved President, Abraham Lincoln, was made what he was largely by the prayers of God's people; and I feel that we ought, in connection with this report, to unite in special prayer for President Johnson.

Rev. Mr. ALLEN, of Massachusetts. No one admires more the comprehensive wisdom of that report than I do; no one was more gratified at the various tributes which were rendered to the different classes who were mentioned in it than I was; but there is one class, it seems to me, that has been neglected, that should have the most earnest tribute of this body; and that is, the women of our country, whose patriotism, whose energy, whose fidelity, whose humanity, whose beneficence, have been unparalleled in the history of the world. [Loud applause.] I hope that a resolution may be incorporated with the rest, significant of that wonderful part of our history and the history of the world.

Rev. HENRY WARD BEECHER, of New York. I am very thankful for those resolutions, — for every word in them; I only ask that there be more such. And especially one resolution, which should cover a ground which I think has not even been alluded to. There have been thousands and thousands of loyal men in all the rebellious States, who have taken their lives in their hands, and have endured incalculable misery. They have been chronic martyrs in this great cause. We ought not to forget them. Besides that, it seems to me, now that the rebellion is broken, that the common people of the South, who have been duped and deceived, by their ignorance made the easy creatures of their leaders, ought to receive from us some assurance of kindness, of hopefulness, that they may not feel that there is rancor in our hearts toward them. While their leaders should be given to justice, it seems to me that we ought to express a kind and sympathetic feeling toward those who have been misled by them in the South. With a recognition of the loyal citizens of the South, and also some kind remembrance of the common people, I know not how that report could be bettered.

Rev. Dr. KIRK, of Massachusetts. I would move that the report be referred back to the committee. There may be some other matters to be rectified, which would be brought to the attention of the committee, if it were recommitted. For instance, it seems to me there ought to be some recognition of the vast amount of work performed in the army by volunteers, for it was invaluable in its influence upon the soldiers and the nation. And then, moreover, I would suggest whether we are not bound to have some reference to our friends in foreign lands, — such men as the Rev. Dr. Raleigh and the Rev. Dr. Massie, who are with us, and who fought our battles in the midst of the opposition of our enemies in Europe. [Loud applause.]

Rev. E. P. MARVIN, of Massachusetts. There is another suggestion. I have heard nothing special about our colored friends at the South, and their remarkable loyalty and fidelity; but if there are any persons in this country to whom we are peculiarly indebted, under God, for our success, it is to them.

Rev. Dr. LINSLEY, of Connecticut. I want to know if this report is presented as the unanimous action of the committee?

Rev. Dr. POST, of Missouri. I will answer that. It was the report of all we could get together this morning. I may be permitted to state, Mr. Moderator, that there is much that ought to be said that can not be said there, unless you write a history of the war. (Laughter and applause.) We can not pay tribute to everybody to whom we owe it, for, I thank the great Giver of helpers to us, we have those to whom we are indebted all the world over. Are not the women of this country included among "the people" to whom we render thanks for their liberality and for their sympathy? I had in view the Christian Commission in the words I employed there; I could not spread out the thought without making a report to which I believed your patience would be inadequate.

Rev. Mr. THOME, of Ohio. As a member of the committee, I desire to say, that I hope action will be taken now. We shall never be better able to act with unanimity and cordiality than we are at this time. I cordially join in the suggestion, that after the adoption of the report, we unite in prayer.

THE MODERATOR (Hon. C. G. Hammond). The chair would suggest, that it is perfectly proper to adopt the resolutions offered, if Dr. Kirk will withdraw his motion, and then, if other parties wish to introduce these other topics, they can do so.

Dr. KIRK said he would withdraw his motion, his object having been accomplished.

Hon. Mr. POMEROY, of Kansas. It is not to be supposed that in a single resolution or two resolutions the committee could report what would be acceptable to everybody. Our only effort was to hit upon some general topics on which we could all agree, and report them to the Council. The fact is, the report would suit me better if we spoke out a little more plainly about hanging somebody. [Applause.] I am very willing to mingle our justice with mercy to the common people of the

South, as has been suggested by our friend Henry Ward Beecher; but it does seem to me it is time somebody was hung. (Applause.) Some wholesome hanging, I think, would have settled this question in the minds of the American people long ago; and I do not believe that a convention, even of this character, composed largely of clergymen,— men who love forgiveness and mercy,—would be harmed if it adopted a little stiffer resolution on this question. I will only say, that I yielded to this report, on that question, for the sake of harmony, because I thought everybody would go for it; I never supposed that anybody would want to temper it more mildly. If the report is adopted, I will take it upon myself to offer a resolution expressing my own views on the subject.

Rev. H. W. BEECHER, of New York. I would inquire if other matters can be added to the report, after it is adopted?

The MODERATOR. Yes, sir.

The question was then put, and the report adopted.

Rev. Mr. Dexter read the following invitation from the trustees of the Pilgrim Society, Plymouth, which was accepted:—

To the Congregational Council:—

GENTLEMEN,—In anticipation of your intended visit to Plymouth, June 22d, in behalf of the trustees of the Pilgrim Society, you are invited to visit Pilgrim Hall. It will be open on that day for your reception, and a committee will be appointed to accompany the different sections to places of interest.

(Signed) TIMOTHY GORDON,
One of the Trustees.

BOSTON, June 19.

Rev. Mr. Langworthy, of the committee on Nominations, reported the following committees, heretofore ordered, and the reports were adopted:—

COMMITTEE ON BOOKS AND TRACTS.

Rev. Henry Ward Beecher, of New York; Rev. Leonard Bacon, D. D., of Connecticut; Lowell Mason, jr., of New Jersey.

COMMITTEE ON COMMUNICATIONS FROM ITALY.

Rev. Edward N. Kirk, D. D., of Massachusetts; Rev. Julian M. Sturtevant, D. D., of Illinois; Rev. Edward Beecher, D. D., of Illinois.

Rev. Mr. Quint, of the Business Committee, offered a report, recommending that the business for to-morrow be the hearing of the report of the committee to whom was referred the report on the Evangelization of the West and South; that the whole day be given to its discussion, if necessary; that all the speakers be limited to twelve minutes; that, if the discussion be not closed at five o'clock, an evening session be held, at eight o'clock; and that the consideration of the subject be ended to-morrow.

The report was adopted.

The moderator then called for the report of the committee to whom was referred the communication from the Massachusetts Convention of Congregational Ministers; and it was read by the chairman, Rev. A. H. Quint, of Massachusetts, as follows: —

REPORT.

"The Massachusetts Convention of Congregational Ministers" requests this Council "to use such language in their proceedings as a Trinitarian Congregational Council, as shall recognize the fact that there are Unitarian and other Congregational churches in this Commonwealth." In addition to this communication there has appeared in the public prints, though not laid before this body, a protest against the terms of the call for the assembling of this Council, as imperiling interests valuable to the members of a body styled a "Ministerial Conference," in whose behalf it is signed. The eminent standing and character of the persons who sincerely feel that a real grievance would be occasioned by the course against which they protest, as well as the respect due to the denomination which this Council represents, requires a just and deliberate avowal of the grounds upon which we use the title of "Congregational Churches of the United States."

Our denomination is the same with that of the first churches of New England. We trace back our lineage in an uninterrupted line to that period. The same fellowship has been perpetuated, based upon a particular system of doctrines and polity, to which we now hold. The denomination which we represent has thus had a distinct and recognized existence, as clear as history can make any historical fact, by all requisite limitations and declarations.

This denomination has always had the distinctive name of "Congregational churches."

It is needless to quote authorities; for, from the days of John Cotton, the name Congregational was used to designate a particular denomination, of a faith well defined and now unchanged, as well as a peculiar polity. Nor did any others, so far as we can learn, though holding the same polity, assume that name while not belonging to this denomination. This distinctive denominational name is still our heritage from the fathers.

It is true that some other churches now hold the same polity, in a greater or less degree of strictness, while differing from us in points of doctrine. In addition to some Unitarian churches, Baptists, Free-Will Baptists, and Universalists hold similar views of church polity. But it is an historical fact, that in America these denominations came into existence after the denomination which we represent had acquired an undisputed right to the title which we still hold.

Some of the churches formerly in our denomination became separated from it early in the present century, by reasons of convictions which led them to renounce the doctrinal principles which were and are essential to the fellowship of this denomination, as declared by our platforms, and established by uninterrupted practice from the days of our fathers. But the separation of a section in Massachusetts, where its chief strength lay, which, in 1820, numbered, so far as can be learned, but a small portion of the denomination, does not, it seems to us, deprive the old and recognized denomination of its ancestral name. That some separating churches may retain the same kind of government does not affect the fact that they do not belong to the denomination which has always kept its distinctive title. Nor does such a secession or separation render it at all necessary that the denomination should either give up its old name, or add any distinctive prefix. When the Wesleyans left the Church of England, the latter was not called upon to modify its title. When the Protestant Methodists separated from the Methodist Episcopal Church, that church took no new name. When several bodies of Presbyterians were separated from the Presbyterian Church in the United States, that body retained unquestioned its old designation, although the seceding bodies held the same views of church polity. The separating portion might well adopt a new title; but the denomination remaining needed no change, nor could any be rightfully demanded.

We find it also to be a fact, that the churches, in whose behalf complaint is made, have as a denomination, deliberately adopted a new title. In their official capacity, a recent convention, representing the Unitarian churches, wholly ignored the term Congregational, and, as "Christian churches of the Unitarian faith," organized a permanent body styled "The National Conference of Unitarian Churches." It is thus evident that there can be no conflict whatever to cause confusion or misunderstanding between the two denominations.

We are also unable to find that the Unitarian churches require adherence to the Congregational platform as a condition of denominational fellowship. Many of their churches are said to be Independent, not Congregational. In some places church organizations have been utterly abandoned, as seems to have been recognized in the call for their recent convention, which asked delegates from societies as well as churches.

While stating that as a denomination we hold a denominational name to which no other lays claim, and which the parties complaining do not assert belongs to any other denomination, we are far from denying that there are other particular churches which maintain the same polity with ourselves. This fact was distinctly recognized in the call under which this Council is assembled. That call was addressed to "those Congregational churches in the United States which are in recognized fellowship and co-operation through the general associations, conferences, or conventions, in the several States." How far this may extend, it is clear that it recognizes that there are Congregational churches other than these. We do not see how any doubt could exist as to what churches were intended. It would be idle to say that any churches are in recognized fellowship through the Massachusetts Convention of Congregational Ministers. Indeed, the fact that only those of our denomination have appeared shows that the call was sufficiently understood.

We see no reason, therefore, why we should prefix the term Trinitarian to the name of our denomination. We are no more Trinitarian than we are Unitarian. If we prefix Trinitarian to distinguish us from Unitarians and Universalists, we must take some other prefixes to distinguish us from Baptists and Free-Will Baptists. We see no need of either.

But inasmuch as it appears that some of those who protest have particularly in view a fear lest, if they adhere to the name of their denomination as recently officially promulgated, and we adhere to the name of ours, some rights of theirs to property, held under the name of Congregational, may be jeopardized, we do now declare that we should deem it dishonorable and unchristian to interfere with any of their present rights to funds or other property under whatever name their holders act, or to attempt to pervert funds given for one kind of religious doctrine to the use of another, whether in colleges, churches, or other bodies. And we distinctly put on record, that, from our retaining our old name of "Congregational," without any modification or prefix, — as we intend to do, — there should be no inference whatever drawn to the legal prejudice of any bodies not in our fellowship, as to any funds or other property to which those bodies lay claim.

We are happy to know that so many of these churches still retain the old polity. And whenever their convictions of duty will allow them to stand on the old platform of faith, of their and our fathers, gladly will we feel that we are one again.

Respectfully submitted.

ALONZO H. QUINT,
W. T. EUSTIS, JR., } *Committee.*
ASA FREEMAN,

Rev. Dr. PATTON, of Illinois. I move to strike out that portion of the report which says, "We are no more Trinitarian than we are Unitarian." It is sure to be misunderstood in some quarters. That is the only objection.

This motion was not seconded, and the question being put, the report was adopted unanimously, and, on motion of Rev. Mr. Eustis, of Connecticut, it was ordered, that it be transcribed, and forwarded to the Massachusetts Convention of Congregational Ministers.

A CONGREGATIONAL HOUSE.

Rev. Dr. Wolcott, of the committee on Business, presented the following resolution : —

Resolved, That the National Congregational Council are pleased to learn that the American Congregational Society has undertaken to erect a Congregational House in the city of Boston, as a suitable memorial of the present meeting, which shall serve as a secure repository for our Congregational literature, in a National Library, — as a place of resort for our brethren, coming to this ancient home of the denomination and the fathers, and also as a convenient center of operations, designed to promote a knowledge of our principles and polity, and the unity and fellowship of our churches throughout the land; and while this object, involving an outlay of $100,000, is commended first of all to the enterprising citizens of Boston and vicinity, with whom it originated, it is also cordially commended to the liberal co-operation of our churches throughout the land.

Rev. Dr. ANDERSON, of Massachusetts. Mr. Moderator, — I do not think, at this stage of the business, that it is proper to enter into any explanation with regard to this object. I ought, however, to explain why I objected to the passage of the resolution proposed just now. I had been detained from the meeting, to discharge the duty of chairman of a committee from the American Congregational Association, and on coming into the house, I was told that there was a proposition coming before this body to raise $100,000 for a church in the city of Washington, and very likely it might be well to have some understanding before these two propositions came before your body. On further explanation, however, I became convinced that there was no reason for objecting to that proposition at all. In regard to this resolution, I do not propose to make any remarks upon it at the present time, but would propose that it be referred to a special committee, to report to this body.

The resolution was so referred.

CHURCH IN WASHINGTON.

The resolution in regard to the establishment of a Congregational Church in Washington, was then taken from the table.

Rev. Dr. STURTEVANT, of Illinois. I only wish to say, that there is a very serious doubt in my mind in regard to entering into this matter of church-building with a view to any particular place, — even Washington city. The question is, whether it would not be much better to take up the matter as a whole, — the subject of church-building in Washington included, — than to take up each place separately. I can not obtain the consent of my own mind, at this present moment, to vote for that proposition, in the shape in which it is.

Rev. Dr. BUDINGTON, of New York. Let me call the attention of

Dr. Sturtevant to this fact: that the passage of the resolution does not commit us to any thing of the kind. I share with him in the feeling to which he has given utterance, and I should have spoken to the same purport if there had been any thing in the resolution conflicting with the sentiments which he has expressed.

On motion of Rev. Dr. Wolcott, of Ohio, the resolution was referred to the committee on Church-Building.

Adjourned.

SIXTH DAY, TUESDAY, JUNE 20.

The Council was called to order at 9 o'clock, A. M., and opened by prayer from the moderator.

The journal of yesterday was read by the scribe and approved.

CIVIL RIGHTS OF REBELS.

Rev. Dr. POST, of Missouri. It was the tacit understanding yesterday, when the resolutions from the committee on the State of the Country were adopted, that I should prepare two or three more which should be subjoined. I have prepared three resolutions for that purpose; but I offer them upon my own personal responsibility, not having had time to consult with the committee.

THE MODERATOR stated that under the rule the resolutions must come before the Council through the Business Committee.

On motion, that rule was suspended.

Rev. Dr. POST resumed. These resolutions relate, first to two classes of society in the revolted States to which the former resolutions made no special allusion, and were therefore objected to. There was also objection because the Sanitary Commission and Christian Commission were not alluded to. That I have regarded as being embraced in the substance of the resolutions. I have thought it proper to add a resolution in regard to the services and sacrifices of the women of the country; not because I did not before design to embrace them among the people of the country. I felt that it was as impossible to separate the services and heroic devotion of our women from our people, in this war, as to separate the sun from the light of day. But as the resolutions were not understood as distinctly ascribing credit and expressing gratitude to this portion of our people, I felt that it would be my pleasure and the pleasure of the Convention that there should be such a distinct recognition; and I have therefore introduced a resolution to that effect. I should feel exceedingly sorry, — I should feel ashamed, living where I have been during the years of this war, witnessing what I have witnessed of the services of the ladies of our State, which have rendered dearer to me the dearest friends I have on earth, if I could be supposed, in this grave body and in this grave crisis, to present resolutions which should omit proper mention and honorable mention of this portion of our brave people.

Rev. Dr. THOMPSON, of New York. At the request of Dr. Post, I will be to him what Hobab was to Moses, — I will be eyes unto him. The resolutions are these: —

Resolved, That we extend to the inhabitants of the late revolted States who have been snared into this rebellion through ignorance, surprise, or overbearing violence of public sentiment, or forced by the power of a merciless conscription, our sympathy and commiseration, and our readiness to welcome them back to civil fellowship and fraternity under the old flag.

Resolved, That those who have maintained steadfast loyalty amid general treason and revolt, undaunted by popular rage or despotic violence, braving, in the cause of the country, the terrors of imprisonment, torture, robbery, and starvation, and of death itself, rank amid the noblest heroes and martyrs of this war, and deserve lasting honor and gratitude.

Resolved, That the heroic devotion and self-sacrifice of the loyal women of the country, during this war, will ever be gratefully remembered as having been of vital efficacy to the triumph of our cause, and will excite the admiration of history, as examples of moral beauty and sublimity, unsurpassed in human story.

Rev. Mr. QUINT, of Mass. I wish that first resolution was expressed a little differently, — at least, the latter part of it. It seems to me a little too strong. For one, I am not prepared to now welcome back those people who have fought against us, to full fellowship. Persons so easily snared through ignorance are not the persons to be welcomed back immediately to full civil rights. If they are, as sure as the sun shines to-day, they will again become the tools of those leaders, again be snared in just the same way, and again support the same sort of men. They are unfit for civil rights until they are a little more enlightened and intelligent. Those men have been fighting through the war against us. They are brave men, — for I have seen something of their work, — but they are uncommonly stupid and ignorant. They do not know any thing near as much as the blacks there. I say that until they repent, they are unfit to come back and be trusted with a vote. Every one of this class ought to be disfranchised for a reasonable time. [Applause.] I move to strike out the last clause.

Hon. Mr. HAMMOND, of Illinois. Why not let it read, "upon evidence of repentance"?

Rev. Mr. QUINT. Because I want their repentance to have years long enough to prove itself genuine. [Applause.]

Hon. Mr. HAMMOND. "On evidence of genuine repentance," then?

Rev. Mr. QUINT. No, — that is not enough; I want it fixed that that evidence shall be by waiting long enough to make the thing clear and safe.

Rev. Dr. Post, of Missouri. I never designed to convey the idea that they should be restored to citizenship or the rights of franchise. I see that the resolution may be misunderstood, and I will strike out the word "civil."

Rev. Mr. Quint. I will not object to that, for one, although it goes terribly against my grain ever to see one of those scoundrels under the old flag again. [Applause.]

Rev. Mr. Bliss, of Tennessee. It seems to me that even with that modification the idea will be that after all they are to be restored to general citizenship. Upon this subject I think the Council should give no uncertain sound. The language, even as it now stands, conveys the idea that we are willing to welcome them back at once to all the rights of citizenship. That we are not ready to do. If I understand the tone of public sentiment, we are not ready to welcome back any man who has borne arms or held a civil or military commission against the government of the United States. [Applause.] The amendments to the Constitution of Missouri, and the amendments to the Constitution of Tennessee, from which State I now come, prescribe a term of years before even the rank and file, with all the evidence of repentance they can bring, can be restored again to the right of suffrage. [Applause.] This is as it should be; and we are safe in no other way. [Applause.] Would that these views might ring through the nation, that we must by a term of years give space for repentance; and even then let there be no general law by which they shall come back, but let evidence be required of genuine repentance. [Renewed applause.] By this course alone can we be safe. I would suggest, therefore, that there be an amendment embodying in the resolution the idea that a suitable term of years should be given as space for repentance before these men should be allowed the full rights of citizenship.

A member moved to postpone the further consideration of this resolution indefinitely.

The motion was rejected by a decisive vote.

Rev. Mr. Allen, of Massachusetts, suggested the addition of a saving clause at the end, "the right of the citizen to franchise excepted."

Dea. Eddy, of Massachusetts, moved to refer the resolutions to a special committee.

Rev. Dr. Dutton moved to amend by referring it to the same committee that had been formerly appointed upon the State of the Country.

The motion to refer to that committee was agreed to.

On motion of Hon. Mr. Douglas, of Connecticut, Rev. Mr. Bliss, of Memphis, Tennessee, was added to the committee.

Rev. Dr. Todd, of Massachusetts, suggested that this resolution should be placed last of the three reported this morning.

FINANCIAL REPORT.

Dea. STODDARD, from the committee on Finance, reported that the amount of funds received from 360 churches was $3,972, of which 176 Western churches contributed $1,479, and 184 Eastern churches, $2,493; being an average of $9 to each Western, and $13 to each Eastern church; the dividing line being an imaginary meridian line through central New York. The total amount of traveling expenses was $7,818; double the amount received. The committee asked for further instructions as to the distribution of the fund.

On mótion of Rev. Dr. Thompson, the matter was referred to a select committee, which, on behalf of the Nominating Committee, he named as follows: —

NEW COMMITTEE ON FINANCE.

Hon. Charles G. Hammond, of Illinois; Hon. Amos C. Barstow, of Rhode Island; Asahel Finch, Esq., of Wisconsin; Daniel S. Williams, Esq., of New York; Rev. Henry Ward Beecher, of New York; Hon. Henry P. Haven, of Connecticut; Hon. Samuel Williston, of Massachusetts; Dea. Samuel Holmes, of New York; Hon. Douglas Putnam, of Ohio; Dea. Sherman S. Barnard, of Michigan; Dea. Simon Page, of Maine; Rev. Samuel G. Buckingham, of Massachusetts; Dea. Philo Carpenter, of Illinois (subsequently added).

The committee, as named, was agreed to.

COMMITTEE ON AMERICAN CONGREGATIONAL ASSOCIATION.

Rev. Mr. Langworthy, from the committee on Nominations, reported the following names for the committee on American Congregational Association: —

Rev. Christopher Cushing, of North Brookfield, Massachusetts; Rev. Ezekiel Russell, D. D., of Massachusetts; Dea. John Smith, of Andover, Massachusetts; Rev. Samuel D. Cochran, of Iowa; Rev. Samuel G. Wright, of Illinois; Hon. Walter Booth, of Connecticut.

ON BOOKS AND TRACTS, — ADDITIONAL.

Rev. Jacob Ide, D. D., of West Medway, Massachusetts; Timothy Dwight, Esq., of Beloit, Wisconsin.

The report was adopted.

RIGHTS OF MEMBERS.

Rev. Mr. Quint stated, in explanation of the action of the Business Committee, that that committee had no discretion as to admitting subjects proposed, but were required by the rule to report all matters referred to them to the Convention.

A member moved to amend the rule, so as to leave it to the discretion of the committee what they should report.

Hon. Mr. HAMMOND, of Illinois. That will never do. We are all elected as peers, and each has a right to bring before the Council what he thinks best, upon his own individual responsibility. This committee was only permitted to be appointed on that condition. If we are foolish, we can not help it; and the churches who sent us are responsible.

Rev. Mr. QUINT. The committee do not ask for a change in the rule, but merely wish to escape censure for reporting unnecessary matters.

Rev. Dr. BACON, of Connecticut. If any thing comes before the committee which strikes them as particularly foolish, they should say so to the gentleman who brings it to them.

UNIVERSAL SUFFRAGE.

Rev. Mr. Quint, from the Business Committee, reported the following resolution: —

Resolved, That a committee of three be appointed to proceed to Washington and present in person to President Johnson the resolutions on the State of the Country, and especially that part in relation to the punishment of traitors and universal suffrage.

Hon. Mr. Child, of Massachusetts, moved to lay the resolution upon the table ; but withdrew his motion.

Hon. Mr. HAMMOND, of Illinois. There are some gentlemen here who feel much interested in presenting to the President the resolutions on the State of the Country; and I understand that they are going to Washington. If we strike out the words "proceed to Washington and," so that they shall merely present the resolutions to the President, I think there will be no objection to the committee.

The resolution was amended accordingly.

Hon. Mr. Child renewed the motion to lay the resolution upon the table.

The motion was rejected.

Rev. Dr. BEECHER, of Illinois, said. I think that the topic mentioned in these resolutions is practically the most important topic before this nation, and one upon which every influence that can be exerted is important to be exerted at this time. I see by the morning papers that the proclamation to reorganize the Southern States, by President Johnson, has gone forth, with reference to at least four States, upon the white basis. It is also reasonable to believe that when a patriotic man takes a course which appears to be dangerous in its results, there must be some considerations for that course. Upon that ground I suspend my judgment with regard to the action of President Johnson in the premises. I have been informed, as I suppose credibly, that President Johnson supposed he should not be sustained by the public sentiment of the nation, if he proceeded upon any other basis, and that he is at least disposed to extend universal suffrage to the colored people.

I feel that if there is any one thing about which we ought to be solicitous, it is that this matter of reorganizing these States on the white basis shall not go so far that the whole we have gained by the war shall virtually slip out of our hands. We are, in my judgment, more in danger upon that point than upon any other point whatever. [Applause.] And we are blind to the interests of the country, if we who have been standard-bearers, — for I say that the Congregational body have had more sagacity and more prominence in holding up the true principles than any other body of men in this country, — if we do not exert the moral influence we can exert by sending a committee directly to President Johnson. If we allow the resolutions to slumber in the pages of a newspaper, perhaps President Johnson to the year's end may never see them; for he does not read every newspaper that is published. I hope that the resolution will pass.

Rev. Dr. STURTEVANT, of Illinois. I do not know but I am going to make a remark that will throw me into the minority in this Christian Council. If it does, I can bear it, for I have been in the minority before. I am opposed to the phrase "universal suffrage," occurring in that resolution; and nobody can ever make me vote for that. I am in favor of striking out from our statute book all disqualifications which depend on color. I am in favor of letting the colored man have the same rights as any other man has. But I am not in favor of universal suffrage; and I suspect that the minority who will be with me, if I am in the minority, will be a very respectable one. I shall therefore want the resolution so amended that the Convention shall not commit itself for universal suffrage through this land. Universal suffrage does not exist in Massachusetts or in Connecticut. Both Massachusetts and Connecticut have set a noble example, which the whole nation should follow, of the limitation of suffrage to intelligent men, of the limitation of suffrage to men that can read and write their own mother tongue. [Applause.] I want the resolution so modified as to be consistent with that view of the case.

Hon. Mr. CHILD, of Massachusetts. I hope the Convention will consider for a moment what is involved in the proposition now before them. If President Johnson and his advisers have settled upon a policy that is to guide them upon this question of voting in the reconstruction of the States, — whether that be right or whether it be wrong, I am not now to say, — is it wise for this Council to adopt a resolution to send a delegation of its members to arraign — for that is the effect of it — the decision of the government upon such an important question?

Again, sir; it says, "in favor of universal suffrage;" and to what does that apply? It applies to all the people of the rebel States. It proposes that this Council should say to the administration, that they should adopt a rule, with regard to these people, admitting them to vote, when they could not to-day vote in Massachusetts or in Connecticut.

I will say that the idea that the word "white" should ever have been in the constitutions of these States, I abominate. A man is not to be excluded because of the color of his skin, nor is he to be admitted to vote because he is black. There are restrictions in Massachusetts. There are restrictions in all the States. I think we are going too far in regard to this matter. All the States have their different qualifications, — in New York, one; in Pennsylvania another; in Rhode Island another; in New Hampshire and Vermont, others and different. And now we propose to declare the sentiment of this Ecclesiastical Council upon a great question of public policy lying at the very foundation of the government. I think it would be better to declare great principles without going into these details. For one I am not willing to vote for the resolution because it involves a principle beyond that adopted even in Massachusetts, and far beyond most of the New England States.

Rev. Dr. BACON, of Connecticut. There is another view of the question which does not seem to have occurred very clearly in any thing that has been uttered here as yet. We are an Ecclesiastical Council. We take cognizance of the things that pertain to the kingdom of Christ. We have a right to take cognizance here of all moral questions, because what is moral is religious. We have a right to say here, in the name of Christ and of the New Testament, that God hath made of one blood all nations of men to dwell upon all the face of the earth; and that all these distinctions which rest upon the color of a man's skin, or the straightness or kink of his hair, are unchristian and impious. We have a right to say that; let us say it.

But is it our province as an Ecclesiastical Council to interfere in what is purely and simply a political question? It is not a question of universal right who shall vote in an election to the legislature. The right of voting is not a right of human nature. I have known men to come from New Hampshire into Connecticut with high-flown ideas of the rights of man, and insist upon voting without the six months' residence which our laws require, without having become citizens of Connecticut, and approach very nearly to a violation of the law in other particulars in order to get their vote into the ballot box of Connecticut. If that were a universal right of human nature, I could justify such men in a measure. But I do not believe that the right to vote is any part of the rights of human nature. The right of suffrage is a right which society confers upon classes of society. The infant of yesterday does not vote; nor does his mother or his nurse vote for him. The right to vote in the State of Alabama is a right to be determined by the laws and Constitution of Alabama, and we are not to dictate to the President of the United States, nor in an ecclesiastical capacity and character are we to send a commission to argue with him upon a question of Constitutional law. I hope this Ecclesiastical Council will not compromise its dignity or its authority as a Council of churches of Jesus Christ by going into this political question. I agree fully and perfectly with all that has been or can be said in behalf of the right of the negro in the Southern States to vote on the same footing and the same terms as the white man, and I believe that the salvation of our country in time to come depends upon their attaining that right fully.

(A member inquired whether this debate was relevant, and the moderator replied it was.)

Dr. BACON resumed: I am speaking against presenting these resolutions to the President of the United States. In order to avoid the misconstructions which continually arise, I was saying that I am ready to concur with everybody here and with every loyal heart in the North, that the salvation of the country depends upon the attainment of the right of suffrage by the black men of the South and upon their standing upon the same political level in all respects with the white men of the South. But I agree with President Sturtevant fully that this principle of universal suffrage is one to which we ought not to commit ourselves. We do not believe in it. There is not a mother's child among us that believes in it.

Rev. Dr. BEECHER, of Illinois, interposed and called attention to the fact that the resolutions offered yesterday said nothing about universal suffrage; and called upon the committee therefore to lay before the President something that did not exist.

The MODERATOR explained that it included the resolutions offered this morning and referred.

Rev. Dr. PATTON, of Illinois, suggested the substitution of the phrase "impartial suffrage."

Rev. Dr. THOMPSON, of New York, moved to strike out the last part of the resolution consisting of the words: — "and especially that part in relation to the punishment of traitors and universal suffrage."

Rev. Dr. BACON resumed: I agree to that entirely; but I do not agree to the idea that we are to tell President Johnson, directly or indirectly, that he has mistaken his business and duty and power; and, furthermore, I do not agree to the idea of those gentlemen who suppose President Johnson to be invested with the power of imperial government over the Southern States. Let him give account of himself to God; let him give account of himself to the people of the United States; to the House of Representatives, to the Senate if the House of Representatives shall impeach him, and to the Supreme Court of the United States; but let us not as an Ecclesiastical Council undertake to guide him, to dictate to him, or even to counsel him on a question which is a law question and not a religious question, not a question of ethics.

Andrew Johnson will proceed, if I understand his nature, in the course in which he has been organizing the governments of the Southern States by the votes of those people, who, under the Constitution and laws of those States as they existed prior to the pretended secession, are the sovereignty of those States under the Constitution of the United States. I believe he agrees with us — I have every reason to believe he agrees with us and with every intelligent and loyal man in the belief that the right of suffrage must be given to the black people of the Southern States upon the same basis and under the same conditions with the white people; but he believes that that thing must be done in a legal way, and not done by the right of conquest. We ought to be careful how we commit ourselves upon questions which are among the deepest and most perplexing and disputed questions of constitutional law, now before, or soon to come before, not only the Houses of Congress but the Courts for adjudication. I have no objection to laying the resolutions upon the State of the Country before the President, but I object to proceeding one inch beyond that, to give him as an ecclesiastical body counsel upon questions of constitutional law.

The amendment was agreed to.

The question recurred upon the resolution, as amended.

A member moved to lay the resolution upon the table.

The motion was rejected.

The resolution, as amended, was then adopted by a decisive vote.

EXCURSION TO PLYMOUTH ROCK.

The committee of Arrangements announced that the train would leave for Plymouth at 9½ o'clock on Thursday morning instead of the earlier hour before reported.

TOBACCO.

Rev. Mr. Quint reported from the Business Committee the following resolution offered by David S. Williams, of Flushing, Long Island: —

" *Resolved*, That the committee appointed by this Council to consider the evil of intemperance be also requested to consider its twin vice, the improper use of tobacco, particularly by ministers and church members; and in case the said committee shall decide to bring in a report or testimony against the former evil, they are hereby instructed to bring in at the same time some suitable report or testimony against the latter."

On motion of Rev. Dr. Wolcott, of Ohio, the resolution was so amended as to leave the subject discretionary with the committee, and then referred to the committee on Temperance.

WESTERN COLLEGIATE EDUCATION.

Rev. Mr. Quint, from the Business Committee, reported resolutions regarding the Society in relation to Collegiate Education in the West; which on his motion were referred to the committee on Colleges.

THE STATE OF THE COUNTRY.

Rev. Mr. Bliss asked and obtained permission, from the committee appointed to revise the additional resolutions offered this morning by Rev. Dr. Post, on the state of the country, to report; and reported the same with a few verbal amendments.

A member moved to insert the words "or forced."

The amendment was agreed to.

The resolutions were then adopted as follows: —

Resolved, That we extend to the inhabitants of the late revolted States who have been snared into this rebellion through ignorance, surprise, or overbearing violence of public sentiment, or forced by the power of a merciless conscription, our sympathy and commiseration, and our readiness, after a suitable time has elapsed, to welcome them, on satisfactory evidence of loyalty, to civil fellowship and fraternity under the old flag.

Resolved, That those who have maintained steadfast loyalty amid general treason and revolt, undaunted by popular rage or despotic violence, braving, in the cause of the country, the terrors of imprisonment, torture, robbery, and starvation, and of death itself, rank amid the noblest heroes and martyrs of this war, and deserve lasting honor and gratitude.

Resolved, That the heroic devotion and self-sacrifice of the loyal women of the country during this war will ever be gratefully remembered as having been of vital efficacy to the triumph of our cause, and will excite the admiration of history as examples of moral beauty and sublimity unsurpassed in human story.

EVANGELIZATION IN THE WEST AND SOUTH.

Rev. Dr. Dutton, from the committee to which was referred the Report upon Evangelization in the West and South, read the following report: —

The committee, to whom was referred the Report on Evangelization in the West and South, would state to the Council that we have carefully examined that report, and have heard many communications from persons specially acquainted with the West and South which confirm and illustrate its positions and reasonings. We commend that report as comprehensive, thorough, and able, and move that it be adopted by the Council.

We see no necessity of using the precious time of the Council by adding to the facts and arguments presented in the report. We would only bring them to a practical issue, by deriving from them, and presenting for adoption by the Council, certain definite recommendations to the churches. We propose, therefore, the following result, namely:

This National Council, in view of the vast and promising fields of evangelical labor opened by the rapid growth of our country toward the West, the North-west, and on the borders of the Pacific Ocean, especially in the mining regions, and opened also by the sublime and awful, yet blessed providence of God in subduing rebellion, and giving their rightful liberty to four millions of bondmen, fields of labor, requiring for their proper culture, and requiring immediately, a large increase of laborers and of funds for their support, do recommend to the churches of Christ whom they represent,—

First of all, that they seek a large measure of the Holy Spirit, to inspire them with the zeal and faith, the courage and self-denial, necessary to make them willing and happy to give all the men and all the money needed to meet this extraordinary and critical exigency of the kingdom of Christ in our land.

Then to the organizations which, in the grace and providence of God, these churches have ready and well fitted to this work, the Council recommend that they devise liberal things: To the American Home Missionary Society — which, according to its constitution, aids feeble churches in sustaining the administration of the gospel, and sends the gospel to the destitute in whatever circumstances found, and by itinerant as well as local preachers, and which, from its beginning many years since, has performed its work with wisdom and fidelity that deserve universal gratitude and honor — $300,000 during the year. To the American Missionary Association — which, by its past fidelity to the rights and spiritual interests of the negro race, and by its evangelical character and comprehensive plans and labors for the education and religious instruction of the Freedmen, is providentially prepared for the great work of their evangelization so suddenly thrown upon the Christian people of the land — $250,000 the present year.

And since there are some places in the country, and especially in that part of the country which has just been delivered from the curse of bondage, and has been impoverished by the war unsuccessfully waged in behalf of bondage, where churches of central influence and of the Congregational polity, that has no guilty implication with slavery to be remembered against it, might at once be prosperously established if suitable houses of religious worship and instruction were built, we recommend that a special fund of $200,000 be raised by the American Congregational Union, and expended under its direction for the building of sanctuaries in such places.

And because of the great importance of occupying such places at once with preachers and pastors of experience as well as ability, we recommend that churches at the North should exercise in some instances the self-denial of relinquishing for that purpose their chosen and beloved ministers, if not permanently, at least for a time.

In view, also, of the ignorance of the great body of the poor whites of the South, who at present form the chief constituency there, according to the precedents of Virginia, North Carolina, and Mississippi, we recommend the plans of the American Union Commission for a universal common-school education, and for a wholesome emigration from the Northern States, with a view to the industrial improvement of society, as worthy the encouragement and support of all Christians and patriots.

But the pecuniary want of the present exigency is not the greatest nor the most difficult to be supplied. To meet the extraordinary call which is now made from these various fields for preachers of the gospel, and which must be met at once, or much will be lost for the country and for Christ, are required (it is not extravagant to say) ten times as many as are now offered by the ordinary process of education for the Christian ministry. The Council therefore recommend that while the churches and ministry do not abate any thing from their zeal and effort for thorough and accomplished theological education, but rather add thereto, and while they use all proper urgency with Christian young men to prepare for the ministry by a thorough or partial course in our theological seminaries, they also commend to the proper ecclesiastical bodies the consideration of the expediency of approving, and if necessary of ordaining with such conditions as they may deem best, laymen residing within their limits whom God has endowed with gifts and grace. And the Council do earnestly invite such Christian laymen to hear the voice of the Lord, and enter into this work.

And because of the woful need of intelligent preachers among the Freedmen, the Council recommend to the churches the speedy establishment at the South of an institution for the training, by a short course, of colored ministers.

Moreover, this Council, while they exhort to the culture and practice of that enlarged catholicity which is according to the nature and habit of Congregationalism, they do also exhort to watchful and thorough fidelity to the church polity and faith of the New England fathers, preeminent, as they believe them to be, in their accordance with scriptural principles and primitive practice, and in their harmony with republicanism in the State; and they would urge that that polity and faith be promoted and extended by all honorable and Christian means, and by no other means.

These recommendations, this Council, under a solemn sense of their responsibility to God, send to the churches whom they represent, beseeching them, and not only them, but all patriotic, philanthropic people in the congregations connected with them, by the love they bear to their country, by their gratitude to God for its recent great and signal deliverance, by their sense of justice to four millions of their fellow-men divinely restored to their natural rights, and by their love to Christ, who has called them into his kingdom, that they might co-operate with him in seeking and saving the lost; that they enlarge their minds and hearts and labors to a thorough and glorious obedience to the commands of his word and his providence.

In behalf of the committee,

S. W. S. Dutton,
Samuel Williston,
Benjamin P. Stone,
L. H. Parker,
D. Clary,
F. D. Parish,
J. Guernsey,
W. Crawford,
J. Bacon,
Geo. H. Atkinson.

The report was accepted.

CHURCH BUILDING.

On motion, the orders of the day were suspended, in order to allow the presentation of the report on the kindred subject of church building.

Rev. Samuel G. Buckingham, from the committee to which was referred the report on Church Building, then read the following

REPORT.

The plan adopted by the Albany Convention in 1852, to aid feeble churches in building houses of worship, was regarded at the time as not the least important result of their deliberations. But the wisdom of this plan could never have been comprehended as it now is, after it has been in operation for thirteen years, and the results are gathered up as they are in the report before us. It has furnished so many churches with sanctuaries; it has been such an efficient aid to home missions; it has proved itself such an economical form of benevolence; it has done so much to promote revivals of religion; it has so spread the faith and church polity of the Puritans, and so stimulated other denominations to take up and prosecute the same Christian work, — that we shall never cease to bless God for the wisdom that conceived of such a plan, and the faith, and enterprise, and liberality that undertook to put it into operation.

But the demand which existed for such Christian work then has greatly increased since that time. Emigration is flowing Westward as fast as ever, while that wall of exclusion which shut it out from the South and the South-west is broken down, and it is likely to overflow and fertilize all that region also. And every consideration that ever urged us to engage in this work does so now, and with increased force. For if it was ever worth while to build sanctuaries for feeble churches, it still is; and there never were half so many that needed to be built as are likely to be called for hereafter. We must therefore assume the duty that is laid upon us, and prosecute the work with becoming vigor. The altered condition of the country may require some modification of our plan and mode of working, but the work is essentially the same, and the duty more imperative than ever.

Your committee on "*Evangelization in the South and West*" call attention to such cities and larger towns as Baltimore, and Washington, and Richmond, and Norfolk, and Wilmington, and Cairo, and Memphis, and New Orleans, and regard them as coming within the scope of this enterprise. As centers of population and influence, they very properly represent them as "strategic points" in our moral warfare, and recommend that no time be lost in taking possession of them in the name of our Great Captain. The wisdom of this recommendation must commend itself to all. But it is equally apparent that appropriations to churches at such points, to be of any value, must be very much larger than any that have hitherto been made. Instead of three or five or seven hundred dollars, it will require some thousands to secure the erection of a house of worship in such a position, and this will be doing no more for them than the former sum has accomplished for a church in some little village. In the mining region, also, where the expense of building is so great, appropriations must be made on an increased scale of liberality to accomplish the desired object. This, however, will require vastly more of funds than we have hitherto raised for any such purpose, and also require some modification of our mode of raising funds, as well as of our scale of expenditure.

We do not regard any new agency as needed to take charge of this work. The Congregational Union, to which it has hitherto been assigned, has labored most assiduously, with the scanty force at its command, to collect funds, and distributed them with wisdom and impartiality. And with our confidence in those who have the charge of this society, and with their experience already acquired in the management of such a charity, we may safely intrust this enterprise with them.

The committee recommend that all applications for aid in church building be made to the Congregational Union; and that, having received their indorsement, special agents shall be assigned to particular fields for their collections, after the manner so successfully followed by the "Society for the Promotion of Collegiate and Theological Education at the West."

We also recommend that we embrace within our plan of church building the affording of aid in the erection of church edifices to feeble churches in the cities and large towns of the South and West, and that our appropriations to them be upon a scale commensurate with the importance of their position and the increased cost of affording such aid.

We further recommend, that in order to meet the increased expenditure which such an enlargement of our plan implies, and also in view of the present demand for church-edifices at the West, and the prospective demand for them in the South, the sum of *two hundred thousand dollars* be raised at once, and that a much larger sum than has hitherto been raised for the purpose be secured annually to carry out the above plan.

In conclusion, we would merely add, that if we can not rear any fit monument to the piety of our fathers, and to God's good providence over them, on Plymouth Rock, let us scatter these sacred and enduring memorials of such faith and grace over the length and breadth of the land, and thus show our appreciation of such faith, and gratitude for such grace.

(Signed) S. G. BUCKINGHAM,
F. B. DOE,
PHILO CARPENTER,
ISAAC JENNINGS,
J. M. CHAMBERLAIN,
EDWIN JOHNSON,
H. P. HAVEN,
Committee.

The report was accepted.

The question was stated upon the adoption of the report.

Rev. Dr. BACON, of Connecticut, suggested that the two reports be referred to a joint committee consisting of the two committees incorporated into one.

Rev. Dr. DUTTON, of Connecticut, stated that this was unnecessary, the committees having already conferred with each other and made their reports to harmonize.

Rev. Dr. STURTEVANT, of Illinois, inquired whether it was in order to consider the two reports together.

THE MODERATOR replied that such appeared to be the understanding of the Convention, although that upon church building was alone strictly before the Convention.

On motion of Dr. Dutton, of Connecticut, it was voted that the two reports should be discussed together.

Rev. Dr. KIRK, of Massachusetts. It appears to me that it is dangerous for us to recommend the organization of African colleges. We do not want African, Irish, or German colleges, but American colleges, without distinction as to the color of the skin. I hope that point will be well considered, because it involves a great deal.

Rev. Dr. DUTTON, of Connecticut. The committee put that in at the urgent request of Mr. Bliss, of Tennessee, and we would like to have him defend his child.

Rev. Mr. BLISS, of Tennessee. In appearing before the committee yesterday, I was led in the course of my remarks to suggest the importance of distinct educational establishments in the South for the training of men as teachers and as preachers of the gospel through that region. There is no question of prejudice of color at all in this matter. Those who know me know that with me that subject was settled full twenty or twenty-five years ago. In looking over the field for nearly two years in Missouri, and the last year and a half in Mississippi, and along down the Mississippi river, I have found that there was a mighty work to be done for the colored people. Any one who has heard these preachers preach and pray will feel distressingly the necessity of training teachers for the four millions of freedmen. This work has not yet been fully entered upon; but already we have at Memphis colored schools containing from 1800 to 2000 people of color; and one high school established with a Congregational minister and his wife at the head of it. There is in that neighborhood an opportunity for training these men for the ministry and for the position of teachers. We must enter into this work early. The colored people themselves demand it; and the times urge it impressively upon us. The question of color is not to be brought in. We do not have any thing to do with it there. We are working for them to the best advantage we can; and we need there an institution which shall be academic, and collegiate, and theological combined, like many of our young Western institutions, so that these young men can enter, and, by perhaps a shorter course than usual, be prepared to preach to their people and to instruct their people.

Memphis is a central point, with railroads running into it from various points, from Charleston in S. C., from Louisville in Ky., and from Little Rock in Ark. Being a central point, it is one of the most important in the whole Southern region. The city of Memphis alone has a population of 40 or 50,000, the colored population amounting to 10 or 15,000, while they are coming there from all points. And you will find there, in the providence of God, an institution now given up, in just the place for just such an establishment as is required for these people.

We can not keep calling upon the North for teachers, for we can not begin to supply the demand. A work must be commenced there, to instruct the preachers who are to teach the people themselves. I look in the same missionary point of view upon the colored people in the South, and think we must pursue the same course with them as is now being pursued with the people of other lands, regardless of color, — the whole question of caste and prejudice being left entirely out of the account. It is not to be considered at all in this proposition.

The colored people there have their own churches and associations without any question of color being raised. There need be no question of that kind. There is no wish to exclude; but they naturally flow together from their social affinities, without any question of color being raised. These things, we trust, are buried for ever in this land.

I introduced that provision with a desire that it might be fairly considered here, and in order that some of the more wealthy men at the North might create such an institution, giving to it a name to immortalize themselves, while at the same time it will prove a blessing to untold millions in that Southern region. This work has grown upon my mind since I have been in the South. The great question how we shall provide instructors and preachers for four millions of people staggers the mind with the attempt to grapple it. We do not begin to reach it by sending a few teachers from the North. There must be raised up men of their own color, and living there among them, for teachers, and for preachers of the gospel among them.

TELEGRAM FROM THE PRESIDENT.

The hour having arrived which had been dedicated to devotional exercises, the moderator read the following telegram received this morning from the President of the United States, to the Council: —

WASHINGTON, June 19.

TO GOV. WM. A. BUCKINGHAM, MODERATOR OF THE NATIONAL COUNCIL OF CONGREGATIONAL CHURCHES, BOSTON,—

I receive with profound thanks the dispatch of your Council. In the arduous and embarrassing duties devolved upon me, I feel the need of the co-operation and sympathy of the people, and of the assistance of the Great Ruler of the Universe. These duties I shall endeavor to discharge honestly and to the best of my judgment, with the conviction that the best interests of civil and religious liberty throughout the world will be preserved and promoted by the success and permanency of our country. Let us all labor to that end, and the mission upon which the people have been sent among the nations of the world will be accomplished.

(Signed) ANDREW JOHNSON.

THE MODERATOR proceeded to say. You all know, my Christian friends, the request which President Lincoln made at the time he left Springfield, that the people would pray for him. In allusion to that subject, in a private interview which I once had with him, he threw out this intimation very clearly, that he felt, that it was in consequence of those prayers, and in answer to those prayers, that he was enabled to bear the heavy burdens which were imposed upon him by the position which he occupied. I am sure that any man occupying a position as prominent as that of Mr. Lincoln during the last four years, must feel his entire incompetency to bear the burden placed upon him, without the divine aid. No man needs it more now than the President of the United States; and surely it is not too much to ask these Christian hearts at this hour to unite in earnest prayer that God would strengthen him still more for the duties which devolve upon him, and give him that wisdom to meet the necessities which the times demand. I will ask brother Carter, of Illinois, to lead in prayer with special reference to the President of the United States.

Prayer was offered by Rev. William Carter, of Illinois, Dr. Adams, Dr. Dutton, and others, and hymns were sung, — these devotional exercises occupying the allotted half hour.

EVANGELIZATION IN THE SOUTH AND WEST.

The consideration of the two reports, that upon Evangelization in the South and West, and that upon Church Building, was resumed, each member being limited to twelve minutes under the rule.

Rev. Dr. STURTEVANT, of Illinois. I take the floor at the opening of this discussion modestly, and at the request of brethren whose request I did not feel at liberty to disregard. How to speak twelve minutes on this subject is to me almost incomprehensible. To speak hours would be easy. We speak of this great Council. When I compare this Council with the work which stretches away before us and around us, it does not seem to me great, but unspeakably small: we have just had — and the Lord in his mercy has delivered us — a mighty physical conflict. That was a conflict for the foundation principle of our political system, the equal rights of man; and how hath it taxed the energies of this great nation! Fathers and brethren, that conflict is only the emblem, and a very feeble emblem, of another conflict which is now before us. We are now to have a mighty conflict for those religious principles which lie down deep at the foundation of our whole structure of civil and political freedom, which are the hope of our own souls, the hope of our children, the hope of our schools, the hope of our nation. If the physical conflict has been a mighty one, what will the religious conflict be? There is just as much necessity, just as stern and absolute a necessity, for carrying through the religious conflict to the complete triumph of those principles of religion upon which the whole rest, as there was for carrying through the physical conflict. Where would we have been if we had not had, or if we had been defeated in, that conflict? Just in that position shall we be if we do not enter upon, and if we do not conquer in, this religious conflict.

What is our problem? To plant over all the West and South such a local church that it will take into its care the entire moral and spiritual wants of the entire community within the boundaries of each and every local church. Do not misunderstand me. If that church owes allegiance to the General Assembly of the United States, if it will do that work I am not the man that will quarrel with it, or plant a Congregational church by the side of it to rival it. Not at all. I advocate our polity simply because I believe it is the best instrumentality to achieve this. But God speed our Presbyterian friends, and God speed our Methodist friends to do all of this work that they can and will do. [Applause.]

There is no such thing as a system of popular and effective universal education that does not draw its life from the local church. We have a fine system of common schools in the State of Illinois. The people of Illinois, in any school district, may have under the State law just as noble a school as they desire. But it is necessary to have a people who are under the influence of moral and religious principles to give life to that system of education; and over vast regions of that State there is no such life-giving power, and therefore that system upon our statute book is a dead letter.

And so it will be every where. The universal diffusion of the Church of Christ is the only condition of the education of our people to be free men, to be intelligent voters, to be men in whose hands the sacred interests of religion and of political freedom can be safely deposited.

How are we to achieve this result? Any one in this assembly may well answer from the depths of his heart, the Lord tell us how. But there is one suggestion I can make with very great confidence. Every one of us sees the necessity of self-denial. What sent these brethren to Illinois, Missouri, Colorado, Oregon, and California? Have golden visions drawn them there? We know the meaning of self-denial for Christ. Brothers and fathers, in the name of the Lord we bring this duty of self-denial and lay the burden of it upon the conscience of every disciple of Christ in the city of Boston, in the city of New York, in the State of Massachusetts, in the State of Illinois, because there is wealth there too that is not consecrated to Christ. We say that whatever stern self-denial this cause lays upon the missionary or the minister, shall be laid right down upon every private member of the church. Brother, sister, the mortgage is upon your homestead; the mortgage is upon your land, upon your son, your daughter. Are we to succeed in this grand enterprise? We are to succeed in it by completely breaking down the perverse distinction so long made between the duty of self-denial in the ministry and the duty of self-denial in the private membership. The Lord has as good a claim upon every disciple of his that lives in these ceiled houses as he has or ever had upon me, or upon that brother who is upon this floor from Colorado. If we are not going to transact the whole business upon this principle, there is no hope for us at all.

I am going to speak plainly. As I have seen how this burden of self-denial and self-sacrifice is laid upon the Christian ministry, — none too much, for we have not borne half what we ought to have been willing to bear for the sake of the Master, — while those who dwell in their palaces of ease and luxury, and press their velvet cushions every Sabbath day, throw those burdens from themselves, my soul has been exceedingly filled with scorn for them that are at ease, and with contempt for the proud. Brethren, there is wealth enough in the church of Christ; not as much as there ought to be, if to-day we would abandon ten thousand of the miserable fooleries and ostentations of fashion, and be far more earnest workers even in our material interests than we are, and practice self-denial and economy, and thus accumulate wealth far more rapidly than we do. But on the other hand I would write "Holiness to the Lord" upon all that wealth; and as to those figures that have been rolled up in this report, $200,000 here, $250,000 there, and $300,000 there — there would be no difficulty at all in the matter.

The difficulty is this: a large portion of our people feel as I once heard a brother say, "I have not volunteered;" "I am on the stay-at-home list; I will give a little, but you must not interfere with my pleasures. My wealth, my home, none of that is mortgaged; the Lord has no hold upon that. I can not part with my luxuries." [The time expired.]

Rev. Mr. PIKE, of Massachusetts, said: I rise but for one moment, and will then leave this discussion for abler hands than mine. It seems to me that the great question before us is not whether we have a large field open, — for that is granted; nor is the question whether this field is to be mainly occupied by regularly authorized ministers instead of any other form of effort to bring the people to Christ, — for that, I take it, is granted also. The main point is whether or not it is necessary for us to have a second tier of ministers. That, I believe, is brought distinctly before us by the report this morning, that such is the necessity of our situation, that our associations or conferences, or whatever body this matter may be intrusted to, are to license and bring in ministers less intelligent and less fitted for this great work. I desire that the remarks of brethren fitted to instruct us may be directed to this point. I regret it, but I do not know but we shall be obliged to come to this. If so, let us come to it in the fear of God and with the earnestness of our hearts. The throwing open to us of this wide field, and raising up so many millions that need to be immediately instructed in the things of the kingdom of God, certainly bring us toward that point. If we have come to the place where we need this kind of ministry, let us enter upon that duty at once.

Rev. Dr. DUTTON, of Connecticut. One word of explanation. That had special reference to the region of the South and West, and had not much reference to New England.

Hon. Mr. POMEROY, of Kansas. I desire only in a few brief words to say that I approve those reports that have been read to the Council. Of course I shall have to leave out vastly more than I can say, and I can not confine the remarks I want to make to the topic just presented. First of all I want to say that I feel called upon to express the gratitude of the churches of my own State for the aid they have had from the Congregational Union; and especially of the church of my own town, of which I am a member, for the $500 contributed and sent to us to aid in building a church. With that aid, we built a church that cost us $8000; and on the 14th of May of this year, it was pronounced completed, and dedicated, at an expense of $12,000; a church out of debt, free, and which I think can be said to be self-supporting. And I will add that if this Council sends to us now for a contribution to aid in building other churches, it will be responded to, and that money can and shall be returned.

I rejoice also to say that in my State there are thirty-two Congregational churches, sixteen having their houses of worship completed, and sixteen more either having them in the process of erection, or being unable to erect. I think Congregationalism peculiarly adapted to a new country, and to all new fields. I remember very well leaving Boston eleven years ago, in a party of two hundred and thirty-one men and two women; and in that company there was a Congregational church, as we found after we planted ourselves in Lawrence, Kansas, on the first Sabbath. We found that we had eleven persons, members of Congregational churches somewhere, and they gathered together in Kansas, a church without a minister and without a bishop. Congregationalism will plant itself wherever believers go. If they are members of churches anywhere, they can come together bringing letters from the churches of which they are members, and naturally and easily form a Congregational church. The Home Missionary Society very soon sent us a missionary, and our church was recognized with other churches. This system of policy is adopted every where. It can go south and so encompass the country and the continent.

On the second topic I would say that I do not suppose that in reference to my own State any extra effort need be made. We are not an inviting field of labor, now that the country is open to us, — the continent almost. We are living "in a grand and awful time," and I wonder if we feel that "to be living is sublime." Never before was this country open to New Englanders, or to men of our sentiments, as it is open to-day.

I want to say, just here, that we have a Capital now. I was in Washington before emancipation, and I have been there ever since; and I want the churches of this country to feel that they have a Washington, — a Capital, from which we are not shut out as we have been. There are ten thousand young men in Washington from the free States, many of them from New England. The clerical help employed in the departments is largely from New England. A Congregational church might be gathered there of two hundred young men to begin with. If we are going South, Washington is the gateway to the South; and there are reasons why a Congregational church should be planted in Washington, that do not so urgently exist in my mind why they should be planted in other places. The city of Washington is peculiarly our field, — the field of the whole nation. Baltimore is in Maryland; Richmond is in what was Virginia — I do not know what it is now; — Charleston, Savannah, and all the Southern cities, must eventually come under some local organization; but there are reasons why a national convention should concentrate some peculiar energy upon the national capital. It is your home and mine. Its very soil has been consecrated to the Union, the government, and, thank God, latterly, to freedom. [Applause.] It is as free a city as Boston. I remember when we used to walk there with weapons, and did not know whether our lives were safe or not. But if we are safe any where, we are to-day safe in Washington. To think that the American Congregational Churches should neglect it, should not have a large representation there, especially since your churches and young men have so large a representation there, seems strange to me. I believe that the resolution in the hands of your business committee, that the Congregational Union should take specific measures to establish a permanent church of our denomination there, should be brought forward and cordially adopted as the sentiment of this Convention.

I know all about the failures we have had in the past. Congregationalism will always fail with slavery. You could not plant a successful organization of our denomination where a part of the church were free and a part were slaves. Our principles would not allow that the few should outvote the many, or that a part should be disfranchised entirely.

I want to say, in conclusion, that this subject commends itself to the Council, because this is a peculiarly favorable time to make the effort. We want a church there that shall reflect credit upon our denomination, and shall accommodate our people. A church in Washington, with such a minister as I could select, could have a congregation there of two thousand every Sabbath. There are more than twenty Congregational ministers, now employed as clerks in the departments, that would go into a church and make useful members; and a Sabbath school could be organized with their aid, such as could be found in no other city. These ministers, broken down in their health or their voice, although no longer competent to labor in the ministry, are good earnest men; and the Congregational church should make the most of them, as teachers in the Sabbath school, and members in the church. And their influence would extend from Washington all through the South.

It is time that we were taking possession of that Southern country. War has desolated it more than the frosts of the North destroy vegetable life. There is a new creation springing up; and we should be there; our seeds should be in the ground.

The doctrine that we are to organize those States again where they broke off to go into the rebellion is a monstrous heresy. Let the governments be inaugurated by those men, coming back as they would now come back, — taking to themselves seven spirits more wicked than the first, — and I assure you that the last state will be worse than the first. [Applause.] Society must be organized by beginning at the bottom and turning it bottom side upward, because it has heretofore been so constructed as to need this overturning. But I will not prolong my remarks upon this point, as there is to be a meeting at Faneuil Hall at 12 o'clock to-morrow, upon the subject of reconstruction, and the rest of my speech in that direction I shall make there.

Rev. J. M. STURTEVANT, Jr., of Missouri, said: I do not know, Mr. Moderator, whether I can say a quarter of what I want to say, in twelve minutes, but I feel that those who have come far, some of them half as far as our foreign delegates, and some quite as far, should say a word at least in this Council. My home is in Missouri. I have seen there some of the work of reconstruction. It has gone further in some respects there than any where else; and I believe that in our experience there are some lessons for the church.

When I went to Missouri, five years ago, it is no violent language to say that there was no such thing as free speech in Missouri, out of a few of the principal cities. I have been told by travelers in England that our English friends can not believe that in a civilized community there ever was such a thing as a suppression of free speech. From the very county where I have my home, Dr. Nelson was chased by men hooting and howling for his life, and that only a few years ago. And in the streets of our county seat, only a few years ago, they burned, — what paper do you think? — for anti-slavery utterances, — the "New York Observer." [Laughter.] I have heard elders of the Presbyterian church and pastors of the same denomination rise before their audiences and confess that they had been silent on the subject of slavery in the State of Missouri, when their consciences bade them speak, and ask God's forgiveness and the forgiveness of the Christian community for that silence which for years they had not dared to break.

But that silence has been broken. It was broken when the chains grew so tight, the demand for subserviency so violent and excessive, that no man could stand it. At last, speech is free there as it is here. But such a change as this could not occur without a thorough visitation of

God's judgment upon those who had suppressed free speech, and a thorough contempt for those who had been suppressed. Their power is gone for ever; and the very organizations with which they were connected are almost in some places refused an utterance in the community. God has turned society upside down. The men who scarce dared say their souls were their own are the leaders of society to-day.

The old churches have been closed, — some of them by the soldiers, because they naturally quartered themselves upon their enemies, and their worst enemies were the old-school Presbyterian and Southern Methodist churches. They have made their homes and their hospitals in those churches, the ministers of which have gone off into the rebel army or fled the country. There is nothing left of the old teachers of the people. These changes have cut people loose from old denominational lines, strict as those lines have been in the West. A community sent word recently, " Brother Turner, wont you send us a real Yankee preacher? " That is what they wanted. They felt that such a man could be trusted.

Besides, the new constitution of the State cuts off from teaching and preaching, everybody that can not swear he has always been loyal to the government. Such has been the change that I verily believe nearly one half the citizens of the interior of the State will move out in the year and a half which commenced last spring; and others must come in and take their places. Those that are left desire, in religion and politics and social life, something entirely different from what they have known before. We feel therefore that this is a glorious time to plant Congregational churches with the new institutions. We began with fear and trembling. We expected to stand alone. We expected to be complained of by men in prominent positions. We supposed it was the work of years to make the people understand what Congregationalism is. To our surprise we had no sooner explained what it was, — an assembling of the people that loved God and Christ, for forming a religious society to be governed by the majority, — than the people rallied around it, and we formed churches in weeks where we expected to be months about it.

Let me be very plain here. We did not form a theological seminary to teach our candidates the catechisms and confessions of faith before we received them. In fact we receive people into the church just as we marry people. We marry people that love one another, and are not already married to somebody else; and we receive people into the church that love God and Christ, and the gospel for Christ's sake, and are not already connected with any other church. [Applause.]

Somebody has accused me of building a church out of Methodists and other denominations. I put no Methodists into the church but what I found lying around loose; and every Christian man that I find lying round loose I propose to build into the church of Christ. All these churches are orthodox. We state in plain terms the fundamental principles of the gospel, and we bring them to unite upon those principles. We have to be careful to state them in simple language, so as to be understood; and if any body is afraid we are heterodox, I can only say that I met upon the Council a man from Maine, one from New Hampshire, Illinois, Iowa, Missouri, and one or two more; and when we came together we found that we agreed very well upon what constituted the church of Christ.

In the present movement, which was rather interrupted by a guerilla movement, we heard from fifteen towns, and in all but one of those fifteen towns there was an immediate call from a Congregational church for a Congregational minister; and that was a failure for special reasons that are not likely to last. And I speak within safe limits when I say that there are fifty more, north of the Missouri river, just as likely to afford places for ministers as those fifteen. But they must be occupied at once, or the opportunity will pass. And these churches, though small in numbers, are promising to have a firm hold upon the community. Many of them are in towns once flourishing, and now so surrounded by fruitful fields and advantages that they must renew their prosperity; and they are oftentimes the only churches in the community where they are planted. We can not wait until a church can be started with all the elements of power and success that belong to an old community. We must make them feel that we bring them the gospel in their weakness. We must say to those men that love Christ, If you are feeble and few, we will help you; and then when men come from the East to the West, we must say to them, Here is a church for you, a small church, but a church of Christ; come with us and we will do you good. This work will make the State of Missouri a thoroughly Christian community so far as the best organizations can go to make it so.

Rev. Prof. BARTLETT, of Illinois. I feel as though we had now just reached the great thing for which we are here together. It is a great thing to declare theoretical principles, — to set forth our faith, or our polity; but the great thing we have now to do, after all, is to go to work and take care of our land for Christ. We feel at the West oppressed with the greatness of the work laid upon us; and we sometimes feel that even the plans laid before you are unworthy and insufficient, when we think of the multitudes of the troops we have sent to conquer the South. What is it that we propose to do? To devote to purposes of church building just about one half the annual cost of a single cavalry regiment; and the whole income of the Home Missionary Society falls far below the annual cost of an infantry regiment. Yet with this preparation we are proposing to conquer the whole South! When we look around upon the churches here, and remember the want of churches in our own vicinity, we feel that our brethren here upon the old homesteads have yet to learn what is the work before them. We want not merely men but money. It has been said this morning that money is not the chief thing we want; but we do want money to do the work. We want institutions, churches; and we can not even plant them, to secure an influence, without money. There are societies to help the churches. The Tract Society, and the Bible Society, the Sunday School Union, and many others, will help the church, when the acorn shall be planted, to grow up into a mighty oak spreading its branches all over our heads. Our want at the West in our vicinity, is largely money. We are poor. We see our churches bought out from under us by men who can come and bid more for them, and can perhaps take up a mortgage upon them. We can not provide for young men who want to be educated for the ministry, because we have not the means. Even our own men have their thoughts largely concentrated upon the old homestead. Two years ago we read the record of some $1,500,000 poured out upon this Atlantic coast, which went into the old institutions that have been planted and watered for two hundred years. I felt that what you were consuming here for your daily bread, might have been, at least a portion of it, our seed corn, which we want and can not do without.

As to the education for the ministry, we find that there is a class of men whom we must employ, — men whom the Master calls, practical business men, of tact and judgment, educated by contact with men, and not always by contact with literary institutions, — men with a life and force in them which men who have gone through a protracted course of study do not often have; and we must still continue to take these men whom the Master honors, and put them into the work.

What we want is to give a true conception of the work opening before us at the West and at the South and to get up something like that spirit of patriotism and loyalty to Christ which our soldiers have exhibited during the campaign. When we look around and see that a million of men have fallen directly or indirectly by the war, who might have had their lives saved, and all the losses of the war prevented, by a band of a thousand, and I might almost say one hundred ministers of Christ spreading the word of truth in its purity and power all over this land, we can not but mourn the lack of foresight that failed to spread the gospel. It was the institutions which you, Christian brethren and fathers, gave to us, which kept the troops of Illinois, Wisconsin, and Iowa from being marshaled in deadly conflict against the men of Massachusetts, New Hampshire, and Vermont. That was the reason why Ulysses S. Grant, instead of leading our armies to victory at Richmond, was not taking your own capitol from you at Washington.

Rev. E. P. MARVIN, of Massachusetts, moved to amend the report by adding the words "and faith" after the word "polity," so as to recommend "to watch carefully over, and protect, and extend the church polity and faith of our New England fathers."

Rev. Dr. DUTTON, of Connecticut. I have no objection whatever to that amendment.

Rev. Mr. MARVIN. The distinction between us and the Unitarians is more in the faith than in the polity; and while I would be willing to go as far as any other reasonable man in this Council to receive those that are weak in the faith, and not to doubtful disputation, still I would not have it go forth in this report that the polity is all we want. We want that which sustains the polity and which has sustained it in all the trying times of the past. I trust it will go forth that we have not lapsed from the faith of our fathers; that the Congregational churches, represented in this great Council, stand by their polity in their faith.

Rev. Mr. ALLEN, of Massachusetts. I hope this question of Christian faith will not be pressed upon this house so suddenly. There is a report upon the subject, and it ought to be known when it is to come up that there may be an expression of opinion upon it.

Rev. Dr. PATTON, of Illinois, read the third article of agreement of the Saybrook platform, as the Western doctrine, —

"That none shall be admitted as members in full communion in all the special ordinances of the gospel, but such persons as are known to be sound in the fundamental doctrines of the Christian religion, without scandal in their lives, but in judgment regulated by the word of God, and persons of visible holiness and honesty credibly professing cordial subjection to the will of Jesus Christ."

The amendment was agreed to.

Rev. Dr. TODD, of Massachusetts, said: when this Council was called together, we hardly knew what the providence of God indicated by its call. I was repeatedly asked what was the object, the central idea, bringing together this great body of men to-day. I think that before we separate we shall all feel that it was the providence of God that brought us together, the spirit of Christ that dwelt in us, and the power of the Holy Spirit that will follow us home. Our brethren at the West can hardly imagine with what joy we meet them, and greet them, and hear them speak, and feel their fire, and see their energy, and rejoice in the soundness of their faith and spirit. I thought yesterday, when our Governor Andrew sat here looking at you, that he must say in his heart that we are a respectable family; that he would feel that here was a house of heads. I wish that he could see the hearts that have made these heads grow old, the cares and anxieties and labors of these dear brethren in that best and holiest of all causes, the cause of our Master.

We are called upon to vote great sums of money. When we met at Worcester last autumn, under the leadership of brother Anderson, we had to vote $600,000 for foreign missions, and he then told us to go home and collect it. Now you are calling upon us for as much more. I don't wonder that my brother Badger's face looks long as he thinks of the thousand home missionaries he has to provide for; or that brother Baldwin, the father of all the colleges of the West, has an anxious heart. We have a great burden laid upon us. I begin to feel it already; and I have no doubt that before we leave this Council, we shall feel that we go home with such a burden resting upon us as we have never had before and can never have again while we live on God's footstool.

I am asked, what are you doing here? What are the results? We can tell fifty years hence, or one hundred years hence, better than to-day. The results will be beyond all that we can to-day describe or imagine. It is not because we vote so much, or speak so much, but it is because we feel so much. It is the moving of the heart under the influences of the Divine Spirit, and the spirit of the Divine Redeemer. These $750,000 — can we get it from our churches? It makes us feel that we have a heavy load to carry, we who are pastors and must take this home and lay it upon the heart of selfishness and covetousness and worldliness. But I want to say one word to relieve this feeling.

When this great rebellion broke out at the South, we felt that there was a power behind the army of the South that we could not meet, — the power of four millions of human hands working to support and sustain the South and their army; and we wondered how in the world we should ever achieve the victory with that power, that reserved army, behind them. We forget that in New England and the free States we have one hundred million of hands behind us, working for us day and night. I mean the machinery in your factories, your mowers, your reapers, your spinners, your water-wheels. The machinery in the free States now is doing every day the work of one hundred millions of hands. That has created the wealth that has carried us through this war. And that wealth, that power, that reserved army, if it is brought in to help us in this cause, will give us the money. I have no fear about that. There is wealth enough. It is being created fast enough. No, sir; it is the great danger of our New England, Northern churches that we shall be swamped through avarice, through worldliness, through the prosperity of this world.

Now we have two things that we want to do. We want consecrated young men to enter the ministry, well educated. If it were in my power, I would send the best man in this house for the purpose to every college in New England. I would have him call together all the pious young men in each college, and talk with them, and pray with them, and get them to pledge themselves to enter the ministry. I was surprised, not long since, upon visiting a college where there had been a delightful revival of religion, to find that that subject had not been brought before them. I could blame nobody for it. But when the subject came to be pressed upon them, there was a response; and there will be a response in every college in New England if we may come to the ear of the young men who there profess Jesus Christ. Let them understand the trials, the self-denial, the labors, and the glory, and they will enter the ministry.

One other thing we want. We must enter upon a new experiment. We must send out half, third, quarter educated men; — a sort of system of lay preachers. We can not help it. The providence of God calls for it; and we, old conservatives at the North, will go as far as any of you in any of these great plans which the providence of God leads us to take up. [Applause.]

One thing more. I feel that when we leave these meetings and go to our homes, we must have a power behind us beyond that which brought us here, or we can never meet the responsibilities of this day and hour. We can never meet these responsibilities unless the Spirit of God rests upon us, and goes with us to our homes. We must carry the Holy Spirit in our hearts; and we must go home to our churches taking hold of the mercy-seat, and asking, expecting, believing that there will be a tidal wave of revival reaching over our churches and over the land, that will prepare us and prepare our churches to meet these awful responsibilities. Dear brethren, believe and you shall receive. Go home expecting and praying for this great revival, and we shall have it.

Mr. PRATT, of Massachusetts. If the raising of $750,000 strikes such a dread and terror to the hearts of the ministers, what must it be to the laymen who will have to raise the money? It has been proposed to erect a Congregational Church in Washington city at a cost of $100,000. Such a project would startle the people of the West and South, for the money proposed to expend for that purpose and for similar objects, would build five hundred churches for the destitute of the West and South.

Rev. Dr. Dutton, of Connecticut, raised the question of order that the subject of the church building in Washington was not under debate, being in the hands of a committee.

The point of order was sustained.

Hon. Mr. HOLTON, of Wisconsin. I was called out of New England by the inviting inducements held out by the West twenty-five years ago, and made my home in Wisconsin. The opening was indeed then very great; and I feel constrained, at this juncture of our meeting, to say a word upon the growth of things in that State under my own eyes. We need sometimes to encourage ourselves by examples from the past, as well as by peering into the future. When I first went to Wisconsin, it had thirty thousand inhabitants only. I have seen the march of the emigration from the East, of men who have come to make their homes in Wisconsin. Following that emigration came the men sent out by your noble Home Missionary Society; and I have seen the gratifying consequences. There grew up two hundred churches of our faith, and two hundred learned and able men came and took their posts there as servants of the Lord to lay the foundations of Christian society. As I have seen coming in, the men from foreign lands, the German with his infidelity, I have paused and said, What shall stay this? It is only God that can stay it.

Fifteen years ago, the Infidels said: Let us have a convention at Watertown, that we may put down the Sabbath. We gave them a severe letting alone. They expected, considering the treatment they had had in the Old World, that we should come there and put them down by force; but we gave them a severe letting alone. They held their convention, adjourned *sine die*, and never came together again. But we went and gathered their children and brought them into our Sunday schools; and thus our system, so silent, so mighty, so potent, has turned aside to a great extent that infidelity; and we have a joyful hope now, that we shall be instrumental in leading this foreign population into right ways, through our system and policy we are pursuing there.

When you of New England have sent aid to our churches in Wisconsin, I can stand here and testify that the results have been noble and encouraging. I am an humble layman myself; but I have seen these things.

Since I have been here I have been sent out upon a committee, and there I met brother Salter. Twenty-two years ago this spring, when the steamer passed the port of Milwaukee, one Saturday night, ten or fifteen of your men, sent out from New England, stopped to keep the Sabbath there, on their way to Iowa. Mr. Salter, then in his primal youth, was one. I might compliment him to-day that he is still a boy; that he has kept that youth. What have these men done in Iowa? They have turned back the accursed influences of the South, which were creeping up from the Southern States. I have marked those men with singular interest. They have filled colleges and schools, and they are they who have by their influence kept back the inroads of slavery, so that to-day Iowa blossoms like the rose.

I point to these glorious fruits of what we have done in a narrower field in the twenty years that are past. But now our rebellion is done, and we have not only the eight millions of men on our own soil, whose eyes are turned upon us; but do you know that there are a hundred million of eyes turned to us from across the water? Do you know that this highway across the sea is to be traversed as it was never traversed before. In Germany, in Ireland, and throughout Europe, their eyes are turned upon us, their hearts bend toward America, and they are coming as they never came before. We must make our calculations not only for the eight millions here in such perilous need, but for twenty millions more from across the water.

I come then and say that we ought to rise and build now, and lose no time. Mr. Beecher said that the foot of slavery is shod with iron, and goes slowly. And if it is also true that the foot of freedom flies fast, we should make haste, when the duty is laid upon us to build the waste places for the cause of our divine Master.

Dea. Shelton, of Connecticut. The practical question appears to be, how the $750,000 are to be raised. There is a single feature of this which presses upon my mind, and I rise with great reluctance and great diffidence, for the purpose of provoking abler minds to bring it before the Convention. It is that the business portion and the wealthy portion of our churches should be brought to adopt the apostles' method of systematic benevolence, in principle, if not literally, laying aside upon the first day of the week according as the Lord hath prospered them; and until this is done, we shall not reach the standard of the gospel, nor shall we be able to meet the necessities of the times. Twenty-five years of observation in regard to the working of this principle, when adopted conscientiously, have tended to deepen the conviction of my mind that this is the great sheet-anchor of our business men, to keep them from drifting away from the spirit of the gospel. I look upon the active business man of the present day as in exceeding danger, in these days of railroads and telegraphs, this age of steam, and in the pressure of business, of losing the spirituality of his heart and life. The remedy appears to me to be that it be laid upon his conscience that once a week, on the first day of the week, every Sabbath, he ask what God hath done for him in a pecuniary point of view, and respond to his duties in that respect, and his obligations to the church of Christ and his Saviour. Those things being brought before him in his closet every week, he changes his Sabbath-day religion to a week-day religion; and he shows that the conversion of his heart to Christ meant the consecration of his property also to the Lord his master. I believe until something like this is adopted by the church of Christ, to put a stop to the absorbing cares of the business of the world, and arrest the current and turn it into the channel of Christ, and a conscientious devotion to his cause, there will surely come up from week to week and from year to year this question with all its pertinency, where is the money to come from? But when this can be done, when our young men can be led to the altar of Christ, to consecrate their talents, their affections, and their money to the Lord, and to inquire week by week how much he demands, then the spirituality of business men will not be consumed by the pressure of their occupations.

FINANCE REPORT.

Hon. Mr. Hammond, from the special committee on Finance, reported the following resolutions, which were accepted and adopted: —

Resolved, That the finance committee be requested to pay the ministers who have presented a statement of the amount of their expenses in attending upon this Council, fifty per cent. of the amount so presented; *provided*, that no person shall receive a sum exceeding $200; *provided, also*, that no one shall be paid any amount toward his expenses who receives an annual salary of $1500 or over.

Resolved, That as soon as the finance committee shall have ascertained the total amount of these expenses, they have permission to make further report as to the manner of securing the needed sum.

The hour of one o'clock having arrived, the Council took a recess, under the rule, until three o'clock, P. M.

AFTERNOON SESSION.

The Council was called to order at three o'clock, the moderator in the chair. The consideration of the reports on the Evangelization of the South and West and on Church Building was resumed.

Rev. Mr. HOWELL, of Liverpool, N. S. (leave having been granted), addressed the Council. He said: —

Mr. Moderator and Gentlemen of the Council: —

I felt a desire this morning, when brother Bliss, from Tennessee, I presume, was addressing the Council, to say a word or two in confirmation of his views in relation to the necessity of a college for the instruction of colored men, to fit them for labor in the Southern field. It was my happy privilege to labor in the Island of Jamaica at the time of the emancipation of the colored people there, from 1836 to 1840; and it was found necessary, in our small field, to introduce a class ot laborers of this order, not only in connection with the London Missionary Society, of which I was the agent, but also in connection with the efforts of our Baptist friends on the same island, and, I believe in other parts of the West Indies; and we have found it work exceedingly well, under the supervision of the missionaries connected with those islands. That supervision, I presume, will long be needful on the part of the various agencies that may be employed in the Southern States.

I am introduced to you as from Liverpool, N. S. I hail from thence at present. I might have hailed, but for my sympathy with Kansas in its suffering, from the State of Michigan; but being denied the privilege of advocating the democracy of the Bible there, and fearing that it might be so in other fields, I removed across the border. But still I have sympathized with the brethren of this body in all their movements. I have met some very dear friends here, with whom I have labored in that State, and many others whom I have seen elsewhere; and I rejoice to meet them here. I want to express the rejoicing that I feel in the prospect that is before you; and to assure you that I have had cause to sympathize with you in the past in relation to your armies. I will mention that two of my sons have been fighting your battles. I rejoice that they have been preserved. I am now laboring in a church planted by descendants of the Pilgrim fathers, in Liverpool, Nova Scotia. We are few in numbers, and exceedingly weak; but our hope is, as yours, to go forward.

Rev. Mr. Turner, of Iowa. I have been long enough in the West to have some knowledge of it. It has been my lot to be with and mingle with the common people. Although my immediate associates in the ministerial associations have been of those who are sometimes called the educated class, the great majority of ministers by whom I have been surrounded all my life have been those whom we call uneducated. The inquiry has come up whether we should put a class of men in the ministry who have not been through college. I should be glad to have all in the ministry educated to the highest degree, if you please; but then, I should be very sorry to have them educated to death [Laughter]; and my conviction is, that a certain amount of education will disqualify them entirely for entering our new fields. If we could have them so educated that they would be willing to go to work in any place, in any position, and use all their powers and capacities, and take things just as they come, why, the more such men we have, the better. But when men are educated above their position, above usefulness and above willingness to labor in the cause of Christ, the less you have of such education the better. [Laughter.] We have had some examples in our little association of Dubuque. We have taken up several whom we have found out there upon the prairies, who have never been in a theological seminary, never been through college, and set them to preaching; — and what has been the result? Why, one of them wandered down here to Massachusetts, and you took him and made him a Doctor of Divinity. [Laughter and applause.] Moreover, you have kept him here! Against this we put in our protest. There are two others, who are laboring with us, who have come on here; and I must confess that I was almost afraid to have them come to your Eastern churches for fear you would keep them. [Laughter.] My conviction is, that if we are to supply ourselves with ministers, we must take such men as we have, and ask God to endow them from on high with the capacity and the ability to preach the gospel.

I wish to say a word with reference to our Congregational polity. I have been an advocate for this polity a great many years. I was its advocate, I believe, before the fathers in Massachusetts were — when they ignored it. I have conversed with a great many men upon the subject, in times past, and I do not recollect a single instance in which the polity was not approved by those before whom it was laid. But while this is true, there is a large class of men, — the majority in our Western States, — who do not know what Congregationalism is. They know what Presbyterianism and Methodism are; they know what Baptist societies are; but speak to them of Congregationalism and they ask, "What is it?" I have heard the question asked whether it was a new denomination, which had sprung up in the West! And then the inquiry is, "What do you believe?" Well, we tell them we believe the Bible, and try to preach the Bible. "Well, where is your book of discipline?" We have never had any thing of that character to show them; and in some aspects, we do not want any thing, while in others we do. I hoped, when the subject of a declaration of faith and a declaration of church polity was proposed for the consideration of this Convention, that there would be a simple, comprehensive, common sense Declaration of Faith, written for the common people, — not written for Andover or East Windsor, or for theologians, but written for the people; something that the people could understand, and feel that it expressed the truth of the Bible; and by the side of that, I hoped there would be put a declaration of polity, so short that it could be read and understood by all, and circulated as a tract among our Western people, so that they would get the great idea of our polity and our doctrines into their minds.

Now, you may think it strange, perhaps, but if a man should go out in many regions of the West, though he should be the President of one of our noblest colleges, or come from one of our theological seminaries, and the people should be told, "He is Dr. Such-an-one" — "He is President Such-an-one," it would not have the slightest influence. "Let us see him, and hear what he has to say, then we will judge of him." There is no respect for titles, there is no respect for a man's standing; but — "What is the man fit for? If he has any thing to say that is common sense, that is Bible, let us hear it!" The mass of the people really believe the Bible, — that is, they give an intellectual assent to it, — and they are ready to hear it, and ready to hear any thing that commends itself to their judgment, and to common sense, and to the Bible. We do not want, in expressing our belief, to tell what our forefathers believed two hundred years ago: that will not satisfy the people of the West. And what our catechisms, or what our confessions of faith are, is of but little consequence to them; they want to know what living men now believe, what living men now preach and teach; and they think that a body as large and as respectable as this, is competent now to tell what we believe. [Applause.] It has been my hope, I say, — but I fear I may be disappointed, — that such a short and comprehensive declaration might be made that we could say, as a Council, "We believe it." We need not put into it *all* we believe, but make a statement of what we actually do believe with reference to the most important doctrines of the Bible, such as we wish to have float down among the common people, and affirm before the world, "Now we believe this." As I have just remarked, we need not tell them it is *all* we believe, and we need not tell them that we shall not make a better creed when we come to have another Council; but if we can agree upon one, which expresses our present belief, and which agrees with the word of God, even if it has no technicalities, even if it will not interest especially those who are guards upon our Zion, my belief is that such a declaration would be of great moment.

Rev. Mr. JOHNSON, of Maryland. The only claim, Mr. Moderator, that I can have upon even a few moments of the time of this Council is found in the fact, that I am here representing, with only one companion, a whole State; and yet that would hardly seem to constitute a valid claim, since we have but a single Congregational church in the State, and that a little one — the very Benjamin of the flock. But you will not on that account despise it, nor despise its representatives.

Congregational Christianity makes its first home in Maryland in a large city, — in the city of Baltimore; and on that account it may be proper that I should say a few words with reference to that part of this report which relates to the work in cities, because, also, there it is a new work, and because there may be more questionings concerning it than any thing else that is recommended. It would seem to be perfectly natural that in this enterprise, as in every other that we should undertake, with a view to extending its ramifications into various parts, we should seize first upon the foci, the centers of trade, and population: and if we look back to the primitive and apostolic days, we shall find that this natural process is precisely in accord with the genius of Christianity itself, and has the sanction of the Master; for the apostles went into the cities of Asia Minor, the cities along the Mediterranean, and the cities of the Roman Empire, not stopping until they reached the great capital itself; and in all these cities they ordained elders over permanent local churches. We are but following their steps, if, entering into a new region of our country, we look to the great cities as the points to be first occupied.

But this work is peculiar. There are special objections that may arise. There are some upon the ground itself. For example, let me come down to that particular field into which I just now entered, the city of Baltimore. Baltimore is, one might almost say, a city of churches. There is more quiet there on Sunday than in Boston. There are no street cars running on Sunday. I think that quite as large a part of the population attend church there as in this city. A great many of the churches are Roman Catholic; then there are Episcopal, Episcopal Methodist, Baptist, and Old-school Presbyterian churches, and one small New-school Presbyterian church. "Why," it may be asked, "go upon this ground, already preoccupied? Why run the risk of collision with these, some of them Protestant, sects?" Well, my friends, we think (not to mention all the matters that might be mentioned in answer to that), that our brethren, our sons, have a right, if there is room, to worship God after the manner of the fathers, in the way of their own choice, and according to the dictates of their own consciences; and though there are Christian churches there, there is room enough in any great city for a new enterprise, and if it has any special excellence about it, then it has as much right to build on that soil as any other Christian denomination. We believe our denomination has some excellences. Here is the matter of church polity, which I do not think we have praised too much, nor are likely to. I hope we are not going to say hereafter, as we have said before, too many of us, that that is a matter secondary and indifferent. It is secondary, and it may be indifferent, if it does not involve a transgression of the equal law of Christ. The denial of that law is just as much heresy as the denial of the doctrine of the atonement, of the trinity, or any similar doctrine. It is anti-Christ. And tell me, from what other source have flowed such streams of corruption and wickedness as the transgression of Christ's principles in the church itself? We are going to put a value upon our church polity, yet not so as to deny the Christian brotherhood and equal rights of our brethren who prefer some other form. We prefer this, and have a conscientious belief that it is the best, and has the sanction of the Scriptures.

Then our methods are different from those of our brethren who already occupy those regions. Our preaching, not superior to theirs, not abler, not more eloquent, is different from theirs, in that it is less technical, less doctrinal, and more practical. It includes, as part of the practical application of Christianity, the duties of men in the State and to the State. We preach politics in a high and true sense. I do not say that none preach it in a wrong, partisan sense; but I believe in preaching it in this sense, that the principles of the gospel of our Lord Jesus Christ are to be applied to man's relations to society and to the state. Our Puritan fathers taught us that the scriptures were composed in large part of politics, — the application of religious principles to politics. We have been taught from that source, and therefore our existence in the South is significant. Most of the churches on that soil (I do not speak with definiteness, for I have not definite knowledge enough) have been, I believe, derelict and false to the Master, in that they have either preached disloyalty and secession, or else remained silent; and our sons and brothers who have been there have felt as our fathers did when, in Holland, they heard strange speech, such as their fathers had not heard, and turned with longing eyes to their old home, and then looked away to a new home, where they could plant the institutions of their own choice and conviction. So do our brethren feel in those Southern cities.

Now there are objections to establishing churches in cities on the score of expense. We can not plant churches in cities without incurring more expense than in rural districts. Here, for example, is a little band of twenty-five people, organized into a church in the city of Baltimore about four weeks ago, by a council called for that purpose, and among them only three or four of any pecuniary means. What can they do? What have they to do? First, pay current expenses, which, with any true economy, will not be less than $2000 a year. Then they must either worship in a hall where to-day there may be preaching and to-morrow dancing, — a place filled with those associations which do not attract devout people, — or go to work and fix somewhere a center around which the church may crystalize, and draw toward itself those who are scattered over a wide field. In the first place, they have got to purchase a lot, and they can not get it for two or three hundred dollars, as they could if it was in the country, but they must pay $100 a foot, the best they can do; and it will tax them ten, twelve, or fifteen thousand dollars to get the lot. What can they do unless they are helped? My brother Gulliver, who preceded me in Baltimore, preaching to this little flock, said to them, "Brethren, go on, and the North will help you. The Congregational Christians of the North will not say, 'Walk alone!' because you are in a city. They will see that you are infants, and can not walk unless you have a finger or a hand stretched out to help you, and they will extend the whole hand to help." I told them so the first time I visited them, when I had no expectation of being identified with them as their minister. I said, "I know by the beating of my own heart how the hearts of the sons of the old Puritans will beat with you and for you, and I know that they will respond to any call that you may make for help." Now, they want a little help. They want to build a little chapel. They do not ask any one to endow them with a great church edifice. If they ever want one, they will grow to it and build it; but they ask for a little chapel now, in order that they may grow. I speak of Baltimore, not because I want to make it a specialty, but because I know it, and because the presentation of the state of things there will disclose to you the condition of things in other places. Maryland and Baltimore have some claim upon you. It was Maryland that first wheeled from the ranks of Secession into the ranks of Liberty, and she ought to have the first Puritan church. More than that, it was in Maryland, in the streets of Baltimore, that the first martyrs of the war, sons of Massachusetts, fell by the hands of Baltimore ruffians. We must retaliate, — in the name of Christianity, we must retaliate, by giving them good for evil; and we must give them the best we have, and that is, the Church of the Pilgrims; — and this we must do over all the South.

Rev. Dr. EDDY, of Massachusetts. I came here charged with a speech; but the twelve minutes' rule has dissipated what little preparation I had made. I do not complain of that rule, because I see that the idea is, that the edifying counsel shall be in the reports, and the hard facts in the speeches. I stand here as a witness. I have recently returned from the city of New Orleans, where I have been in very familiar intercourse with various individuals and classes, and I believe I can state some facts which will be of importance to the Council, in connection with the subject under discussion.

I will say, first of all, — it is due to the band of noble men and women there who have applied for assistance to the American Home Missionary Society, — that I was very cordially received; that I found them ready, so far as they could, to co-operate in any enterprise which had for its end the establishment of a loyal Congregational church in that city. There were some obstacles, however, which I need not enumerate here. I propose simply to call your attention to a few facts bearing upon this question. Is there a call for a church of our order in the city of New Orleans? (which is a representative city.) If there is, what is the method proper to be adopted for the accomplishment of that end? That there is a call for such a church, I would infer from this. The Northern people there, and the loyal people who have long resided in the city, imbued with evangelical views, look around them in vain among all the old churches of the city for a single place in which they can, with comfort, I had almost said in which they can without a violation of their consciences and the compromise of their sacred convictions, worship God. Our New England people would look naturally first to the Presbyterian churches, of which there are three. The first of these churches is famous all through the land, and its former pastor, — its present nominal pastor, — the Rev. Dr. Palmer, is known wherever the rebellion has been heard of. He still remains the pastor of that church; the people still pray for his return; and I was assured by several members of the congregation, that he would be most cordially welcomed when, in the providence of God, he should be restored to them. The acting pastor of that church is a Northern minister, I believe a Scotchman by birth; and in order that you may understand the kind of preaching that they now enjoy in those Presbyterian churches, I will give a short account of my own attendance upon a single service. It was on the Sabbath which had been set apart by the military authorities for a public thanksgiving, in view of the great national successes which resulted in the capture of Richmond. Having no engagement in the morning, I went to the First Church, — the most elegant and commodious church edifice in Louisiana. The Psalm that was read was the twenty-third Psalm; and especial emphasis, the significance of which could not be missed by any, was laid upon the words, "Thou preparest a table before me, in the presence of mine enemies." The prayer, which ought to have been a thanksgiving, was a prayer that God would give his people there, and throughout the land, a spirit of submission to his righteous judgment. The tone of the prayer, from beginning to end, evidently rose from the feeling, that they had been called as a people to endure very severe chastisements. Then followed the sermon, — an Orthodox sermon of approved staple in that respect from beginning to end. But what struck me in the sermon, — in which there was no allusion to national victories or national trials, — was one remarkable display of courage. In the midst of the sermon, the venerable minister was about to assert a truth, as it would seem from his manner, under imminent danger of martyrdom. He said, with uplifted hands, "If I were to be led to the stake for saying it, if I were to lay my head on the block for saying it, I would still assert *that man is a sinner, and must be saved by the grace of God.*" [Loud laughter.] I have given you, not an exaggerated, but a perfectly candid description of that religious service; and there is no church in the city, of the Presbyterian order, which holds out greater attractions than that church to our New England people. There remain, it is true, two Methodist churches, occupied now by ministers under a military order, and a Baptist church, given over, by a military order, in the same way, to a loyal minister; and many of our New England people have very properly, with great earnestness and zeal, thrown themselves into those churches, and are doing what good they can in connection with such ministrations as they there enjoy. The substantial gospel, doubtless, is preached, but you can well understand that those who have been trained up in our New England churches are hardly satisfied with preaching, the substance of which, to say the least, is Arminian. There is a call, therefore, by the loyal Christian people of New Orleans for an evangelical church; and I think the preference among them is very decidedly (although it must be said the majority have been formerly Presbyterian) for a church order which has not been compromised by any connection with slavery or with the great rebellion.

There are difficulties in the way of the organization of such a church. One of the principal is want of a church edifice. I believe to-day, that if you would give me $35,000, I could establish, in the city of New Orleans, a Congregational church, the influence of which would be felt all over the Southern States. A church edifice can be bought now for less than half its original cost, which would amply accommodate all who might desire to attend upon a Congregational ministry for years to come.

In regard to the colored people, of whom there are about 40,000 in the city, I will say that I formed a very close acquaintance with them; and I enjoyed my intercourse with the colored ministers and my attendance upon the colored churches more than any other labors which I performed or any other privileges which I enjoyed. Much has been said of the ignorance of the colored people. I want frankly to say, that the colored people of New Orleans, with whom I had such large acquaintance, did not strike me as so extremely ignorant. Many of the free colored people of that city are very thoroughly educated, and several of their ministers are very well qualified to instruct them, not only in religious matters, but in their rights and duties and privileges as citizens. The very best address I heard in the city on the assassination of our beloved President, was by an aged colored minister, — an address which thrilled me from head to foot, and made my eyes overflow with tears. There is not a colored person in the city who is not loyal. [Loud applause.] And however much I might assent to the general principle, that the exercise of the elective franchise ought to be conditioned upon a certain degree of education, — looking over the population of Louisiana, I believe that those who are at present best qualified for the exercise of that privilege are the free colored people and the freedmen. [Applause.] I went down South a bit of an old fogy; but I came home greatly changed in that respect. [Applause.]

The colored people need thorough instruction of a moral even more than of a religious nature. Their ideas and conduct, in regard to two or three of the cardinal virtues, are perhaps somewhat questionable; and, if I can have the time, I would like to relate two incidents, in as few words as possible, for they illustrate the very vices which prevail among them, and which must be uprooted by proper instruction. A colored woman, regarded as eminently pious, who had been long an inmate of a Christian family, was sent, on one occasion, to the market. There she saw a fat goose. She had a craving for the goose, and slipped it under her apron and carried it home. She was detected; and when, the next Sunday morning, she asked her mistress if she had permission to go to church, her mistress said, "Mary, you know you stole that goose the other day; how can you go to the sacrament? Don't you remember that goose?" "Lor, missis, do you think I'd turn my back on my blessed Jesus for dat old goose?" [Great merriment.] The other fact is not an amusing, but a significant one. While I was in the city, a quadroon woman, splendidly dressed, having a nurse with a baby in her arms, stood up in the colored church to offer her infant for baptism; and a white man, with whom she had lived for years, appeared with her. The child was his. The minister was asked afterward by a friend of mine, — "Were those persons husband and wife?" "Oh, yes, husband and wife." "But I mean, have they been married?" "Oh, I don't know about that," said he; "probably not." That answer will suggest to the minds of this Council a great deal of solemn, and perhaps very sad, reflection.

Rev. Mr. THOME, of Ohio. *Brethren of the Council,* — I may be permitted to say that I belong neither to the East nor to the West, but to the North and to the South. To the latter, originally, natively, and therefore by ties which can never be wholly sundered, let the South do as she may. I am very strongly reminded, on being in Boston now, that thirty-one years ago, this month, then a youth from Kentucky, and just emancipated from the trammels of a slave-holding family, I had the honor of speaking in this city on the then rising, and since great question of the land and of the world, — the emancipation of the enslaved. Now, after the lapse of thirty years, I meet here, not a handful of the citizens of Boston, but a great multitude of the representatives of the numerous churches in the East and in the West, who have come here to look down from their elevation upon the South, and to entertain the great, and, as it seems to me the paramount inquiry, "What can we do — we who dwell in those States that have been blessed by the institutions of the Puritans, and have seen their blessings springing up in the institutions of the church, the family, and society, — what can we do to disseminate our hallowed institutions in the South?"

I wish to speak for the South; not for Baltimore; not for New Orleans; not for a few prominent metropolitan positions in the South, — but for that great field, that magnificent empire which the war has opened to us — opened to US, pre-eminently, among all the Christian peoples of this land. I find myself, sir, as representing that great field before you in an humble capacity, between two great peoples there, in both of whom we ought to feel a profound interest. On the one hand is that class who are known as "the poor whites," who have been more or less involved, indeed, in the war of the rebellion, but who, after all, have but little of the criminality of that rebellion resting upon them, and who, in their ignorance, in their religious destitution, in their utter distrust of the religious establishments which have hitherto been in operation among them, look now, they scarcely know whither. They look by a divine guidance, no doubt, to us, for religious institutions that shall be adequate to their necessities. I speak for them to-day; and I speak in their behalf with intense earnestness, that we may heed the call of Providence, and, seeing by the eye of faith their outstretched hands, asking us to come to their help, may avail ourselves of this opening of Providence, and introduce the Christianity which we represent into and among the families of this poorer class of the whites of the South, — always poor, rendered poor by slavery, and now rendered doubly poor by the rebellion, which has desolated their country, and crushed them under the heel of a military as well as a civil despotism.

Then, sir, on the other hand, I see millions of the lately oppressed, redeemed from their oppression, liberated from their bondage, — oh, how strikingly, and how gloriously, — by a sudden stroke, the stroke of war and the stroke of the President's pen; liberated from oppression and bondage! — and yet, not liberated from the dark bondage of ignorance, of religious demoralization and debasement. Now, the query with me is, how shall that people be elevated most rapidly? With all the advantages that may be secured to them by political action, or by the magnanimity, generosity, or justice of the government elevating them to the position of citizens in this land, and introducing them as rapidly as practicable and expedient to the fullest privileges of citizenship, — after all this, which may be a question of time, and, indeed, which may await, in part, our action, — there still lies at our door a work of a religious and educational nature, which they are calling earnestly upon us to render to them; and as I have studied their wants, their necessities, — their most pressing present necessities, — I have felt that the providence of God had most manifestly convened this Council at this time, more especially that it might look upon this degraded and outcast people, now being lifted up into view, and that it might provide for them those religious institutions which are so well calculated to elevate them. Our churches are local churches; that is the prominent idea in our system of church polity; and the establishment of churches, not merely in the cities of the South, but all over the Southern country, where on the one hand the poor whites, and, on the other, the poorer blacks, may find true Christian nurture, and a position of equality, if not in the State, at least in the church, where they shall be self-governed, and have the charge of their own religious affairs, would be the very best and most rapid means of preparing them, as we well know for the discharge of their political duties and their civil duties also.

It is on this ground, Mr. Chairman, that I wish to urge the importance of that work which is now being done by the American Missionary Association and kindred bodies, — but especially by that body. In one of our reports to-day, honorable allusion has been made to this Association, as a body which has rendered its claim paramount to our support and countenance in its endeavor to diffuse a true Christian polity and true Christian faith among the colored people of the South. Let us labor through this instrumentality, not discouraged, not with faint hearts, but with strong confidence that God, having opened this field to us, will permit us to occupy it.

Rev. Dr. POST, of Missouri. *Mr. Moderator and brethren of the Council*, — I do not know that I should occupy your time at all, but that I have thought you might think it a little strange that one who has been for many years an out-*post* [Laughter] of your denomination, — toward the extreme of your denominational watchmen to the South and West, — should not add a word in regard to the experience of the years which he has there spent, and which furnish some results that may guide in the present crisis of affairs.

When I first took charge of a Congregational church that had established itself in St. Louis, the question was asked by many, "What is the need of a Congregational church in this city, and what call is there from Providence for it?" — such questions as have been propounded to us by my brother from Baltimore. I have lived long enough to see that God had an end in view in planting that church there, in the focus of this great moral strife, and at a time in the history of this country when a power such as gathers round the principles of your polity and your faith, has had a most beneficent vocation and influence; and I believe that the existence and action of this church (I may say it without challenging any thing for myself), have had much to do with the condition of Missouri to-day, as a loyal State, and one that has decreed the abolition of slavery. I therefore believe that it will be found to be of moral profit to aid the beginnings of churches in cities, after the apostolic plan. Not that the country should be neglected; but the idea has been entertained by some that no aid was required in such places. You never render aid where it will produce more important results. Graft a church upon a growing metropolis, and it grows with the metropolis, and it acquires power as the men gathered in it have power; it becomes a progressive thing, and at last a mighty thing.

One word about the obstacles in Missouri. The obstacles that have been thrown in the way of the progress of that church have not been so much opposition to us on the ground of our anti-slavery, as hostility, for some strange reason, to the church principles that we have advocated. And I will say, too, that it comes from your own children, — because they are your own descendants. Those who have been nourished by your money, and sent forth from the bosoms of your families, from your churches, and from your seminaries, have regarded Congregationalism

and Abolitionism as two isms too full of vague evil and odium to carry through that country.

I wish to say one thing here. We are, brethren, very glad to welcome members of your churches there, but I hope, if they come there, they will understand something of the difference between your church polity, so dear to your fathers — for it was regarded as one of the greatest gifts of God to them — and all the other forms that come in to lay claim to them and draw them to themselves. There was a time when I felt this more bitterly than I can tell. We do not need your help now, but there may be others in the same situation, and remember them.

There is in Southern Missouri a vast field for the enterprise that we are now projecting, or talking of; and I wish to put in one protest in regard to the churches that may be there formed. Brethren, do not require of us that we be exactly correspondent to the old type of the church in New England. There are many communities there where the old ecclesiastical organizations have been broken up, and the disintegrated fragments have been scattered, with no principle of union. They stand looking each other in the face, none of them strong enough to form an organization, — their children growing up in barbarism; and when they would unite, some string of dissent or malice draws them apart. Now, some Christian man with great common sense will rise up, eventually, and say, "Brethren, what do we here? Shall our children grow up in barbarism? Shall we have no Christianity, no preaching of the gospel? Why not come together on common-sense ground? Cleaving to the essential principles of the gospel of Christ, and laying aside those which distinguish us from each other, let us come together on the principles of brotherly equality, one man possessing the same franchise as another. You have a Congregational church in consequence, and you have the great articles of faith, which may not be a very complete system of theology, but which, if they were more complete, would be incomplete and imperfect for the object for which such a system is there required.

I wish to say one other thing in connection with that. Do not be alarmed at it. Do not be afraid we shall go to wreck and ruin and destruction in consequence of it. There is less danger of it now than there was years ago. The reason is, we have been placed in circumstances where work has been required; and I wish to say, that I hail this rolling by the Almighty of a burden upon our denomination as a great blessing this hour, a great means of preserving us pure in doctrine and keeping us to the principles of our church polity, keeping us in proper order; and under this influence, aiming to convert men, the churches will grow in orderliness. The ships sailing toward the same port, guided by the same star, will find that they are not very far off, though they do not stop to consider each other's latitude and longitude as they pass.

One word more here. Although I feel grateful to those who present complete systems to us, — the symbols that represent us before the world, — I do not have any apprehension for the loss of Christian faith or true orthodoxy, while the church is doing its great work, is practically awake,

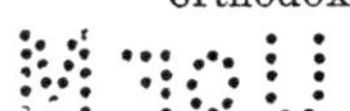

any more than I have of the loss of the theory of Copernicus, or the theory of gravitation, while men are working amid the great dynamics of the outer world. [Applause.] While rivers roll, and masses fall, and the stars are wheeled in their spheres, men will hold to it, without a set of philosophers getting together every few years, and resolving that the Copernican system is true. [Applause.] Now, Christian brethren, this great system of our dynamics is alive; it is no theory; no logic can prove it; no words can evolve it; it is a thing into which men and communities grow, and you might as well attempt to carve out a populous city of beauty and life from northern icebergs, under the eternal winter, — you might as well undertake thus to create a living city, as, standing still, without doing the Lord's work, by your logic and theses, and comparison of the various forms of theologic thought, hope to build up a Christian church. The eternal ice will not waste under the light, however brilliant, of the aurora; but call the sun into the heavens, let him strike down into the germs of life, let him wake up the seeds of vitality there, and they will grow into beauty, and the ice-fields will change themselves to paradise. So it will be with the ecclesiastic world. The great work to which God calls us to-day is the force of moral gravitation which draws his church toward one mighty center. As water, when standing still, becomes stagnant and breeds pestilence, but when brought under the influence of the great forces of nature, becomes a living, vitalizing power, and scatters bloom, life, and health along its track, so it must be with the great stream of life which flows through the church of God. [Applause.]

Rev. Dr. Beecher, of Illinois. I speak, not to make a speech, but because there is something I want to say, — something that I feel deeply. I had great anxiety with regard to this meeting of the Council, when I perceived, from the doings of the committee at New York, that the declaration of a creed, and a declaration in regard to church polity, were included among the matters to be brought before it. Not because I did not feel the importance of both these items, but because I was deeply convinced that the original idea of this movement, in the Triennial Convention at Chicago, and further South, where it originated, was simply *practical;* it was simply and only to promote the work of evangelization; and I have felt, ever since I have been here, afraid that there would be a disposition to spend the time in talk, in remembrances of the Pilgrims, in visitations, and in the many things which are very agreeable, in themselves considered, but which, in the end, amount to nothing, unless they are connected with distinct and definite enterprises, clearly laid out and resolutely undertaken. If I were asked to state what I consider to be the essence of this assembly, I should say, — *Three hundred thousand dollars to the Home Missionary Society, — two hundred and fifty thousand dollars to the American Missionary Association, — two hundred and fifty thousand dollars to build churches.* When you have stated that (you may put more on, if you please, and include other objects), and fairly put your shoulders beneath it, with a resolute purpose to raise that amount of money; if you separated and did nothing else, you would have done the thing for which this body came together. [Applause.] That is what I wish to burn into the minds of this assembly. We all know that in mechanics, if you undertake to lift a heavy weight, you must put your force beneath the center of gravity, and when you do that, you lift the weight. You may apply the force so that the weight will revolve upon its axis, and there will be a great deal of motion, but you do not lift it; and we all know, too, that if you undertake to move a tree, and only take possession of the root, the top branches will go with the root. So it is with regard to this question which we are met to consider to-day. The root which will carry the branches is this $750,000. I have been more interested in the $750,000 than I have in all the reports. [Laughter.] Not that I have undervalued the reports. I consider them in the light of material to make steam, if they are properly used; but it is the $750,000 that we are after in this movement, [Applause,] and if we gain it, we gain the end for which we have come together, and if we do not gain it, we do not gain the end. There is no power to move these great masses of men, there is no power to move these great enterprises, unless we can place our power beneath that which is the center of gravity, and lift that; unless we can place our power beneath that which is the root, and lift that, — we carry the branches with it, of course. Who does not know that men are needed in the ministry? Who does not know that we need men of a lower grade of education? Why, the other day, when I went to ordain a man in Iowa, a brother of Mr. Thome — a practicing physician — came to me and told me that the grace of God was burning in his heart; that there was a field in Missouri, and he felt he must go and preach the Gospel; but he was not an ordained minister, and how could he go? Well, half a dozen pastors said, "We will give him a written recommendation to go and preach;" and we gave him a recommendation to go into Missouri and preach and gather churches as fast as he could. [Loud applause.] I gave him a letter of recommendation, also, to brother Turner, who is the agent in that field; and, by-the-by, he is a sprout that came out of the college at Jacksonville, where brother Sturtevant is President.

Now, the question is, how can you get up that enthusiasm, how can you get up that earnestness, how can you get up that resolution in New England that shall bring out the power there is here? The agent who went through New England in behalf of Iowa college, Dr. Holbrook (and I imagine he is the person brother Turner referred to when he spoke of somebody who was stolen from the West), succeeded very well in his enterprise up to a certain point, and then, for reasons best known to himself, but no doubt valid, located himself where he is now, — a very useful man, I have no doubt, — in the central part of New York. But what I have to say with regard to all such movements is this: that just as surely as New England shall retain an amount of wealth within herself which is enough to produce corruption, or in so far as the principle of self-denial to which brother Sturtevant referred is not made really to go down to the depths of the property there is in this State, we shall fail of our object. That brother said, it was perfectly astonishing what wealth there was in the churches of Massachusetts alone. Now, what I say is, if we have a power of Christianity, if we have a power of conviction, if we have a power of persuasion and faith, that shall not only warm but heat all this mass of mind, and go down and take hold of this wealth, and take hold of it enthusiastically, we can raise the $750,000. [A VOICE. "Make it a million."] Add on $300,000 more, if you please; it can be carried! It is the easiest thing in the world to raise it, if we only have the power. It is just as it is with those prodigious steam-engines that we have in our Western steamers. You go on board one of those boats, and while the engine is cold it has no power. But kindle a fire under the boiler, and make it burn, and then you see the smoke coming out of the pipe, you hear the steam hissing through the cracks, and presently the boiler is full, and the piston begins to rise and fall, and the whole machinery is instinct with life; the steam plays with it as though it were a mere plaything, and the vessel moves on triumphantly. Now, what we want is that steam power; we want that pervading, that penetrating earnestness of conviction, with regard to these great interests, that shall not only make New England willing, but shall make New England truly unable to do otherwise than to pour forth its power, its energy in this great work. Oh, what is money worth, if it is not to be used for such work as this? Such a country to save! such a society to reorganize! such a future as there is within our reach, just as certainly as cause follows effect, if we apply the proper means! What is the worth of money when God thus, as it were, hangs up in heaven these great signs, these great omens; and when God thus calls, as it were, from heaven, — what is the worth of money, except to respond to such a call, to save such a country, to penetrate and fill with the pure light of the gospel all those vast regions that are open to us, and which are to affect the country even down to the millennial age, and beyond it, to eternity.

Dr. Kirk, in behalf of Gardiner G. Hubbard, Esq., of Cambridge, presented an invitation from that gentleman to the Council to take tea with him to-morrow evening, at 5½ o'clock. The invitation was accepted.

Mr. BOWEN, of New York. *Mr. Chairman,* — when this great rebellion broke out, one of the first questions that came up was the money question. I was delighted when the Rev. Dr. Beecher introduced that question here, for I think it very opportune that it should come up at the present time. The fact is, we must go to business now, and go to the raising of the $750,000, or we shall fail of the great work, the practical work, that has brought us together. I have had some acquaintance with the working of the $50,000 fund which was raised in Albany a good many years ago. I well remember when that convention came together, and when the committee was appointed (of which I was a member), to consider the question of church building, and it was proposed to raise $50,000 for that object, they said it could not be done, and recommended a smaller sum. But when the brother from the West, who has been referred to, who has lately gone to the State of New York, to settle, presented his argument to the committee and told his story in regard to the wants of the West, and we had heard also from brother Turner, who spoke earnestly in behalf of raising that money, we decided that $50,000 could be raised, we resolved that it should be done, and it was done. Sixty or seventy thousand dollars were raised in one day by a collection in all the churches for that object. That collection, Mr. Chairman, and brethren, was one of the best gifts that the church of Christ, in my judgment, ever gave to the cause of this country; and now we are called upon to do a much greater work, and yet a work which, if we think of it properly, and with a right spirit, will be a small work for us to do. There are six hundred delegates present, if I remember right. These six hundred delegates, representing the Congregational churches of this nation, can settle that question before they return to their homes. There are various ways to raise money. Business men find out, when money is to be raised, where money is to be had, and they come at that point. I propose to make a few remarks in regard to the method to be taken to raise this money. Suppose any of you, from however poor a district, perhaps from one receiving aid from the Home Missionary Association, were asked to raise a thousand dollars, would you not say, whether layman or minister, if that work was put upon your shoulders, "Yes, if it must be raised, I can raise it in my district." Now, if each one of you will raise a thousand dollars, you will have $600,000. There is a proposition for you to think of. If we pass this resolution to raise $750,000, we must take hold of it in earnest. And that reminds me of a little story that I heard when I came into town. A friend went to the Lunatic Asylum to see a very estimable and formerly very useful woman, that he might report to her friends what her condition was. She appeared very sane, and he did not see any traces of insanity about her. She talked, he said, like a lady and a Christian, and as he got up to go away, he could not help making the remark, "My friend, I am surprised to see you here; I think you ought to go home to your friends." "Oh," said she, "you don't understand me; you don't know what is the matter." "Why," said he, "what is the matter?" "I will tell you what is the matter — I have got a hobby. Don't you know what a hobby is?" "No," said the minister. "Well, there are two kinds of horses. If you get on a four-legged beast, that has got flesh, and blood, and bones, you can get off when you please; but if you get on a hobby, you can't get off. I have got on a hobby." That was her difficulty. I think there is a good deal of instruction in that. No great work was ever accomplished without a persistent determination to carry out that work. What could the Home Missionary Society have done, if they had not had men who made it a hobby — made it a life-work to take hold of the matter and carry it through? What would the Foreign Missionary Society have done, if men had not taken hold of it as a hobby? Now, let us make this a hobby for the time being; we can get off when the work is done. Let us devise some plan by which we can raise this $750,000.

We can do it. It may stagger you to think of it; it is a very large sum of money to raise in these times, but, brethren, it can be done. The nation is roused as never before, and we ought to be aroused as Christians, to do the work which God has placed upon us; and I call upon you, brethren, and fathers, every one of you, to take hold of this matter, and to carry it through. Relying upon the blessing of God, we can carry it through, and who of us can tell the results? — who of us can estimate the good that would be accomplished by raising $750,000? Why it would shake the nation; it would shake the world. Christendom would rejoice and give thanks to God; we should have a day of thanksgiving, and we ought to have one. It is not a great work, after all; we can do it; and therefore I say, that I hope the question of how to raise funds to carry out the objects concerning which we have had such able reports, will be carefully considered. When we go home, brethren, this matter in regard to the raising of the $750,000 will be about the only thing that we shall remember of the Convention. What can you remember that occurred at the Albany convention except that the $50,000 fund originated there? If that fund had not been raised, there would have been scarcely any thing about it, that we should remember now. Let us do this work, and we shall have something to remember and praise God for as long we live.

Rev. Dr. Budington, of New York. I would like to ask what the distinct question is that is before us? What do we commit ourselves to when we vote?

The Moderator. The first question to be presented to the Council will be the adoption of the Report on Church Building.

Rev. Dr. Budington. Is that question still before us?

The Moderator. That is the question still before us. I will state the position of the business before the Council. There was, in the first place, the Report of the Committee on Evangelization, which was accepted, and therefore before the Council. Then it was moved, and carried, to suspend action on that report, and the Report on Church Building was introduced. The question on that was one of acceptance, which was carried. The question then was, on the adoption of the report. It was afterward moved, and voted by the Council, that the two reports should be considered as one in the debate; so that, when the debate shall close, the question will recur on the adoption of the Report on Church Building.

Rev. Dr. Budington. I beg pardon; I do not exactly understand, and I think the brethren around me are in the same state of mind that I am. When we debate a report which ends in a series of questions, the adoption of the report, I believe, according to our rules, signifies that the Council becomes responsible for the principles embodied in those resolutions only. Now, what I want to get at is this: How much, when we come to vote on the reports, will this Council commit themselves to in the way of approbating the principles here set forth? I have observed, in the reading of these reports, that very important principles are commended to the adoption of the Council in the body of the report. I do not think that the distinction has been observed in drafting the reports, which our rules have presupposed. Now, there are several points of principle, which have been alluded to by the various speakers, upon some of which I feel a personal and special interest, and, before the vote is taken, I wish to have them distinctly brought up before the minds of the Council. I should be very sorry if we should vote blindly, generically, so as not to commend to the churches, distinctly and understandingly, the principles that have been incorporated in these reports.

THE MODERATOR. If I understand the position of the business, it is that these two reports are still before the Council, and are to be considered together, but they are not to be acted upon, or voted upon as if they were one, but they will be separated, and when the vote is taken, the question will be on the adoption, first of the Report on Church Building, and then of the Report on Evangelization. When adopted, the Council do not adopt the principles laid down in the report, but simply the recommendations contained in the resolutions.

Rev. Dr. PATTON, of Illinois. The brother confuses the reports of the preparatory committees with the reports that have just been read.

Rev. Dr. DUTTON, of Connecticut. The report of the committee is in the form of recommendations to the Council, which constitute the whole body of the report.

Rev. Dr. BUDINGTON. When I took my farewell of my church, I told them I expected to present to them, on my return, a deliverance, on the part of the Council, as to their duties as a church, in regard to the evangelization of the country, and in regard to the development of the lay talent in our church. Now, I want to carry out my plan, and to be able to say what in the opinion of this body, is the duty of the churches in regard to the development of the slumbering lay talent in our churches, which I understood Dr. Todd to say was demanded in order to occupy the outlying stations of Christian effort, which are the germs of distinct churches, round about that ancient Puritan church. The case is the same with my own church. I believe there are men in my own church, who, for their own spiritual good and for the growth of religion in the city of Brooklyn, need to have this urgency brought upon their understandings and hearts, and I, as their minister, desire to be instructed, that I may bring this conscientious obligation upon them; and I have risen for that purpose, — to know whether this Council are delivering themselves now upon that one point of Christian polity.

Hon. Mr. WALKER, of Michigan. I have been interested in hearing the gentlemen who have spoken of the value of Congregational churches in our frontier cities. I have had something to do in planting churches in some of the frontier cities of the West. I am a Western man, in the matter of experience, and what I have to say will be concerning collegiate institutions, and that method of propagating Congregationalism; — in my opinion, after an experience of forty years, the most effective method of all in advancing the principles of the Puritans, and their forms, throughout the West, the North, and the South. I mean to speak but a very few moments in regard to the question of promoting Congregational interests in the North, the South, and the West by emigration.

The very best centers of Congregationalism, in the West, — the centers from which have been diffused almost all the Congregational power that has been built up at the West, — have been the centers that were colonized from New England, by New England men, by New England women, who have planted in those centers their institutions of learning, and they have gathered about them New England Congregationalists, their children have been educated by the institutions, and they have sent forth large numbers of men to preach the gospel, and of women to teach in the schools of the West; and they have carried with them spiritual Christianity, and other institutions which are dear to this body to-day, — dearer than they were some years in the past.

To illustrate the matter, let me refer to the institution with which I have been connected recently. That institution has sent four hundred teachers into the schools of Ohio, and one hundred ministers of the gospel into Ohio and the West in five years; it has gathered about it men from New England, who have brought their children there to be educated. I need not name the institution, but I have no hesitation in saying that it has revolutionized the politics of the State of Ohio, and through that institution, two-thirds of the Congregational churches that are planted in the State of Ohio were originated.

Now, fathers and brethren, go from Ohio into Michigan, and there you will find a nucleus of Congregationalists settled in the townships. When they settle in a township, they bring in the school, the academy, and the college, and from that center goes forth the influence that propagates Congregational forms and Congregational forces through the wide West. It is not from the isolated churches in the country, it is not even from the isolated churches in the cities, that Congregational principles are diffused, — it is from these centers of power.

The last words I have to say are these: I went into the pulpit from business as a layman, and I have endeavored by experiment to learn what was the best method of evangelizing the West and South. I have left the old places, and old associates, and the old dwelling, and have gone and lived in a log cabin in the extreme northern parts of the southern peninsula of Michigan, and I have settled five townships, and organized a Congregational church in each of those townships; and in three of those townships there was nothing else but Republican votes cast at the last election. We expect to organize three more townships this year, and at the center of each of these townships will be a Congregational school; and in the center of Bay county, where there was not an inhabitant six years ago, we expect to establish a college that will propagate Congregational principles, and be the means of furnishing teachers through the south-western part of Michigan. We have now the means of accomplishing that end, in part, throughout that region. I see men here — men whom I respect as highly as any man here, though I respect every one of them with all my heart — who know that Congregational churches have been planted there. I see Dr. Beecher here; I see the agent of the Home Missionary Society here; and they know that to be the fact. We were on the ground first. We brought in Congregational forms from New England, and planted them in the center of the townships of Southern Michigan; and we have made Congregational townships in Northern Michigan, and in the center of those townships we will plant the churches and schools which will disseminate Congregational principles away up in the mining region, where there is not a Congregational church, but which is now teeming with population, waiting to be visited by Congregational teachers.

Dr. Todd presented an invitation from Hon. J. Z. Goodrich, collector of the port of Boston, to make an excursion down the harbor, in the U. S. steamer Pawtuxet, at such time as might suit their convenience. [See p. 384.]

Rev. Mr. CLARK, of New Hampshire. I want to say just one word. The difficulty with us in this part of the house is, that we do not know what all this talk is about. We have had some good speaking, but we were all ready to vote, and could have come to a vote just as well at eleven o'clock as now, and saved our time for other purposes.

Rev. Dr. WOLCOTT, of Ohio. Permit me to say, that there has been a departure from what has been regarded as the order of business for to-day; to wit, that the report should be read, and discussed, and no vote taken until the last man had said his last word. We lost an hour in discussing the amendment this morning.

The reading of the Report on Evangelization was called for, and it was again read.

Rev. Dr. BUDINGTON, of New York. Is it in order to take a vote on this subject?

THE MODERATOR. Both the reports are open for discussion, but when the debate shall cease, and we come to vote, we vote first upon the question of the adoption of the Report on Church Building.

Rev. Dr. BUDINGTON. I move that the debate now cease.

Rev. Dr. DUTTON, of Connecticut. I hope we shall not have the previous question in this body. I wish, sir, you would allow me one word of explanation. I desire to say, that there appeared before the committee a great number of gentlemen, representing various institutions of the West and South, and various destitute parts of the country. We told them we could not embody their details in our report, but that the substance of what they had to say was what should be said before this Council, to stir up our minds to the work which it had been doubted whether we should enter upon or not. Therefore the committee made their report that this matter should be laid before the Council, and the debate continued through the day, and into the evening, if necessary, that these deliverances might be made to stir us up, and that then we should vote.

Rev. Dr. BUDINGTON. Well, I am stirred up now — I am ready to vote. [Laughter and applause.] Mr. Moderator, *cui bono?* We are a nation of speakers, or have been, our English friends think, and can talk without limit. I am willing to hear talking if any brother has any thing fresh to say; and if any brother desires an opportunity to address the Council, I will not press the motion I have made.

Rev. Mr. TWINING, of California. I hope, brethren of the Council, that what I have to say will not seem to come from one who is not interested in this subject, or who has nothing to say that is worth saying. The churches of California, who have sent me here, desire that you and the churches you represent should be informed of the peculiar state of things upon that coast, and that, in consequence, they should have the benefit of your prayers, of such deliberations as you engage in here, and of such plans as you adopt.

The churches of California full well understand the great importance of that field which is now opening in the South. They would do nothing whatever, in urging their claim, to the prejudice of the claims of the churches in that field. They fully understand, and have always understood, the great claims which the churches of the West, and which the new fields of the West, have upon the Christian public. But they feel that there has risen among them a new state, — a state and a civilization which are to be developed under new conditions, and which, as surely as the sun continues to roll over those lands, will be a great, rich civilization; that there will grow up there a population most numerous and most powerful, and which is destined to act a most important part in the future of this country; and they feel that upon them is rolled a great burden of responsibility, in the time to come, to possess this field and to win it to Christ.

I can not go through here, in the very few moments that remain, with all the details and statements which I should like to make; but there is one view and one idea which I wish to present to you, and that is this: that this California sphere, and this whole Pacific sphere, and all the churches connected with that sphere, are distinct and separate from the churches in the East. It is away off toward the setting sun, and there is no connection between you and it. When the churches of the West fall back from the outposts, they fall back upon an older country, upon stronger churches, upon more numerous churches, upon colleges, and at last they come back to Plymouth Rock, — to what we consider the foundation of New England. But when Californians fall back from their cities, when they move away from San Francisco, they fall back upon the wild Indian and the wilderness. There is a distinct, separate State, which has its own center, and in one sense is far away by itself, and yet which is to be the germ of a new civilization, and a civilization developed under peculiar circumstances, and differing from any thing else upon this continent. It is of the utmost importance that a State so growing, that a State so separated from the other parts of our country, and from the churches of our country, should have the fullest benefit of all the plans of evangelization which are adopted by this Council. They feel that they must have help, and the principal help which they want at this time is men. It is men to preach the gospel; it is men to occupy the vacant posts; it is men to stand up amid the mining population in the new towns and in the new cities, and to preach Christ in such a way that they shall be heard, and shall have an effect in shaping the growth and giving character to that people. They are greatly thankful for such pecuniary help as has been or may be sent; but what they want, and want most of all, is men, — men to pray and labor with the people, and preach to them. I recollect receiving a call from my brother Atkinson, when I had the fortune to be in Oregon. He did not know, at that time, that he should be here, and be able by his own word of mouth to urge his plea, and the burthen, the refrain of what he said to me was, — "Send us men — good, faithful, earnest pastors — to fill these pulpits, to do this duty;" and the very last words that were spoken to me, as I was on board a steamer in the harbor of San Francisco, were, — "Remember, there are six or eight new churches that are without pastors, and that will look to the East and to the older churches to send them men; and we will give the promise that we will support them." Now, brethren, there stand, to my certain knowledge, within the boundaries of California, eight churches, in communities that will support the men, if they shall be sent there. They want these men to come to them and labor, and if they come, they will support them. Therefore, what I have to say is, that the great want, the first petition of those churches is, that you will send them men, who shall be MEN, living men, to work with them, among them, and for them.

Rev. Dr. Patton, of Connecticut, moved that when the Council adjourn, it be until eight o'clock in the evening, and that the debate continue until half past nine, and then the vote be taken. After some discussion, the question was put and the motion lost.

Rev. Mr. WEBB, of Massachusetts. I want to occupy one moment of the time of the Council, to say this. We are here proposing to give men to this work of evangelizing the continent. We are proposing to raise $750,000 for the same thing. How are you going to do it? Do you expect to get any thing out of my pocket? There isn't much there. I thought this morning, when these resolutions were read, that I was ready to vote; but the more I think about this, the less I am ready to vote. I am not nearly so ready as I was this morning; and why? Because I am beginning to feel a personal responsibility in this matter; and if you vote this thing, if I have a son or a daughter, I don't see but I am committed to give that son or daughter for a teacher; and if I have a hundred dollars, I don't see but I am committed to give that. I don't want to vote, until, with a new consecration, a new baptism, I can do it. If you are ready for that, let us vote. [VOICES — "We are ready."] Then I say one thing more, and only one. When this Council was called, it was proposed that the churches that sent delegates here, should take up a collection to defray the expenses of this Council. We have heard what the result of that was. Now, it is easy to vote money; it is not quite so easy to get it. Not one half the money has been raised that is necessary to pay the expenses of this Council; not one half the churches have responded to that vote with a dollar. It is idle for us to vote, and go away and say, "Well, the church at Hartford, or the church at Chicago, or somewhere else, may raise this money." The simple question is, Are you ready, brother, to give your thousand dollars for this purpose? That is the feeling I want to find in me, before I vote, and pledge myself before Almighty God and my brethren here to accomplish this thing.

A motion was here made that the vote be taken, which was lost. A motion to adjourn was also lost.

Rev. Dr. PATTON, of Illinois. *Mr. Moderator,* — Dr. Beecher, in the remarks which he addressed to the brethren, properly stated that this money question is the great practical question; by which he did not mean that there should be a unanimity of sentiment in this body with reference to the propriety of raising the money, but that there should be a unity of determination on the part of this body to secure that money. I wish to say one thing, which is a practical illustration of the spirit of the West. I think I have a right to say, of the characteristic spirit of the West, where the movement for the assembling of this Council was initiated. A layman of the city of Chicago, feeling a deep interest in the objects proposed by this body, assured me, that if the proposition now before this body to raise the money specified in this recommendation could be carried out, he would give $10,000 toward the amount. [Loud applause.] I have been waiting all the afternoon for an opportunity to state this fact, in the hope that it would stir up other laymen to follow suit, and the pastors of laymen to manifest a kindred spirit, so that we might electrify one another and go home to rouse our congregations to take hold of this work in earnest. That is the reason why we need to prolong the debate; but I see the brethren are more disposed to vote for a sentiment than to take measures to have that sentiment carried out.

Some discussion followed on a proposition to have an evening session, and a motion to that effect passed, but was subsequently reconsidered, so many members being entertained out of town that it was thought inexpedient to hold evening sessions.

At six o'clock the Council adjourned, after singing the Doxology in long meter.

SEVENTH DAY, WEDNESDAY, JUNE 21.

The Council was called to order at nine o'clock, and prayer offered by assistant moderator Hammond. The minutes were read and approved.

On motion of Hon. Linus Child, of Boston, the resolution adopted yesterday, authorizing a committee to proceed to Washington, to present to the President the resolutions on the state of the country, was reconsidered, for the purpose of amendment.

Mr. Child then moved to amend by substituting, that the resolutions, attested by the officers of the Convention, be transmitted to the President of the United States by the moderator of this Council.

The amendment was adopted and the resolution passed.

Rev. Mr. Quint, in behalf of the business committee, presented the order of business of the day recommending, —

That the discussion be continued on the subject before the Council yesterday afternoon until quarter before eleven o'clock, and that the vote be then taken; and that each speaker be limited to twelve minutes. The committee also recommended, that at the close of the devotional exercises, the first business be the report of the committee appointed to prepare a response to the foreign delegations, to be followed by the report on the letter from Italy, and the report of the committee to whom was referred the paper on the Declaration of Faith.

Rev. Mr. Adams, of New Hampshire, moved to amend by inserting eight minutes, instead of twelve, and the amendment was carried.

A motion was made to amend by substituting quarter after ten, instead of quarter before eleven, but the motion was lost, and the report adopted.

EVANGELIZATION AND CHURCH BUILDING.

Rev. Mr. Burr, of Connecticut. I think, sir, that we may safely venture to assume that the gentlemen of this Council possess a competent knowledge of the religious condition of the South and West. We fully recognize the importance of that work, and the need of promptly planting in all those regions religious institutions of the right sort. But how? — that is the point to be considered. Will the building of a Congregational House in the city of Boston do very much toward that end? Will the building of a showy Congregational church in the city of Washington help this matter very much? Will it be well, sir, to open the doors of the Christian ministry to an untrained crowd of Christian laborers, to meet the demands of the South and West? Allow me to say, that I think this is not the wisest plan. No one shall exceed me in the desire to have lay labor in the church, and in the service of God. I should be very glad to have our Christian laymen, by thousands and tens of thousands, go every where, teaching the religion of Jesus Christ, telling the story of Jesus, establishing Sabbath schools, establishing prayer-meetings, and reading excellent sermons, under the title and with the distinction and standing of "Bible readers," or "lay evangelists." I should be exceedingly glad to see this, and, if it were necessary, I would invoke a persecution, to scatter our Christian laymen abroad on this Christian business, as it scattered the primitive laymen. Oh, yes, sir, I am in favor of multiplying the Christian force in the service of Christ by the whole multiplication table. At the same time, I must confess I am not in favor of admitting to the full standing and status of the Christian ministry an untrained throng of even good men. Sir, "with a great price have we obtained this freedom;" and if there are any persons who are put upon us as free born by the dispensation of Providence, — men who are born at the point which we have reached only by patient study and culture,— why, sir, we will take them by the hand, as we would take the hand of Mr. Spurgeon, or of Mr. Whitefield, and introduce them into the gospel ministry. But, sir, it seems to me it would lower the standard and the standing and the influence of the sacred profession immeasurably to introduce this class of men, in the manner proposed, into the ministry.

Rev. Dr. Dutton, of Connecticut. Will my brother allow me to interrupt him one moment. He loses sight of one phrase in the report. It authorizes the licensing of laymen "by the proper evangelical bodies with such conditions as they may deem best."

Rev. Mr. Burr. But I am not sure that it would be wise even to send abroad a class of non-ministerial laymen, to be supported, even in a modest way, by a board established for this purpose. I confess that yesterday I had a different view of the case, and I was prepared to say I would do all I possibly could for the purpose of securing a body of lay evangelists to go forth; but on mature reflection, it seems to me it is inexpedient. I am persuaded that we have agencies enough. God bless the American Home Missionary Society, which has done so much for the West! God bless the American Missionary Association, which is able to do so much for the South! Sir, if we place $750,000 in the hands of these organizations, to spend on the platform of Christianity, and are prepared to do our work, it strikes me we shall do more and do it faster for the cause of evangelization in the South and West, than can be done by any new scheme that may be proposed.

Rev. Mr. Atkinson, of Oregon. *Mr. Moderator, fathers, and brethren*, — I have not occupied your time one moment since I came into this Council. I am sorry that I am here alone from Oregon, but you sent me out alone, in 1847, when we had Oregon only on the Pacific, — then a territory containing 300,000 square miles. We had no California, or Nevada then. Oregon has now 100,000 square miles only, because you have taken off three territories from it, that are to be three States, — Washington, Idaho, and Montana; but I may claim, perhaps, properly, to represent what was originally Oregon. The present Oregon will still be divided, leaving about 30,000 square miles in the Willamette valley, and another State between that and Idaho, a mining region; so that I may say, in brief, we shall have five States in the area originally called Oregon; — an important fact, politically, certainly; when it is felt in the senate, it will be felt as an important fact in the councils of the nation. But, sir, the time which you give us does not allow me to touch upon but one point. I must leave the agricultural capabilities of the Willamette Valley, where we have a few churches, and a college started; I must leave the great lumber and coast region of Washington Territory, west of the Cascade Mountains, from which your Maine lumbermen are carrying timber all over the Pacific, — to California, the Hawaiian Islands, the Society Islands, the whole Polynesian group, — and supplying even Calcutta, and sending their spars to England and France, — a region destined to become the great lumber field of the whole world; I must leave all that region, — where we have not a Congregational church or minister and only one in Washington Territory, and he but three miles north of the Oregon line, — I must leave all that region, and speak briefly of one simple interest which I have felt to be a growing interest, and one marking a feature in God's present dealings with us as a nation. I refer to the mining interest. That came upon us suddenly, and we of the West felt it more than you did. I was then preaching in a little church in Oregon city; a great room was filled night after night, and Sabbath after Sabbath, when news came, "There is gold in California." Some of us tried to discredit it. It was repeated, — "There is gold in California, that you can pick up by the handful." Our men started, and they left me with only women and children to preach to. It was said, "You can't get to California except by sea." These men, who had crossed the Rocky Mountains, said, "We will go to California." The Fur Company's men said, — "You can never get there; there is only a track;" but they said, "We will go." They loaded what provisions they had upon their wagons, and they rolled down the mountains, and reached Sacramento, traveling seven hundred miles, where never a wagon had gone before. And they came back, and said, "There is gold in California," and others started. I attempted to stop some of my church with the text, "He that maketh haste to be rich shall not be innocent;" but the text was not sufficient to check them; they went over it; and for seventeen years, we have had an excitement that has taken the church members and all classes of men, and left us the women and a few men, who could not go very well, to sustain our church operations. I was almost necessarily obliged to examine this question, and ask myself, "What does God, in his providence, mean, by sending us out here to form churches, and then taking away our followers?" — and, sir, I have learned this lesson, that God had a mighty magnet in the Sierra Nevada, and Blue Mountain regions, and I have learned that our people have just as much right to go mining as your Cape Cod fishermen have to go fishing. What has been the result? They have discovered, not only the mines of California, but the silver mines of Nevada, and they have made a noble State within the last five years, — the first to adopt the amendment to the constitution. [Applause.] We are loyal upon the Pacific. I would not forget that; and you have helped us some. We had slavery in Oregon, but your home missionaries stood up for the " higher law," for freedom and liberty, and their influence has been felt, and we are loyal there as yet.

Well, sir, those men, tempted by the riches of California, have not only discovered mines in that State, but thence annually *raid*, so to speak, into the mountain regions of Oregon, — those barren, God-forsaken regions, which, apparently, had no compensation in them for their discoverers, — and they have discovered mines over a range five hundred miles in length and four hundred and fifty in width. These mining spots are developing gold and silver in large quantities. I was told, by an agent of Wells, Fargo, & Co's Express, that we are now sending two millions a month of the precious metal from Oregon; and those men who have lately discovered silver mines north of Nevada are now investing hundreds of thousands of dollars in stamp mills, without the least fear. I have conversed with men who are ready to invest all their property in stamp mills, for the development of the silver and gold in these mines.

Now, what is the meaning of this immense mining magnet? It means that God intends to draw population there. He has made a California, a Nevada, and an Oregon there; he is making an Idaho and two other States there. What is this population? It is heterogeneous. It comes from all the States of the Union; and, lest I forget it, let me say, it comes now very largely from the South. [At this point, the rule limiting speakers to eight minutes was suspended, and Mr. Atkinson was allowed twelve minutes, in order that Western missionaries might be put upon a par with their Eastern brethren.] We have in Oregon, people from Missouri, Arkansas, and the extreme pioneering regions of the West. It was hard work to labor among them, — it is yet, though they know now, as they did not when I first went there, what a Congregationalist is. We are drawing somewhat largely from the North now, but more largely, as I have said, from the South. After the battle of Pea Ridge, in which Price was defeated, the men who could get away from the Southern army, went over to Oregon and Idaho, and they changed the delegate of Idaho last fall, and came very near changing the electoral vote of Oregon. The brother from Missouri told us that the central counties of that State are to be depopulated. He did not tell us where the people are going, but he knew, and I know, where they are going. They are going to Idaho and Oregon. You have the whole North to take care of the South; you send the whole South out to Idaho and Oregon, and you send half a dozen men to take care of them. Not even that! I came here for six men, and I fear I shall not get one to go to that coast. We have also an enterprising population. It takes an enterprising man to start with his family and cross two thousand miles beyond the outposts of which Dr. Post spoke so well yesterday; and it takes enterprising men to open new countries so distant from any bulwark of strength to fall back upon. They are enterprising men; they are noble men, in many respects; they are liberal men. They are earnest men — those miners; they are men in an unsettled condition, to a certain extent, but if you will only give them a stand-point around which they can cluster, give them any kind of organized institution which commends itself to their common sense and Christian convictions, and they will gather around it with characteristic energy and zeal.

Now (as I must be very brief), what we want in this mining district between the Cascades and the Rocky Mountains is a few men to go in there and be sustained, and we want church buildings. We will do our part. We want men to go to Ruby city, and Carson city, and Le Grand, and Boise, and Idaho city, and the other principal points in the mining regions and put down their feet and say, "Here is a church, here are men who will help you, and I will start the matter and preach the gospel to you, and establish a common school and a Sunday school, and get matters well organized." That is what we want; and I came here for nothing else but to say to you that God has put upon us, who have been laboring with those little churches, a tremendous burden, and that we feel, more strongly than I can express in words, that we must have help; and to ask this Congregational Council to feel with us, that we must have help, and must have it now.

Rev. Mr. KEDZIE, of Michigan. I understand that when we get through with the business of this Council, and pass a vote of thanks to the good people of Boston for their kind hospitality, and to the officers for the faithful discharge of their duties, there is to be proposed a vote of thanks to the brethren who have *not* said any thing. [Laughter.] I had hoped to come in for my share of that, but I shall have to forfeit it, because there is one point that ought to be brought up; and as it has not been, I want to speak to it.

We have been perfecting our scheme, lubricating our machinery, and now the question is, whether we can get force enough into it to make it go — whether we can raise this sum of $750,000. In order to stimulate our friends to this, we have been looking at the needs and wants and greatness of the work. We have had brethren from Oregon and the South and all around the country, laboring to create a vacuum, to see if we can not suck this money out of the churches; but it don't come in that way. It may help some, but there is another force needful. How is it that during these last years of the war, we have been able to get, for the Sanitary and Christian Commissions, millions of dollars? It is because there has been patriotism in the hearts of the people, including the women; and because there has been a sympathy with our soldiers who have gone forth for the defense of our country. This power, this propulsive power of patriotism, has secured large sums. It is not by creating this vacuum in front of us that we shall be able to raise this amount; there must be a propulsive power of a higher character working within us. In our meetings at home, before we came here, there was a looking upward, with the eye of faith, for a special and remarkable outpouring of God's Spirit, and it is by the power of that Spirit, by the revival of His work, by the power of piety in our hearts, by the indwelling of God's Spirit in the churches, that this money is to be brought out. It is by "the propulsive power," as Dr. Chalmers says, "of a higher affection." And now, whether that shall be the case, whether an outpouring of God's Spirit shall flood this country, leading all to feel that they live only for the great work of evangelizing the world, will depend upon the spirit of faith and the spirit of prayer in the churches. Whether there shall be that, will depend upon the spirit of faith and the spirit of prayer in the ministry. Whether there shall be that, will depend upon the spirit of faith and the spirit of prayer in this Council. Here, then, we can decide the question whether that money shall come. I know it is of God's own sovereign free grace and mercy that his Spirit ever comes; but when it comes, it comes by this preparation of prayer and faith in the churches and in the ministry. When that Spirit comes, when the Spirit of the Lord shall do for us what patriotism has already done (and it can do what patriotism never has done), then shall this work be accomplished, and all shall feel that they are not their own, but that every thing they have belongs to Christ. I have laid up during some fifteen or twenty years in the ministry, a little fortune for my children. I have got three, and I have laid up a hundred dollars for each of them; and I believe that the time may come when it will have to go into the treasury of the Lord. We have got to wake up to new conceptions of the power of God and the claims of God, and a new experience of what God can do for us. [Applause.] The gospel was meant to save just such a world as this, and it can do it, and God has organized an agency adequate to do it; and when these ministers shall be thus imbued with the spirit of the Lord, and shall show the churches what God gives them money for, and instruct them liberally on that point, there will be no difficulty.

Rev. Mr. Bliss, of Tennessee. It is with no desire of my own to occupy the attention of this Council that I speak at this time. I was requested to come here and bear testimony to the wants of the South, and I have come from Memphis for that purpose. I first began my missionary work in the northern part of Missouri, as the exploring agent of the American Home Missionary Society; and having some little part in doing a work there, I was requested to visit Memphis, by the same Society. I went there, certainly feeling that there might be an open door, and that something might be done, but I did not expect to stay there. I found, however, that, having driven the nail, I must clinch it on the spot, and I therefore remained two months, and secured the organization of a Congregational church almost in the very center of the rebellious territory. This is an important point, and we have felt that the wants of the South were the wants to be specially considered by this Council (not to the exclusion of others), for there is a wide and effectual door open in that great region, and we want to know what is to be done.

We have, at the outset, met with opposition, — just as we expected, — because we are Congregationalists. One man intruded himself upon the platform after I had preached a sermon to a large audience on the subject of Christian Union, and commenced his remarks by saying that he endorsed every word I had uttered, and then said, "After all, what is a Congregational church? Why Universalists, and Unitarians, and Spiritualists, and Come-outers, and every other form of ism is Congregationalism." These are the things we have had brought up to oppose us at the outset; but these things did not avail. We have organized a church numbering forty members; we have a congregation of from one hundred and fifty to three hundred; we have a Sabbath school of one hundred members; and we raised last year for the support of the church and incidental purposes, $2500. They have delegated me to represent them here, and to secure, if possible, the means for erecting a church. We purpose to be very modest in our request. We do not ask for any $100,000 or $50,000, but we want a few thousand dollars to give us a start. In other words, we do not ask you to do our work, but simply to give us a lift. We have been self-sustaining so far. We have had no help from the American Home Missionary Society. Land is very high in Memphis. We shall have to pay $10,000 for a building lot. It is the great central point in the valley of the Mississippi; it is a place to be occupied as the base of operations, — as the secretary of the Home Missionary Society wrote me again and again, — and we are entering upon that work. Not only have we organized a Congregational church there, but measures have been taken to secure preaching to the colored people. We have also secured the appointment of a district secretary of the American Tract Society; we are planning a religious depository, and endeavoring to secure there various agencies, so that we may be an effective base for that whole region.

Society in the South is in a perfectly chaotic state: lay that down as an axiom. Where our soldiers have gone in and occupied the field, Northern men go in and occupy the ground. They already control two-thirds of the business of Memphis, and some of the merchants are extending branches into the country. The old slave-holders in the country will tell you, "You can not raise cotton, you can not raise produce, with free labor." One old slave-holder told me, "You can't raise cotton enough with free labor to make night-caps for the old women." That idea fills the minds of these people, and they feel there is nothing for them to do. Property is changing hands; the great plantations are to be cut up into farms, and then what is to become of the old settlers? Why, sir, they are all moving like a great tidal wave, across Missouri, into Idaho, Colorado, and Nevada, and that whole Western region; and, as one gentleman recently from Matamoras told me, there is a steady stream setting forward into Mexico. The tide of events leads them to move away, to change their old associations. They feel, now that the rebellion is cast down, that they must go about in that community and in the nation with the curse of Cain upon their brows. We are to go in and occupy the great central points. They must be occupied immediately and effectively, and we ask your sympathy, your prayers, and your pecuniary assistance; for we can not enter that great field and occupy those large cities without much pecuniary assistance.

Let me say now one word in regard to the colored people. They are in a most interesting condition. A great many evil reports are started with regard to mutinies. It was said there was a great mutiny in Fort Pickering. I inquired of the commandant, and he told me that there was not the shadow of any thing of the kind. Yet that story went through all the Northern papers, with the design of prejudicing your minds. Beware of these stories. The wonder is, that these blacks have behaved so well as they have. [Applause.] The wonder is, that, after all the provocations they have received from their old masters, who have marked their backs with stripes, and sold their children before their eyes, — the wonder is, that they can keep their hands off of them. But we bless God that they have been so forbearing, and now we must beware of prejudice against them. Do not listen to the evil reports that come to you, for very few of them have any foundation. The schools for colored children are flourishing. There are already two thousand scholars in the colored schools of Memphis. We have already a high-school established among the colored people. We want an academy, a theological seminary, and a college established there, to train these high-school scholars for preachers and teachers of the gospel, to four millions of colored people. This is a work of great interest, and it must be done. While the demands are great from all parts of the country, here is the whole Southern region, with four millions of people in darkness and ignorance to be lifted up and enlightened and blessed by the gospel and the free institutions of the North.

And here let me say one word in regard to our own church order. We need in the South the breaking of the manacles on pulpit and press and speech and free institutions generally, just as much as the slave needed to have his manacles broken. This is as simple as an axiom. You find that the curse of slavery has worked everywhere, and poisoned every drop of blood in the social system. Every single church in Memphis was swept overboard by the tide of treason; and what was true there was true in most of the Southern cities. Now, we must plant there the institutions of New England, and among them, our own liberty-breathing and liberty-loving Congregationalism. I believe, under God, it is to this church order, so free, so liberty-loving, so careful of the rights of the churches, that New England owes her first and chiefest superiority among the States of this nation.

Rev. Mr. GUERNSEY, of Iowa. That report says that our chief want, after all, is not money; and I think there is more truth in that statement than some of the brethren have seemed to admit. We want *men*, too, who will be willing to undertake a work that no amount of money would ever persuade any man to undertake. Since I have been here some brother said in this Council or elsewhere, speaking of a particular field, "We don't want any six-hundred-dollar men for that place." Sir, we have scores of men on our prairies, whom we would not exchange for your two-thousand-dollar men [Applause], who are living on salaries of four, five and six hundred dollars. If they are six-hundred-dollar men, it is not certainly on the ground of the measure of influence they have exerted in behalf of Christ and in behalf of the country. If they are six-hundred-dollar men, it is not on the ground that they could not command in their profession a higher compensation than that. They occupy the fields in which God has placed them, because it seems to them that the preaching of the gospel is needed there, and that it is their duty, in response to God's call, to preach it with such compensation as the church shall give. In the State of Iowa, which, as brother Bliss said to me a few moments ago, is an old field, — it is *almost twenty-five years old*, and we have one hundred and sixty churches, — in the State of Iowa, there is territory larger than the whole State of Massachusetts put together, lying in a body without a single Congregational church and without a single Congregational minister engaged in the work of preaching; and there are some fifteen or twenty counties in which there is scarcely any preaching at all. Send us your six-hundred-dollar men, if you have them, and we in Iowa will make two-thousand-dollar men of them in a little while. [Applause.] In Iowa, in any new country, where things grow by the jump, men grow in the same way.

I have had application, since I have been at this Council, from a dozen brethren, perhaps, for opportunities to labor in Iowa, but they want just such fields of labor as are supplied, or as we could supply every day in the year, while we have scores of fields for which no application comes. Send us your men. A year ago, a good brother in Massachusetts, a classmate of mine, — and a noble fellow he is, too, — wrote me that he wanted to come to Iowa. But what sort of a parish do you suppose he asked for? He wanted, first, a village of some two or three thousand inhabitants; and we have plenty of them where the gospel is needed; he wanted an academy; he wanted a meeting-house; he wanted as good society as he should leave behind him in New England. Those are all very pleasant things, and no man is to blame for asking for them; but he might as well have asked me to locate him in Paradise as to make such a proposition in relation to my field. [Laughter.] That portion of this report which refers to the employment of lay talent in preaching, seems to me to present the only prospect for any thing like an adequate supply of laborers in our field. We want to take such men as we have in our churches, — and there are not a few of them, — lawyers and physicians, and give them the sanction of Associational approbation, and send them out to preach the gospel (even while they continue in their secular business), in the destitute neighborhoods that lie in the regions of country, ten, fifteen, twenty, or fifty miles between our several churches. We want such men; and if now and then we find one among them who proves to be skillful in the work, and shows by his efficiency in it, and by the education he gets in it, — and that is the best sort of education we have, in some respects, — that he is adapted to make the ministry of the gospel his life-work, then we will ordain him, in accordance with the recommendation of this report. And that is no new thing with us. We have done it over and over and over again; and we have from one to two thousand men of that stamp at work in Iowa, and all we ask of you is, that you will let them work on, with their salaries of four, five, or six hundred dollars, and not tempt them away, as has sometimes been the case with your offers of two thousand dollars.

One thing more. I believe in the importance of the Southern work. I believe that all the impression that brother Bliss and others who have spoken here can make will be all too small in behalf of it. But I believe, also, that the only way to carry on that work to a final and successful consummation is to take care of that great field through which the influences are to pass which are to reach and mold the South in the future. Something has been accredited to us in the work of subjugating the South in connection with the rebellion; and that has been largely due, as has been already said, to the influences of our Home Missionary Society. Now, take care of that field, and we will roll a tide of moral power into the South, in years to come, that shall be as resistless as were the hosts that marched under the command of Grant and Sherman. [Applause.] We have there one college planted by Home Missionary efforts, and in that college we have already trained teachers who are at work in the South, and we will gladly train more of them, — all we can raise up on that ground, and all you will send us; and we will train the black teachers, if brother Bliss will give them to us, for their work. While, then, we seize these important points at the South, and press the work there as rapidly as possible, let us have the men for our work at the West, and let us prosecute that as a part of the work of the South — for a part of the work of the South it is.

THE MODERATOR. I propose to make a very short speech, which is all ready to my hands, and which I think will be acceptable to the audience: —

The Moderator then read a note from a friend of Southern Evangelization, expressing his interest in the cause, — signed "A Friend of Liberty." [1] The Moderator proceeded : —

Accompanying this note is a bond of the city of Boston for $1000. [Loud applause.] I beg leave to say to other gentlemen, similarly situated, that in spite of orders of the day, or any motion to adjourn, the moderator will entertain such motions. [Laughter.]

Rev. Mr. CRAWFORD, of Colorado. (The rule was suspended to allow Mr. Crawford to speak twelve minutes.) Coming as I do a distance of two thousand miles, — seven hundred of it by coach, — to attend this Council, I feel as though I might presume upon your attention for a few moments. Coming at an expense of $500, more than half of which I expect to pay from my own private purse, I feel as though I would like to get, partially, at least, the worth of my money.

A day or two since, the question was put to me, "How far do you live from Nowhere?" [Laughter.] I replied, that my home was in Central City, seven hundred miles west of Atchison, forty miles west of Denver, one hundred miles north of Pike's Peak, six hundred miles east of Salt Lake City, and eight thousand feet above the level of the sea. [Laughter.] Standing on this watch-tower, and looking abroad over the mountains, I will tell you what I behold. In the first place, looking west, I see the new State of Nevada. I see there Virginia City, containing a pop-

[1] Neither the note, nor a copy of it, appears in the phonographic report, nor in the official record of the secretaries. Inquiries in various directions have proved unavailing, and it is necessarily omitted.

ulation of from ten to fifteen thousand, and Rees' River Mines containing as large a population; and we have no Congregational minister in that State. Looking at Mòntana, north of Colorado, I see there an immense population, and one city, Virginia City, again, containing a population of from six to ten thousand. I know we have many New England brethren among the Congregational people there. I know that among them are the families of the governor and attorney-general of the territory. I have heard of two ministers in that great city; one a Baptist minister, who is clerk of the court, and cook of a boarding-club, and the other a Methodist minister, who, I believe, attends more strictly to the Lord's business. Now, we want Congregational ministers at once in that territory. Looking west again, I see the State of Utah, and I have been interested of late to know that we have now, in the very metropolis of Mormondom, a Congregational church of eighteen members. [Applause.] When Dr. Kendall, secretary of the New School Presbyterian Board made his overland tour, last summer, he made a visit to Brigham Young, at Salt Lake City, and put to him this question, — "Have you any objection to my sending a missionary to the Gentile population of this city?" for the Gentile population there now numbers from six hundred to one thousand people. He said, "None at all; and you may send missionaries among the Mormons, if you like." President Blanchard (of Wheaton College) said there should be a minister there at once, and, coming to Denver, spoke to Mr. McLeod. With the enthusiasm of a western man, Mr. McLeod fired up at the prospect of preaching Christ where he had never yet been heard. I told him to go and God would be with him, and I would get another man to supply Denver. He went, and has organized a church of eighteen members. He has a congregation of three or four hundred people, of whom many are Mormons, and has a Sabbath school of four hundred and fifty. He also preaches at Camp Douglas. The people have raised for the support of the church $2000 a year. Mr. McLeod wrote to me that he desired me to represent him in this Council.

Now let me come to Colorado. The first city which meets you after you have crossed the plains is Denver, — a city covering an area a mile and a half long and three-quarters of a mile wide, regularly laid out with large brick buildings, three or four stories high, built with considerable architectural beauty, and which would do no discredit to your Washington street. There are firms in Denver, which in the spring season will sell not less than $10,000 a day, day after day. There is in that city a Methodist church building that cost over $20,000; an Old School Presbyterian church which cost over $5000; an Episcopal church which cost some three or four thousand dollars; and the Baptist minister has lately raised $8000 at the East, to which he will add some $5000 there, to build a Baptist church; and we have a little Congregational church, with a flock of twelve members. In the year 1859, a Congregational church might have been organized there of twenty-five members, and if a man could have been found to occupy the field, we should have had there a large structure, and a self-supporting church, giving their money into the foreign and home missionary treasuries. Dr. Beecher can tell you the story. There are men there to-day who blame him for not sending ministers there, when in truth there were no ministers to be found. I had the honor of founding the first Congregational church established on the slopes of the Rocky Mountains, and since then, I have organized, with the help of others, another church. My church numbers twenty-nine members, and for the past year has been self-supporting, raising $2000. We have also raised $6000 for a church edifice, which will cost not less than $14,000; we can raise $4000 more; and if I can raise $4000 more here, the work is done. My people are liberal, but there are impossibilities which they can not accomplish. At Boulder City, we have a church of fourteen members, and they have been calling for a minister. We want a minister for Denver, another for Empire City, and another for Cañon City. We have a population at Denver City of five thousand; at Central City, within a circle of four miles, a population of from seven to ten thousand; at Boulder City, nearly ten thousand; at Cañon City, where there are large oil fields, nearly fifteen thousand, and those places must be manned.

One single word in regard to ways and means. One of the purposes of this report is to secure men. Now, there are many here who can leave their old fields and go into new territory. We don't want sticks; we want men of ability, devotion, and energy; and if there are any such men here to-day who covet the opportunity of laying the foundations of a church and preaching Christ in a new country, let them make application to Dr. Badger, who sits here before me, and whose crown of glory can always be seen from every part of the house. [Applause.] That is a practical suggestion.

Another thing. We want money. And let me tell you that this church building enterprise is the most desirable on your list. Brother Langworthy said to me, "I fear our cause is not to have any place in the plans and affections of our churches." Let me say to you, brethren, that you must pay just as freely to him as to any other cause. Give us a church, and we can support it ourselves. You may keep a home missionary in the field for five years, at an expense of $300 a year, and a church will have to be built at the end of that time; but give to that field one or two thousand dollars, and a church building is put up at once, and the church becomes self-supporting at once. That is the more economical way.

Another thing. If you are going to help us at the West, you must preach upon our church polity. Our Congregational brethren do not understand this, and when they go to the West, they go into Methodist churches and Presbyterian churches, and say that they wouldn't turn their hand over for the difference between them. Now, if our principles are true, if we are standing on the right ground, if we have found the "old paths," let us stay therein. [Applause.]

One word more and I am done. The question has often been asked me, "How did you happen to start off to that distant region?" I will tell you. Two years ago, I heard a voice crying, "Whom shall we send, or who will go for us?" and after waiting and hearing no response, I said, "Here am I; send me." I am not a pioneer from choice, but from necessity. Are there any other men who feel the same necessity to preach the gospel where Christ has not been named?

Rev. Mr. GAYLORD, of Nebraska. You have been hearing reports of great interest, and claims are pressing upon you with great weight from the vast territories that lie stretching off toward the setting sun; territories that are filling up, as I can bear testimony, from the vast stream of population that is flowing annually through the region where I live, with a rapidity that challenges the earnest attention of every friend of his country, and of the cause of Christ. I came to speak to you of a territory that lies in the very heart of this great country, between the States and these mountain territories, that are opening up with so much promise, and with such demands upon your attention and your interest. The field which I represent is the great valley of the Missouri, lying north of the State of Kansas and the State of Missouri. The Missouri river runs directly through the great heart of my home missionary district; and that is a very important section of the country, not for its mining resources, but because it is the section from which the mining population are to draw those supplies that sustain physical life, while they are engaged in unearthing the hidden riches of the mountains; and, as my brethren from Iowa and from Colorado have said, so I can reiterate. Our great want is men; men to occupy the opening fields; men to man our towns and villages; and men to go forth with hearts warm with the love of Christ, and of souls, to take our scattered population and lead them to Christ, the Lamb of God, that taketh away the sins of the world. On the whole line of the Missouri river, for two hundred miles in our territory, we have but one stationed minister at this present time. I occupy the position of agent of the American Home Missionary Society. We have at Nebraska city the only Congregational minister on the whole line of the Missouri river for two hundred miles on our eastern border; and it is a region of country rich in its natural resources. It is fertile, it is productive, and is to be filled with an active and enterprising population. After I left home, I received a letter from Sioux City, in reference to Yankton, the capital of Dacotah Territory, asking for a Congregational minister, and saying that the Congregational element was in advance of all others, and stronger, probably, than all others put together; yet the only minister they have is an Episcopalian, with whom the people are not in sympathy. A few weeks ago, I was way up the valley, to Platte, eighty miles west of Omaha, on the line of the great tide of emigration that pours over, year after year, to the Pacific coast and the mountain territories; and there, at the central point of the United States, is an opening for a Congregational minister, who might be the center of influence in the place if he were there to-day; and within twelve months, the cars of the Union Pacific Railroad will be running from Omaha city to that place. In all probability, it is destined to be the future capital of the territory or State of Nebraska, — the center of a wide section of country, that will be filled with an enterprising population.

Thus the fields are opening on every hand. We need men who are willing to endure hardness, who are not looking for fat places, such as brother Guernsey described, but who are willing to go out on the frontier, who are willing to drive the first stake, and to preach if need be, in a log cabin, or a private room, or on the open prairie, and are willing to sleep there, upon a bed of down or a bed of husks, or if necessary, upon the grass itself.

Dea. BRYANT, of Delaware. *Mr. Moderator*, — This subject of Evangelization in the South is one in which I am deeply and personally interested; for, if there is any part of our land that needs Evangelizing or Unionizing, it is that part which I represent. I come before you as the representative of the only Congregational church in the State of Delaware. We are the pioneers in the *Emigration Enterprise*, inaugurated two years ago by the Delaware Improvement Association, and which is rapidly filling the State with Northern men of energy and enterprise. We have heard, sir, much of the West and its pressing wants, and there seems to be enough there to engage all our attention; we have heard, too, from the South, — and a vast field looms up before us in that direction, which must be occupied; and I can not allow this discussion to close without calling your attention to my own State, which has so long been under the blighting influences of slavery, that not only have the people become IGNORANT, destitute, and many of them rebellious, — but the very soil seems cursed and almost refuses to yield to the demands of the husbandman. Delaware is in great need of and is worthy to receive from the North that "Gospel which makes men free;" — the Diamond State is ripe for New England institutions. We want the church, with its sacred ordinances, its means of grace and religious instruction; — we want the School-house, too, as well, — so that the light of intellectual as well as moral and religious truth may penetrate the darkness, if it can not dispel it, which envelopes many a noble mind; and I ask you to-day, that in considering the wants of other sections of our land, you will remember that if Delaware has not been as faithful in this great crisis as she ought to have been, it is only because she has been deprived of the religious privileges and blessings that you enjoy. In 1860, the population of Delaware was 112,216, of which 90,589 were whites, and 21,627 were blacks; there were at that time, 1798 slaves in the State; but at this time, there are not probably 100 slaves, the majority having either been drafted or enlisted in the service of the country, and the balance have run away, so that the State is practically free. Of the whole population of the State, it is safe to say that three-fourths are without any religious instruction. We have no Sabbath school organization in the State and but few Sabbath schools outside of Wilmington. Over 500 families from the North have moved into the State within three years; — and still they come, — and by the first of November next, enough will be there to change the political character of the State; — and our copperhead legislature evidently see the "handwriting on the wall," which foretells a grand funeral celebration (if I may use the expression), on next election day over the last vestige of copperheadism and slavery in our State.

We are establishing a Northern rural village in the center of the State, and enough are already there to feel the want of religious and educational privileges to which we were accustomed in our Northern homes. New England, New York State, and Pennsylvania, are contributing principally to our settlement. Although strongly urged to organize a Presbyterian church, with the promise of assistance, yet we clung to the Congregational form as the one best suited to the wants of that growing community; — and, as there will be a demand in that section for other Congregational churches, we feel that most important results, in the extension of the Redeemer's Kingdom in that South-eastern portion of our country, rests upon the success of this enterprise in Canterbury. Our church consists of twenty members; we should have a congregation of two hundred, if we had a house of worship; but we are obliged to hold religious services in our houses, — our means being too limited to build and furnish a church. We have no pastor at present, but have one in view; — and we think, — with a little help now, — our church will soon be self-sustaining. We want to build a neat village church that will seat three hundred persons, and the estimated cost of which complete will be $3500. We have strained every nerve in the raising of $800 in money and materials among ourselves; the Congregational Union gives us $500, and a friend $200, with which to pay last bills; so that we have $800 to begin with, — but we must raise $2000 more before we can get the $700 which will complete our building; — and we are obliged to appeal to our Northern brethren to lend us a helping hand. We come to you in His name who said "Ask, and ye shall receive," believing that you will cheerfully assist us in planting in Delaware a branch of the true vine, — and promising on our part to be such faithful workers that, with the blessing of God, that now barren waste will, in due time, become a fruitful vineyard of the Lord. Oh, that I could ring such an appeal in the ears of my Northern brethren, as would move their pure minds and open their full pockets. A gentleman who has just given me $50, says he will be one of twenty to give $100 each, to make the amount required. Can we not raise this amount on the spot, and let it be a part of the $750,000 which we are going to raise? If obliged to wait until that amount is raised, we shall starve and die; but give me $2000 *now*, and I will have the first Congregational church in Delaware, ready to dedicate by the first of next November.

We have put our "shoulders to the wheel;" Christian brethren of the North, will you not give us a lift?

Rev. JAMES MASSIE, D. D., LL. D., of England. *Mr. Moderator*, — I have listened with deep and intense interest to the statements concerning the West and the South; and I would not have obtruded myself on this platform had I not felt that I had a message to you and a word of encouragement. I will not dilate upon any of the points, but endeavor as briefly as possible to express what is in my heart.

It has been my privilege to spend the last twelve months mostly on behalf of your freedmen, in the service of the Freedmen's Association, formed at London. I have traveled between three and four thousand miles, and attended more than thirty meetings, in company with an American from Cincinnati, — Mr. Levi Coffin, identified with the underground railroad. [Applause.] I have thus been brought into connection with the Friends, or Quakers, as they are better known, throughout England, Ireland, and Scotland, and have found their sympathies ready to be awakened concerning your country, and especially the benevolent portion of your work in the South, if not also in the West. We have worked together in connection with the Freedmen's Association of London on this principle. The London committee, consisting of members of the Society of Friends, clergymen, and members of the established church, ministers and members of non-conformist churches, welcomes and entreats the assistance of all classes of society in its object, and only seeks to give such aid, physical and educational, and to apply such moral and religious culture as shall, under the divine blessing, enable the once down-trodden and degraded slave to act for himself, and to give evidence of his capacity for the blessings of freedom. That society has sent off to America more than £4000, — and sent it so that the friends in America might have the benefit of the exchange. [Applause.] It has been identified with a congenial institution formed among the Society of Friends, and the two together, with the society of the Midland counties, working at Birmingham, have sent £25,000 in money and goods, to your Freedmen's Associations. [Applause.] I believe that, since I left, as much as £5000 more have been prepared to be sent, if not already sent.

I should like to read the principle on which these friends operate in your behalf. It is well that you should know what is felt concerning you in the country from which I come. Speaking of your efforts in the Sanitary Commission, in the Christian Commission, and in the Freedmen's Associations throughout the country, our friends say: —

"With all these efforts, the work is so vast, that it altogether overtaxes their strength. THIS IS THE TIME OF AMERICA'S NEED. SHE HELPED US IN OUR NEED. SHALL WE NOT HELP HER IN HERS? We speak not, of course, of her need in war. With that we can have nothing to do. And it is with no feelings of political partisanship that we now address you. But the hundreds of thousands of freedmen in her midst, who need food, clothing, nurture, and Christian instruction, and who are the helpless victims of circumstances over which they have no control, are as really a burden cast upon her, and claiming and deserving our sympathy and help, as the starving thousands of Ireland and of Lancashire were a burden cast upon us, and deserving (and obtaining too, be it remembered, to a vast extent), AMERICAN sympathy and help."

Then follow some paragraphs, which I pass over, proving that there was received from America, more than £200,000, in money and goods, to help Ireland and Lancashire, during the distress of those two periods. And now they say: —

"In issuing a revised edition of this appeal, after the fall of Richmond, the surrender of Lee, and the awful assassination of President Lincoln, — at the eve, we had trusted, of the return of peace to the United States, — we have felt that, so far from damping our zeal, these events are in themselves a call for redoubled efforts to meet the increasing scale which the work is likely to assume.

"May England answer to the call! May her ministers and statesmen especially feel that the expression in Parliament of national sympathy with America in her struggle to remove such an evil as slavery, is no less a duty now, than was the expression of national gratitude to America in 1847 for her generosity to Ireland. It may be that various opinions have been held in England with reference to the war; but with the return of peace, every fair and generous critic will feel that the condemnation of acts which seemed to him blameworthy, constitutes in itself an obligation to recognize those which he can not deny to be worthy of praise."

I feel I ought not to trespass upon your time after reading these extracts; but I wish to say, that I think it is in your power, as a Council, to secure the co-operation of the Congregational Union of England and Wales in your missionary enterprises among the colored people of this country. I know not what your response will be to the delegation who have come from that Union, — a Union of which I am a member, and in which I had the honor to propose the appointment of the delegation, and the nomination of one of the best of our men, who is amongst you; but that Congregational Union will regard the missionary organization sanctioned by this Council as one in which they can have confidence. I believe the Society of Friends will aid you in your efforts without reference to sectarianism in any sense.

Rev. Mr. ALLEN, of Massachusetts. *Mr. Moderator*, — It is with extreme reluctance that I rise in this assembly at this time; or it would be, did I not feel it to be an imperative duty. I regret the occasion, but willingly assume the responsibility, under the circumstances.

The two papers which are before this body seem to be united in the debate. They are the joint-stock property of this Council, and I regard myself as a stockholder in it, and therefore have a right to speak. I have rejoiced in all the testimony which has been given, and in all the sympathy which has been expressed, in relation to the two great objects which have occupied the attention of this house. However much others may feel on this subject, I can say that no one feels more than I do; and I have been exceedingly unwilling to interrupt the strain of feeling that has been so often expressed and listened to with such constant interest by this assembly. But, sir, there is one clause that has been introduced into the report of Dr. Dutton, to which I object, and against which I protest, and that is, that we declare our consent to, and belief in, the doctrines of our fathers, as they have declared them, in respect of what may be called the substance of doctrine. There is one great doctrine which is regarded as fundamentally true by a considerable portion of this body, as a cardinal doctrine, which is regarded by another portion of this assembly, and that a large one, as cardinally and fundamentally false, — and that is the doctrine of "original sin," as held by our fathers, and by those who were in agreement with them in the country from which they came. I say, sir, if you send forth that document, with that declaration in it, you send forth a declaration to all our Congregational churches, that is not true; and you send forth to all other denominations of Christians, you declare before the whole world, and you make it the record of history, to be read in all coming time, — a sentiment which carries a lie in its right hand. This is a subject that is greatly misunderstood by many in this body. Though I would not assume anything for myself, I will say here that I have examined that subject historically with great care and for years; that I have read much, thought much, and given it my most deliberate and earnest and conscientious consideration; and I say, sir, that the public mind in our churches and among our ministers has been obfuscated upon this subject; that that state of things, sir, has been brought about by those high in position as teachers of theology; and that, to accomplish this end, they have interpolated the catechism itself, — they have changed its language, and given it a form and expression that do not belong to it. I will say, sir, that on this subject, I feel prepared to meet the question anywhere and everywhere, and that I intend to meet it on another platform, broader than this, and to show historically that that declaration of sentiment is false. And, sir, did not the brother who introduced it know that he has been contending on that very subject, — contending earnestly, as for "the faith once delivered to the saints," — contending that the Congregational churches in the land were divided extensively on this subject, — that it was a controverted point? Who does not know it?

Rev. Dr. Bouton, of New Hampshire, called for the order of the day, to wit: the question on the adoption of the report on Church Building, and, the vote having been taken, it was declared adopted.

A motion was then made that the recommendations of the report on "Evangelization in the South and West" be taken up separately; which was lost.

Rev. Dr. Dutton, of Connecticut, moved that the report be divided into three parts, and that the vote be taken first on the portion preceding the recommendation in regard to the employment of Christian laymen; next on that recommendation; and then on the balance of the report. This motion prevailed, and the first part of the report was adopted.

Rev. Dr. Barstow, of New Hampshire, moved that the sentence in regard to "rail-splitters and tailors" be stricken out of the next recommendation; and the motion was carried.

Rev. Dr. Patton moved to strike out the word "license," and substitute the word "approve," which was carried.

Hon. Mr. Child, of Massachusetts. I wish to suggest another amendment. This is a very important matter, I apprehend. Indeed, it is upon a subject very delicate; and I should prefer that, instead of seeming to decide, as the recommendation now stands, on the propriety of approving and ordaining laymen, it should be so altered as to refer that question, — the question of its expediency, — to the local associations.

Rev. Dr. DUTTON, of Connecticut. That is so, sir.

Hon. Mr. CHILD. I beg pardon of the chairman of the committee. The report reads, — "They also recommend to the proper ecclesiastical bodies that they license for the needed work, and if necessary ordain, with such conditions as they deem best, Christian laymen," &c. The amendment I would suggest is, "that this Council commend to these local associations the consideration of the expediency of licensing, or approving laymen within their bounds." I fear, sir, that if it goes out from this Council that that class of men —

Rev. Dr. HOLBROOK, of New York. I rise to a question of order. Is this question debatable? If it is I have something to say on the other side.

THE MODERATOR. (Mr. Hammond.) Debate is not in order. The question must be taken on amendments without debate.

Hon. Mr. CHILD. I move to amend by striking out the words, "They also recommend to the proper ecclesiastical bodies that they license for the needed work, and if necessary ordain," &c., and inserting in their stead, "They also commend to the proper ecclesiastical bodies the consideration of the expediency of approving, and, if necessary, ordaining with such conditions as they may deem best, laymen residing within their respective limits."

The amendment was adopted.

Mr. Child moved further to amend by striking out the words, "and the Council do earnestly invite such Christian laymen to hear the voice of the Lord and enter into this work." The motion was lost.

The recommendation was then adopted.

Rev. Mr. JENNEY, of Illinois. I move to amend the passage which speaks of the use of "all other honorable means," by erasing the word "honorable,"— as if there were any other than honorable means that we could use!

Rev. Dr. DUTTON, of Connecticut. There are other means, and Congregationalists sometimes use them.

Rev. Mr. JENNEY, of Illinois. If that be so, let us not publish it to the world.

The motion to amend was lost, and the remainder of the report adopted.

Rev. Dr. Bouton, of New Hampshire, moved the adoption of the report as a whole, and as amended, and it was adopted.

A recess of five minutes was then taken and spent in devotional exercises.

RESPONSE TO FOREIGN DELEGATIONS.

Rev. Dr. BACON, preliminary to reading the report of the committee appointed to prepare a response to Foreign Delegations, said: I am bound to say that to one of the members of the committee this report has not been read since its preparation. It has been unanimously accepted and approved by the others. The mover of the resolution to prepare such a response (Rev. Henry Ward Beecher), at my request put into my hands an outline of what he conceived could best be said. If the report, as I have drawn it up in conformity with that outline is found too long, let him bear part of the blame.

Rev. Dr. Bacon, then read the following

REPORT.

This Council has been honored with the presence of brethren who have brought us friendly and fraternal greetings from various Christian bodies in foreign countries. Our neighbors beyond the St. Lawrence have sent to us the Rev. Edward Ebbs, the Rev. Henry Wilkes, D. D., the Rev. John Wood, the Rev. E. J. Sherrill, the Rev. A. Duff, the Rev. D. C. French, and Theodore Lyman, Esq., who appear as delegates from the Congregational Union of Canada. Brother W. H. Daniels comes to us from the Congregational Union of Nova Scotia and New Brunswick. From the Evangelical churches of France, a youthful brother, bearing a beloved and honored name, the Rev. Theodore Monod, delegated by the Union of those churches, has stood among us, and from his eloquent lips we have received a new assurance that the Evangelical Protestantism which in that great country was so long persecuted and oppressed, is yet to be a power in the conquest of the world for Christ. The Congregational Churches of Wales, worshiping God in their own ancient language, and inheriting that primitive British Christianity which is older than the name of England, have been represented by the Rev. John Thomas, C. R. Jones, Esq., and J. Griffith, Esq., deputed for that service by the Glanmorganshire Association. From the Fatherland of our own Pilgrim Fathers, two distinguished ministers, the Rev. Robert Vaughan, D. D., and the Rev. Alexander Raleigh, D. D., commissioned by the Congregational Union of England and Wales, the Rev. S. R. Asbury, commissioned by the North Staffordshire Congregational Union, and another, who needs no letters of recommendation to us, the Rev. Dr. James W. Massie, have come to renew and confirm the alliance which ought ever to be firm and intimate between the Congregationalism of England and the Congregationalism of America. The presence of these brethren in our National Council gives us the opportunity of testifying the Christian fellowship of our churches with all in every land who are sincerely seeking to advance the kingdom of Christ.

To our brethren in the neighboring British Provinces, we need only respond with grateful recognition of their interest in us and in the work committed to us. Their peculiar work is in some degree co-ordinate with ours. It is for them, though under many discouragements, to maintain and propagate in their country those religious ideas and organizing forces which our fathers brought with them to New England, and which, whenever they have had free course upon this continent, have made the wilderness rejoice and blossom as the rose. May God give them enlargement and prosperity!

The salutations of the French Evangelical churches remind us of the many points of contact between the history of their country and the history of our own. Here in Boston there was once a congregation of French Protestants exiled for their religion. The Huguenot migration to New England and to all the English colonies was one of the streams that made up by their confluence the American race and nationality. Names that were once French, and that were brought hither by fugitives from persecution almost two hundred years ago, are borne by thousands of our people, and some of them are illustrious in our history. The relation of France to the achievement of our national independence can never be forgotten by the American people while the memory of Lafayette is blended with the memory of Washington. From the earliest stages of the French Revolution to the present hour, our people, more intently perhaps than any other, have watched the vicissitudes of liberty, and especially of religious liberty, in that country. Our churches have watched with prayer and with praise to God the rekindled life in the dying remnants of French Protestantism, and gladly have they contributed something of substantial aid to a movement so full of hope for Europe and for the world. Yet when the terrible storm of adversity burst upon our country four years ago, and we looked to all parts of the world for sympathy from the wise and the good, we little expected that from a Protestant Frenchman there would come, to invigorate our confidence in God, and to reassure the consciousness of our relation to his work who is making all things new, such a tribute to the grandeur of our cause, and such an appeal to the Christian world in our behalf, as came from the illustrious Count Ajenor de Gasparin. We were in a position which made us know with lively sensibility what was said of us and what was thought of us in every country of the civilized world. It gave us no discouragement to find that everywhere the enemies of liberty and the upholders of military and priestly despotisms were in full sympathy with our enemies. But to know, as we knew from the beginning, that the friends of liberty and progress throughout Europe, and especially in France, were our friends, and that they recognized the identity of our cause with theirs, gave added courage to all our loyal people. To know, as we know, that the religious aspects of the conflict, and its relations to the work and kingdom of Christ, were understood and appreciated by the revived Protestant churches of France, and that their prayers were unceasingly offered for us, was to all our churches a fresh inspiration of faith and hope. From our experience of what their words of cheer have been to us in our darkest hours, we would learn, for our own guidance in all future time, how much good the Christian people of one nation may do to the Christian people of another nation, in times of peril and of trial, by speaking to them and speaking for them, words of Christian sympathy and confidence, in the free, clear tone of Christian manliness.

Our brethren in the principality of Wales assure us, by their delegates, that, in the great struggle of our nation for civil and religious liberty, their sympathy with us has been constant and outspoken, and that their prayers have been offered to God for us in the time of our calamity. It would hardly have been strange, if, in the seclusion of their ancestral mountains, they had felt that a conflict on the other side of the globe, though all the world beside should be shaken with the Titanic struggle, was no concern of theirs, and that the military neutrality proclaimed by the government of their country required them to suppress their moral and religious sympathies. But the mountains are ever the home of free and brave hearts; and the ocean over which adventurous Madoc is reputed to have sailed seven hundred years ago, has been crossed in more modern times by thousands of Welshmen who have retained in their homes among us their own language and their communications with their kindred in the land of their fathers. The Welsh settlements in our country are settlements of Congregational Calvinists, and everywhere they have been thoroughly loyal to their country and to liberty. To them in part we owe it that the Congregational churches in Wales have so well understood the merits of our cause, and have so frankly given to us, in our conflict with oppression and with treason, the Cambrian steadfastness of their sympathy, and the Cambrian fervor of their prayers.

In England, too, our country and our churches have had, from the beginning of the great agony, firm and enlightened friends. Perhaps it was a fondness on our part, but, in that love for old England which so many ages of separation had not extinguished, we have cherished the belief that the sovereign lady, whose womanly and queenly virtues have so adorned the throne of her ancestors, has not forgotten with what enthusiasm of hospitality her royal son was received by the American people, and has freely given the homage of her personal sympathy and regard to the grandeur of the sacrifices which God has required of us for our country and for the welfare of mankind. In the highest rank of the British aristocracy, one at least was found (alas that we can not join the name of Shaftesbury with the name of Argyle!) who at the first perceived and openly declared the necessity that was upon us, as patriots and as men, to defend in arms and at all hazards, not our national inheritance only, but our national life. Among the foremost statesmen in the British House of Commons, such men as Bright and the lamented Cobden, — whose names, like that of Hampden in his day, are greater than titles of nobility, — among philosophic thinkers in the sphere of political science, such men as Stuart Mill, and Goldwin Smith, have been the champions of our cause before their countrymen. But notwithstanding all this, the prevalent opinion of England and of Scotland has been notoriously adverse to our cause. Though we had able defenders among those who control the journalism of Great Britain, the most powerful of the organs that sway and express the public opinion of Great Britain, the most ponderous reviews, the most popular magazines, the most widely circulating and authoritative newspapers, whig and tory, conservative and radical, high-church and infidel, if they could agree in nothing else, were well agreed in their hostility to us and in their sympathy with the rebellion.

This was not what we expected. It struck the hearts of thousands of our countrymen with a pang like that which any man might feel when some friend whom he loved and trusted has suddenly become his enemy. Yet this is what we might have expected if we had adequately considered the infirmities of human nature and the forces by which national antipathies are generated and determined. Our kindred in Great Britain had seen with mingled pride and apprehension the portentous growth of the United States, and had been sometimes disgusted with that boastful and vain-glorious habit which has hitherto entered so largely into our national character. We can not wonder that the British nation had some feeling of relief and satisfaction at the apparent downfall of a power that had seemed likely to rival "the mistress of the seas," and that might have attempted some day to wrest the trident from her grasp. The political institutions of the United States, though in some sense an outgrowth of ancient English law and liberty, had no place for the theoretical monarchy and the actual and powerful aristocracy of the British constitution. We can not wonder that thousands of loyal subjects in Great Britain accepted with a cheerful feeling the apparent ruin of our federal democracy, and made haste to infer with joy the impossibility of any political welfare without a powerful aristocracy. In the United States there was no established Church; but all forms of worship were alike protected by the law, and alike dependent upon the voluntary offerings of the people. We can not wonder that in England, where the Established Church is ubiquitous in its presence and its power, and where all church parties, High Church, Low Church, and Broad Church, and all theologies in the church from ultra Calvinism to ultra Rationalism, agree in venerating the sanctity of tithes and in abhorring the impiety of a nation without a church by law established, there was a religious feeling, widely diffused, which devotedly interpreted our national calamity as a revelation from heaven of God's wrath against our national impiety. Nor was this all. The island of Great Britain is one great hive of manufacturing industry; and British commerce has been for many ages the cynosure of British statesmanship. But on the other hand the people of the United States have shown a determination to enrich their own country by a large development of manufacturing industry; and the commerce of the United States had seemed likely to rival the world-wide sweep, and to surpass the daring enterprise of British commerce. We can not wonder that the nation which the first Napoleon, in the insolence of a robber, thought to stigmatize by calling it "a nation of shopkeepers," and in which the great manufacturers and traders already share with the ancient aristocracy of land-owners the actual sovereignty of the empire, was moved with something like a national joy at what seemed to be the final paralysis and ruin of a great commercial rival. Yet there was one class in the population of Great Britain which surprised the world by standing firmly and bravely for us.

The operatives in the manufacturing districts were the first to suffer from the effects of the American conflict. But as if by some instinct divinely given, they felt and knew that the conflict was a conflict for the rights of labor and the liberty of all mankind; and from first to last they steadfastly resisted all attempts to bring them through their sufferings into any sort of fellowship with the impious power that was struggling to found an empire on the principle that the proprietors of land and capital ought also to be the proprietors of their less fortunate fellow-men. Let us give due honor to the humble operatives in the mills and forges and countless workshops of Great Britain, whom God enabled to stand firm in the day of their calamity and of ours.

From our brethren of the Congregational churches in England, we expected at the first an unequivocal and constant declaration of sympathy with the American people. Were they not our brethren, inheritors with us of the faith and order for which the martyrs of Congregationalism suffered under Queen Elizabeth? Did they not glory in our Pilgrim Fathers? Was not our history their boast? Was not our religious prosperity, our civil liberty, our marvelous progress among the nations, the most powerful of arguments for their principles? Were they ashamed of Milton and of Cromwell, or of the position which Britain held among the nations when a Congregationalist Lord Protector reigned in the place of the perjured and persecuting Stuarts? Was not our cause "the good old cause" of the Puritan against the Cavalier, acknowledged and proclaimed as such by our enemies? Had they not in the freedom and fidelity of Congregational fellowship, rebuked us at sundry times and in divers manners, publicly and privately, through the press and by official communications, for the lukewarmness of our zeal and the imperfection of our testimony against the wickedness of slavery? And when at last the American people, roused in part by such remonstrances as theirs, and moved by the pressure of a purely religious feeling throughout the free States, — a feeling to which the Congregationalism of New England and the North contributed more than its full share of glow and impulse, — rendered, in the unequivocal form of a national election, its purpose to arrest the extension of slavery and to resist the insolent demands of the slave-holding and slave-trading interest, though at the hazard of war and national dissolution, — was it not to be expected that the Congregational churches and ministers of England, with one voice of no uncertain sound, would testify for the righteousness of our cause, not only as the cause of order against anarchy, and of constitutional government by votes against government by violence and arbitrary power, — not only as the cause of religious liberty and the universal diffusion of knowledge against a system which made the Bible an incendiary book and the teaching of the alphabet a crime, — but also as the cause of personal freedom, and of every man's right to his own limbs and faculties, against the hideous atrocity of subjecting a race to perpetual servitude, hopeless and unrewarded, and the impiety of perverting the Christian religion into a divine warrant for that atrocity.

Our brethren who bring to us in this assembly the congratulations of the English Congregational Union must not be permitted to return under any impression that we have not felt deeply and sorrowfully, through these four years of national agony, the actual position of English Congregationalists. We know that among them there have been some, whom it might be invidious to name, because we could not name them all, who have been from first to last, our most constant, devoted, and faithful defenders. We frankly and gratefully acknowledge, on the testimony of the honored delegates here present, that the majority of the Congregational ministers and churches in England have sympathized with us, and have prayed for our deliverance from our enemies, and our victory over the Antichrist that rose up to destroy us. But faithfulness to them and to Christ forbids us to forget that the dominant influences in the Congregational Union, and the ostensible organs of Congregational opinion in England, were against us, or that honored brethren who went from us to them, for the purpose of explaining our position, and asking for their sympathy and their prayers, were refused a hearing. Yet while we remember this, we remember it not as retaining any unkind remembrance of an injury to us. We accept the presence of the beloved and honored delegates who have stood in our assembly as a proof that they now understand us, and that the ancient fraternity and unity between them and us shall be perpetual, and as a hopeful omen that between these kindred nations there shall be peace, ever growing more intimate and indissoluble by co-operation in all works of beneficence to mankind and of glory to God.

LEONARD BACON,
HENRY WARD BEECHER,
J. M. STURTEVANT, } *Committee.*
RUFUS ANDERSON,
J. B. WALKER,

Rev. Mr. QUINT. I make the motion to accept and to adopt this report. I feel easier and breathe easier than I have since last week. I have had the sound of those cheers weighing down upon me ever since the reception of our foreign brethren, and I am glad now to hear this manly and clear utterance.

We have felt the position of England toward us. I have felt it myself particularly, because I have seen its effect. England is now, I suppose, converted and on our side; for England is like Providence, "always on the side of the strongest battalions," always ready to follow the powerful, and always ready to crush the weak [A few hisses]; robbing in India, plundering in Ireland, and in connection with our affairs worse than that.

Some of you think I feel strongly upon this. I am willing you should; and when you have earned the right to feel as strongly as I do, and earned it in the same way, by a three years' devotion of your life in the service of your country, and have had England to fight all the way, then you may hiss if you please; you will then be entitled to the respect which I am, and which I claim. [Applause.]

When those cheers were given the other day I could not help thinking that, notwithstanding they were intended for the adroit eloquence of the venerable brethren whom we welcomed, they could not vindicate by that eloquence the facts which have been brought out in this report.

When I went to settle in the place where I live I found that my people's property, being upon the sea, had been given to the flames by British pirates, vessels of war, built in England, manned, and supplied there. But when I was in the service of my country and saw my comrades dead, when I saw friends from Wisconsin, Indiana, and New York dead side by side, I knew that they fell by British bullets, from British muskets, loaded with British powder, fired by men wearing British shoes and British clothing, and backed up by British sympathy. [Applause.]

But now they are converted. Yes! Their attention was arrested at Atlanta. Their convictions were awakened at Savannah. They were very strongly convicted of sin at Petersburg, and tolerably converted at Richmond; and I hope they will not fall from grace by the sin there was in the skirts of Jeff Davis. [Laughter and applause.]

When I heard those cheers the other day, and I say it with the utmost kindness of feeling toward these brethren, I wanted to cheer them, too, but I thought I heard in the sound of those cheers [Referring to Dr. Vaughan's speech before the Council, on Thursday the 15th], the whiz of the bullet, the crash of the bursting shell, the groans of the wounded, the weeping of the orphan, and the wailing of widows at home, made so by British sympathy. Brethren, I could not cheer!

But what did our own brethren over there do? How did they feel? How did they talk? I quote extracts from their leading periodical [British Quarterly:]

"We have no faith in the doctrine, *that the continuance of the colossal Union which has grown up over that vast territory is desirable.* We feel convinced that some division, and perhaps more than one, would be favorable in many ways to the progress of international harmony, and of Christian civilization.

"The most self-governed people in the world have become the most ill-governed. The world, it seems, was to see how a colossal republic may become a colossal Napoleon; how the former may become as ambitious as the latter, and fully as heedless in regard to the costs of its ambition.

"The manhood of seven millions of people reduced to *that.* If this be anything like true, has the world ever witnessed a carnage so deliberate and so horrible? And all for what? That slavery may be annihilated, is the answer of some well-meaning but *mistaken* men. For the perpetuating of empire is the answer from the majority of the Northern people. Disguise it as we may, it is that America may be the seat of a Republic as large as Europe, and that it may be strong enough to issue maritime law to Europe.

"The issue is narrowed to a single point. Independence is the one word, comprehending everything at the South. Submission is the one word comprehending everything at the North,— a submission, however, which means the future rule of a vanquished minority by a conquering majority. Wise men must be as alien from the spirit of the *invaders* in the struggle as from the slave element of the invaded."

When I heard those abominable tory principles of suffrage, which I ached to oppose, advocated yesterday, I expected something different *here;* I did not as to England. But while I felt this with regard to England, and with regard to the Congregationalists there, and the position they took, after having attacked us so much on slavery on every occasion, I felt also in my heart that we could afford to be generous to them, if they were *frank to us.*

It has been said in some of the remarks that "we do not want war." I do not want war. I know what war is; and I tell you, brothers, give yourselves to peace always, if you can do it without dishonor. But we want it understood we are not afraid of war,—we have had two with that country; the last ended at *New Orleans*, and if we begin again, we can begin from that point, and with the vantage ground of Grant, Sherman, and Farragut too. We shall say to England we have got a bill for you to settle, and if you don't, these are the sheriffs we send after you,—that's all. "We could sweep from the ocean each other's commerce," one of the brethren says. Brethren, they swept away ours; but then their pirates ran into ports where we could not follow them; the next time, we follow them.

Now, whatever this Council does, I plant myself on the record that in the present position of English Congregationalism I do not hold myself responsible for any fraternal fellowship; but when they express their repentance for the past, it is different. I would say that "While the lamp holds out"

[Time expired.] [Laughter and applause.]

Rev. Dr. THOMPSON, of New York. I rise to second the motion upon grounds altogether different from those upon which the adoption of it has just been advocated. I like every word of that report. I like its truth; I like its candor; I like its manliness; and I like its kindness. I think this body is prepared to adopt it unanimously, and therefore I shall be extremely brief.

When we are thus just, as I think we are to our English brethren, let us not forget to be just to ourselves. An Englishman has ten reasons to study the political geography of continental Europe and the East, where, prior to this war, he had one to acquaint himself with the geography and institutions of the United States. His relations to us were for the most part simply commercial. If you will look into the school-books of Great Britain, and see how small a portion is assigned to American affairs, you will find some excuse for our brethren for their non-acquaintance with our institutions.

When President Buchanan was called to confront secession from his official post, he announced to the world the impossibility of coercing a state. As the representative of the United States, he declared to all mankind the right of secession, and denied any constitutional or material power on our part to prevent it. It was a monstrous crime in him, equivalent to a participation in treason [Applause], but he did it. Then when our honored and lamented and beloved Lincoln came into office, in his inaugural address, in the vain hope of soothing the excited feelings of the South, he went out of the way to say, and it was true as he understood it, "I have no right and I have no disposition nor intention to interfere with slavery in the States where it exists." Now put these two things together, and judge an Englishman by the declaration of our two presidents; President Buchanan's declaration that we had no right to coerce a state, and President Lincoln's that he had no thought of interfering with slavery, and can you wonder that he should say, what in the world then are you fighting for? Is it wonderful that they suspended their judgment?

Then there came the unfortunate Trent complication, exciting blood in them, and exciting blood in us. I think this much is due to them. They made a sad mistake; they lost a grand opportunity — those Congregational brethren of ours. We have labored with them. I have myself been in constant correspondence with the leading paper of the Independents in London; and the brethren who have read those letters can testify whether I tried to deal faithfully with their consciences upon this subject. They have done me the justice to print every line I sent, except an exposition of General Butler's conduct in New Orleans, which may have failed to reach them, and which did not appear.

I know that the silence in their Congregational Union is not a token of an explicit want of sympathy in our cause, because they have had to study, as we have had to study here, those nice balancings of policy so as not to create a division among themselves, and interfere with their great work of the salvation of souls. They have had to watch against dividing, disturbing causes among themselves; and knowing that they did not all cordially agree and see eye to eye, they have forborne to have a contest upon that ground. Dr. Budington, as a Committee of the Congregational Union, wrote to them about the Bi-Centenary Association, and made a declaration of principles concerning the war; and they sent back a complimentary letter about the Bi-Centenary Association and ignored the war. It was wrong; it was a mistake; and we felt it; but I do not think we should stand here to-day and criminate them because we have given them so good an excuse for it. Have we not as a nation been in such complicity with the system of slavery as to blind our brethren across the sea? Now, that our hands have been washed of that guilt in the most precious blood of the land, shall we stand up before God and man and say, "We have washed our hands in innocency; stand by, for we are holier than you"?

Rev. Dr. VAUGHAN, of England. I think I can disabuse your minds a little on this subject. I am one of the very few men now living who had to do with the formation of our national representation — the Congregational Union of England and Wales. When we set about that work, we found it, to our surprise, a very difficult work. Many of our old and most influential men stood aloof from it, and were opposed to it, under the impression that it might grow into an organized invasion of the liberty of our independent churches. Our Presbyterian brethren, too, were not slow to taunt us with having found out the weak places of Congregationalism, with taking a leaf out of their book, and being about to come over to them. Our Congregational Union has outlived all that. It has come to be for us of vast importance. It has given us a place and a power in the eyes of our country which Congregationalism has not possessed in England since the days of the Commonwealth. It has been seen from its history that it is very possible for institutional independency to be allied with a very effective organization. The independency of the churches may be allied with all the advantages, within certain limits, of concentrated action.

How have we done this? It has been by a determination not to allow any question, relative to which there is a strong division of opinion among ourselves, to come up as a question to be decided in our Union. Had we allowed questions producing excitement and narrow divisions to be carried by bare majorities, or it may be by impatient and boisterous majorities, our Union would have been anything but what it is. A large portion of our more thoughtful and influential men would have withdrawn from it, and it would have become the representation of a part,— a section,— and not of British Congregationalism. We may have been in error in adopting this course, but that is the course we have pursued.

Now, in not allowing the discussion of the events of your war, to come up in our Congregational Union, we have done by you just as we have been doing for the last thirty years by ourselves. God's law requires that a man should love his neighbor as himself; but I do not know that it requires that he should love his neighbor beyond himself. We were divided, not as to being friends and enemies of your country, because there has not been an enemy to your country to my knowledge within the range of Congregationalism since these troubles have come upon you; and I think I know more of English Congregationalism than any other Englishman. If there has been such a *rara avis* as an English Congregationalist opposed to your country, it has not come under my notice. There has been diversity of opinion, but not of that kind. When you remember what has been said by my esteemed friend, Dr. Thompson, when you consider the three thousand miles of ocean rolling between you and us, and that we were not likely to have had our attention drawn to these things, you will see that we had some reason for hesitating to risk our union for the sake of giving expression to our opinion what the results of the war ought to be.

Our press was open to you everywhere. Scores and hundreds of our pulpits were open to you if you chose to occupy them. They were occupied in your behalf by many of our ablest men. We simply required that our Union should restrict itself to the reiteration of its emphatic utterances against the slave system. Now I leave it to your candor. Condemn us if you think fit; but I hardly think you will.

Now, sir, a word for myself. Since I have come to this country I have been in many instances, relative to this question, rather severely criticised. I have been so under this roof to-day. It is quite true, my brethren, that at the outset of your troubles, I was one of those who had the impression that from the nature of the country and from other causes, the conquest of the South was not practicable. My impression further was that, if it should be practicable, it would be at the cost of such a fearful amount of suffering, both in the process and consequent upon conquest, that it was hardly to be warranted that even the extinction of slavery should be sought for at such a terrible price.

If I was a sinner for thinking thus, I can assure you that I was a sinner in company with many of our most enlightened and of your most warm-hearted friends in our country. I can say here, in your presence, and in the presence of the Searcher of hearts, that I have not uttered a sentiment concerning your affairs at any time that has not been a solemn conviction of my mind according to the evidence that has been before me at the time. I have never said a word that could be painful to you that was not connected with much more pain in my own mind than it was likely to bring to you. My affection for your country is, and ever has been, next to the affection that I bear my own. [Applause.] My brethren in England all know that; you may not know it, but they do, and they have grounded the wisdom and justice of sending me here upon what they know relative to my feeling toward you.

I have been represented as being a great check to the Congregational Union, preventing its speaking for you on more than one occasion. I think in the course of four years I have in two instances uttered a few sentences, a very few, relative to it; to the effect that I thought we would better go on as we had been, and avoid the hazard of wrecking our union by introducing what would be a divided question.

Then I think I may venture to say, without the fear of contradiction, that I have done more in my country for the exposition and defense of our common principles as Congregationalists, than any other Englishman; and I think I have done more for the defense and exposition of your Congregationalism than any other Englishman has done. It is only three years ago, when we were engaged in our Bi-centenary controversy, when our Episcopalians were ransacking your annals, and bringing out of them all the instances they could select to show the ignorance and intolerance of your forefathers, and thus attacking your Congregationalism, that I was able to put an end to it; and I did. [Applause.] I gave the story as it is, — not garbled as they gave it; and there was an end of that kind of warfare.

It is because my brethren know my heart has been with you, and I have been as ready to fight your battles as theirs, that they imagined it would be a fitting thing for me to stand here to-day in your presence, and bid you God-speed. [Applause.]

Then as to this war, and as to what is said to have taken place at our last annual meeting of the Congregational Union; I am said to have breasted opinion, to have opposed the expression of opinion in your favor. With submission, that is just the reverse of the truth. Instead of that, I consented to the passage of resolutions drawn up, calling for sympathy in your behalf; and said then, in the presence of all my brethren,—without the slightest idea of coming here to say anything like it,—the substance of what I said the other day in your hearing. My brethren know this; and on those grounds they sent me.

Then I wish just to say that I have not become converted, as the reverend gentleman who has addressed the Convention just now, in the course of his remarks seemed to imply, from some cowardly motives changing my views. I am no coward; not a bit of it. [Applause.] And I think I am not a selfish man either. I have said what I have said when I have been obliged to speak against you, frankly and honestly; and I say everything I say to you, that is kindly and acceptable to you, just as frankly.

Now, what I have seen, from what has been brought before my mind during not merely the last year but the whole of this struggle, I have certainly received, with regard to your affairs, light I had not before. I now believe that those Southern provinces that you have vanquished, were the homes of a society that were so corrupt that there was no other way of effectually dealing with it besides that you have taken. [Great applause.] And I do thank God and congratulate you on the triumph of the Northern armies over that portion of your country. [Renewed applause.] I would say again that I think if you could have drifted those Southern States a thousand leagues off into the Atlantic, to take their pest-house with them, and left them there, it would have been a good thing for you to do. But you could not do it. They must be side by side with you; and for them to be side by side with the systems at work at the North, I see clearly, would have been to entail upon you mischiefs perpetual, and mischiefs the most complicated. Providence has dealt with this matter, I believe, in the way intended for your general good, and for the good of humanity. I sincerely congratulate you on this account.

Why have I said this? Not that I might win favor of those who have cast their sneers upon me. I do not ask them for favor. I do not ask them for justice. I leave them to what may be pleasing to them. But I am very anxious that you should see this matter as it is; that you should see the case of our Congregational Union as it is; that you should see on what ground it is that they have sent me here into your midst. And I make no secret of saying, that though I shall never perhaps look upon any face among you again, after a few days more, I should like to live in your hearts with the character of an honest man. [Great applause.]

The hour of taking the recess having arrived, and Mr. Beecher being loudly called for,

On motion of Rev. Mr. Allen, the order of the day requiring a recess to be taken at one o'clock, was suspended.

Rev. Henry Ward Beecher. When I landed in England last year, not far from this time, no man could well have persuaded me, from what

I saw, and felt, and observed in others that felt, that England in any of its parts, had either direct or remote sympathy with us. It seemed to me that they were given up to believe a lie that they might be damned; and I felt incensed when any man told me there was a deep feeling of sympathy for our country two years ago. After I had cooled myself off in Switzerland, and come round through phlegmatic Germany, when I came back to London, some of the brethren were kind enough to deal with me; and as the result of their faithfulness, and my more intimate acquaintance with things, I at last had the eyes of my understanding opened, so that I felt, — "Confound those Englishmen, I love them in spite of myself."

I could not deny that the allegations that we made on our side, were founded, as we looked on things, in justice and in truth. And I could not deny, when I saw the interior working of things in England, that for the most part the brethren there had reasons and motive causes of action which we neither understood on this side, nor, from the nature of our institutions and customs, could be made well to understand. But I did come to feel, while I was in England, that while there was great discrepancy of judgment among even those who were our friends, and still more among the lukewarm and our enemies, there was a cordial, influential feeling among the Dissenters of England, for our strife and our cause in America; and I have never had any occasion to change the conviction that I brought with me from my father-land. I loved England before I went there with a kind of romantic and poetic love; and it was not decreased, although I was tossed a night and a day upon the sea there, and had some fights with the wild beasts at Ephesus; for I think my feelings came back to my father-land with just as much enthusiasm and with deeper veneration than before the insurrection broke out.

I do not say these things to smooth over the matter. I think they are an excuse, a palliation, but not a justification. I think they ought to have taken a different course. Their convictions were sincere; they were thoroughly honest; they believed they were doing their duty; but I differ from them in judgment very seriously in this regard. The Frenchmen had just as many reasons for mistake; and I felt thoroughly ashamed that in a nation speaking another language, they could see like daylight through all our difficulties and appreciate our position so well, while those from whom we borrowed our customs, our polity, and most of our ideas of government, speaking our own language, stumbled and could not see. I felt bad about that; and as for their teachers I did not feel that there was any palliation or justification. It was their place to see. They were appointed for seers, and put upon the mountain-top, to distinguish between good and evil the world over, to draw the lines the world over; and if they have no function for that, what is their function? [Applause.]

But that is all past. We felt it needful in receiving these brethren they should understand that we saw, and that they should see, the facts of the past, and that they should know that we were not in any manner deceived. But that is all; there is nothing more to say; and now let the past bury the past; let the dead bury the dead. There is no enmity between England and America to-day. [Applause.] I do not believe there will be any cause of offense given by the English government. If that which I understand to be the demand of our government, as unquestionably it will be, reparation for the losses we have suffered through their malfeasance and defective administration, is denied both to be valid and to be just, let it be referred to some just and disinterested party. [Applause.] I think I may say that the Christian population of America are perfectly willing to refer our losses to arbitration; and that if a just arbitrator is found, and if he decides against us, we will repeat one of the sublimest spectacles the world has ever seen, — our action in the case of the Trent. The moment our Secretary of State said — and it was said to the hot heart and fierce zeal of this enkindled nation — that we were in the wrong, and we must take such a course, there never was a single word pronounced against it by newspaper, caucus, or people. We say that this people, by virtue of their liberty, and intelligence, and by virtue of their civil and religious polity, are a nation loving law better than any other nation on the earth can. It is the glory of our institutions that it makes the people at once the fountain of the law, and then the mothers and nurses of that law they themselves bring forth. Nowhere else is there a disposition so universal to observe that which is found to be just by the proper tribunals. And if the tribunal to which we shall jointly refer this, shall determine that these losses are not the fault of England, and she must not be held responsible, we never shall say another word on the subject. [Applause.]

More than that; we have an account to settle with England. There is a reckoning between us, and we tell these brethren they have got to come to that and can not shirk it. We are bound to do more for the world than they can. [Applause.] We are bound to send two missionaries where they send one; and better fellows too. We are bound to work more for the education of the common people of the globe. I should not wonder if we sent missionaries even to England yet. [Laughter and applause.] We acknowledge the tie that binds us to you. It is not a vain saying that we are proud of our origin. It is for no offense that I say that our greatness arises in our own judgment from the antagonism of England. Some have thought that we dominated them. They know not our feeling toward them. During the time that Southerners swaggered in our councils, we did; but never, since the days of Washington, when Northern counsels prevailed. We are not a warlike people, although capable of war on a just occasion. It is not to our taste. It is not in consonance with our polity, the current of our thoughts or the occupation of our minds. Where did you ever see so large a war so successfully carried on? Where did you ever see so large an army dissolve as the snows of March dissolve when April gives advice to them. They have gone back to the forge, and the field; and now, everywhere, east and west, we are bent again upon the arts of peace and civilization; and in an enthusiastic spirit we are bent on evangelization. And New England to-day, the most hated of all the parts of the continent, New

England that has been hated, kicked at and cursed everywhere, goaded and pursued for the last fifty years, — what is New England doing to-day? Councils, and caucuses, and conventions are working to procure money to pour school-books into the South, to support missionaries and teachers there, and considering how we shall bind up the wounds we were obliged to make. While the South is in trouble, we have stood like the father of the whipped boy, crying as much as the boy did. Every blow smitten upon them was smitten upon ourselves as well. For myself I never felt as much yearning affection for the South as I feel to-day, as a part and parcel of us. To labor for the South is to help not the South alone but all mankind. We feel that God has given us to-day this large territory, unobstructed with old hereditary institutions, with the evils of past generations cleared out of the way, as a field inexhaustible for us to cultivate. It is not that we may pride ourselves, or enjoy luxury or leisure, but that we may work harder and do more for the regeneration of the world than those nations tied up and hampered by institutions that have come down to them from barbaric ages. And in this great work I throw down the gauntlet to you and defy you to outdo us; while, in the name of your Christian brethren in America, I extend in greeting, the right hand of fellowship, to you, brother Raleigh, whom I knew across the seas, and to you, brother Vaughan, whom I met for the first time here. [At this point, Rev. Mr. Beecher, shook hands cordially with Dr. Raleigh, and Dr. Vaughan, amid tumultuous applause, cheering, and waving of handkerchiefs, concluding with three hearty cheers for "England and America forever."]

Go back then; tell your brethren what we have honestly said; that if we have spoken to your blame, it is not because we are angry, or cherish animosity, not because there is lurking in us any warlike feeling, but that we are in the full spirit of fellowship and Christian love with you, and long to go on with you side by side in the great work of the civilization and Christianization of the globe. For though the French people have sympathized with us and better understood us in this great struggle, after all "blood is thicker than water." [Applause.] I would rather have an Englishman back me in a difficulty than any other man on the face of the globe, unless it be a Scotchman or an Irishman, and I count them all three to make only one Englishman. [Laughter.] In this country it takes but one man to make a man. [Renewed laughter.] And now, sir, I hope there is peace among us; and all I ask is, that if there is, and if I have helped to make it, I may have some of the blessing promised to the peace-makers. [Applause.]

Rev. Dr. RALEIGH, was greeted with loud applause, and said: I have but one word to say; I think it will be better to say but one word, and not even to attempt anything that might be regarded as "adroit." [Laughter.] I bethink me of an old minister in Scotland who had the habit in teaching his people, — and a very good habit let me say, — of expounding the Scriptures book by book and chapter by chapter; and of course the good man sometimes came to passages hard to be understood; and his way of getting over a difficulty, — just such a difficulty I think as we have on hand this morning, — was very convenient, to say the least of it. He would say, "No doubt, my Christian brethren, there is a great difficulty here, as all the commentators are agreed upon that; so let us look the difficulty boldly in the face, and — pass on." [Great laughter.]

A MEMBER. Isn't that "adroit"? [Renewed laughter.]

Rev. Dr. R. proceeded: We must pass on, sir. We must pass on into a new time, to higher and holier duties that are awaiting us, through all the chequered experiences which come to us as to you in the service of our Master. I have, as I said, but one word to utter now; and that is, in the spirit of all I have said among you, that I hope we shall pass on hand in hand. May God bless you for the kindness, abundant and continual, manifested to us in your homes, and the kindly reception given to the poor words we have uttered in your sanctuaries and meetings. May God bless you, and make you a blessing; and in the memory of the suffering you have passed through, and in the prospect of the work waiting for you to do, may he make you patient and loving, even as he has made you strong, and fearless, and free. [Applause.]

A member moved to amend the address by striking out the expression, "With the insolence of a robber." [Referring to the Emperor Napoleon.]

Rev. Dr. BACON objected. He had thought of putting it, "with the insolence of a slaveholder;" but he preferred the expression as it stood.

The amendment was rejected.

Rev. Mr. GULLIVER. I move that the passage characterizing the nation as "boastful and vainglorious," be omitted. I think that was true of us when the slave-holders governed and were the mouth-piece of the nation, and gave tone to its public sentiment; but I hope that we shall not say that it is true of us now.

The passage was read.

Rev. Dr. BACON. I submit that that is true, every syllable of it; and that it is very becoming in us to say it under the circumstances. It is not the habit of our government under the administration of Northern freemen to be vainglorious and boastful; but it is the habit of our democratic people to-day; and how much of it we have on this platform now.

Rev. Dr. KIRK, of Massachusetts. John Bull boasts down in the belly, and we in the mouth. He feels as large as anybody.

Rev. Mr. GULLIVER. Every traveler in Europe has this thrown in his face; and I say it is not true of this nation that we are more boastful or vainglorious than other nations. It would be wronging ourselves to adopt that expression, and it would be quoted against us everywhere.

A MEMBER. I hope it will be qualified by adding "in common with all nations." [Laughter.]

Dr. BACON. The passage reads: "Our kindred in Great Britain had seen, with mingled pride and apprehension, the portentous growth of the United States, and had been sometimes disgusted with that boastful and vainglorious habit which enters so largely into our national character," "and which we inherit from them," — suppose we put that in. [Laughter.] If that clause is stricken out, this very sentence will be an instance of the vice. They "had seen with mingled pride and apprehension the portentous growth of the United States." There is Jonathan for you. It is necessary that some clause of voluntary humility should be added.

The amendment was rejected.

On motion of Rev. Dr. Bacon, the word "hitherto" was inserted, so as to read "which has hitherto entered so largely," &c.

The report was then adopted.

It was now half past one o'clock.

Hon. Linus Child, of Massachusetts, moved that the Council meet this afternoon at half past three, instead of three o'clock, and continue in session for two hours.

The motion was rejected, upon division; ayes, 75, — noes, 82.

The Council then took a recess until three o'clock, P. M.

AFTERNOON SESSION.

The Council were called to order at three o'clock, P. M., by Hon. C. G. Hammond, First Assistant Moderator.

Rev. Dr. BUDINGTON, of New York, moved that the Business Committee be instructed to prepare the remaining business of the Council, with the view to adjournment at 5 o'clock, P. M., on Friday. If the business was not completed by that time the Council would be kept over another Sabbath. Many delegates would be unable to remain; and rather than have the business left to be transacted by a small minority, he would prefer to hand the subjects remaining over to committees to prepare reports, to report at an adjourned meeting six months or a year hence; or to refer them to committees representing all shades of opinion, to prepare reports, with foot-notes, expressing the various opinions; such reports to be printed and distributed to the Council.

Rev. Messrs. SAVAGE, of Illinois, and GULLIVER, of Connecticut, opposed the motion, on the ground that the business of the Council would require the session to be continued over the Sabbath.

The motion was rejected.

FREE ITALIAN CHURCH.

Rev. Edward N. Kirk, D. D., Chairman of the committee on Italy, reported the following resolutions:

Whereas, The Spirit of the Lord has breathed on the people of Italy, and rekindled the fires of godliness extinguished by the Roman hierarchy; and

Whereas, The providence of God is leading this people out from the bondage of superstition and of a tyrannic priesthood; therefore,

Resolved, 1. That this Council recognize with fraternal sympathy, and with thankfulness to God, their attainment to the blessings of civil and religious liberty.

2. That this Council entertains a lively sympathy with every soul, however obscure, there and elsewhere, earnestly searching God's word to learn the character and will of God.

3. That this Council congratulates the various little bands of believers who are striving to organize themselves into churches of Christ under any of the several forms adopted in our Protestant countries.

4. That this Council regards with peculiar interest those who are founding free Italian churches, independent of foreign control or dictation; seeking to rebuild on the foundation of apostles and prophets, Jesus Christ himself being the chief corner-stone.

5. That the Council request the Rev. Messrs. Clark of Milan, and Hall of Florence, to convey to our Italian brethren the expression of our sympathy, and the assurance that, by prayers and pecuniary contributions, we will do what in us lies to promote the advancement of Christ's kingdom in their beautiful and classic land.

Rev. Dr. KIRK, said: Rev. Mr. Walker having just returned from Italy, will present to the Council a very succinct and impressive view of the religious condition of Italy. I will merely say that the progress of free government has liberated the consciences of the Italians from priestly domination. The Bible is now extensively circulated in Sunday schools on our plan, and the gospel extensively preached. There are three classes of converts; 1st, those who have embraced the gospel under the influence of the British Wesleyan missionaries, who are the first missionaries who preached the gospel to them, but who are now drawing the lines tightly round them to organize them as a part of the Methodist church; 2d, the Waldensians, who are trying to form Waldensian churches; and 3d, a body organized upon Congregational principles, and called the Free Italian Church. They know nothing of our principles; but they have studied the Bible, and do not want to be British Christians, or Waldensians, but Italian Christians. One remark they make requires a word of explanation, that the Waldensian supreme body is called the Waldensian Table. These men say they have left the Papal Chair, and do not want to be covered by the Waldensian Table.

Rev. EDWARD A. WALKER, of Massachusetts (recently from Italy). I come bringing you the news that there is at present going on in Italy a movement which for power, extent, and spiritual purity, has scarcely been equaled in the history of modern Christianity. You may not be aware that at the present time there is being convened in the ancient city of Bologna what might be called a national council of the Congregational churches of Italy. There was some talk when I left of calling this meeting the Alliance; but whatever the name of it may be, the tendencies of this movement are distinctively Congregational. You may hear through Presbyterian and Church of England channels, these churches stigmatized as Plymouthists. The Plymouthists, as you may know, do not recognize a ministry. Their ministers are tradesmen or mechanics during the week, who go into the pulpit on Sunday. These men in Italy are not Plymouthists; for there evangelists are set apart to preach to them, and nothing would more fully meet their feelings and principles than the establishment of a theological seminary for the training of an efficient ministry.

Again, these are not independent churches; but in all matters which concern the brotherhood of churches they co-operate with one another. They recognize this to be a duty as fully as we do. Again, they are not Presbyterians, because this mutual government is only advisory in its nature. They plant themselves on the Congregational principle that sovereignty in the church as well as in the State is vested in the people and can not be delegated by them to a synod, any more than it can be usurped by a hierarchy of priests. Thus those free Italian churches are distinctly Congregational.

With regard to the extent of this movement and its power, I am justified in saying that it is one of the most important that the Christian world has ever seen. In the first place, it is a popular movement. It is not carried on by the influence of a few individual minds, but it is rather the flowing together of many individual currents of thought and feeling forced out of the hearts of the people by the fear of papal oppression. It is not an intellectual movement. No new statement, as to doctrine, has been brought out by it. It is not a sentimental phenomenon, resulting from extensive revivals. But it is a determination on the part of a priest-ridden people, that they will have their rights, that they will throw off for ever the power of priestcraft, that they will have the Bible in their own hands, and interpret it with their own minds, and govern themselves according to its precepts.

Hence this movement is popular. It is a favorite with the people and spreads among them with great rapidity and power. In the city of Milan, there is at the present time a church of fifteen hundred members, as good Congregationalists as we are. And in Bologna, Cologne, and other cities of Northern Italy, are churches already founded and established upon this basis. We only need men and means to establish a Congregational church in every city and town in that land. Let me say here that this movement is especially popular with the middle classes, the working men of Italy.

With regard to the spiritual power of this movement, it is strong and full, because it is a movement with the Bible in hand. At a meeting which I attended a few weeks ago in the city of Milan, I was struck with the fact that almost every person present had a well-worn copy of the Bible; and whenever a quotation was made from the Scriptures, every one at once found the passage in his own book. They seemed to be unwilling to take anything from the lips of a preacher, without confirming it by the word of God.

I asked whether the members of these churches were spiritually converted men in every sense of the word; and was assured that they were. In that respect they differ from the Waldensians, and the other church; for those churches are national institutions, and multitudinous. Everybody belongs to a church there, either Catholic or Protestant; and partakes of the communion once a year for the sake of securing his civil rights. But in these churches, it is not enough for a man to hate the pope and priests; he must love the Lord Jesus Christ, or he can not be a member of the church.

When we look at this movement, thus spontaneous and national in its character, we are struck with this fact, that these people, left to themselves, in their reaction against the power of papacy, and taking the Bible in their own hands to be governed by its precepts, naturally come down into Congregationalism; and we have every reason to believe that they will be true to the Congregational principles upon which they now stand.

It is in this movement that lie our strongest hopes for the regeneration of Italy. When we contrast this movement with the other agencies at work there, we shall see this more clearly. When Italy was first thrown open to the gospel, many agencies went to work to plant the Bible throughout the country. These agencies are all of them feeble, and to a certain extent they operate against one another. The Wesleyans try to bring in their own peculiarities and force them upon the Italian people. The Episcopalians try to force upon them the *sine qua non* of a prayer-book. The Waldensians must bring everything under the control of their synod. These different agencies have done an immense amount of good; and yet there is a want in the hearts of the Italian people which they have not reached. The Italians do not want to be Wesleyans, Church of England people, Scotch Presbyterians, or Waldensians. They want to be Italians; to preserve their own national peculiarities, and not accept any of those foreign peculiarities which these agencies have tried to bring upon them. Thus this movement has come out of the free hearts of the people, — a free Italian church, a Congregational church; and it is upon this movement that the people everywhere rely.

Now, I love the Waldensians. You all love them. You know their history. There is a romance about them; and in their historic antiquity, there is something that satisfies the cravings of many of the Italians themselves. But after all, these Italian Congregationalists, in their reaction against Papacy, go back of the question of historic legitimacy, as they are bound to do. They fall back upon the archaic principle that the government of the church belongs to the members of the church; that the servants of Christ are to reign priests and kings with him; not the clergy with gowns and bands, but all the members of the church. This is the principle. It is older than the apostles. It is as old as creation. Men fell from it in Adam, and were restored to it in Christ. And although the seed long slumbered in the ground, it has at last become a tree with healing in its leaves for the healing of the nations. [The allotted time here expired.]

The report was accepted, and the accompanying resolutions were adopted.

BOOKS AND TRACTS.

Rev. Dr. Bacon, of Connecticut, from the committee on Books and Tracts, read the following report: —

The committee to whom was referred the subject of *the relation of our denomination to Books and Tracts* respectfully report :

They have considered the subject in the following order: I. What are the existing relations of the denomination to literature? II. What are the disadvantages of the present order of things? III. What measures, if any, may wisely be introduced to obviate these disadvantages?

I. The Congregational churches, in all systematic operations by means of books, stand practically related to literature mainly through six different book-manufacturing and book-selling corporations; namely, 1. The American Bible Society. 2. The American Tract Society, Boston. 3. The American Tract Society, New York. 4. The American Sunday School Union. 5. The Massachusetts Sabbath School Society. 6. The Congregational Board of Publication.

Our method of operation through these corporations is simply this: to pay our charitable contributions (amounting to a very large sum annually) to the treasuries of these corporations, by which they are expended, partly in the preparation of stereotype plates and the manufacture of books; partly in the donation of books to missionary societies, churches, Sunday schools, and other distributing agencies independent of the publishing societies; and partly in the maintenance of a system of bookselling or distribution, through depositories or colporters, by the publishing societies themselves. But our contributions for doing good by the circulation of good literature all pass through the hands, and are subjected to the discretion, of those concerned in the manufacture and sale of books, and are necessarily more or less complicated with their business arrangements.

II. *Disadvantages of our present method.* 1. Literary and Moral. 2. Economical.

1. The literary and moral disadvantages of our present method of benevolent operation by means of books may be stated briefly thus: that it shuts us up almost wholly to the use of the books issued by the societies which are the recipients of our contributions. The narrow classes of literature, to which we have been thus disastrously restricted, may be thus defined: (1.) A negative religious literature, from which all character-

istics of any individual or party have been scrupulously eliminated. (2.) A merely sectarian literature. And even within these very narrow limits we have had no access in our benevolent operations to the general field of such literature, but have been debarred from the publications of all private firms, and of societies other than those through which we have operated.

Some of the sorts of literature from the public use of which we have thus suffered ourselves to be excluded are these: (1.) Christian *secular* literature. For certain religious and philanthrophic uses, — as for instance, for ship, and garrison, and hospital libraries, — an exclusively religious literature is inadequate. (2.) Generally the works of men characterized by the highest force and originality, whose writings cannot, without an excess of mutilation, be brought within the prescribed limits of the publishing societies, whether on the denominational, or on the "catholic," basis. (3.) The works of good men of other denominations which are marked by any of their denominational peculiarities. (4.) The books from the publication of which our own societies have been forestalled by the activity of other societies or private firms, or from which they are debarred by copyright; and this class includes a large proportion of the best productions of our own time and country.

It can not be doubted that one of the most serious disabilities with which Puritan principles have been crippled in their progress has been the bondage under which they have been placed to publishing societies, and especially to those which have been constructed on that fallacious "catholic basis," which presumes that the condition of Christian union is the repression of individual convictions.

At the same time, it must be considered that in some cases, being debarred from the use of the *best* literature, we have been paying lavishly for the circulation of much that is second-rate or third-rate. It is especially true in the case of the old publication societies, the New York American Tract Society, and the American Sunday School Union, that their catalogues are cumbered with many works proved to be unsalable, or grown obsolete and superseded by better works on the same subject, which, nevertheless (the stereotype plates being on hand), continue to be manufactured, because, although they can not be sold, they can be given away at the expense of the churches.

It is by no means the least of our present moral disadvantages in this matter, that the essential and recognized inadequacy of the system of publishing societies to supply the books needed, especially for Sunday-school libraries, has brought in among us a mixed multitude of books that have passed no responsible revision, and from which the majority of purchasers have no means of making wise selection. The mixture of pernicious books in Sunday-school libraries is a grievous evil, to which our present arrangements afford no remedy.

2. *Economical Disadvantages* of our present system.

It is *theoretically* bad economy to intrust large sums of money for the purchase and distribution of goods to the discretion of the same concern, which manfactures the goods and keeps them for sale. *Theoretically,* it would be better that if various concerns, public or private, have undertaken to produce good books and tracts, and offer them for sale, the charitable gifts of the public should go into the hands, not of these interested parties, but of other and disinterested parties, who shall expend them wherever they can get the best books for the least money.

We should not press this theoretical point against a system which, on the whole, was found to work well. But, in fact, the very evils which might have been predicted from this system are widely believed to exist. *This* evil, certainly, has occurred, — that in consequence of their double position, as being at once the buyers and the sellers, the publishing societies have been subjected to constantly renewed *suspicions*, which, however undeserved, have been to them an annoyance and a hindrance. If they had been either buyers only, to give away, or manufacturers only, to sell, they would have escaped these imputations. If our donations had been intrusted to disinterested parties, with liberty to go into open market for the goods, they would have brought to bear on these various manufacturing corporations the healthful influence of competition, both with each other and with private enterprise. Private booksellers have constantly declared, that, if they were allowed equitably to compete with charitable corporations, they could undersell them. There could be no imaginable loss or disadvantage to the Christian public in giving them the chance.

3. *What measures, if any, may be wisely introduced to obviate existing disadvantages?*

We will not undertake, in this place, to lay out the details of a better system than the present. What we want is some arrangement by which the church may reach forth her hand into every department of literature, and take the best books for her use, and place them wherever they are needed, distributing mainly by the hands of her servants, as an incident in the main work of spreading the gospel. Such an arrangement we do not believe to be beyond the wit of man. It would require a board of Christian scholars and critics, who should thoroughly winnow the vast mass of books and tracts that are offered to the public by societies of every sort and sect, and by private firms, and present the public with a new catalogue, made up only from the best among them all; and a board of capable business-men, who should see that the alms of the churches were not spent to disadvantage, and who should undertake to apply donations according to the intent of the donors. It would be a simple and inexpensive institution.

The committee take pleasure in announcing the fact, that these considerations have been for some time before the minds of some of the best and wisest men in the country, and that preliminary steps have already been taken, under the auspices of President Woolsey, of Yale College, President Hopkins, of Williams College, and others, which, it is hoped, will result in supplying this desideratum.

(Signed) H. W. Beecher,
Leonard Bacon,
Lowell Mason, Jr.

Rev. Dr. BACON, remarked, while reading the above: The chairman of the committee (Rev. Henry Ward Beecher) stated to me that he found, a year or two after his settlement in Plymouth Church, Brooklyn, that in the Sunday-school library they had complete sets of the works of Captain Marryat and of Bulwer's novels. I told him that if he were to make that statement here, there would be surprise, first, at the books being there, and second, at his having objected to them. [Laughter.]

Hon. Mr. HAMMOND, of Illinois. Will you tell us what reply he made?

Rev. Dr. BACON. I think I had better not say. He intimated that he had not so much objection to them as I thought he ought to have had.

The report was accepted.

The question being upon the adoption of the accompanying resolution, several members objected to it, especially upon the ground that it was indefinite and incomprehensible.

THE MODERATOR. (Hon. C. G. Hammond in the chair.) If the resolution were omitted, the report would go to the churches for what it was worth.

On motion of Rev. Dr. Eddy, of Massachusetts, the resolution was stricken out.

The report was then adopted.

DECLARATION OF FAITH.

Rev. J. O. Fiske, of Bath, Maine, chairman of the committee to whom was referred the report of the preliminary committee on a Declaration of Faith, read the following report:—

PRELIMINARY REMARK.

The committee, on presenting the following report to the Council, regret that time and circumstances would not allow them to prepare a condensed statement of the doctrines held by our denomination. We desire it to be distinctly understood that the brief confession of the faith which we hold in concert with the great body of believers, is in no sense designed to be regarded as a creed for our churches.

REPORT.

When the churches of New England assembled in a general synod at Cambridge, in 1648, they declared their assent, "for the substance thereof," to the Westminster Confession of Faith. When, again, these churches convened in a general synod at Boston, in 1680, they declared their approval (with slight verbal alterations) of the doctrinal symbol adopted by a synod of the Congregational churches in England, at London, in 1658, and known as the "Savoy Confession," which in doctrine is almost identical with that of the Westminster Assembly. And yet again when the churches in Connecticut met in council at Saybrook, in 1708, they "owned and consented to" the Savoy Confession as adopted at Boston, and offered this as a public symbol of their faith.

Thus, from the beginning of their history, the Congregational churches in the United States have been allied in doctrine with the Reformed churches of Europe, and especially of Great Britain. The eighth article of the "Heads of Agreement," established by the Congregational and Presbyterian ministers in England in 1692, and adopted at Saybrook in 1708, defines this position in these words: "As to what appertains to soundness of judgment in matters of faith, we esteem it sufficient that a church acknowledge the Scriptures to be the word of God, the perfect and only rule of faith and practice, and own either the doctrinal part of those commonly called the Articles of the Church of England, or the Confessions or Catechisms, shorter or larger, compiled by the Assembly at Westminster, or the Confession agreed on at the Savoy, to be agreeable to the said rule."

In conformity, therefore, with the usage of previous councils, we, the elders and messengers of the Congregational churches in the United States, do now profess our adherence to the above-named Westminster and Savoy Confessions for "substance of doctrine." We thus declare our acceptance of the system of truths which is commonly known among us as Calvinism, and which is distinguished from other systems by so exalting the sovereignty of God as to "establish" rather than take away the "liberty" or free-agency of man, and by so exhibiting the entire character of God as to show most clearly "the exceeding sinfulness of sin."

At the same time we re-affirm the fundamental principle of Congregationalism, that the Bible is "the only sufficient and invariable rule of religion;"[1] that, in order to attain a faith which is "right and divine, the word of God must be the foundation of it, and the authority of the word the reason of it."[1] We "ought to account nothing ancient that will not stand by this rule, and nothing new that will."[1] "It was the glory of our fathers, that they heartily professed the only rule of their religion, from the very first, to be the Holy Scripture."[1]

Besides thus expressing the faith which we hold as a denomination, we deem the present a fit occasion to express the earnestness of our sympathy with all those Christian churches who are agreed with us in the essential truths of the gospel; especially as our common faith is now assailed by popular and destructive forms of unbelief, which deny the living and personal God, which reject the possibility of a supernatural revelation by Jesus Christ, which exclude the fact of sin and the hope of redemption.

Against these dangerous errors, we, in common with all Christian believers confess our faith in God the Father, the Son, and the Holy

[1] Preface to the Savoy Confession as adopted at Saybrook in 1708.

Ghost, the only living and true God; in Jesus Christ the incarnate Word, who is exalted to be our Redeemer and King; and in the Holy Comforter, who is present in the church to regenerate and sanctify the soul.

With the whole church, we confess the common sinfulness and ruin of our race, and acknowledge that it is only through the work accomplished by the life and expiatory death of Christ that we are justified before God and receive the remission of sins; and that it is through the presence and grace of the Holy Comforter alone that we hope to be delivered from the power of sin and to be perfected in holiness.

We believe also in the organized and visible church, in the ministry of the word, in the sacraments of Baptism and the Lord's Supper, in the resurrection of the body, and in the final judgment, the issues of which are eternal life and everlasting punishment.

We receive these truths on the testimony of God, given originally through prophets and apostles, and in the life, the miracles, the death, the resurrection of his Son our divine Redeemer. This testimony is preserved for the church in the Scriptures of the Old and New Testament which were composed by holy men as they were moved by the Holy Ghost.

We affirm our belief that those who thus hold "one faith, one Lord, one baptism," together constitute the one catholic church, the several households of which, though called by different names, are the one body of Christ; and that these members of his body are sacredly bound to keep "the unity of the spirit in the bond of peace," and to dwell together in the same community in harmony and mutual fellowship.

We hold it to be a distinctive excellence of our Congregational system that it exalts that which is more, above that which is less, important, and by the simplicity of its organization facilitates, in communities where the population is limited, the union of all true believers in one Christian church; and that the division of such communities into several weak and jealous societies, holding the same common faith, is a sin against the unity of the body of Christ, and at once the shame and scandal of Christendom.

We bless the God of our fathers for the inheritance of these doctrines which have been transmitted to us their children. We invoke the help of the divine Redeemer, that, through the presence of the promised Comforter, he will enable us to transmit them in purity to our children. We rejoice, that, through the influence of our free system of apostolic order, we can hold fellowship with all who acknowledge Christ, and act efficiently in the work of restoring unity to the divided church, and of bringing back harmony and peace among all "who love our Lord Jesus Christ in sincerity."

We believe that these truths and this free spirit have blessed our country in the past, that they have made New England what she is in the present, and have carried her principles, by other denominations as well as our own, throughout the Union, while, in our recent struggle, they have largely contributed to redeem and save the nation.

In the critical times that are before us as a nation, times at once of duty and of danger, we rest all our hope in the gospel of the Son cf God. It was the grand peculiarity of our Puritan Fathers, that they held this gospel, not merely as the ground of their personal salvation, but as declaring the worth of man by the incarnation and sacrifice of the Son of God; and therefore applied its principles to elevate society, to regulate education, to civilize humanity, to purify law, to reform the church and the State, to assert, to defend, and to die for liberty; in short, to mold and redeem by its all-transforming energy everything that belongs to man in his individual and social relations.

It was the faith of our fathers that gave us this free land in which we dwell. It is by this faith only that we can transmit it to our children, a free and happy, because a Christian commonwealth.

We acknowledge the duty that is laid upon us by the Redeemer to carry this gospel into every part of this land and to all nations, and to teach all men the things which he has commanded us to observe and to do. May He to whom all "power is given in heaven and in earth" fulfill the promise which is all our hope: "Lo, I am with you alway, even to the end of the world." To him be praise in the church for ever, Amen.

For the Committee,

JOHN O. FISKE, *Chairman.*

The report was accepted.

Rev. Dr. Wolcott, of Ohio, moved its adoption.

Rev. Mr. Balkam, of Maine, moved to substitute the original paper, read by Rev. Dr. Thompson.

Rev. Dr. THOMPSON, of New York. I hope that amendment will not prevail. I will give you my opinion on that subject in a very few words. Notwithstanding the services rendered by Dr. Lawrence in preparing the report for the committee, that report cost us no little thought and labor and care. But I am sure that I speak the sentiments of my brethren upon the committee, as well as my own, when I say that we have not the least personal desire that that particular document which we prepared should be adopted by this body in preference to any other. Our aim in the preparation of that document was, not to bring forward our own opinions specifically, and to urge them upon any body, but to prepare, as we were instructed to do, a declaration of the faith commonly received among our churches. And we met and prepared that declaration upon a basis which, by anticipation, might be acceptable to the great and most respectable body of brethren and fathers who would be here convened.

I have given this but a hasty reading here, but it strikes me as, in several particulars, a decided improvement upon the document which I had the honor, as chairman of the other committee, to submit. It is based upon the same general principle; and I am sure that we can agree to a declaration of faith upon no other principle. We canvassed that matter so thoroughly, I am sure we were not mistaken. We said, The Council may do as they please with the words, but they must come back to the two essential ideas: maintaining the historic unity of our body in that grand system of theology which has been the life of our churches here, and which our Western brethren need to-day, more than our fathers needed it two hundred years ago; and, on the other hand, we must, in these present times, reach forth widely the hand of fellowship to all who love our Lord Jesus Christ, by avoiding any offensive statement of peculiarities of doctrine. We prepared our paper upon that principle, with such measure of wisdom and grace — and we humbly thought and felt that the grace of God was with us — as was vouchsafed to us.

This declaration adheres to that principle. It is an improvement to place it in the form of confession, "We believe," instead of the abstract form of declaration which we had followed. This comes from practical gentlemen, theological professors, and not from such speculative gentlemen as were engaged upon the other. [Laughter.] But whatever may be the verbal comparison we may institute between these two documents, the fact that we have had upon the committee which made this report, a large representative body of pastors and deacons of all schools — if it is worth while to talk of schools here; I do not belong to any myself — and from all parts of the country; and we have added to these a representative from every one of our theological seminaries. They have sat upon this document carefully and prayerfully, in whole committee and by subcommitee, as I understand, for these many days; for which they largely deserve the thanks of this Council; and some of us know how tedious and responsible that sort of work is. They largely deserve thanks from us for denying themselves the pleasures and excitement of this meeting to attend to this work. Their work is well done, and I should be very sorry, although I acknowledge the complimentary courtesy of the mover of this amendment, to have any other declaration brought up here to impede the passage of that which this committee have to-day reported to us.

Rev. Dr. WOLCOTT, of Ohio. I should not have risen to advocate any motion upon this subject, had I not felt constrained, at an earlier stage of our proceedings, to offer a resolution relative to this general subject. As my vote will rest not alone upon my conviction of the excellence of the declaration now submitted, nor alone upon my conviction of the wisdom of issuing such a declaration by this Council, I can not explain it without a brief recurrence to the steps by which the Council has been brought into its present relations to this subject; and I think the consideration of this may bring those who have not been in favor of issuing any declaration, to the unanimous conclusion to adopt the paper before us.

The preliminary meeting of the State committees in New York, sent, in the letters missive to the churches, a proposition, that, among other topics, we consider the expediency of issuing a declaration of our faith. So far as the Ohio delegation is concerned, and I suppose it is true of other State committees, that preliminary meeting was authorized to call a National Council, if thought advisable, for certain specific reasons, of which this was not one. They were pleased, however, to include this in their letters missive; and it has been responded to by all the churches, and they all came up to consider the expediency of issuing such a declaration.

The paper submitted to us by the committee appointed at the preliminary meeting did not argue that question. It assumed it. The whole paper rested upon the assumption that the issuing of such a paper was expedient. There were considerations bearing upon the expediency of the thing, wholly irrespective of the merits of any paper that might be presented here. We could not do what was asked here, without taking that question into account. The committee on Church polity did discuss it, and gave reasons in favor of the adoption of such a document. Therefore, under the rule which precluded the discussion of a paper, but left us entirely free to instruct a committee, I moved the reference to a committee with instructions.

I was understood, I find, by more than one in favor of that motion for instructions, to argue in favor of a certain view and opinion upon the general measure, which I could not have conscientiously done, because I had not, at that time, any opinion upon the general subject which I wished to maintain respecting the paper, or the expediency of issuing any declaration. I urged that the committee should be thus instructed for the valid reason, that this topic did not enter into the original conception of this Council; that it was one upon which our churches were traditionally sensitive — naturally and justly so. And, if we accepted the issuing of the paper as a foregone conclusion, without considering the expediency of it, I felt that the result would not be satisfactory to the churches. But, as able a committee as the body could raise have taken the whole subject under advisement, and have thought it expedient to issue a declaration, and have united in the declaration which is now before us. My individual opinion is, that the faith of our churches never stood in a fairer light before the world than at the time this Council came together; and that what we wanted was not so much to declare our faith, as to prove our faith by our works, — making more account of the fact that we are Christians than of the fact that we are Congregationalists, though by no means overlooking the latter; but coming together as members of the Church of Christ, to occupy the field which the providence of God has given to us, to lay our plans for taking possession of it in the name of the Lord. I thought it desirable, if we could, to come together as a National Council, for this practical work, without discussing the faith and polity of the churches; because, if that is understood to be the work of a National Council, we can not meet oftener than once in a century, or, perhaps, two centuries; while, upon the other plan, we might secure the benefit of occasional, and, perhaps, stated meetings of this kind.

But whatever may have been my opinion originally upon the question of the expediency of issuing such a declaration, I certainly think we should now be liable to grave misconception, if we should fail to send one forth at the stage which the matter has now reached. I heartily join in the adoption of the paper now submitted, although I regarded the former paper as a very able document, and could have voted for it. I give the preference to that which has been read this morning, for this reason among others, that I observe in it a hearty recognition of other churches of Christ, churches of other denominations; and I feel that we are bound as Congregationalists to recognize as true churches of Christ these local companies of believers connected, according to their own ideas, with national organizations which we ignore. To the churches themselves, as Christian brethren, we ought to extend the right hand of fellowship; and as far as permitted, we should co-operate with them in our work of faith and labor of love.

Rev. Mr. BALKAM, of Maine. I trust that this Council may be expected to vote for the paper which it prefers, and not out of deference to any committee. In moving the adoption of Dr. Thompson's report, I did not move it as anything complimentary to him, or to the committee of which he was chairman; but because I preferred his report and believed that it was right, and that it expressed in a remarkable degree the convictions of this Council. I can not doubt that the Council, if it will follow its own convictions, will prefer the first report.

There are some things in the report which has just been read which I like very much indeed. I thought it was great felicity in the admirably conceived and admirably expressed report of Dr. Thompson, that it did pursue what it characterizes as the abstract form; that it did not say, "We believe." I thought the Congregational churches were independent churches, and were jealous of having any council, even a national council, prescribe forms of faith to them. I thought this original report very ingeniously avoided any objection of that kind, by saying, "We bear testimony to these doctrines; we do not prescribe them; we do not enjoin them upon anybody; but this Council, an assembled body of Christians, meeting in Boston, begs leave to bear its testimony so and so." I submit that it was admirably done; and if the Council prefer the original report, I hope they will adopt it.

Rev. Dr. BACON, of Connecticut. It is with regret that I obtrude any thought of mine upon the Council at this time; but I feel constrained, — being such an one as the apostle Peter speaks of as "Paul the aged," for I am a little of an old man, — I feel constrained to say a few words upon the subject now before the Council. It has seemed to me from the beginning that the whole scheme of an advance and aggressive action in this country, and especially of our aggressive action upon the States recovered from the late rebellion, is dependent upon being able to declare with one heart and one voice what our faith is — what is our united faith as a Christian body.

I must say here, and I hope I may be found to be in error, that I have had some apprehension that some of our brethren in some parts of the country have an idea of Congregationalism that it consists in believing nothing in particular. I remember a brother who read here yesterday, as a sufficient declaration of our faith, the ancient and present condition of membership in our churches. We all of us hold, I trust, that every disciple of Christ, however weak his faith, if he have intelligence enough and faith enough to make it manifest that he believes in the Lord Jesus Christ, and trusts in him for the salvation of his soul, and intends to follow him, has a right to come to the Lord's table, and be recognized as a fellow-disciple, and be a member of any of our churches.

I believe all our schools, so far as we have any schools, are agreed upon this. But I do not believe that a profession of personal faith in the Lord Jesus Christ, be it ever so satisfactory, is a sufficient profession of faith for a church to make that offers itself for the more intimate communion and fellowship of the Congregational churches; nor do I believe it is a sufficient profession of faith for a man to make, who, at the call of any church, is presented before an ecclesiastical council as a candidate for ordination for the work of the Christian ministry. I believe that for the Christian ministry we are to require also a general declaration, not simply of personal faith and repentance, — repentance toward God, and faith toward our Lord Jesus Christ, — but such a profession of doctrinal belief as shall show the competence of the man rightly to divide the word of truth.

I believe, furthermore, — I am making something of a declaration of faith myself, — that it is the right and the duty of any such body of representatives as those representing the Congregational churches of the land, to stand up, and with one heart and one voice to say what we believe, — what we unitedly believe, and not what this or that particular colleague believes or would like to have other people believe; not what a few perhaps would like to impose by some sort of force or coercion upon people that do not believe it, but what we ourselves believe; because we who are here assembled know that, one and all, there is a great body of Christian doctrine upon which we are unanimous; not unanimous, perhaps, in any possible statement of it, but unanimous as to the substance of it, and which we know our churches hold as the basis of their special fellowship and communion, and co-operation in the advancement of the kingdom of Christ.

We are not Arminianists, and we do not want to invite the body of Arminian clergy, or the Arminian Methodists, to come in and be as one with us. We should fall out by the way very speedily. But I am willing and desirous to make such a declaration of our common faith as shall disarm the hereditary prejudices and antipathies of other bodies of Christians, and show them, if possible, in its attractiveness and beauty and power, our common system of faith.

There is this difference to be observed, which I think the brother who spoke last did not adequately realize: there is a difference between a profession of faith made, and a confession of faith imposed. It is the history of Congregationalism to protest everywhere against imposed confessions of faith. I protest against them everywhere. An imposed prayer-book I protest against. An imposed confession of faith I protest against. I protest against that entire Presbyterian system of imposing confessions of faith. I hold it to be not only inconsistent with the highest freedom and purity of the churches, but actually and absolutely demoralizing. It is an idol set up in the church of God. I go any length in opposition to that whole system of imposed confessions of faith which a man does not make for himself, which he does not understand, about which judicatories dispute and wrangle, and which every man, under penalty of losing his living, shall swear by, through thick and thin. It is an idol, and contrary to the second commandment. [Applause.]

Let me make my own profession of faith, and I can make as good a one, and, if need be, as long a one, as anybody else. But we do not want to make a long profession of faith here; and no profession of faith we may make can by any possibility be imposed upon anybody. No profession of faith we may make can bind anybody's conscience. Surely, if we can unite in adopting a report like that placed upon your records, we can unite in adopting a report like that now under consideration. We can say as a Christian assembly, as a representative assembly of Christian pastors and messengers, that we do hold in substance to that great, strong, iron-ribbed doctrine which was the common faith in the Reformation; which has come down from Paul, through Augustine, and Calvin, and, among us, through Edwards and Hopkins. We can say that we hold the substance of that; not that we swallow the whole of Hopkins' body of divinity at a gulp; not that we swallow even Dwight's more diluted system of theology; not that we swallow the entire Westminster Catechism, in every angle of it,—but the great body of the doctrine; and, like the New Orleans minister, we will hold it, though we die for it.

At the same time we can say, as this last report says, here is a body of doctrines which we do not profess to be peculiarly ours, but which are held by all evangelical Christians with whom we co-operate or desire to co-operate, which we hold in common with them. I hope — I am confident, that when the question is put to this Council, "Will you accept this report, and adopt this declaration of your faith?" the yea will be unanimous; and we shall unite, as the Council or Synod of 1648 united, in an anthem of praise to God for the unanimity.

Professor PORTER, of Yale College. I rise for the purpose of saying a few words in order to put the committee right with reference to the previous report, and also to express the view taken by the committee of the document now presented. We understood, when we were called together, that it was the desire of the Council that some change should be made; and we have acted under that impression. For aught that I know, every individual of us would have been willing to accept the declaration reported by the preliminary committee. I certainly, for one, was entirely ready to receive it. We acted rather as the servants of the Council in preparing this report. I can assure you that we did not act to please ourselves. I presume that not a single individual of the committee would say that the document is such a one as he for himself would have prepared. But as the servants of the Council, we desired to construct a document which would meet the varying views of the representatives of 2,500 or 3,000 churches. We accordingly abridged the historical statement, and changed in form, somewhat, our adherence to the old confessions. Then it seemed desirable that we should, in a more devotional form, — in the form of a confession, — express the common faith we held in all our churches, at a time when the common foundations of all Christian faith were openly assailed and secretly undermined in all our communities.

With reference to this condition of things, which it will not do for us to ignore, however much we would like that it should not be, we thought it proper that all who believe with us should confess our common faith, in a personal God, in a God incarnate, in a Redeemer, — the great truths without which Christianity is nothing, and the church itself can not exist. It seemed not only proper, but our bounden duty so to do. It seemed desirable to do it in somewhat briefer terms, and in a somewhat different manner, from that which was adopted by the preliminary committee.

Then it seemed desirable to confess our faith concerning the church,— which also is one of the great questions of our times, — concerning the church, the house of God. There is in all our communities a great moral and Christian movement, with which I confess I sympathize, toward the restoration of the divided body of Christ. We must recognize that movement. We, of all the so-called sects, are alone prepared to throw ourselves upon it, to guide it, to assert our vantage with respect to it. Congregationalism, with all the rigor of its Calvinism, with all the energy of its theology, with all the directness and manliness of its piety, is yet the only denomination which is truly in its principles unsectarian. So was it from the beginning. The five dissenting brothers, — among whom were those two conspicuous stars, John Owen and Thomas Goodwin, — the five dissenting brothers in the Westminster Assembly, were set apart, among the rest, as asserting this great truth. We are true to our traditions, and true to our spirit. Acting in that spirit, we have given away to other denominations hundreds upon hundreds, which might have been our churches. We might have had hundreds more here represented, churches which are now Presbyterian, if it had not been that we cared more for the gospel than we cared for a form of polity. This it seemed right to assert, to assume for ourselves this vantage position, and place it before the world. Our order is apostolic, and therefore it is unsectarian.

In addition it seemed proper for us to assert, in a word or two, the fact which is notorious, that the truths, the forms in which we have held Christianity, Calvinism, has been eminently favorable to the reformation of men. The Puritans, who pre-eminently were Congregationalists, have held Christian truth in all possible applications to reform; and that is one of our peculiarities.

These are the special points which you will find expanded in this declaration. It seemed desirable, as this declaration will be looked at with great interest, that in language which could be understood, which though condensed might be followed, we should express our faith in these various aspects; our faith as Calvinists, our faith as unsectarian, and our faith as reforming Puritans.

Rev. Prof. Lawrence, of Connecticut. I stand in a peculiar relation to the motion now before the Council, inasmuch as my hand was in the formation of the first report made to this body, and also of the second. I am rather a father to both. They are my children, and I am ready to recognize that relation. I do not regard them exactly in the light of Esau and Jacob, and yet I have a decided preference for the younger. I am not very new-school in my theology, yet I prefer this because it is the newest, as well as because I think it is the best. It propounds some of the modern issues of the times more distinctly, more livingly, and, I am persuaded, more satisfactorily to the body, and to the whole denomination. I like both the reports on this ground, because there was the old and the new, and because they were combined in one, having this attribute of our holy Scriptures, an Old Testament and a New Testament. It should be remembered that our fathers have fought the great battles of truth and freedom on the basis of the old. Our distinctive denomination under Calvin obtained deliverance in Geneva. Cromwell and the Independents of Old England fought against the Royalists upon this ground, and conquered. Edwards, in the last century, and Hopkins and Bellamy, "fought it out on this line" to victory. In the opening of this century, Morse and Worcester and Woods and Stuart and Beecher fought Unitarianism and conquered, as we believe, though the victory is claimed on the other side, and we allow them the victory. Here then in this Council, after one hundred and fifty years and a little more, we resume our standing upon this time-honored ground upon which our fathers have stood.

Then I like the new, because we have defined clearly our position as a denomination. We step upon the high platform of faith with the other denominations, and we invite them to a unity of faith against Romanism, Heathenism, and all other isms that assail our common foundation. I like both the old and the new. I like both my children, the elder and the younger; but I like the younger better, and I hope this Council will adopt it and make it its own, and that the denomination will adopt it and make it its own.

Rev. Mr. Balkam, of Maine, withdrew his motion to amend, and the question recurred upon the adoption of the report read by Rev. Mr. Fiske.

Rev. Dr. Leavitt, of New York. I move as an amendment to this document, to strike out from the third paragraph the words "which is commonly known among us as Calvinism," &c. I make this motion, not because I am not a Calvinist, as the word is generally understood, for I am so, and have always been so. I am so firmly a Calvinist that I have never been afraid that the system which is called Calvinism could not stand alone and take care of itself without being continually dinned into people's ears under the name of Calvinism. The historical preliminary statement need not be altered, because it is historically true that our fathers did accept those confessions of faith in substance of doctrine. It is also true that they have always adhered to those systems of faith in substance of doctrine. But by allowing the denomination to be characterized by adhesion to those confessions of faith, we have lost the country which was once ours.

Those systems of faith we do not hold as systems. As systems they were devised and formed for organized churches, not for free churches like ours. As systems they are characterized by qualities, and have been the cause of consequences which are injurious, which are deleterious to our well being as a body of Christian churches. As long as you persist in calling yourselves in this way; characterizing yourselves as Calvinists, which you are not in the sense in which the word is understood by those outside of ourselves, so long you have the whole of that system of faith continually thrown in your teeth, and brought up for your destruction. While this is true, — while we have seen our congregations melting away from under us by the use which has been made of these ancient, worn-out, obsolete confessions,— it is also true that the system of doctrines which you teach, and hold, and preach, has made itself felt, is almost openly adopted, is certainly realized in the inmost convictions of large bodies of those who consider themselves bound by their position to reject the name of Calvinism.

I am familiar with ministers and members of Methodist Churches, and I say they hold this system of doctrine, the greater part of it, as tenaciously and as intelligently as we do ourselves, with the only exception of some technical terms, and the name of Calvinism. If we are to bring them to the test of Calvinism, they can not come to us without a greater strain than is naturally to be expected from poor human nature. I have known instances where able men, and better preachers than the average of us have been deterred from accepting invitations to become the pastors of our churches, simply by the dread of the scrutiny and screwing to which they might be subjected by an examining council to see whether they were Calvinists or not.

Rev. Dr. PATTON, of Illinois. I wish to say a word in support of that motion, not upon the ground upon which it was made by our brother, but upon the ground that our Lord Jesus told us to call no man father.

A MEMBER. Master.

Dr. PATTON. Master and father both. I consider it a great blessing that I was not born in the Lutheran denomination, to bear all my life long a man's name in connection with my religion. I consider it a happy thing that the Congregationalists, although we hold the substance of his doctrines, do not bear the name of Calvin. I think we ought to avoid falling into that snare; and while we retain the acknowledgment of the doctrines, we should strike out the human name.

Rev. Dr. DUTTON, of Connecticut. I give my hearty concurrence to the two brethren who have just spoken. It is time that we ceased to call ourselves by any human name. Why not call ourselves Edwardians as well as Calvinists. We propose to take the Bible as our rule of faith, instead of Calvin. It is customary with other sects to put horns and hoofs upon Calvinism; and if we adopt the name, they put the horns and hoofs upon us and veritably believe they belong to us.

Rev. Dr. STURTEVANT, of Illinois. I am not prepared to vote for this document unamended; but I do not know that I can find any considerable number to sympathize with my views. I agree with Dr. Bacon entirely that we wish to propagate all over our country and the world a great, unique, definite system. I have no misunderstanding on that point at all; and I testify for all my western brethren that they think so too. If Dr. Bacon or any other man supposes that there is any lukewarmness on that subject at the West, he is simply mistaken.

What I want is, that if we are to have any declaration of doctrine at all, — and I have pretty nearly come to the conclusion that we ought to have, although I doubted it very much at the outset, — I want a declaration of doctrine that goes the whole length of stating, in original living words of our own, in this year of grace 1865, what our view of that system is. If those brethren who have reported this document will take the language back again, and put their heads, and their hearts, and their prayers at work for six months, and draw up for us such a document, I will come from my home to another meeting of this Council, and bear my own expenses, that we may have such a document as will actually express the faith of these churches here and now, with no reference whatever to any past formula, that shall be the Boston Confession, if you please; that shall be the sentiment of the Congregational churches in the year 1865, in words of their own choosing.

One word more. I am sorry for these references to the old standards. I do not know how many will agree with me there. I will tell you why I am sorry. There is language in every one of those old standards which not a man upon this floor receives.

A MEMBER. "Substance of doctrine."

Rev. Dr. STURTEVANT. I wish to be excused from that phrase when I make a confession of faith. I want a confession of faith to express what I mean; and it will be hard work for me to vote for it if I know there is phraseology in it which I do not mean. In all my controversies with the Presbyterian Church, they insisted upon my subscribing their formula for substance of doctrine. I wanted to be simply an honest man; and I want these brethren to be simply honest men, and to accept a confession of faith which every one of them does in his heart and soul believe, without any phraseology or statements in it which we could wish were away, with no expression to be a stumbling-block to every professor of theology and to every man in this house. I have sat here and doubted and doubted whether to make this speech or not; but I have made it, and here I stand.

Rev. Dr. BARSTOW, of New Hampshire. I hope we all hold to the old formula of the Westminster Assembly's Catechism, and the Savoy Confession of Faith, and I hope every member will be ready to reaffirm it.

SEVERAL MEMBERS. No, no.

Dr. BARSTOW continuing. The same phraseology our fathers used in 1648. We say we believe for substance of doctrine the confession of the Westminster Assembly. I stand upon that ground now, and I hope the brethren of this body will.

Rev. Prof. PARK, of Massachusetts, said: I do not feel able to say a word this afternoon, in consequence of my having been kept in a cellar[1] for two or three days [Laughter], and being now quite feeble in health. But, sir, we are Calvinists, mainly, essentially, in all the essentials of our faith: and the man who, having pursued a three years' course of study, — having studied the Bible in the original languages, — is not a Calvinist, is not a respectable man. I have a high respect for this Council. I have a great reverence for this Council; and although I have been immured in a cellar for so long a time, yet when I have seen members of this Council, I have seen that they were intelligent and able men, — such men as are very seldom assembled in any one body. But I should alter my opinion of it at once and totally, if it should discard the name of Calvinists. I confess I should be utterly and perfectly ashamed to have this amendment pass. I should be ashamed to see it published in the newspapers. We should be a hissing and a by-word among the people; because we are such in substance of doctrine, and we avow ourselves to be such in the main and in the essentials. We use these expressions very frequently. And if we can not go before the world, and say we are such, then I think we have misunderstood the nature and the spirit of this great system. This is an historical name; and I would not be cut off from our historical connection with the great fathers of our churches. I hope by all means that this amendment will not pass this afternoon at this late hour. If the brethren insist upon considering it further, I hope that the subject will be deferred until to-morrow.

Rev. Mr. Allen, of Massachusetts, rose to speak, desiring to occupy but one minute.

The hour of 5 o'clock having arrived, the Moderator stated that it would not be in order.

On motion, the order was suspended to allow Rev. Mr. Allen two minutes.

Rev. Mr. ALLEN stated, and appealed to Professors Park, Lawrence, and others, to sustain him, that the doctrine of the imputation of Adam's sin was not to be found in Calvin's writings. He believed in total corruption, but not in imputation. Those who believed in imputation, therefore, were not Calvinists.

The question being taken upon the amendment, upon division, there was manifestly a large majority opposed to it, and it was declared rejected without a count.

Rev. Mr. Ferrin, of Vermont, moved to lay the report upon the table.

The motion was rejected.

[1] The basement of Mount Vernon Church, in attendance upon committees.

Rev. Dr. Eddy, of Massachusetts, moved to adjourn.

The motion was rejected.

Rev. Mr. Byington, of Vermont, raised the question of order, that the Council must be declared adjourned, unless this order was further suspended, without a motion.

The Moderator ruled that the Convention had just, by its vote, declared otherwise.

Rev. Dr. EDDY, of Massachusetts. I protest against having a confession of faith imposed upon us.

A member moved to postpone the further consideration of the report until the next session.

The motion was rejected.

Rev. Mr. Quint, of Massachusetts, moved to suspend the order fixing the hour for adjournment until further vote.

Rev. Mr. Balkam raised the point of order, that even that motion was out of order after 5 o'clock.

The point of order was overruled by the Moderator.

The motion to suspend was agreed to.

Rev. Dr. Leavitt, of New York, moved to amend the report by inserting after the word "above-named," in the third paragraph, the words, "Doctrinal Articles of the Church of England."

Rev. Dr. WOLCOTT. I should deprecate exceedingly pressing this matter to-night to a decision of the Council. I move that we hear some notices from the Business Committee, and then adjourn.

Rev. Mr. Dexter, of Massachusetts, suggested as a modification of the motion, that it be to meet to-morrow morning, at 11 o'clock, on Burial Hill, in Plymouth, unless it be rainy, in which case, to meet in Rev. Dr. Kirk's Church.

Rev. Mr. Wolcott accepted the modification, and the motion as modified was agreed to.

Rev. Mr. Quint, of the Business Committee, introduced various papers, which were appropriately referred; as follows: —

(1.) *Whereas*, The use of tobacco is a great and growing evil in our land, and large treasures are wasted in forming and cherishing a habit that is not only expensive but highly injurious; therefore

Resolved, That this Council do, in the most solemn and decided manner, raise a voice of warning against this evil, and exhort our churches and our people everywhere to set their faces like a flint against it, that our precious youth may be saved from its baneful influence, and the fairest portion of our earthly heritage from foul desecration.

Accepted, and referred to the committee on Temperance.

(2.) *Resolved*, That we recommend to all the churches represented in this Council the observance of the —— day of —— as a day of special fasting and prayer for the outpouring of the Holy Spirit upon the land, to crown with success the results reached by this body; and that we send a brief address to those churches, to be laid before them on that occasion.

Accepted, and reference ordered to a special committee to be appointed.

(3.) *Whereas*, Our Pilgrim Fathers regarded the strict observance of the Sabbath as a duty they owed to God, and also as indispensable to the formation of a free Christian republic; and

Whereas, The desecration of the Sabbath is proverbial, both by the nation and by individuals, and thereby one of the fundamental principles on which our fathers reared this mighty nation is greatly imperiled, and the God who ordained the Sabbath dishonored: therefore

Resolved, That we as a Council greatly deplore the general desecration of the Sabbath in our beloved land, and feel called upon to use all proper efforts, in the pulpit and by the pew, by prayer, and if necessary by our petitions to Congress, to restore to the nation the sanctity of the Christian Sabbath, once so dear to our fathers.

Reference ordered to the committee on the "Declaration of Faith."

(4.) *Whereas*, This Council is informed that a band of Christians in Baltimore, many of whom are known to have been first among the foremost in the great movements in Maryland during the last four years for liberty and the Union, have recently been organized into a Congregational Church; and

Whereas, These representatives of the New England polity and spirit have with great self-sacrifice devoted themselves and their property to the enterprise of building, upon a commanding hight in that city a church edifice worthy of their cause, and of gathering from the large number of intelligent and liberty-loving citizens of that emancipated metropolis a vigorous and influential church; and

Whereas, We have reason to believe that the success of one such enterprise would lead to the early establishment of other strong churches in Baltimore, and that such a church, standing in the gateway of the South, would insure the organization of many more in the regions beyond, and would itself become a light and a power over the whole land: therefore

Resolved, That this National Council commend this initial enterprise at the South to the sympathy and most liberal aid of our whole denomination, as one of the highest importance to our country, to the interests of liberty, and to the cause of Christ.

Accepted, and referred to the committee on the Evangelization of the West and South.

(5.) *Resolved*, That it is inexpedient and improper that pastors of Congregational churches should assume, or retain, membership in another denomination.

Accepted, and referred to the committee on Church Polity.

(6.) *Resolved*, That a committee be raised to devise ways and means to raise the $750,000 voted as expedient for national evangelization.

Reference ordered to a special committee to be appointed.

(7.) *Resolved*, That this Council will adjourn *sine die* on Saturday next, at 12, M.

Reference ordered to Business Committee.

(8.) *Whereas*, The expeditious securing of the $750,000 which our churches have been recommended to raise is of the first importance to our land and the Church; and

Whereas, An equitable apportionment of this sum among the churches of our several States, according to their several ability, would greatly facilitate the obtaining of the entire sum:

Resolved, That a committee be appointed to make as equitable an apportionment as possible of the sum to be raised, among the different States, and in due time to inform the churches of each State what portion of the fund it properly belongs to them to furnish.

Accepted, and reference ordered to the special committee on Ways and Means of obtaining the $750,000 fund, previously ordered.

The special committee to whom was referred the report of the Finance Committee reported by resolutions, as follows:

Whereas, The failure of a large number of churches to respond to the call made by the preliminary meeting, for contributions to meet the expenses of this Council, has resulted in a lack of means to meet the just demands upon our treasury: therefore

Resolved, That the Finance Committee be authorized to call upon the more wealthy of those churches which failed to make contribution, for a sum not less than one thousand dollars to meet such deficit; and that said committee be directed to pay over any balance which shall remain in their hands, after discharging all just claims against this Council, into the hands of the Congregational Union.

Resolved, That the delegates to this Council, representing the churches to which this call shall be addressed, be requested to aid the committee in their collections.

Accepted and adopted.

After singing the Doxology, the Council adjourned, at half past five o'clock, P. M.

EIGHTH DAY, THURSDAY, JUNE 22.

The Council met on Burial Hill, Plymouth, on the spot where the first meeting-house of the Pilgrims stood, at 11½ o'clock, Assistant Moderator Hammond presiding.

On motion, the reading of the minutes of yesterday was omitted.

Rev. Mr. QUINT, of Massachusetts. I have been directed by the Business Committee to read a paper which is in their hands. The idea was entertained that it might possibly meet the views of all present. If it did, well; if it did not, it could be quietly dropped. The paper is as follows:

DECLARATION OF FAITH.

Standing by the rock where the Pilgrims set foot upon these shores, upon the spot where they worshiped God, and among the graves of the early generations, we, Elders and Messengers of the Congregational Churches of the United States, in National Council assembled, like them acknowledging no rule of faith but the word of God, do now reiterate our adherence to the faith and order of the Apostolic and Primitive Churches as held by our fathers, and as substantially embodied in the Confessions and Platforms which our Synods of 1648 and 1680 set forth or reaffirmed. We declare that the experience of the nearly two and a half centuries which have elapsed since the memorable day when our sires founded here a Christian commonwealth, with all the development of new forms of error since their times, have only deepened our confidence in the faith and polity of these fathers. We bless the God of our fathers for the inheritance of these doctrines, which have been transmitted to us, their children. We invoke the help of the Divine Redeemer, that, through the presence of the promised Comforter, he will enable us to transmit them in purity to our children.

In the times that are before us as a nation, times at once of duty and of danger, we rest all our hope in the gospel of the Son of God. It was the grand peculiarity of our Puritan Fathers that they held this gospel not merely as the ground of their personal salvation, but as declaring the worth of man by the incarnation and sacrifice of the Son of

God, and therefore applied its principles to elevate society, to regulate education, to civilize humanity, to purify law, to reform the Church and the State, to assert and to defend liberty; in short, to mold and redeem, by its all-transforming energy, everything that belongs to man in his individual and social relations.

It was the faith of our fathers that gave us this free land in which we dwell. It is by this faith only that we can transmit it to our children a free and happy, because a Christian, commonwealth.

We hold it to be a distinctive excellence of our Congregational system that it exalts that which is more, above that which is less, important, and, by the simplicity of its organization, facilitates, in communities where the population is limited, the union of all true believers in one Christian Church; and that the division of such communities into several weak and jealous societies, holding the same common faith, is a sin against the unity of the body of Christ, and at once the shame and scandal of Christendom. [Inserted on second reading.]

We rejoice that, through the influence of our free system of apostolic order, we can hold fellowship with all who acknowledge Christ, and act efficiently in the work of restoring unity to the divided Church, and of bringing back harmony and peace among all "who love our Lord Jesus Christ in sincerity."

But recognizing the unity of the Church of Christ in all the world, and knowing that we are but one branch of Christ's people, while adhering to our own peculiar faith and order, we extend to all believers the hand of Christian fellowship upon the basis of those fundamental truths in which all Christians may agree. With them, we confess our faith in God, the Father, the Son, and the Holy Ghost, the only living and true God; in Jesus Christ, the incarnate Word, who is exalted to be our Redeemer and King; and in the Holy Comforter, who is present in the Church to regenerate and sanctify the soul.

With the whole Church, we confess the common sinfulness and ruin of our race, and acknowledge that it is only through the work accomplished by the life and expiatory death of Christ that we are justified before God, and receive the remission of sins; and that it is through the presence and grace of the Holy Comforter alone that we hope to be delivered from the power of sin, and to be perfected in holiness.

We believe, also, in an organized and visible Church, in the ministry of the Word, in the sacraments of Baptism and the Lord's Supper, in the resurrection of the body, and in the final judgment, the issues of which are eternal life and everlasting punishment.

We receive these truths on the testimony of God, given originally through prophets and apostles, and in the life, the miracles, the death, the resurrection, of his Son, our divine Redeemer, — a testimony preserved for the Church in the Scriptures of the Old and New Testaments, which were composed by holy men as they were moved by the Holy Ghost.

Affirming now our belief that those who thus hold "one faith, one Lord, one baptism," together constitute the one catholic Church, the several households of which, though called by different names, are the one body of Christ, and that these members of his body are sacredly bound to keep the "unity of the spirit in the bond of peace," we declare that we will co-operate with all who hold these truths. With them, we will carry the gospel into every part of this land; and with them we will go "into all the world, and preach the gospel to every creature."

May He to whom "all power is given in heaven and earth" fulfil the promise which is all our hope: "Lo, I am with you alway, even to the end of the world." Amen.

Rev. Dr. BACON, of Connecticut. I want to make a suggestion, which I think will meet the entire approval of the Council.

When we adjourned last evening, I felt that a providence of God had intervened to prevent the adoption, at that time and place, of the Declaration of Faith that was then before us. I felt that on this consecrated spot, to us "the holiest spot of all the earth," we should become, all of us, more deeply and fervently conscious of our relation to the past, and of our relation to the boundless continent, and to the boundless future, than we could be even there, and that there was a fitness in our here uniting in giving our testimony to the faith and to the order which our Pilgrim Fathers brought with them when they came to this spot and laid the foundations of empire, in their humility, and their unconsciousness of the grandeur of their destiny. I wish to suggest then, Mr. Moderator, that in adopting this paper which has now been laid before us, we are to be understood as adopting it according to the old forms, the old use of language, *substantially*; adopting it, not as if every one of us was going to swear by those *ipsissima verba*, but adopting it in its essence, in its meaning, and in its scope. Then, if it be fit, we may adopt the other also, — although I do not perceive any deviation in this from the other; — and then, for the sake of perfecting the document, grammatically, rhetorically, and in respect of logical arrangement, — although I think this is an improvement upon the first one in that regard, — it may be referred to a large and representative committee, who, by a sub-committee of their own appointment, shall make it as perfect as possible, in all respects, and shall then certify to the world, in giving it out, that this is the Declaration of Faith which was made on this sacred spot, by this Council. I believe the suggestion is understood, and trust it will receive the unanimous approval of the whole Council here assembled.

Rev. Mr. ALLEN, of Massachusetts. In the name of our fathers, I protest, from this consecrated hill, against that Declaration. It is sectarian.

THE MODERATOR. Any protest against our action may be filed with the Secretary, and put upon the record in the proper way.

Dea. STODDARD, of Massachusetts. I hope the Declaration will be adopted, in accordance with the suggestion of Dr. Bacon.

Rev. Prof. PORTER, of Connecticut. I have no very special objection to most of the paper which has been read, which is taken, in substance, from the document that was before us yesterday; but it seems to me scarcely in keeping with the traditions concerning order which we have received from our fathers, that a paper should be presented under circumstances like these, in which all debate must be necessarily excluded, in order to carry a point which, perhaps, on deliberation, might be agreeable to us all. I noticed, still further, the omission of what I deem to be an important paragraph in the paper reported by the committee, and that is a paragraph which is near the bottom of the second page, where we assert the value of our system in promoting what I consider a very great movement at the present time, — the unity of the Church. I think that paragraph ought to be retained; and, if it is, I have no objection to the paper.

Rev. Dr. BACON, of Connecticut. My intention was to move that the substance of the paper which was before us last evening, and of that which has now been read, be adopted, and that the two papers be referred to a committee, to be perfected.

Dr. Dutton moved that the paragraph referred to by Prof. Porter be incorporated in the paper which had been read by Mr. Quint; but the Moderator ruled that the motion was unnecessary, as Dr. Bacon's motion included the substance of both papers.

Rev. Dr. EDDY, of Massachusetts. I felt yesterday that we were crowded to a vote; I felt the tyranny of a majority. I feel the impropriety of this proceeding this morning; but, under all the circumstances, I feel constrained, in conscience, all things considered, to second the motion which has been made, and hope we shall adopt the substance of these papers.

Rev. Mr. COCHRAN, of Iowa. I have not had a word to say in the Council on any of these questions. I supposed, when we separated last evening, that this matter was laid over until Friday, and I think that was the general impression. I have not heard this paper, and a number did not get here in time to hear it read; and I desire to hear it before I vote upon it.

Mr. Quint again read the paper, and at its conclusion, said:

The idea in preparing this document was, honestly and heartily to endeavor to avoid the points on which we seemed to split yesterday. I, for one, think we are all of one heart, but there may be some differences of expression. Now, this paper has been prepared to embody, briefly, the *essential* parts of yesterday's paper, with certain new parts in a new framework, and thus to avoid, if possible, any difficulty or conflict. I think it will not be best — although I do not care to argue the matter — to adopt the *two* papers, when this was intended to avoid some difficulties growing out of the other. It seems to me that it would be better, on several accounts, to adopt only one paper, and that, this paper. Further than that, I would say that I am not ready to give to any committee, which shall sit after this Council adjourns, power to promulgate any creed they please.

[Right!] I am ready to give a committee the privilege of making such verbal alterations as may be necessary, which will not affect the sense, or interfere with the feelings or prejudices of other persons, — nothing further than that; but even that should be reported for the action of the Council. I would also have the paragraph referred to by Prof. Porter inserted, for I think it extremely valuable, and am sorry it was inadvertently omitted, and, if permitted, will insert it.

I move to amend the motion before us, so that it read that the Council adopt the paper now read; and that a committee be appointed to suggest such verbal alterations, not affecting the sense, as may seem needful.

Rev. Dr. BACON. I accept his amendment; that is, that we now adopt the paper which has been read, including that paragraph, with the understanding that the whole paper is to be referred to a committee of revision, to perfect the diction, and to report to this body before its final adjournment.

The question was then put, and the motion adopted with but two dissenting voices.

On motion of Rev. Mr. Dexter, of Massachusetts, it was —

Voted, That the first business to-morrow morning be the election, by a ballot, of a committee, consisting of one from each State represented, to whom the paper just adopted shall be referred for revision.

Rev. Dr. Daggett, of New York, then addressed the Throne of Grace in a fervent and most impressive manner, concluding with the Lord's Prayer, in which the members of the Council audibly joined.

Edward S. Tobey, Esq., of Massachusetts, then made some statements in regard to the arrangements for the remainder of the day, after which, it was, on motion,

Voted, That when the Council adjourn, it be to meet at the Mt. Vernon Church, Boston, at 9 o'clock, to-morrow morning.

The Doxology "Praise God from whom all blessings flow," was then sung, and the Council adjourned.

After the adjournment, the members of the Council proceeded, in a body, to Forefathers' Rock, and to Pilgrim Hall, to inspect the various memorials of the Pilgrims there sacredly preserved. They were then hospitably entertained according to arrangements by the preliminary committee, and the collation was followed by addresses.

ADDRESSES AT THE TABLE.[1]

ADDRESS OF REV. A. L. STONE, D. D.

Fathers and Brethren of the Council, — The Committee of Arrangements have offered you this excursion not simply as a pleasant railroad trip, — not simply as a day of rest and recreation amidst the arduous and weighty cares of your protracted session, nor merely as a pleasant visit to one of our fair New England towns, with its quiet bay and its green islands, but with a deeper intent and purpose regarding the fitness of things. It was fitting, we thought, that the apostles and confessors of our faith and order, — gathering from every part of the land to look upon one another's faces, take one another by the hand, and strengthen one another to enter in and possess that magnificent future of our heritage for God and the old Puritans, — should have their reunion in the old Cradle of the Puritan city, the metropolis of the commonwealth and of New England. And now it is fitting, in the second place, that we, children of the Pilgrims, tracing back the steps of our forefathers with love and veneration, should not suffer our feet to pause until they come quite to the memorable Bay and to Forefathers' Rock. This is the earlier and the holier shrine. To have come so near and not to have reached it, not to have touched it, not to have clustered around it, to renew our vows of everlasting fealty to our religious faith, in its doctrines, in its order, in its memories, in its inspirations, would have been such a mistake and blunder as history — the history that writes the doings of these days that we are freighting so deeply for the future, — would have deemed incredible. Now, it will be regarded as one of the grand reminiscences of this hour, as congruous and chiming in well with the spirit, and calling, and work, of this Council, that we came hither that we might, by contact with the electric forces of this scene, thrilling through every mind and soul, put ourselves into closer communion with the fathers and their ever-living principles. It is well that we follow the stream back to its fountain, that we may drink again at the ancient spring fresh and pure, — drink, every man of us, until our souls overflow, — drink until we ourselves become channels, brimming full, in which the external and religious life of the past, cherished in our hearts, shall flow forth to all the saints of the common family.

Oh, how good it is to stand on Plymouth Rock once more! — to feel something solid beneath our feet! Amid all the fluctuations of the present, amid the tossing billows of that storm of war, and the agitations that succeed, which show that the great sea is not quiet yet, to find that our feet are on the immovable granite, where nations, ages may build, and no flood can overflow! [Applause.]

It is not mine, I will not ask that it shall be mine, to name even one element of that firm-supporting faith, on which, as on an everlasting rock, our fathers planted their feet, and on which our feet have come to

[1] Though not a part of the official proceedings, the exercises after the collation are recorded, on account of their peculiar interest.

be planted too; for we are sons of those sires by more than natural descent; we are one with them by more than the bond of a common faith, though that bond be so mighty, so indissoluble. We are one with them by a common experience now. What they saw we have seen, and the more clearly; what they heard, we have heard, and the more audibly. We have seen the mighty hand of God in our personal story; we have heard his voice near to us again, here, in the old Puritan commonwealth. Nay, more: in all the land, men walk and talk and sit and commune with a present, living God, as our fathers walked and talked and sat and communed with him. God is nearer from the bending heavens to all the children of the Puritans to-day than ever since the old Puritan days. We are at one with the fathers by that common and blessed experience. Our souls will keep fresher for our visit to this scene; and it will grave every line of that earlier scene deeper into mind and heart and memory.

In most of the pictures, you know, that artists have given us of that earlier scene, they drew largely upon the imagination. Art steered the Mayflower at first into this harbor, and anchored her in the background; art rowed a boat-load of living, breathing men, women, and children, arrayed in festal attire, to the sacred Rock; art grouped the wild Indian, in picturesque costume, in the background of the wood. But history tells the story differently, — that the Mayflower found her first anchorage in Provincetown Bay, on the eleventh of November; and three expeditions, you know, were sent out from the Mayflower, the third of which came to this point. One, on foot, moved as far as Wellfleet; another, by boat, entered Pamet Bay, Truro; then the shallop, that bore the sacred seed of a grand harvest, — the shallop came in on Thursday night: the first keel that ever parted these waves, over which only the light canoe had skimmed, and the wild fowl of the ocean. It came, not at first to this rock, but to that green island across the bay, — Clark's Island. There the Pilgrims passed Friday and Saturday (perhaps in repairing their boat; for they came in, in a fierce north-easter, their rudder gone, and the boat steered with difficulty by two oars, their mast overboard, in three pieces), and there they kept the sacred Sabbath; and, on Monday morning, the 11th of December, 1620, — the 11th, old style, the 21st, new style, — that shallop came to the rock and unloaded its freight of precious life thereupon, and the continent was ours. [Loud applause.]

I am trespassing upon a rule which I shall shortly impose upon all who follow me [Laughter], — to be very brief, and to remember all who are to come after them. But the welcomes of this occasion will not be made complete until you have heard, on behalf of the people of this town, whose pleasant faces and gala attire and thronged streets and winning smiles, are one, and not the least memorable, part of our welcome [Applause], — until you have heard, on behalf of this town and on behalf of the Pilgrim Society, doubly represented here by a gentleman to whom I shall presently refer, and by this gentleman [Dr. Timothy Gordon], whom I shall ask to complete my welcome, in the name of the town. From these gentlemen you will have other and perhaps warmer words of welcome. Will you listen to Dr. Gordon, of Plymouth, a member of the Pilgrim Society, and the gentleman at whose instance Pilgrim Hall was opened to us to-day, and to whose active instrumentality so much that is pleasant in this scene is due?

REMARKS OF DR. TIMOTHY GORDON, OF PLYMOUTH

Fellow-citizens and Friends, — I rise simply to show you my face, for I can have no expectation of interesting you, after the words of eloquence and beauty to which you have just listened. I will merely say, that the citizens of Plymouth bid you welcome, and that the Pilgrim Society, also, bid you welcome, thrice welcome to these shores whereon our Pilgrim Fathers first set their feet. I trust that what you have seen to-day will make such an impression upon your minds that you will be disposed to come again and to send your children and children's children to view the same spectacle which you have seen on the shore of Plymouth. [Applause.]

Rev. Dr. Stone. This salutation is from the citizens of Plymouth, and, in part from the Pilgrim Society. The president-elect of that society is present, and being a very modest man, as all Bostonians are [Great merriment], he is afraid I am about to introduce him to the audience; and unless I take him by the hand, and lead him to the chair [" suiting the action to the word"], I have no expectation of overcoming that difficulty, so that he can address you. I will whisper to you softly, the name of Edward S. Tobey, Esq., President-elect of the Pilgrim Society.

REMARKS OF HON. EDWARD S. TOBEY.

Mr. Chairman, and Gentlemen of the Congregational Council, and Ladies and Gentlemen, — I am highly gratified, in the first place, at the exceedingly proper estimate which the distinguished chairman has formed of your speaker [Laughter] ; but I am more than vexed at the thought that he expects me to make complete what he was pleased to consider incomplete. I beg leave to differ from him. I consider his speech so complete, that but little can be expected from me. And yet, ladies and gentlemen I should feel that I had hardly performed the duty which you had a right to expect, even from a president-*elect* of the Pilgrim Society, should I fail to add my most cordial welcome in behalf of that time-honored institution represented in every part of our land. I have the privilege of saying to you, that, not only in the name of that association, but in the name of the people of this town, I bid you a most cordial welcome to this sacred spot. And yet, in doing this, we do not wish to have it understood that we have any exclusive rights in this spot, either as the Pilgrim Society or as the people of Plymouth. We shall not consent that one fragment of that rock shall be taken from this place, but we shall ask you, all of you, to draw fresh inspiration from that consecrated spot, and transmit it throughout our land; and we believe it will be transmitted to the end of time. We have heard it said that the time is not distant when even our erring sister, South Carolina, will claim a part of Pilgrim Rock. [Applause.] I believe we shall need to transplant the principles of Pilgrim Rock, and it should be our chief concern to propagate those views throughout our country.

It is a sublime thought, that we are assembled in this peculiar period of our country's history. Perhaps at no time since our fathers first planted their feet on that spot, has there been seen a more grand, a more expressive representation of all that is valuable or likely to be valuable to this nation, than the present occasion. A most singular providence of God has ordained that the blood of the chief magistrate of our nation should be the last shed in sealing the liberties of our land. The last drop of blood shed was that of our beloved and revered chief magistrate, Abraham Lincoln; and it is fitting and proper that we here, at this early day, should come to renew our vows of fidelity to the principles for which this civil war has been waged, and to pledge ourselves, from every portion of our land, to go forth to our respective homes, and there, in every way, to disseminate the true principles of civil and religious freedom.

But, ladies and gentlemen, I do not feel at liberty to enlarge on this topic. We have been very kindly admonished by the chairman, by the very lengthy speech he made himself, that we are not to talk long, [Laughter] and I will conclude by simply repeating that the Pilgrim Society will gladly have you cherish in your memories this interesting occasion as one of the brightest spots of your lives; and while I feel myself the great privilege of extending this welcome to people from the remotest parts of our land, — even from Colorado, and Nevada, from Oregon and from California, — I am equally glad to extend the right hand of fellowship to those from what we are compelled to call a foreign land, but what we had better, perhaps, call our fatherland. The time has come when we can welcome to this spot those of our friends who represent religious liberty on the other side of the water; for, be it remembered, whatever course may have been pursued by a portion of the people from whom we descended, we have had a vast number of friends, who are represented here to-day by those who are ready to extend to us the congratulations of that country, and to join hands with us in seeking to carry forward the great work of Christian civilization the world over.

Rev. Dr. Stone. Thrice over have we had the hand of welcome extended to us, and perhaps you would like the privilege of interchanging greetings with our friends, and saying whether you accept these salutations. His Excellency, Governor Buckingham, the Moderator of the Council, could not be here to-day, and I will ask Colonel Hammond by what voice it shall please him to respond to these salutations.

REMARKS OF HON. CHARLES G. HAMMOND, OF ILLINOIS.

Mr. Chairman, — The system which we recognize and which we intend to perpetuate is one of order. Order is its first law; and that says, that there is a place for everything, and everything should be in its place. As it was not the place of any to talk of war in the presence of Hannibal, so it is not my place to address you in the presence of my colleague; and therefore you will permit me to introduce to you the Rev. Dr. Joseph P. Thompson.

REMARKS OF REV. JOSEPH P. THOMPSON, D. D., OF NEW YORK.

Mr. Chairman, — Should I attempt to express our gratitude and admiration for the well-ordered and munificent hospitality which has been extended to us from our first assembling as a Council to this hour, I should transcend the boundaries of all space and all time; [Laughter] for I am to-day the mouthpiece, not only of my own burning, responsive heart, but of five hundred hearts and voices, who wish to speak through me. [Applause.] It will devolve upon His Excellency, the Governor, or, in his absence, I insist that it shall devolve upon my military superior, Colonel Hammond, to return the thanks of the Council to you in Boston, in Mt. Vernon Church, for the totality of this reception; but I wish to-day, in a few words, to express our thanks to you, sir, the chairman of the Committee of Arrangements [Rev. A. L. Stone], to you, gentlemen, who have represented the town and the society of the Pilgrims, for bringing us to this particular spot. I remember, when I first saw a cathedral in England, — I remember when, back of that, I saw the remains of the old Roman walls, there was an oppressive sense of antiquity. When I went to Greece, the weight was heavier. When I went to Egypt, it was so vast that it disappeared in the infinity of space. I walked with Abraham and the patriarchs. Well, sir, when we came up to the Old South, I experienced the same feeling. When we went to Mt. Vernon Church, though that does not have the same odor of antiquity, yet we were led back to the old fathers by that earnest, loving disciple, who carried us back so far that he only stopped short of original sin. [Laughter.] Then, sir, we were led out to Charlestown, and there felt ourselves in sympathy with the early founders of that church. And now, to-day, we are brought to the most hallowed and most ancient spot, where all our local associations of antiquity merge themselves in that grand past that lies beyond the sea, and we feel ourselves linked, on this spot, with the holy men of old from across the waters, and, far back, with the whole church of God, through all the ages of time.

Some may have come here — I have been here before — expecting to find Pilgrim Rock a dead old fossil rock, or, perhaps, an utterly inorganic rock. Instead of that, we have found it a most lively *Stone* [Laughter and applause], and we desire to join ourselves thereunto, and to build with this living *Stone* from this time forward. [Renewed applause.] Our friends in the western part of the continent, having rich ores of their own, desired to transport this polished *Stone* to build into their temple. You refused us that gift; but now you shall not prevent us from carrying back from this spot Pilgrim Rock. We shall carry it with all its grand memories, with all its inspiring associations, back to the busy marts of commerce in New York and Chicago; we shall carry it across not only the Alleghanies, but the Rocky Mountains. It shall be planted, with all its living associations and power of truth and grace, upon the far shore of the Pacific. Henceforth, Pilgrim Rock is ours; Boston is ours. You have nothing hereafter apart from every one of us. [Applause.]

We have to-day caught the very spirit of the fathers. That scene, in which we engaged on the hill yonder, was a beautiful reproduction and illustration of their very spirit and methods. Some thought we were in a hurry. I remember reading, in a preface to the old Savoy Declaration, — which, you know, we have now reaffirmed, verbatim, and literally adopted, — I say, I remember reading in a preface to that old declaration, which was prepared by a committee of six, — Drs. Owen, Goodwin, and Nye, Bridge, Caryl, and Greenhill, — that they were engaged only eleven days, excluding Sundays, in preparing that momentous document. By way of apology for not spending more time upon it, they said it was prepared by men accustomed to think for themselves, who knew what they thought, who could communicate to the Council what they thought and believed, and who thought and believed all alike. Now, how beautifully we have reproduced that thing! We have had a committee of five hundred men examining their faith for themselves; we have compared our views, and we have found that we all feel exactly alike. Why, Mr. Chairman, the able document prepared in the first instance by two city pastors, with the concurrence of two very highly esteemed theological professors, was found to be altogether too abstract and metaphysical. Then we remanded that document to a large committee, and on that committee we had, I think, seven living professors of theology.

Rev. Dr. Bacon, of Connecticut. Do you mean seven professors of living theology? [Laughter.]

Rev. Dr. Thompson. I did not say that, sir. It was apprehended, on all sides, that when that document was brought in, we should have collisions between the various schools, and that everybody would want to alter it. But when it was brought in, we found we were all agreed, "for substance of doctrine;" and this document, which has been carefully elaborated by seven theological professors, is remanded to a committee, — for what purpose? To eradicate any lurking heresy? No; to correct a few grammatical mistakes. [Laughter.] Now, Mr. Chairman and gentlemen, I believe this Council to be orthodox, and I have a right to certify to it. If any man tells you your faith is not up to the old standard, there are just two men who can stand up in your vindication. There are two men whose Calvinism is unimpeached and unimpeachable, — Dr. Park and myself [Laughter]; and just as surely as any man tells you your faith is not orthodox, Prof. Park will open his great gun in the "Bibliotheca Sacra," and I, with the permission of brother Dexter, will fire my little squibs in the "Congregational Quarterly;" and with that assurance of your Calvinism, we will carry it through, even to the Pacific coast.

Now, sir, we are here, as I have said, catching the spirit, and intending to illustrate the principles, of the fathers; and how well have we not only rehearsed and renewed their faith, but illustrated their order! It was a meeting acting in order. Those men who came to these shores taught us another lesson. We do not need walls around us to give us a sense of order. No; when the living men touched this soil from the Mayflower, there was a State; and when the living souls, joined to Christ, came from that ship to these shores, there was a Church, without walls, without roof; and they have taught us that the principle of order and of organic life and unity is in ourselves, and not in the external arrangements of the hour. We therefore met in order; we acted in order; we illustrated the other grand principle, the conservative principle of the polity of our fathers, that, wherever, with a believing faith, men are convened for the work of Christ, there is the spirit of Christ, and there is the order of the Lord's house; and I maintain that no confession has ever gone forth from any Council prior to this, under circumstances of more grand and imposing order and solemnity than were witnessed on yonder hill to-day.

Sir, we shall go now, in the spirit of this polity and this faith, remembering that the first act of those noble men, before they built their own houses, was to put up a rude house in which to worship God, and, when threatened by enemies, to make it a battlement for their defense. You know that they did not dare (ah! this is why we can not identify the resting-place of those honored dead!) — they did not dare to put up the rude monument or raise a mound upon their graves, lest the Indians, counting the number of the fallen, should come and lay waste the whole settlement. Brethren, what, after all, have we known of sacrifice, of consecration, and the baptism of blood! Let us take upon our souls, — God hearing and blessing us in this hallowed hour, — let us take upon our souls the faith and the duty of the fathers, and over their uncounted, nameless graves, of which we can only know that here they who gave themselves for their country lie, let us move forward in the grand march of God and humanity, for the redemption of this land unto Christ, and the building here of a temple that shall overarch the continent. [Applause.]

Rev. Dr. STONE. These are the home-voices to which you have listened; these the greetings, these the salutations of those who know one another here. But stranger voices, foreign voices, speaking in our own mother tongue, and speaking in our own hereditary faith as well, will not be discordant with these home salutations. We are glad that Englishmen should see the house upon which the winds came and the rain fell, and against which the torrents roared, and it fell not, because it was founded upon a rock. [Applause.] The first Indian salutation, when the wandering feet of the dusky race came over yonder hill to the Pilgrim encampment, near Burial Hill, was also in our own native tongue, to the surprise of our fathers; and that first salutation, from the lips of Samoset, was, "Welcome, Englishmen!" We are prepared to give that greeting to our visitors from abroad.

Sir [addressing Dr. Vaughan], I ask you to stand upon your feet, that I may have you by the hand. We have welcomed you to our shores and to our hospitality, and I think we have become tolerably familiar with you. We have opened our whole heart to you. [Laughter and applause.] We have said everything that was down in the bottom of our heart; it is all said; we have made a clean breast of it [Laughter]; it is all out; there is nothing more hidden there, you may be sure. We feel a great deal better about it, and I dare say you do. [Loud laughter and applause.] The relation between us is now a thousand-fold more cordial. We ask you not to carry away any grudge, and we know you will not. [Applause.]

REMARKS OF REV. ROBERT VAUGHAN, D. D., OF ENGLAND.

They talk about English fervor sometimes; but to get up to American fervor, I feel is a very difficult thing to do. [Applause.] I am very glad of it.

It is now one-and-twenty years ago since I started a periodical in England, intended to vindicate the principles of Congregationalism, and the first article in that periodical was upon the Pilgrim Fathers. At that time English non-conformists were thinking but very little about the Pilgrim Fathers, and, I am sorry to say, very little about American Congregationalism; but they have learned to think a great deal more of them since that time. In writing that article I had a map of this neighborhood before me. I studied it in all its details, to the best of my ability, and pictured to my imagination the scenes that I supposed to have taken place in the year 1620. You will readily understand that I have come to this spot to-day with a good deal of interest, remembering how I felt in relation to it in those distant times. I have tried to picture to myself that boat which came off from the Mayflower; the dark clouds, as they floated through the sky; the descending sleet, as it came upon the men who rowed the boat, and upon all who were within it, and coated them over with ice, as if they were dressed in mail; and how they landed upon that spot, and there, amidst the cold, wintry night, with difficulty kindled their first fire upon the soil, and offered up their first evening prayer. It is pleasant now to be able to see, that though there were things they hoped to realize here that they did not, Providence was accomplishing by them results greatly beyond anything they dared to ask or think. They did, as you are accustomed to believe, lay the foundations of empire for this continent; and it is delightful to me to feel assured, that what was done by them and those who came in their track, and which has become embodied in your institutions, and enshrined in your religious faith, formed the elements that are to leaven your whole country, in ages to come, to a far greater degree than now. It is a delightful thing to be able to see, that the seeds that were then sown, are seeds which we can fully anticipate are to achieve great things. Christianity itself grew up in the world without observation. It did not make its way through the earth from senates and monarchs downward; it made its way through the earth from the people downward. [Applause.] We get our tailoring and our millinery from court pageants; we get our opinions from ourselves. [Applause.] And this is God's way of carrying on his work in the world.

I feel sure, my friends, that you have a very imperfect impression of the feeling that has prompted my brethren in England to send myself and my valued brother, Dr. Raleigh, into the midst of you. I am quite sure they are counting the days until we get back again, that they may hear what we have to say about you; and I am thankful that we shall be able to tell them that which they will be glad to hear. [Applause.] I am confident that I see about me, in your midst, the budding influences that are to achieve great results in the new circumstances in which Providence has placed you. When Christianity came into the world, two thirds of the human race were slaves to the other one third. Christianity was to sweep away that. The serfdom of the middle ages was another form of servitude that came into the place of the ancient; and the last vestige of that servitude has been swept away, to his infinite honor, by the Emperor of Russia. [Applause.] And now, the last link of the slave in Christian nations may be virtually said to have been struck off by you. [Applause.] It is a great thing to have been called by Providence to bring that great evil to humanity to the issue to which we have reason to believe it is now brought. It would seem a sad thing, indeed, that eighteen hundred years should have been needed thus far to regenerate the great mass of society; but God's ways are slow; it has been accomplished in his time; and there is no chapter in your history that will be more to your honor than your having recorded your inextinguishable antagonism to that institution, as unchristian, unrighteous, and inhuman. [Applause.]

I would just say, further, the good men who came over here from England came, as you know, not merely as a church, but to found a state. The necessities of their circumstances were such that they were obliged to do so. They are charged with having enacted exclusive laws; with having become great persecutors. I am quite sure that portion of their history is but very imperfectly understood. They came, at indescribable cost, to secure for themselves the settlement which they obtained on this soil; and when that was accomplished, having made their church-membership their franchise, and founded their little state, — the church and state being carried on by the same men, — they said to all the world, "We have founded this state at great charge and peril to ourselves. Any man wishing to have the benefit of it is open freely to take that benefit, but he must respect the conditions on which we have founded it. If he wishes to introduce something different from what we have regarded as right toward man and acceptable to God, the world is before him; let him go and found a state according to his fancies. [Applause.] Let us have that which has cost us much, which is properly our own, and have it we will; no one shall invade it. If the attempt be made to force disorder into our community, we will force that element out of it." Now, sir, if I had lived among those men, I should have done just that. [Applause.] I should have taken precisely that course; and instead of its being a course at variance with what was wise and good, it was the very course that that patriarch of Congregationalism, John Robinson, laid down as grave counsel for these early settlers. He told them they could not afford to have their little settlement rocked in every direction by all varieties of opinion; that they should settle their system for themselves, and uphold it until it could bear a different policy; and that was the course they pursued. It is a mistake, therefore, to charge these men with having been narrow-minded persecutors. They were wiser, by far, than the dilletanti critics who presume to sit in judgment upon them. [Loud applause.]

Now, my friends, I am looking upon you here about Boston for the last time. I am about to go home to my own people to live and die among them; and I think I shall be able to do a little more good in God's world than I should otherwise have done, from having come into this neighborhood, and being able to return with the report of you that I can take. [Applause.] My countrymen shall know what has taken place here to-day. They shall know what has taken place in that Council of yours. There shall be a clearing out of my heart, as well as yours. [Loud applause.] I respect the man who does that, — the man who gives out what God has put in him to-day, as God has given it; and if he has something different to bring out to-morrow, gives that out to-morrow. [Applause.] I was in the midst of an *elite* assembly the other day in London, consisting of a grand gathering of our literary men, who all got at loggerheads about something that was to be done; and after I had sat and heard the quarrel for a long time, I said to them, "Well, now, you have had a pretty good clearing out all round. Are you Englishmen? Are you willing, after all this, to shake hands and go to work and do the thing that is to be done?" That simple putting produced at once a laugh; and then they said, "Really, that is the best way;" and the thing was done. Let it be so here. Let there be a clearing out. I have nothing in me that you don't know now [Laughter]; and I am glad that you have called it out. I shall go home quite confident that you do give me the place of an honest man, and that we shall love each other all the more for all this coming to pass. Our hearts are with you. [Applause.]

Rev. Dr. STONE. Nothing that has been said needs confirmation; but you know it is written, that "out of the mouth of two or three witnesses every word shall be established;" and we must go according to Scripture. I shall therefore call upon the colleague of Dr. Vaughan, Dr. Raleigh, from England, Scotland, Wales, and Ireland, — *and the whole of Great Britain.* [Laughter and applause.]

REMARKS OF REV. ALEXANDER RALEIGH, D. D., OF ENGLAND.

I shall be very happy to take my part, on returning to England, in the telling of all that has happened to us here; and in telling our English brethren who have sent us, that we feel that all that has happened has been, as we trust, for the furtherance of the gospel. I shall be very happy to see any of you on the English shores; and if I knew the ship by which that gentleman who spoke first yesterday morning [Rev. A. H. Quint] would come, I would go to the shore to meet him and bid him welcome.

I did not know until to-day that it was the shortest day of all the year, the 21st of December, — a cold, bitter, wintry day, — when the Pilgrims landed down yonder. It is rather a singular coincidence that we are assembled here on the longest day of all the year, — the 22d of June, — in the bloom and hight of mid-summer. "The winter is past, the rains are over and gone, the flowers appear upon the earth, and the time of the singing of birds is come." [Applause.] They landed down yonder, a few men, comparatively, representing principles rather than any great number of persons. We here to-day may be said to be the representatives of a great multitude, which could hardly be numbered, out of many nations, and peoples, and tongues. They fled, not from persecuting England, but from England's persecuting government; and there is rather a difference between these two things, remember. [Applause.] We are here to-day, Englishmen and Scotchmen, representing, however imperfectly, yet truly, the best part, and, I take leave to say, — although that is not according to the document that was carried yesterday morning, — the greatest number of the English people, uniting with you, in cordially honoring the memory and adopting the principles of those men in the main. [Applause.] They fled for shelter and for safety in the wilderness; and now the wilderness has been changed into a fruitful field, and you have made this place now more than ever an asylum and home for the oppressed of all the world. What a change! And yet, I bethink me to-day, "that which hath been is now, and that which is to be hath already been; and God requireth that which is past." I look around upon you, American citizens, who have struggled and fought and bled in your representatives and servants, and I say, Are you not standing to-day in that shadow of Calvary in which the Pilgrims stood, and which is over all the earth? Have you not been drinking of their cup? Have you not been baptized with their baptism? Have you not been fighting, under different conditions, and in a wider field, the same battle of freedom which they fought in their expatriation and life-long endurance? I feel it an honor to-day, — I speak solemnly, and as in the presence of God, — I feel it an honor to be permitted to stand here in your presence, and to assert my solemn belief that you never so much as now were worthy to call yourselves the sons of those great fathers. That social state which they founded you have guarded, you have defended, you have preserved, you have laid, if I mistake not, on a more solid if not wider basis than at first. You have fought, as I said, the self-same battle, — a battle extending over a wide continent, continuing, without interruption, through four long, weary years; but the fruits of it who can number or tell? Liberty to the slave, — elevation to the South, — the hand of true brotherhood to all free nations, and all nations that wish to be free! Your own part, in short, and that not a little part, in that benediction from on high, "Glory to God in the highest, on earth peace, and good-will among men!" [Loud applause.]

Rev. Dr. STONE. May it please the court, — we desire to swear in one more witness to this point. You will hear the testimony of Dr. Massie, who is invited to take the stand.

REMARKS OF REV. JAMES W. MASSIE, D. D., LL. D., OF ENGLAND.

I wish I were qualified to do justice to the subject, to the scene, and to my own feelings. But "I am no orator, as Brutus is." [Applause.] I can not "put a tongue in every wound" of your country, and make it speak as it ought to speak, to stir you on, not to a "flood of mutiny," but to a flow of love between yourselves, and between America and England. [Applause.] I have met many during the proceedings of this Council who have taken me by the hand and have asked if I was indeed Dr. Massie, and expressed their thanks for the humble services that I tried to render your country two years ago, and that I have been trying to render to your cause during the interval of my return to England until the present hour. [Applause.] I know what England is. I have met the operative classes, and the skilled mechanics of the country, in all parts of England, and in that part of the kingdom of which my friend Dr. Raleigh is so proud, and to which I belong as well as he, — for I am of the good Scotch blood that he so rejoices in, — I say I have met the mechanics of that country, even to the shipwrights, and some of them building vessels that were designed to run the blockade, or to fight the battles of piracy, and I have challenged them to come upon the floor and answer for it whether they, with their hard hands, could sympathize with the ministers of oppression, who only sought to establish the Confederacy that they might put down labor and its rights amongst men. [Applause.] I know what the middle classes of England are, for I have been engaged by them, sustained by them; I know their benevolence and liberality; and I say that the men who are the cream of the middle classes of England are with America. I have said to Dr. Raleigh to-day, that my firm conviction is that three fifths of the population of England, Ireland, and Scotland are with the North, and have been with the North, through all its struggle until this hour. [Applause.] I went to the borough of Mr. Lindsey, the member of Parliament who stood up in the house and confessed that he had been guilty of the folly of going to Louis Napoleon, in order that they might confer for the recognition of the South. I went to his borough, and met a committee of his representatives, and defied them to sustain him in his infamous conduct; and they felt that it was needful he should go down to soothe them, to speak sweet words to them, after I had had two full meetings of his constituents, and lectured for an hour and a half on America; and then they did not dare to put a resolution in his favor to the audience.

Do not, therefore, suppose that we three individuals are the representatives of a fraction only of England, Ireland, and Scotland. I dare say there is another fifth who are for you now. [Applause.] I dare say the "Times" will tell you that Jefferson Davis has sacrificed his party by stupidity [Laughter]; that Gen. Lee, after all, was no great general [Renewed laughter]; and that, in fact, the Southern party have altogether failed because they were not fit to be an empire! [Merriment.] Take the "Times," and you will take a lying slanderer for your witness, only fit to be the companion of your own "New York Herald." [Laughter and applause.] Nay, it is fed upon the garbage that has flowed through the sewer of the "Herald" office. Don't suppose that it represents the English public opinion; it may try to catch it sometimes, and try to misrepresent it. The "Daily News," the "Morning Star," the Manchester "Examiner and Times," the Leeds "Mercury," the "Caledonian Mercury," the "Spectator," of London, and a dozen other papers that I could name, would tell you what England is a thousand times better than the "Times" does. [Applause.]

But I am not here to talk of these things, as if you needed to be persuaded toward our country; nor am I here to speak on behalf of my brethren, who have so well spoken for themselves. I am sure, however, that Dr. Vaughan never would have set his foot upon the American shore, if he had not been satisfied it was his duty to come, and if he had not been determined to do his duty to you, as a faithful witness and friend of liberty, and the champion of the truth everywhere. [Applause.] I can not pretend or profess to describe what I have seen during the last ten days. I have been to Niagara and marked the Falls there, and read descriptions of them, and I have wondered that men would attempt to describe Niagara. Why, they might as well attempt to fathom every foot of the ocean deep. And I rather think my friend, Dr. Vaughan, will find it a task to tell what he has seen and what he has yet to see in this vast country. [Applause.] He is going to New York, to Washington, to Richmond, to Chicago, to the Mississippi. Let him roll the waters of the Mississippi back again, and then he will be able to describe a country whose arms stretch out to the farthest heavens, whose riches go down to the deepest depths, and whose population are destined, in my humble judgment, to be the mightiest people in the earth. [Applause.] I wish we could get a united banner. [Applause.] I wish the Union Jack might be in the right corner, and the stars — I wont say in the left [Laughter] — the stars in their own proper places [Applause] — that England and America might be one in the missions that are to be conducted amongst your colored people, — missions that are, I trust, to be conducted with the same efficiency and fidelity that characterize the management of your foreign missions. I have divided my bread with the American missionary. I have been welcomed as a guest in the American Mission House, in India; I have traversed that country in company with American missionaries; I went forth with Gordon Hall in the last journey that devoted servant of God took, when he died upon the way, serving his Master; and I tell you, that as far as I can judge from my reading and from my personal intercourse, there is not, in all the branches of the church of God, a more faithful, a more efficient body, a body more worthy of the confidence of those who send them, and of those who meet them, than the men and women who are missionaries from America to heathen lands. [Applause.]

Rev. Dr. Stone. There was a blending, in the earlier days, the old days of storm and strife, of a foreign flag with ours. We shall never forget that the flag of France was blended with the stars and stripes in those early days. Old France was with young America then; and though America is a little older now, she is still youthful America; and young France is, in her heart of hearts, with us. And, on this shore, no person could more fitly represent young France than our young brother Monod, from Paris.

REMARKS OF REV. THEODORE MONOD, OF FRANCE.

Mr. Moderator, Ladies and Gentlemen, — It is with great joy and with honest pride that I find myself here to-day, the representative of the land of Lafayette in the land of Washington; and, what is higher yet, the representative of the land of Calvin in the land of the Pilgrims. [Applause.] What I feel this day, I will not even attempt to describe to you. I cannot describe it to myself. But this one great thought seems to underlie all the others, — that we are brought face to face with what is the very source of all your greatness and of all your influence, — yea, of your very life. We have been hearing and we have been talking, during these last days, of that great war into which and through which and out of which the hand of God has led you; and although our minds were lifted up so high, and our hearts glowed with such warmth of feeling, that it seemed as though there could hardly be a higher or a warmer feeling, yet I do feel that all this, — the overthrow of this rebellion, the future that lies before you, the work that you have in your hands, is comparatively a small thing, if you put it side by side with what we see, or, rather, what we think of to-day. What would your nation be worth without the faith of the Pilgrim Fathers? That monument on Bunker Hill is a great monument, and 1776 is a glorious year; but all that, even, fades away before the glory of the light that shines from this place. [Applause.] What would liberty itself be worth without the faith of the Pilgrim Fathers? Liberty is nothing but an instrument; and what is liberty good for unless it has the grace of God to inspire it, — unless it has the glory of God for its aim, and the laws of God for its bounds? [Applause.]

Here, then, we are brought face to face with these Pilgrim Fathers; and when we reach them, — ah! we have not reached the foundation yet; and they would be the first to tell us so, — we reach to God in them. And if there is a feeling to-day in our hearts, it is the feeling that God is here; that God who was here, who is here, and who will be here, "the same yesterday, to-day, and for ever." And if you would (and you know this far better than I do) carry on the work that lies before you, if you would remain the home of liberty and the hope of mankind, if you would remain as a light-house on the ocean shore to all the people of the earth, be true to the faith of the Pilgrim Fathers, who are our fathers also; for did they not bring from us, — not only from England, but from us over in Holland and in France, from Calvin and others, — the glorious truth that they brought with them here? This is what I need not say here; but oh, how I need to say it in France! Oh, that I may say it with more intelligence and earnestness than ever before! We have some intelligent writers in Paris who speak of America, and who say, "There is liberty there, and every man respects the rights of every other man, and that is a very fine thing;" and they want us to have

American institutions as far as we are able. Then they say, "In America, they have a great many inventions, — they have the sewing-machine, and many other things. Why, they read the Bible in the morning and the evening in their families, and they have a great deal of preaching." They just dispose of the whole subject of Bible preaching as they would tell that you have rocking-chairs in your houses. They seem to take it as an incident of American life; they do not look upon it as a vital principle. That is what we want to learn from you. And in order that we may learn from you, you must continue to teach us, and teach us more and more. You must go on and on, in view of the great work you want to do, "seeking first the kingdom of God and his righteousness, and all things else shall be added unto you." [Applause.]

But I will not preach to you myself. I will read to you a sentence that I copied from the grave of Robert Cushman. "You," he says, "my loving friends" (and I may well call you "my loving friends"), "the adventurers to this plantation, as your care has been first to settle religion before either profit or popularity, so, I pray you, go on." You go on; be true to yourselves; be true to George Washington; be true to Abraham Lincoln. [Applause.] Aye, more: be true to the Pilgrim Fathers; be true to the world that looks upon you. And you will do all this, if you are true to the Lord Jesus Christ. [Loud applause.]

Rev. Dr. Stone. Now we come back from over the sea; and I am going to cross the breadth of the continent, to the very shores of the Mississippi, that the tide of the "Father of Waters" may answer back to the voice of "the bay where the Mayflower lay." While I am stepping over the Alleghanies for Dr. Post, I will ask Dr. Adams, of Maine, to sing the "Battle Hymn of the Republic."

Mrs. Julia Ward Howe's popular hymn was sung by Dr. Adams with thrilling effect, the audience very generally joining in the chorus.

Rev. Dr. Stone. While Dr. Post is coming over the Alleghanies, I will say that we have just twelve minutes to remain here, which will give us an opportunity to hear four speeches of three minutes each. [Laughter.]

REMARKS OF REV. TRUMAN M. POST, D. D., OF MISSOURI.

Mr. President, Gentlemen and Ladies, — I feel oppressed as I stand in this place, and am called upon in three minutes to say anything worthy of the position; but I will say, in the first place, that I am glad, I rejoice, that at these portals, through which History entered this new world, we commune together to-day, not only with each other, but with representatives from the old world; and I feel that it is fitting we should do it here, rather than in Boston harbor.

We have been engaged for two hundred and fifty years in a mighty experiment. When, from the storm and conflagration of war that enveloped the old world, like a frightened bird emerging from the tempest was seen the Mayflower hovering off your coast, when it furled its sails within the harbor of Plymouth, it seems to me, in looking upon that scene, that I see emerging from that ship, not simply human personalities, but the representatives of mighty principles, vast ideas, that, emerging from the conflict of the old world, the baptism of blood and tears, and the storms of the great deep, touched these hills, and sent a thrill that is to stretch through the ages and through the length and breadth of this continent, till time shall be no more. [Applause.]

To-day we inquire, what has been the history of those principles since that hour; and I seemed to see, as we stood upon that hill, forms that were not walking among us or of us, that came from other times and inquired of us what we were doing with that which they brought to work thus mightily here. And we could point to states and empires that have been gathered and built up in the far West; we could point to the achievement of the liberties of a great nation; to mighty works wrought in the name of civil and religious liberty and the rights of man. But, alas! a bloody gulf rose up before us, and in it there was another form emergent; and that form had well-nigh stricken down those ideas which came forth in the persons of Winthrop and Bradford and Brewster,— and that were represented, too, by the lovely Rose[1] that came so soon to wither in the frosts of the new world. There had been a struggle between the light and the darkness, and from that struggle the principles of light had at last come forth triumphant, and we could point this day with exultation to the fact, not only that from the shores of the Atlantic to the golden coast of the Pacific, yonder beauteous and glorious emblem lifted its folds to the breeze triumphant, but that with it had gone their principles and their ideas, and they were this hour ascendant.

I will not detain you longer, brethren, with my three minutes' speech; but I bid you, in the presence of the genius of this place, in the midst of these friends that are around us, in the presence of friends from other parts of the world, and of those who have come up here from other ages to meet us in the light of this descending sun, farewell. Brothers, let us stand together, and not only cover this continent with our institutions of liberty, but with those principles of eternal truth that this day we have sworn to again upon the graves of our fathers. [Applause.]

Rev. Dr. STONE. It would be pleasant to have at least one voice from the Capitol. There is a United States senator somewhere in the grounds, whose voice has always been true to liberty, and the first principles of an old Puritan faith, against any and every antagonism. [Voices— "Wilson"—"Wilson."] As you have introduced him, I need not name him.

Senator Wilson not appearing, the chairman continued,—

While Senator Wilson is trying, timidly, to approach,— as he also is known to be a sensitive and shrinking man [Laughter]—I will cover his approach by asking you to listen to a voice from New Haven, Conn.

[1] The wife of Captain Standish died Jan. 29, 1621, a month after the landing.

REMARKS OF REV. LEONARD BACON, D. D., OF CONNECTICUT.

What is the use of a man, who is essentially long-winded, undertaking to make a speech in three minutes?

Rev. Dr. STONE. You shall have five.

Rev. Dr. BACON. Well, I have only one thing to say, and I will say it in short meter. I would like to make quite a circuitous approach to it, but I will come right up. [Laughter and applause.] We sometimes, heretofore, have talked of the mother country, and have recognized our English friends as the elder branch of the family. This late war of ours, in the providence of God, was a war of independence. Our political independence was recognized in the year 1783; but our social, moral, and intellectual independence has not been recognized heretofore, and we have not been conscious of it ourselves. I said to some of our English friends, four years ago, "At the end of this war, when we come out victorious over all the powers of evil, and this broad continent is never more to be cursed with the footstep of a slave, we shall set up to be the elder branch of the family" [Applause]; and what our brethren have been saying to us to-day and yesterday, gives the explanation of that prophecy. You know the prophets always spoke in a double sense, and didn't know the extent of what they said. The principles that came in at this gate of history are victorious not only here, but henceforth in England; and not this "boundless continent" alone is theirs, but that boundless continent also is theirs, by a predestination that is at last revealed. The principles of liberty, civil and religious; the principles of indefinite progress; the principles of universal human welfare, that, in the providence of God, were embarked on board the Mayflower, and that began to be planted here two hundred and forty-four years and six months ago this day, — those principles are yet to receive the homage of all aristocrats, of all imperial thrones, for those principles are the Gospel of our Lord and Saviour Jesus Christ; and the day is dawning when a voice shall be heard on high, saying, "The kingdoms of this world are become the kingdoms of our Lord, and he shall reign for ever." [Voices — "Amen!"]

As I came in sight of this harbor this morning, — I never saw it before —

A VOICE. You ought to be ashamed of it.

Rev. Dr. BACON. I am not, because I have been, all my life, a laboring man, and never had time to indulge in the pleasures of sentimentality. Forty years ago, for the first time, I entered Boston; and I have been in Boston a great many times, and have passed through Charlestown a great many times; but the first time I ever saw Bunker Hill was last Saturday; the first time that ever I stood within the walls of Faneuil Hall was yesterday; and to-day is the first time I ever was at Plymouth. I am going, by and by, to a better Plymouth than this.

I was about to say, that I was thinking, as I came in sight of this harbor, and the spot was pointed out to me where the shallop rounded the point and came so near being wrecked, why it was that they were saved. It was because of Calvinism. That explains it all. The destiny of the world was in that shallop. Cæsar was a bit of a Calvinist when he told the pilot not to be afraid, for the boat in which he sailed carried the fortune of Cæsar. That shallop could not be wrecked, because the destiny of the world — God's purposes — were in that boat. And so it rounded the point in the darkness, shot into the calm and tranquil waters of the harbor; and the destiny of the world was safe, because it was in the hollow of God's hand; safe until

"The waves of the bay where the Mayflower lay
Shall foam and freeze no more."

Rev. Dr. STONE. Now, is that lost senator here? [Voices — "No, sir."] Then shall we not, before we join in the Doxology, have a voice from Brooklyn Hights? Mr. Beecher is not here; but we can have a voice from those Hights, if you desire it. I will call upon the Rev. Dr Budington.

REMARKS OF REV. WILLIAM I. BUDINGTON, D. D., OF NEW YORK.

I will say one word, brethren and friends. I will say this: that I understand to-day, as I never did before, that our Congregationalism is a spiritual power, a history. Multitudes, who have gone to Niagara, say that they were disappointed. Multitudes, who have come to Plymouth, have said they were disappointed; that Plymouth Rock, of which we have heard so much, has disappeared in the soil of America. It scarcely crops out above ground; while the graves of the fathers are not to be found. John Robinson's house, in Leyden, can not be made pilgrimages to; the graves of the honored and beloved dead here can not be made a pilgrimage to. Why? Because the cause of truth, which the Pilgrims bore to our shore, is a spiritual one; and that spirit is now taken to the very ends of the continent. And I claim to-day Abraham Lincoln as the main agent who has consummated the Puritan spirit and Puritan history. [Applause.] It fell to me last autumn, as the mouthpiece of the Congregational Association of New York, to carry loyal resolutions down to Washington, and lay them before our now martyred president. I told him that I came to him with principles that landed more than two centuries ago on Plymouth Rock; that I came to him in the name of the advocates of those principles that were now spread across the continent; that we believed the war then raging, and over which he was presiding, was a war that had grown distinctly out of the cause that landed on Plymouth Rock; and that every man, woman, and child of the sons of the Pilgrims was with him. And what do you think our president said? Looking me steadily in the eyes, and elongating that form of his, his eyes flashing upon me, he said, "Sir, I think that is exactly the state of the case." [Applause.]

The Doxology, "Praise God from whom all blessings flow," &c., was then sung, after which, the company hastened to the cars, and returned to Boston, having spent a most delightful and profitable day.

NINTH DAY, FRIDAY, JUNE 23.

The Council was called to order, and opened by prayer, at 9 o'clock, A. M., by the First Assistant Moderator, Hon. C. G. Hammond, of Illinois.

The Scribe read the proceedings of the last two days, and the record was approved.

DECLARATION OF FAITH.

The first business in order was the appointment, by ballot, of a committee to revise the Declaration of Faith in its phraseology.

On motion of Rev. Dr. Dutton, of Connecticut, the vote requiring the committee to be nominated by ballot was reconsidered.

On motion of Rev. Dr. Eddy, of Massachusetts, a committee of three, to be appointed by the Moderators of the Council, was substituted.

FINAL ADJOURNMENT.

Rev. Mr. Quint, of the Business Committee, reported that, according to present appearances, a day or two of next week would probably be required to finish the business of the Council.

Rev. Dr. Holbrook, of New York, moved that the committee be instructed to arrange matters if possible so as to adjourn to-morrow at the usual hour. A large proportion of the members, to his knowledge, would leave this week, and the important matters should first be acted upon.

Rev. Dr. Wolcott, of Ohio, stated that the business could not be finished without restricting debate to an extent the committee did not feel authorized or disposed to recommend.

Rev. Mr. Gulliver and Rev. Dr. Bacon were opposed to the motion.

Rev. Dr. Holbrook modified his motion, so as to instruct the committee to present the more important matters for action first.

The motion, as modified, was laid upon the table.

MISCELLANEOUS.

The thanks of the Council were tendered to the Hon. Collector

Goodrich, for his polite invitation to the Council to make an excursion down the harbor.

The Business Committee reported the order of business for the morning session of to-day.

On motion, the order was amended so as to bring the report upon systematic benevolence before the report on the Congregational House; — ayes 85; noes 49.

Rev. Dr. Bouton, of New Hampshire, moved that a committee be appointed to express the views of the Council in regard to the first report upon the Declaration of Faith.

The motion was laid upon the table.

PROTEST.

Rev. Mr. ALLEN, of Massachusetts. I rise to a question of privilege. At Plymouth, yesterday, on Burial Hill, I entered my protest against a paper then read by Brother Quint, and was specially desired by the Moderator to present the same in writing after the adjournment to this place. When I entered my protest, it was, on my part, unexpected, unpremeditated, and entirely extemporaneous, growing out of the character of the paper as then and there presented. I now take the earliest opportunity to present that protest in the entire spirit of it, and, as nearly as I can recollect, in the exact words:

"Standing over the ashes of the Pilgrim Fathers, and on the summit of this hill consecrated to their memory, I solemnly protest against the adoption of the paper here and now presented, as being too sectarian for their catholic spirit, and too narrow to comprehend the breadth of their principles of religious freedom."

On motion of Hon. Mr. Hammond, of Illinois (the Moderator having taken the chair),

The protest was accepted, and ordered to be placed on the minutes of the Council.

The following members were appointed as the committee upon verbal revision of the Declaration of Faith:

Rev. WILLIAM A. STEARNS, D. D., of Massachusetts.
Rev. WILLIAM W. PATTON, D. D., of Illinois.
Rev. JULIUS A. REED, of Iowa.

MINISTERIAL SUPPORT.

Hon. EDWARD D. HOLTON, of Wisconsin, chairman of the committee on the paper on Ministerial Support, made the following verbal report:

The committee felt themselves embarrassed by the magnitude of the question submitted to them, and the subject matters that were perpetually pressing upon them. They drew up sundry resolutions, which at one time they adopted; but finally reconsidered them, and laid them all aside. There came before them complaints of the meager and inadequate support of the ministry. There was testimony as to the meanness and narrowness of societies, to a degree that was truly painful. But upon the whole, looking carefully over the admirable paper of Dr. Shepard, we concluded that we could add nothing to what he had said upon that point. That report recommends the system of ownership of the property, so that the pews can be rented for the support of the ministry. But in new communities this can not exist, or must be meager at best, and the old method of subscription must still be resorted to. The report of Dr. Shepard deprecated resorting to festivals as a method of eking out the support of the ministry. Your committee, while they would not discard this pleasant method of contributing to charitable objects, agree with the original report in deprecating its use in the support of the ministry.

Your committee are also of opinion that the societies of our denomination who may hereafter build churches, should not, by the selection of a miserable place, and the erection of a wretched house of worship, unsightly to behold, entail upon their societies a living death, and such circumstances that it will ever be almost impossible to establish or sustain a ministry in such places. The papal churches select the sightly and beautiful places throughout the land to erect their edifices upon; and make them commodious and handsome, that the youth of the community may be attracted there. So should we pay such attention to the external surroundings of the house of worship, and make the associations so pleasant, that the minister may be able to call around him those of sufficient ability to contribute to his support. But considering this subject as rather belonging to the Committee on Church Building than to themselves, they left it out of their report.

Your Committee testify to the nobleness and great-heartedness of many brethren scattered through the churches, through the length and breadth of the land, and hope that it may incite a like-minded liberality among them everywhere. The question of extravagant salaries paid by some churches also came to the attention of the Committee; and they recommend that while good salaries be given, the societies give more to missionary associations, instead of inciting undue ambition among the ministry in that direction.

But after all, your Committee considered that this Council was not one of cardinals and popes, to give direction and instruction to Congregational bodies, how they should act, and they therefore laid aside all their resolutions, and present the following report:

"The Committee to whom was referred the paper submitted to this Council by the preliminary committee through its chairman, Rev. George Shepard, D. D., on the subject of Ministerial Support, have had the same under careful consideration, and beg leave to report it back to this body with their cordial approval, and with the recommendation that it be adopted by the Council, and that at least 10,000 copies be printed, if within the province of the Council so to do, and circulated among our churches as an approved compendium of the relative duties existing between pastor and people.

EDWARD D. HOLTON,
WILLIAM SALTER,
HIRAM ELMER,
EDWIN N. LEWIS,
SELDEN M. PRATT,
MARSHALL S. SCUDDER,
DAVID S. WILLIAMS."

CONVENTION AT CLEVELAND.

The Moderator read the following telegram from the Convention of Non-Episcopal Methodists now in session at Cleveland, Ohio:

"CLEVELAND, OHIO, 22D JUNE, 1865.

"TO THE MODERATOR OF THE CONGREGATIONAL COUNCIL:

"The Convention of Non-Episcopal Methodists, in session at Cleveland, send their fraternal greeting to the Congregational Council at Boston.

(Signed) W. H. BREWSTER,
J. KOST,
JOHN SCOTT."

Rev. Dr. WOLCOTT, of Ohio. That is a very important convention, consisting of three ecclesiastical bodies, — Protestant Methodists, Wesleyan Methodists, and Independent Methodists, — that have seceded from the Methodist Episcopal Church, and have dropped the Episcopal features. I move that the Moderator be authorized to respond to this telegram, in the name of this Council.

The motion was agreed to.

The following reply was sent by them, viz.:

"TO THE MODERATOR OF THE CONVENTION OF NON-EPISCOPAL METHODISTS, AT CLEVELAND, OHIO, CARE OF REV. H. B. KNIGHT:

"The National Council of Congregational Churches, standing upon the basis of Christian Union, and Catholicity in faith, cordially responds to the fraternal greeting of the Convention at Cleveland.

W. A. BUCKINGHAM,
CHARLES G. HAMMOND,
JOSEPH P. THOMPSON.

"BOSTON, 23d June, 1865."

COMMUNICATION FROM BOSTON, ENGLAND.

Rev. Dr. Thompson, of New York, read the following communication, dated at Boston, Lincolnshire, England, certified in due form with a seal, and beautifully engrossed.

The Pastors and Delegates *of the Independent Churches of the County of Lincoln assembled at their half-yearly meeting in the Town of Boston, to the President and Members of the Convention of Congregational Pastors and Churches assembled in the City of Boston, Massachusetts, U. S.*, Greeting:

Dear Brethren, —

Having learned that the Transatlantic Churches of our Faith and Order are to assemble by their representatives, in the City of Boston, almost concurrently with the half-yearly meeting of our own County Association in the old town of Boston; — we deem it fitting to address to you a message of fraternal affection and sympathy.

It would have afforded us a high satisfaction to have been able to depute one of our own brethren from our County to your Assembly, charged to express with the living voice, the deep interest we take in your prosperity, and especially in this the hour of your Country's mingled triumph and sorrow. The ties by which the mother Town and her daughter are connected, have in various ways been recognized, but in no previous instance, that we can discover, have the Congregationalists of Lincolnshire addressed the descendants of the illustrious John Cotton, and those "of the Congregational way," who with him sought, in the wilds of Massachusetts, that freedom to worship God, which was denied them in their own land.

We therefore eagerly avail ourselves of the opportunity which your gathering presents, to assure you how much we rejoice in the large measure of success, which the Redeemer has vouchsafed to your Churches; and how earnestly we pray for its continuance and increase. We are not discouraged by the recollection of the sore trial through which the great Republic has been called to pass. We believe that you have been engaged in a struggle for right against wrong, — for freedom against slavery; — and we entertain the most profound conviction, that both your Political and Religious institutions will be stronger, and more powerful for good, because of the discipline through which you have passed. We have watched the evolutions of your mighty drama with the most intense anxiety. But amidst all its varying fortunes, we have held firmly to the belief, that however it might be protracted, it *must* issue in the triumph of righteousness and mercy.

We were stunned by the blow which deprived *you* of your noble President, and the world of one of its Kings of Men. But already it has become apparent, that Abraham Lincoln, the martyr, is rendering to the cause of his Country and of humanity, by his death, a more signal service than would have resulted from his prolonged life.

Go on, then, Honored Brethren, in your work. May it be given you to secure for our principles a development higher, and more comprehensive than has ever been attained in the Mother Country; — to reconcile the fullest individual liberty with the most perfect order in the Churches of the Saints; — to maintain inviolate the sovereignty of the Redeemer over his Church; — above all, by the preaching of the Gospel in your own Country, and amongst the Heathen to extend the blessings and augment the triumphs of the Common Salvation.

That your meeting in Convention may tend largely to promote these great ends is the Prayer,

Dear Brethren, of

Yours most fraternally and affectionately,
in the bonds of the Gospel of Christ,

Signed in behalf of the Lincolnshire Associated Pastors and Churches of the Congregational Order.

JOSEPH SHAW, Pastor of the Church, Red Lion Street, Boston, *Chairman.*
JOSEPH RUSTON, *Treasurer.*
ENOS METCALF, Pastor of the Church, High Street, Lincoln, *Secretary.*
THOMAS DAVEY, Pastor of Grove Street Church, Boston.

BOSTON, June 1st, 1865.

REPLY.

BOSTON, U. S., February 14, 1866.

The Pastors and Delegates of the National Council of Congregational Churches in the United States of America, assembled in Boston, in the State of Massachusetts, June 14, 1865, *to the Independent Churches of the County of Lincoln, in England,* GREETING:

DEAR BRETHREN, —

It was a great gratification to the members of the National Council of Congregational Churches assembled in this city, in June last, to receive from the "old Town of Boston," in England, from which the city of our own solemnities derived its name, a letter of Christian salutation and encouragement from the Pastors and Delegates of the Independent Churches of the County of Lincoln.

If the undersigned, as a Committee of the Pastors and Delegates of our American Churches, to whom the pleasing duty of answering your "message of affection and sympathy" was assigned, have not returned an earlier reply, it has been on account of special circumstances in which the Chairman of the Committee has been placed, and not from any want of heartfelt thankfulness and joy, on the part of the Council and its Committee, in receiving such an assurance of your affectionate interest in the objects and acts of your American brethren.

The words of your message show that you fully sympathize with us in appreciating the blessings of Christian liberty inherent in our mutual forms of church government; and that your minds expand with the benevolence and wisdom of the gospel of our common Lord, in comprehending the momentous interests connected with our late national struggle for liberty and law.

You have mourned with us over the loss, by assassination, of our late excellent President; you have felt and expressed the deep and grateful conviction that God has graciously made his death the occasion of good to our country; you have, with the fervor we have long known to be glowing in the hearts of our Congregational brethren in England, rejoiced in the advancement of human freedom connected with our victory over rebellion; and the widened field for the advancement of the gospel, in the forms of our mutual church polity, throughout our country, and in heathen lands, opened by the blessed results of our late civil conflict.

All these encouraging events, so wonderfully ordered by the good providence of God, amid the conflicts of human passion, you have rejoiced in with us. And, we are happy, and, we trust, grateful to God, as we assure you, that their increasing developments, since we had the pleasure of receiving your letter, have exhibited the loving-kindness of our heavenly Father the more brightly to our eye of faith, and called the more loudly for corresponding works, on our part, to meet his mercies with the action of our thanks.

We are happy, also, in assuring you, that the results of the Council, since its session, have been cheering to our hearts; — that a fresh and increased interest has been awakened, throughout the Congregational Churches of our land, in the adaptation of our ecclesiastical system to our republican forms of National and State governments; and that we are advancing, as one of the great Christian denominations, in gathering churches to shine as lights, and hold forth the word of life in all parts of it, — not forgetting the duty of striving to have the Word of God "sounded out" from us to "the regions beyond."

At this time, there are very strong and encouraging indications that the special influences of the Holy Spirit of God are accompanying the means of grace used by the churches, and giving blessed promise of revivals of religion in many parts of our country.

We take encouragement, also, from "the signs of the times," dear brethren, to hope confidently that we may rejoice together in the passing away from the political sky of those clouds which have made us, sometimes, fear lest the tempest of war might break the harmony which has now, for so many years, existed between England and the United States. And we heartily congratulate you and ourselves in the pleasing prospect thus spread before us of yet closer ties of Christian love and fellowship, that we may, with one mind and one spirit, strive together for the faith of the gospel.

Yours, dear brethren, most affectionately,
in the gospel of our Lord and Saviour, Jesus Christ.

GEORGE W. BLAGDEN,
EDWARD N. KIRK,
HENRY M. DEXTER, } *Committee.*

Rev. Christopher Cushing, of Massachusetts, chairman of committee on a Congregational House, read the following report:

REPORT.

First. The Desirableness of a Congregational House. Without attempting to present an exhaustive statement on this point, we would call attention to a few considerations.

(1.) A Congregational House is rendered desirable by the necessities of the Congregational Library.

(a.) The American Congregational Association have already in their possession a library of over five thousand bound volumes, and over fifty thousand unbound pamphlets, many of them exceedingly rare, and most of them of great value as illustrative of Puritan history, and of the faith and polity of the Puritan churches.

This library, as it is now situated, is liable any day to be consumed by fire; and it is an imperative necessity, which as Congregationalists we can not fail to appreciate, that this treasury of knowledge should have a safe place of deposit.

(b.) There are many individuals who have carefully selected private libraries, or at least a few books, of special historic interest, and pamphlets rescued from the paper-mill, that great foe to antiquarian researches, who would gladly contribute them to the American Congregational Association, if a fire-proof building were furnished to guarantee their permanent preservation.

Thus, in a few years, this library could be made richer in ecclesiastical literature than any other in our land.

We owe it to our own denomination to provide a place where those who love our order, and possess relics of the fathers, may come and present their gifts.

(2.) Again, a Congregational House is rendered desirable as the means of increasing our devotion to our own denomination.

We all *know*, our Western brethren *feel*, that we have not properly discriminated between sectarian zeal and denominational interest. In avoiding the former, we have neglected the latter. The American Congregational Association desires, by procuring essays and lectures on questions of a denominational character, to promote our appreciation, as a branch of the Church of Christ, of our distinctive peculiarities; and they would be greatly aided in this work by a house in which such essays may be read and lectures delivered.

(3.) We need a place where those societies which are doing the work of our denomination may have their centers of operations, whether they make provision for the feeble churches, publish theological works for ministers, Sabbath-school books for children, or tracts for the congregations.

(4.) We need a *home* to which, as Congregationalists, we may resort.

This city, as the home of our fathers, is endeared to us by the most sacred associations — the most hallowed memories. It is on this account that we are convened here on the present momentous occasion.

We need a home here to which we can repair, not as a Council once in a century, but as individual members of the Congregational family, as often as God in his providence shall favor us with the opportunity.

Such a home will give "a local habitation" to what might otherwise have only "a name." It will serve to promote union among the churches of our order in this city, and thus strengthen the denomination where it was first established. It will give fresh interest to our anniversaries. It will also promote union between the East and West. It will enable the sons of the Pilgrims, the adopted sons, and the sons-in-law, when they come from their distant homes, to rekindle the torch at the old fireside, and bear forth its light to any Egyptian provinces where they may be called to sojourn.

It may, in this connection, be well to call to mind that the erection of such an edifice by us will be nothing peculiar.

The Presbyterians, of both assemblies, have such houses in Philadelphia; the Methodists in New York; and our Congregational brethren in England have just raised by subscription two hundred thousand pounds sterling, as their bi-centennial fund, out of which, among other objects important to their denomination, they propose to erect such a building, for purposes similar to those which we contemplate, with the title of the "Memorial Hall." It will be a happy circumstance if we can have such a memorial, not only of the Fathers, but of the meeting of our present National Council.

Second. The Agency for the erection of a Congregational House.

We have no occasion for any new organization. The American Congregational Association, incorporated in 1854, under the title of the Congregational Library Association, which name was changed in 1864, is authorized to hold property to the amount of $300,000, and "to do such acts as may promote the interest of Congregational churches, by publishing works, by furnishing libraries and pecuniary aid to parishes, churches, and Sabbath schools, by promoting friendly intercourse and co-operation among Congregational ministers and churches, and with other denominations, and by collecting and disbursing funds for the above objects."

This society, already in the field, is everything, so far as respects an agency to secure a Congregational House, which could be desired.

Third. What has already been accomplished.

The American Congregational Association have at the present time property in real estate to the amount of about $10,000, and have recently secured a subscription of $20,000 in Boston and vicinity toward the erection of a Congregational House; and such is the facility with which this has been accomplished, that the conviction is expressed that it will not be difficult to secure an increase of this subscription, in this city and vicinity, to $50,000.

Fourth. The plan proposed.

It is thought that $100,000 will be needed for this object, and it is suggested that, should the subscription in this city and vicinity be increased to $50,000, the remaining $50,000 should be secured chiefly from Massachusetts, or at least New England.

Fifth. Objections.

(1.) It may be objected to this proposition that the raising of this amount of money for this object will interfere with the raising of the $750,000 already proposed for other objects. To which we reply, that the raising of the $750,000 proposed is not so formidable as at first appears, for we have been accustomed to raise large sums for the American Home Missionary Society and the American Missionary Association, and something also for the American Congregational Union. And the past year we have raised a very large amount for the Freedmen; and as the $750,000 includes the objects of all these societies, the portion of the $750,000 which is over and above what we have been accustomed to raise is not appalling.

Again, as the Congregational House is designed to conserve and foster an interest in our own denomination, its erection will be the means of rendering it easier in the end to raise money for other denominational purposes.

(2.) It may be objected that the existence of such a house will involve continued annual expenses; but this it is estimated will be met in part, or entirely, by the rents which such a building will yield. With the understanding that the money shall be raised chiefly from persons in New England, and particularly in Massachusetts, who are able to contribute large sums, and that the Congregational House shall not be a "House of Bishops," nor the source of a centralized power for the control of Congregational bishops or churches, but a home for all the brethren, to form or renew acquaintance, promote Christian fellowship, and the interests of the great denominational family to which we belong, we commend the American Congregational Association and its enterprises to the confidence and co-operation of our churches.

(Signed) CHRISTOPHER CUSHING,
EMERSON DAVIS,
E. RUSSELL,
S. D. COCHRAN,
S. G. WRIGHT,
WALTER BOOTH,
} *Committee.*

BOSTON, JUNE 21, 1865.

The report was accepted.

Rev. Dr. ANDERSON, of Massachusetts. I have no such special connection with this enterprise as involves the duty of addressing this body; but it seems desirable that a few things should be said in relation to it, that the body may feel prepared to give their sanction to the enterprise. It has been suggested to me that there are some persons who feel that the sum desired for erecting this building, and putting it into working condition, would be so much taken out of the amount otherwise to be contributed to the funds of the Council. In my opinion the reverse is the fact; and this portion of your enterprise is just what we need here to develop the spirit of Congregationalism among our churches in the East, and especially in this city and vicinity.

I have felt that we have not realized at all the importance of the denomination to which we belong, not only in New England but all over the country, not as a sect, but as a portion of Christ's visible kingdom. I have had in view for a number of years the object contemplated by this enterprise; to wit: something in Boston to bring forth the spirit of our churches, and make us feel that it is important for us to extend the denomination over the far West, and now, if may be, over the far South. I can not think of any one thing that is so likely to accomplish the object as this particular enterprise, so ably brought before us by this report that I need not go into the subject in detail.

We had in this city, not long since, a meeting of merchants, the largest and best meeting of merchants for an object that contemplated a subscription, that I have seen in this city for twenty years past or more. We brought the proposition before them to raise $50,000, which was as much as we thought it would do to ask for an object not fully comprehended. But the enthusiasm of the meeting was such, based upon a clear understanding of the facts brought before them, that it was thought best that we should aim at raising $100,000, in order to obtain a building adapted to our purpose. Toward that amount five merchants have subscribed $2,500 each, with the understanding that it shall be payable as soon as $50,000 have been pledged. Another gentleman in the interior sent us $2,000; and I have no doubt at all, as he is a member of this Council, that, if necessary, he will add to that sum. Others are ready to contribute $1,000, and others $500. There has been no object proposed in Boston for a long time in the importance of which religious men have been so united as in this.

We have obtained from the legislature the power of holding $300,000, in property; which will include all that is needful to carry out the objects as they are contemplated by the directors.

I do not think it necessary for me to go further into the subject, as there are others, living in other parts of the country, who will say something upon it. I will close by stating my own conviction that our Western brethren, by giving their sanction to this enterprise, are doing the best thing they can to raise a working power which will bring to them more than half a million dollars in a very few years. I rejoice that the American Congregational Union have been authorized to raise $200,000 for the building of churches. New York is our great commercial center, and that is the best place, I have no doubt at all, for that society to operate in; but Boston is the place for the Library, and Boston is the place from which to issue Congregational literature; and this society, which does not contemplate to become a purchasing institution, would be the best to advise Sabbath schools and churches of our denomination throughout the country what are the best books for them to purchase.

Rev. Dr. Wolcott, of Ohio. The Senior Secretary of the American Board, who is known to many of us to have taken a very deep interest in the subject, and to have devoted a great deal of time, and thought, and solicitude to it, before rising, appealed to me, as the representative of the Western Conference, to confirm, if I could, by a word or two, his impression respecting the sympathy, or rather, the identity, of the interest between the West and the East with regard to this subject. I do this with the greatest pleasure. I regard this as one of the most important practical suggestions which has been brought before this Council. I do not deem it an exaggeration to say that the success of this project is essential to the full success of every other measure which has been proposed here.

Now, sir, with reference to the West. While our faith and polity have, during the last thirty years, made wonderful progress, we have not yet, in many localities, obtained that social vantage ground which is occupied here. We are overshadowed by churches of another denomination that have drawn their strength from New England, made up mainly of emigrants from New England, and their descendants, sons and daughters of the Pilgrims, and of the Puritan faith and polity. Some of our own churches, comprised of those who have adhered to our polity, which is as well adapted to the West as to the East, and is as much needed at the West as at the East, are overshadowed by the older churches; while others have become as strong as they. Others are becoming stronger, and amid great difficulty and discouragement are attempting to hold up the banner for Christ that it may be displayed for the truth.

These churches first of all lift their eyes to the eternal hills whence cometh their help; but they do also lift their eyes occasionally to the hills of New England, the monument of our polity combined with evangelical faith; and it strengthens and cheers us to be able to turn to New England as a specimen of what such a faith and such a polity, under God, can accomplish.

The Western delegates to this Council have come up here, able and strong; and it was a special pleasure to them to meet in this National Council, because it was to meet in this home of our youth, in this Jerusalem of our Congregational Israel, which is free and gendereth not to bondage. I find that a large number of my brothers in the West have never visited Boston before; and it does them good to walk about, seeing how tall are her towers, to mark her bulwarks, and consider her palaces, that they may tell to the present as well as to the following generation who are to people the broad West in the future, where must be derived so largely the strength of our churches.

I believe that the interest which is felt in this cause by the churches of the West, is fully as great as that which is felt in the East, and that they will gladly respond to this proposition, and, according to their ability, will cheerfully subscribe. I hope some steps will be initiated before the Council shall dissolve, by which the suggestions of this able paper shall be realized, and that a subscription paper will be started here which will give us some reasonable assurance that, in the good providence of God, the object here proposed will be accomplished.

Rev. A. P. Marvin, of Massachusetts. This is a subject in which I have felt the deepest interest from the beginning. Living as I do some seventy miles from the city, I have never been able to be present at any of the meetings of the Association; but I have found no man here who has felt more interest than I in that subject. I never had an opportunity to consult with any person about it except the late most excellent and lamented Rev. Joseph Clark. When I saw such a meeting called, my first impulse was to come here, simply from the interest I felt in it; but knowing that I could do nothing to aid the movement, I concluded to stay at home. I am glad now to be able to be here. I only regret that the sum has been put at $100,000; for I do not see how the object can be accomplished, as it should be, for $100,000. Perhaps the business men here can understand that. They may hope, from the rents of the building, to be able to do what is necessary; but for a building so large, and architecturally so beautiful as I desire, it seems to me that $100,000 will not be enough.

I wish to speak only on one point, the relation of this institution to our history; not only to Congregational history, but to New England history. I believe this point has not yet been touched upon. Brethren who have not turned their attention to it, may wonder what good this is going to do; how a library and a great collection of manuscripts in Boston will be of any use to all the churches between here and Oregon. I suppose if there is any information gathered here, it will be easy to communicate it. This will be the center where all the facts of our history will be stored up; and we shall have a librarian who can answer any question with regard to it, upon any topic which may be interesting connected with our history, or our polity, and our local as well as our general history.

You know we have been, I was about to say, "damned like Cromwell to everlasting fame," almost infamy, in a certain sort of literature current in England, and beginning to be in this country. The fact is, that our forefathers, and the friends of our forefathers in England, were all covered over and blackened by the poets and letter-writers in England; and it is only in recent days that we have been getting this black rubbed off, so that we begin to shine out and to be understood by the world. We have ourselves men rising up, poets, novelists, editors, lyceum lecturers, ready to throw out their slanders and their misrepresentations of the character and history of our ancestors. I want simply to collect the facts and have them ready to answer all these misrepresentations.

One of the designs of Mr. Clark was this very thing. He said there were continual misrepresentations going out, of writers in Boston, or Massachusetts, or other parts of the country, which could be corrected by the facts which we were beginning to collect. I recollect the remark of one formerly noted lyceum lecturer, who said, "Yes, the Puritans were a noble people; but I am glad they lived 200 years before I did." He was full of prejudice, from his want of knowledge of the history of New England. Mr. Palfrey has done a great thing for us, as well as for himself, in his candid and noble history. But if we can have a library here, and a suitable building properly conducted, and a librarian who understands his duties, and who is not merely a custodian of books, it will change the current of opinion, and will do very much to make our name honored, as it only needs to be known to be honored; and our brethren and friends, and our posterity, in the West and in the South, will be proud of the name of their ancestors.

Rev. Mr. Quint, from the committee on Business, stated that the committee on the Declaration of Faith were prepared to report.

On motion of Hon. Mr. Hammond, of Illinois,

the report was made the special order for 12 o'clock.

Half an hour was then spent in devotional exercises, prayer being offered by Rev. Dr. Dutton, a hymn being sung, and remarks being offered by Rev. Dr. Kirk, of Massachusetts, Rev. G. S. F. Savage, of Illinois, Dea. Charles Stoddard, of Massachusetts, Rev. Dr. Adams, of Maine, Rev. Dr. Sturtevant, of Illinois, Rev. Dr. Gates, of Iowa, and others.

The Council then resumed the consideration of the report of the committee on a Congregational House.

Hon. Mr. HAMMOND, of Illinois. I wish to say a word or two in reference to this report, and perhaps my remarks may be a little wider than the report. I very much approve of this building in Boston, and wish it had been done long ago. I think it ought to have been done; and that it would have been done, if the ministry of New England had preached to their people on the subject of their polity as much as they ought. I think if the people of New England, with all her money, and intelligence, and refinement, had been made, by the watchmen upon the walls, to understand the value of their church polity, they would have poured out their money and built the house, and we should have had that home. Still more, if we had had that home, as the result of that conviction, the polity would have been carried to the West by those who have come there, and they would have lived by it; whereas, in the town I came from, the larger number of our Presbyterian ministers came from the Congregational ministry of New England. Instead of their being the most efficient leaders of the Presbyterian church, we should have had them to assist us. When we have had but a little band, in want of sympathy as we have been, I have thought, "Oh, that the people of New England loved their polity, and would teach it to their children, and teach them to love it!" I am sure that if New England — rich in money, thought, and education, and all that makes New England glorious — loved this policy as they ought, and had been taught it as they ought, they would long ago have built this house.

I have been distressed since I came to this Council, and before I came here, by the fear that we should separate and only skirmish round about, and not come to meet the enemy face to face and conquer. What have we to do? What did we come here for, Christian fathers and brethren? Did not we come here for the purpose of devising ways and means by which to enlist a thousand men, and by which to equip and drill a thousand men, and to furnish the commissariat for a thousand men or more to go forth and bear the glad tidings of the gospel to those regions in which there is now so much desolation? Is there before us anything else so important as to determine how to raise these men, how they are to be equipped, drilled, and supported in carrying forward this holy war? If there is anything else so important, I will sit right down and let any brother state what it is. No; there is nothing else.

The fact is patent to every one of us, that the reason why the gospel does not extend wider and farther, and does not bring more to its support, is that its privileges are not sufficiently appreciated; it is because we undervalue the gospel. Do you not know that some persons, who profess to be godly men, say there is such a thing as paying too much for the gospel; and they can not afford to part with so much of their money as they are called upon to do, to support the gospel? Let me tell you that, whatever it costs to support the gospel, it costs a great deal more not to do it. I have seen that as a business man, in the different towns which have grown up alongside of each other in the West. I have seen one town planted upon a whiskey-barrel, and another planted upon the gospel of our Saviour. Commencing with the same advantages, the one has become a light to all around, while the other has gone out in darkness. This is true, and will always be true.

Now, what is the reason that there is such an undervaluing of the gospel? I verily believe that the gospel is undervalued quite as much by the ministry as by laymen. How many of the ministry — the reverend fathers before me, and those we have left behind — are willing to come up to the laymen, and tell them that no farther than they consecrate their property to God have they the means of grace? How many will tell them that never, until it is all sacrificed, have they the evidence that they are Christians? How often do you hear faithful sermons to rich men? How often are we laymen, who are so apt to be covered up in the world, and buried in the care of the dollars and cents, met by one who will look us square in the face and tell us to consecrate all to God? How often are we told that the only privilege is to hold so much property as is necessary in the performance of the duties of our calling or profession? One man may be a merchant, requiring a capital of $500,000; another may require $50,000, and another $5,000; another may be a manufacturer, and God only knows how much he needs. But he knows, and God knows, how much income he should reserve. And he knows, or ought to know, — and if he does not know it, you ought to tell him, — that he owes all that he makes over and above the necessary support of his family, and laying up sufficient to educate his children, and what is necessary to keep up the tools of his profession, as the library of the lawyer, to God. Do you believe that if you talked thus, with all the earnestness with which you ought to teach us, we should want for $750,000? Do you believe we should want for the money which is necessary to raise and educate these men, to establish these schools and colleges, and to carry out these great objects which must be accomplished, or we shall sink with a weight of guilt upon us which no one can estimate? He who reads the Bible is taught to consecrate himself and all he has to God.

I know some of you say, We must not talk about money to our people. You do not estimate the laymen aright. They require this teaching above all things. They are, for six days in the week, wrapped up in their business, and are very likely to overestimate the value of the good things of this world. If you only speak to us about faith, and patience, and hope, and justification, and these glorious truths; if you say nothing about the particular duty of daily consecration of all that we can make, aside from what I have said may properly be excepted, do you believe the brethren will be ready to consecrate this money to God? It is not so. God has ordained that by the foolishness of preaching he will save those that believe; that by the foolishness of preaching he will prepare us for salvation; that by the foolishness of preaching he will instruct us in our duty and bring us up to it.

How difficult it is for a man to know, and then to be brought up to his duty! You know you can not bring us up to this, unless we see your soul in it; unless we see you so determined to do it, that you will not be afraid to offend a rich man because he is covetous. That sin of covetousness, — O Lord, deliver us from it! If we could but be delivered from that, we should want but a very few moments so to arrange our plans as to be sure of extending the gospel of God. When we reach the practical sacrifice of consecrating all to God, then we may be assured that the glory of God and the extension of his kingdom is secured through this broad land — yea, throughout the world. [Applause.]

Hon. Mr. DOUGLAS, of Connecticut. Some of us had the pleasure and gratification yesterday of visiting the old consecrated ground at Plymouth, and the opportunity of looking on what our immediate fathers have done toward laying the foundation, there of memorials of those goodly men. There we saw the foundations of an immense monument to the memory of our Pilgrim fathers. We saw the foundation also for another over that holy rock, — that sacred spot where first they placed their feet. A canopy is to be erected to protect that from the wearing drops of the storms of heaven, and from ruthless hands that might endeavor to gather fragments from that precious rock to carry to their several homes to look upon. The grand forethought of our immediate fathers and friends in laying these foundations to preserve these sacred relics, and in the erection of Plymouth Hall for the preservation of the memorials handled by our godly fathers, which to look upon did our hearts good, may well be imitated by us to-day. If it strengthened us to see things which our fathers looked upon and handled, is not the same thing true of our old Congregational church, especially here in this Puritan city, its early foundation? Shall we not put up some monument here to commemorate their labors, their prayers, their tears; — something that our children in future time, as they come to this business mart, may look upon, to see what their fathers did to preserve the memory of their church? Shall we not erect here the monument of the Congregational church here founded, so near the old rock upon which our fathers landed?

I think we have neglected these things far too much. The Congregational church has been truly a pioneer church. We have marched our armies through the fields, over the territory, conquering city after city; but we have failed to garrison the cities as we have gone through. What would have been thought of Sherman, if, in his triumphal march, he had marched from city to city and failed to garrison them? We must garrison the cities, not against other sects of orthodox persuasion, but against the enemies of Christ's kingdom. I think the best way to garrison this old city of our fathers is to erect here a memorial building for our children to look upon.

I think, with the gentleman who has just spoken, that our clerical friends have been too tender-hearted in this matter, too mealy-mouthed, too afraid to ask us — the laity — to contribute to these objects. It has been often spoken of among the laity, that upon this matter of calling for contributions the clergymen are backward; that they are afraid of hearing what has been called the "Judas jingle" in our churches. I like to hear it. There is nothing which does me so much good as to hear the church-plates go round. Do not be too mealy-mouthed; pass round the plates, and we will give the money.

Hon. Mr. BARSTOW, of Rhode Island. I wish for a little light before I vote for this. I should like to be informed of the number of the corporators, and their locality, and whether the matter is perfectly guarded, so that we may be sure that this building will represent our polity in future generations. We have seen such things slip out sometimes.

Rev. Mr. QUINT, of Massachusetts. The association, although incorporated by the Legislature of Massachusetts, is composed of members of Orthodox Congregational churches without regard to locality, each paying one dollar or more into its treasury, and thus becoming a life-member. The number of corporators, therefore, is the whole number of those church members, who choose to become such by the payment of one dollar. There is an annual meeting held in Boston at the time of the anniversaries in May. The list of officers will show the names of those connected with it. The officers are elected annually by ballot.

Hon. Mr. BARSTOW. I think the corporation is too open, if the payment of one dollar makes a man a member for life. No matter what his change of faith may be, he is still a voting member.

Rev. Mr. DEXTER, of Massachusetts. That is guarded against. He must be and remain a member in good and regular standing in an Orthodox Congregational church, or he can not vote.

The report was adopted.

DECLARATION OF FAITH.

The hour of 12 o'clock having arrived,

Rev. Dr. STEARNS, on behalf of the committee to revise the language of the Declaration of Faith, said: Your committee have confined themselves strictly to the duty intrusted to them. They have not attempted to introduce any new matter whatever, or to modify any old matter, so as surreptitiously or by any possibility to introduce new matter which was exceptionable. Nor upon a review of this document did they desire, all things considered, to introduce anything of that kind. They confined themselves simply to modifications of language, regarding somewhat euphony, but more especially perspicuity, in order that the sentiments here expressed may go out intelligently and satisfactorily — so far as the document itself is satisfactory — to all.

In paragraph 1, substitute "declare" for "reiterate"; "substantially as embodied," instead of "as substantially embodied"; strike out "as" after "primitive churches." In the sentence commencing "We bless the God of our fathers," make it read "We bless God for," etc., and strike out all after "doctrines."

In paragraph 2, after "the state," insert "and."

In paragraph 6, change "But" to "Thus" for the first word; and read "should agree," instead of "may agree."

In paragraph 7, before "are justified," substitute "believers in him" for "we"; after "before God," strike out "and"; after "remission of sins, and," strike out "that it is"; after "Comforter," strike out "alone that we," then substitute "are" for "hope to be"; and strike out "to be" before "perfected."

In paragraph 8, substitute "the" for "an" before "organized."

In paragraph 9, strike out "originally."

Rev. Dr. Stearns then read the revised Declaration of Faith, as follows:

Standing by the rock where the Pilgrims set foot upon these shores, upon the spot where they worshiped God, and among the graves of the early generations, we, Elders and Messengers of the Congregational churches of the United States in National Council assembled — like them acknowledging no rule of faith but the word of God — do now declare our adherence to the faith and order of the apostolic and primitive churches held by our fathers, and substantially as embodied in the confessions and platforms which our Synods of 1648 and 1680 set forth or reaffirmed. We declare that the experience of the nearly two and a half centuries which have elapsed since the memorable day when our sires founded here a Christian Commonwealth, with all the development of new forms of error since their times, has only deepened our confidence in the faith and polity of those fathers. We bless God for the inheritance of these doctrines. We invoke the help of the Divine Redeemer, that, through the presence of the promised Comforter, he will enable us to transmit them in purity to our children.

In the times that are before us as a nation, times at once of duty and of danger, we rest all our hope in the gospel of the Son of God. It was the grand peculiarity of our Puritan Fathers, that they held this gospel, not merely as the ground of their personal salvation, but as declaring the worth of man by the incarnation and sacrifice of the Son of God; and therefore applied its principles to elevate society, to regulate education, to civilize humanity, to purify law, to reform the Church and the State, and to assert and defend liberty; in short, to mold and redeem, by its all-transforming energy, everything that belongs to man in his individual and social relations.

It was the faith of our fathers that gave us this free land in which we dwell. It is by this faith only that we can transmit to our children a free and happy, because a Christian, commonwealth.

We hold it to be a distinctive excellence of our Congregational system, that it exalts that which is more above that which is less, important, and, by the simplicity of its organization, facilitates, in communities where the population is limited, the union of all true believers in one Christian church; and that the division of such communities into several weak and jealous societies, holding the same common faith, is a sin against the unity of the body of Christ, and at once the shame and scandal of Christendom.

We rejoice that, through the influence of our free system of apostolic order, we can hold fellowship with all who acknowledge Christ, and act efficiently in the work of restoring unity to the divided Church, and of bringing back harmony and peace among all "who love our Lord Jesus Christ in sincerity."

Thus recognizing the unity of the Church of Christ in all the world, and knowing that we are but one branch of Christ's people, while adhering to our peculiar faith and order, we extend to all believers the hand of Christian fellowship upon the basis of those great fundamental truths in which all Christians should agree. With them we confess our faith in God, the Father, the Son, and the Holy Ghost; in Jesus Christ, the incarnate Word, who is exalted to be our Redeemer and King; and in the Holy Comforter, who is present in the Church to regenerate and sanctify the soul.

With the whole Church, we confess the common sinfulness and ruin of our race, and acknowledge that it is only through the work accomplished by the life and expiatory death of Christ that believers in him are justified before God, receive the remission of sins, and through the presence and grace of the Holy Comforter are delivered from the power of sin, and perfected in holiness.

We believe also in the organized and visible Church, in the ministry of the Word, in the sacraments of Baptism and the Lord's Supper, in the resurrection of the body, and in the final judgment, the issues of which are eternal life and everlasting punishment.

We receive these truths on the testimony of God, given through prophets and apostles, and in the life, the miracles, the death, the resurrection, of his Son, our Divine Redeemer — a testimony preserved for the Church in the Scriptures of the Old and New Testaments, which were composed by holy men as they were moved by the Holy Ghost.

Affirming now our belief that those who thus hold "one faith, one Lord, one baptism," together constitute the one catholic Church, the several households of which, though called by different names, are the one body of Christ, and that these members of his body are sacredly bound to keep "the unity of the spirit in the bond of peace," we declare that we will co-operate with all who hold these truths. With them we will carry the gospel into every part of this land, and with them we will go into all the world, and "preach the gospel to every creature." May He to whom "all power is given in heaven and earth" fulfill the promise which is all our hope: "Lo, I am with you alway, even to the end of the world." Amen.

Rev. Prof. PORTER, of Connecticut. I move that the report be adopted. I was somewhat disturbed, I must confess, at the proposition that the report should be passed so suddenly yesterday morning. The reason why I was disturbed was this. When I came to this body, and especially, when I became acquainted with the committee to whom was entrusted the preparation of this document, I felt it to be my Christian and sacred duty to prepare a document which would represent every phase of faith held by members of this Council in such language as they could conscientiously accept, and in such form that they could cordially unite in putting it forth as a confession of their united and common faith. I felt sacredly bound to act truly and faithfully in the interest of every phase of doctrine here represented. Under the pressure of this acknowledged duty, all the committee acted in presenting their report, the result of three days' deliberation. They were so happy as to find that the report was generally and cordially accepted.

A certain portion of the assembly, however, objected to two or three paragraphs, in which the name of that most eminent reformer and theologian, John Calvin, occurs, whom we are proud to honor as one of the ablest theologians and noblest thinkers that Christendom has ever produced. [Applause.] In the objection, however, to the introduction of that name, both representative wings of doctrine united. Those who held to the extreme forms of Calvinism, and some individuals more Calvinistic than Calvin himself, objected to the introduction of any human name.

When, then, it was found the next morning, that the proposition to pass at once a modified report was to be acted upon, I felt hurt, pained, disturbed, grieved; for I feared that a portion of the Council — that portion which may be said to be most strenuous for the characters and the names of the fathers — might feel that their rights were not respected. For that reason I interposed my objection.

I was afterwards so happy as to learn that the whole project originated in the brain of an individual who represents that phase, if he represents any school, — the suggestion of a happy or unhappy inspiration, — and that it did not originate with any of those who might be supposed to tend in a looser direction. The knowledge of that fact removes all my objection to passing the document as modified. I am now prepared to vote for it, and think we are all as well prepared to vote for it now as we shall be after two days of discussion. [Applause.]

Rev. Dr. BARSTOW, of New Hampshire. What is the meaning of the expression, "all who acknowledge Christ"?

Rev. Dr. ADAMS, of Maine. Is it proper for the committee to make any explanation of the meaning of the report?

Rev. Dr. BARSTOW. A great many say they "acknowledge Christ," whom we do not acknowledge.

Rev. Prof. PORTER. We have professed Christ in a certain form, and we say that we can hold fellowship with all who acknowledge Christ in this way.

Rev. Dr. BARSTOW. Say that, and we will go for it.

Rev. Prof. PORTER. That is implied. It was intended to state our faith in the shortest and most devotional way. Let the critic whine and the objector cavil. No honest man will misunderstand the meaning of the Council. I stand upon my responsibility before all classes of theologians in this Council, and before the Christian world, that there can be no misconstruction in language of this sort.

Rev. Dr. BARSTOW. My object is answered, if this explanation goes out with the Declaration of Faith.

Rev. Prof. PORTER. I think it will. We are here as a Council representing all phases of Christian doctrine, including those theologians irreverently called the "twice-baked crackers," and also if there be any like "cakes unturned," who need to be put into a theological seminary and baked again, we include them. We include representatives from the Eastern shore of Maine to the Western shore that is washed by the Pacific; and now from each beach let there go up in the face of heaven our united speech "We are one." [Prolonged applause.]

Rev. Dr. Stone, of New Hampshire, moved to amend the clause confessing faith in God, the Father, the Son, and the Holy Ghost, in Jesus Christ, and in the Holy Comforter, so as to read, "we confess our faith in one only living and true God, *consisting* in God, the Father, the Son, and the Holy Ghost."

On motion of Rev. Mr. Bliss, of Tennessee, the amendment was laid upon the table.

On motion of Rev. Mr. Bliss, of Tennessee, it was ordered that there be no further debate upon this report.

On motion of Rev. Dr. Adams, of Maine, it was ordered that the Declaration of Faith be again read, that prayer be then offered, and the question be then taken upon the adoption, not only of the report, as to verbal amendments, but of the Declaration of Faith, as a whole, as reported by the committee this morning.

The Declaration of Faith was accordingly again read, in a distinct and impressive manner, by Rev. Dr. Stearns.

Prayer was offered by Rev. Dr. Palmer of New York.

The vote was then taken by rising upon the adoption of the above Declaration of Faith, and it was adopted, *nem. con.* [Applause.]

At the suggestion of Rev. Prof. Porter, it was agreed to sing "My faith looks up to thee," to be followed, at the suggestion of Rev. Dr. Stearns, by the old doxology, "To God the Father, God the Son;" and, at the suggestion of Hon. Mr. Hammond, the Council rose while singing.

The Council then took their usual recess until 3 o'clock P. M.

AFTERNOON SESSION.

The Council met at 3 o'clock.

Rev. Mr. Quint, from the Business Committee, submitted some resolutions, without any recommendation, which were, on motion of Dr. Dutton, referred back to the committee, to be disposed of by them as they should think proper.

Rev. Mr. Quint also submitted the following resolution, which was referred to the committee on the Erection of a Church in Washington:

Resolved, That this Council recommend, that from the amount raised for church building in central localities at the South, a sum not exceeding $50,000 be appropriated by the American Congregational Union, for the establishment of a Congregational church in the city of Washington, D. C., provided that an amount equal to the sum appropriated by the American Congregational Union aforesaid be received from other sources.

The following order was also submitted by the Business Committee:

Ordered, That a committee be appointed to report to this Council a brief paper on the subject of worship — not an *order* of worship — but worship both in public and private.

Rev. A. P. MARVIN, of Massachusetts. I will say to the Council that this does not propose the adoption of an order of worship, or a form of worship. It is no crotchet about altering our forms of worship, but simply *worship;* and it is brought in in consequence of a conversation with Dr. Kirk. As he has not brought it in, I have; and if I may be allowed a suggestion, without interfering with the business of the nominating committee, I would suggest that Dr. Kirk be the Chairman of the Committee.

The order was adopted.

The following resolution was also presented by Mr. Quint, in behalf of the Business Committee:

Resolved, That as our Lord Jesus Christ always spoke openly, and said nothing in secret, and is alone entitled to the unqualified faith of his followers, this Council hereby utters its solemn testimony against all secret associations which bind their members by extra-judicial oaths or obligations.

The resolution was laid upon the table.

Rev. Dr. BACON, of Connecticut. May I interrupt the reading of the report of the Committee on Business with one suggestion? Is it not time for us to instruct the Business Committee not to bring any new business before this Council? We may sit here longer than the Council of Trent, if we are to entertain every pet notion that anybody may choose to lay before that committee.

Rev. Dr. DUTTON, of Connecticut. I wish Dr. Bacon would modify the motion, so that the committee be empowered to use their discretion about submitting matters to this body. There may something come before them that the Council would like to act upon.

Rev. Dr. BACON. The order could be suspended, if anything extraordinary came up. But I would move that the Business Committee be instructed to present no new business.

Rev. Dr. DUTTON. We shall not save ourselves in that way. These matters will force themselves through the body, if we shut up the Business Committee in that way; but if we empower the Business Committee to use their discretion, we shall have no new business that is not important. I move that amendment.

Rev. Dr. Bacon accepted the amendment, and the motion, in that form, passed.

Rev. Mr. Quint presented another resolution regarding raising money, which, on motion of Rev. Dr. Holbrook, of New York, was referred to the committee already appointed on that subject.

Mr. Quint also submitted the following resolution from the Business Committee, stating that it originated from the question raised in the morning whether unlimited membership was perfectly consistent with the security of the property of the American Congregational Association, and was prepared by Hon. Mr. Barstow, of Rhode Island.

Whereas, this Council has recommended that the sum of $100,000 be raised for the purpose of erecting, in the city of Boston, a suitable building for an American Congregational House, therefore,

Resolved, That said association be requested to seek such change of its charter, or make such change in the 3d article of its Constitution, as shall better secure the property held thereby to those who represent our faith in coming generations.

Rev. Dr. ANDERSON, of Massachusetts. I would move that the name "Congregational House" be substituted for the phrase, "building erected for the Congregational Association."

Rev. Dr. BARSTOW, of New Hampshire. I hope that alteration will not be made. The name in the preamble is exactly what the Association bears; and, whatever name we give to the house, it will be controlled for ever by the Association to which we give the name. It is a house to be erected for the American Congregational Association.

Rev. Dr. ANDERSON. I want to say that there are conveniences in having the name retained, if you retain the other name. I would suggest that it read, "A Congregational House, for the use of the American Congregational Association."

The amendment was adopted and the resolution passed.

The Business Committee also submitted the following resolutions, which were referred to a special committee: —

Resolved, That this Council desires to record its sense of the importance of the worship of God's house, independently of the sermon, usually and justly holding with us so conspicuous a place, while there is reason to apprehend sufficient attention is not always given to reading, prayer, and praise, with a view to make them, in the highest practical measure, attractive, awakening, and edifying.

Resolved, That our mode of public worship, especially of prayer, — so plain and simple, but happily affording scope for the utmost variety of thought, and beautiful adaptation to the ever-changing experience of life, — should be conducted, not with reference to instruction, or assertion of doctrine, or notification to men of passing events, which is a degradation, but with a view pre-eminently to the producing of devout emotion, and the commingling of all hearts in one spirit of confession, supplication, and praise.

Resolved, That we recommend to ministers to give much more attention to this part of divine service, and to teachers in our theological seminaries to endeavor to impart a better preparation for this part of a minister's service.

The following preamble and resolutions, also presented by the Business Committee, were referred to the committee on Devotional Exercises: —

Whereas, We, the members of the National Council, recognize in our deliberations a degree of unanimity and cordiality which was hardly to be expected in view of the wide separation of our churches in space, and the diversity of experiences and influences under which they have been trained in the Providence of God. Therefore,

Resolved, 1st, That we do hereby cordially and unanimously assert our assent to the general course of action in this Council.

2d. That we devoutly thank God for the evidence developed in this assembly that we are harmonious in our views of the teachings of God's word, and the leadings of his providence in our times.

3d. That before the close of this Council we will unite in the observance of the Lord's Supper (at such time and in such manner as the committee on Devotional Exercises may deem best), whereby we trust all our minds may be turned to Him who is the source of all our hopes and convictions as Christians, and all our hearts united in the love of our Saviour, the great Head of the Church.

Mr. Quint stated that the Business Committee recommended that the session be extended until half-past six, in the hope that the business might be finished by to-morrow noon. The recommendation was adopted.

Rev. Mr. Langworthy, from the Committee on Nominations, offered the following report: —

COMMITTEE ON THE APPORTIONMENT OF THE $750,000.

New York. — Deacon Samuel Holmes, Rev. John C. Holbrook, D. D., Rev. L. Smith Hobart.

Maine. — Charles A. Lord, Rev. Uriah Balkam, Rev. Seth H. Keeler, D. D.

New Hampshire. — Rev. Alvan Tobey, Rev. Henry E. Parker, Hon. Thomas J. Melvin.

Vermont. — Rev. Lewis O. Brastow, Rev. George P. Tyler, Hon. Ira Goodhue.

Massachusetts. — Rev. Ariel E. P. Perkins, Hon. Allen W. Dodge, Marshall S. Scudder.

Connecticut. — Rev. Davis S. Brainerd, Rev. Hiram P. Arms, D. D., Deacon George W. Shelton.

Rhode Island. — Hon. Amos C. Barstow.

New Jersey. — Lowell Mason, Jr.

Pennsylvania. — Rev. Edward Hawes.

Delaware. — Deacon Abner H. Bryant.

Maryland. — Nathaniel Noyes.

Ohio. — Rev. Thomas Wickes, D. D., Rev. John C. Hart.

Tennessee. — Rev. Thomas E. Bliss.

Indiana. — Deacon A. G. Willard.

Illinois. — Rev. Richard C. Dunn, Rev. William Carter.

Michigan. — Rev. Herbert A. Read, Rev. Hiram Elmer.

Wisconsin. — Rev. Edward G. Miner, Rev. Isaac N. Cundall.

Iowa. — Rev. Jesse Guernsey, Seth Richards.

Minnesota. — Rev. Charles Seccombe.

Missouri. — Rev. Julian M. Sturtevant, Jr.

Kansas. — William H. Watson.

Nebraska Territory. — Rev. Reuben Gaylord.

Colorado. — Rev. William Crawford.

California. — Jacob Bacon.

Oregon. — Rev. George H. Atkinson.

COMMITTEE ON PRAYER AND FASTING.

Rev. Leonard Swain, D. D., R. I.; Rev. Geo. A. Oviatt, Conn.; Rev. Erastus Maltby, Mass.

Rev. Dr. BACON, of Connecticut. I want to ask what the first of these committees is for?

Rev. Mr. LANGWORTHY. I was not present, and, so far as I can learn, neither of my colleagues were, when this committee was ordered.

Rev. Dr. DUTTON, of Connecticut. It was to apportion the $750,000.

Rev. Dr. BACON. If that is the meaning of it, I say the raising of the $750,000 becomes an impossibility the moment it is attempted in that way.

Rev. Dr. THOMPSON, of New York. I would ask if we have not just now passed a resolution covering that whole ground, and defining that that was not an amendment, but a reconsideration?

Rev. Dr. HOLBROOK, of New York. I understand this committee to be a committee to devise ways and means for raising the $750,000.

Rev. Dr. BACON, of Connecticut. I understand that the idea is (and if I am wrong, I desire to be corrected), to assess, in the form of a recommendation, the $750,000 among the several States. That being the motion before us, to appoint a committee who shall consider that method of raising money, I want to say that, supposing a programme comes out, saying, specifically, that the churches in Massachusetts should pay a certain portion of it, and the churches in the State of California pay a certain portion, and the one church in the State of Delaware pay a certain portion, if the one church in the State of Delaware don't pay that portion, it never will be paid; and if the churches in California don't pay their portion, no other State will make it up; for the utmost that you can expect, when you make such an assessment, is that any church or State on which a certain amount is apportioned, will raise that amount. A good many will inevitably fail to make up their part, and it will be impossible to secure the $750,000. The only way of raising the money is to appeal to the universal sympathy, love, charity, and zeal of the whole body of our churches.

Rev. Dr. Thompson, of New York, raised the point of order that the Council had already voted to appoint a committee to consider this subject, and that the committee just nominated by the Nominating Committee was the committee thus ordered, and the chair so ruled. The report of the committee was then adopted.

Rev. Dr. Dutton, from the Committee on Evangelization at the South and West, reported, in reference to a church in Baltimore, that they would move that this Council commend the object, and refer it to the special consideration of the American Congregational Union. Adopted.

On motion of Rev. Dr. Badger (representing California), Hon. Samuel A. Chapin, of Virginia City, Nevada, was admitted as an honorary member.

Rev. William A. Stearns, D. D., of Massachusetts, from the committee to whom was referred the paper on Systematizing Benevolent Contributions, submitted their report, as follows: *—

REPORT OF COMMITTEE ON BENEVOLENT SOCIETIES.

The committee to whom was submitted the paper entitled "Systematizing Benevolent Contributions" ask leave to report, that they have given as much time to the consideration of the subject of the paper as your intervals of business and their other engagements would allow, and see no reason to dissent from the general views and statements presented by the original committee.

They were evidently embarrassed, as all who give attention to the facts and circumstances of the case must be, by the number of existing organizations engaged in important enterprises, and by the difficulty of connecting those organizations by any wise and practicable plans of concentration. If the authors of the paper had any such end in view when they commenced the work assigned them, they were evidently brought to despair of its accomplishment. Your committee fully agree with them in the opinion that much less can be safely attempted towards reducing the number of benevolent associations, and giving greater breadth and power to a few which might be specially recommended to public confidence, than the inexperienced in such an effort would naturally imagine. Most of these societies have long since attained to the dignity and stability of years and experience, and have acquired confidence by valuable services. Most of them have their own charters, their own endowments, their own special patrons and friends, and their own specific works. They have also a history and a life, and would be destroyed only by undesirable pressure and violence. The work of evangelizing the heathen and nominally Christian nations abroad, and of converting the population of our own country wholly to Christ, is the one work, generally speaking, which as Christians and Congregationalists we are all interested, in connection with the upbuilding of our own churches, to achieve; and we suppose it to be an established fact that this work must be carried on among us through the agency of the great missionary and other benevolent associations which have been established for the purpose.

It must not, however, be forgotten that new and great opportunities for Christian effort have been opened to us by the results of the war. The colored freedmen, the long neglected whites of the South, the inrushing, enterprising, diversified populations of the West, even more than before, all demand Christian sympathy and assistance, which can

* The report is here printed as finally adopted, — the original paper not being obtainable. The slight alterations made from the original will be easily gathered from the discussions.

be best afforded, sometimes by the old organizations, and sometimes perhaps by temporary associations formed expressly for their benefit. We can not restrict the liberty of the churches in selecting the fields of their labor, the objects of their benevolence, and the channels through which they would bestow their contributions.

Your committee, therefore, in view of the whole subject, would limit themselves to a few simple suggestions, and those chiefly in accordance with the sentiments of the paper before them.

1. They suggest that it is exceedingly desirable that the disposition to Christian giving should be greatly intensified and extended—that all the members of our larger churches should be educated and accustomed to it, and that pains should be taken to interest not only the smaller, but the smallest churches in it. Of this last character, it is believed that there are large numbers which are rarely visited by the agents of benevolent societies, for the reason that such agents do not find this work pecuniarily remunerative to the associations which employ them. In consequence of this neglect, while the pecuniary loss to the kingdom of Christ is great, the loss of Christian growth, through the disuse of giving, is far greater and deplorable. We would call the attention of ministerial associations, church conferences, agents of benevolent societies, pastors, and churches, to this subject, that they may inquire, in their respective localities and relations, what can be done to develop the benevolence of all churches and Christians within the reach of their influence.

2. Your committee suggest, that it may be safe and wise to presume that intelligent Christians, in selecting societies, will naturally give their preference to those whose work, as defined, come nearest to that "foolishness of preaching" by which Christ saves those who believe.

3. Your committee suggest, that without infringing upon the liberty of the churches and of private Christians, in their selection of societies, and because we are afraid that many churches, especially at the West, would esteem it a great favor to be informed of the facts, it may be well for this body to say that the American Board of Commissioners for Foreign Missions, the American Home Missionary Society, and the American Missionary Association, have the confidence of our churches, and have been accustomed to receive and disburse most of the charities intended to subserve the ends for which these societies were formed; that the American Education Society, for the increase of the number of Christian ministers; the Society for Promoting Collegiate and Theological Education at the West, having the same general object in view; the American Bible Society for the translation and distribution of the Word of God; the American and Foreign Christian Union for diffusing the simple gospel among nations and communities whose Christianity has been sadly corrupted, and in some instances almost destroyed by human additions and superstitions; the old and well-established societies for the benefit of seamen, and for the gathering and improving of Sabbath Schools, and the Christian education of children in them; the Congregational Board of Publication, and the American Congregational Asso-

ciation,—have all been sanctioned by the customs of the churches, and by the recommendations, often repeated, of numerous religious bodies among us; also that the objects for which the American Tract Societies were instituted, namely, the distribution of religious books and tracts, especially in settlements supposed to be destitute of them, are considered by this Council as of great importance, and are cordially recommended to the churches; also that, whereas there are many associations for the benefit of the freedmen,—the paper under consideration says at least twelve, others say as many as eighteen within their knowledge,—it would seem desirable to concentrate such agencies, so far as *our* contributions are concerned, into some one responsible body sufficiently known and approved to be worthy of our confidence; and as the American Missionary Association has undertaken this work, we are happy to say that in our judgment there is no existing organization which has better adaptations to the successful performance of it; also, and as a matter of special importance, that an effort to encourage and aid church building, especially at the West and South, should be earnestly carried forward by the Congregational Union, which has undertaken this enterprise.

4. Your committee suggest, that while it is not expedient for this Council to attempt constrained conjunctions of societies, nor in their power to furnish perfect systems of Christian giving which may be applicable to all cases, it is the legitimate business of each church, and would conduce greatly to its order and comfort, to decide, after full consideration for themselves, what objects they will patronize, what societies they will employ as their organs, and at what times they will make their contributions. They can adopt either of the plans suggested in the paper before us, or construct a plan each for itself, always regarding the ability of the church, and adopting such courses as may be most conducive to good order and most fruitful in good works. Your committee can not think that impulsive giving to irresponsible solicitors, when the circumstances can not be well understood, is either required by our Lord, or is conducive to the edification of his church. New objects of high importance will often demand consideration; but it entertained at all, they should be regarded only as occasional and extraordinary.

Finally, your committee suggest that it would be a great saving of expense and confusion, and for the edification of the churches, if the pastors would undertake, as far as may be practicable, to act themselves as agents in behalf of the several objects for which the churches under their care may choose to contribute; and that while agents may be invited when necessary to communicate information, the systematic efforts of pastors and churches should be our main reliance for securing those stated contributions which our churches may choose to bestow.

W. A. Stearns,
J. H. Linsley,
Wooster Parker,
Calvin B. Cady,
H. A. Miner,
Jeremiah Butler.

Rev. Mr. ADAMS, of New Hampshire. I would suggest a single verbal alteration. In the place of "The Foreign Evangelical Society," what I suppose the committee meant was "The American and Foreign Christian Union."

The amendment was accepted.

A MEMBER. I notice the omission of any reference to the Congregational Board of Publication, which is to our denomination what similar boards are to other denominations. It has a fund, and is prepared to issue tracts to supply missionaries at the West, to a certain extent.

Rev. Mr. LANGWORTHY, of Massachusetts. I would like very much, Mr. Moderator, with your permission and the permission of the Council, to say a word, as I could not get the floor when the subjects of Evangelization at the South and West and Church Building were under discussion.

After sixteen or twenty other good societies, — they are all good, brethren, — I have not a word to say against one of them, — after these other societies have reaped the field, the committee kindly suggest that the American Congregational Union is a very good society through which to aid in building houses of worship at the South and West. Now, I do want, exceedingly, an expression from this body in regard to church building. There was a general "omnibus bill" passed here the other day, saying that it would be a good thing to raise $200,000 to build churches. I have very little hope from that expression. It does not reach the point. Not one half of the churches have ever recognized this object. They have looked upon it as a very clever thing in its way to do something toward building meeting-houses, but they have never lifted a finger to help. I have worked at this matter for eight years, and I have said a good many things — some of them, perhaps, not very wisely. The brethren of the West have felt themselves very dependent upon this aid; and I say, if this matter is passed over in this way, we shall not raise the $200,000, nor even $20,000. If you make this object dependent upon putting another month into the year, — as one minister told me, he would take up a collection for the Congregational Union if I would make thirteen months in a year, — I say, if you make this object dependent upon that, nothing will be done.

All these commercial societies are doing a good work, but are they first, second, or third in importance to our churches at the present time? If you so decide, let this matter slide; let it take care of itself; I certainly do not want to press it upon you. To me it is a very important and vital thing. It seemed to me that if there could be two or three short resolutions passed, something to this effect: "That we will do our utmost to double our contributions to the American Home Missionary Society and the American Missionary Association, and go on in the same way year after year," (for these societies will need double); and then if you would say, "We will put the church building work of the American Congregational Union on our calendar for annual contributions, and recommend others to do the same,"—I say, that if some such resolutions could be passed, something would be done. We never shall raise one half or one quarter of $200,000 unless this society comes nearer to you than the fifteenth or sixteenth to which you are called upon to contribute. Can there not be something said that will make this report a little more decided, and so that we shall know the opinion of the Council on this church building work?

I feel keenly on this subject. It is my specialty, you say; but I have been called upon to make it so, and I believe it is vital to our denomination that this matter should be acted upon by the Council. Do you ask me how many of the churches in Massachusetts and Connecticut contribute to this object? About one in twenty; and most of these only at my importunity. Not fifty churches in New England have it on their calendar, and make regular contributions to it.

I ought to say now, that since this Council commenced its session, I have received letters which assure me that, if the good work of the Lord shall prosper in Southern Missouri for twelve months, as it has for the last three months, our receipts of last year, and our prospective receipts for the year to come, would not meet the demands for church building in Missouri alone. Perhaps there will be a cessation, but if brother Turner goes on as he has been going on for three months, we shall not have enough to meet the wants of that State; and that, too, without appropriating more than $500 to any one church. And yet, from all the South and West are coming floods of letters asking for contributions.

Rev. Dr. Holbrook, of New York. I sympathize very much with the remarks of Mr. Langworthy, but I will not add anything except to say that this subject will come up again in connection with the report of the committee which has just been appointed for devising ways and means for raising funds. It was my purpose to propose a plan, if nobody else did, by which that sum of $200,000 should be raised for church building. When that committee shall report, the whole subject will be before us.

Rev. Dr. Stearns, of Massachusetts. A word of explanation. The committee, in preparing this report, did not overlook the importance of this society, and did not intend to put it in an inferior position. We hardly thought it was best to begin with that society, and we thought the next best place was the end, as the beginning and the end are more likely to attract attention than any other parts. [Laughter.] We thought we gave this society a good position,—not the highest, but perhaps what might be next to it. Besides that, we supposed there might be a special resolution on the subject, and I should be very glad, for one, to vote for one presented by the secretary of that society, or by some committee which should urge this object with as much eloquence as it is proper to introduce into a resolution. But we could not do everything in a little report like this.

On motion, the report was amended by the insertion of the "Congregational Board of Publication."

Rev. Dr. THOMPSON, of New York. I move to amend the report by omitting the paragraph referring to the two Tract Societies. I don't wish to discuss the question. I have no desire that the Council should express itself in favor of either of these societies. There are obvious reasons why we should specially urge the claims of the society whose center is in this city of Boston, and whose history has been one of unswerving fidelity to the cause of freedom and humanity. [Applause.] But I do not care to discuss the matter. As it stands now, the two societies are evenly balanced, and while neither is specially commended, they are thrown out before the public as having, equally, the sanction of this body. I much prefer that we should say nothing about either.

Rev. Dr. BUDINGTON, of New York. I would ask if the motion contemplates striking out the reference to the N. Y. Society in the original report?

Rev. Dr. THOMPSON. Not at all. I hope the original report will remain, to be printed with the various documents before the body. That involves no action on our part. The action now proposed is action by this body on that report.

Rev. Dr. BUDINGTON. I am perfectly willing that no reference should be made to the two Tract Societies — perfectly willing; but, for one, I should feel as though the courtesy which is due to the various opinions of this denomination was violated if we should, directly or indirectly, put the seal of our approbation as a Council upon either of those societies. I stood by the side of my brother, Dr. Thompson, at the time of the revolutionary proceedings in the Brick Church, and in Lafayette Square Reformed Dutch Church, and I am free to say that my sympathies were strongly with the policy that enforced upon the original society the introduction of those topics that were then agitated. If I understand the matter now, both societies are based upon the same principles, and doing the same work of patriotism, in the spirit of a common catholicity and Christianity. I am quite sure that this Council, — in view of the course it has taken hitherto, of respecting not only the opinions of the minority upon all points of theological sentiment, but the opinions and feelings of the smallest minority among us, — would not be willing, but on the contrary would take special pains not to throw its influence against any organization which at the present time is the cherished organ of persons who, hand in hand and heart to heart, are doing the common work alike of patriotism and of religion.

The object I have in rising is simply to say this: that if Dr. Thompson contemplates the erasure from the original report of that unkind, and, as it seems to me, unchristian and uncourteous reference to a society in which I have no special interest, and with which I did not sympathize at the time of the agitation to which I have referred, but with which I feel obliged to sympathize now, if I can sympathize with the society at Boston, — as I cordially do, — I can have no objection to his motion. But I am not willing, as a member of this Council, that we should commit ourselves to a censure upon a body of men who, by their action during the past four years, have shown themselves to be as cordial, as intelligent, as whole-hearted in the work of the world's evangelization and the redemption of our country from the sin and curse of slavery as any body that is recognized by our Congregational churches. All I wish, sir, is that this society be let alone.

Hon. Mr. HAMMOND, of Illinois. Let them confess their penitence. [Great applause.]

Rev. Dr. BUDINGTON. Very well, sir. I have heard that the difference between the societies comes at last to this : we acknowledge that, at present, as those societies are working, they are working for our Lord and Master, and there is no difference in spirit or action between them ; but we require of the old society that they humble themselves before us in a confession of the wrong they have done. Now, Mr. Chairman, I do not feel that this Council, or any other of the representatives of Christ's church, is called upon to ask any such act as that. Does the fact that they are not willing to go back over the heated and angry disputes of that period, and renew the flames of that spent controversy, constitute any reason why we should censure them ?

Sir, I will say again, in closing, that I speak the more freely on this subject, inasmuch as my sympathies were with my honored and beloved friend, Dr. Thompson, all through that controversy ; that is, I felt that the society should adopt those principles of action, the non-adoption of which led to the split. But when, in the providence of God, there rises up throughout this land one common spirit of patriotism and Christianity, which, like the great flood of Noah, submerges every division line upon the face of the earth, I am mistaken very much with regard to the feelings and character of this body, if now, when we want a union that shall be a union of heart and of hand in the great and more difficult work of reconstruction, we are again to renew the heart-burnings, and alienations and divisions of that period, which seems now to be indeed like the period before the flood. If it is the intention to strike out all reference to both Tract Societies, so that this Council can, neither really nor constructively, be understood as passing a censure upon either one or the other, I heartily endorse it.

Rev. Dr. THOMPSON, of New York. I do not intend to debate the question for one moment, but simply to explain, in reply to my friend, Dr. Budington's, inquiry.

This Council has not yet determined what shall be the final disposition of the several documents presented to it by the preliminary committees. If those documents are ordered to be published, they do not commit the Council to any of their statements or sentiments, beyond the action of the Council in its own reports or resolves thereupon adopted. For example: if the Council shall see fit to print, in an appendix, the Declaration of Faith that I had the honor to submit, nobody can present that as the Declaration of this Council. It goes for just what it is worth, nothing more, with the names of the committee subscribed to it. So with each and every one of those reports. The intent of my motion is to strike out all reference to the Tract Societies, and just leave it an open question. The report as it stands expresses too much confidence in one of those societies.

Rev. Mr. WELLMAN, of Massachusetts. I hope this motion will not prevail. If I understand it, the committee have recommended to the Council that these two Tract Societies be commended to our churches. The motion now is to erase this recommendation, which would place both these societies upon the same level. Whatever of odium, therefore, there is in the motion comes upon both societies alike. For one, I make a distinction between these two societies. My personal wish is, that we should commend the Boston Tract Society to the churches. I am not willing to commend the New York Tract Society to the churches. [Applause.] I do not believe, as the brother who has spoken does (Dr. Budington), that the New York Tract Society is yet worthy of the confidence of the churches of our denomination. [Voices — "No."] I took pains, at the time of conflict to which reference has been made, to go to New York to be at that meeting; and, having witnessed the action of the New York Tract Society at that time, I have not seen any action on their part since that seemed to me to make them worthy of the commendation of this Council; and I do hope that we shall not, at the end of this conflict, say that the Boston Tract Society, which has been true from the beginning to liberty and humanity, shall be placed on the same level with the New York Tract Society. [Applause.] For one, my wish would be that we should make a discrimination; that we should erase from the report the New York Tract Society, but not the Boston Tract Society.

Rev. Mr. SAVAGE, of Illinois. It seems to me that the simple question is this: Are we willing to sustain those who, at the cost of large sacrifices to themselves, took a stand, previous to the war, in favor of truth and righteousness; or shall we take a stand for those who delayed their action until they were compelled to it? [Applause, and cries of "Hear, hear."] Our churches at the West feel strongly on this matter; and I believe that every Congregational association in the Western States has passed resolutions indorsing fully the American Tract Society of Boston, upon the ground that it is worthy to be sustained by Congregational churches, both for the principles avowed and sustained, and for the great work which it is doing; and I am sure that we should do a great wrong if we should say, that all this in the past is to be entirely obliterated, and go before our churches throwing the influence of this great Council against the society that has, as I have said, in the face of opposition, and when it cost largely of self-denial and of self-sacrifice, taken its stand on the side of right and truth.

Rev. Dr. STEARNS, of Massachusetts. I wish to explain. I believe none of the committee had any strong feeling on this subject; I do not know that any of them were in any sense partisans of the New York Society; but a paper was put into their hands, on which they were called upon to report. On examining that paper, they found these words: "The American Tract Society at Boston is worthy of the confidence of our churches for many reasons, and should be specially commended for the manner in which its business affairs are managed, and for restricting its operations to its own appropriate sphere." Now, it may be true, or it may be false, that it should be commended for such things; but there is a strong and sharp intimation that the other society does *not* conduct its business operations in a manner worthy of the confidence of this body; and, moreover, that it does not confine its operations to its own appropriate sphere. Whether they do or not, I do not know; I am not called upon to judge. It seemed to the committee, that if this paragraph was to remain untouched, unnoticed in any way, we should arraign the society and condemn it without a trial. If this were a proper Council, and proper witnesses could be summoned, and it could be ascertained that the society at New York does not conduct its business operations properly, and, moreover, that it does not confine its operations to its appropriate sphere, and if, after a full and fair investigation, that should be the opinion of this Council, and this body was the proper body to take action upon it, then I say, it would be all right. But to have these statements come in here and receive the sanction of this body, without their knowing anything about it, did not seem to the committee to be right, and therefore they presented their report as it is, saying that these bodies have the sanction of this Council, without specifying the peculiarities of either of them; not denouncing either of them; but proposing that what is in the original report censuring one of the societies should be stricken out; and we did that partly to meet the views of the friends of the Boston Society. One gentleman, a friend of that society, came and said, "If that paragraph goes in, I shall turn my contributions to the other society, for it is an act of impropriety and injustice."

Now, in view of this explanation, if the Council decide to leave that paragraph in, so be it.

Rev. Mr. Bliss, of Tennessee. It seems to me that the difficulty can be very easily obviated. If the two societies are to be commended to the confidence of the Christian public, it might be expressed in a few words, and then special confidence expressed in the Boston Society, in view of its fidelity in the hour of trial. I think some little testimony like this should be paid to the Boston Society for its faithfulness to its principles. This is due to it, due to us, and due to all the interests at stake in this matter.

Rev. Dr. Dutton, of Connecticut. Confidence in the New York Society is what I can not express. "Confidence is a plant of slow growth." That society forfeited our confidence at one time — at any rate it did mine, and my confidence has not yet grown so that I can express it. Dr. Budington is more generous in his nature, and his confidence has grown very rapidly. But I choose to exercise more caution than is involved in his position. If we are going to express confidence in either of these societies, for myself, it must be expressed only in the Boston Society.

Mr. Wellman moved to amend the motion of Dr. Thompson, so that the name of the New York Society should be erased, instead of both societies, and Dr. Thompson accepted the amendment.

Rev. Dr. Wolcott, of Ohio, asked that the sentence might be read, and the chairman of the committee, Rev. Dr. Stearns, read it.

THE MODERATOR. The name, "American Tract Society" does not appear. The amendment is really not applicable.

Rev. Dr. DUTTON, of Connecticut. I move to amend by striking out the whole paragraph.

Rev. Dr. KIRK, of Massachusetts. I want to know if that strikes out the Boston Society?

Rev. Dr. STEARNS. It leaves the report of the original committee, recommending the Boston Society, "for the manner in which its business affairs are managed, and for restricting its operations to its own appropriate sphere."

Rev. Dr. Thompson, of New York, moved to amend by substituting, for the paragraph referred to, the following:

"That the object which the American Tract Society, originally founded in Boston, has in view, in the manufacture and distribution of religious books and tracts, in settlements supposed to be destitute of them, is considered by this Council of great importance, and is cordially commended to the churches."

Rev. Dr. BACON, of Connecticut. I did not intend to say a word on this matter, but the course of discussion constrains me just to throw out a suggestion or two. Is the American Tract Society, in the first place, a missionary society? Is it not formed on the catholic basis of issuing nothing but what the Publishing Committee, composed of four or five different denominations, unanimously concur in? Is it, therefore, congruous for a society, formed on that catholic basis, to employ missionaries to go abroad and preach the gospel? That is the first question. And, in the second place, is it worth while for a society with a capital of about $750,000, at present rates, — all that we ask for in this great year of jubilee, — to be commended to our churches as an object of charity? [Loud applause.]

Rev. Mr. BODWELL, of Kansas. I would ask the privilege of reading the resolutions which the General Association of Kansas passed on this subject:

Resolved, That this Association views with surprise and grief the conduct of the American Tract Society, of New York, in that the course they once declared forbidden by their constitution, they now pursue, with no Christian acknowledgment of the wrong they *then* did, or are *now* doing, to the feelings of "Evangelical Christians." [Laughter and applause.]

Resolved, That in once suppressing the publication, even of Bible denunciations of man-stealing and oppression, and in rudely preventing free discussion in their great annual gatherings, we do hold them guilty of encouraging the growth and insolence of that power, which, by sword and starvation, has slain scores of thousands of our best citizens; has filled the land with widows and fatherless children; and has wasted the treasures of the nation in a long and bloody war. [Applause.]

Resolved, That we ask the older and more influential associations of our order to join us in calling upon this society for such an expression of penitence, for the wrongs done the country and the cause of Christ, as shall warrant a restoration of that confidence, which, by upholding the wrong, it has justly forfeited. [Great applause.]

Rev. Mr. HURD, of Michigan. I wish simply to bear my testimony on this matter. The New York Tract Society could not get into any one of our one hundred and forty churches in Michigan, unless they stole their way in.

A VOICE. So in Illinois.

ANOTHER. So in Iowa.

ANOTHER. So in Wisconsin.

Rev. Dr. WOLCOTT, of Ohio. I hope the amendment of Dr. Thompson will pass. For one, I have no desire, as a member of this Council, to utter any word of censure or reflection on the American Tract Society of New York. That society missed an opportunity which God in his providence seldom sends more than once to any individual or to any organization, in my judgment, to place itself in a position in which it could go down to the future with moral power. I do not doubt that that society is now, and has been for the past three years, doing a very patriotic work; but I have a lively remembrance of the experience of some of the beloved brethren of this body who attended its public meetings with all the rights and responsibilities of members, who had to fight their way through amid interruptions and despotic decisions so numerous, that the man who was anciently condemned to walk blindfold among burning ploughshares had an easy time compared with them. [Laughter and applause.] But, sir, I leave that society to God, and to the providence of God; I have no vindictive feelings in regard to it; but I do feel that we ought to commend that society which, like the seraph Abdiel, was "faithful among the faithless found." [Applause.]

Rev. Dr. BLODGETT, of Rhode Island. I have not opened my mouth in the Council. I prayed, before I left home, that I might not do any harm here, and I have found grace, so far, to keep silent; but I do feel constrained to say, now, that with whatever protestations of friendship brethren may come, with the proposed action, the result of that action will be to reflect dishonor upon the New York Society, and draw an invidious distinction between the two societies, which, it seems to me, if I may be allowed to say it, is not in accordance with the spirit of the times, and with the spirit of the discussions in which this Council has been engaged. Neither does it look with an aspect of favor to the great work of home evangelization, which we are called upon as a Council to undertake, to begin this new dispensation by placing a brand upon one of the great instrumentalities of evangelization which God has thus blessed; and I am sure that, when it is very doubtful whether a rebel of the last four years, except Jefferson Davis, — and a little doubtful whether he proves an exception, — will be hung, it is no time for this Council to go, as it were, for hanging the American Tract Society. It seems to me that, when the whole spirit of the times, coming out of such a terrible conflict as we are now, is that of large forbearance, we should look with leniency, so far forth as we can in conscience, upon the shortcomings of any of our associations in times that are past. It is no time to stand on points of ceremony and of difference of measures, such as formerly existed between these two great associations that have, under the force of events that are stronger than men, been brought to march side by side in the great work of seeking the salvation of souls throughout this land. It is no time in this Council to interpose and say, "We can not, by implication even, approve the course of the American Tract Society of New York;" and we do say this if we adopt the line of action that is contemplated. If I understand it, I should be very, very sorry to have anything go out from this Council of that character.

Rev. Mr. BRADSHAW, of New York. I wish to inquire to whom the American Tract Society belongs?

Rev. Dr. BUDINGTON, of New York. It is a catholic society, as Dr. Bacon says. I am under the necessity, very much to my grief, indeed, of leaving this house in a few moments, and if any brother thinks I am obtruding, I throw myself upon his mercy, while I say a few words.

I came up to this assembly with some fears and many hopes, and my fears have all disappeared, and my hopes have risen into one jubilant thanksgiving to Almighty God. That independent men, having among them different sympathies and lines of action, should come up here, and, respecting one another's feelings, tastes, preferences, prejudices, locality, and everything of that kind, still meet in the spirit of one catholic Christianity, prepared to unite in an aggressive movement upon all the forms of atheism in this country and the world, seemed to me the culmination of the grand principles of Congregationalism. Let me appeal to the Council through you, Mr. Moderator, not to dissolve the charm of that union which I believe is the outgrowth of the Spirit of God in the hearts of these brethren, kept alive and glowing there by that half hour of prayer every forenoon. Do not, I beseech you, in a moment of angry haste, stab the reputation for Christianity, and for patriotism, of men who love their country as much as any other men — men who have given —

A MEMBER. I protest against the words, "angry haste."

Rev. Dr. BUDINGTON. I will take them back; I am sorry I used them. I did not mean to say any word which any brother could misconstrue. I respect, sir, with all my heart, that steadfast loyalty to principle that animated my brethren of New England throughout that controversy; but I do desire, for the cause of our common country and our Union hereafter, that we may not rake up that old controversy. These resolutions from Kansas arraign our brethren in New York as having done an unchristian thing; so unchristian that, in order to the restoration of confidence, they should come forward and confess it. [VOICES. — "True,"—"true."] I have only a word or two to say. My grand desire is the unity of our churches in a life-long work for the conservation of the interests of this country; and I ask you, in God's name and in the name of our Redeemer, not to divide brethren who love the same cause, and who are pursuing the same cause by the same methods, simply because, in times past, they differed, and as brethren differing do, said hard things about one another.

I do wish to say, brethren, that those gentlemen, who have been arraigned here on this platform, were many of them, I know, as anxious to do what was desired in the matter of publication as any gentlemen in Boston were, but they felt themselves bound by that constitution of catholicity which I understand Dr. Bacon to comment upon, — and in his comments I cordially agree. I think it is not the organization for us; and I agree cordially in that report, which seems to have been forgotten by some of us, which has reviewed the whole underlying policy of both these Tract Societies. I beg you, brethren, do not arraign men because they felt themselves bound by the constitution under which they were acting, and, under that constitution, felt themselves unable to publish anything which any section of any evangelical church, co-operating in that united society, objected to. Do not arraign gentlemen who felt themselves bound in honor and in conscience to the course which they pursued.

Brethren, we had Dr. Vaughan here before us; we had brother Beecher a short time afterwards, endorsing what Dr. Vaughan said in regard to the position of England toward our country; although in the first instance he could not understand it; but having cooled himself among the glaciers of Switzerland, and come round through phlegmatic Germany, he did understand the feelings of those brethren who, sympathizing, as Dr. Vaughan tells us, with this country, thought the constitution of the "Union" forbade them to introduce the vexed question of the American war, and realized that it was only as a matter of self-preservation, and not as casting any censure upon us, that they pursued the course they did. Will you have charity for a "Union" over the water, and refuse it to a "Union" among your own brethren, engaged in doing the same work with you? I beseech you, brethren, for the sake of harmony and efficiency in our efforts for the consummation of the work to which we are now giving ourselves, do not, directly or indirectly, arraign the character for patriotism of your brethren in New York.

Rev. Mr. BRADSHAW, of New York. I inquired to whom the N. Y. Tract Society belongs. Does it not belong to us as much as to any other people in this land? We argue that we are so zealous to have a force to go into the West and South that we are ready to recommend the licensing, and perhaps ordaining, of men uneducated. Now, the American Tract Society have done things that we did not approve; but are we going to rake up that? That society is a power, a great power,—$750,000, Dr. Bacon just told us. Now, why should we alienate that society? Why should we throw ourselves into an attitude so that we cannot appropriate that to the great work we have in hand, after a little, if not now? One half of these brethren are members of that society. In the name of common sense, of good policy, and of our Saviour, for whom we labor, let us not repudiate that society.

Rev. Dr. BACON, of Connecticut. I want to say a word or two, in the hope that this question will be disposed of immediately and kindly. There is a brother [Dr. Dutton] whom I love as I do my own soul. He has a very forgiving spirit, and so have I. He has forgiven Gen. Butler, and yet I have never heard that Gen. Butler made a confession of his sin. He was as big a sinner, before Fort Sumter, as the American Tract Society, and has never said to this day that he has repented. We have forgiven ever so many men who never made any confession, and I am willing to forgive these men—every mother's son of them. [Laughter.] I am perfectly willing to forgive them, and hope I shall remember nothing against them of what happened "before the flood," as the brother said. I want to dispose of this matter in such a way as shall leave no scar and no unkind feeling anywhere, either in the mind of brother Budington, or Dr. Kirk, or any of us. Can we not say that the object of doing good by the distribution of books and tracts is commended to our churches? That I am ready to say. I do not permit the representative of brother Kirk's society, nor of any Tract Society, to stand in my pulpit, and ask money for a manufacturing and trading corporation.

Rev. Dr. KIRK, of Massachusetts. We don't ask it.

Rev. Dr. BACON, of Connecticut. No, you don't ask it. But your representative goes round among my people,—and I am glad to have him,—and solicits money for an increase of the capital, or for the charitable operations of your society; and the other man comes, whether I am glad or not [Laughter]; he knows the beat; he got the track long ago; but sometimes he has complained, of late years, that he has got more kicks than coppers; and I am sorry for the kicks he gets, and a little sorry for the coppers [Laughter and applause]; because my judgment—my private and personal judgment—does not go along with the scheme of doing good which is prosecuted especially by that society. The publication of books, whether by the Carters or by this excellent Publication Society here in Boston, is a good thing; and the giving away of books is a good thing; and I have a contribution taken in my church every year to buy books for the purpose of giving them away, and we buy them of this society, but not exclusively; and what we can not give away in our own parish, and to the Germans and others in New Haven, we put into the Home Missionary barrels, and send them to the home missionaries to give away; and we put in these books of the American Tract Society, and all sorts of societies, taking a little pains to see that the books are worth the freight. [Laughter.] Now, let us get rid of this difficulty, and say nothing of either of these societies, but merely say, that the object of doing good by the distribution of books and tracts is commended to the churches.

Rev. Dr. STEARNS, of Massachusetts. I will not object to the amendment, provided the passage in the original report is stricken out, and provided these words shall be put in: "without passing judgment on other organizations."

The amendment was accepted.

Rev. Mr. BLISS, of Tennessee. There are some here who know my interest in the Boston Society. I attended the three days' session at New York, and when at last it was concluded to draw off, I may be pardoned if I state that I made the first motion to that end. Three amendments were offered, which I moved to lay on the table, which brought the matter to an issue. I am just as cordial a friend of the Boston Society as any man can be; but while thus friendly to that society, I should dislike to introduce anything like a firebrand to divide and alienate the brethren of this body. Sir, there is no call for it, no demand for it, whatever. We have a large interest in the New York Tract Society. We have not come up here as a Council to call upon that society to make confession and pay obeisance to us. That is not our province. It is a matter of small moment, in view of the grandeur of the work before us, whether they shall in so many words confess their sins, or whether they shall, "forgetting the things that are behind, press forward to the things that are before." That is the great question before us ; and while that is so, I would not throw a straw in the way of that society ; I would not do a thing in this Council to alienate one brother. There is no need of it ; there is no call for it. All I would say, would be simply to commend both these organizations in common, for they are both doing a great and blessed work in our day. Only look over the literature of that New York Tract Society. What a treasure of religious truth, — what a treasure of the richest gospel and Christian experience is to be found in their publications! Why need we do anything here that shall seem to cut us off or alienate us one moment from that society ? There is no need of it. We have a large interest in that organization, and now that they have righted themselves, let us do nothing that shall cut us off from that society or prevent our drinking largely from their fountains of love and Christian truth and experience. No man could grieve more deeply than I did over the terrible fault, mistake, or error (the *sin*, I call it, for it seemed to me a dreadful sin), of that society in neglecting and persistently refusing to testify on the great question of American freedom. Those were my feelings then; but they have at length "righted themselves," as we express it at the South; and now, doing God's work as they are, let us not alienate or divide brethren on this question. But it seems to me, that while commending that society, a reference ought to be made to the faithfulness of the Boston Society in the hour of emergency, when it still stood forth and testified for the great principles of freedom and righteousness in the land. It seems to me that this would be wise, kind, forgiving, and loving.

Rev. E. P. MARVIN, of Massachusetts. I will not detain you long; and having voted with the Boston Society throughout all that time of division, I am sure I shall not be misunderstood in the remarks I am about to make. I am feeling exceedingly anxious in the line of thought that Dr. Bacon suggested. Does this Council wish to throw $750,000, with all the New York Tract Society can raise in New York and throughout the country, into the hands of the Presbyterians? Do we want to make the same mistake which they have made, — a sad one for them, too, — in regard to the Home Missionary Society? Men who do not forgive, who are not kind and cordial, when everybody must be forgiving, are very sure to make mistakes; and while I believe that the Tract Society in Boston ought to be commended, I do not wish to say a single word in this Council which shall alienate that society. If you do, you will find rich men and rich societies and ministers and men of influence throughout New England, — a great many of them, — who will give their money to that society, and it will go against the interests of the Congregational denomination. Here is an argument which, to my mind, is perfectly conclusive. Do not alienate that powerful society, which will command money by hundreds of thousands of dollars in New England, in spite of any action which you can take here to-day. Let us have what commendation you choose for the Boston Society — though I do not think it needs it, where there have been so many local commendations; but I beg you not to say anything that shall be construed into opposition to that great society, and especially into opposition to it on the ground of the management of its business affairs. If we are to say anything on that subject, even by implication, we ought to call upon some of our shrewd business men to decide that question, for there is a dispute about it. I understand that some of our own friends do not wish that we should put that to the test, because good men differ in regard to it. I have been somewhat behind the scenes, and I know that the question has been submitted to a committee of business men in New York, and I know a proposition was once made here in Boston to submit it to business men here; and while I would not wish to intimate at all what the decision would be, I beg of you not by implication to censure that society.

Rev. Mr. MILLS, of Michigan If we had any special responsibility as pertaining to this matter, I should favor a thorough, sharp discussion of the question, and some thorough, sharp decision; but we represent independent bodies of Christians all over this land, who are able to form their own judgments, and have, for the most part, formed them. We have no special responsibility with reference to the manner in which they shall give to this object. If there was a necessity for making a sharp declaration, I should be willing to make one. I have my own judgment, my church has its own judgment, and I presume it is a good one; and it is clear that the great mass of the churches represented here have their own judgment.

Now, sir, I am exceedingly anxious that nothing shall be said which shall be felt as a hardship by any single member of this Council. We are independent men, we are independent churches, and we have no right in a matter where we are not called upon to act, to be a hardship to any one. Inasmuch as we gain nothing by a positive utterance, I am in favor of the manner in which the thing was put by Dr. Bacon, — and I wish he had presented it as an amendment, — that the *cause* of the societies be commended to the churches, leaving it to the churches themselves to judge between them. Why do we need to get into heat and embarrassment by discussing this question, and by sharp divisions on this matter?

Rev. Dr. BARSTOW, of New Hampshire. I wish this report might be recommitted to the committee. We are doing infinite mischief by this discussion.

Rev. Mr. ALLEN, of Massachusetts. I think the house could be harmonized by introducing an amendment to this effect: after passing what has been suggested, adding, "without judging any other society, but bidding God-speed to every society having the same object as our own."

Rev. Dr. KIRK, of Massachusetts. I beg the privilege of saying a word. I think that, just as Satan, when he saw Adam and Eve in Paradise, happy, contrived some way to get in there and tempt them to eat the apple, so he has done here. It is ten thousand pities that we ever got on this track; and I must say, that Dr. Budington did it.

Now, let me say, as an official of the Boston Tract Society, that all we wish is, that you shall not put us out as if we were not one of your societies. Only refrain from that, and we shall be satisfied. We are not a court of justice, and are not trying the brethren of the New York Society; and I pray God and my brethren that we shall end this afternoon as we ended this morning, in the spirit in which we shall go to heaven.

A motion was made, that the report be recommitted to the committee, and carried.

Rev. Mr. Langworthy, from the committee on Nominations, reported the following names as the

COMMITTEE ON PUBLIC AND PRIVATE WORSHIP.

Rev. Abijah P. Marvin, Rev. Nathaniel H. Eggleston, of Massachusetts; Rev. Jonathan L. Jenkins, Rev. Orpheus T. Lanphear, of Connecticut; Rev. Joshua Leavitt, D. D., of New York.

The report was accepted.

A recess of five minutes was taken, after which, Rev. John P. Gulliver, of Connecticut, read the following as the report of the committee on Church Polity:—

REPORT ON CHURCH POLITY.

The committee to whom was referred "the statement of Congregational Polity" respectfully report.

Your committee found it necessary, in the opening of their consideration of the subject referred to them, to fix definitely in their own minds the precise limits of the functions of a Council like this in issuing a statement of Church polity. These limits are defined,—

1. By what we have a *right* to do.
2. By what we have *time* to do.
3. By what it is *expedient* for us to do.

In respect to the first question the answer is plain. We have a right to issue as complete and comprehensive a statement as we are able to secure, for the consideration of the churches whose representatives we are, so long as, in the language of Richard Mather, we claim no more authority for such statement "than there is force in the reason of it."

In respect to the question how far it is possible for a body of five hundred men, in the time at our command, to issue a perfected statement concerning a subject so extensive, and embracing such variety and number of details, your committee were soon convinced that only an *approximation* could possibly be made to that precision and comprehensiveness and conciseness which must characterize such a document, if it shall be worthy of this National Council or generally acceptable to the churches we represent. Your committee, therefore, became convinced, early in their deliberations, that all that this Council could possibly do, under the most favorable circumstances, would be to give a general approval to the documents reported to it, and that it would be compelled at last to commit them with such emendations and additions as it might direct, and such as might be brought out by open discussions, or private suggestions by members of the Council to a committee, for final revision and publication.

And in these *necessities* of our position we found an answer to our *third* question, as to how much it would be *expedient* for us to do even if we should have at command all the time we could desire. On this point your committee have been led to the conclusion, that inasmuch as the action of this Council is to go forth over large portions of our country, in which the idea of church authority and ecclesiastical legislation prevails, to the nearly entire exclusion of the conception of our free Congregational forms, it would prevent much misconception and misrepresentation, if such a document, after receiving the *general* approval of this Council, should go forth to the world with the *full* indorsement only of the gentlemen whose names shall be appended thereto.

In this manner we might hope to find a middle course between the two extremes of too great authority on the one hand, and of the entire absence of authority on the other. We might hope, in other words, to avoid all appearance of legislation *for* the churches, while at the same time we might commend *to* the churches a statement of polity which should carry with it *primâ facie* evidence of its correctness: first, from having received the general approval of this National Council; and, secondly, from the minute and absolute approval of a large committee carefully selected by this body, who shall have received the benefit of an extended discussion of the papers now under examination, for months to come, by the whole body of our ministers and churches.

Having settled in their own minds these general principles, your committee applied themselves to the close and careful study of the two papers presented to them.

They found the longer of these papers to be an able, comprehensive, and, in their view, a generally correct statement of the principles of the Congregational polity, and well worthy to be the basis of the platform which we now desire to take the place of the ancient Cambridge Platform. They found a close similarity to that long-revered work of our fathers, large portions being little else than a substantial reproduction of that document.

They found the shorter of these papers to be concise and yet comprehensive, and in these respects well calculated for ordinary use in our churches, and for insertion in our church manuals.

A careful examination on the part of the committee of the detailed statements contained in these documents, and of written suggestions sent in to us by members of this body, reveals the fact that special attention is necessary in the final revision to the following points:

1. The insertion of *proof-texts*, after the manner of the Cambridge Platform, and also of references to standard works on Congregationalism.

2. The definition of *Church Polity.*

3. The definition of the *Church Visible*, and the whole arrangement of the definitions of the church, local and universal, visible and invisible, militant and triumphant, with reference to the question of genus and species, and of logical consistency.

4. The statement concerning *councils*, as to their action in certain cases as *boards of referees;* as to the propriety of admitting persons as *corresponding* members not invited in the letters-missive; as to the propriety of sending *stated supplies* to act as pastors on councils; as to the propriety of using the word "*Synod.*"

5. The relation of *ecclesiastical societies* to the churches, and the degree and kind of control which such societies should have over Church property, and also as to the recognition and commendation of the practice of dispensing with the "ecclesiastical society" altogether, when the civil law allows.

6. The relation of baptized children to the church.

7. The designation of the church members who may properly vote in church meetings.

8. The more distinct recognition of the aggressive and missionary functions of the church, and the question of a more direct control by the church of the various benevolent enterprises which they maintain.

9. Sundry questions concerning *ministers* and the *pastoral office*, such as these: — Should a minister be a member of the church of which he is pastor? Are the statements of the platform under consideration, concerning the eldership and the presbyters, on page nine, correct? What should be the office of the pastor in inaugurating and administering discipline in the church? Is a pastor, *ex officio*, the moderator of all the meetings of the church? Are the *rights* and *powers* of a pastor correctly stated? Should the pastor have entire control of the service of *teaching* or *preaching* in his own pulpit? Should a *church* ordain and depose from the ministry, or only a *council?*

10. The grouping of all the churches of a city or town into one church, page six.

11. The scriptural requirement that the Psalms be used in public worship.

12. A more precise specification of the only mode of separation from the church.

13. The importance of introducing more fully the doctrines of the Cambridge platform, concerning the withdrawal of fellowship from a disorderly church by its sister churches.

14. The importance of sharply defining, in a separate chapter, the distinction between the church polity of Congregationalists and the polity of other denominations.

15. The principle and law of fellowship through councils and the proper functions of ex-parte councils.

16. The statement made on page thirteen, article six, concerning the treatment of excommunicated church members.

17. The statement made on page eighteen, section twelve, respecting the confederation of churches, and the question whether there should be a recognition of standing councils.

18. The expediency of securing the preparation of a catechism upon the cardinal principles of our faith and polity, for the use of the churches.

Such your committee have found to be the general character of the two documents submitted to them, and such are the points which seem to require special attention and revision.

In conclusion, your committee recommend the following action on the part of the Council:

Resolved, That this Council, having received and duly examined the two statements of church polity presented to them, hereby express their approval of the general principles and scope of the same.

Resolved, That these documents be referred to the committee reporting them, consisting of Rev. Leonard Bacon, D. D., Rev. Alonzo H. Quint, and Rev. Henry M. Storrs, D. D., which committee shall be enlarged by the addition of twenty-four members, of whom six shall be professors selected, one from each of our six theological seminaries; viz., Bangor, Andover, New Haven, East Windsor, Oberlin, and Chicago, to be nominated by the committee on Nominations, and appointed by this body, who shall revise and publish the same under the following instructions:

1. All members and ministers of Congregational churches, either in an individual or associated capacity, and especially the committee who framed these documents, shall be invited by the committee of twenty-five to indicate such additions, emendations, and omissions as they may judge proper.

2. The committee shall take into special and careful consideration the points to which attention is now called in this report, and in general shall be empowered to make such changes and additions to the documents in their charge as they may deem advisable, and as may not be inconsistent with the general principles now approved.

3. In cases where, without a violation of the cardinal principles of Congregationalism, the usages of Congregationalists differ, the mode preferred by the committee shall be inserted in the text, and the varying usages shall be indicated in a foot-note.

4. The origin and history of the document shall be set forth in a preface, to which shall be appended the signatures of the committee.

5. An appendix shall be added, containing such ecclesiastical formulas as the committee may deem expedient.

John P. Gulliver,
Edwards A. Park,
Samuel Harris,
S. C. Bartlett,
N. Bishop,
Chas. C. Salter,
J. Guernsey,
J. S. Hoyt,
J. G. Davis,
J. D. Liggett,
E. F. Burr.

Rev. Dr. Leavitt, of New York, presented a minority report, as follows: —

MINORITY REPORT ON THE STATEMENT OF CHURCH POLITY.

The undersigned, a minority of the committee of the National Congregational Council, to whom was referred the statement of Congregational

Polity presented by the Committee of the Provisional Conference at New York, respectfully report: —

That the Council, and the churches they represent, are under obligations of gratitude to the Provisional Committee for the pains and study they have bestowed in the preparation of this document, which is both instructive and valuable as a presentation of the ancient principles of Congregationalism in their application to modern circumstances. Should it be published, as it ought to be, either among the doings of this Council or in a separate work, or in both these ways, it will add one more to the many attempts of wise and good men to reduce these principles and their applications to the form of a consistent and harmonious code. As the latest in the order of time, it will be found among the most complete and useful of similar compilations in our language. But valuable as all must admit it to be in its general character, and worthy of high respect as a comprehensive statement, it is quite beyond both the province and the capacity of this Council to determine, with the needful deliberation, the innumerable points of detail of so extensive a work. And it would be neither right nor wise for the Council to seem to attach the authority of its sanction to statements which it has neither formed nor considered in their minute expression and multifarious application. What is rather appropriate for this Council, would be such a statement of the general principles of Congregationalism, and such an exposition of the bearing of those principles upon the civil and religious liberties of the country, upon our free institutions, and upon the growth and character of our American civilization, as would be fitted to commend their principles to the respectful consideration of those that are not Congregationalists, and illustrate the benefits which would accrue to churches and Christians of every name from the general adoption of the simple methods of church government exhibited in the New Testament. If Congregational principles are destined to meet with general prevalence throughout our country, I apprehend that it will not be done by the present slow process of training up Congregational ministers in Congregational seminaries, who shall gather Congregational churches, forcing their way in antagonism to all the other churches, so much as by ministers and churches of other denominations coming by convincement of fact and conscience to the belief of the soundness of our principles, and the safety and good effects of maintaining church life and efficiency with such simple machinery.

The Congregationalists of England and Wales, some of whose churches are older than our own, and whose numbers and efficiency, the learning and orthodoxy of their clergy, and the general intelligence and piety of their members, entitle their views and practices to great weight, and with whom we hold equal fellowship, have published a general statement of their principles of faith and order, which may afford a useful hint in regard to the business before us. It was prepared at the annual meeting of the Congregational Union of England and Wales in 1832, submitted to the ministers and churches of the respective county and district associations, and, having met with general approbation, was unanimously adopted in 1833, "with the distinct understanding that it was not intended as a text, or creed, for subscription." Of this document, the "Principles of Church Order and Discipline" occupy about one page, and this has been found, for more than thirty years, to be a sufficient exposition of the nature of their church order and discipline. The most important parts of this declaration may be given with still greater brevity, omitting such portions as relate to their particular circumstances, and with such changes of phraseology as may give to the principles a greater distinctness of expression.

1. They hold it to be the will of Christ that believers should assemble together to observe religious ordinances, to promote constant edification, to perpetuate and propagate the Christian religion, and to advance the worship and glory of God; and that such society of believers, having these objects in view, is properly a Christian Church.

2. That the New Testament contains, either in the form of express statute or in the example and practice of apostles and apostolical churches, all the principles of order and discipline requisite for constituting and governing the churches; so that human traditions, fathers, and councils, canons and creeds, possess no authority over the faith and practice of Christians, and all questions are to be settled by appeal to the Scriptures.

3. That the New Testament authorizes every Christian church to elect its own officers, to manage all its own affairs, and to stand independent of all authority, saving that only of the Lord Jesus Christ.

4. That the only officers placed by the apostles over individual churches are the bishops or pastors, and the deacons, in numbers according to the necessities of the church; and to these, as the officers of the church, is committed respectively the administration of its spiritual and temporal concerns, subject to the approbation of the church.

5. The power of admission into any Christian church, and rejection from it, is vested in the church itself, and to be exercised only through its officers.

6. That no persons should be received as members of Christian churches but such as make a creditable profession of Christianity, are living according to its precepts, and attest a willingness to be subject to its discipline; and that none should be excluded from the fellowship of the church but such as deny the faith of Christ, violate his laws, or refuse to submit themselves to the discipline which the word of God imposes. . . . . .

10. That it is the duty of Christian churches to hold communion with each other, to entertain an enlarged affection for each other as members of the same body, and to co-operate for the promotion of the Christian cause; but that no church nor union of churches has any right or power to interfere with the faith or discipline of any other church, further than to separate from such as in faith or practice depart from the gospel of Christ.

11. That it is the privilege and duty of every church to call forth such

of its members as may appear to be qualified by the Holy Spirit, to sustain the office of the ministry; and that Christian churches unitedly ought to consider the maintenance of the Christian ministry in an adequate degree of learning, as one of its (*sic*) especial cares; that the cause of the gospel may be both honorably sustained and constantly promoted.

12. That church officers, whether bishops or deacons, should be chosen by the free voice of the church; but that their dedication to the duties of their office should take place with special prayers, and by solemn designation; to which most of the churches add the imposition of hands by those already in office.

13. That the fellowship of every Christian church should be so liberal as to admit to communion in the Lord's Supper all whose faith and godliness are on the whole undoubted, though conscientiously differing in points of minor importance; and that this outward sign of fraternity in Christ should be co-extensive with the fraternity itself, though without involving any compliances which conscience would deem sinful.[1]

In comparing these passages with the document referred to this committee, or any other accredited publication on American Congregationalism, several considerable differences are apparent, both in the presentation and the application of the practical rules drawn from the one fundamental principle which is common to both countries, the perfect autonomy of the local church. For instance, they do not require the strictness of an actual covenant to the being of a church, but take practical union in worship as a sufficient basis of church power and church responsibility, which is all that can be clearly proved from Scripture. They give the binding force of law to no custom or inference not clearly found in Scripture. They give more distinct and express prominency to the tenet that the church is "independent of all authority" but Christ's. On the other hand, their requirement, that all church action should be "through its officers," would not be well received among us, where all our people are accustomed and trained to take an active part in the management of affairs.

A still more important difference appears in their broader presentation of the rights and relations of churches, so as to include, not Congregational, but all "Christian churches," alike in their claims and responsibilities. Has not the time come, and is not this Council the appropriate agent, for American Congregationalists to take this elevated ground, and, looking away beyond the narrow bounds of a denomination, proclaim to all Christian churches our recognition of their right to all the liberties which we enjoy, and our readiness to embrace in our fellowship of the churches all who give evidence that Christ acknowledges them for his?

This view of the possible duty of the Council suggests another reason why the document referred to us is not quite appropriate to the occasion. It is based upon the Cambridge Platform of 1648, and is a transcript of

[1] See Hanbury, Historical Memorials, vol. iii. pp. 599, 600.

much of that famous and valuable record, including as well its antiquated phraseology as its uncouth and lumbering logic. But that platform was an outgrowth of the circumstances in which our Pilgrim Fathers then found themselves, only twenty-eight years after the first settlement at Plymouth; and it is submitted that the circumstances in which this Council convenes call for an utterance as different in tone and aim as our present situation, duties, and responsibilities differ from theirs. If we throw ourselves back into their case, we shall find a synod summoned and authorized by the civil power, embracing the representatives of thirty or forty feeble churches, the only Christian lights of about as many thousand civilized inhabitants, sprinkled through the dense wilderness from Salem to Hartford. They were pressed down with two great anxieties which they looked to the synod to allay. First, their hearts longed, even to bursting, in their solitude and weakness, to feel the fellowship and confidence of the churches of the Old World, so large and so strong. And secondly, they felt that the future welfare and even life of their whole enterprise depended upon the preservation of entire unity among themselves. And their utterances naturally took the forms calculated to meet these their greatest necessities. As the churches of the Old World with whom they were in correspondence were all Calvinistic, and mostly Presbyterian, the synod gave full and emphatic assurance of their own adherence to the Calvinistic formularies, but only "for substance of doctrine;" and were also careful to put such a face on their own Congregational usages as was best fitted to make them appear as good as Presbytery. And on the other point, they made the cords of their unity fully as stringent as could possibly appear consistent with the cardinal principle of the autonomy of the individual church. And from that time to the present, Congregationalism has suffered itself to be shut up in a corner of the country, and has presented itself as on the defensive in the presence of the more organized and governed bodies of Christian churches in this country; and all its utterances have been more or less apologetic in their tone. And in like manner, it has been the great care of our leading minds to cherish the spirit of unity among ourselves; to consolidate our ranks as a sect among sects; to tone down diversities, and repress everything out of the ordinary course; often sacrificing efficiency to uniformity; trying to elevate usage into the rank of law; and to lower the sacred sympathies of fellowship into the character of a code with despotic power. This first meeting in a National Council, of the Congregational churches, naturally calls us to take an account of the results of this whole restrictive policy. And what do we find? Why, just this, that we have kept our churches in unity and order, but have lost our hold upon the people. Whereas, at the beginning of our national existence, Congregationalism embraced the whole population of New England, except in Rhode Island, and a few congregations of Episcopalians and of Baptists elsewhere, at the present time we are in a minority in every county and almost every township of New England. Why should we take measures to spread ourselves over the whole country by pursuing a policy which has not enabled us to keep what we once had firmly in hand ?

The very circumstances under which this Council assembles, by their strong contrast with those of the Cambridge Synod, might well suggest to us that the time has come for a trial of a different policy. The population of the country has increased well-nigh a thousand-fold, and even our Congregational churches have multiplied about a hundred-fold. The glorious issue of a glorious war for the defense of our national existence has placed our nation in the fore-front among nations, and laid upon us a proportionate responsibility in reference to the establishment of Christ's kingdom. The same social convulsion which has thrown down the hitherto impenetrable barrier to the extension of our principles in one half of the country has deprived the great organized and governed bodies of churches of no small share of their strength, both of members and of vivifying energy. Let us now realize our opportunity, raise ourselves up to the hight of our privilege, look beyond the narrow field of denominational aggrandizement, and see what we can do in giving to the great fundamental principles of Congregationalism the influence they deserve, and which the interests both of religion and of the country so perilously need. We do not now need to seek the guidance of Europe, or court its favor; for Europe now comes to us with its explanations and professions, and asks of us the good-will which we are ready to give, and the example which they will be glad to follow. We no longer stand on the defensive in the presence of presbytery, or prelacy, or itinerancy; but are able and bound to stand upon our pure scriptural basis, and let *them* apologize as well as they can for their unscriptural usurpations, and their imposition of unlawful burdens which the churches are unable and ought not to bear. With our order and unity as fully recognized and firmly established as the Union and government of the nation itself; with our doctrinal soundness and harmony in the great principles of Christianity, and freedom and divinity in the modes of presentation; with our learned ministry and numerous colleges and seminaries; with our educated population and the vast wealth diffused among the people; with our benevolent Boards and Societies which have been and are the exemplars of all others; and with the kind favor of God in giving so great prosperity, as well as in pouring out his Spirit upon our congregations, — surely it is not becoming for us to offer any other explanation or apology for our faith or order than to point at their fruits, "known and read of all men." In what remote country or in what benighted corner is it necessary to raise an argument or adduce vouchers to prove that the Congregationalists of the United States of America are a body of evangelical Christians, enlightened and benevolent, and worthy of as much respect and confidence as any other body, of any other name, or in any other country? With abundant reason to be humble before God that our good fruits are so far below our obligations, we stand up before all Christian men, and offer and demand a perfect and equal reciprocity of respect and confidence and coöperation. Neither is it becoming for us, after the scenes we have passed through, and the experience we have had in two hundred and fifty years, to cherish or allow the continuance of distrust and harassing and captious anxiety, lest our freedom of thought, controlled only by the government of opinion, should be unable to preserve the soundness of the faith, or lest our allowed diversity of gifts and methods of action should at length prove incompatible with the Christian unity which is practically necessary for our highest usefulness and honor. It is our duty now to assume the sufficiency of our ecclesiastical system by boldly commending it to others as tried and trustworthy; to commend our way to the confidence of others by writing as if we believed it ourselves; to spend as little time or strength as possible in the indulgence of cavils and fears; and, in the assurance that we are right, to go forward in the most unreserved manner to give the widest influence to our principles, and aim to secure at the earliest period the universal adoption of our ecclesiastical order by all churches of every name and diversity that have a right to be called Christians.

With this view, and without asking of the Council their publication of this report, or any sanction of its statements and reasonings, the undersigned recommend that, besides ordering the publishing of the provisional report, the following resolutions be adopted as embracing the declarations and indicating the policy which this body might appropriately put forth in place of the lengthy document referred to the committee: —

Resolved, 1. That the laws of Christ, which give to the individual or local societies of believers alone the right of self-government, including the election and continuance of their own officers, and the admission and retention of members, and the power of discipline for deliquency, necessarily make such churches alone responsible for the exercise of these important functions, and the discharge of these solemn trusts; and from this responsibility they can neither discharge themselves, nor is any human authority competent to absolve them, with or without their own consent.

2. That the existence of these rights and responsibilities, and all the consequent duties and privileges, does not depend upon any compact, usage, or human recognition, but solely upon the fact that any society is in reality a Church of Christ.

3. That the duty of individuals or other churches to recognize such society as a church of Christ arises from the reasonable evidence they have that Christ himself so regards and treats it.

4. That the relations of fellowship between churches are established by the laws of Christ, and do not depend at all upon any agreement among themselves, any modes or forms in their organization, any name they may assume, as Congregational or any other, or the presence or absence of any peculiarities whatever, but arise and attach inseparably to every Church of Christ in respect to every other Church of Christ, and can neither be remitted by a church, nor dissolved by any human authority, usurped or otherwise.

5. That this Council, representing the body of churches in the United States commonly called Congregational, bound together by strong sympathies and hallowed memories, desire to lay aside all claims, all usages, and all sentiments, inconsistent with these principles, solely because they are not in accordance with Christ's laws; and we hope to shape our future course of action as nearly by this standard as human infirmity will allow.

6. That we cordially invite all other Christian churches in this country, by their love to Christ and regard for the interests of religion among us, to adopt a similar course; to renounce all human authority over them, whether presbyterial, prelatical, or itinerant, which would hinder them from the exercise of these rights, or the maintenance of these principles; so that we may all stand together and act together as one united brotherhood and host of the Lord.

7. That it is the natural right of the churches, as it is of individuals, to form special intimacies, either transitory or permanent, with those to whom they are drawn by similarity of views, objects, and habits; but this should never be allowed to interfere with the duties of justice, kindness, and friendly aid, which they owe alike to all who are entitled to the name of Christian Churches, irrespective of any peculiarities or differences whatever. As surely as they belong to Christ, the things in which they agree are immeasurably greater than the things in which they differ. And we are all one in Christ Jesus, churches as well as persons, and our unity of relation and consequent duties of fellowship with all depend not upon human volition.

JOSHUA LEAVITT.

Rev. Mr. GULLIVER, of Connecticut. Before this report passes from the hands of the committee, by its acceptance, it seems to me necessary that a brief statement should be made of the principles upon which the report of the majority has been founded. The simple effort has been, to enable this Council to do as much as it was possible for them to do, by way of propounding to the churches a system of church discipline. The committee became convinced, at a very early period, that it would be utterly impossible, physically impossible, — I think myself, *morally* impossible, — for this Council to go over the whole of this extended document, covering twenty-seven large and closely-printed pages, and examine every item, every expression, every word, noting all omissions, and making every emendation that might be deemed desirable, and do this work in a manner satisfactory to themselves, or that would be likely to be satisfactory to the churches to which it is to be presented. We all know how much trouble there has been in bringing to perfection that very brief Declaration of Faith, which I understand was adopted this morning, and we can easily understand the very great difficulty there would be in perfecting such a document as this, — so multitudinous in its details, and so extended in its bulk, — by an assembly of this kind. The committee, therefore, gave that up as impossible. They, however, decided that the following things were possible for the Council:

In the first place, that it was possible for this Council, in the opinion of the committee, to form a general estimate of this document; to know whether they are prepared to adopt, and to commend to the churches, the general principles upon which it is founded. The members of this Council are prepared, after having had this document in their hands for nearly a week, to say whether they will adopt and commend the principles contained in it, or whether they wish to discuss, to propound, and to indorse the principles which have been so ably presented in the minority report at this time. We can do as much as this. We can give our general approval to the general principles and scope of the document now before us.

The committee thought the Council could take another step: that it could appoint a committee of twelve (as it has done), which committee, in their name, should give that attention to the subject which the great body of the Council could not possibly give. That committee was announced just a week ago, I believe, and since that time, they have been in almost constant session and labor, hardly taking time for sleep, depriving themselves of the enjoyment of nearly all the public proceedings of this Council; and they have, collectively and individually, gone over that document, article by article, item by item, — some of us going over it repeatedly, and with very great care and deliberation. The Council could, we thought, through such a committee, designate the points which need attention. We did not believe that the Council, through its committee, nor any committee in behalf of the Council, could settle all those points; but we did think the committee could do as much as this: they could cull out the points that needed further attention, and present them to the Council as possibly requiring revision.

The committee thought the Council could do another thing: that it could indicate to the committee such emendations and omissions as individuals should think needful. Accordingly, public invitation was given in the Council, that such emendations should be suggested to the committee. They have been suggested, and they have all been at least substantially embraced in the statement which we have made of those points in this document which we considered worthy of further attention.

Then we thought that, after the Council had done all in these various steps which it could possibly do at its present session, in its present capacity, it might still, for the future, go one step further. It might appoint, by its own selection, and by its own authority, a committee, — a large committee,— a committee that should represent the current leaning of our denomination in regard to this subject of church polity; and that committee, being so appointed by the Council, might complete the work which the Council itself could not do; and that the completion of the work, the perfecting of these minuter details, could be made known to the world under the name and by the authority of the committee thus appointed by the Council.

In this manner, your committee have endeavored to lay out, as distinctly as they could, what was possible in regard to this matter on the part of the Council, and what was impossible in respect to it, and to recommend the adoption of a plan which embraces all that is possible, so far as we are able to form an opinion concerning it, and excludes all that is impossible to you. This is the basis and principle upon which the majority report, which has been made in your hearing, is founded.

Rev. Dr. LEAVITT, of New York. I should be glad to make a single word of explanation. The document referred to the committee is of the nature of a code of practice; so it would be called by lawyers, I think. Having had in my youth some little familiarity with law-books and their use, I have endeavored to imagine to myself a convention of lawyers, delegated in the proportion of one to every ten from all parts of the United States, assembled together to construct a code of practice. Those who are familiar with the matter can imagine for themselves what sort of a book it would be. Books of practice, with which lawyers are familiar, are necessarily the product of individual minds, and there are, perhaps, a score of them in use, more or less, among lawyers. Some of them are small books — duodecimo; some octavo; some two or three volumes octavo; more or less extensive, and of greater or less authority, according to their estimated worth.

Now, we are not wiser than the children of this world. We can not make a code of practice by a convention, nor by a committee, — it is not possible. If it is made at all, it will be the product of one, or, possibly, of two or three minds, or else it will be a hodge-podge that will make its authors a laughing-stock in future generations. I predict that.

Now, sir, a desire is evidently felt to get a code of practice in Congregationalism that shall possess authority, when all we have said here, during all these ten or a dozen days, has been to prove that we have no authority in Congregational churches except that of the Scriptures. I look upon this proposition, — the least injurious that could be made, — to appoint a committee of twenty-five leading and learned men to form that code, as an attempt to clothe the product, which that committee shall bring forth, with authority.

A MEMBER. I rise to a question of order. Is it in order to discuss the merits of this question, before a motion is made?

Rev. Dr. LEAVITT. I don't know that I am going beyond the precedents.

THE MODERATOR. The question is one of acceptance. I believe the speaker is in order.

Rev. Dr. PATTON, of Illinois. I hope he may be heard.

Rev. Mr. QUINT, of Massachusetts. I move that the reports be accepted.

This motion was carried.

Rev. Dr. Eddy, of Massachusetts, moved that the report of the majority be adopted.

Rev. Mr. QUINT, of Massachusetts. While not differing very materially from the conclusions to which the committee have come, I would like to take a little time to explain a few things in regard to the report of the preliminary committee, which I think ought to be understood. I should not presume to do it, in the presence of the venerable man who is so much better able to do it than I am, were it not that, as it is well known that the main statement was written by him, with scarcely a touch by any other hand, he will feel, with his instinctive modesty, a delicacy in saying some things about it, which I can say.

Allusion has been made to the production of a code of practice, &c. I want to say, that the principle on which these documents was prepared was not that of making a new code of practice, or anything of the kind; it was simply to put upon paper, in the clearest way, the principles, and, connected therewith, the present usages of the denomination; not to legislate or make anything new, but simply to record what is the practice of the churches.

It has been said, in substance, that it is well for us to show what we believe in our present system, that people may see it, instead of arguing to establish it; but is it any harm for us to put on paper what that system is? I can not see that it is. There is no attempt here to introduce a novelty; I want that understood. Lest brethren should be frightened with the idea that there is an attempt to force something new on the churches, I will say that there is not a single point in that report that is not believed to be the simple, healthy principle of our churches. The starting-point was this. There are two principles in our polity. One is, the entire completeness of each local church for its own government; and the other is, the principle which relates to all those duties and privileges which grow out of the relation of one church to another. Everything that conforms to those two principles, everything consistent with them, is good Congregationalism; everything opposed to either of them is bad Congregationalism. We believe that in this paper there is nothing that interferes with either of these principles.

Our system allows flexibility; it is adapted to every place where it is needed; but, at the same time, there are fundamental principles which will always keep it, in practice, from going far out of the way. These are the two principles that have been followed in the report of the preliminary committee.

Then the Cambridge Platform has been followed, to a great extent. I do not agree with the feeling manifested by Dr. Leavitt, when he speaks of its "uncouth phraseology." I do not object to the language because there is an antique ring to it; I rather prefer it, — very much as I prefer King James's version of the Bible to Sawyer's translation. [Laughter.] I don't think that a little spice of antiquity will hurt us, any more than I think that the gray hairs, which are quite plenty in this congregation, now injure the appearance of this body. As to those fathers not being qualified to explain what Congregationalism is, because of their leaning to Presbyterianism, I am sorry to say, I differ historically from the brother who has spoken of that matter. Some years before that platform was eunciated, the fathers of Congregationalism were defending Congregationalism against Presbyterianism, not leaning to it. There were one or two ministers who did, but not the bulk. I have books in my own library written against Presbyterianism by those very ministers. They did not attempt to court it.

Then I don't think these men were ignorant, if they did live two hundred years ago; and in reiterating our love for the doctrine and faith they held, and for their polity, I don't believe there is any harm in following that platform. I have felt it was best that this body should assert some such thing; and I felt it the more strongly when I took up the "Independent" of this week, where I found an article from the eloquent brother from Connecticut [Rev. J. P. Gulliver], in which he says:

"Why then, we must still ask, do we need a platform of discipline, emanating from this National Council, and the product of its combined wisdom?

"It is that the polity which now exists may be distinctly *enunciated*, with all the modifications which an experience of more than two centuries can give.

"It is that the polity, which is now so well understood by New England men, may challenge the attention *of all*, and command the respect *which is its due.*

"More than all, it is that the polity which is so abhorrent of the letter which killeth, and so instinct with the spirit which giveth life; the polity which is so tolerant of minute variation, and so flexible in its practical details, may yet live in its *great principles.*"

I could not, if I talked all day, find expressions that come closer to the truth than these.

This body could not consider all the details of the report; therefore they appointed a committee to consider them fully. I am inclined to think that committee was too large. If it had been a committee of three, I think they would have come to a conclusion three or four days ago. We have seen how it operated in regard to the Declaration of Faith. The larger the committee was, the worse we were off, until we got rid of all committees on that subject, and then we settled down on something. If this committee had been smaller, I think they would have agreed. I know, if I was one of a committee of twelve, I should have my pet hobby, and ride him very thoroughly. These large committees remind me of the story of two deacons, who were supposed to be somewhat obstinate. They had a controversy about the location of a school-house, and a great deal of alienation arose. At last, after months of trouble about it, one of the deacons went over very early one morning to his brother deacon's, and said he, "Brother, I haven't slept all night for thinking about this matter. It isn't right to differ so about it; we must agree; and, brother, *you have got to give up, for I can't.*" [Laughter.] That is very much the way with large committees. The result is, that instead of agreeing about details, they see any number of questions rising about this matter and that. I was amazed at the variety of petty things that were brought up by this committee. Nine-tenths of them ought to have been settled in ten minutes. Many of them are perfectly explained in the paper itself. If the original committee had been consulted in regard to them, they could in two minutes have swept off two-thirds of them. When a document has been thoroughly studied for months, and extensive correspondence had, there may be some expressions that would seem natural to those who prepared it, that would not to others; yet a committee not tenacious of mere expressions I think could have shown why they should agree in a little time.

This body, as I said, could not examine all the details, therefore they appointed a committee to examine and report about them, which they have not done. Little matters about *ex parte* councils and the like are objected to. The very statements that are questioned have passed under the eyes, not only of students of these matters, but of legal men, well versed in ecclesiastical history, and familiar with our usages. Then, it is questioned whether a minister should be a member of his own church. That question should not be settled. There are things that we want to remain in doubt. We don't want to be tied down in reference to all these petty details. While I think a minister better be and ought to be a member of his own church, I am not going to complain of any man who thinks it is not best, and say he has got to be, or not be a minister. There is one thing that might offend somebody, and that is to say that a Congregationalist minister ought to be and must be a member of a Congregationalist church, not of some other church. Such a declaration, I can well imagine, might stir up some people. [Laughter.]

There are a great many of these things; and I only want to say, that this formidable list of questions could be swept off very easily in a few moments, and I think they ought to have been swept off. I say this without any disrespect to the committee. It was too large; there was the great difficulty. This difficulty of working together reminds me of a mule team that I saw down near Atlanta last year. There were six of them, and when the two in front were pulling, the other four were not; and when the two in the center pulled, the two in front and behind stood still; and when the two on the pole pulled, the others backed. [Laughter.] That is just the way with large committees; you can't get them to pull together.

Now, this committee recommend that we repeat this error. They recommend that a large committee — a committee of twenty-five — be appointed, to whom this matter shall be referred. Now, if it took them eight days to get through, and you appoint this committee of twenty-five, you may go home; you will never see that document again in this world. [Laughter.] Dr. Leavitt need not be at all alarmed.

Rev. Dr. LEAVITT. I'm not.

Rev. Mr. QUINT. If you appoint a committee at all, appoint a small one. Twenty-five men, scattered all over the country, — when can they get together?

Rev. Prof. BARTLETT, of Illinois. The committee were not divided; they were substantially agreed.

Rev. Mr. QUINT. I take it back. The committee were agreed. Here are twenty-five questions that they couldn't settle, but—the committee were agreed. If you appoint this large committee, you may order them to report to the National Council that will be held one hundred and eighty-five years from now, — it would be of no use to expect it sooner. [Laughter.] If this report is to go out in the way suggested, appoint a committee of five, and they will be able to agree, and accomplish the work.

And I will venture to suggest another thing. I do not like the suggestion in this report, that the chairman of that preliminary committee, learned as he is in this whole matter, shall be deliberately excluded from this committee.

I will close by moving, as an amendment, that instead of a committee of twenty-five, there be a committee of five appointed, to whom this whole matter shall be intrusted.

Rev. Prof. BARTLETT, of Illinois. I wish merely to say a word or two in regard to our course. It is very evident from the speech just made, that if there had been a very small committee, and that a committee of one, and that committee the speaker, the whole thing would have been settled.

It is, perhaps, courteous, Mr. Moderator, for these remarks to be made in reference to "mule teams," and things of that kind; and it may be modest for an individual to speak in this way of a committee who have labored carefully upon this document, and now present the result of their deliberations; — I leave that to the body to judge. Our report is not founded upon disagreement; it is founded upon a careful examination of the document, article by article, conjointly and individually. I do not wish to open the whole subject of the document, with all its contents; but we deliberately concluded that the matters requiring revision were not superficial. We stand in that judgment eleven men, with no parental or personal relation to it. Our deliberate opinion is, that while it is an able document, of great depth and comprehensiveness, — no doubt as able as any three gentlemen in this body could have prepared, — it still contains omissions that are, in the judgment of each of these eleven gentlemen, important omissions; and we have specified those points. We also thought that some of the statements, — important fundamental statements, too, — required careful revision. We found some of them questionable, some loose, some contradictory. As, for example, in the second chapter, where it is stated, in the first paragraph, that "The visible church consists of those who belong to Christ;" declaring them to be, "in the phrase of our ancient platform, 'saints by calling,'" whereas the Cambridge Platform declares that they are those who, "*in charitable discretion* may be accounted saints by calling." And the next article declares the visible saints to be those who "make a credible profession of religion." And so I might go through the document. Our judgment was unanimous, that there were several articles which needed revision. These twenty-five points enumerated include a great many other points, so that they amount to forty or upwards. We found that we could not put these matters into proper shape at this time, and it seemed to us that any document which we could lay before you, which might then be passed, would be passed very unintelligently and unadvisedly. It seemed to me, for one, that that would not be in accordance with our Congregational usage. It seemed to me that a document so voluminous, not to say luminous, — twenty-seven solid pages, — could not be adjusted by us as it ought to be done. There were brethren who thought it could be done, and we entered upon the trial. We labored together five or six days, and then those brethren who were most enthusiastic in the belief that this could be made all right, and polished for acceptance and adoption here, were convinced it could not be done. Some of us felt, too, that, under the circumstances, it was more congregational, after having expressed our view of the substance of doctrine, to refer this document to a committee, carefully selected, who should then put it forth, not as the authoritative utterance of this whole Council, which would be an entire revolution, but as the utterance of able men, carefully selected, deliberately considering, and also deliberately and protractedly consulting together. That was our idea: that these individuals should take time; consider profoundly; go to their friends and invite suggestions; gather all these thoughts, and then come together as a whole, and take a week, or two or three or four weeks; and then, having got the voice of the committee, in conference with these able men as well as others, get the united voice of the churches as far as might be, and then produce a document which should bear all the weight to which it was entitled from the character of the men and the deliberation they had expended upon it, and no more. That, in my judgment, is the true theory of Congregationalism.

Rev. Prof. PARK, of Massachusetts. I have only one word to say. I know that I speak as a "mule;" my only hope is, that I may speak as a respectable one. [Laughter.]

Rev. Dr. PATTON, of Illinois. Does that mean a Calvinistic mule?

Rev. Prof. PARK. I don't know how any one could be more respectable than that. I am glad that the Council have been informed that these questions are not proposed because the committee could not agree upon the topics alluded to. We did not wish to express our disagreement with the preliminary committee in a bold manner, in a *mulish* manner, and therefore we have suggested our opinion on topics to be considered. And one reason why some of the questions were proposed is this: that there are varieties of usage, and great varieties of opinion with regard to some of them. The question which has been alluded to is one: "Should a minister belong to his own church?" There are some councils which will not ordain a minister unless he will promise to belong to the church over which he is pastor; and there are some councils which will not ordain a minister if he *does* belong to the church over which he is pastor. Now, this is an apparent difference of opinion! [Laughter.] It appears to the committee, Mr. Moderator, that where such great diversities of usage exist, they should be stated, and the reasons for one usage and the reasons for another usage be stated, and preference be given to one over another, provided there be any such preference found in the minds of the able men who may be appointed to present this document to the world. They think, sir, that there are many instances in which there are the greatest diversities among the churches, and that those instances may very properly be specified in the document that this Council may issue.

I think, sir, that whatever document is published under the express or implied sanction of this Council will have very great influence. It will have, doubtless, more influence than our opinions as a Council really merit. We are a multitudinous body; we are in Boston during the heat of summer; and it is impossible for us to give that attention to that document which we might give individually, each one in his own study. Still the document will be considered as having the authority of the Council. Now we propose that it be published under the superintendence of a committee appointed by this Council; but yet, this committee will not be considered as having the authority of the Council for all their utterances. We desire it to be a large committee in consequence of the great variety of usage in the country, and in consequence of the great variety of opinions in different parts of the country; and we have supposed that the different parts of the country would consider themselves better represented by this large committee than if we had a small one. Then, sir, there may be, as it appears to the committee, many references to be made and books to be consulted in regard to it, and it is no small labor to impose upon any one man, or any two or three men, to collect these references and properly adjust them. We supposed that the work might be divided and sub-divided, in such a manner that the labor would not be so great but that each one of the committee could easily endure it. We thought, also, that the influence of the document would be greater on our missionary stations, and in courts of law, if it came under the careful supervision of a large committee, who will have the benefit of the suggestions made by all the members of this Council, and by the different churches to whom this document, prepared by the committee, and under consideration by the Council, may be sent, and who may direct to the committee of twenty or twenty-five their hints and suggestions.

Rev. Dr. BACON, of Connecticut. Although I have very little sensibility, parental, in regard to the fate of this document, I think, at the same time, I might be excused for having a great deal; for I may say it has cost me a great deal of labor, and if, instead of bringing it here, I had kept it, the copyright of it, I think, would have been worth $500 to me. At any rate, the labor I have bestowed upon it I might have bestowed in a way to make it worth all of that to me. I might, therefore, perhaps, be excused if I had a little parental sensibility in regard to its fate.

I took my first lesson in Congregationalism, in reality, from the author of this minority report. The whole modern development of Congregationalism, as I conceive, even that which has resulted in the convocation of this assembly, really proceeded from an article which was written by that brother, and published in the "Quarterly Christian Spectator," at New Haven, in the year 1830. Prior to that, I, having been educated at the feet of Gamaliel, (Dr. Woods), at Andover, had no more conception of Congregationalism than other people educated in the same way. [Laughter.] But I have from that time to this been profoundly and increasingly interested in the Congregational church order, in its natural growth and development from its roots, which are its first principles, and in the distinction between the Congregational form and conception of church order and polity, and that of every other sort and name; and the great incumbrance upon Congregationalism, almost from the time when the Cambridge Platform was shaped and laid down, — almost the greatest incumbrance upon its progress has been that the working of it has been confided to the hands of a ministry who either did not understand it or did not believe in it. I go back (not in my personal recollection exactly) to the time when, in Connecticut, the Congregational churches and ministers were called Presbyterian. I think I could take down in the Congregational Library a volume of sermons, or some such work, by the immediate predecessor of Dr. Hawes, who styled himself "Pastor of the North *Presbyterian* Church in Hartford;" and I recollect seeing, a few years ago, a certificate signed by Dr. Nathan Strong, and Dr. Nathan Perkins, of West Hartford, and another D. D., or a person of the same standing, certifying that the churches of Connecticut were Presbyterian. That is where we were a few years ago; and for a long time we have been trying to tinker up Congregationalism by borrowing, — and the process is not ended yet; — borrowing a usage or a principle from Presbyterianism; borrowing some little bit of ritual, perhaps, from Episcopalianism; — borrowing in this direction and borrowing in that, instead of developing our system from its original ideas, in which it has its whole being, as the chicken is in the egg and the oak in the acorn.

I think the work of that Cambridge Synod which produced the platform of 1648 was not adequately represented by the author of the minority report at all. That synod met first in 1646. That, by the way, Mr. Moderator, was the only *National* Synod or Council of the Congregational churches that ever met in America. The subsequent synod — that of 1662 — was a *Massachusetts* Synod, and neither Connecticut nor New Haven was represented in it. Nay, under the influence of John Davenport, my predecessor, the whole colony of New Haven sent a remonstrance against the aim and objects of that memorable body. So the synod of 1680 was a Massachusetts Synod, as much so as that of 1708, which made the Saybrook Platform, was a Connecticut Synod. That Cambridge Synod met first in 1646, continued in session about a fortnight, discussing matters, elaborating, making its preparations, and then, at the end of that time, appointed a committee to draw up a platform. They met again in 1647, but remained in session only a very short time, the prevalence of an epidemic disease throughout New England breaking up the synod, — an epidemic of which, that very season, Thomas Hooker died at Hartford. Then it met a third time in 1648, and after sitting as long as we have now, it resulted in that memorable and most important document, the Cambridge Platform. The same synod, at the same time, declared its assent to the substance of doctrine contained in the Westminster Confession. It was not with the idea of conciliating Presbyterianism that that synod was called, I apprehend. The Congregational element was just beginning to be developed.

At this point, the hour of adjournment (6½) having arrived, Dr. Bacon yielded the floor, and after singing the Doxology, the Council adjourned.

TENTH DAY, SATURDAY, JUNE 24.

The Council met at 9 o'clock, and prayer was offered by the Moderator.

The minutes were read, and, some corrections having been made, approved.

Rev. Mr. Quint, from the Business Committee, reported the order of business for the day, with a recommendation that speeches be limited to eight minutes. This was amended by reducing the time to five minutes, and the report adopted.

Rev. Dr. THOMPSON, of New York. Yesterday, sir, the duty of replying to that admirable document from Boston, England, was intrusted to yourself, with the Assistant Moderators; and now, in the name of us all, I beg to move that the document be referred, instead, to a committee of pastors in this city, in order that the local references from old Boston to new Boston may be properly considered. I would suggest the names of Dr. Blagden, Dr. Kirk, and the Scribe, Mr. Dexter, who will give an official signature for the body.

This motion was carried.

Dr. Sweetser, chairman of the committee on Ministerial Education, presented a resolution, recommending that the resolution submitted to them in reference to collegiate and theological institutions at the West be referred to a special committee. Adopted.

CHURCH POLITY.

Rev. Mr. GULLIVER, of Connecticut (Dr. Bacon yielding the floor). There are two or three points that need to be brought up here, and I think they will very much facilitate the business we have now before us. A paper was referred to this committee, by vote of the Council, which never came before the committee, in reference to the preparation of a Catechism; and the committee desire, so far as I have been able to see them, — and I know it will be their unanimous desire, — to amend their report by inserting that as one of the items, if there is a general assent thereto.

There is another point. The committee, in the report which was presented to them yesterday afternoon by their sub-committee, found a provision that Dr. Bacon and Mr. Quint should constitute a joint committee with the committee of twenty-five, having certain powers superior to that committee. That proposition was considered very objectionable, and the result was, that in the haste of our deliberations, at the close, they appear to have been cut off from that committee entirely. I am not able to speak now in the name of the committee, but I can as an individual member of that committee, with the approbation of all whom I have been able to see, make this suggestion, which I do in the form of an amendment to the proposition to appoint a committee of twenty-five, — that this Council re-appoint the committee previously appointed by the meeting in New York, — Dr. Bacon, Mr. Quint, and Dr. Storrs, — and that that committee be enlarged by the addition of those members.

Another point. Brother Quint [absent in committee] wishes me to say that, upon explanations, he has changed his view with regard to the number of which this committee should consist, and desires me to withdraw, in his name, the amendment he proposed. That brings us back to the original proposition, that a committee of twenty-five be appointed, and the amendment to that, namely, that the original committee be re-appointed and added to the committee of twenty-five, making twenty-eight in all. I am prepared to give reasons, which I think will be entirely satisfactory to this Council, as they have been to brother Quint, why there should be a committee of this size.

Rev. Mr. Burr, of Connecticut. I would inquire whether it is intended that Dr. Bacon shall be chairman of that committee?

Rev. Mr. Gulliver. That follows, necessarily.

Rev. Prof. Bartlett, of Illinois. I would inquire whether that is a correct statement, — whether it is not always in the power of a committee to choose its own chairman?

Rev. Mr. Gulliver. That is the way it struck my mind; that is the expectation.

The Moderator. In reply to Prof. Bartlett, I will say, that I understand that it is competent for any committee to appoint its own chairman, unless the body appointing that committee designate the chairman.

Rev. Dr. Bacon, of Connecticut. I am altogether at a loss. I find a rule that every speaker shall be limited to five minutes, and I don't see that I can do any good whatever by speaking five minutes, or help anybody to a conclusion.

Rev. Dr. Dutton, of Connecticut. I move that that rule be suspended in the case of Dr. Bacon, who was chairman of the committee and wrote the report, and certainly has a right to explain it.

This motion was passed.

Rev. Dr. Bacon. Gratefully acknowledging the kindness of the Council toward me, I desire to be interrupted if my remarks are protracted beyond any reasonable limit, as there is danger that they will be, because I can not judge as well as the brethren can as to the amount of what I say nor the pertinency of it.

I was speaking, last evening, about the Cambridge Platform — the origin of it and the meaning of it; and I have taken the liberty to bring here this morning the record of the Massachusetts Colonial Government, which called that synod; and the intention with which that synod was assembled is upon the record, and will be suggestive to us in relation to the business now before us. It reads thus:

"The right form of church government and discipline being a good part of the kingdom of Christ upon earth, the settling and establishing thereof by the joint and public agreement and consent of churches, and by the sanction of civil authority, must needs greatly conduce to the honor and glory of our Lord Jesus Christ, and to the settling and safety of church and commonwealth where such a duty is duly attended and performed; and inasmuch as times of public peace, which by the mercy of God are vouchsafed to these plantations (but how long the same may continue we do not know), are much more commodious for the effecting of such a work than these troublesome times of war and of public disturbances thereby, as the example of our dear native country doth witness at this day, where, by reason of the public occasion and troubles of the state, the reformation of religion and the establishing of the same is greatly retarded, and at the best can not be perfected without much difficulty and danger; and whereas divers of our Christian countrymen and friends in England, both of the ministry and others, considering the state of things in this country in regard of peace and otherwise, have sundry times, out of their brotherly faithfulness, love, and care of our well-doing, earnestly by letters from thence solicited and called upon us that we would not neglect the opportunity which God hath put into our hands for the effecting of so glorious and good a work as is mentioned, whose advertisements are not to be passed over without due regard had thereunto, and considering withal that through want of the things here spoken of, some differences of opinion and practice of one church from another do already appear amongst us, and others, if not timely prevented, are like speedily to ensue, and this not only in lesser things, but even in points of no small consequence, and very material, to instance" — then follow some particulars.

"Therefore, for the further healing and preventing of the further growth of the said differences, and upon the other grounds, and for the other ends aforementioned, and although this Court make no question of their lawful power by the Word of God to assemble the churches, or their messengers, upon occasion of counsel for anything which may concern the practice of the churches, yet because all members of the churches, though godly and faithful, are not yet clearly satisfied, it is therefore thought expedient for the present occasion not to make use of that power, but rather hereby declare it to be the desire of this present General Court, that there be a public assembly of the elders and other messengers of the several churches within this jurisdiction, who may come together and meet at Cambridge upon the first day of September now next ensuing," &c. (Records of the Colony of Massachusetts Bay, vol. iii. pp. 70–72.)

Afterward, there is a section inviting the plantations under the jurisdiction of Plymouth, Connecticut, and New Haven, to send there the leaders and messengers of their churches also.

It appears plainly enough from what I have just read, that one object which the framers of the Cambridge Platform had in view was to give light and help to their friends in England, who were then contending against the Scotchmen or Presbyterians — against the attempt to bring the "Solemn League and Covenant" into England, and by the force of that "Solemn League and Covenant," to establish what was called a "covenanted uniformity" of doctrine and of discipline throughout the three kingdoms, England, Wales, and Scotland. That "covenanted uniformity" is sought for, quarreled for, and suffered for to this day. Congregationalism was spoken of, in old England, as "the way of the New England brethren." It was understood that there was a way they had in Scotland, which they had borrowed from Geneva and the continent, and there was another way, which the brethren who had moved from the Old World into the New, for the purpose of practicing, as they expressed it, "the positive part of church reformation," had struck out here in the wilderness; and it was for the sake of setting out that way, in a clear light, not only for themselves, but also for their friends in England, that this Cambridge Synod or National Council was called. And I may say here, that the whole history of the Congregationalism of England, and the present status of it, as compared with the history and present status of the Congregationalism of New England, have not been such as to induce me to seek, as yet, for the model of Congregationalism in old England, as the report of the minority of the committee seems inclined to do. Our Congregationalism is not Brownism. Brownism is older than Congregationalism, in one sense; older, except as Congregationalism is as old as the apostles. Brownism was the great step forward in the discussions and inquiries which resulted in that boon that was given to our fathers, — free Congregationalism; and Brownism is essentially the scheme that is set before us in the report of the minority as that which will bring in the millennium straightway. Brown hit upon a capital idea, — the idea of the duty of church reformation, — to be practiced by everybody, without waiting for government. There was the point of division between the "Separatists," or "Brownists," as they were called, indiscriminately, and the Puritans. The Puritans were waiting and waiting for the government to reform the church. That was their position. The "Separatists" took up Brown's principle, namely, that every man was to reform for himself, and that the State had nothing to do with it. In that principle lies the germ of Congregationalism, and the germ of all our liberty to-day, civil and religious, — in the idea that every man was to practice for himself the reformation of the church, — in the idea of the freedom of the church, not by asking leave of Cæsar or of Elizabeth, but by asking leave only of the Lord Jesus Christ; and that is where we stand.

But it is not given to any one man to discover the whole continent of truth. Columbus discovered the West India Islands, and we call him the discoverer of America, — and he was buried in Cuba. It is one of his followers who is said to have discovered the continent which bears his name. Brown only discovered an outlying island, as it were; a continent lies beyond it, and we acquired the continent. I have no notion, for one, of going back, with the author of that minority report, to the little island where Brown was. [Applause.]

Now, not to take up too much time, let me suggest, briefly, this: The report has in it, I may say, three leading ideas or principles, and I want a distinct expression of the Council as to the correctness of those three leading principles. The first is the principle of the autonomy of every particular church or worshiping assembly of Christians, permanently embodied and organized; that there is no church other than the parochial Congregational church, organized for government; that no church censure, or admonition, or excommunication, no ordination of a minister, no inauguration or deposition of church officers, can be had by any other authority than that of the particular or local church. That is the first principle, out of which our whole moral system proceeds; but that is not the only principle. That is the principle of the minority report, in reality; there is a word or two said of fellowship.

The next great principle is the principle of the communion of churches one with another; and the development of that principle, added to the development of the first, makes Congregationalism. And there lies the difference between the Congregationalism of New England and the Congregationalism of Old England — in the development or application of the principle of the union of churches one with another. Do we hold that principle? The brethren in England hold it vaguely, generally, obscurely, in a sense, as it is held forth vaguely, obscurely, indefinitely, and in a manner incapable of application, in the report of the minority. It is the definiteness with which we hold that principle which makes us one body, and which gives us power to recognise one another, and to act together as a common body, in mutual confidence. In the Cambridge platform, that principle of the common union of churches one with another is developed theoretically. When that synod met, less than twenty years from the landing at Charlestown, the question of the communion of churches one with another was the great theoretical question before them, the great question of the future, the great question for England as well as for themselves, and they developed that principle as well as they could in their one chapter on "The Communion of Churches one with another." In this new draft which has been submitted to the Council, that chapter is extended into one distinct part or division of the entire scheme, the parts being — first, some few general principles and definitions; second, the autonomy of the particular or local church; thirdly, the communion of churches one with another, and their mutual responsibility. First, *the theory*, which is essentially the same with that of the Cambridge platform; second, *the development of the theory*, which gives occasion (1.) for a chapter on Councils, (2.) a chapter on Conferences, and (3.) a chapter on National Councils.

Now, I want to secure the attention of the brethren, before we take a vote upon the subject, to this question : Do we believe in the importance of the communion of the churches one with another, as that idea has been developed and applied in the experience of the two hundred and seventeen years that have elapsed since the Cambridge platform was formed ? Do we believe in it ? I do, for one ; and I believe in it so firmly that I will have nothing to do with any body or (as the word is here) denomination, — I do not like the word, but I use it because it seems to be intelligible, — I will have nothing to do with any denomination of Congregationalists in which that principle of the communion of churches one with another, and their responsibility to give account of their proceedings one to another, in all matters of common interest, is not recognized and acknowledged. [Applause.]

Now how do our brethren in England ordain their ministers ? According to my understanding of it, a church elects its pastor and ordains him, and it is nobody's business who he is or what he is. According to our principle, the church elects its pastor and ordains him, and it is the business of all the churches who he is and what he is ; and the church that ordains him is responsible to all the churches to give an account whom it is that they elect to that office, and of his ordination — what he is, what theology he holds, what faith, what principles of order, — what qualifications he has by nature, by education, and by the grace of God for the performance of that duty ; and if a church, falling back on its reserved rights, its extreme powers, says : "We will have nothing to do with other churches, we will elect whom we please to be our minister, and we will turn him away when we please," we say, "Very well, only you don't ride in our troop, that 's all." [Applause.]

So if the Mt. Vernon Church excommunicates a man, and the Old South Church takes that man into its communion the next Sabbath, there is a breach of fellowship between those two churches. There is no remedy or redress in such cases among our English brethren, as I understand their system — no help ; but these churches must stand frowning over one against the other, and stand in perpetual opposition and hostility until Time comes to heal the wound. Our system is otherwise. We say, that if a man is excommunicated from this church, he shall not be received into any other church in fellowship with this, without the intervention of a council to examine the case, and to give advice to this church, and to give advice to the person who has been excommunicated ; and if this church refuses to follow the advice, then the person has his redress, and may be received into the Old South Church, or any other church that sees fit to receive him — not because the council has put him in there, but because the council has examined into the case, and is of opinion that the fellowship of the churches will not be broken by one of them receiving that man to communion. . . . .

I refer to these things for the sake of showing what our system is. We have no power over a particular church but the power of the church of Christ and the authority of the Scriptures ; and then these individual churches, all responsible to Christ alone, all deriving their powers directly from Christ, recognising the obligations of good neighborhood and mutual fellowship, and recognising their duty, whenever called upon in an orderly way, to give an account of any of their proceedings to each other.

I have been a member, in my life-time, I believe, of three *ex parte* councils. One was in this wise. A man had been expelled from a church in Brooklyn, New York. He thought he was unjustly and unscripturally dealt with, and had a long argument to show it. He asked the church to unite with him in calling a council, and the church said the case was plain enough, they didn't want any help in it, and they wouldn't call a council. He called an *ex parte* council, and the church was courteous enough to appear before us, and explain its proceedings. It turned out that the man was a very troublesome church member; he was always making motions; he didn't like the minister, and was very troublesome indeed, — and if I had been the minister I should have wanted to get rid of him very much. At last the church got out of patience with him, and a motion was made that he be excommunicated, and that he have ten minutes to reply to that motion [Laughter]; so that he was excommunicated after the fashion of a drum-head court-martial. Was that right? According to the report of the minority of this committee, the man would have had no redress whatever, and it would have been no interruption of order, no violation of any comity to a brother, for that church to have voted in that way.

Another instance of an *ex parte* council was in this wise. A church (there are a good many members here who will recollect the case I now refer to), had got into trouble — lots of it — and had been wrangling, and going like a machine when one of the principal wheels is broken; and at last, by calling in all the women and children to vote, they voted out just about a moiety of the members of the church, without trial, if I recollect the story right; but whether it is right or wrong, it is good enough for an illustration. Then they said, "We are independent, and don't want any council about this; we are an independent church, and wont have any council." Now, I say, if a church says it is independent, and wont have any counsel, then it don't belong to us — we have nothing to do with it [Applause]; and wherever that church is, whether it be in Boston, in New York, in Chicago, or in San Francisco, it don't belong to what we call our denomination. . . . .

Then we had another instance quite recently, in the place where I live, where there was a similar division of a church, and the majority, which was constituted by calling in the women and children to vote, having settled a minister in defiance of the communion of the churches, who assumed to call himself pastor of the church and all that kind of thing, refused to recognize the right of the claim to be heard by a majority of the brethren on the ground. Well, the council decided — and it was a large council, called from all parts of the State — that a church which proceeded in that manner and fashion was not, in the common acceptation of the word, a Congregational church, and the churches of Connecticut have followed the advice of that council, so far as I know, without a dissenting voice. That church claimed to be an independent church, and so it was; but independency, in that sense, is not Congregationalism.

There is one point more in the scheme of discipline, of order and fellowship, which is laid down in the report which was submitted to this body; namely, that there is recognised among us a ministry, a professional ministry, consisting of men devoted and consecrated by ordination to the work of preaching the gospel. That is not in the Cambridge Platform. It was not really in the theory of the founders of the New England churches, for they did not see, in all respects, the working and application of their own principles. They held to lay preaching — what they called "prophesying,"— but they did not see how to recognise any man as a minister of the gospel who was not an officer of the church. That distinction is clearly made in the document under consideration. A man may be a minister of the gospel who has received the right-hand of fellowship. He may be employed in the work of the ministry in foreign missions. Eliot, the apostle to the Indians, was pastor of a church over here in Roxbury as long as he lived. The churches at that time had no idea that a man could really be an ordained missionary, a missionary having the powers of a minister of the church, unless he was an officer in the church.

We have outgrown that, and it is an inevitable necessity for us to outgrow it. We have none of the fear which they had, that a ministry would be a hierarchy. Our churches have grown to age, and can take care of themselves. There is no danger of a hierarchy; and the fact that Dr. Leavitt is a minister of the gospel gives him no power or jurisdiction in the church of which he is a member, but that which belongs to his judgment, intelligence, learning, and personal character; and so of any other minister. Dr. Anderson here, is a minister, and a member of a church, but he is an officer in no church, and has no more power in the church of which he is a member than any other member. That is the distinction which is clearly laid down and insisted upon in the document under consideration.

Now, are the members of this body, as a body, ready to adopt these principles: first, that a church is a church, and there is no other; no church but a congregation of believers, ordinarily consisting of those who can meet for worship in one place, and whose affairs are managed by one administration; no church government including a great many congregations, governed by a representative assembly; no church governed by a synod; no church governed by a prelate, and stretching over a diocese; no national or ecumenical church, governed by a pope or by a council; but only the local church? Are we ready for that? Are we ready for this — that the local church has no power but what it has a warrant for from Christ? — that no church has a right to enact any rules or by-laws which are inconsistent with or additional to the New Testament? If we are not, we can not go on. If we insist that the local church may make itself something besides a church of Christ, if we insist that it can undertake to run an india-rubber factory, for example, or that it may undertake to mine and "strike ile" [Laughter], or anything of that kind, then, so far forth, it ceases to be a church; and if it assumes to be anything other than a New Testament church of Christ, it is guilty of usurpation over its members.

That is the first great principle: that a church is a *church*, and derives its power and authority from Christ, — not from a voluntary compact, — mind that! Not that a certain number of men may come together and say, "We will be a church, and we will be a political organization, too; we will be a church, and we will build a railroad at the same time; we will be a church, and we will be something else." That kind of voluntary compact does not make a church. A church is made simply by the members of it agreeing — expressly or impliedly agreeing — to walk together in one assembly, under the rules of the New Testament, trusting in Christ, doing his work together, helping one another, administering the Word and the sacraments. We hold that. Do we also hold the communion of churches?

Do we also recognize a ministry — a ministry with no powers, no prerogatives, no jurisdiction or authority over the churches? If we do, then we have got the essential things of the platform before us; and I hope that the Council will so far adopt the platform (if I may call it so) that has been submitted here, as to be understood distinctly as sanctioning these three principles. If so, the matters of detail will be easily adjusted.

I will say here, that some of the things which seem to have stumbled the committee are misprints, — clerical or typographical mistakes. For example: there is a word left out in the first part of chap. i. part 2. "The visible church consists of those who belong to Christ," &c. It should read, "The visible church consists of those who *visibly* belong to Christ." That was commented on yesterday, and very properly. It is simply a case of omission. I mention this as an illustration of similar errors which have crept into the report that lies before you; and for that reason alone, even if it were adopted entire, and without qualification, it ought to be referred to some such committee as is here proposed, to be perfected. — I ask pardon for having spoken so long.

Rev. Mr. ALLEN, of Massachusetts. I wish an explanation from Dr. Bacon himself, lest we should misunderstand him on an important matter; and that is, in relation to the position of unsettled ministers. Are they regarded by the principle laid down by Dr. Bacon as still ministers of the gospel, or as brethren only? The ministers don't all know where they belong. This body, according to the call, was to be composed of pastors and delegates from the churches, — meaning those not pastors. Now, the question has risen repeatedly in this body, whether ministers were authorized to be chosen under that call.

Rev. Dr. BACON. Certainly.

Rev. Mr. ALLEN. If that is admitted, that is all.

Rev. Dr. BEECHER, of Illinois. There are special reasons why I made an effort to obtain the floor; I will state what those reasons are.

Before the National Council had been called, the General Association of the State of Illinois put in operation a train of measures designed to produce or procure a work on Congregationalism, adapted to the wants of the West, — adapted to the field in which they were laborers. I was chairman of the committee the first year, and made a report to the meeting at Quincy, which report was accepted. In that report, I laid before them the outline of two works, — one a large work, the other a manual based upon the large work. Both were adopted by the General Association, and I was requested to finish the large work on my own responsibility, and to finish the manual and report it to them. I reported the manual to the General Association of Illinois, at their meeting at Peoria, just before the meeting of this Council. The report was accepted and adopted, but, at my suggestion and request, was recommitted, in order that I might attend the meeting of the National Council, and hear what should be presented there. A proposition was also made to instruct the representatives of that association to request this body to have the manual, which had been laid before the Association, read before this Council. To this I objected, inasmuch as there was a course inaugurated, and I felt, from the ability of the committee that had been appointed, that it would be thoroughly carried out, and I preferred not to seem to interfere or to commingle myself with that movement. I am now called upon to vote with regard to the proposition that is before you; and in order that I may justify the vote which I feel it is important to have passed in this assembly, I ask the liberty of stating, in brief, what it was that the General Association of Illinois instructed me to do, and what, in the opinion of the Association, it is important should be done. A part of that work would be accomplished by that report; a part would not be accomplished. To meet the wants of Congregationalism at the West, which, after a residence there of twenty-four years, I think I understand, it is important that certain things should be done, and they should be done in a way in which they would not be likely to be done by an individual who has grown up in the midst of the Congregationalism of Massachusetts and Connecticut, and has not resided at the West. As the new fields — missionary fields — are specially important at this time, so it is specially important that Congregationalism shall be contemplated in reference to aggressive movements; or, if not aggressive, that they shall be movements in which the system shall be so presented as that it shall be best adapted to carry the convictions of those to whom the document shall be presented.

The five minutes having expired, on motion of Dr. Patton, the Council voted to allow Dr. Beecher fifteen minutes more, in view of the relations sustained by him to the whole subject at the West.

Rev. Dr. BEECHER resumed: In order, then, that I may distinctly bring before this body those things which it seemed important to the General Association of our State should be done, I will in the first place read an outline of the large book I reported to them, and upon the basis of which outline the manual was prepared, which was reported at the last meeting of the Association. After having, in the first place, given a general view of the works on Congregationalism which have authority among us, both in England and in this country, coming down as late as the correspondence and works by Brother Dexter and by Brother Quint, and others who have written in the "Congregational Quarterly" (covering the ground up to that date), I proceeded:

"There is reason to believe that the providence of God demands, and has prepared the way for, a more complete and comprehensive work than now exists, not, indeed, for the introduction of novel speculations or theories, but to unite what the spirit and providence of God have developed in the wide range of discussion and argument of which an outline has been given.

"Your committee will give an outline of what such a work ought to contain, and make suggestions as to its preparation. It should contain,

"1. A statement of the teaching of Scripture as to the principles and facts of the original ecclesiastical organization and government of the churches, free from modern additions and extensions, confirmed by authorities and concessions; and also a tracing of the recognition of these facts and principles by history into the first and second centuries. These scriptural facts and principles are too often commingled with subsequent ideas and practices; as, for instance, councils, mutual and *ex parte*. This scriptural portion should be wrought out with care, discrimination, and impartiality.

"2. An investigation of the scriptural philosophy of Congregationalism, so developed. By this is meant a view of its end, relations, adaptations, and place in the system which God is administering in this world, taken as a whole, and considered in the light of his Word. Here different views have been taken. The fathers of modern Congregational development took the ground of a *jure divino* system of Congregationalism. Others in modern times have called all other systems organizations of Satan. From this, some recoil to the idea that the scriptural facts involve no enjoined system, but contrarywise; that there is a providential room for diverse modes of organization, in a pliant indefiniteness as to outward organization. The question is, was not the divine original adoption of the Congregational, that is, of the anti-hierarchal, system, based on reasons common to all ages, and is it not essential to the full development of the kingdom of God, which is foretold? If it is, then this adaptation and its reasons should be developed and set forth as a means of giving tone to the feelings of the professors and defenders of the system, and of securing that final result.

"3. A statement of the modern development of Congregational principles, including what is not taught by express command or example in the Bible, but what is introduced on the ground of the light of reason, viewed as a divine revelation; for the early fathers of the system agreed in the propriety and necessity of an appeal to this standard, as well as to scriptural principles, commands, and examples. Punchard and others state the case too strongly of an appeal to the Bible alone. Upham and others, especially the fathers, take the true ground of an appeal to the light of nature, as the voice of God.

"This statement should include two parts: 1. The local church, viewed individually, as to its materials, formation, powers, and organizations. 2. The relations of Congregational churches, taken in the aggregate, to each other on the principles of church fellowship. Here will be found to be the widest field for an appeal to the light of nature.

"4. A development of the system in action, that is, a description of actual Congregational usages and precedents as to the mode of organizing churches, receiving or dismissing members, electing and ordaining officers, administering discipline, calling and conducting councils. Of this kind are Cotton's Way of the Churches of New England; Mather's Ratio Disciplinæ; most of Upham's work by the same name; the fourth part of Punchard's work; the third part of Crowell's; and of other works a part.

"5. A historical outline of the modern revival and development of the system, with a reference to the causes affecting it during this progress, both in England and America, and the errors for a time held and at length eliminated. Designed also to expose the dangers to be guarded against in its use, in the light of experience, and to give cautions against its perversions or corruptions, and suggestions as to what should be done to perfect its development and action."

I attach very great importance to this point. The subject of councils in Massachusetts has been considered in a very able article, which is to appear in the July number of the "Boston Review," by the Hon. Woodbury Davis, a lawyer, and is entitled, "Congregational Polity, Usages, and Law." He introduces the decisions of civil courts, and endeavors to make out what he calls Congregational usage as an existing fact. But there are no principles stated by which Congregational usage, as an existing fact, can be judged of, and by which the question can be answered, "Is that usage right or wrong?" "Ought that usage to be abolished or not?" Existing usage may tend to evil, and there is need of principles to know whether it does tend to evil or not; and in Massachusetts, in particular, it is a matter of very great moment. Any one who knows anything in regard to the original introduction of councils,— of which the most satisfactory account I know of is given in Palfrey's "History of New England,"—knows that they were introduced under peculiar circumstances, and that there were then peculiar influences operating upon councils. The Constitution of the Civil State of Massachusetts was such, at that time, that none were voters but those who were members of the church. The formation of a church was then, of necessity, the introduction of so many voters into the civil State. No church could be formed that did not affect the question of voting; and therefore it was ordered in the civil State, that certain regulations should be introduced with regard to councils in the formation of churches; and the whole development of Councils was affected by that relation to the civil State. It is incumbent upon us to be capable of judging with regard to this development, and therefore we need a calm historical analysis of the origin and progress of the system, and the causes that were operating at the time of its development, while it took the form in which it actually revealed itself, and we shall never understand anything of New England Congregationalism as we ought until we do this.

I would state, still further, that I have been called, in Massachusetts especially, to act on *ex parte* councils. One *ex parte* council occupied me for months, in laborious investigations. The council met and adjourned and a report was made out, and that report was afterward accepted. The main object of that council was to correct certain modes of abusing Congregational councils, or abusing the interior structure of the Congregational church — of abusing the influence of ministers who had been upon a council subsequently to that council. I might enumerate five or six modes which have been practically adopted in the churches of Massachusetts of perverting and abusing the system of Congregationalism; and I say deliberately, at this time, from my knowledge of it, that the danger in Massachusetts is, of tying up the churches and reducing them to bondage under the name of fellowship, — which is a sacred name, a holy name[Applause], — so that they shall be beneath a power indefinite, which Presbyterianism is not, and yet doing the very things which Presbyterianism does — doing them without its guards, doing them without its definiteness.

This historical outline, therefore, of the modern revival and development of the system, with reference to the causes affecting it during its progress, and the errors for a time held, and at length eliminated, is of fundamental importance at this moment, and in this attempt to extend the Congregational system and augment its power, that we may have it free from local influences, free, if I may say so, from New Englandism, — for New England, in its past history, you know, was a commingling of church and state, and it has not been until very lately that New England has worked itself clear, and we are bound to work Congregationalism clear from all the corrupting influences that have come into it from this or any other source.

The last point is a statement of the advantages of Congregationalism, in itself, and in comparison with other systems, and answers objections; and for the practical purpose of spreading Congregationalism, this is of very great moment. A mere naked statement of what Congregationalism is, you may find in many works, but if we are intending, as a body, to carry out this movement to spread Congregationalism, we must put it in a form to spread.

The manual reported to the General Association of Illinois is a carrying out in part of the points in this outline, and it was my purpose, according to the recommendation of the General Association, to prepare a larger work, upon my own responsibility, on this general plan.

I would say now, in applying these statements, that I myself could not consistently vote for the report of Dr. Bacon, as though it were sufficient to accomplish all that for which I feel that such a work ought to be prepared. I feel that the manual of Dr. Bacon is a very able and valuable one, and that it does a given work well, but not all that is required at this time. If the powers of the committee shall be so construed as to include the right to introduce whatever in their judgment the present exigency demands, I shall cordially vote for the appointment of the committee, and for the reference of Dr. Bacon's manual to them.

Rev. Dr. PATTON, of Illinois. *Mr. Moderator*, — The brethren at the West, as is well known, feel a special interest in this topic; and the interest they feel in it is not, as I suppose, because they have any quarrel with New England, or any antagonism with New England, — nothing of that sort, — but because they wish to have the polity which prevails in New England more thoroughly known, and understood, and practiced at the West. I think that is the general feeling of the brethren at the West. We know the value of this polity. We love it, because, when we lived at the East, we lived under it. We have desired to take it with us in removing out to the West, and we desire to have it presented to the Western mind as free as possible from all objections. Now, our difficulties are these. In the first place there are multitudes who come from the East to the West who do not understand their own polity, — and that is not strange when we find facts coming to our notice, in Connecticut and Massachusetts, such as these. When I was a lad, I used to go to Stonington sometimes to recreate. There is a Congregational church in that place, but the people all supposed they had a *Presbyterian* church, and called it so. They talked about the *Presbyterian* minister, and I dare say they talk so there still. I had occasion, shortly after I was settled in Hartford, to exchange with a good brother in West Hartford. I went into the pulpit and took down the Bible, and saw this inscription upon it: "Presented to the West *Presbyterian* Church of Hartford," by so-and-so. Why, the brethren in Connecticut didn't know but what they were Presbyterians, a few years ago, and some of them haven't found out to the contrary yet, we have reason to fear. [Laughter and applause.]

Now, sir, when material of this kind floats out West, you can easily see why it does not always go into Congregational churches, and why it very naturally deposits itself in Presbyterian churches. We think it desirable, therefore, that there should emanate from this body something that should be for the instruction of the East as well as of the West. It is not merely a boon which we desire for our own people, but we desire that it may go out and draw the attention of the brethren, ministers, and laymen at the East, to the Congregational polity and its advantages, in order that they may be prepared intelligently to adopt it when they remove to the West; and of course still more do we need such a manual for the instruction of the churches at the West, composed of very heterogeneous materials, and increasingly so, because we stand in great favor at the West. Inquire of almost any denomination in the West, and they will tell you that, next to their own, they love the Congregational denomination, and that, if they were to make a change, — and some of them intimate that perhaps they will, — the change would be into Congregationalism. That is exceedingly common testimony.

Now, sir, many are coming to us from all quarters in the laity and the ministry, and they are ignorant of our usages, and, to some extent of our principles, especially of the great second principle enunciated by Dr. Bacon, that of the communion of churches. I have been battling, ever since I have been at the West, this principle of introducing men as acting ministers of churches, who live on, year after year, without any ordination, as a violation of one of the fundamental principles of Congregationalism. It is pure Independency. The brethren in Chicago generally share these views, and they desire that some document shall go out to instruct our brethren throughout the West as to the true doctrine of Congregationalism on this point.

Prof. E. A. LAWRENCE, D. D., of Connecticut. I think, Mr. Moderator, in view of the lucid explanation, — I may say, exhibition, — which has been given us this morning of our polity, from the chairman of the committee, there are a good many who feel, as is suggested by my brother on the left, that we are likely to "save our *Bacon*," and that we must have our Bacon upon the committee to help save it. [Laughter.]

The principles which have been proclaimed, namely, — first, of a church distinct from Presbyterianism, from Episcopacy, from Romanism, is a fundamental principle; the second principle, the community of churches, is equally fundamental. The two distinguish between what is confounded by all the other theories. They give us the church and the churches; they give us independency and fellowship; they give us a ministry and they give us pastors; and from these principles we can never depart and maintain our denominational integrity. We can never secede from them, any more than from Plymouth Rock, where we stood a day or two since. Our whole history is based on those principles; our councils are based on them; our experiences are identified with them. We can never blot out Bunker Hill. We can take down that mouument, if you please, but we cannot erase Bunker Hill. We can never blot from our recent history the names of Gettysburg and Richmond, though those places themselves might be destroyed; they are wrought into our language. So these principles, and the history they throw light upon, have become part of our existence as a denomination. I therefore wish to indorse the proposition that the old committee be placed upon this new one.

Rev. Dr. ELDRIDGE, of Connecticut. In the interesting speech, Mr. Moderator, made last evening by Mr. Quint, our attention was drawn, in terms of deliberate commendation, to an article contained in the last number of the "Independent," written by the chairman of the committee to whom the documents on polity were referred. That article was spoken of, as I say, in terms of deliberate and strong commendation. Having great respect for the views of Mr. Quint, my attention was drawn to this article, and I found in it the following statement: — "It has mattered little that the Consociationism of Connecticut has striven for long years to extinguish one of the two cardinal principles of Congregationalism — the absolute independence of the local church in matters pertaining to its internal affairs."

I was entirely content to say nothing upon the report, most able and lucid, of Dr. Bacon, although he alluded to the Consociation system of Connecticut very briefly, yet respectfully, cautioning the Council to be on their guard against pushing it so as to override, in any way, the fundamental principles of Congregationalism; and I do not rise now with any purpose of propagandism, but simply in an attitude of self-defense. The friends of that system are charged with the intention of uprooting one of the fundamental principles of Congregationalism. Now if there is any man in Connecticut who is exposed to that charge, I am that man. I have been working that system, in the same locality, for thirty-four years, and I am the oldest pastor, I suppose, in the State, who has been located there and on the same ground continuously. I have too much regard to my own comfort to be very easily provoked, and therefore I do not avail myself of every opportunity to be indignant, when indignation might be justifiable. I entertain, also, very great respect for the chairman of the committee. He is one of that class of men who see very clearly objects that are not too large [Laughter], and who pursue, with great energy and perseverance, individual objects, not always taking into sufficient consideration the bearings and the relations of the object. I impute to him no intention of injury, and I rise now not to vindicate Consociationism, or myself as one of its representatives and friends in Connecticut, but there are gentlemen from the far West for whose good opinion I entertain a regard.

A MEMBER. Is this discussion in order?

THE MODERATOR. Perhaps not, strictly.

Rev. Mr. GULLIVER, of Connecticut. I wish to say that I shall claim the privilege of reply, if personal attacks are to be made on me on this floor, and I don't know how long that will take.

Rev. Dr. ELDRIDGE. I am not going into any discussion.

A MEMBER. All these views and ideas can go before the large committee of twenty-five.

Rev. Dr. EDDY, of Massachusetts. I hope we shall not choke down Dr. Eldridge; he has not opened his mouth before.

Rev. Dr. ELDRIDGE. I am entirely at your disposal. It is true that I have not opened my mouth before, but I will close it now, if you say so. I was going to say this: that if those who work this system are engaged in overthrowing or uprooting one of the fundamental principles of Congregationalism, they are engaged in it innocently and unconsciously. We are not desirous of being despots, and we do not mean to be slaves.

Now I will state, in a very few words, just how the thing is, that those who never have heard anything about Consociationism, except in terms of reproach, may get some glimmering idea of what it is. The churches within a certain boundary, say twenty in number, meet together and form a constitution developing the very principles of comity that are supposed to exist. They say, "There may be cases in churches where individuals shall be aggrieved; there occur instances where churches will not permit a pastor to be settled, and there may be difficulties occurring among the churches themselves. Now, we agree, whenever any such question shall arise — whenever an individual or a church shall be aggrieved, whenever a pastor is to be settled or dismissed, whenever anything of that kind is to be done, — we agree to invest this Council with power to act, and we will consider it invested with all that authority which properly belongs to a council. There may be, in some of these constitutions, verbal expressions that are unadvised; but the practical working of the system is, that we do by this organization, say, what councils do otherwheres.

Now, as to the advantage of it. It is known; it is permanent; it is responsible. We have a printed constitution, which has been accepted by every church, who feel bound to abide by it until it is changed. We keep a record of our proceedings, and every precedent is recorded; and if any church is disposed in any way to abuse other churches, that abuse is recorded, and operates as a principle to be applied to them in return. The effect of our action is under our own eyes; we see it, and are responsible to the community for it. We have worked that system for thirty-four years in my locality. I have attended more than two hundred meetings of the organization, and I have never seen oppression or abuse. There have been many mistakes, doubtless, as there will be; but I can confidently point to that portion of the state as comparing favorably with any other community in the purity of its ministers, the intelligence, piety, and liberality (according to their means and opportunities), of its churches, and their freedom from spiritual and doctrinal errors.

Rev. Mr. GULLIVER, of Connecticut. I claim the privilege of replying.

Rev. Mr. BLISS, of Tennessee. I move that the rules be suspended for five minutes, to hear Mr. Gulliver. Carried.

Rev. Mr. GULLIVER. I don't propose to make any reply to the remarks of the preceding speaker, for I don't think the matter of importance enough, although I entertain the very highest possible respect for Dr. Eldridge, as he very well knows. I take the floor to thank you for giving me the opportunity to reply, and yield it to Prof. Park, that he may submit an amendment to the amendment which I have proposed, which will greatly facilitate the business before us. [Applause.]

Rev. Prof. PARK, of Massachusetts. I wish to propose, as an amendment to the amendment, the following resolution: —

Resolved, That this Council recognizes as distinctive of the Congregational polity —

First, The principle that the local or Congregational church derives its power and authority directly from Christ, and is not subjected to any ecclesiastical government exterior or superior to itself.

Second, That every local or Congregational church is bound to observe the duties of mutual respect and charity which are included in the communion of churches one with another; and that every church which refuses to give an account of its proceedings, when kindly and orderly desired to do so by neighboring churches, violates the law of Christ.

Third, That the ministry of the gospel by members of the churches who have been duly called and set apart to that work implies in itself no power of government, and that ministers of the gospel not elected to office in any church are not a hierarchy, nor are they invested with any official power in or over the churches.

I would simply remark, that this is an enlargement of the first resolution which was proposed in the report.

The question was put, and the amendment carried unanimously. The report was then adopted, as amended.

Rev. Mr. Langworthy, in behalf of the Nominating Committee, submitted the following names to constitute the

COMMITTEE ON EDUCATION AT THE WEST.

Rev. Edwards A. Park, D. D., of Massachusetts, Rev. John P. Gulliver, of Connecticut, Rev. William De Loss Love, of Wisconsin.

RAISING THE FUNDS.

Deacon Samuel Holmes, of New York, asked and obtained leave to offer at this time, from the Committee on Ways and Means, the following report and resolutions: —

The committee to whom was referred the question, "By what means to raise $750,000 for the Evangelization of the West and South?" beg leave to suggest, that the sum named, as it can not be reckoned *large*, when compared with the grandeur of the *object* and of the *opportunity* which God in his providence has set before us, so *neither* is to be regarded as *extravagant* in comparison with the *ability* which divine munificence has bestowed upon *us*, the Congregational churches of America.

Were we standing higher upon the mount of vision and of consecration, we should be startled not at the *greatness* but at the *littleness* of our plans for answering the appeal made to us at this signal moment in the history of our nation.

The one thing necessary in order that the amount named, and even more, may be realized the ensuing year, and from year to year hereafter, is that the benevolent spirit of our Master be more fully present in the churches, and that we be prompted to exercise broader and clearer views of the work to be done.

It will be understood that the present is not a proposition to raise for the three societies a special fund of $750,000 over and above their ordinary receipts. It does propose to *double* the annual revenue of the American Home Missionary Society and that of the American Missionary Association, while for church building it aims to do, through the

American Congregational Union, a special service, plainly demanded *now*, and to a greater or less degree likely to be demanded for years to come.

We esteem it a fortunate circumstance, that the new campaign for Christ's cause finds our denomination provided with the three distinct and harmonious agencies that correspond to the three departments of labor into which the direct work of evangelization divides itself — an agency to assist in planting and sustaining churches; an agency to secure the building of houses of worship; and an agency to care for the comfort, education, and religious well-being of the lately enslaved blacks.

We desire to take no labor *off* from these societies, but rather to lay *more upon* them, and encourage them to put *more* upon the churches in Christ's name.

In accordance with these views, the committee recommend to the Council the passage of the following resolutions: —

1. *Resolved*, That each of the several benevolent societies named in the report of the committee on the Evangelization of the West and South be desired and *enjoined* to adopt the most efficient means in its power to secure the sum proposed, as *its* quota of the $750,000.

2. *Resolved*, That, regarding this as the most significant of all the practical measures that have occupied the attention of the Council, we do hereby *pledge* ourselves to our Father, our Saviour, and to each other, to co-operate with the secretaries and agents of the societies referred to in any effort they may wisely and zealously adopt.

3. *Resolved*, That the Council recommend to the American Congregational Union, without arresting or delaying the special efforts now in progress or ready to be put forth in behalf of the churches needing aid for the erection of houses of worship, to call for a simultaneous collection on the Sabbath preceding Forefathers' Day, December 17th, when every Congregational church, large or small, from the Atlantic to the Pacific, shall contribute what it can towards the $200,000 for church-building. Let the good work be finished in a day, and give the proper punctuation to this memorable meeting.

4. *Resolved*, That an appeal be issued from the Council, and placed, so far as may be, in the hands of every member of every Congregational church in the country — urging the duty and privilege of self-denying benevolence, with immediate reference to the object contemplated in this paper.

5. *Resolved*, That we undertake this work, not in our own strength nor for our own glory, but with humble dependence upon Him whose are the silver and the gold and the hearts of men; and in humble imitation of Him who said, "It is more blessed to give than to receive," — to Him be glory by the church throughout all ages.

In behalf of the committee,

SAMUEL HOLMES, *Chairman*.

Rev. Mr. Allen, of Massachusetts. We are prepared to adopt those resolutions without debate.

Rev. Dr. Holbrook, of New York. I ask that the question be taken by a rising vote.

Dea. Samuel Holmes, of New York. I move that the question be taken by a rising vote, to be followed by a prayer consecrating our vote, and that we then at once proceed to our usual prayer-meeting.

Rev. Mr. Webb, of Massachusetts. Shall we not incorporate this idea,— that we not only pledge ourselves to our Father, and our Saviour who has redeemed us, but to each other, that we will carry out to the letter this recommendation in all the churches throughout the land? I make that motion.

The motion was agreed to.

The question being taken upon the resolutions, they were adopted *nem. con.* by a rising vote; and prayer was offered by Rev. Flavel Bascom, of Illinois.

DEVOTIONAL EXERCISES.

The Council then proceeded to the usual devotional exercises, a hymn being sung, prayer being offered by Rev. Dr. Beecher, of Illinois, Rev. George Allen, of Massachusetts, and others, and remarks being made by Rev. J. C. Holbrook, and others.

CONSOCIATIONISM.

The Council having resumed the consideration of the report upon Church Polity,

Rev. Dr. Field, of Connecticut, moved that at least one of the members of the committee recommended should be a pastor of a consociated church.

Rev. Mr. Gulliver, of Connecticut. I object very much to that recognition of schools among us. We have already recognized our six theological seminaries in the resolutions; and a distinguished lawyer upon this floor has said that that fact would convince any court of law in the country that every possible interest was represented. If we begin by recognizing Consociationists, we must go on and recognize Hopkinsians, and Old School and New School theologians. I should deprecate it very much, as distinguishing me from the rest of my brethren. There is no disposition to crush down members who belong to the consociated churches. There will be every disposition to have them represented. I hope there will be no intimation that there is a disposition to crush them, for it does not exist.

REPORT ON WORSHIP.

On motion of Rev. A. P. Marvin, of Massachusetts, the order of business was suspended to enable him to offer a report.

Rev. A. P. Marvin, from the committee on Worship, read the following report, which was accepted and adopted:

The committee to whom the order on the subject of *Worship* was referred, having given it what attention was possible in the short time since the matter was referred to them, respectfully submit the following report: —

To avoid all misapprehension, the committee would begin by saying, that the subject before us is *worship;* not *forms* of worship, nor the *order of service* in the house of the Lord, but simply worship. It is quite true that the dividing line between our denomination and some other bodies of Christians is not liturgical. Congregationalists might have a prescribed order of service, with written forms of prayer, without infringing any of their peculiar principles ; but that subject is not now before us ; and we desire to say, so distinctly as not to be misunderstood, that we do not wish to raise any agitation in regard to it within this body. Our mode of worship is well established, and is satisfactory to the great mass of our fellow-worshipers.

The point to which we call especial attention, and would impress with emphatic earnestness, is this, that in our devotions, both public and private, we should bring in much more of the element of worship. Prayer, as generally defined, consists of several parts, as invocation, confession of sin, petition, thanksgiving, and praise. Any one, however, who gives attention to the custom in our public and private devotions, will be struck with the fact that the larger part of our prayers is taken up with petitions ; confession of sin comes next in frequency and prominence ; thanksgiving is not entirely forgotten ; but praise, worship, adoration, are often entirely omitted. In saying this, we do not mean to intimate that we, as a denomination, in comparison with other Christians, are deficient in reverence ; but that there is a general want of the element of worship which we share in common with others. A skeptical philosopher and statesman in a former generation ridiculed the practice of worship as if it consisted in flattering the Almighty ; and we have heard Christian ministers inquire, in the same strain, why we should tell God in our prayers how old he is, and how great. This error comes from apparent unfamiliarity with the practice of ancient saints, as seen in the Psalms ; and also from profound ignorance of the design and effect of worship. The Psalms of David, of Asaph, and the other sacred poets, are replete with the spirit of worship.

In commencing their service, they were accustomed to say, " O come let us worship ; let us bow down before the Lord our Maker ! " . . . " Let us enter his courts with thanksgiving, and his gates with praise ! " They thought of the eternity, the self-existence, the power, the truthfulness, the justice, the mercy, and the holiness of God, until their hearts were full, and then their feelings burst forth in the highest strains of adoration and praise.

Let it always be borne in mind that no one can worship God unless his soul is in love with infinite excellence; and that in proportion as his love for perfection increases, will be his desire to render unto God the worship which is due. And in the act of worship the soul is enlarged and purified. No exercise of the human heart is so elevating and improving as that of meditating, with adoring feelings, upon the character of the ever-blessed God. As we study him in his works, and especially in his words, as revealed in his perfect laws, we are "changed into the same image from glory to glory."

We do therefore earnestly call upon all with whom the proceedings of this Council will have weight, to make the element of worship more prominent in their devotions, both in public and private religious services. To the objection that the endeavor to effect this end would prolong devotional exercises to an undue length, we would reply, that prayers are sometimes tedious because they have not the variety which meets all the wants of the devout soul, and are made up of "vain repetitions" in the form of petition for blessings. It is believed that our devotional services, both in the house of God, in social meetings, and in the family, would be made far more interesting by being more complete, while by the same means they would be rendered more acceptable to the Hearer of prayer. Those who render earnest and sincere thanks for divine favors, will thus enforce their prayers for new mercies in the presence of the prayer-answering God; and those who, by high and holy expressions of adoration, draw near to the great white throne, will be thereby fitted to make a good use of all the blessings which God may be pleased to bestow upon them. Our petitions will be more pleasing to our heavenly Father when we worship him in the "beauty of holiness."

A. P. Marvin,
N. H. Eggleston,
J. L. Jenkins.

CONSOCIATIONISM.

The consideration of the report on Church Polity was resumed.

Rev. Dr. Eldridge, of Connecticut. I hope that the amendment proposed by Dr. Field will not be accepted. I have no disposition at all to intrude consociationism upon this Council. I wish to leave the committee entirely untrammeled. The question seemed rather to be drawn before the Council by the reference to that document by Mr. Quint. We are entirely satisfied with the system. We are not afraid of its being overturned, and have no disposition to propagate it against anybody's wishes.

Rev. Mr. GULLIVER, of Connecticut. I would suggest that the Professor from East Windsor will necessarily be from a consociated church.

The motion of Dr. Field was laid upon the table.

Rev. Mr. ALLEN, of Massachusetts. No one perhaps more respects the gentlemen spoken of to be classified in the committee, as professors, than myself. I have not only a very respectful but a very affectionate regard for them, so far as I personally know them. But I object to a class of men being taken and placed upon this committee as a class; and particularly upon the ground that has been verified by the opinion of an unknown but distinguished lawyer, who may well understand the business of his own profession, but certainly does not so well understand ours.

And, sir, I will here say, that the greatest difficulty that has arisen since any of us were born, in regard to the subject of Congregationalism, has been made by perhaps the most distinguished and influential professor of theology in New England, if not in the country; and that that individual did more, in the course of thirty years, to uncongregationalise and Presbyterianise Congregationalism, than any other man, or all other men in New England; and that from his position as professor of theology in an institution of high character, and from his own celebrity, because of his influence, there are now a multitude of churches in this country that are Presbyterian, notwithstanding he was a professor of theology in the earliest and most distinguished theological institution of this land. I would add that there are men in this body, and they are numerous, that understand that subject better than theological professors, a great deal, and who have studied it with great care and know its bearings, better far.

The amendment by Mr. Gulliver was then adopted.

Rev. Dr. Eddy, of Massachusetts, desired that the mode of appointing the committee should be amended.

On motion of Mr. Gulliver, the adoption of the amendment was reconsidered in order to meet Dr. Eddy's views.

Rev. Dr. Eddy, of Massachusetts, moved that the committee be appointed by the Moderators of the Council (the Moderator and First Assistant Moderator, the Second Assistant Moderator being absent.)

The motion was agreed to.

The amendment of Rev. Mr. Gulliver was adopted, and the report as amended was adopted.

COLLEGIATE AND MINISTERIAL EDUCATION.

Rev. Seth Sweetser, D. D., of Massachusetts, chairman of the committee to whom was referred the paper presented by the preliminary Committee on Collegiate and Ministerial Education, read the following report: —

The Committee on Collegiate and Ministerial Education respectfully recommend that the resolution submitted to them in reference to Collegiate and Theological Institutions at the West be referred to a special committee.

They also recommend the adoption of the comprehensive, clear, and well-arranged report on the education of young men for the ministry presented to this Council by the committee appointed at the preliminary meeting to consider that subject.

And in order that some of its more weighty suggestions may be distinctly impressed, and be carried out in the practical application they deserve, the committee beg leave to submit to the Council for their adoption the following statements:

1. As it is an admitted fact that in the providence of God the high religious character, the Christian energy, the sound and intelligent patriotism, and the wide and salutary influence of New England in the past have depended to a large extent upon the existence and continuous work of an educated and devoted ministry, so it must be admitted, that in the future within New England the perpetuation and enlargement of such character and influence, and beyond New England the training of communities to a similar character and influence, depend, and will ever depend, upon the existence and continuous work of a ministry in like manner devotedly pious, and generously educated.

2. Inasmuch as the present emergency is pressing, and the condition of the West and South imperatively demands immediate attention, it is eminently desirable that our theological seminaries should provide for the education of earnest-minded and vigorous young men, whose hearts are in the Lord's work, by arranging a course of instruction not requiring a previous collegiate training, in order that, with as little delay as practicable, they may engage in preaching the gospel to the many thousands who wait for it in our land.

3. As the duty of consecration to the spreading of Christ's kingdom is not laid exclusively upon those who minister the word, and as it is not salutary nor right that those who go into the warfare equip themselves at their own charges, the obligation should be recognized by all members of the Church of our Redeemer, to help young men in their education for the ministry, by assistance rendered directly to individuals, by supplying ample funds to education societies, and by generously endowing scholarships in colleges and theological seminaries.

4. Notwithstanding the often presented discouraging aspect of the Christian ministry, arising from an alleged insecurity and insufficiency of pecuniary support, young men of the requisite ability and good disposition should be encouraged to devote themselves to preaching the gospel, in the cheerful exercise of a simple faith in the promise of our Lord Jesus

Christ to his messengers, "Lo, I am with you always!" trusting with all good assurance and hope in the Word of the Lord, that all necessary things shall be added unto them.

By vote of the committee,

S. SWEETSER, *Chairman.*

June 23, 1865.

Rev. Dr. Sweetser proceeded to say: I was instructed by the committee to explain why so brief a report upon so great a topic, is presented. It is done, first, because some of the special points brought to view in the report submitted to the committee have already been presented in other reports, and acted upon; and, secondly, that by concentrating attention upon a few special points of vast importance, those points may be impressed more vividly upon the minds of this Council.

In the opinion of the committee, this is one of the fundamental matters for the consideration of the council. We have passed, with great unanimity, and with expressions of gratitude to God, votes recommending the raising of large sums of money to meet the exigencies of our nation at the present time. We have voted to advise the churches to pay $300,000 into the treasury of the Home Missionary Society, and $250,000 to aid those who shall go to preach to and instruct the freedmen, and $200,000 more to build churches. But where are the men who are to receive this sum in doing the service of the church. We were told yesterday that we needed a thousand men to-day, trained, and disciplined, and drilled, for what God is calling upon this church to do. The report of your committee says that there are 800 more churches than there are men. Where are these men to come from, and how are they to be furnished?

Are we to expect our young men to prepare themselves for the work of the Lord at their own charges? I believe the whole history of our church shows that those who have entered into the sacred office have come in a very small degree from families well supplied with wealth. Experience seems to demonstrate that it has never been the will of God that young men nursed in luxury and abundance, should be the pioneer men in doing God's work. We have now, and we always have had as pioneers, men in moderate circumstances and even in hard necessity, who have been kept from self-indulgence, and have grown up under the teachings of necessity to a manhood that was equal to the demand when they came into the service. If we were to-day to exclude from our ministry the men that have been helped to come in, and if we were to exclude from our missionary labors the men that have had help from the churches, we should erase from our record the best, the ablest, the most devoted and most energetic men that have been in the service of the Lord for the last century.

The allotted time having expired, on motion Dr. Sweetser was invited to proceed.

I do not ask this for myself; but it seems to me that it is a subject that ought to be more fully considered. Unless there is something done to meet the necessity of bringing men forward, what we have already done, in advising the raising of funds to carry on the work, will be in vain.

The beginning of the struggle is in the preparatory course. I submit to this Council whether it is good economy, to say nothing more, to leave our young men to struggle against poverty, and against debt, while they are preparing themselves to preach the gospel; to waste their strength and their time in furnishing themselves with the means of living, when they ought to be devoting all their energy of mind and body to the great work of preparation.

When Napoleon wanted to reinforce the armies of France, and make them superior to any other force that could be brought against them, he laid the whole kingdom under a system of education, holding out inducements to young men of energy and ability to go into the army, by the payment of all their expenses of education; and he was a wise man in all his proceedings in that direction.

Our churches need to see to it that their own young men who are fit to go to this work, shall not be left to hesitate because they can not see their way clear through this process of education. I take it, that it is the opinion of this body that the ministry, as a general thing, must be educated according to the old standard; that that is to be the rule, and that the partial course is the exception. If that is so, we must make a strong effort to provide the means to keep our young men in our own schools and in our own seminaries, and send them into the work under Congregational influence. Let us do it in a manly, Christian spirit, coming up to the demand, under the full conviction of the greatness of the necessity. Let every pastor undertake it in his own church, that means shall be set in operation, at once, to bring this great question before our young men in the colleges and seminaries, that they may not withhold themselves when God is calling for such multitudes to go and enter the field which in his providence he has opened.

I want to say a word more — I am aware your time is precious — in regard to the principle of going into the ministry, which is embraced in that last statement. We have heard over and over again, that there are great discouragements to young men, because their salaries are so stinted, and their means of support are so uncertain. I wish it were in the heart of this Council to put that obstacle for ever out of sight, and that we might ask our young men to go into the ministry from a higher motive; that they should understand that the question is not whether they shall have a large salary, and a conspicuous position, and an honorable place. I submit, sir, if every place where a man can serve Christ is not an honorable place. And I submit whether the promise of Christ to be with us always even unto the end of the world, is not sufficient security for any young man, if he is called of God to go into his service. As I have heard again and again these appeals made, I have almost wished that I could be a young man, — that I could again to-day, as a young man, buckle on the armor and go into this warfare. I would not ask any man to insure me a support. I do not believe there is the slightest danger of any faithful servant of Jesus Christ suffering want, so long as he is faithful to the word which he is called to proclaim. [Applause.] I do not believe the history of our churches shows an instance in which a man, who, in the simplicity of his heart, with an earnest faith, and with fidelity, did the work that God gave him to do, has been left to suffer; and all coming time will not show an instance. Our young men ought to be delivered from this slavery to the money question.

I do not mean to exonerate the churches. It has been settled, by high authority, that the servant is worthy of his hire. We do not want to unsettle that principle; but that is another question to be pressed in another quarter. What I desire to say here to our young men is, if Christ calls, do not you hesitate. The note of some of our merchant princes is reliable; but I submit that the promise of Christ, "I am with you always," is a better pledge. I would go into the work with no other promise, if, in the promise of God that was the only promise I could get. I want our young men to feel that that is the way to settle the question, and to come to the work of the Lord with the feeling that we are not to be paid for it. We are not paid. I never thought that I was paid for my services. I should be ashamed of myself if I should hesitate for one moment to do the work God calls upon me to do, because in a commercial point of view, and according to the standard by which men of the world are paid, I am not paid. I do not ask my people to pay me. I want them to give me a support. There is a promise for us all, "Trust in the Lord and do good; so shalt thou dwell in the land. Verily thou shalt be fed." Brethren, bread and water are sure. "The earth is the Lord's and the fullness thereof." God has messengers, and God has servants, and he will take out of his own abundance, and will feed any man that in his work is in necessity. I hope that a voice will go out from this Council to all our colleges, and all our seminaries, to set aside the question of place and salaries and honor, and to act upon the question, "Does the Lord call me?" And let him who hears the voice of the Lord calling him, in all joyfulness and hope say, "Here, Lord, am I, — send me."

SYSTEMATIZING BENEVOLENCE.

On motion of Rev. Mr. Cushing, the orders of the day were suspended to enable him, at the request of Dr. Stearns, to report certain verbal alterations to be made in the report of the committee on Systematizing Benevolence. Rev. Mr. Cushing then read the proposed changes.

Rev. Dr. Bacon, of Connecticut. It is not in the power of this body to alter a report which has been submitted to it and subscribed by a committee, any more than to alter a note of hand, unless they adopt it as their own.

Rev. Dr. PALMER, of New York. I think that view is correct; but I have no doubt the committee will assent to its modification. I move that it be recommitted.

The motion was agreed to.

After consideration by the committee, Rev. Dr. Palmer, in their behalf, reported that the committee preferred the statement as it stood, but consented to the alteration.

On motion of Rev. Dr. Wolcott, of Ohio,

The name of the "American Congregational Association," which had been inadvertently omitted, was added.

The report as amended was then adopted.[1]

APPEAL TO THE CHURCHES.

Rev. Dr. Beecher, of Illinois, moved that an appeal be issued by this Council, and placed, so far as possible, in the hands of every church member in the country; and that a special committee be appointed to prepare and issue this appeal.

This motion was agreed to.

MINISTERIAL EDUCATION.

The Council resumed the consideration of Rev. Dr. Sweetser's report on Collegiate and Ministerial Education.

Rev. Dr. LEAVITT, of New York. I think that this report touches the marrow of the case in regard to the future progress of Congregationalism. We are told that we want eight hundred ministers now, with our present extension; and we are told that we must exhort young men to disregard the question of support, and trust to Providence. That is very good doctrine. I remember seeing a picture in the window of a shoemaker's shop, of a customer trying on a boot; and while he is groaning with pain the shoemaker very politely and earnestly assures him that it is not possible for that boot to hurt his feet. But the man who had the boot on knew where it pinched; and I think there are a good many ministers who know where the shoe pinches.

I do not think the report of the committee has touched the core of the difficulty after all, that ministers suffer for the want of sufficient support. There is a keener suffering which educated and generous men are

[1] As on pp. 410-412.

capable of feeling, and which drives men away from the ministry. If you want to increase the number of ministers, you must call off your dogs from them. John Newton, after he had graduated in a slave-ship, felt the necessity laid upon him of going into the ministry, and took orders in the Established Church of England, although his sympathies were all with the Congregationalists; and he says in a letter which is in print, that he did it for the sake of enjoying freedom. I have known valuable and earnest ministers to go into other denominations, — Methodists, Baptists, Presbyterians, and Episcopalians, — for the sake of enjoying freedom; — freedom to worship God, and freedom to preach his gospel and administer his ordinances in the way they thought conformable to the will of Christ. We must enlarge our charity and treat ministers as they deserve. We must respect them as ministers; and not, when any one steps over his line, hunt him down as with hounds.

REGARDING FINAL ADJOURNMENT.

Rev. Mr. Quint, in behalf of the Business Committee, desired the Convention to decide whether they would adjourn to-day, or on some day next week. If the Convention considered it necessary to adjourn to-day, the remaining papers might be read, and the business concluded, by extending the session to half-past two o'clock, unless the time should be occupied by debate.

Rev. Dr. Wolcott, of Ohio, moved that the business be finished by half-past two o'clock, the session being extended until that time, and that then the Council adjourn without day.

The motion was agreed to.

MINISTERIAL EDUCATION.

The Council resumed the consideration of Dr. Sweetser's report.

Rev. Prof. Fisk, of Illinois. I dislike to take a moment of the time of the Council at this late day; but it is the first time I have opened my mouth here. I am delighted with the report, as able as it is brief; and I am also greatly pleased with the remarks of the chairman of the committee. I wish now to comment upon one or two points which have been brought up in that admirable report.

First, let me say in regard to the short course, I am a convert to the opinion expressed in the report. When I was appointed Professor of Rhetoric in the Theological Seminary at Chicago, eight years ago, I hesitated for nearly a year; and one great reason was because of the special course which was marked out for certain young men who had not had a collegiate education. I beg to say that my views have undergone an entire change in this respect; and that some of our ablest and best young men, — yes, some young men on this floor to-day that you only know to honor and to love — are men who have been through the three years' special course in the Theological Seminary at Chicago. I shall not trespass upon the proprieties of the occasion if I mention a young man upon this floor now, who came, a carpenter, from Iowa, sent to us by brother Guernsey, and went through our course. When offered $1500 to stay in Chicago, he said, "I came from Iowa, and I go back to Iowa to labor there among those brethren;" and he went back with a salary of $400, and was sent by the churches there to represent them before you. Such cases are not rare with us.

If you take the railroad at Chicago and pass through those magnificent empires opened to Christian civilization, and see what a moral waste lies around us, and what need there is of Christian missionaries to go on the front tide of emigration, swelling on over rock and mountain; if you look South and get some apprehension of the great needs there; you will see how much we need men. No tongue can tell, no pen can describe it properly. We have sent out forty men from our seminary in five years. If we had had five hundred, we could have sent them out. One missionary agent said to me, "I will take all you have got for one State." And we have seven States centering upon us and turning to us.

Much as we need men, we need, more than all, the men who have the spirit of Christ, and are willing to go where they are sent. I have received sixty letters within the last two months from people at the East. One man says, "I have married into a very intelligent family, and I have a very delicate wife, and I must have a refined circle into which to introduce her." Another says, "I have a poor constitution, and I fear the fever and ague." Another wants to be upon a railroad. I always send back to these men, kindly, "We have room enough, but we have not room for you. Much as we want men, what we want is men who will go anywhere, do anything, sleep in an upper chamber, or on the ground like our brave men who went South to defend the country; and we want no man west of the Hudson River, who is not willing to go anywhere that he can, and to live as his Master did, who did not seek for places where there was no fever and ague. We take all the men you can send us of that kind." We want to raise up such men. We want such men as the brother who came out there, and who said to me, "I have sold my homestead to pay the funeral expenses of my wife; but I bless God for putting me into the ministry." If we can get such men, we shall have men enough to do the work. [At this point the allotted time expired.]

Rev. Mr. GAYLORD, of New Hampshire. I find nowhere in the report beyond a brief passing allusion to the consecration by parents of their children to the ministry. I move to add, on the fifteenth page of the preliminary report, near the end of the thirteenth line, the words, "and a deeper and more general consecration, on the part of Christian parents, of their children to the work of the gospel ministry." I believe this is one of the most important things in connection with this whole subject. When Christian parents realize the duty of consecrating their children specially to the ministry, we shall have attained one of the conditions of this important work.

A member inquired whether the report could be amended.

Rev. Mr. GAYLORD, of Nebraska. The report of Dr. Sweetser, as I understand, recommends the adoption of this preliminary report, consequently I understand it to be competent for the Council now to amend the report of the preliminary committee.

The amendment was agreed to.

The report was then adopted.

Rev. Dr. Wolcott, on behalf of the Business Committee, reported the following resolution, submitted by Rev. J. A. Thome, of Cleveland, Ohio: —

Resolved, That for the supply and proper training of a ministry adequate to the wants of the West and the South, and for the spiritual preparation of the Lord's people East and North to respond suitably in money, measures, and men, to the calls of Providence to enter and occupy the land which late events have opened to our faith and polity and evangelical enterprise, and to plant churches among, and furnish all requisite means of grace to, the freed people and the inhabitants generally of the South, *Revivals of Religion* in our colleges and theological seminaries, and throughout our churches, Sabbath schools and families, leading to the renewed consecration of the wealth and the youth of our Zion to the Redeemer, are now the pre-eminent necessity:

And that this Council does conjure the pastors and churches of our order, from the Atlantic to the Pacific, to employ promptly, and in faith, the measures they may deem most efficient, under God, in promoting a general and genuine refreshing from on high.

And would God this work of grace might begin at this Jerusalem.

The resolution was adopted.

AMERICAN PROTESTANT ASSEMBLY.

Rev. Dr. Taylor, of Connecticut, on behalf of the Committee on the American Protestant Assembly, read the following report:

The papers brought before this body in reference to a Protestant Assembly, and referred to a special committee, emanated from two sources having the same general object in view. The Young Men's Christian Association which recently held a convention in the city of Philadelphia, regarding the signs of the times as indicating greater harmony among brethren, recommended that measures be taken for securing a concert of action on the part of all Protestant denominations, to resist the encroachments of infidelity, in its varied phases of bold opposition to the gospel; as well as to promote harmony and love among those who belong to the household of faith. The General Assembly of the Presbyterian Church, which held its late session in the city of Pittsburg, Pennsylvania, had a more definite form given to the subject in the following resolutions, which were presented for its consideration : —

Resolved, That the wide-spread influence of infidelity, in its varied phases of bold atheism and rationalistic philosophy, which is now putting forth redoubled energies for its dissemination throughout every section of our land, calls for the prompt and united action of evangelical Christians, in a clear, honest, and uncompromising enunciation of the great cardinal doctrines of grace, and a bold defense of the truth as it is in Jesus.

Resolved, That in the providence of God we believe that a solemn responsibility is now laid upon the Church of the Lord Jesus Christ in this country to manifest her loyalty to the Great King, by maintaining inviolate and steadfast, both by the enunciation of the pulpit and the issues of the press, the great principles of the gospel, which are designed to elevate the cross, establish the kingdom of Christ, and ultimately overthrow the whole system of error.

Resolved, That the fearful growth of the Papacy, both as an ecclesiastical and civil power in this land, is well calculated to awaken the fears and arouse the mightiest energies of the entire Protestant community, and calls imperiously for the adoption of measures at once timely and adequate to the emergency, so that we may, under the divine blessing, be enabled to counteract the secret and malign influence of the man of sin, and present an unbroken front of the army of truth against this system of corruption which is hourly girding itself for the approaching conflict.

Resolved, That it is our candid judgment that the present is an auspicious moment to inaugurate such a measure, and that, while we would not presume to dictate, we would most respectfully request the General Assembly of the Presbyterian Church, now in session in this city (Pittsburg), to put forth a suitable deliverance upon these important subjects, and to take steps to have such action concurred in by other branches of our American Protestant Church, so as to bring about the formation of a great national Protestant league, which, by its constitution, shall be fully up to the urgent demands and necessities of the times.

Resolved, That a committee of four ministers and three laymen be appointed by this meeting to present this subject to the General Assembly, and to be associated with a similar committee to be appointed by that body in devising plans by which a general and concerted movement of all the Protestant force in the land may be brought about, and bold, continuous, and vigorous protest, by word and act, shall be enunciated against both infidelity and Roman Catholicism, the arch-enemies of truth in the midst of the professing Church of God, and arch-traitors to civil and religious freedom throughout the world.

These resolutions elicited the warm approval of the Assembly to that degree that they appointed a large committee to carry out the spirit of them in co-operation with committees which may be, or have been, appointed by other denominations for a like purpose. The subject has been urged also on the attention of this body, by private letters entitling it to serious consideration. Your committee, therefore, recommend the passage of the following resolution by this Congregational Council :—

Resolved, That a committee, consisting of five clergymen and an equal number of laymen, be appointed, to act in concert with other committees similarly appointed by other evangelical denominations, for the purpose of giving expression to our desire for more outward fellowship, and more vigorous co-operation for the defense of Protestant Christianity against the encroachments of Roman Catholicism and infidelity in our land.

For the Committee,

JEREMIAH TAYLOR, *Chairman.*

The report was adopted.

TEMPERANCE AND TOBACCO.

Rev. Dr. Blodgett, on behalf of the committee on Temperance, read the following report : —

The special committee to whom was referred the subject of temperance, under the form of an inquiry, "whether any, and, if so, what deliverance should be made on the subject by the National Council," make the following report : —

It is eminently fitting that the Council send forth to the nation a distinct and solemn testimony in favor of the principles of temperance. The subject is too tenderly associated with the labors and "blessed memory" of many of the fathers in our ministry who gave to it their labors and their prayers ; and it too deeply concerns the interests of morality and religion for the present and for the future of our blood-bought country to allow us to refrain from giving it an open and hearty indorsement.

Intemperance is a sin against God, a curse to society, a foe to the purity of the Church and its ministry, a corruption of the young, a hindrance to the profitable hearing of the word of God, and so to the conversion and salvation of men. Under various pretenses of health and hospitality, and by various influences of appetite and gain, and those growing out of the late war with rebellion, drinking usages are widely prevailing, to the *danger* of all, and to the *destruction* of many of our young men, the late defenders, and the future hope, of our country.

That the alarming progress of the evil may be arrested, and our country saved from a more disastrous doom than that in which the late rebellion threatened to involve it, in the name of humanity, patriotism, morality, and religion, yea, in the name of God, we earnestly invite the co-operation of ministers and Christians, of teachers in our schools, of officers in our colleges, of our legislators and our ministers of justice, of our physicians and lawyers, and of our rulers in all departments of government, that our nation may be saved from the dangers which impend from the increasing prevalence of intemperance.

We would give the trumpet that certain sound which such men as Lyman Beecher and Justin Edwards gave, when the nation was aroused from its guilty slumber, and marshaled under God for that great moral battle, in which the friends of temperance so signally triumphed.

The committee submit for the adoption of the Council the following resolutions, namely :

1. *Resolved*, That this Council hails with satisfaction and gratitude to God the renewal of temperance efforts, in a Christian spirit, and on the scriptural principle of self-denial for personal safety and the good of others, efforts long successfully urged by wise and good men in our own ministry and churches, and in the ministry and churches of other denominations ; and that we regard the family, the Sunday school, the Church and the congregation, and above all the ministry, as the fitting channels of influence, on this as on all other great moral questions.

2. *Resolved*, That while we accept with thankfulness the aid of legislation, in the conflict with intemperance, we must still rely mainly upon moral and spiritual appliances for progress and final triumph ; and that we hold the temperance enterprise thus prosecuted to be just *one method* of that home evangelization in which this Council is so deeply and so properly engaged, and that, too, a method indispensable to the complete success of that divine work of evangelization.

3. *Resolved*, That, while we acknowledge with great satisfaction the eminent services of many of the medical profession in the cause of temperance, we hold it to be matter of regret that such numbers prescribe intoxicating beverages for convalescent and other patients : and we would earnestly inquire if the superior science and wisdom of the profession can not find substitutes for such inebriating tonics, the use of which will be attended with less peril to those who are under the power of an incipient or confirmed appetite for intoxicating drinks.

4. *Resolved*, That we receive with satisfaction the invitation to send a delegation to the National Temperance Convention to be holden at Saratoga, New York, August 1st, 1865 ; and that we respond to that invitation by appointing six delegates, headed by our respected Moderator, to that convention, with the desire to add the testimony of this national

body to that of the many State and local bodies to be represented in that convention,

(Signed)

C. BLODGETT,
Z. S. BARSTOW,
WILLIAM THURSTON,
LORENZO D. DANA,
C. A. STACKPOLE,
J. COLLIE.

Rev. Dr. BACON, of Connecticut, moved to amend the resolutions by striking out the words, "in the form and to the extent of prohibition," and said: I think it will be unfortunate, and to an extent disastrous, to commit this Council to that particular style of legislation; for it is my most solemn conviction, which I utter here knowing that it will cost me something, that the temperance cause was wrecked on the rock of the Maine law; that the quackery of such legislation has been the ruin of the cause, from which it can not be rescued until we cut ourselves clear of the whole scheme of legislating alcohol out of the creation of God.

Rev. Mr. GULLIVER, of Connecticut. I hope we shall retain that word. We have all made up our minds upon it, and I hope we shall have a deliberate vote upon it.

Rev. Dr. WOLCOTT, of Ohio. I am ready to vote for it, not because I am opposed to prohibition, but because the omission will strengthen the sentence.

The amendment was agreed to.

Mr. WILLIAMS of Flushing, New York, said: I have been a very interested spectator of these proceedings for the last ten days, but have not let my voice be heard before. I do it now with diffidence; but I feel constrained to move to add the following resolution:

Resolved, That this Council while it bears its solemn testimony against the evil of intemperance, would also bear its testimony against its twin vice, the improper use of tobacco, particularly by ministers and church-members.

Rev. Mr. DEXTER, of Massachusetts, raised the question of order, that the resolution should come through the Business Committee.

Rev. Dr. BLODGETT, of Rhode Island. Certain resolutions upon the subject of the use of tobacco were referred to the committee. The committee agreed that these papers belonged to a different category, and did not think it within their province to ask for any action respecting them. We had already prepared our report upon the subject of temperance.

Rev. Dr. WOLCOTT, of Ohio. I should probably vote for the amendment; but I know it would lead to a long discussion, for there are members here who would speak at length against it. And therefore, with no unfriendliness to the object of the mover, I move to lay the amendment upon the table.

The motion to lay upon the table was rejected.

Rev. Mr. WEBB, of Massachusetts. It will kill the whole thing if we load it down in this way. If one member objects to tobacco, another will object to tea and coffee, and another to something else, and the whole will be defeated. That is my reason for voting against the amendment.

Rev. Dr. BLODGETT, of Rhode Island. I think the committee were unanimous in the judgment that we should not indulge in the use of narcotics; but we were of one mind that it would be unwise to marry this special reform to the great temperance question; and it was certain that I would not be the instrument of marrying the two in this Council; and I ask the Council not to compel me to stand in that attitude.

Rev. Mr. QUINT, of Massachusetts. So far as the resolution goes, it meets my views precisely, and I should be, under proper circumstances, ready to vote for it. But I do not think it is a proper question to be brought before the National Council of Congregational Churches.

Furthermore, this Council has four times summarily put out of the way such resolutions, when they were fully represented. It would hardly be proper to have it now passed upon in a very thin house, suddenly sprung in this way at the close of our session. These are my reasons for voting against this particular resolution. The other three I should have voted against upon principle, because they were wrong. This one is not; it is right, so far as it goes; but I do not think it is right to adopt it in this way.

The amendment was rejected.

Rev. Mr. WEBB, of Massachusetts. There is an expression in the resolution that I should be glad to see stricken out, that we hold temperance to be one of the methods of home evangelization. We gain nothing by identifying temperance with religion, and making one seem the other. I hope the question whether it is home evangelization or not, will be left for us to decide individually. I move that that clause be stricken out.

Rev. Dr. EDDY, of Massachusetts. I hope that will not pass, because moral reform is a part of home evangelization. I do not want to divorce temperance from religion. I think they have been married by God himself, and ought not to be put asunder.

Rev. Mr. WEBB, of Massachusetts. Temperance is the fruit of evangelization, but it is not itself evangelization. You may make a man temperate, and yet he may go to hell if you can not make him pious, too.

The amendment was rejected.

Mr. Thurston, of Massachusetts, moved to amend by striking out everything relating to legislation; for if we can not have prohibitory legislation it is better not to have any, and not to have legislation for licenses.

Rev. Dr. WOLCOTT, of Ohio, suggested that the amendment was

unnecessary; that the resolution referred to the "aid" of legislation, which could not mean legislation against temperance, and which did not exclude prohibition.

Rev. Dr. BLODGETT, of Rhode Island, said that the cause had received great aid from legislation in times past, and that it was proper to acknowledge, under God, although we might not rely upon it for the future.

Gov. BUCKINGHAM (Mr. Hammond in the chair), said: "I beg leave to say one thing on the question of legislation on the subject of temperance. I believe we want all the aid we can secure from any and every proper source to aid in the cause of temperance. There are men to be restrained by persuasion; there are other men to be held in check by positive legislation. [Applause.] We want both. I do not ask and I would not have an amendment in that report requiring prohibition; but I do ask that there shall be nothing stricken out to show that this Council are ready to reject all the co-operating influences of legislation. The best comment that I have known upon the prohibitory law has been before this nation within the past few days. I had the pleasure of being in Washington during the great review, and having been there forty-eight hours, and seen those streets thronged with tens of thousands of men, women, and children, and more than one hundred and fifty thousand soldiers, I saw not one intoxicated — not one. [Applause.] That was under the power of the military law, for every grogshop and every bar was closed by military authority. But no sooner was that military authority removed, no sooner were those grogshops and those bars opened again, than there was a scene of confusion and rioting which required military force for its suppression; and in order to prevent disorder in the city of Washington, orders were again issued by military authority that those places should be closed from seven o'clock at night until seven in the morning. Then again peace and order were restored. In view of these facts, I ask that this Council shall not utter a word that shall prevent proper legislation upon this subject. I do not ask for a prohibitory law. Let men judge as circumstances may determine. [Applause.]

Rev. Mr. GULLIVER, of Connecticut. I am persuaded that this Council did not properly measure the consequences of the vote passed just now, striking out the clause relating to "prohibition." I think if that clause had never been put in, it would have been a very different matter. But we have deliberately excluded that clause, upon the ground stated by the Rev. Dr. Bacon, that he believed that prohibition had killed the cause. We have, in a degree, indorsed that opinion.

SEVERAL MEMBERS. No, no.

Rev. Mr. GULLIVER, of Connecticut. I think we have; and I think a great many will so understand it. I appeal to some gentleman in the majority to move a reconsideration of that vote, that we may not even appear upon the record as opposed to a prohibitory law.

Rev. Mr. WEBB, of Massachusetts. For the gratification of the gentleman, I move a reconsideration, although I shall certainly vote against it. Whatever reason Dr. Bacon may have assigned for his motion, we adopted it upon our own deliberate judgment.

The motion to reconsider was rejected.

Rev. Dr. DUTTON, of Connecticut. I am afraid we are doing something rash in adopting that part of the report pertaining to medicines. Does not that imply that, in our judgment, intoxicating drinks are not to be given to convalescent persons?

SEVERAL MEMBERS. No, no.

The report of the committee was adopted.

LINCOLN COLLEGE.

Rev. Prof. Park, from the committee on Collegiate and Theological Education, reported the following resolutions: —

Resolved, That in order to the raising up of an educated ministry for the supply of the churches of the new States, now becoming filled by the advancing tide of population, and to meet the large demands of those States which recent events have opened to Christian influence, it is a fundamental necessity that well-endowed and well-manned collegiate and theological institutions should be established, and that, too, in the best positions.

Resolved, That the society for the Promotion of Collegiate and Theological Education at the West — in rendering efficient aid to fourteen Collegiate and Theological Institutions, scattered from Eastern Ohio to the Pacific coast, so placing them on sure foundations, and in so managing this whole subject, as at once to have saved the churches from annoyance, and to have given a wise direction to their charities — has accomplished a work of great and enduring benefit, which this Council recognize with gratitude to God, by whose help it has been wrought.

Resolved, That in view of the great work remaining to be done, both at the West, and in the South, and the admirable adaptation of this society to the accomplishment of it with the least possible friction and expense — this Council do heartily commend it to the increased confidence and larger liberality of the churches represented here.

RESOLUTION ON LINCOLN COLLEGE.

Whereas our brethren in Kansas are laying the foundations of a Congregational College, which shall, on the field of its early victory, be a monument of the triumph of freedom over slavery; a memorial of that Christian emancipator, whose name it bears; a source of ministerial supply for the Missouri valley and the regions beyond: Therefore,

Resolved, That we commend the enterprise to the confidence, sympathy and liberal support of all friends of New England principles and polity, of civil and religious liberty, and of home evangelization; and yet that their appeal to the public be only through and in accordance with the rules of the Society for the Promotion of Collegiate and Theological Education at the West.

Rev. Dr. Sturtevant, of Illinois, moved to strike out the last resolution, upon the ground that the Council should not make discriminations among the various institutions in the West that are claiming aid.

Rev. Prof. PARK explained that the friends of Lincoln College desired the passage of the resolution because another college had been organized, bearing the same name, and founded upon no religious principles.

Rev. Mr. BODWELL, of Kansas. Our object is not to place ourselves in an invidious position with reference to other colleges; but there is a movement to establish another college upon an unchristian basis, to bear the name of Mr. Lincoln. We think that Kansas is as good a place to build that monument as anywhere else. It is there that the first blood was shed; it is there that the conflict commenced. You talk of your Massachusetts martyrs who fell in the streets of Baltimore. The grass was growing upon the graves of our martyrs before they fell. We have sent, too, the most men into the army of the Union in proportion to our numbers. We think we are entitled above all other places to build a monument to Mr. Lincoln. We took this name before it became a power, before the death of Mr. Lincoln, and we think Providence has indicated that we are to build that monument. We want this indorsement, not to aid us in going before the churches, but to avoid being forestalled by another monument that from its greater nearness to the centers of wealth might overshadow ours. We are small, weak, and unknown. We wish, therefore, to place the name of our institution upon the records of this body, so that any attempt to forestall our movement may be suppressed.

The amendment was withdrawn, and the report was adopted.

Rev. Mr. Langworthy, from the committee on Nominations, reported the following committees; and the report was adopted.

Delegates to Temperance Convention. — Hon. William A. Buckingham, of Connecticut; Hon. Edward D. Holton, of Wisconsin; Dea. Charles A. Stackpole, of Maine; Rev. Henry M. Dexter, of Massachusetts.

On the Special Fund. — Rev. Edwin B. Webb, of Massachusetts; Rev. Thomas P. Field, D. D., of Connecticut; Rev. John C. Holbrook, of New York; Rev. George S. F. Savage, of Illinois; Rev. Richard Hall, of Minnesota.

On the American Protestant Assembly. — Rev. Jeremiah Taylor, D. D., of Connecticut; David S. Williams, of New York; Rev. William Carter, of Illinois; Hon. Edward D. Holton, of Wisconsin; Rev. John

Patchin, of Michigan; Richard J. Patterson, M. D., of Iowa; Rev. Charles Shedd, of Minnesota; Rev. Ezra Byington, of Vermont; Dea. Sampson W. Buffum, of New Hampshire; Dea. Jacob Blanchard, of Maine.

COMMITTEE ON STATEMENT OF CHURCH POLITY.

Hon. Mr. Hammond, of the special committee appointed to nominate a committee on Church Polity, reported the following:

Rev. Leonard Bacon, D. D., of Connecticut; Rev. Alonzo H. Quint, of Massachusetts; Rev. Henry M. Storrs, D. D., of Ohio; Rev. Edwards A. Park, D. D., of Massachusetts; Rev. Samuel Harris, D. D., of Maine; Rev. Samuel C. Bartlett, D. D., of Illinois; Rev. George P. Fisher, of Connecticut; Rev. James H. Fairchild, of Ohio; Rev. John P. Gulliver, of Connecticut; Rev. Benjamin Labaree, D. D., of Vermont; Rev. Mark Hopkins, D. D., of Massachusetts; Rev. William Barrows, of Massachusetts; Rev. Julian M. Sturtevant, D. D., of Illinois; Rev. Truman M. Post, D. D., of Missouri; Rev. Edward Beecher, D. D., of Illinois; Rev. William Salter, D. D., of Iowa; Rev. James S. Hoyt, of Michigan; Rev. David Burt, of Minnesota; Rev. Joseph P. Thompson, D. D., of New York; Hon. Woodbury Davis, of Maine; Hon. Henry Stockbridge, of Maryland; Hon. John H. Brockway, of Connecticut; Rev. Nathaniel A. Hyde, of Indiana; Rev. Leonard Swain, D. D., of Rhode Island; Rev. Richard Cordley, of Kansas; Asahel Finch, of Wisconsin; Warren Currier, Esq., of Missouri; and,

On motion, Rev. Rufus Anderson, D. D., of Massachusetts, was added to represent the missionary cause.

The report was adopted.

PAROCHIAL EVANGELIZATION.

Rev. Mr. Robinson, of Massachusetts, on behalf of the committee on Parochial Evangelization, presented the following report:

The committee, to whom was submitted the paper on Parochial Evangelization, presented to the Council, would respectfully report.

The relation which the work of Parochial Evangelization bears to other objects of Christian enterprise will be obvious at a glance. It is preliminary, and, as a condition of ultimate success, indispensable. How, for instance, can the great work of evangelization at the West and South, which has occupied so large a portion of the time of this Council, be carried on, unless our home communities are pervaded and permeated by the spirit of the gospel? How are foreign missions to be sustained, if heathenism is intrenched on our own shores? Whence are to come the future ministers and missionaries of the cross, if there are no Christian homes, and young men consecrated from their infancy to Christ and the church? How are collegiate and theological institutions to be established and endowed, unless the wealth of the land is in the hands of men, who, having first given themselves to God, acknowledge his claim upon all that they possess? How are the treasuries of our various benevolent societies to be supplied, if there are no springs of piety and Christian sympathy to feed the channels of benevolence, and swell the streams that make glad the city of our God? We do not say that no foreign work is to be done until the whole home field is cultivated, and made as the garden of the Lord,—that, until our own parishes are thoroughly evangelized, the heathen must be left to perish; but what hope can we have of final success in converting the world to Christ, unless his kingdom be established in the hearts and homes of our own people? The stream will not rise above the fountain. The fruits of the Spirit must somewhere be grown before they can be transplanted and propagated. What advantage will it be to build new churches at the West and South if the churches of New England are to die out and disappear? Why plant a Christian empire in the heart of Asia or Africa with a heathen population at our very doors? Let not the church, "who is the mother of us all," ever be obliged to say, "They made me the keeper of the vineyards, but mine own vineyard have I not kept."

Your committee are more and more impressed with the importance of this work. They have carefully examined and considered the report submitted to their inspection. They indorse substantially the recommendations appended at the close, and commend the report as a whole to the earnest and prayerful consideration of the churches represented in Council.

The committee do not feel called upon to discuss anew the general subject; this is not necessary. But there are certain fundamental truths or principles brought to view in the report, to which they would call special attention, that it may be understood what is the precise work, and what substantially are the measures, to which the Council virtually pledge themselves, should the report in question be adopted.

1. *The Church in its Design.*

The church is a brotherhood of believers, united in the bonds of Christian fellowship, for the upbuilding of Christ's kingdom among themselves and throughout the world. In its very nature and design, the church is aggressive; nor will it have done its work until every man, woman, and child is brought under the power of the gospel.

2. *The Parochial Relations of the Church.*

Every local church is the center of a parish, more or less extended, as the case may be. Geographical limits can not always be assigned, nor is it necessary that they should be. Two or more parishes may come within the same bounds, and cover much the same ground. The parish of each church consists of all the families not belonging to other congregations within its reach. For the evangelization of these, it is held of God responsible. There may be outlying districts, neglected neighborhoods, on the borders of towns and villages. These also are to be cared for. In some way, by systematic visitation, by neighborhood prayer-meetings and occasional preaching services, by mission Sabbath schools and the distribution of religious books and tracts, by the circulation of the Scriptures and the employment perhaps of Bible-readers, the people of such outlying neighborhoods are to be made acquainted with the truths of the gospel. And these movements are to be under the supervision of the church; not spasmodic, but steady; not philanthropic simply, but Christian; the forth-putting, on the part of the church, of its activity and power. All effort in the work of parochial evangelization that is not connected with the local church, and does not bring the evangelized masses within the fold, and under the watch and care of the church, will prove futile.

3. *Church Accommodations and Worship.*

Ample accommodations are to be provided for all who are disposed, or who can be persuaded, to attend upon the services of the sanctuary. The style of church architecture should be such as to bring the pew sittings within the reach of the poorer classes. The sanctuary should be made attractive also, not by costly embellishment, but by a clear and winning exhibition of the truth as it is in Jesus. There is no such power to sway the hearts of men as is found in the simple preaching of the doctrines of the cross. In "the service of song in the house of the Lord," it is the duty and privilege of all, so far as they may, to participate. There is devotion in such singing more than in the performances of a few hired singers. The Scriptures, whether read or chanted, should have prominent place in any church service; while the offering of prayer should be, not a prescribed form, but the free out-breathing of a soul in habitual communion with God. With such a service, however humble the structure in which it was held, the people would be drawn to the house of God, and they who came to scoff, perhaps, remain to pray.

4. *The Duty of Ministers.*

It is the duty of every minister of Christ to explain to his people the nature and methods of this work of parochial evangelization, and to direct them in it. He is himself, so far as health and other circumstances may allow, to take the initiative. Like his divine Lord, he is to *seek*, as well as to attempt to save, the lost. In going forth to the remoter sections of his parish, and preaching the gospel from house to house, in the patient endurance of toil and hardship and self-denial in this blessed work, he is to be an ensample to the flock. More especially is he to lay upon the hearts and consciences of the people to whom he ministers the responsibility that properly devolves upon them. He is to make them see and feel that they have something to do; that they were called into the kingdom of Christ to labor, and not to rest. He is to guide them, teach them, show them how they may be useful. He is to inspire them, to animate them, with his own spirit of self-denial, and devotion to the Master's cause. If he is not equal to this, he is not fit for his place. "Behold," says the prophet, "I have given him for a witness to the people, a leader and commander to the people." And such should every minister of Christ be among the people of his charge, — a leader as well as a witness.

5. *Lay Preaching.*

The duty of laymen, in their own way and sphere, to preach the gospel of Christ, is now acknowledged. All are to spread the glad tidings. A personal responsibility rests upon every member of the church to engage in this work. Ministers are no more called of God to win souls to Christ than laymen. "Let him that heareth say, Come." One may preach in the pulpit, and the other just as really, and perhaps more persuasively, in his warehouse or workshop. "Lord, what wilt thou have *me* to do?" is the question which every professed disciple of Christ should raise from day to day. "Where can I be most useful?" "How can I most honor him who loved me, and gave himself for me?" The church is supposed to be a body of workers, not of drones. "We, then, as workers together with him," says Paul. If any man will not work, neither shall he eat of that spiritual bread which came down from heaven. The question has been raised, whether the time has not come for setting apart an order of lay evangelists. And this matter is certainly worthy of consideration. Let no man run before he is sent; but when he is sent of God, then let him not stay.

6. *Special Efforts for the Young.*

Efforts are to be made for the conversion of all, but more especially for the children and youth. They are the hope of the flock. Let them be gathered, one and all, into the Sabbath school, under competent teachers, "wise to win souls to Christ." Let the old system of catechetical instruction be revived, or some substitute be found, which shall be equally crowned and blessed of God. Let more prominence be given to the rite and doctrine of infant baptism. Let Christian parents be instructed as to their duty and privilege in this particular, until they shall come to see the preciousness of covenant blessings, proffered to them and their seed after them. Let the hearts of the fathers be turned unto the children, and the hearts of the children unto the fathers, that the curse may be averted, and the pains and penalties of the Old Testament be converted into the promises of the New. Children should be brought to the house of God also. The Sabbath school is no proper substitute for the regular church service any more than for household religious instruction. Sermons to children should be preached occasionally, and other means devised to instruct them in the truth and the gospel. He who said, "Feed my sheep," said also, "Feed my lambs."

7. *The Home Prayer-Meeting.*

The committee attach great importance to this. The object of the meeting should be to devise ways and means for reaching the neglected classes of the community; those who live under the very eaves of the sanctuary, and yet have never been persuaded to enter. Prayer should be offered with special reference to this object. Reports should be received from visiting committees, tract distributers, Bible readers, when such have been appointed. The pastor should give some account of his labors, of the encouragements he has met, and the discouragements and obstacles with which he has to contend. The main point should be, not so much to make the meeting interesting as useful. Then it will prove both interesting and useful; a meeting which the churches will not be willing to forego.

8. *The Social Element in the Church.*

How can we make the most of the social influence and power of the church? is a most important inquiry. There is felt to be a want in all our churches, — a want of sympathy and mutual love. We are not one as Christ prayed that we might become. There are lines of division in the church which ought to be obliterated. How to obviate this difficulty is the problem to be solved. It is related of one whose name and memory are indissolubly associated with this church edifice,[1] whose hands helped to build these walls, and whose spirit still lingers about the sanctuary in which he so long worshiped (the late Deacon Safford), that he "regarded the family of Christ as his own family." It was his custom to keep a list of the members of the church, and to cultivate a personal acquaintance with each, — loving those united with him in these sacred bonds "with a pure heart fervently." This sheds light upon the subject so far as the officers of the church are concerned. Something can be done also in the way of social gatherings, meetings of sewing societies, etc. What is wanted is simply to bring those who are members of the mystical body of Christ heart to heart. Then also will they see "eye to eye." There ought to be no tie so tender and strong as that which binds one church-member to another; no feeling of love like that which wells up in the heart of every believer from that common fountain whence we draw our spiritual life. Over the portals of our churches, that all who enter there may read, should be inscribed, "Love the Brotherhood."

9. *Higher Standard of Piety in the Church.*

We might almost say that the whole work of parochial evangelization resolves itself into this. Let the standard of piety be elevated; let every church-member feel that he is called of God and consecrated to the work of serving Christ in saving lost men; that this is his mission, and not to get money or achieve a high social position, — the work which is given to him as a Christian man to do, and by which he is to prove that he is a Christian man, — and there would be no further need of discussion as to the methods of parochial evangelization. A way would be opened, a broad highway, in which every consecrated believer in Jesus would delight to walk. What we want on the part of the membership of the churches is more humility, more brokenness of spirit, a deeper and truer penitence for sin. We want a stronger love for Christ, a more abiding sense of obligation to him. We want, as ministers and laymen, more of the spirit of self-denial and self-sacrifice, the spirit of the cross, — a willingness to be anything or do anything if only God may be glorified, and we glorified in him. The evangelization, not of our parishes simply, but of the world, is an easy problem when contemplated from this point of view.

[1] Mt. Vernon Church.

10. *The Abiding Presence and Power of the Holy Ghost.*

We live under the dispensation of the Spirit. This fact is never to be lost sight of in all our plans and efforts. The doctrine of the Holy Ghost, of his personality and power, should be made very prominent in the preaching of ministers at the present day. There have been three grand epochs in the history of the world. In the first, God the Father was the principal actor. In the second, God the Son. Now appears God the Holy Ghost, to whom it is given to complete the glorious work. He is the source of all spiritual life and strength. Without him we are nothing. And just here is our danger in this work of home evangelization. We mature our plans, we organize our forces, we enter upon the work. The machinery is perfect, and we expect great results. But the spirit of power does not rest upon us, and we can accomplish nothing. How different is it when the Spirit is poured out from on high!

But we need the continued presence of the Spirit in our churches, and this was the promise of Christ: "And I will pray the Father, and He shall give you another Comforter, that He may abide with you for ever." We have our seasons of refreshing followed by seasons of spiritual declension. How can we constrain the blessed Spirit to *abide* with us? The question still remains to be answered. One thing, however, is certain: when that time shall come, the problem which now seems so difficult will have been solved. "Then will the Lord create upon every dwelling-place of Mount Zion, and upon her assemblies, a cloud of smoke by day, and the shining of a flaming fire by night; for upon all the glory shall be a defense." Then every house will have its altar, and from every hearthstone will ascend incense and a pure offering. "Then judgment shall dwell in the wilderness, and righteousness remain in the fruitful field. And the work of righteousness shall be peace, and the effect of righteousness, quietness and assurance for ever." May the Lord hasten it in his time!

R. T. Robinson,
A. S. Chesebrough,
J. M. Holmes,
H. M. Goodwin,
D. Burt,
R. Cordley,
J. T. Ford.

The report was accepted.

Rev. Dr. Adams, of Maine. I would make a request, rather than a motion, that the phrase, "and not by artistic singing from hired choirs," be stricken out; not but that I am heart and soul, from top to toe, in sympathy with the sentiment, but that many of our churches do employ hired singers, and I would not reflect upon them.

Hon. Mr. Hammond, of Illinois. I would ask if we are for ever to be striking out things which we believe from the bottom of our hearts to be true.

At the suggestion of Rev. Dr. Dutton, of Connecticut,—

Rev. Dr. Adams modified his request, and formally moved to amend so as to read, "There is devotion in such singing *more than in* the performance of a few hired singers," etc.

The amendment was agreed to.

On motion of Rev. Dr. Leavitt, of New York, the word "supervision" was substituted for "control," in speaking of the efforts in evangelizing parishes, &c., so as to read that they "should be under the supervision of the church."

The report was then adopted.

CHURCH IN WASHINGTON, D. C.

Rev. Mr. Buckingham, from the committee on the Church in Washington, D. C., read the following report:—

The Committee preferred that no specific sum should be recommended, but that the whole matter should be referred to the Congregational Union, and therefore recommend the adoption of the following resolution:

Resolved, That the trustees of the American Congregational Union, be advised and requested to take into consideration the importance of a well-sustained Congregational Church in the city of Washington; and, having ascertained what facilities there are for the establishment of such a church, and what aid will be necessary to institute the arrangement, according to their best judgment and discretion, to build or purchase a suitable edifice in the National Capital in which a Congregational Church may maintain the preaching of the gospel and public worship of God.

The resolution was adopted.

FAST-DAY.

Rev. Dr. Swain, of Rhode Island, read the following report of the committee upon a Day of Fasting and Prayer:—

The committee would recommend that Thursday, the 14th day of September next, be observed by the churches represented in this Council as a day of fasting and prayer to Almighty God for the outpouring upon them of his Holy Spirit, so that this great convocation may be speedily followed by those good effects which were aimed at in the beginning, by a close union and a warmer mutual sympathy both among ourselves and with all who love our common Lord; by a deeper and more intelligent grasp of the principles of our own faith and polity; by a more earnest personal consecration to Christ and his kingdom; by a new spirit of missionary zeal both in behalf of the work to be done abroad, and the new and important fields to be occupied at home ; so that, having, like the primitive disciples, tarried at Jerusalem for "The promise of the Father," the ministry and the churches may go forth beneath a new and mighty baptism of the Holy Ghost to preach that gospel which brought our fathers to these shores, which is sent for the healing of the nations, and which is destined to lead the whole world unto Christ. The committee would also recommend that a committee of three be appointed to prepare, and issue to the churches as soon as possible, a circular to this effect, embracing also an appeal to the churches in behalf of the 750,000 dollar fund.

A member stated that the Massachusetts Conference holds its Convention upon Sept. 14th, the day recommended by the committee.

After consultation, Friday, the 15th of September, was appointed as the day of fasting and prayer.

The report as amended was adopted.

It was now half past two o'clock, and on motion of Rev. Mr. Quint, of Massachusetts, the hour of adjournment was postponed for half an hour.

Rev. Dr. ANDERSON, of Massachusetts. There were a few mistakes as to matters of fact in the answer to the foreign delegations, which it was Dr. Bacon's intention to ask permission to correct. He is not here, and, as the hour of adjournment is at hand, I would move that the chairman be authorized to make such corrections in that report as shall make it correspond with matters of fact since ascertained.

The motion was carried.

Rev. Mr. Langworthy, from the committee on Nominations, reported the following names as the

COMMITTEE TO PREPARE A PASTORAL LETTER.

Committee to prepare a Pastoral Letter.—Rev. Edward N. Kirk, D. D., of Massachusetts ; Rev. Oliver E. Daggett, D. D., New York ; Rev. Asa Turner, of Iowa.

THE ROLL.

Rev. Dr. Beecher, of Illinois, from the committee on the Roll, presented their report, embracing the list of delegates, and in submitting it, said :—

"In addition to this report, I wish to state certain things that should be understood in connection with the result of our labors, and which, unless there shall be an indication to the contrary, we shall consider as sanctioned by the assent of this body.

"The names in the list are arranged in alphabetical order, beginning with California and ending with Wisconsin. The mode of arrangement will be this: — At the National Council of the Congregational Churches of the United States of America, convened by letters missive issued by committees of the General Association, Conference or Convention of Maine, New Hampshire, etc. — specifying the States that in fact issued the letters, — were present from Maine, etc., delegates from the following churches: —then specify the churches that acted in the conference, and opposite put the names and residences of the delegates, by whom they were represented, and pursue that order through.

"There was passed, subsequently to the appointment of this committee, an order, 'That the committee on the roll be instructed to report the names of those members only who furnish a list of the churches that actually participated in the vote, by which they were chosen.' To this vote the committee were obliged to give a liberal construction in some cases, to wit, in the cases of Maryland, Delaware, and Tennessee, in which 'churches' did not participate in the action, inasmuch as there was but one church in each of those States to act. In these cases, the church and delegate are reported, and the committee, in making out the roll, assumed that the proceedings in these cases were satisfactory, and to be considered as coming within the spirit of the invitation.

"I would also state, that in some cases we accepted parole testimony as to the action of certain churches. For example: Here are certificates from three churches in Oregon that they elected G. H. Atkinson as a delegate to this body. The document which he brought was simply an appointment by the General Association of Oregon, which, according to the principles adopted, would not be satisfactory credentials. But there are, from three churches in Oregon, testimonials that they met as churches and elected him; and he gave parole testimony that three other churches did the same. We have accepted that statement, and reported six churches from Oregon, instead of the three from which we had formal credentials. In other cases, where that principle applied, we have not reported the names of the churches, unless there were credentials that covered the case, or that which was considered satisfactory evidence that the churches had acted in the case, and were truly represented.

"I would also state that one church, which was not present by delegate deserves notice, for the sake of the moral impression, and that is the church in Utah. The facts in regard to this church are these: An invitation was sent by Dr. Bacon to the church, and a reply from the pastor located there received, stating that the letter had come to hand, and at the same time stating some very interesting facts with regard to that church — the only church in the territory of Mormonism, in the Salt Lake City; and we felt that in some way this church, which does not properly come upon the roll, should be presented and commended to the sympathy of the Congregational Churches of the United States; and in connection with the proceedings of this Council, and with the consent of the body, the committee will in some way bring this to pass."

The report of the committee was accepted.

APPLICATION FOR THE OPENING SERMON.

Rev. Dr. Leavitt, of New York, stated that the publishers of the "Independent" desired to print the sermon of Dr. Sturtevant in next week's paper, and moved that the manuscript be returned to the preacher for that purpose.

After some explanatory statements in regard to the matter by the scribe, Rev. H. M. Dexter, the motion was laid on the table upon the motion of Rev. P. R. Hurd, of Michigan.

MISCELLANEOUS MATTERS.

Rev. Mr. Quint, of Massachusetts, from the committee on Business, stated that there were a few papers still remaining in the hands of that committee, and submitted them to the Council, as follows: —

Resolved, That this Council recognize with thankfulness the blessing of God upon the instruction and influence of Sabbath schools, and commend this instrumentality to the deeper interest and more earnest prayers of the churches.

Adopted.

Resolved, That the following minute be entered upon the records of this Council: That the Council declares that no action that has been taken by this body is to be taken as adverse to any prohibitory action on the subject of temperance.

Adopted.

Resolved, That the official proceedings of this Council be published in the "Congregational Quarterly," and that the sum of two hundred dollars be appropriated toward the expense of printing, and that the publishers be requested to issue as many copies of the same proceedings, in a separate form as shall be called for, at cost price.

Adopted.

Resolved, That the original records and papers of this Council, with the phonographic report, be, after the final adjournment, placed on perpetual deposit with the directors of the American Congregational Association, never to be removed from its library room; and that the directors be authorized to publish a volume of proceedings and debates.

Adopted.

Resolved, That when the work of the committee on a Platform of Polity is concluded, it be published under the care of a committee, by the directors of the American Congregational Association, who shall retain the copyright.

Adopted.

Resolved, That the Declaration of Faith adopted by this Council, and the Confession of Faith adopted by our Synod at Boston, in 1680, be printed with the report that the committee on Polity may make, that our doctrine and polity may go out together, and be easily obtained by every one of the churches.

Adopted.

The committee on Business recommended that the duty of compiling these documents be entrusted to the committee on Polity, and this recommendation was adopted.

On motion of Rev. Mr. Davis, of New Hampshire, it was ordered, That the committee on Church Polity be authorized, if they think best, to issue an epitome or digest of their large work for use and circulation among the churches, the copyright to be held in trust by the Directers of the American Congregational Association.

Adopted.

FINANCES.

Dea. STODDARD, of Massachusetts. I do not understand how the matter of finance is left. Mr. Henry Hill is Treasurer, but he has never been appointed by this body. There is but little money in the treasury, probably not more than enough to pay expenses ; but, suppose money should come in after this body adjourns, who is to be the custodian of it ? I don't see that there is any provision made for that.

Rev. Mr. GULLIVER, of Connecticut. I move that Mr. Henry Hill be the Treasurer of this body, and dispose of the money in his possession under the rules.

Dea. STODDARD. Do I understand that the functions of the committee on Finance cease when this body adjourns?

THE MODERATOR. Like all other appointees of this body, I think their duties are then at an end.

Hon. Mr. HAMMOND, of Illinois. There is a resolution upon the subject, which was brought in by Mr. Barstow, which fixes the status of that committee. [The resolution was read by the scribe.]

Dea. STODDARD. Then the committee lives after this body dissolves?

Hon. Mr. HAMMOND. Yes, sir.

Rev. Dr. ANDERSON, of Massachusetts. I think it would be well to appoint the treasurer upon that committee.

Hon. Mr. HAMMOND. I would move that Mr. Henry Hill be added to the committee on Finance, with Dea. Stoddard.

Adopted.

MEMORIAL TO JOHN ROBINSON.

Rev. Mr. DEXTER, of Massachusetts. I desire to state that the house in which John Robinson lived, in Leyden, has been identified in the square opposite the cathedral of St. Peter's, and our American Minister at one time intended to insert a stone in the wall, calling the attention of the traveler to the fact that he once lived upon that spot. I thought it would be a pleasant thing if this Council would authorize the placing of a slab in the wall of that house, with a suitable inscription, testifying to the traveler, and to the students of the University, which is very near the house, that the representatives of three thousand churches — fruits of the seed that was in the ground there for a little while — gratefully remember that John Robinson once dwelt and taught on that spot. It can be done without any expense to the Council. I move that a committee be appointed, and authorized to prepare a proper inscription for a slab to be placed in that wall.

The motion was carried, and Rev. Messrs. Dexter and Wellman, of Massachusetts, were appointed that committee.

CLOSING PROCEEDINGS.

Rev. Mr. QUINT. The business of the Council, so far as the committee know, is closed, with this exception, that two brethren desire to offer resolutions. Over forty committees have reported, and a great number of papers have been acted upon. We move now that all business be closed, except to hear motions from the Hon. Mr. Hammond, and Rev. Dr. Wolcott.

Carried.

Hon. Mr. HAMMOND. The resolutions which I hold in my hand were placed there by Mr. Eustis: —

Resolved, That this Council declare their high appreciation of the time and labor which have been expended by the committees appointed by the preliminary meeting at New York, to prepare business for this Council, and especially to the committee of Arrangements at Boston, to whom they are indebted for innumerable attentions, and for that excursion to the spot where our forefathers first brought that Catholic Church whose order we maintain. They would also gratefully notice the invitations from individuals and corporations, most of which we regret to have been obliged to decline.

Resolved, secondly, That this National Council of the Congregational Churches of the United States do hereby return their thanks to the citizens of Boston and its vicinity for the generous hospitality which has been so munificently provided for the members during this session, and to the churches whose sanctuaries have been freely opened for their accommodation ; and pray the Lord who does not forget even a cup of cold water given a disciple, to reward with the richest spiritual blessings this community, for their abounding kindnesses and entertainments.

The resolutions were adopted unanimously.

Rev. Dr. Wolcott, of Ohio, offered the following resolution, which was unanimously adopted : —

Resolved, That the Council tenders its thanks to His Excellency, Gov. Buckingham, our honored Moderator, for the dignity, urbanity, and courtesy with which he has presided over its deliberations, to which, in part, we ascribe the pleasant cordiality of feeling, unmarred by bitterness or harshness, which has prevailed throughout its earnest discussions ; and as a National Council we express the satisfaction with which we are reminded by this assembly of the early days of our Puritan history, when the chief magistrates of the colonies were the servants of the churches, and the honors of the State were humbly laid at the foot of the cross.

The Moderator replied as follows : —

Mr. Moderator : I am not prepared — not able — properly to reply to that resolution. I remember, by history, that one hundred and fifty-seven years ago, my paternal ancestor presided as the Assistant Moderator at that synod which adopted the Saybrook Platform. [Applause.] For me to occupy such a position as I do to-day, through your partiality, is a high privilege. I believe I occupy it, in part, in consequence of the partiality which has been manifested by the citizens of Connecticut toward me, in placing me in a position which has linked my name, for the few years past, with the government of that little State so intimately connected with the cause of liberty and civil government. [Applause.] This, also, has been an unspeakable privilege, occurring, as it has, during a period when all the interests of civil government have been, as it were, concentrated upon the events of the passing hour or year. No events have ever transpired, in the history of this world, of such importance to civilization, to civil government, to morality, and to religion, as the events which have transpired before us. It is a privilege to live at such a time; and it is a privilege to be the chief magistrate of a State whose patriotism goes down to the very depths of love, and offers her sons and her fathers as sacrifices on the altar of liberty. [Applause.]

But there are still higher interests than those of merely civil government ; there are higher interests than those which are merely temporal ; for they will pass away. This Council binds us to those higher interests, reaching from this, on to another, life ; and to be connected with a body like this, which takes action for the promotion of those interests, is a higher privilege than is enjoyed by any man whose duties relate merely to earthly things. I rejoice in it. I am grateful to you ; I thank you for your forbearance toward me. I am grateful to God who grants me this privilege. [Applause.]

Rev. Dr. Wolcott also presented the following resolution, which was adopted, unanimously: —

Resolved, That the ability with which the occasional and special services which have devolved upon our respected Assistant Moderators have been performed, and the promptness and thoroughness with which our Scribes have discharged their various duties, are entitled to special recognition. And to all these officers, also, the Council tenders its thanks for their faithfulness and efficiency.

Hon. Mr. HAMMOND. In the absence of Dr. Thompson, I can only say we sincerely thank you for the kindness with which you have received all we have attempted to do to carry forward the business of this Council. I would say one other word, and that is, that to the latest day of my life, I shall with gratitude and with joy look back to the doings of this Council, hoping, as I do, that all future generations will with us rejoice that this Council has met, — that it has met in Boston, and that it has done what it has. And may the Lord bless us all! [Applause.]

The minutes of the day's proceedings were, at this point, read and approved.

THE MODERATOR. I understand that the Synod which was summoned in 1648 closed by singing the "Song of Moses and the Lamb." What version it was, I know not; but I propose that we now sing three verses of that song, as it is found in the 159th hymn. Sing the first and the last two verses.

The verses referred to are the following, and they were sung by the entire Council, the congregation also uniting: —

"Awake, and sing the song
Of Moses and the Lamb;
Wake, every heart, and every tongue,
To praise the Saviour's name!

"Soon shall we hear him say,
'Ye blessed children, come;'
Soon will he call us hence away
To our eternal home.

"Soon shall our raptured tongue
His endless praise proclaim,
And sweeter voices tune the song
Of Moses and the Lamb."

Rev. Rufus Anderson, D. D., of Massachusetts, then offered a fervent and solemn prayer, after which the Doxology was sung, —

"To God the Father, God the Son,
And God the Spirit, Three in One,
Be honor, praise, and glory given,
By all on earth, and all in heaven !"

The Moderator then declared the Council adjourned, without day.

(Signed)

WILLIAM A. BUCKINGHAM, MODERATOR.
JOSEPH P. THOMPSON, FIRST ASSISTANT.
C. G. HAMMOND, SECOND ASSISTANT.
HENRY M. DEXTER,
PHILO R. HURD,
M. K. WHITTLESEY,
SAMUEL HOLMES,
E. P. MARVIN,
SCRIBES.

THE NAMES OF THE MEMBERS OF THE NATIONAL CONGREGATIONAL COUNCIL WHICH CONVENED IN BOSTON, JUNE 14th, 1865, WITH THEIR PLACES OF RESIDENCE AND THEIR BIRTHPLACES, AS ALSO THOSE OF THEIR FATHERS AND MOTHERS.

PREPARED BY REV. INCREASE N. TARBOX, BOSTON, MASS.

NAME.	PLACE OF RESIDENCE.	BIRTHPLACE.	BIRTHPLACE OF FATHER.	BIRTHPLACE OF MOTHER.
Dea. Charles Adams,	Litchfield, Ct.,	Litchfield, Ct.,	Roxbury, Mass.,	Litchfield, Ct.
Rev. George Eliashib Adams, D. D.,	Brunswick, Me.,	Worthington, Mass.,	Canterbury, Ct.,	Sherborn, Mass.
" George Moulton Adams,	Portsmouth, N. H.,	Castine, Me.,	Pembroke, N. H.,	Bucksport, Me.
" Harvey Adams,	Farmington, Iowa,	Alstead, N. H.,	Franklin, Mass.,	Franklin, Mass.
Ebenezer Alden, M. D.,	Randolph, Mass.,	Randolph, Mass.,	Stafford, Ct.,	Randolph, Mass.
Rev. Ebenezer Alden, jr.,	Marshfield, Mass.,	Randolph, Mass.,	Randolph, Mass.,	Newburyport, Mass.
" Walter Scott Alexander,	Pomfret, Ct.,	Killingly, Ct.,	Killingly, Ct.,	Killingly, Ct.
" Asa Smith Allen,	Black-Earth, Wis.,	Medfield, Mass.,	Medfield, Mass.,	Walpole, Mass.
" George Allen,	Worcester, Mass.,	Worcester, Mass.,	Boston, Mass.,	East Hartford, Ct.
" Joshua Wing Allen,	Franklin, Mich.,	Jefferson, N. Y.,	State of N. Y.,	State of Vt.
" Rufus Anderson, D. D.,	Roxbury, Mass.,	North Yarmouth, Me.,	Londonderry, N. H.,	New Gloucester, Me.
" Israel Ward Andrews, D. D.,	Marietta, Ohio,	Danbury, Ct.,	Ellington, Ct.,	North Adams, Mass.
John Swain Andrews, M. D.,	Ashby, Mass.,	Fitchburg, Mass.,	Ipswich, Mass.,	Ashby, Mass.
Rev. George N. Anthony,	Marlborough, Mass.,	South Kingston, R. I.,	South Kingston, R. I.,	South Kingston, R. I.
" Hiram P. Arms, D. D.,	Norwich, Ct.,	Windsor, Ct.,	Deerfield, Mass.,	Goshen, Mass.
Dea. Horace Armsby,	Millbury, Mass.,	Paris, Me.,	Foxborough, Mass.,	Northbridge, Mass.
Caleb Brooks Atkins,	Glenwood, Iowa,	Chelsea, Mass.,	Wellfleet, Mass.,	Chelsea, Mass.
Rev. George Henry Atkinson,	Portland, Oregon,	Newburyport, Mass.,	Newbury, Mass.,	Newbury, Mass.
Albert Austin,	Suffield, Ct.,	Suffield, Ct.,	Suffield, Ct.,	Suffield, Ct.
Rev. Frederick D. Avery,	Columbia, Ct.,	Groton, Ct.,	Groton, Ct.,	Groton, Ct.
Marshall Ayres,	Griggsville, Ill.,	Truro, Mass.,	North Brookfield, Mass.,	Templeton, Mass.
Rev. Rowland Ayres,	Hadley, Mass.,	Granby, Mass.,	Granby, Mass.,	Granby, Mass.
Jacob Bacon,	San Francisco, Cal.,	Bath, Me.,	North Yarmouth, Me.,	North Yarmouth, Me.
Rev. James Monroe Bacon,	Essex, Mass.,	Newton, Mass.,	Wayland, Mass.,	Charleston, N. H.
" Leonard Bacon, D. D.,	New Haven, Ct.,	Detroit, Mich.,	Woodstock, Ct.,	Bethlem, Ct.
" Milton Badger, D. D.,	New York City, N. Y.,	Coventry, Ct.,	Coventry, Ct.,	Coventry, Ct.

Rev. Smith Baker, jr.,	Veazie, Me.,	Bowdoin, Me.,	Litchfield, Me.,	Litchfield, Me.
" Uriah Balkam,	Lewiston, Me.,	Robbinston, Me.,	Attleborough, Mass.,	Norton, Mass.
" William Macleod Barbour,	South Danvers, Mass.,	Scotland,	England,	Scotland.
" Davis Robert Barker,	Guy's Mills, Pa.,	Hope, Me.,	Kennebunk, Me.,	Concord, Mass.
Dea. Sherman Sergents Barnard,	Willsborough, N. Y.,	Marlborough, Mass.,	Amherst, Mass.,	Glastenbury, Ct.
Rev. Stephen Alfred Barnard,	Detroit, Mich.,	New Hartford, N. Y.,	Marlborough, Mass.,	Boston, Mass.
" William Barrows,	Reading, Mass.,	New Braintree, Mass.,	Thompson, Ct.,	Sudbury, Mass.
Hon. Amos Chafee Barstow,	Providence, R. I.,	Providence, R. I.,	Scituate, R. I.,	Providence, R. I.
Rev. Zedekiah Smith Barstow, D. D.,	Keene, N. H.,	Canterbury, Ct.,	Canterbury, Ct.,	Canterbury, Ct.
" Alexander Bartlett,	Austinburg, Ohio,	Salisbury, Ct.,	Plympton, Mass.,	Salisbury, Ct.
" Joseph Bartlett,	Buxton, Me.,	Salisbury, N. H.,	Salisbury, N. H.,	Salisbury, N. H.
Rev. Prof. Samuel Colcord Bartlett, D. D.,	Chicago, Ill.,	Salisbury, N. H.,	Salisbury, N. H.,	Salisbury, N. H.
Rev. Flavel Bascom,	Princeton, Ill.,	Lebanon, Ct.,	Lebanon, Ct.,	Colchester, Ct.
" Henry Bates,	Grass Lake, Mich.,	Charlton, Mass.,	Bellingham, Mass.,	Mendon, Mass.
" Edward Beecher, D. D.,	Galesburg, Ill.,	E. Hampton, L. I., N. Y.,	New Haven, Ct.,	Guilford, Ct.
" Frederick W. Beecher,	Kankakee, Ill.,	Jacksonville, Ill.,	E. Hampton, L. I., N.Y.,	Biddeford, Me.
" Henry Ward Beecher,	Brooklyn, N. Y.,	Litchfield, Ct.,	New Haven, Ct.,	Guilford, Ct.
Hon. James Dean Bell,	Walden, Vt.,	Walden, Vt.,	Lyme, N. H.,	Hardwick, Mass.
Rev. Henry S. Bennett,	Wakeman, Ohio,	Brownsville, Pa.,	Chester Co., Pa.,	Brownsville, Pa.
" George Bent,	Burr Oak, Iowa,	Middlebury, Vt.,	Rutland, Mass.,	Holden, Mass.
" Thomas Curtis Biscoe,	Grafton, Mass.,	Cambridge, Mass.,	Watertown, Mass.,	Framingham, Mass.
" Nelson Bishop,	Windsor, Vt.,	Manchester, Ct.,	Bolton, Ct.,	Columbia, Ct.
" George Washington Blagden, D. D.,	Boston, Mass.,	Washington, D. C.,	England,	England.
" Amos Blanchard, D. D.,	Lowell, Mass.,	Andover, Mass.,	Wilton, N. H.,	Andover, Mass.
Dea. Jacob Blanchard,	Blanchard, Me.,	Cumberland, Me.,	Cumberland, Me.,	Cumberland, Me.
Rev. Thomas Eliakim Bliss,	Memphis, Tenn.,	Brimfield, Mass.,	Brimfield, Mass.,	Belchertown, Mass.
" Constantine Blodgett, D. D.,	Pawtucket, R. I.,	Randolph, Vt.,	Stafford, Ct.,	Monson, Mass.
" Lewis Bodwell,	Wyandotte, Kansas,	New Haven, Ct.,	Simsbury, Ct.,	Durham, N. Y.
Hon. Walter Booth,	Meriden, Ct.,	Woodbridge, Ct.,	Woodbridge, Ct.,	Woodbridge, Ct.
Rev. Nathaniel Bouton, D. D.,	Concord, N. H.,	Norwalk, Ct.,	Norwalk, Ct.,	Norwalk, Ct.
Henry C. Bowen, Esq.,	Brooklyn, N. Y.,	Woodstock, Ct.	Woodstock, Ct.,	Dudley, Mass.
Edson Boyd, M. D.,	Ashville, N. Y.,	Carroll, N. Y.,	Wilmington, Vt.,	Halifax, Vt.
Hon. John Boyd,	Winsted, Ct.,	Winsted, Ct.,	Little Britain, N. Y.,	Boston, Mass.
Rev. Charles Boynton,	Watertown, Wis.,	Watertown, N. Y.,	Concord, N. H.,	Deerfield, N. Y.
Dea. William T. Bradbury,	Westminster, Mass.,	Hollis, N. H.,	Haverhill, Mass.,	Hollis, N. H.
Joseph Russell Bradford, Esq.,	Roxbury, Mass.,	Watertown, Mass.,	Billerica, Mass.,	Boston, Mass.

Rev. John Bradshaw,	Crown Point, N. Y.,	Potsdam, N. Y.	. . . . . .	. . . .
" Davis Smith Brainerd,	Old Lyme, Ct.,	Haddam, Ct.,	Haddam, Ct.	Haddam, Ct.
" Lewis Oramond Brastow,	St. Johnsbury, Vt.,	Brewer, Me.,	Brewer, Me.,	Brewer, Me.
" Loren W. Brintnall,	York, Ohio,	Windham, Vt.,	Windham, Vt.,	Francestown, N. H.
Dea. Albert G. Bristol, M. D.,	Rochester, N. Y.,	New Haven, Ct.,	Hamden, Ct.,	State of Ct.
Rev. Edward Brown,	Zumbrota, Min.,	Colebrook, Ct.,	Canton, Ct.,	Norfolk, Ct.
Josiah Brown,	Bethel, Me.,	Bethel, Me.,	Waterford, Me.,	Norway, Me.
Stephen Brown,	Kensington, N. H.,	Kensington, N. H.,	Kensington, N. H.,	Salisbury, Mass.
Dea. Abner H. Bryant,	Canterbury, Del.,	Buffalo, N. Y.,	Chesterfield, Mass.,	Northampton, Mass.
Rev. Samuel Giles Buckingham,	Springfield, Mass.,	Lebanon, Ct.,	Saybrook, Ct.,	Old Lyme, Ct.
His Exc'y, Gov. Wm. A. Buckingham,	Norwich, Ct.,	Lebanon, Ct.,	Saybrook, Ct.,	Old Lyme, Ct.
Rev. William Ives Budington, D. D.,	Brooklyn, N. Y.,	New Haven, Ct.,	Fairfield, Ct.,	New Haven, Ct.
Dea. Sampson Wilder Buffum,	Winchester, N. H.,	Lancaster, Mass.,	Richmond, N. H.,	Lancaster, Mass.
" Orrin Bugbee,	Lake Village, N. H.,	Hartford, Vt.,	Enfield, Ct.,	Enfield, Ct.
Rev. Henry Lewis Bullen,	Durant, Iowa,	East Medway, Mass.,	East Medway, Mass.,	Framingham, Mass.
" Enoch Fitch Burr,	Lyme, Ct.,	Westport, Ct.,	Westport, Ct.,	Norwalk, Ct.
" David Burt,	Winona, Min.,	Monson, Mass.,	Norton, Mass.,	Sutton, Mass.
" Jeremiah Butler,	Fairport, N. Y.,	Onondaga Hill, N. Y.,	Durham, Ct.,	Shaftsbury, Vt.
Dea. Philander Button,	Greenwich, Ct.,	North Haven, Ct.,	Groton, Ct.,	North Haven, Ct.
Rev. Ezra Hoyt Byington,	Windsor, Vt.,	Hinesburgh, Vt.,	Waterbury, Ct.,	New Haven, Vt.
Dea. Asa Cady,	East Cleveland, Ohio,	Stafford, Ct.,	Killingly, Ct.,	Somers, Ct.
Rev. Calvin Brainard Cady,	Alburgh, Vt.,	Fairhaven, Vt.,	Windsor, Vt.,	Fairhaven, Vt.
" Cornelius Sydney Cady,	Maquoketa, Iowa,	Orwell, Vt.,	Windsor, Vt.,	Fairhaven, Vt.
Charles Carpenter,	West Charleston, Vt.,	Derby, Vt.,	Randolph, Vt.,	Windsor, Vt.
Rev. Elbridge G. Carpenter,	Houlton, Me.,	Foxcroft, Me.,	Sutton, Mass.,	Merrimac, N. H.
Dea. Philo Carpenter,	Chicago, Ill.,	Savoy, Mass.,	Rehoboth, Mass.,	Savoy, Mass.
Timothy Walker Carter,	Chicopee Falls, Mass.,	Brimfield, Mass.,	Ware, Mass.,	Holland, Mass.
Rev. William Carter,	Pittsfield, Ill.,	New Canaan, Ct.,	New Canaan, Ct.,	New Canaan, Ct.
" Joshua Metcalf Chamberlain,	Des Moines, Iowa,	West Brookfield, Mass.,	Westborough, Mass.,	Westborough, Mass.
Hon. Samuel A. Chapin,	Virginia City, Nev.,	. . . . . .	. . . . . .	. . . .
William C. Chapin,	Lawrence, Mass.,	Providence, R. I.,	Uxbridge, Mass.,	Uxbridge, Mass.
Rev. Edward Daniel Chapman,	Sinclearville, N. Y.,	East Haddam, Ct.,	East Haddam, Ct.,	Portland, Ct.
" Louis Emile Charpiot,	Stratford, Ct.,	France,	France,	France.
" Benjamin Chapman Chase,	Foxcroft, Me.,	Cornish, N. H.,	Cornish, N. H.,	Claremont, N. H.
Dea. Russell Cheney,	Emerald Grove, Wis.,	Thetford, Vt.,	Hartford, Ct.,	Springfield, Mass.
Rev. Amos Sheffield Chesebrough,	Glastenbury, Ct.,	Stonington, Ct.,	Stonington, Ct.,	Stonington, Ct.

Hon. Linus Child,	Boston, Mass.,	Woodstock, Ct.,	Woodstock, Ct.,	Woodstock Ct.
" Henry H. Childs,	Pittsfield, Mass.,	Pittsfield, Mass.,	Deerfield, Mass.,	Wethersfield, Ct.
Dea. Horace Childs,	Henniker, N. H.,	Henniker, N. H.,	Henniker, N. H.,	Hopkinton, N. H.
Hon. James Webster Childs,	Augusta, Mich.,	Henniker, N. H.,	Henniker, N. H.,	Henniker, N. H.
Dea. William H. Childs,	Niagara Falls, N. Y.,	Lovonia, N. Y.,	Henniker, N. H.,	Henniker, N. H.
Rev. Erastus B. Claggett,	Lyndeborough, N. H.,	Newport, N. H.,	Portsmouth, N. H.,	Litchfield, N. H.
Dea. Charles Clark,	Cuyahoga Falls, Ohio,	Waterbury, Ct.,	Waterbury, Ct.,	Middlebury, Ct.
Rev. Edward Warren Clark,	Claremont, N. H.,	Tewksbury, Mass.,	Tewksbury, Mass.,	Woburn, Mass.
Rev. Nathaniel Catlin Clark,	Elgin, Ill.,	Benson, Vt.,	Northampton, Mass.,	Hebron, Ct.
Rev. Dexter Clary,	Beloit, Wis.,	Conway, Mass.,	Leverett, Mass.,	Greenfield, Mass.
Dea. John Clary,	Conway, Mass.,	Conway, Mass.,	Sunderland, Mass.,	Deerfield, Mass.
Rev. Samuel Davies Cochran,	Grinnell, Iowa,	Congruity, Pa.,	Frederick, Md.,	Ireland.
Dea. Orris Kirtland Coe,	Watertown, Wis.,	Trenton, N. Y.,	Durham, Ct.,	Torringford, Ct.
Rev. George H. Coffey,	Jackson, Mich.,	Ireland,	Ireland,	Ireland.
" Albert Cole,	Cornish, Me.,	Cornish, Me.,	Sanford, Me.,	Sanford, Me.
" William Lewis Coleman,	Mitchell, Iowa,	Mount Hope, N. Y.,	Bloomingrove, N. Y.,	Mount Hope, N. Y.
" Joseph Collie,	Delavan, Wis.,	Scotland,	Scotland,	Scotland.
Edward Conant,	Randolph, Vt.,	Pomfret, Vt.,	Pomfret, Vt.,	Bridgewater, Vt.
Rev. Richard Cordley,	Lawrence, Kansas,	England,	England,	England.
Hon. William I. Cornwell,	Weedsport, N. Y.,	Stamford, N. Y.,	New Haven, Ct.,	Brantford, Ct.
George Horatio Crane,	Northfield, Vt.,	Williamstown, Vt.,	Williamstown, Vt.,	Brookfield, Vt.
Rev. Robert Crawford, D. D.,	Deerfield, Mass.,	Scotland,	Scotland,	Scotland.
" William Crawford,	Central City, Colorado,	Barre, Mass.,	Oakham, Mass.,	Barre, Mass.
Dea. Walter Crocker,	West Barnstable, Mass.,	Barnstable, Mass.,	Barnstable, Mass.,	Barnstable, Mass.
William Crosby,	Grasshopper Falls, Kan.	Hampden, Me.,	Hampden, Me.,	Castine, Me.
Rev. Isaac Newton Cundall,	Rosendale, Wis.,	West Killingly, Ct.,	West Killingly, Ct.,	Attleborough, Mass.
Warren Currier, Esq.,	St. Louis, Mo.,	Walpole, N. H.,	Billerica, Mass.,	Washington, N. H.
Rev. Christopher Cushing,	North Brookfield, Mass.,	South Scituate, Mass.,	South Scituate, Mass.,	South Scituate, Mass.
Samuel Cushman,	Black Hawk, Colorado,	Attleborough, Mass.,	Attleborough, Mass.,	Attleborough, Mass.
Rev. Temple Cutler,	Skowhegan, Me.,	Lynn, Mass.,	Hamilton, Mass.,	Ipswich, Mass.
" Edward Francis Cutter,	Rockland, Me.,	Portland, Me.,	Yarmouth, Me.,	Yarmouth, Me.
" Oliver Ellsworth Daggett, D. D.,	Canandaigua, N. Y.,	New Haven, Ct.,	Attleborough, Mass.,	New Haven, Ct.
" John Jay Dana,	Cummington, Mass.,	Poultney, Vt.,	Newton, Mass.,	Roxbury, Ct.
Dea. Lorenzo D. Dana,	Morrisville, N. Y.,	Fenner, N. Y.,	Holland, Mass.,	Swansey, Mass.
Rev. Malcolm McGregor Dana,	Norwich, Ct.,	Brooklyn, N. Y.,	Owego, N. Y.,	Rhinebeck, N. Y.
" Henry Metcalf Daniels,	Winnebago, Ill.,	Franklin, Mass.,	Franklin, Mass.,	Franklin, Mass.

Name				
Rev. George Darling,	Hudson, Ohio,	Sterling, Mass.,	Marlborough, Mass.,	Sterling, Mass.
" Edward Davies,	Waterville, N. Y.,	New York City, N. Y.,	Wales,	Wales.
" Thomas W. Davies,	Youngstown, Ohio,	South Wales,	South Wales,	South Wales.
" Emerson Davis, D. D.,	Westfield, Mass.,	Ware, Mass.,	Ware, Mass.,	Ware, Mass.
" Josiah Gardner Davis,	Amherst, N. H.,	Concord, Mass.,	New Ipswich, N. H.,	Goffstown, N. H.
" Oliver Stone Dean,	Roxbury, Ct.,	Patterson, N. Y.,	Patterson, N. Y.,	Roxbury, Ct.
George B. Delamater, Esq.,	Meadville, Pa.,	Whitehall, N. Y.,	Whitehall, N. Y.,	Granville, N. Y.
Rev. Andrew Clark Denison,	Portland, Ct.,	Hampton, Ct.,	Hampton, Ct.,	Pomfret, Ct.
Joseph Addison Denny,	Leicester, Mass.,	Leicester, Mass.,	Leicester, Mass.,	Leicester, Mass.
Rev. Henry Martyn Dexter, D. D.,	Boston, Mass.,	Plympton, Mass.,	Rochester, Mass.,	Freetown, Mass.
" John Dinsmore,	Winslow, Me.,	Anson, Me.,	Auburn, N. H.,	Stark, Me.
Hon. Allen W. Dodge,	Hamilton, Mass.,	Newburyport, Mass.,	Hamilton, Mass.,	Newburyport, Mass.
Rev. John Dodge,	Harvard, Mass.,	Brooksville, Me.,	Haverhill, Mass.,	Brooksville, Me.
" Franklin Bradley Doe,	Appleton, Wis.,	Highgate, Vt.,	Newbury, Vt.,	Corinth, Vt.
Hon. Benjamin Douglas,	Middletown, Ct.,	Northford, Ct.,	New Haven, Ct.,	Wallingford, Ct.
Rev. Edmund Dowse,	Sherborn, Mass.,	Sherborn, Mass.,	Sherborn, Mass.,	Fitchburg, Mass.
" Andrew Jones Drake,	Atlanta, Ill.,	Morristown, N. J.,	Morristown, N. J.,	Sussex Co., N. J.
Dea. Samuel Fletcher Drury,	Olivet, Mich.,	Spencer, Mass.,	Spencer, Mass.,	Townsend, Vt.
" Archibald Harris Dunlap,	Nashua, N. H.,	Antrim, N. H.,	Bedford, N. H.,	Antrim, N. H.
Rev. Richard Chapman Dunn,	Toulon, Ill.,	Augusta, Geo.,	England,	Savannah, Geo.
Elnathan Freeman Duren,	Bangor, Me.,	Boston, Mass.,	Billerica, Mass.,	Portland, Me.
Rev. Samuel W. Southmayd Dutton, D.D.,	New Haven, Ct.,	Guilford, Ct.,	Watertown, Ct.,	Watertown, Ct.
" Theodore M. Dwight,	Putney, Vt.,	Westfield, Mass.,	Northampton, Mass.,	Wethersfield, Ct.
Timothy Dwight, Esq.,	Beloit, Wis.,	New Haven, Ct.,	Stratford, Ct.,	Northampton, Mass.
Rev. Solomon Ashley Dwinnell,	Reedsburg, Wis.,	Lee, Mass.,	Millbury, Mass.,	Springfield, Mass.
" Morgan Lewis Eastman,	Lisbon, N. Y.,	Fairfield, N. Y.,	Arlington, Vt.,	Northampton, Mass.
Dea. Nathaniel Eddy,	E. Middleborough, Mass.,	E. Middleborough, Mass.	Middleborough, Mass.,	Middleborough, Mass.
Rev. Zachary Eddy, D. D.,	Northampton, Mass.,	Stockbridge, Vt.,	Middleborough, Mass.,	Lyme, Ct.
" John Edgar,	Falls Village, Ct.,	. . . . . .	. . . . . .	. . . . . .
" Nathaniel Hillyer Eggleston,	Stockbridge, Mass.,	Hartford, Ct.,	Windsor, Ct.,	Granby, Ct.
" Joseph Eldridge, D. D.,	Norfolk, Ct.,	Yarmouth, Mass.,	Yarmouth, Mass.,	Yarmouth, Mass.
" Hiram Elmer,	Clinton, Mich.,	West Hartford, Ct.,	East Windsor, Ct.,	East Windsor, Ct.
" Alfred Emerson,	Fitchburg, Mass.,	Beverly, Mass.,	Hollis, N. H.,	Bradford, Mass.
" Joshua Emery,	No. Weymouth, Mass.,	Newburyport, Mass.,	Atkinson, N. H.,	Plaistow, N. H.
" Samuel Hopkins Emery,	Quincy, Ill.,	Boxford, Mass.,	Atkinson, N. H.,	Plaistow, N. H.
" George R. Entler,	Meredith, N. Y.,	Shepherdstown, Va.,	Shepherdstown, Va.,	Martinsburg, Va.

Constantine C. Esty, Esq.,	Framingham, Mass.,	Framingham, Mass.,	Newton, Mass.,	Framingham, Mass.
Rev. William Tappan Eustis, jr.,	New Haven, Ct.,	Boston, Mass.,	Rutland, Mass.,	Charlestown, Mass.
Benjamin Fairchild, M. D.,	Milton, Vt.,	Georgia, Vt.,	State of Ct.,	State of Ct.
Rev. Prof. James Harris Fairchild, D. D.,	Oberlin, Ohio,	Stockbridge, Mass.,	Sheffield, Mass.,	Richmond, Mass.
Rev. Minor Wenn Fairfield,	Lyons, Iowa,	Parkersburg, Va.,	Pittsford, Vt.,	Winchester, Va.
Dea. Andrew Atherton Farnsworth,	Peterborough, N H.,	Bakersfield, Vt.,	Sterling, Mass.,	New Ipswich, N. H.
Rev. Franklin Ebenezer Fellows,	Kennebunk, Me.,	Weathersfield, Vt.,	Weathersfield, Vt.,	Windsor, Vt.
" Clark Ela Ferrin,	Hinesburgh, Vt.,	Holland, Vt.,	Londonderry, N. H.,	Litchfield, N. Y.
Dea. Phinehas Field,	E. Charlemont, Mass.,	East Charlemont, Mass.,	Northfield, Mass.,	Northfield, Mass.
Rev. Thomas Power Field, D. D.,	New London, Ct.,	Northfield, Mass.,	Northfield, Mass.,	Boston, Mass.
Asahel Finch, Esq.,	Milwaukee, Wis.,	Genoa, N. Y.,	Walden, N. Y.,	Durham, N. Y.
Dea. Allen Fish, jr.,	Port Huron, Mich.,	Montreal, C. E.,	Sandwich, Mass.,	Hartford, Vt.
Rev. Prof. George Park Fisher,	New Haven, Ct.,	Wrentham, Mass.,	Franklin, Mass.,	Wrentham, Mass.
Luther P. Fisher,	Oakland, Cal.,	Scotland, Ct.,	Princeton, Mass.,	Canterbury, Ct.
Rev. Prof. Franklin Woodbury Fisk,	Chicago, Ill.,	Hopkinton, N. H.,	Wilmot, N. H.,	Manchester, Mass.
Rev. John Orr Fiske,	Bath, Me.,	Bangor, Me.,	Northborough, Mass.,	Merrimack, N. H.
Dea. John A. Fitch,	Hopkinton, Mass.,	Hopkinton, Mass.,	Hopkinton, Mass.,	Hopkinton, Mass.
Allen Folger,	Gardner, Mass.,	Nantucket, Mass.,	Nantucket, Mass.,	Nantucket, Mass.
Dea. John Graham Foote,	Burlington, Iowa,	Middlebury, Vt.,	Simsbury, Ct.,	Suffield, Ct.
Rev. James Thomas Ford,	Stowe, Vt.,	Abington, Mass.,	Abington, Mass.,	Hanson, Mass.
Hon. Asa Freeman,	Dover, N. H.,	Hanover, N. H.,	Mansfield, Ct.,	Norwich, Ct.
George Foster French,	Lunenburgh, Vt.,	Lunenburgh, Vt.,	Tamworth, N. H.,	Lunenburgh, Vt.
Jonathan French,	Braintree, Mass.,	Braintree, Mass.,	Braintree, Mass.,	Braintree, Mass.
Rev. Nahum Gale, D. D.,	Lee, Mass.,	Auburn, Mass.,	Westborough, Mass.,	Westborough, Mass.
" Charles Henry Gates,	Oskaloosa, Iowa,	Palmer, Mass.,	Monson, Mass.,	Wales, Mass.
" Reuben Gaylord,	Omaha City, Neb.,	Norfolk, Ct.,	Norfolk, Ct.,	Norfolk, Ct.
" William Luther Gaylord,	Fitzwilliam, N. H.,	Woodstock, Ct.,	Ashford, Ct.,	Pomfret, Ct.
" Heman Geer,	Wayne, Ohio,	Richmond, Vt.,	Kent, Ct.,	Richmond, Vt.
" Edwin R. Gilbert,	Wallingford, Ct.,	Hebron, Ct.,	Hebron, Ct.,	Hebron, Ct.
" James Boardman Gilbert,	Lansing, Iowa,	Pittsford, Vt.,	Pittsford, Vt.,	Dorset, Vt.
Hon. Robert Goodenow,	Farmington, Me.,	Henniker, N. H.,	Marlborough, Mass.,	Gloucester, Mass.
Hon. Ira Goodhue,	Westminster, Vt.,	Westminster, Vt.,	Dunstable, Mass.,	Westminster, Vt.
Rev. Henry Martyn Goodwin,	Rockford, Ill.,	Hartford, Ct.,	East Hartford, Ct.,	Wethersfield, Ct.
Timothy Gordon, M. D.,	Plymouth, Mass.,	Newbury, Mass.,	Brentwood, N. H.,	Newbury, Mass.
Dea. Jabez R. Gott,	Rockport, Mass.,	Rockport, Mass.,	Rockport, Mass.,	Rockport, Mass.
Rev. Griffith Griffiths,	Utica, N. Y.,	North Wales,	North Wales,	North Wales.

Rev. Leverett Griggs,	Bristol, Ct.,	Tolland, Ct.,	Tolland, Ct.,	Pittsfield, Mass.
Dea. Abram Griswold,	Gustavus, Ohio,	Windsor, Ct.,	Windsor, Ct.,	Granby, Ct.
Rev. Henry Martyn Grout,	West Rutland, Vt.,	Newfane, Vt.,	Westminster, Vt.,	Brattleboro, Vt.
" Jesse Guernsey,	Dubuque, Iowa,	Watertown, Ct.,	Watertown, Ct.,	Watertown, Ct.
" John Putnam Gulliver, D. D.,	Norwich, Ct.,	Boston, Mass.,	Taunton, Mass.,	Reading, Mass.
" Richard Hall,	St. Paul, Min.,	New Ipswich, N. H.,	Mansfield, Ct.,	New Ipswich, N. H.
Hon. Charles G. Hammond,	Chicago, Ill.,	Bolton, Ct.,	Bolton, Ct.,	New Haven, Ct.
Rev. John Wheeler Harding,	Longmeadow, Mass.,	Waltham, Mass.,	West Medway, Mass.,	East Medway, Mass.
Ivory Hovey Harlow,	Middleborough, Mass.,	Middleborough, Mass.,	Halifax, Mass.,	Middleborough, Mass.
Hon. Milan Harris,	Harrisville, N. H.,	Nelson, N. H.,	Medway, Mass.,	Dublin, N. H.
Rev. Prof. Samuel Harris, D. D.,	Bangor, Me.,	East Machias, Me.,	Boston, Mass.,	East Machias, Me.
Rev. John Clark Hart,	Kent, Ohio,	Cornwall, Ct.,	Cornwall, Ct.,	Cornwall, Ct.
Jacob Haskell,	Fitchburg, Mass.,	Harvard, Mass.,	Harvard, Mass.,	Pepperell, Mass.
Hon. Henry P. Haven,	New London, Ct.,	Norwich, Ct.,	Wrentham, Mass.,	New London, Ct.
Rev. Prof. Joseph Haven, D. D.,	Chicago, Ill.,	Dennis, Mass.,	Holden, Mass.,	Orleans, Mass.
" Edward Hawes,	Philadelphia, Pa.,	Topsham, Me.,	Yarmouth, Mass.,	Vassalboro, Me.
" Josiah Taylor Hawes,	Bridgton, Me.,	Yarmouth, Mass.,	Yarmouth, Mass.,	Yarmouth, Mass.
Dea. Henry Haynes,	Sturbridge, Mass.,	Millbury, Mass.,	Somers, Ct.,	Millbury, Mass.
Rowland Hazard,	Peace Dale, R. I.,	Newport, R. I.,	South Kingston, R. I.,	Bristol, Pa.
Rev. Henry Martyn Hazeltine,	Sherman, N. Y.,	Jamestown, N. Y.,	Wardsboro', Vt.,	Wardsboro', Vt.
" Henry Allen Hazen,	Plymouth, N. H.,	Hartford, Vt.,	Hartford, Vt.,	Danville, Vt.
" Joseph Warren Healy,	Milwaukee, Wis.,	South Hero, Vt.,	Washington, N. H.,	Washington, N. H.
Dea. Willis Hemingway, jr.,	Fair Haven, Ct.,	East Haven, Ct.,	East Haven, Ct.,	East Haven, Ct.
Levi Tomlinson Hewins, M. D.,	Loda, Ill.,	Burton, Ohio,	West Stockbridge, Mass.	Derby, Ct.
Henry Hill, Esq.,	Roxbury, Mass.,	Newburgh, N. Y.,	Saybrook, Ct.,	Marlborongh, N. Y.
Dea. William E. Hinsdale,	Blandford, Mass.,	Meriden, Ct.,	New York City, N. Y.,	Newark, N. J.
Homer Owen Hitchcock, M. D.,	Kalamazoo, Mich.,	West Westminster, Vt.,	West Westminster, Vt.,	Ashfield, Ct.
Rev. Loammi Ives Hoadley,	Craftsbury, Vt.,	Branford, Ct.,	Branford, Ct.,	New Haven, Ct.
" L. Smith Hobart,	Syracuse, N. Y.,	Potter, N. Y.,	Townsend, Mass.,	South Kingston, R. I.
" John Calvin Holbrook, D. D.,	Homer, N. Y.,	Brattleboro, Vt.,	Weymouth, Mass.,	Shrewsbury, Mass.
" John Milton Holmes,	Jersey City, N. J.,	England,	England,	England.
Dea. Samuel Holmes,	New York City, N. Y.,	Waterbury, Ct.,	Waterbury, Ct.,	Cheshire, Ct.
Hon. Edward D. Holton,	Milwaukee, Wis.,	Lancaster, N. H.,	Ellington, Ct.,	Haddam, Ct.
Charles Hopkins,	Norwich, N. Y.,	Rutland, N. Y.,	Stratford, Ct.,	Rutland, N. Y.
Rev. James Seymour Hoyt,	Port Huron, Mich.,	New Canaan, Ct.,	Stamford, Ct.,	New Canaan, Ct.
Rev. Geo. B. Hubbard,	Aurora, Ill.,	New Haven, Ct.,	Meriden, Ct.,	New Haven, Ct.

Dea. George W. Hubbard,	Hatfield, Mass.,	Philadelphia, Pa.,	Hatfield, Mass.,	Hatfield, Mass.
" Hiram Hulburd,	Stockholm, N. Y.,	Stockholm, N. Y.,	Rupert, Vt.,	Richmond, Mass.
Rev. Philo Ruggles Hurd,	Romeo, Mich.,	Rhinebeck, N. Y.,	Monroe, Ct.,	Brookfield, Ct.
" Azariah Hyde,	Pawlet, Vt.,	Randolph, Vt.,	Norwich, Ct.,	Oakham, Mass.
" Nathaniel A. Hyde,	Indianapolis, Ind.,	Stafford, Ct.,	Stafford, Ct.,	Stafford, Ct.
" Jacob Ide, D. D.,	Medway, Mass.,	Attleborough, Mass.,	Attleborough, Mass.,	Rehoboth, Mass.
" Alfred Eaton Ives,	Castine, Me.,	New Haven, Ct.,	Branford, Ct.,	New Haven, Ct.
Dea. Galen James,	Medford, Mass.,	Scituate, Mass.,	Scituate, Mass.,	Scituate, Mass.
" Samuel James, jr.,	Weybridge, Vt.,	Weybridge, Vt.,	Weybridge, Vt.,	Amherst, Mass.
Rev. John Lord Jenkins,	Kokomo, Ind.,	Kirby, Vt.,	Hinsdale, N. H.,	Ware, Mass.
" Jonathan Leavitt Jenkins,	Hartford, Ct.,	Portland, Me.,	Barre, Mass.,	Greenfield, Mass.
" Elisha Jenney,	Galesburg, Ill.,	Fairhaven, Mass.,	Fairhaven, Mass.,	Fairhaven, Mass.
" Isaac Jennings,	Bennington, Vt.,	Trumbull, Ct.,	Fairfield, Ct.,	Trumbull, Ct.
Charles A. Jessup, Esq.,	Westfield, Mass.,	Richmond, Mass.,	E. Hampton, L. I., N. Y.,	North Guilford, Ct.
Rev. Edwin Johnson,	Baltimore, Md.,	Plymouth, Ct.,	Cheshire, Ct.,	Plymouth, Ct.
" Samuel Johnson,	Chenango Forks, N. Y.,	England,	England,	England.
" David M. Jones,	Arena, Iowa,	South Wales,	South Wales,	South Wales.
" Lemuel Jones,	Bellevue, Iowa,	England,	Wales,	Wales.
" Thomas Jones,	Olivet, Mich.,	Wales,	Wales,	Wales.
William Wallace Jones,	La Crosse, Wis.,	Marlborough, Ct.,	Hebron, Ct.,	East Haddam, Ct.
Dea. Guerdon Judson,	Raymond, Wis.,	Simsbury, Ct.,	State of Ct.,	State of Ct.
Rev. Adam Stewart Kedzie,	Somerset, Mich.,	Stamford, N. Y.,	Scotland,	Cambridge, N. Y.
" Seneca McNeil Keeler,	Guilford, N. Y.,	Ridgefield, Ct.,	Ridgefield, Ct.,	South Salem, N. Y.
" Seth Harrison Keeler, D. D.,	Calais, Me.,	Brandon, Vt.,	Pittsfield, Mass.,	Deerfield, Mass.
" Lysander Kelsey,	Columbus, Ohio,	Sudbury, Vt.,	State of Ct.,	Athol, Mass.
Dea. Freeman Keyes,	Newbury, Vt.,	Vershire, Vt.,	Warren, Mass.,	Thornton, N. H.
Rev. James Parker Kimball,	Falmouth, Mass.,	Townshend, Vt.,	Bradford, Mass.,	Groveland, Mass.
John M. Kinsman,	North Potsdam, N. Y.,	Shrewsbury, Vt.,	Hubbardston, Mass.,	Templeton, Mass.
Rev. Edward Norris Kirk, D. D.,	Boston, Mass.,	New York City, N. Y.,	Scotland,	Princeton, N. J.
Hon. William C. Kittredge,	Fairhaven, Vt.,	Dalton, Mass.,	Tewksbury, Mass.,	Dalton, Mass.
Andrew Jackson Knapp,	Wauseon, Ohio,	Homer, N. Y.,	Goshen, N. Y.,	Monson, Mass.
Henry Martyn Knight, M. D.,	Salisbury, Ct.,	Stafford, Ct.,	Monson, Mass.,	Monson, Mass.
Rev. Benjamin Labaree, D. D.,	Middlebury, Vt.,	Charlestown, N. H.,	Charlestown, N. H.,	Charlestown, N. H.
" Daniel Lane,	Eddyville, Iowa,	Leeds, Me.,	New Gloucester, Me.,	Bridgewater, Mass.
Dea. Samuel M. Lane,	Southbridge, Mass.,	Sturbridge, Mass.,	Wrentham, Mass.,	Sturbridge, Mass.
Rev. Isaac P. Langworthy,	Chelsea, Mass.,	Stonington, Ct.,	Stonington, Ct.,	Westerly, R. I.,

Rev. Orpheus Thomas Lanphear,	New Haven, Ct.,	West Fairlee, Vt.,	Columbia, Ct.,	Bradford, Vt.
" Edward Alexander Lawrence, D. D.,	East Windsor Hill, Ct.,	St. Johnsbury, Vt.,	Winchester, N. H.,	Winchester, N. H.
" Robert Coit Learned,	Plymouth, Ct.,	New London, Ct.,	New London, Ct.,	New London, Ct.
" Joshua Leavitt, D. D.,	Brooklyn, N. Y.,	Heath, Mass.,	Charlemont, Mass.,	Charlemont, Mass.
" Edwin N. Lewis,	Ottawa, Ill.,	Enfield, N. Y.,	Lenox, N. Y.,	Philipstown, N. Y.
" Elisha M. Lewis,	Nebraska City, Neb.,			
" James Donaldson Liggett,	Leavenworth, Kansas,	Warren Co., Ohio,	Rockbridge, Co. Va.,	Rockbridge Co. Va.
" Joel Harvey Linsley, D. D.,	Greenwich, Ct.,	Cornwall, Vt.,	Woodbury, Ct.,	Woodbury, Ct.
Charles Austin Lord,	Portland, Me.,	Kennebunkport, Me.,	Kennebunk, Me.,	Kennebunkport, Me.
Rev. Charles Lord,	Buckland, Mass.,	Williamsburg, Mass.,	North Killingworth, Ct.,	Williamsburg, Mass.
" William DeLoss Love,	Milwaukee, Wis.,	Barre, N. Y.,	Bridgewater, N. Y.,	Bridgewater, N. Y.
" Erastus Maltby,	Taunton, Mass.,	Northford, Ct.,	Northford, Ct.,	Northford, Ct.
" Abijah Perkins Marvin,	Winchendon, Mass.,	Lyme, Ct.,	Lyme, Ct.,	Lyme, Ct.
" Elihu Parrish Marvin,	Medford, Mass.,	Romulus, N. Y.,	Lyme, Ct.,	Hackensack, N. J.
Dea. Thomas Marvin,	Walton, N. Y.,	Cambridge, N. Y.,	Simsbury, Ct.,	New Canaan Ct.
Lowell Mason, jr.,	Orange, N. J.,	Westborough, Mass.,	Medfield, Mass.,	Westborough, Mass.
Dea. Nelson Mason,	Sterling, Ill.,	Paislee, Scotland,	Scotland,	Scotland.
Hon. Seth May,	Auburn, Me.,	Winthrop, Me.,	Attleborough, Mass.,	Sandwich, Mass.
Rev. James Tomb McCollom,	Bradford, Mass.,	Salem, N. Y.,	Derry, N. H.,	Ireland.
" James Adolphus McKay,	Lamont, Mich.,	Skaneateles, N. Y.,	Dover, N. Y.,	Northampton, Mass.
" Silas McKeen, D. D.,	Bradford, Vt.,	Corinth, Vt.,	Londonderry, N. H.,	Chester N. H.
" Charles T. Melvin,	Elk Grove, Wis.,	Chester, N. H.,	Chester, N. H.,	Chester, N. H.
Hon. Thomas J. Melvin,	Chester, N. H.,	Chester, N. H.,	Chester, N. H.,	Chester, N. H.
Rev. William Edward Merriman,	Ripon, Wis.,	Hinsdale, Mass.,	Hindale, Mass.,	Peru, Mass.
Dea. Abel Kimball Merrill,	Haverhill, N. H.,	Warren, N. H.,	Plaistow, N. H.,	Rumney, N. H.
Rev. Orville Willard Merrill,	Anamosa, Iowa,	Orford, N. H.,	Salem, N. H.,	Windham, Vt.
" James Browning Miles,	Charlestown, Mass.,	Rutland, Mass.,	Rutland, Mass.,	Rutland, Mass.
" Milo N. Miles,	Geneseo, Ill.,	Sharon, Ct.,	Watertown, Ct.,	Sheffield, Mass.
Hon. Samuel Miller,	New Haven, Ct.,	Williston, Vt.,	West Springfield, Mass.,	Wallingford, Vt.
Rev. Samuel Miller,	Eaton, N. Y.,	Augusta, N. Y.,	Marshall, N. Y.,	Rutland, Mass.
" Charles E. Milliken,	Littleton, N. H.,	Fitzwilliam, N. H.,	State of N. H.,	Keene, N. H.
" Henry Mills,	Kalamazoo, Mich.,	Kingsville, Ohio,	Livermore, Me.,	Norfolk, Ct.
" Edward Goddard Miner,	Whitewater, Wis.,	Roxbury, Mass.,	Northfield, Mass.,	Roxbury, Mass.
" Henry Austin Miner,	Menasha, Wis.,	Halifax, Vt.,	Stonington, Ct.,	Halifax, Vt.
" Thomas Edwin Monroe,	Mount Vernon, Ohio,	Plainfield, Ct.,	Rehoboth, Mass.,	Stonington, Ct.
Hon. Henry Morris,	Springfield, Mass.,	Springfield, Mass.,	Wilbraham, Mass.,	Springfield, Mass.

Rev. David Murdoch,	New Milford, Ct.,	Glasgow, Scotland,	Scotland,	Scotland.
" John Conrad Myers,	Saugatuck, Mich.,	Weisslenreuth, Germany,	Germany,	Germany.
" Osborne Myrick,	Provincetown, Mass.,	Orleans, Mass.,	Orleans, Mass.,	Brewster, Mass.
Dea. Lorenzo Smith Nash,	Granby, Mass.,	Hadley, Mass.,	Hadley, Mass.,	Hadley, Mass.
Rev. John Hesler Nason,	Smyrna, N. Y.,	Homer, N. Y.,	State of Me.,	State of N. Y.
" George Benton Newcomb,	Bloomfield, Ct.,	Allegany, Pa.,	Thetford, Vt.,	Thetford, Vt.
George K. Newcomb, Esq.,	East Saginaw, Mich.,	Westfield, N. Y.,	Thetford, Vt.,	State of Ct.
Rev. Wellington Newell,	Brewer Village, Me.,	Pembroke, N. H.,	Brookfield, Mass.,	Pembroke, N. H.
" Prof. Daniel James Noyes, D. D.,	Hanover, N. H.,	Springfield, N. H.,	West Newbury, Mass.,	Andover, N. H.
Rev. Daniel Parker Noyes,	Boston, Mass.,	Byfield, Mass.,	Byfield, Mass.,	Byfield, Mass.
Nathaniel Noyes,	Baltimore, Md.,	Abington, Mass.,	Abington, Mass.,	Abington, Mass.
Rev. John Keep Nutting,	Bradford, Iowa,	Groton, Mass.,	Groton, Mass.,	Groton, Mass.
" Richard Osborn,	Champion, N. Y.,	Greenwich, N. Y.,	. . .	. . .
" George Alexander Oviatt,	Somers, Ct.,	Bridgeport, Ct.,	Milford, Ct.,	Bridgeport, Ct.
" Abel Kingman Packard,	Anoka, Min.,	No. Bridgewater, Mass.,	No. Bridgewater, Mass.,	No. Bridgewater, Mass.
" Theophilus Packard,	Sunderland, Mass.,	Shelburne, Mass.,	No. Bridgewater, Mass.,	Abington, Mass.
Deacon Simon Page,	Hallowell, Me.,	Readfield, Me.,	Kingston, N. H.,	Readfield, Me.
Levi Leonard Paine,	Farmington, Ct.,	East Randolph, Mass.,	East Randolph, Mass.,	Bridgewater, Mass.
Rev. William Pomeroy Paine, D. D.,	Holden, Mass.,	Ashfield, Mass.,	Hatfield, Mass.,	Northfield, Mass.
Dea. Thomas Wilcher Painter,	Weymouth, Ohio,	Weymouth, Ohio,	Plymouth, Ct.,	Bristol, Ct.
Charles Winslow Palmer, Esq.,	Cleveland, Ohio,	Norwich, Ct.,	Jewett City, Ct.,	New London, Ct.
Hon. Julius Aboyneau Palmer,	Boxford, Mass.,	Little Compton, R. I.,	Little Compton, R. I.,	Little Compton, R. I.
Rev. Ray Palmer, D. D.,	Albany, N. Y.,	Little Compton, R. I.,	Little Compton, R. I.,	Little Compton, R. I.
" William Stratton Palmer,	Wells River, Vt.,	Orford, N. H.,	Warren, Ct.,	Fairlee, Vt.
Hon. Francis Drake Parish,	Sandusky, Ohio,	Naples, N. Y.,	Canterbury, Ct.,	Hartland, Ct.
Rev. Prof. Edwards A. Park, D. D.,	Andover, Mass.,	Providence, R. I.,	Newton, Mass.,	Wrentham, Mass.
" Charles Carroll Parker,	Waterbury, Vt.,	Underhill, Vt.,	Richmond, N. H.,	Dudley, Mass.
Dea. Daniel H. Parker,	Dunbarton, N. H.,	Dunbarton, N. H.,	Bradford, Mass.,	Bradford, Mass.
Rev. Henry Elijah Parker,	Concord, N. H.,	Keene, N. H.,	New Ipswich, N. H.,	Keene, N. H.
" Lucius Parker,	Palmyra, Wis.,	Southborough, Mass.,	Southborough, Mass.,	Hopkinton, Mass.
" Lucius Hubbard Parker,	Galesburg, Ill.,	Woodstock, Vt.,	Groton, Mass.,	Tolland, Ct.
" Wooster Parker,	Belfast, Me.,	Underhill, Vt.,	Saybrook, Ct.,	State of Ct.
" Ebenezer Greenleaf Parsons,	Derry, N. H.,	Westport, Me.,	Westport, Me.,	Westport, Me.
" George C. Partridge,	Batavia, Ill.,	Hatfield, Mass.,	Hatfield, Mass.,	Hatfield, Mass.
" John Patchin,	Owosso, Mich.,	Newbury, Ohio,	Fairfield, Ct.,	Derby, Ct.
Richard J. Patterson, M. D.,	Mount Pleasant, Iowa,	Mt. Washington, Mass.,	State of Vt.,	Rensselaer Co., N. Y.

Rev. William Weston Patton, D. D.,	Chicago, Ill.,	New York City, N. Y.,	Philadelphia, Pa.,	Waltham, Mass.
Dea. Oliver Pendleton,	Wabasha, Min.,	Westerly, R. I.,	Westerly, R. I.,	Stonington, Ct.
Rev. Philip Peregrine,	Blossburg, Pa.,	Brecon, South Wales,	South Wales,	South Wales.
" Ariel Ebenezer Parish Perkins,	Ware, Mass.,	Royalston, Mass.,	Topsfield, Mass.	Byfield, Mass.
" Sydney Keith Bond Perkins,	Glover, Vt.,	Braintree, Mass.,	No. Bridgewater, Mass.,	W. Bridgewater, Mass.
" Ralph Perry,	Agawam, Mass.,	Manchester, Ct.,	Vernon, Ct.,	Colchester, Ct.
Dea. Moses Pettingill,	Peoria, Ill.,	Salisbury, N. H.,	Salisbury, N. H.,	Salsbury, N. H.
Rev. Philo Columbus Pettibone,	Beloit, Wis.,	Stockholm, N. Y.,	Norfolk, Ct.,	Norfolk, Ct.
" John Pike,	Rowley, Mass.,	Newburyport, Mass.,	Newburyport, Mass.,	Newburyport, Mass.
Joseph Greeley Pollard,	Woburn, Mass.,	Wilton, N. H.,	Hudson, N. H.,	Bedford, N. H.
Rev. Lemuel Pomeroy,	Wethersfield, Ill.,	Southampton, Mass.,	Southampton, Mass.,	Southampton, Mass.
Hon. Samuel C. Pomeroy,	Atchison, Kansas,	Southampton, Mass.,	Southampton, Mass.,	Southampton, Mass.
Rev. Giles Meigs Porter,	Garnavillo, Iowa,	Farmington, Ct.,	Farmington, Ct.,	Middletown, Ct.
Dea. John Porter,	Cedar Falls, Iowa,	Ashfield, Mass.,	Ashfield, Mass.,	Ashfield, Mass.
Rev. Prof. Noah Porter, Jr., D. D.,	New Haven, Ct.,	Farmington, Ct.,	Farmington, Ct.,	Middletown, Ct.
" Samuel Fuller Porter,	Wheaton, Ill.,	Whitestown, N. Y.,	Abington, Mass.,	Plainfield, N. H.
" Truman M. Post, D. D.,	St Louis, Mo.,	Shoreham, Vt.,	Rutland, Vt.,	Rupert, Vt.
George Washington Pratt,	River Falls, Wis.,	Braintree, Mass.,	Braintree, Mass.,	Braintree, Mass.
Dea. Selden Mather Pratt,	Center Brook, Ct.,	Essex, Ct.,	Saybrook, Ct.,	Saybrook, Ct.
Zebulon Pratt,	N. Middleborough, Mass.	N. Middleborough, Mass.	N. Middleborough, Mass.	Bridgewater, Mass.
Elliot Beecher Preston,	Rockville, Ct.,	Eastford, Ct.,	Ashford, Ct.,	Hempstead, L. I., N. Y.
Hon. Douglas Putnam,	Harmar, Ohio,	Harmar, Ohio,	Pomfret, Ct.,	Plainfield, Ct.
Rev. Alonzo Hall Quint,	New Bedford, Mass.,	Barnstead, N. H.,	Parsonsfield, Me.,	Barnstead, N. H.
William Ramsdell,	Milford, N. H.,	Salem, Mass.,	Lynn, Mass.,	Salem, Mass.
Rev. Herbert A. Read,	Marshall, Mich.,	Attleborough, Mass.,	Attleborough, Mass.,	Attleborough, Mass.
Dea. Edgar Hodges Reed,	Taunton, Mass.,	Taunton, Mass.,	Taunton, Mass.,	Norton, Mass.
" Josiah Reed,	South Weymouth, Mass.,	So. Weymouth, Mass.,	Boston, Mass.,	S. Weymouth, Mass.
Rev. Julius Alexander Reed,	Davenport, Iowa.,	South Windsor, Ct.,	South Windsor, Ct.,	Vernon, Ct.
" Samuel T. Richards,	Spencerport, N. Y.,	Haverford, Pa.,	Springfield, Pa.,	W. Nothingham, Md.
Seth Richards,	Bentonsport, Iowa,	Enfield, Mass.,	Bridgewater, Mass.,	Truro, Mass.
Rev. Alden Burrill Robbins,	Muscatine, Iowa,	Salem, Mass.,	West Cambridge, Mass.,	Salem, Mass.
Nathaniel Crafts Robbins,	Salem, Mass.,	Salem, Mass.,	Roxbury, Mass.,	Salem, Mass.
Daniel C. Robinson, Esq.,	Brooklyn, Ct.,	Brooklyn, Ct.,	Windham, Ct.,	Tolland, Ct.
Dea. Henry Wright Robinson,	Johnson, Vt.,	Greenville, N. Y.,	Poultney, Vt.,	Benson, Vt.
Rev. Reuben Totman Robinson,	Winchester, Mass.,	Exeter, N. Y.,	Barre, Mass.,	Barre, Mass.
" Edward Warren Root,	Springfield, Ohio,	Conway, Mass.,	Conway, Mass.,	Taunton, Mass.

Rev. Thomas Henderson Rouse,	Jamestown, N. Y.,	Pittstown, N. Y.,	Pittstown, N. Y.,	Bennington, Vt.
" Joseph Edwin Roy,	Chicago, Ill.,	Martinsburg, Ohio,	Baskinridge, N. J.,	Conn. Farms, N. J.
" Moses Thurston Runnells,	Orford, N. H.,	Cambridge, Vt.,	Vershire, Vt.,	Waltham, Mass.
" Ezekiel Russell, D. D.,	East Randolph, Mass.,	Wilbraham, Mass.,	Wilbraham, Mass.,	Stoughton, Mass.
" Isaac Russell,	Bowen's Prairie, Iowa,	Perth, Scotland,	Scotland,	Scotland.
" Lewis Sabin, D. D.,	Templeton, Mass.,	Wilbraham, Mass.,	Stafford, Ct.,	Ellington, Ct.
" John Safford,	Bellevue, Ohio,	Perry Lake, Ohio,	Pawlet, Vt.,	Braintree, Vt.
" Charles Cotton Salter,	Minneapolis, Min.,	New Haven, Ct.,	New Haven, Ct.,	New York City, N. Y.
" William Salter, D. D.,	Burlington, Iowa,	Brooklyn, N. Y.,	Portsmouth, N. H.,	Portsmouth, N. H.
" George Slocum Folger Savage,	Chicago, Ill.,	Middletown, Ct.,	Middletown, Ct.,	Middletown, Ct.
" William Thomas Savage,	Franklin, N. H.,	Bangor, Me.,	York, Me.,	Plymouth, Mass.
Dea. Charles C. Sawyer,	Saco, Me.,	Saco, Me.,	Saco, Me.,	Biddeford, Me.
Rev. Rufus M. Sawyer,	York, Me.,	Otisfield, Me.,	Westbrook, Me.,	Westbrook, Me.
Joel K. Scarboro,	Payson, Ill.,	Brooklyn, Ct.,	Brooklyn, Ct.,	Brooklyn, Ct.
Marshall Sears Scudder, Esq.,	Grantville, Mass.,	Boston, Mass.,	Hyannis, Mass.,	Chatham, Mass.
Rev. Charles Seccombe,	St. Anthony, Min.,	Salem, Mass.,	Danvers, Mass.,	Danvers, Mass.
" Seth Willard Segur,	Tallmadge, Ohio,	Chittenden, Vt.,	Chittenden, Vt.,	Williamstown, Vt.
Dea. Edward David Selden,	Brandon, Vt.,	City of N. York, N. Y.,	Haddam, Ct.,	City of N. York, N. Y.
Rev. John Smith Sewall,	Wenham, Mass.,	Damariscotta, Me.,	Chesterville, Me.,	Chesterville, Me.
" Charles Shedd,	Wasioja, Min.,	Rindge, N. H.,	Rindge, N. H.,	New Ipswich, N. H.
Dea. George Wellington Shelton,	Birmingham, Ct.,	Huntington, Ct.,	Huntington, Ct.,	Huntington, Ct.
Rev. Prof. George Shepard, D. D.,	Bangor, Me.,	Plainfield, Ct.,	Plainfield, Ct.,	Plainfield, Ct.
" David Shepley,	Yarmouth, Me.,	Solon, Me.,	Pepperell, Mass.,	Pepperell, Mass.
Rev. John Collins Sherwin,	Barre, Wis.,	Penfield, N. Y.,	State of Maine,	State of Pennsylvania.
" William True Sleeper,	Patten, Me.,	Danbury, N. H.,	Andover, N. H.,	Salisbury, N. H.
" Samuel P. Sloan,	McGregor, Iowa,	Whiteoak, Ohio,	State of Md.,	Cane Ridge, Ky.
" George W. Smiley, D. D.,	Philadelphia, Pa.,	Carlisle, Pa.,	Carlisle, Pa.,	Harrisburg, Pa.
Dea. Brainerd Smith,	Normal, Ill.,	Sunderland, Mass.,	Sunderland, Mass.,	Sunderland, Mass.
His Exc'y Gov. James Gregory Smith,	St. Albans, Vt.,	St. Albans, Vt.,	Barre, Mass.,	Troy, N. Y.
Dea. John Smith,	Andover, Mass.,	Brechin, Scotland,	Scotland,	Scotland.
Ralph Dunning Smith, Esq.,	Guildford, Ct.,	Southbury, Ct.,	Brookfield, Ct.,	Easton, Pa.
Rev. Aaron Snow,	Miller's Place, N. Y.,	Saybrook, Ct.,	Saybrook, Ct.,	Saybrook, Ct.
" George Soule,	Hampton, Ct.,	Willington, Ct.,	Middleborough, Mass.,	Quincy, Mass.
" George Spaulding,	West Eau Claire, Wis.,	Frankfort, Me.,	Lowell, Mass.,	Dracut, Mass.
" Charles Spooner,	Greenville, Mich.,	Keene, N. Y.,	Petersham, Mass.,	Hardwick, Mass.
Charles Augustus Stackpole,	Gorham, Me.,	Portland, Me.,	Harpswell, Me.,	Hingham, Mass.

Fitch B. Stacy,	Stacyville, Iowa,	Dekalb, N. Y.,	Cooperstown, N. Y.,	Marshall, N. Y.
Rev. Alanson St. Clair,	Croton, Mich.,	Greene, Me.,	Gorham, Me.,	North Yarmouth, Me.
" Josiah H. Stearns,	Epping, N. H.,	Epping, N. H.,	Epping, N. H.,	Milton, Mass.
" William A. Stearns, D. D.,	Amherst, Mass.,	Bedford, Mass.,	Epping, N. H.,	Andover, Mass.
Dea. John Stevens,	Cromwell, Ct.,	Haddam, Ct.,	Killingworth, Ct.,	Haddam, Ct.
Stephen B. Stinson,	Sandwich, Ill.,	Boston, Mass.,	Dunbarton, N. H.,	Dunbarton, N. H.
Dea. Charles Stoddard,	Boston, Mass.,	Northampton, Mass.,	Northampton, Mass.,	Northampton, Mass.
Rev. Andrew Leete Stone, D. D.,	Boston, Mass.,	Oxford, Ct.,	Madison, Ct.,	Lyme, Ct.
" Benjamin Perkins Stone, D. D.,	Concord, N. H.,	Reading, Vt.,	Groton, Mass.,	Leominster, Mass.
" James Woodward Strong,	Faribault, Min.,	Brownington, Vt.,	Brownington, Vt.,	Norwich, Vt.
" Julian Monson Sturtevant, D. D.,	Jacksonville, Ill.,	Warren, Ct.,	Warren, Ct.,	Warren, Ct.
" Julian Monson Sturtevant, jr.,	Hannibal, Mo.,	Jacksonville, Ill.,	Warren, Ct.,	Canaan, Ct.
" Leonard Swain, D. D.,	Providence, R. I.,	Concord, N. H.,	Pittsfield, N. H.,	Amherst, N. H.
" Francis Keyes Swan,	Calais, Me.,	Winslow, Me.,	Groton, Mass.,	Augusta, Me.
" Seth Sweetser, D. D.,	Worcester, Mass.,	Newburyport, Mass.,	Charlestown, Mass.,	Charlestown, Mass.
Dea. Gilbert Mortier Sykes,	Dorset, Vt.,	Dorset, Vt.,	Dorset, Vt.,	Cavendish, Vt.
Henry Walbridge Taft,	Lenox, Mass.,	Sunderland, Mass.,	Montague, Mass.,	Sunderland, Mass.
Hon. Henry G. Taintor,	Hampton, Ct.,	Hampton, Ct.,	Colchester, Ct.,	Colchester, Ct.
Nathaniel Tobey Talbot,	Rockport, Me.,	Turner, Me.,	Dighton, Mass.,	Berkley, Mass.
Dea. Chester Talcott,	North Coventry, Ct.,	North Coventry Ct.,	Vernon, Ct.,	North Coventry, Ct.
Daniel Smith Tarr,	Gloversville, N. Y.,	Rockport, Mass.,	Rockport, Mass.,	Rockport, Mass.
Rev. Chauncey Taylor,	Algona, Iowa,	Williamstown, Vt.,	Bolton, Ct.,	State of Ct.
" Lathrop Taylor,	Farmington, Ill.,	Buckland, Mass.,	Ashfield, Mass.,	Middleborough, Mass.
Judge Lester Taylor,	Claridon, Ohio,	Hartland, Ct.,	Chatham, Ct.,	Durham, Ct.
Rev. James Franklin Taylor,	Chelsea, Mich.,	Benton, N. Y.,	New Windsor, N. Y.,	Lycoming, Pa.
" Jeremiah Taylor, D. D.,	Middletown, Ct.,	Hawley, Mass.,	Yarmouth, Mass.,	Yarmouth, Mass.
Joseph J. Taylor,	Newcastle, Me.,	Jefferson, Me.,	Newcastle, Me.,	Whitefield, Me.
Rev. Sewall Tenney, D. D.,	Ellsworth, Me.,	Bradford, Mass.,	Bradford, Mass.,	Bradford, Mass.
" Thomas Tenney,	Plymouth, Iowa,	Bradford, Mass.,	Bradford, Mass.,	Bradford, Mass.
Hon. William W. Thomas,	Portland, Me.,	Portland, Me.,	Portland, Me.,	New Gloucester, Me.
Rev. James Armstrong Thome,	Cleveland, Ohio,	Augusta, Ky.,	Lancaster, Pa.,	North Ireland.
" Joseph Parrish Thompson, D. D.,	New York City, N. Y.,	Philadelphia, Pa.,	Stratford, Ct.,	Coleraine, Ireland.
" Eli Thurston,	Fall River, Mass.,	Brighton, Mass.,	Westboro', Mass.,	Roxbury, Mass.
Dea. Wm. Thurston,	Newburyport, Mass.,	Sedgwick, Me.,	Rowley, Mass.,	Boxford, Mass.
Rev. Joseph Titcomb,	Kennebunk, Me.,	Kennebunk, Me.,	Kennebunk, Me.,	Kennebunkport, Me.
" Alvan Tobey,	Durham, N. H.,	Wilmington, Vt.,	Berkley, Mass.,	Brimfield, Mass.

Edward S. Tobey, Esq.,	Boston, Mass.,	Kingston, Mass.,	Berkley, Mass.,	Kingston, Mass.
Rev. John Todd,	Tabor, Iowa,	West Hanover, Pa.,	West Hanover, Pa.,	East Hanover, Pa.
" Horace Toothaker,	New Sharon, Me.,	Old Town, Me.,	Deer Isle, Me.,	Belfast, Me.
" Charles Cutler Torrey,	Chester, Vt.,	Salem, Mass.,	Salem, Mass.,	Salem, Mass.
" Charles William Torrey,	Madison, Ohio,	Canandaigua, N. Y.,	Kingston, Mass.,	Scituate, Mass.
" Henry Martyn Tupper,	Waverly, Ill.,	Hardwick, Mass.,	West Stafford, Ct.,	West Stafford, Ct.
" Asa Turner,	Denmark, Iowa,	Templeton, Mass.,	Templeton, Mass.,	Templeton, Mass.
" Kinsley Twining,	Hinsdale, Mass.,	West Point, N. Y.,	New Haven, Ct.,	West Point, N. Y.
" George Palmer Tyler, D. D.,	Brattleboro', Vt.,	Brattleboro', Vt.,	Boston, Mass.,	Watertown, Mass.
" George Leon Walker,	Portland, Me.,	Rutland, Vt.,	Woodstock, Ct.,	Concord, N. H.
Hon. James Barr Walker, D. D.,	Benzonia, Mich.,	Philadelphia, Pa.,	North Ireland,	North Ireland.
Joseph Pierce Walker, M. D.,	Cincinnati, Ohio,	Wilton, Me.,	Rindge, N. H.,	Acton, Mass.
Rev. Cyrus Washington Wallace,	Manchester, N. H.,	Bedford, N. H.,	Bedford, N. H.,	Dracut, Mass.
Evander Smith Warner,	Kellogsville, Ohio,	LeRoy, N. Y.,	Roxbury, Ct.,	Otego, N. Y.
Rev. Warren William Warner,	Lawrenceville, N. Y.,	Vernon, N. Y.,	Cambridge, N. Y.,	Bath, N. H.
" Leroy Warren,	Elk Rapids, Mich.,	Pittsfield, Ohio,	Tyringham, Mass.,	Sheridan, N. Y.
" William H. Watson,	Leavenworth, Kan.,	. . . . .	. . . . .	. . . .
" William Watkins,	Newburg, Ohio,	Cardiff, South Wales,	South Wales,	South Wales.
" Edwin Bonaparte Webb, D. D.,	Boston, Mass.,	Newcastle, Me.,	Newcastle, Me.,	Augusta, Me.
" John Calvin Webster,	Wheaton, Ill.,	Hampton, N. H.,	Chester, N. H.,	Pelham, N. H.
Albert E. Wellman,	Cornish, N. H.,	Cornish, N. H.,	Cornish, N. H.,	Cornish, N. H.
Rev. Joshua Wyman Wellman,	Newton, Mass.,	Cornish, N. H.,	Cornish, N. H.,	Cornish, N. H.
Dudley R. Wheeler,	North Stonington, Ct.,	Stonington, Ct.,	Stonington, Ct.,	Stonington, Ct.
Josiah Burley Wheelock,	Coventry, Vt.,	Sanbornton, N. H.,	Sanbornton, N. H.,	Sanbornton, N. H.
Rev. John Wesley White,	Morrison, Ill.,	Weathersfield, Vt.,	Ireland,	Charlestown, N. H.
Dea. Albert D. Whitmore,	Housatonic, Mass.,	Binghampton, N. Y.,	Killingly, Ct.,	Castleton, Vt.
Rev. Elisha Whittlesey,	Waterbury, Ct.,	Salisbury, Ct.,	Washington, Ct.,	Coventry, Ct.
" Martyn Kellogg Whittlesey,	Ottawa, Ill.,	Stockbridge, Mass.,	Stockbridge, Mass.,	Newington, Ct.
" Thomas Wickes, D. D.,	Marietta, Ohio,	Jamaica, L. I., N. Y.,	Fishkill, N. Y.,	Jamaica, L. I., N. Y.
" Moses Hale Wilder,	Gaines, N. Y.,,	Winchendon, Mass.,	Wichendon, Mass.,	Winchendon, Mass.
Dea. Albert G. Willard,	Indianapolis, Ind.	Charlton, Mass.,	Dudley, Mass.,	Dudley, Mass.
Rev. John Willard,	Fairhaven, Mass.,	Hartford, Ct.,	Newington, Ct.,	Newington, Ct.
" Samuel G. Willard,	Willimantic, Ct.,	Wilton, Ct.,	Chester, Ct.,	Wilton, Ct.
" William Henry Willcox,	Reading, Mass.,	New York City, N. Y.,	Newport, N. H.,	Clinton, Ct.
" Benjamin Glazier Willey,	East Sumner, Me.,	North Conway, N. H.,	Lee, N. H.,	Durham, N. H.
David S. Williams,	Flushing, L. I., N. Y.,	Mexico, N. Y.,	Florida, N. Y.,	Salisbury, Ct.

Rev. Edwin Erastus Williams,	Warsaw, N. Y.,	Clinton, N. Y.,	Lebanon, Ct.,	Littleton, Mass.
" Edwin S. Williams,	Northfield, Min.,	Elizabeth, N. J.,	Huntington, L. I., N. Y.,	Hatfield, Mass.
" Francis Williams,	Chaplin, Ct.,	Ashfield, Mass.,	Ashfield, Mass.,	Cummington, Mass.
" Roderick R. Williams,	Pittsburg, Pa.,	Glynn, South Wales,	South Wales,	South Wales.
Hon. Samuel Williston,	Easthampton, Mass.,	Easthampton, Mass.,	West Haven, Ct.,	Stratford, Ct.
Rev. Thomas Wilson,	Stoughton, Mass.,	Paisley, Scotland,	Scotland,	Scotland.
" Horace Winslow,	Binghampton, N. Y.,	Enfield, Mass.,	Berkley, Mass.,	Belchertown, Mass.
Samuel Dutton Winslow, 2d,	Townshend, Vt.,	Dummerston, Vt.,	Putney, Vt.,	Rockingham, Vt.
Rev. Samuel Wolcott, D. D.,	Cleveland, Ohio,	South Windsor, Ct.,	South Windsor, Ct.,	South Windsor, Ct.
Bartholomew Wood, Esq.,	Newton, Mass.,	Newburyport, Mass.,	Italy,	Newburyport, Mass.
Rev. Horace Wood,	Ossipee, N. H.,	Orange, N. H.,	Alstead, N. H.,	Canterbury, Ct.
Dea. John Beach Woodford,	Windsor, Ct.,	Avon, Ct.,	Avon, Ct.,	Hartland, Ct.
Hon. Arden Woodruff,	Strykersville, N. Y.,	Farmington, Ct.,	Farmington, Ct.,	Farmington, Ct.
Alfred Woods,	Iowa Falls, Iowa,	Charlton, Mass.,	Roxbury, Mass.,	Dedham, Mass.
Luther Wright,	Easthampton, Mass.,	Easthampton, Mass.,	Easthampton, Mass.,	Northampton, Mass.
Martin Wright,	Lee Center, Ill.,	Northampton, Mass.,	Westhampton, Mass.,	Westhampton, Mass.
Rev. Samuel Guild Wright,	Dover, Ill.,	Hanover, N. H.,	Hanover, N. H.,	Lebanon, N. H.
Dea. William Wheeler Wright,	Oberlin, Ohio,	Tallmadge, Ohio,	Winsted, Ct.,	Hanover, N. H.
Rev. John Kimball Young, D. D.,	Laconia, N. H.,	Dover, N. H.,	Madbury, N. H.,	Dover, N. H.

NAMES OMITTED IN THEIR PROPER PLACES: — Moses Howe, Haverhill, Mass.; Rev. Thomas F. Hicks, Alpena, Mich.; Rev. John Todd, D. D., Pittsfield, Mass.

SUMMARY.

The Council consisted of 516 members, including the 14 honorary members, and not including delegates from other bodies. The following shows the

MEMBERSHIP FROM DIFFERENT STATES.

Maine,	39	Rhode Island,	4	Maryland,	2	Iowa,	32	Kansas,	6
New Hampshire,	33	New York,	41	Michigan,	26	Wisconsin,	26	Nebraska,	2
Vermont,	34	Pennsylvania,	6	Ohio,	30	Minnesota,	10	Oregon,	1
Massachusetts,	98	New Jersey,	2	Indiana,	3	Tennessee,	1	Colorado,	2
Connecticut,	55	Delaware,	1	Illinois,	39	Missouri,	3	California,	4

BIRTHPLACE OF MEMBERS.

Maine,	42	Connecticut,	100	Ohio,	11	New Jersey,	2	Foreign lands,	23
New Hampshire,	43	Rhode Island,	8	Michigan,	1	Georgia,	1	Unknown,	3
Vermont,	59	New York,	60	Illinois,	2	Virginia,	2		
Massachusetts,	142	Pennsylvania,	10	District of Columbia,	1	Kentucky,	1		

BIRTHPLACE OF THE FATHERS OF THE MEMBERS.

Maine,	27	Massachusetts,	183	New York,	22	New Jersey,	2	Foreign lands,	30
New Hampshire,	58	Connecticut,	140	Pennsylvania,	6	Virginia,	2	Unknown,	5
Vermont,	29	Rhode Island,	6						

BIRTHPLACE OF MOTHERS.

Maine,	29	Massachusetts,	189	New York,	24	Georgia,	1	Foreign lands,	29
New Hampshire,	53	Connecticut,	125	Pennsylvania,	7	Virginia,	3	Unknown,	5
Vermont,	35	Rhode Island,	6	New Jersey,	4	Kentucky,	1		

INDEX OF SUBJECTS.

INDEX OF NAMES OF PERSONS.

www.ingramcontent.com/pod-product-compliance
Lightning Source LLC
LaVergne TN
LVHW021258110826
845150LV00003B/421

* 9 7 8 1 4 2 5 5 6 0 4 1 6 *